Minnesota

Wisconsin

Michigan

Iowa

Illinois   Indiana   Ohio

Missouri

Kentucky

West Virginia

Tennessee

Arkansas

Mississippi   Alabama   Georgia

Louisiana

Florida

Maine

Vermont
New Hampshire

New York

Pennsylvania

Massachusetts
Rhode Island
Connecticut
New Jersey

Delaware
Maryland

Virginia

North Carolina

South Carolina

Plant
Hardiness
Zone Map

**Approximate range
of average annual
minimum temperatures**

Zone 1 Below − 50°F

Zone 2 − 50° to − 40°F

Zone 3 − 40° to − 30°F

Zone 4 − 30° to − 20°F

Zone 5 − 20° to − 10°F

Zone 6 − 10° to 0°F

Zone 7 0° to 10°F

Zone 8 10° to 20°F

Zone 9 20° to 30°F

Zone 10 30° to 40°F

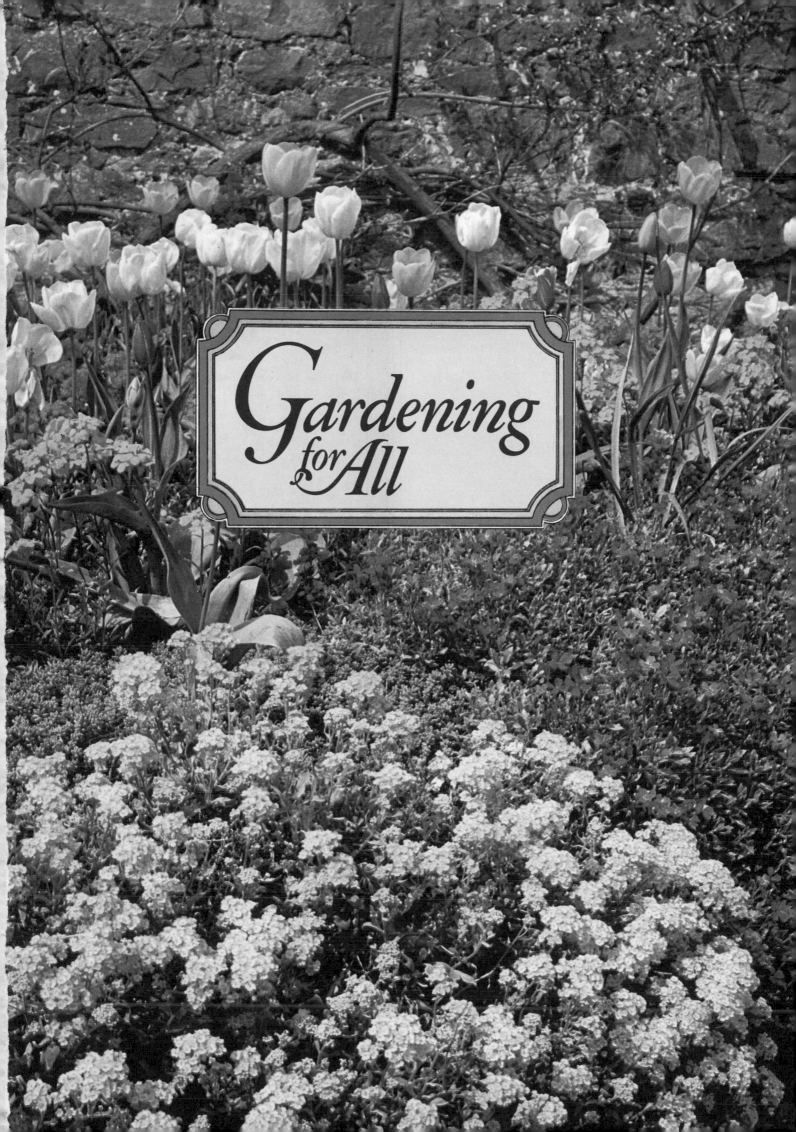

Gardening for All

Edited by
Peter Hunt FLS

Contributors:

Harold Bagust

Alan Bloom VMH

Ann Bonar

P R Chapman

T K Colledge

H G Witham Fogg

Brian Furner FLS

John Garrity BA

Richard Gorer MA

Miles Hadfield

Ray Hanson

Denis Hardwicke

Cyril Harris

Gay Hellyer BSC

Will Ingwersen VMH

Rev E Morley Jones

Christine Kelway

F J Martin

Margaret Martin

F R McQuown MA FLS

A du Gard Pasley AILA

Ray Procter AHRHS

Tony Venison

First published in the USA 1977 by
Chartwell Books, Inc.
a division of Book Sales, Inc.
110 Enterprise Avenue
Secaucus, New Jersey 07094

© 1973 Octopus Books Limited

ISBN 0-7064-0326-6

Produced by Mandarin Publishers Limited
22a Westlands Road
Quarry Bay,
Hong Kong

Printed in Hong Kong

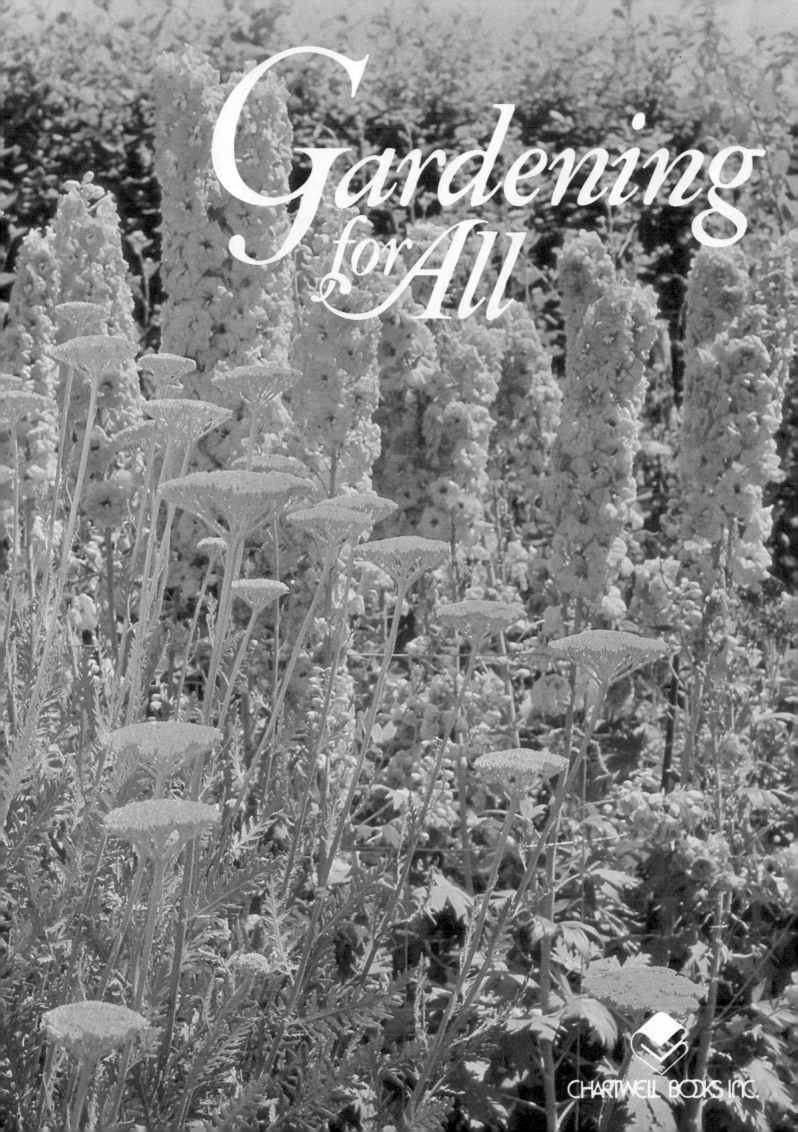

Gardening
for All

CHARTWELL BOOKS INC.

Contents

Introduction

Gardening books of one sort and another have been published for centuries, during which time every conceivable aspect has been dealt with. Books range from step-by-step guides for the complete beginner to highly specialized monographs, to slim pamphlets describing particular methods of gardening. The price range of these publications is equally wide.

In GARDENING FOR ALL we bring you an encyclopedic work which covers in detail not only all the main gardening subjects but many other ancillary features such as *The Gardener's Year*, which covers the plants in season and the work to be done month by month throughout the year.

As its name suggests, this book caters for everyone. If you are a beginner you will find that each chapter presents its subject matter as clearly and completely as possible. If you are more experienced and delight in growing particular plants such as chrysanthemums or dahlias to exhibition standard, then you will find much of value, provided by expert growers and exhibitors.

In fact all of the chapters have been written by gardeners who are well known for their ability to pass on their knowledge to others in easily understood terms, knowledge which has been handed down and added to over the centuries, all of which goes toward making this book an accumulation of gardening wisdom and experience.

A word more about this publication. Few people would think of building a house without preparing plans beforehand, yet far too many create gardens without adequate prior planning and, in the end, are dissatisfied with the results of their endeavours. For this reason GARDENING FOR ALL starts with a most important chapter on *Planning your Garden* in which it is shown that plans, simple or elaborate, can be drawn up for any size or shape of garden, provided the planning is done on the right lines. It is not necessary to have professional surveying instruments; most plans can be prepared by using such simple materials as pieces of string, a measuring tape, pegs, laths, a spirit level, a few large pieces of paper, plus some previous ideas of what you want your garden to look like and to provide for you in the way of flowers, fruit and vegetables, etc.

Plant categories are dealt with in separate chapters. You will find, for instance, chapters on Annuals; Hardy Perennials; Roses; Bulbs of all kinds; Trees and Shrubs (with particular emphasis on those that are suitable for the smaller garden); and Rock Gardens and Pools. Greenhouses are becoming increasingly popular and you will find much information on the various types and what you can grow in them. For those who like to grow plants in the house there is a chapter on Indoor Plants, which deals with the wide range of foliage and flowering plants, as well as cacti and other succulent plants, that are now so popular.

If you need guidance on which jobs to do each month and which flowers, fruits and vegetables are in season, you will find it in *The Gardener's Year*.

Finally, you will find that GARDENING FOR ALL is crammed with color pictures. Many of them illustrate the best varieties of garden plants, others are detailed drawings which will enable you to carry out essential tasks or construct various features.

Peter Hunt

A new garden is at once a challenge and an opportunity. The very sight of some barren or weed grown plot brings out our latent desire to impose order and create our own particular version of paradise on the wilderness. Without much thought the ground is cleared, cultivated, grass seed sown, odd beds prepared for plants gathered in a haphazard manner, a path, and storage buildings appear as needed. Then, instead of fulfillment, there is a feeling of unease. Paradise was never like this? Perhaps a pergola, a rockery, a pool, a patio would improve things. Books, newspaper articles, magazines all suggest a new answer and more and more elements appear on the ground, unrelated to one another and to the needs of the owner. Small saplings, planted near the house, grow into large trees and darken the rooms, the various beds contain no color and too many weeds, mud tracks are worn across the lawn because the paths do not lead in the right direction, there is no room for chairs on the terrace, the vegetables will not grow, and disillusion sets in. One can see all the stages of this kind of garden, in which one kind of chaos merely replaces another, on any train journey through a residential area. But what went wrong?

In almost every case these gardens were made without a plan, or at best with a few hazy ideas scribbled on an envelope. The makers did not really know what they wanted, had no clear idea of the finished product towards which they were working and inevitably the result was a muddle.

Years of growing time—and even in this period of instant gardening, time is still important—and endless labor have been wasted for very little result. And curiously enough it is the smallest gardens which need the most careful planning because every inch is vital and the slightest lack of decision can be seen immediately. So, faced with a barren plot full of debris, or a neglected wilderness, how does one set about preparing a plan which will satisfy all the needs of the family in a practical way, however long it may take to complete?

The Site

First of all there is the site itself, and as this is the raw material with which you have to work, it merits very careful consideration. Although there are many aspects of it which will have to be considered and noted down, you will need a scale drawing which will form the basis of your work. There is very seldom any plan available, because the plans which form part of the title deeds of the normal house are on too small a scale to be very helpful, so you will have to provide one yourself. Unless your site is very large and very complicated you will not find the survey difficult.

You will need only very simple equipment. If it is possible to borrow two 100-ft. tape measures you will find them very useful but, if not, you will have to take some strong cord

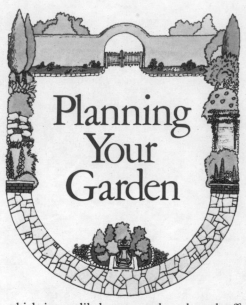

Planning Your Garden

which is not likely to stretch and mark off into units of 5 ft. and 10 ft. As you will be using this cord to take long measurements, be sure that the divisions are accurately made and try to mark the 10 ft. divisions by means of differently colored tags so that you can tell immediately where you have got to without counting along from the end every time. All the shorter measurements you can take with a steel tape. If the survey is large or you are working alone, an ordinary metal spike fixed to the free end of your long tapes or cords will be useful, as you can fix it in the ground at key points and take several measurements from that position.

Make a rough sketch of the site—or just one part, if it is too large to do all at once—big enough to write in neatly all the measurements you are likely to need. This sketch does not have to be very accurate but it is as well to keep the general proportions—for instance the length of the house compared to the length of the garden—correct. But even that is not essential because the measurements will enable you to plot the work correctly afterwards.

Decide on a base line from which to work. A straight, simple object like a boundary wall or fence, uncluttered by obstructions, is best although one sometimes has to invent a base line formed by one of the tapes laid down and fixed in position. Measure this base, working away from the house, and mark with bamboo canes any significant distances, such as the 50 ft. mark, from which you may want to take subsequent measurements. Always try to take all your measurements in the same direction—say from the house outwards—because it makes it easier to plot the survey afterwards. Then measure an adjoining boundary or the other line more or less at right angles to your base line; 'more or less at right angles' because you should never assume that any apparent right angle is in fact true. The eye can accept quite wide variations in this. Having measured these two lines, complete a triangle by measuring the distance between the two free ends.

Starting again from the base line, fix the position of the other boundaries by forming

another triangle or triangles if the plot is not a basic rectangle. At this stage it is best to treat the house as a simple block or even run a line straight across the back, picking up only the positions of the corners if the shape of the building is complex.

You have now the basic details of the plot shown as a series of triangles, each related to one another and all tied back to your essential base line. At this stage you could draw up the ground plan if you wished, but generally speaking it is as well to continue and fill in all the detailed information at the same time. The position of features which are close to boundary lines, or directly on the diagonal lines forming the sides of triangles, can be positioned as these main lines are measured. Even if the object is a foot or two away from the line, it is quite easy to judge a right angle over a short distance, and to measure outwards with the steel tape.

Objects inside the site—for instance existing trees or groups of shrubs—are measured separately by a series of small extra triangles and it is at this point that the intermediate measurements marked on the base line with bamboo canes can be useful, as they can form known points from which these smaller triangles can be measured. The small triangles may be linked together but they must always be tied back to the base line or other points whose position has already been measured.

This leaves the details of the house itself, and it is often more convenient to take these

Far left: Small town gardens on the street using every available inch of space
Left: A colorful garden of annuals
Above: A small town garden carefully planned for privacy, color and interest over a long period. Permanent shrubs such as roses are augmented with spring and summer bedding plants and annuals. Paving makes for easy maintenance

on a separate piece of paper, as a large number of separate measurements will need to be written down. Starting at one corner, work along the face of the house, noting the measurement to the outer edge of each window and doorway, width and number of steps, position of leaders, manhole covers, etc. If there are projections or recesses, these will have to be measured separately and triangulated back to the corner of the house or some other measured point to make sure that they are really at right angles to the main structure.

If the site is large or of a complex shape it may be easier to divide it into sections, measuring each section separately. But you must ensure that the measurements of each section are complete in themselves and tied closely back to those of the adjoining section, or you may find that the total work is not accurate. One or two check measurements taken from the beginning of the base line, right through the sections to some fixed and measured point are often helpful in these cases.

Now to put this rough data into some definite and accurate form. The easiest base material to use is probably graph paper since it is already covered by a grid giving both a means of scale measurements and vertical/horizontal lines to work against. But it is not essential and large sheets of lined paper can also be used. If possible pin the paper to a large, smooth board of suitable size, as it will be very much easier to work on, and decide the scale at which you are going to work. In

other words, at what size will each foot measured on the ground, appear on the paper? The scale should be some standard unit, easily measured with a ruler. For small gardens a $\frac{1}{4}$ in. to equal 1 ft. is a convenient measurement. For larger areas an $\frac{1}{8}$ in. to 1 ft. is easier because otherwise the size of the finished plan might become unmanageable.

Having seen from your notes roughly how the size of the garden will fill out the paper at the chosen scale, draw your base line, mark on it any intermediate measurements you took along it, and you are ready to begin. At this point you will need a large compass, possibly with an extending arm, so that you can measure the other two sides of your first triangle and strike them off as two arcs which will bisect at the point of the triangle. This will then give you the length and position of the second boundary. It is not necessary to draw in the diagonal lines forming the third side of each triangle because the bisecting arcs giving you the various fixed points, are all the reference you need. In the same way all the triangles can be plotted and the existing features drawn in. Finally the details of doors, windows and projections can be filled in on the block of the house. You will now have a representation, to a standard scale, of your plot, drawn on a flat sheet of paper.

But although your paper may be flat, your site is probably not, so it is time to think about levels. Surveyors use sophisticated leveling equipment but although this can sometimes be hired it is not easy for the amateur to use without instruction. Some levels can be

found by direct measurement – the number and depth of steps from a door to outside ground level for instance, or the difference in the number of courses of brickwork exposed when ground level slopes past a brick wall. Others may be worked out by using two laths, a spirit level and your steel tape. Take a convenient fixed point, such as a manhole cover, to act as a datum point to which all your measurements will refer and rest the larger lath on edge across it. Hold the lath steady against a shorter lath held upright and adjust the level of the long lath by using the spirit level. Then measure the difference between the upper edge of the lath and the ground, using the steel tape. Drive a peg in level with the surface of the ground at the point you took the measurement, then repeat the process. The position of the pegs can afterwards be measured and plotted onto your survey and the various differences in level worked out. It is possible – though tedious – to take a whole grid of levels in this way, but usually only a few will be needed to give you the basic differences in level within the area of a normal garden.

Basic Information At this stage it might be useful to make one or two copies of the plan, as you will begin to collect basic information which might be applied more easily and clearly on separate sheets. If these extra copies were drawn on tracing paper, you could slip one or more of them over your basic plan sheet to give you the additional data you need when thinking of the final design for your garden.

Consider the question of sunlight and shadow, both in summer and winter. It is easy to plot their movement across your site on any given clear day, and to sketch in this pattern of movement on the plan. Ideally the movement at midsummer and midwinter should both be shown, as both will influence the final placing of trees and shrubs, and the choice of plant material for the different areas. If you cannot wait for six months to complete the two operations, you will have to plot one season and approximate the other, but this method is not so satisfactory unless you are very observant and have noticed the amazing effect of change in elevation of the sun at different seasons.

At the same time, make notes of areas which are particularly warm and sheltered, where heat is reflected from house walls and hard surfaces, those always shady and damp or permanently cold where frost and snow lie long after they have melted elsewhere.

Winds and drafts are another important element. Although we are mostly aware of the prevailing wind, this may not have the greatest effect on your particular garden. Often trees, hills or other buildings deflect the wind, bringing it in from some unexpected quarter while in urban areas downdrafts, wind tunnels between buildings and even minor whirlwinds in apparently sheltered courtyards can all cause havoc. These too can be noted on the plan as they are often very localized and may affect only part of quite a small garden.

Although most gardens will have the same amount of topsoil—or lack of it—over the whole area, this is not always so, and it is worth digging one or two trial holes to find out. Often builders fill in hollows with subsoil taken from foundations, or spread a layer of infertile subsoil over the ground near buildings. The most astonishing things are done to the soil and levels of new housing developments, and the unwary owner is to be pitied if he should attempt to make a garden without investigating what lay beneath. If there is any significant variation the areas concerned should be noted on the plan and numbered soil samples sent off for analysis of pH value (to see whether it is acid or alkaline, which affects the types of plant you can grow) and mineral deficiencies.

Many new gardens are quite bare, but when an old garden has been split up into smaller plots, or some other site redeveloped, there are generally some existing trees and shrubs whose position, level in relation to surrounding ground and general size, shape and species (if known) should be carefully noted. Never destroy an existing plant, however poor or common it may seem, until you are quite sure that it cannot be incorporated in the new plan. Even if the final scheme does not require it, an existing shrub or tree, already established and probably capable of improvement by careful pruning and shaping, can give an immediate air of maturity while the new planting grows up. After five or ten years, if it is no longer needed, it can be removed.

Even an old, overgrown hedgerow in the wrong position will often yield a few saplings of interesting shape which will soon spread out and form nice trees when freed from the surrounding jungle. If you have inherited an existing garden, however neglected, do not do more than minimal tidying and lawn mowing for the first year, as all kinds of treasures may come to light which would otherwise be destroyed unseen. This year of limited activity will give you time to prepare a detailed survey, and get the feel of the place, so that the ensuing new garden will be far more interesting and practical than it could otherwise have been.

Then there are factors outside your own site which may nevertheless have an important bearing on your final design. If you are lucky you may have a view, either spectacular or merely pleasant, which can be seen from some parts of the garden and not from others. The best viewing positions should be noted, as these may affect the placing of seats or the shape of terraces. Often the good points are less obvious: a church spire glimpsed between two buildings, an old tree in a neighboring garden, an interesting grouping of gables and chimneys seen against the sky are all features which could be used to draw the eye outside the garden and make it seem larger than it is. Again, the best views of these should be noted, together with the places where planting is needed to hide less desirable features and so draw attention to good ones. And there are the neighbors' windows which may dominate some parts of the garden while other areas are relatively private.

All open spaces are extrovert or introvert in character. In other words they can be outward looking, depending for all or part of their effect on views and objects beyond their boundaries, or they are inward looking with no views, or only bad ones, outside and needing to contain all their interest within themselves. It depends entirely on these outside factors what kind of garden you can have.

All this preparation may seem elaborate and complicated but if you consider the physical effort needed to make the garden, and the time it will take to grow, the planning stage falls into perspective as a small but vital part of the process.

❧ The Zone of Influence ☙

The first thing to do is to consider the site in relation to its surroundings. Every site has a zone of influence which may extend as far as the next street or even the next hill top if it happens to be in the country and can be seen as part of a larger landscape pattern in which hills, woods and fields form major elements. One must always remember that far more people will see a garden from outside looking inwards, either at short range or from a greater distance, than will ever see it in detail from within. It can be an interesting experience looking at your potential garden from outside and realizing how much you can improve the general view for others. A care-

The first three stages of a survey. *Above left:* a sketch of a 'minimal' garden (front and back of house), drawn freehand and ready for survey measurements; *center:* this sketch has the detailed measurements. Some features which will be altered have not been measured. *Right:*

this drawing shows the garden before any changes are made. Notes about ground conditions, views etc., have been included. Right: a simple method of levelling. *Top:* a long lath is laid on edge across a fixed point, e.g. a manhole cover. Hold this lath steady against a shorter, upright lath, and use a spirit level to adjust the level of the longer lath. *Center:* measure the distance between the top of the lath and the ground and drive a peg in level with the fixed point. *Bottom:* repeat the process as often as necessary and plot the differences in level on the survey.

fully placed tree might hide leaders, or break up the long perspective of a dull street to make it seem more interesting. An urn or a patch of bright color seen through a gateway might make all the difference at the end of a dead end, while in the wider view careful planting to conceal the hard lines of boundaries might help to blend a new garden into the countryside. Often visiting an unfamiliar area, it is the minor, unexpected touches which please most. A sudden cascade of roses over the top of a wall, the spray of a fountain in a patch of sunlight, an inviting garden path framed by trees. We forget that these effects were planned by someone and that we are often in a similar position to give pleasure to others.

Human Needs Once you have become familiar with the site and noted down all its physical characteristics both good and bad, it is time to consider very carefully the exact role the garden is to play in your life. Everyone has different priorities but it is very important at this stage to get these in the right order, because it is unlikely that any modern garden can fulfil all the needs and wishes of the various members of the family.

First there are the obvious needs: a place for children to play, room to sit in sun or shade, a vegetable patch, space for flowers for cutting for indoor decoration, an area for compost heaps, a workshop or a building for storing tools and equipment, are just a few of the many varying elements which go to make up a family garden.

Then there are the more elaborate requirements: a swimming pool, a tennis court, a croquet lawn, a sauna cabin, a greenhouse, a rose garden, rock garden, orchard, lily pool. Each of these is a major element round which a whole scheme might be evolved.

Less obvious, but still vitally important, are other basic human needs which are often forgotten today with fatal results in terms of human happiness. The need for privacy, not just from neighbors but from other members of the family, however harmonious our family life, there is from time to time a need to be alone and the garden is an ideal setting for solitary thought.

With privacy go seclusion and the pleasures of the imagination. Children love to play in a world of make believe, hidden from grown up realities by a few shrubs or a spreading tree which will form the basis of any number of adventures. And it is not only children who need the pleasures of make believe. As the grown ups make their own world more and more intolerable, they too need a comforting touch of illusion to support them.

So what do you really want? Only you can make the decision. Prepare a list of elements and place them in order of priority, but unless you actually do this you are likely to find eventually that something important has been forgotten. So much depends on the way you live, the amount of time and money you are prepared to spend on maintaining the garden afterwards, the specific problems with which only you have to contend.

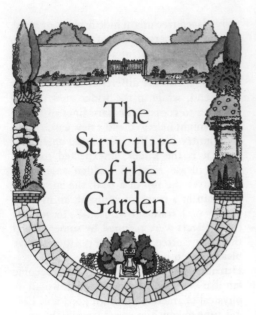

The Structure of the Garden

While deciding on the various elements which the garden must contain, it is as well to consider the structure which should form the basic outlines of any garden, large or small. So often the lack of this underlying structure results in the garden being a formless jumble rather than the satisfying composition which we subconsciously need.

Any garden, or landscape, consists of an arrangement of masses and voids. The masses may be formed by hills and or by buildings and banks of shrubs, while the voids are represented by lakes, rivers and fields or lawns, pools and beds of low-growing flowers. Basically a mass is formed by objects at or above eye level, while a void can be anything upon which one looks down. Voids are largely horizontal, masses are vertical and it is the balance between open void and closed mass, the contrast between horizontal and vertical which gives any garden its shape.

Masses do not have to be solid. A pergola, an avenue, a group of trees standing on a lawn, even a single tree with wide spreading branches, all give an effect of partial inclosure which still allows the eye to penetrate to open spaces beyond. It is this feeling of space flowing onward, flooding like water between the tree trunks, forming pools when held up by plant masses or buildings, which can give to the garden a sense of movement, interest and the illusion that the area is much larger than it is.

Illusion is important and the smaller the garden the greater the need to use all available arts to make it seem larger and more interesting than it really is. Bad proportions can be improved, ugly features hidden, small spaces enlarged and apparent privacy achieved by simple means. Once the basic principles are understood, they can be applied, varied and improved according to circumstance.

Space A small garden without defined boundaries, in a large open area will appear very small indeed, whereas if the boundaries are emphasized by strong vertical elements reaching above eye level, the space at once seems larger.

You have only to think of a house in the course of construction to see this fact emerge. When the foundations are first laid out on the ground, the whole house appears no larger than a reasonably sized room. When the walls are about waist height, the individual rooms emerge but appear very small. Once the walls have reached ceiling height the rooms are seen in their true proportion and may seem quite large. In the garden the same rule holds good, although there one has the ability to change the proportion by altering the heights of the walls and creating internal divisions by means of trellises or a series of large plants in pots which will contain a series of interlocking spaces of different kinds.

The partial division of a small area can make it seem larger and more interesting by emphasizing the half seen, allowing the eye to penetrate further in one direction than another and leaving the feeling all the time that there is something beyond.

Light and Shade Another means of altering proportion and apparent size is by the careful use of light and shade. Shadow can conceal a great many bad points without using means which in themselves draw attention to what is being hidden. Take the obvious case of garbage containers in a courtyard garden. You can put them into a neat brick box with doors in front for easy access and flower boxes on top to brighten the effect. Certainly the containers are hidden and everyone will think 'How clever, that is where they hide the garbage containers'. Alternatively you can have black containers, either bought that way or painted, and put them in the shadow of a large evergreen shrub or a slightly drooping bamboo. A dark painted trellis covered with ivy in front of which bright flowers are grouped in sunlight, completes the illusion. The eye is drawn to the sunlit flowers, everything beyond is vague and mysterious. The garden may extend for some distance but it is difficult to tell and the black garbage containers stand unseen in the shadows.

Climbers Again, faced with a walled town garden many people start by painting the garden walls white. This is fine if you wish your garden to be a white box of sharply defined shape. Certain very formal types of garden rely on such emphasis for part of their effect, but if you feel confined and want an impression of greater space, this treatment is fatal. Better by far to overplant the walls with vines and creepers, not trained too neatly, which will swing forward in curtains of greenery, masking the boundaries in shadow and producing the feeling of a forest clearing.

The Uses of Water Water, even in the form of a tiny pool or fountain basin, can be a tremendous help to illusions of all kinds. Apart from the pleasure which the sound of moving and falling water always gives us, the greatest use of water in the garden is reflection. For this reason pools should always be painted black inside, for not only do they appear of limitless depth but they also produce the best reflections. Blue pools may be used to achieve special effects in that color, but all the other benefits of water are thereby lost.

Dark pools of this kind, in positions such as town courtyards where the lateral rays of the sun are cut off, can bring a brilliant patch of sky down to lighten what may otherwise be rather dark and dank surroundings. Larger pools can often be built to reflect objects in the garden or even outside it, giving double importance to some feature which you wish to emphasize. For instance, a long canal has been used in a town garden to mirror exactly a church spire which was the only redeeming feature of an otherwise very bleak outlook.

Because of its powers of reflection, the level of water in relation to the surrounding ground is very important. Try always to keep water level and ground level as close as possible. Water only 1 in. below ground level will appear to be 2 in. down because the depth of the edge is reflected – if it is 6 in. below it, therefore, appears to be 1 ft. down and the appearance already begins to be that of a well rather than a pool. For this reason you should always make pools slightly larger than you intend them to appear and the lower the intended water level the larger the actual water surface required to compensate.

Unless heavily masked by planting, water strongly emphasizes the exact form by which it is contained. This does not matter, indeed can be a positive asset, where a formal pool is concerned, provided that the shape is well proportioned, but it does lead to problems with the design of informal pools and water features. A brief study of pools and ponds in areas where these occur naturally will show that the more eccentric curves of garden ponds are largely an invention of their makers

Above: In a successful garden design, the balance between masses (vertical elements) and voids (largely horizontal features), is an important factor. It is often possible to make a small garden seem much larger than it is by the correct placing of trees, shrubs and other features in relation to open spaces. *Below:* In this small town garden there are no well-defined boundaries. *Right:* The wall here is well related to the house. The illustration also shows the proper use of climbing plants

rather than an imitation of natural forms. In this, as in so many other aspects of garden design, when in doubt simplify. One large pool of simple shape is worth half a dozen contorted puddles joined by an unconvincing stream.

Ground Shaping   Water, which looks happiest in a slight hollow, either natural or man made, leads to the consideration of ground shaping and levels. Few gardens are exactly flat and even in those which are, quite a minor excavation will produce enough soil to create interesting modulations of the ground surface. But do not undulate just for the sake of doing so. A slight valley formation will emphasize what lies at the end of it, whether a seat, a view, or an urn on a stand. A very gentle mound will give point to a group of trees standing on a lawn or alternatively a lawn slightly saucer shaped, surrounded by banks of shrubs, will appear intimate and secluded. A terrace raised only 6 in. above the rest of the garden will give the house much greater importance than if the two were on the same level. But if the terrace is too narrow for its length, the fault will be magnified if it is at a higher level.

Exterior proportions are not the same as those used indoors, simply because the scale of everything outside is larger. Many mean looking and unsatisfactory features have arisen because internal proportions have been used out of doors. When in doubt, make it larger, the steps wider and shallower, the terrace broader, the borders deeper. Our natural inclination is to design things which are too small, and are reduced to insignificance by the size of the outdoor world or the exuberance of the plant material which soon swamps our little beds and invades the narrow paths.

Structural Elements

Now, having considered some of the effects we can achieve, it is time to think about the various elements concerned in greater detail.
Harmony of Materials and Shapes These fall into two classes, vertical structures including walls, fences, screens, gateways, pergolas and garden buildings, and horizontal structures of drives, paths, terraces and steps. Before examining any of these, one should look for a moment at the relationship of objects. Certain shapes and materials relate to one another, others do not and if we are to create satisfying gardens it is essential to achieve an underlying unity which will hold our designs together. To take some extreme examples, one would not choose to use precast concrete slabs as the terrace for an ancient brick farm house, or lay paths of rustic crazy paving to a steel and concrete building. Both would look incongruous and would irritate rather than give pleasure. But equally ridiculous things are done every day of the week.

Before deciding on any type of structure or material, study your house, the buildings which surround it, the materials and methods used in the locality, so that your own structures can become a part of their setting rather than something introduced and obviously alien. You may not particularly care for the materials and style of your house or the neighborhood, but it is still wiser to employ these, even in some slightly different form, than to change the subject altogether. Of course there are gifted people who can mix the most dissimilar elements with success, but the remainder of us would be wiser to play safe. One does not need to make an exact copy of any particular feature, provided that the general feeling and intention of the new work blends in with what is existing

Always try to make your new structures seem an inevitable outcome of the old by linking them firmly to the house or adjoining buildings, emphasizing the major features of these by carrying their lines and shapes out into the garden. For instance, where the upper half of a house is faced with tiles, the edge of the facing will form a strong horizontal line which should be extended at the same level when a boundary wall joins or runs close to the building. This may mean a high wall, but the level can change at the next significant point such as the junction between house terrace and lawn. Never change the level unnecessarily or at some point which has no importance in the general design. Nothing is more irritating than a wall which descends in a series of pointless little jumps which do not relate in any way to the remainder of the garden.

If the façade of the building has a strong rhythm – for instance a series of columns of the same size between windows – these might be reflected in the paving pattern of the terrace and expressed as strips of stone crossing some other hard material such as brick or gravel. Arched glass doors opening onto a courtyard could be faced by brick arches of the same size, framing views of the garden or countryside.

Even on the most simple level, steps from lawn to terrace should lead obviously to a garden door or at least to some major architectural feature, rather than being directed straight at a blank piece of wall just because this happens to be in the middle of the terrace. If such a solution has to be arrived at, then at least let there be an important seat or urn placed to give apparent point to the arrangement.

Boundaries All too often boundaries and space divisions are made of materials whose only apparent virtue is cheapness, giving an air of meanness to the garden which no amount of subsequent care and planting can ever dispel. Nor are they cheap in the long term, as flimsy woven panels are impermanent and require frequent replacement, while trellis and rustic work last just long enough to become covered with climbing plants before collapsing in a tangle of broken woodwork and earwigs.

Much better, if these structures are to be expressed visually, or even used as supports for climbing plants, to construct them properly with appropriate materials at the outset, even if the cost means delaying completion of other parts of the garden for a year or two.

Walls are best made of brick or stone to match the house, although given really solid foundations and suitable design, either in staggered panels or with sufficient piers to give support, the brickwork need only be $4\frac{1}{2}$ in. instead of the normal 9-in. thickness, which will help to keep down the cost. Different types of wall have different characteristics. A run of wall with a flush face

emphasizes length, walls of staggered shape or with frequent piers, especially if these are related to the ground plan, can make a narrow plot seem wider. Pierced walls, or those made of open concrete blocks, can suggest distance and depth, but such openwork elements are best used in short lengths or as panels framed in solid walling, as used alone in any quantity they can seem to dominate and have a rather irritating effect.

Painted walls in the garden, though sometimes necessary to relate to a painted house, create problems because they become quickly streaked with dirt and climbers make re-painting difficult. It is better to give them a broad coping to throw off the rain, and to use them as a background to bold groups of foliage plants rather than plant directly against them.

Walls built solely as a background and support for climbers can be made of inexpensive concrete blocks, possibly with a brick coping to match the adjoining building. But remember that you will have to plant climbers on both sides of such walls if they are to be suitably concealed.

Where wooden fences, or panels of well-made hardwood trellis, are used near the house they can be given a much more architectural character by being set on a dwarf brick wall between brick piers so that they appear to have been designed as part of the general structure rather than added as an afterthought.

Gateways One of the most exciting things to come upon while exploring a strange town is a solid wooden door set in a high garden wall. The desire to turn the handle and look into the garden beyond is irresistible. Although we do not often have the chance to own such a door in a wall, it does teach us the importance of entrances of all kinds, each of which has a different character. Tall and narrow openings of this kind are exciting and mysterious. A broad opening in a high wall is expansive and hospitable, as though designed for a party, especially if emphasized at either side with finials of some suitable kind.

The character of the gates and doors themselves is important. Solid woodwork of good design is always useful, particularly on boundaries. Even the best wrought-iron work will only show to advantage against an absolutely plain background of grass, water, sky or simple paving. When a gate or door of open design is required to be seen against a complex background, then an arrangement of upright bars in wood or metal is generally best, as the repetition forms a grid of reference, giving point to the details beyond it.

Gates and walls which are below eye level are more difficult to deal with as they seem to imply an irritating obstacle to one's progress rather than a feature of consequence in themselves. Where they are necessary as a protection for (or against) dogs and children they are best made of simple vertical elements, not too closely spaced and painted black, to appear as unobtrusive as possible. The standard London cast-iron railing, which

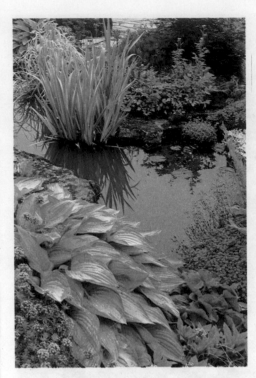

Above: A pool can often be used as a mirror to reflect objects inside or outside the garden *Below:* Two kinds of pierced walls: at the bottom, one made with modern pre-cast concrete sections; at the top, ridge tiles have been used to obtain the same effect. *Right:* Clematis and other wall plants used to conceal the hard boundary of a modern house. *Below right:* An effective way of growing roses, against a pillar or pyramid gives protection while not impeding the view, is quite a good model to take, even though the scale and materials employed may not seem the same.

Anything of complicated design, whether castellated brick walls, wooden gates in the form of cartwheels or rising suns, or 'wrought-iron' fencing seemingly made from portions of cans painted black and stuck together, should all be avoided like the plague. And although ranch type fencing of painted horizontal boarding can look quite effective, it requires a great deal of maintenance to keep it in order.

Garden Buildings Garden buildings – sheds, summer houses, greenhouses and conservatories – create a number of problems which are not easily solved. Basically to have such structures designed and built specifically for any given position – as they should be – is very expensive whereas they can be obtained in prefabricated form quite cheaply. Naturally there are any number of designs and makers, and some of these may be more suitable than others for your given position. Unobtrusive siting and the use of matching materials – for instance the brick base of a greenhouse or conservatory should match the adjoining house or garden wall – can help considerably. So can matching major horizontals, such as the line of the top of window frames, to similar elements on the façade of the house.

Pergolas The pergola is designed to give protection from the sun and create a shady walk. It also provides an excellent way of growing many types of climbing plants and can be visually very useful by extending the structure of the house into the garden and possibly linking it to some other building such as the garage or summer house which might otherwise appear as an isolated element. Here, too, proportions need to be generous, the width always being greater than the height, the structure sound and the materials used for its construction related to the adjoining house, if the effect is to be completely satisfactory.

The isolated pergola, unrelated to other structures, is seldom successful, especially if it begins and ends at nothing in particular, which is too often the case. Pillars built in brick or stone, precast classical columns of simple shape, or slender metal uprights are all suitable in their place. Heavy beams set directly above the supports, or a more closely spaced pattern of lighter ones on continuous cross members, can form the roofing which should not be too solid or the finished effect when planted will tend to be dark. At all costs avoid structures made from flimsy rustic poles – if you can afford nothing better it would be wiser to forget about having a pergola and grow your climbers on pyramids made from three or four poles stoutly braced, which can look quite effective.

The Types of Hard Surface

Paths, drives, courtyards and terraces have all to be covered with hard wearing materials which will take vehicles, foot traffic, chairs and tables while remaining clean and easy to use at all times of year. Builders tend to put down a drive and path of plain concrete and leave it at that, but there are a great many more interesting materials which are equally suitable. Which you use, of course, depends on the style and material of your house, but the main possibilities are these:

Precast Paving This, the most easily obtainable paving material on the market is simple to lay because sizes and depths of slab are fairly standard, whichever make is chosen. The disadvantages lie mainly in the hard mechanical finish and extraordinary colors produced. But many types have a pleasantly rough texture—which is also nonslip—and if quiet buffs, browns and cream colors are chosen the finished effect can be pleasant. Most colors weather down to softer tones and in appropriate settings some of the new slate-gray and purplish colors could be used successfully. At all costs avoid the crude raspberry reds and poison greens which look wrong everywhere, and do not use a large number of colors to achieve 'variety'. A fruit salad contains variety both of form and color, but you do not necessarily want to look at it every day. A random mixture of the larger sizes is generally best, although in a small, formal area such as a courtyard, one of the stylized patterns suggested by the makers can look well. On the whole these rigid patterns tend to emphasize the machine-made form of the slabs, which is seldom a good thing.

Bricks As the unit is small and regular, these are ideal for small scale work—narrow paths, parterres, designs involving curved lines, and panels which may be inset as part of a composition of stone or precast paving. It is best to use brick paviors specifically made for the purpose and only 2 in. thick, but these are not so easy to obtain today. Over baked bricks, obtainable from some brickworks, are good although dark in color, but

are hard to lay as they are often warped and uneven in size and shape. Otherwise, really hard building bricks are suitable, but it is wise to get the suppliers to admit that they are suitable for outdoor paving before purchase. On no account use any kind of soft brick as these will crumble on exposure to frost.

Stone Paving Various types of stone paving are obtainable in different parts of the country with pleasing textures and color variations which can be had in slabs large enough to provide a good sense of scale and fairly easily cut to pattern if required. They are best laid in a random pattern.

Granite Setts At one time when all the roads, quay sides, tramways and other places laid with these square or oblong pieces of granite were being taken up, setts were easily obtainable. Nowadays they are hard to get and have always been hard to lay because the greater part of the sett is hidden below ground. They look effective as panels in a large stone terrace, or as a surface for an arrival or garage court largely used by wheeled rather than foot traffic.

Cobbles This is another surface which is difficult to lay and uncomfortable to walk on, although this fact can be put to advantage to keep people away from certain areas, such as the edge of a retaining wall or a pond. They are best used as decorative panels in a setting of brick or stone. Only the end, or in some cases one edge, of the cobble stone is exposed; the remainder is buried to keep the stones in place. They need to be very closely set so that none of the supporting cement is visible, because nothing looks worse than a mass of concrete in which cobble stones are set singly, looking like currants in a plum pudding. Swirling all over patterns can be made, using the variation in color of the stones, and the different shapes of ends and edges, in a simplified version of those elaborate pebble pavings one sees sometimes in foreign gardens.

Gravel The 'Prim gravel walks which ever winding go' of the Victorian garden have been out of favor for a long time. However, gravel properly laid and firmly held in place—preferably with brick or wood—is an excellent, hard-wearing and comparatively inexpensive surfacing material. With modern weed killers even keeping the gravel clean is no longer a problem. The matt texture, quiet coloring and possibility of laying to any shape all give gravel the advantage over other materials.

Concrete Concrete by itself is not an attractive material for the garden. However, it has certain advantages and much can be done to improve its cold coloring and unpleasantly smooth finish. By using different colored sands, different aggregates and coloring agents which can be obtained for the purpose, the color of the concrete can be changed from the usual hard gray/white to warm buff, tan and brownish shades more suitable to a garden setting. If an interesting aggregate is chosen it can be exposed before

the concrete is absolutely dry, giving a pleasantly varied surface, or different textures can be applied while it is still damp by ribbing with a wooden lath, pressing coarse burlap on to the surface, or something similar. On no account draw paving patterns in the damp concrete with a pointed stick. They convince no one and merely look absurd. The fact that large areas of concrete cannot be laid without expansion joints to avoid cracking, can be turned to advantage by using patterns of wood strips, bricks on edge, panels of cobble stones, or similar materials to form an element in the design.

The Use of Hard Surfaces

Just as gardens are formed by the contrast of mass and void, open and closed spaces, so they need a proper balance between hard and soft elements. Either they can be largely soft with just enough hard surface to make them practical, like most country gardens, or the proportions may be reversed as they generally are in city sites. Where they are more nearly equal, the design is more difficult to handle and an exact 50:50 ratio seldom looks well. One should decide on the general intention before thinking of the detail, so that the completed work does not suffer the timidity and lack of purpose evident in many gardens.

Paths The first essential of any path is that it should be convenient to walk on and should take you where you want to go. If it fulfils these requirements comfortably it is of practical value and the exact form it takes will be dictated by the intended character of the garden of which it forms a part. Too many paths criss-crossing the ground can produce a restless and busy air, particularly as some of them are not needed. If dry walks are required in all directions it may be better to cease to think of them as paths, but to have a general pattern of interlocking hard and soft surfaces which together make a complete composition. Wherever practicable it should be possible for two people to walk comfortably abreast on a path and if the design demands that it should be curved, the curves must appear natural and inevitable, not forced and arbitrary.

Stepping Stones For casual use, where the line of a formal path would interrupt the flow of grass or planting, carefully placed stepping stones can provide an answer. They should be so spaced that a regular, easy pace will bring the foot well down on to each stone, rather than on to the edge with the risk of damaging the soft surface between them. Because grass or plants will tend to spread across the stone, the individual slabs should be large, so that there is not a constant edging problem, and where they cross lawns the stones must be set $\frac{1}{2}$ in. below the level of the turf to insure that the mower blades can pass unharmed over the top. One should never use stepping stones where they will be used by wheelbarrows, because the wheel will wear a runnel of mud in the soft surface between them.

Mowing Stones Where grass abuts a vertical element such as a wall or step, it is essential to have a narrow strip of some hard

material, once again sunk $\frac{1}{2}$ in. below the surface, to allow for easy mowing. The strip can be as narrow as a single brick, which will be almost invisible or it can be a broad band of stone or concrete forming part of an overall design. These wide bands are invaluable, also, between lawn and flower border, as they do away with the need for constant edging, which is always such a chore, and at the same time allow the plants to flop forward so that they can grow freely without the risk of being cut by the mower.

Terraces Most terraces are generally too wide for paths and too narrow for their proper purpose of forming a base to the house and a general area for sitting, entertaining and viewing the garden. No building looks its best rising straight from hard surface, so that a bed should always be left between house and terrace to give space for a foundation planting of low shrubs, foliage plants, bulbs and climbers if these are appropriate to the style of architecture. The material used for the terrace will naturally be influenced by the material of the building to which it is attached. Because the terrace is the first link on the horizontal plane between house and garden it must partake strongly of the character of both if it is to be effective. The architectural details of the house can often be reflected in the patterning and surface treatment of the terrace also, giving a further close link between the vertical and horizontal elements. Proportion is important and the classical width for a terrace is that it should equal the distance from ground to cornice (or in our

case the eaves) as though, indeed, the face of the house were reflected again upon the ground. Although, where a bungalow is concerned the terrace would need to be wider to compensate for the low wall of the house behind. If you have not the space to allow for a terrace of this width, you should seriously consider whether a terrace is appropriate at all, or whether the whole of the garden should not in effect be the terrace in the form of an outdoor room directly related to the house. Not all this space needs to be paved, of course, because it can contain a certain amount of planting either in beds or carefully grouped containers. The terrace needs a well defined edge, but unless there is a considerable drop it is better to avoid little hedges or irritating dwarf walls which cut up the view with little advantage. A single step, the full width of the terrace either up or down on to the lawn can be very effective, and even two or three long steps on which groups of easily changed pot plants can stand, will be very effective. The long horizontal lines of the steps will add greater importance to the house or give stability to the details of the garden beyond.

Steps Steps can be very much more than a means of proceeding from one level to another since they can provide interest, excitement, dignity and sculptural form. However, they must be comfortable to use. The formula for step design is that twice the rise plus the width of the tread should equal 26 in. and that, except very occasionally for some specific reason, the rise should never be more than 6 in. An easy proportion is a tread of 17 in. and

Bricks may be laid in various patterns to form pathways, such as the basket-weave pattern (1) and the herring-bone pattern (2). Stepping stones (3) make an interesting and unusual path across a lawn. *Below:* When using precast paving it is best to choose the quieter, muted colors and to use one color only. *Right:* Bricks laid in running bond pattern to form a paved area a rise of $4\frac{1}{2}$ in., but a rise of less than this can be dangerous because it is difficult to see and easy to trip down. In general, the shallower the steps, the broader they should be, but final decisions on both these points will be influenced by the scale and proportions of their surroundings. The form of the step can either be that of a solid block, whether of hewn stone, shuttered concrete or brick, or formed from two distinct parts, the riser (which can be of brick or stone) and the tread formed from stone or precast concrete slabs. In this case the tread should overhang the riser by about $1\frac{1}{2}$ in., to give a deep line of shadow under the edge.

Retaining Walls Although these are strictly vertical features, they seem to belong with steps and terraces and so find their place here. Retaining walls should usually be made of (or at least faced with) the same material as the house to which they belong. If for some reason this is not possible they should be constructed from local stone or other material, or failing that be designed to be completely hidden by climbing and trailing plants. It is naturally essential that retaining walls should retain, and they must, therefore, be built on very solid foundations and can often be helped by a backing of rough concrete and reinforcing bars. Drainage holes must always be left at the base of such walls to prevent water from being trapped behind and undermining the foundations. There was an unfortunate fashion in the earlier years of this century for making stone walls with earth joints. In the cracks were grown suitable plants and ferns but unless they were faultlessly made and maintained they either tended to collapse or become infested with deep-rooted weeds impossible to dislodge without demolishing the wall. Even worse was a fashion for leaving odd holes in the face of walls in order to grow tufts of trailing plants which merely resulted in the face of the wall having a spotty appearance.

Drives and Forecourts These features are the first introduction to house and garden and they should partake strongly of the character of the house to which they belong and should make an appropriate setting for it. The normal pattern of front garden, with a concrete garage run, a narrow bed, a path of some other material and then a patch of lawn and flower beds is very unsatisfactory. Often it could be better replaced by a forecourt, perhaps patterned in brick and paving, which would provide the hard standing needed for the automobile, dry access to the house, and space for planting, in one unified composition. This arrangement of strips of paving making a simple pattern with square or rectangular panels filled with some other hard surface where people and vehicles will pass, and with planting in the outer areas, is very satisfactory and capable of infinite variation. Naturally very solid foundations must be laid where automobiles will stand, but lighter ones can be employed for foot traffic. Long drives, of course, are best made with bound gravel, firmly edged, or with blacktop

with grit or fine gravel carefully rolled in to conceal the black surface.

Decoration

Although the main decoration of the garden will naturally consist of living material, even the smallest garden can absorb one or two decorative objects, particularly if they are also useful. The temptation to have too many things, and to scatter them about as though a place had to be found for them somehow, must be sternly avoided if the garden is not to look like a cross between a junk dealer's yard and a garden center. The placing of any object whether seat, urn or fountain must appear the inevitable outcome of the garden design, rather than an afterthought.

Urns Under this heading one can include all kinds of plant containers from the simple

half-barrel stained or painted, to the most elaborate marble urn on a pedestal. The first consideration must be whether the principal attraction is to be the container or the planting. If the latter then simple shapes and generous provision for soil and good drainage are all-important. When possible choose containers which do not require maintenance in the form of painting, nor have to be taken into the house or under cover to preserve them from winter frost which is necessary with much earthenware and pottery imported from abroad. Pleasing groups can be built up using pots and bowls of contrasting form, some old and others new, or other appropriate materials (but hard shiny plastic is not appropriate in outdoor settings). Such groups might have a permanently planted backbone of small shrubs and foliage plants, leaving space for seasonal bedding which can be

Left: A wide band of paving stones between the border and the lawn allows the plants to trail freely over the edge and the grass may be mown easily. *Below:* Informal steps made from stone slabs well cemented together for safety *Above right:* A well-placed seat in a quiet corner. Hostas provide color and interest. *Right:* Plants in various containers. *Far right:* Colorful petunias in a half barrel augmented with the addition of plants such as lilies in normal pots, set out while they are blooming and then removed to make way for something else. If the urn is to be considered as a decoration in itself it may require no planting or only some quiet trailing plants of a recessive nature. Again a simple design is best, chosen to blend with the general character of the garden. Good reproductions of antique pieces cast in reconstructed stone are obtainable.

Statues It is unfortunate that there is so little good modern sculpture available for the garden although an approach to the local art institute might produce interesting results. However, there are some good reproductions of antique pieces available in reasonable materials and visits to demolition sales and antique dealers can be rewarding. One does not have to stick to figures as such – a coat of arms on a stone panel, a large finial from a roof top or even a broken column tactfully draped in ivy would all be acceptable in the right setting. Primarily the intention is to draw the eye to a certain point, or to add an element of scale or punctuation to a part of the design. Both the placing and the object must appear inevitable in the given setting – if not, then the thing is irrelevant. Fine detail and materials are wasted in the garden, and provided that the balance, proportion and outline are good, one seldom looks more closely. Pale materials such as

stone or marble are best against dark simple backgrounds, for example an alcove in a yew hedge, whereas bronze or lead figures are better in the open, seen against sky, water or mown grass. Elaborate carving or molding needs to be placed in full sunlight against shadow, simple shapes or openwork modern 'constructions' in metal are most effective when viewed in silhouette against the light.

Fountains Much the same remarks apply to fountain figures as to other sculptures although seen in full sun with reflected light playing round them and themselves reflected in the waters of the pool, they need to be of higher visual quality than a statue half hidden in a shadowy grove. What is more we are always attracted to water, particularly when it is moving, and will examine its source carefully. If no suitable figure can be found, a simple shell or bowl, fixed to appear floating on the surface of the water, with a plain jet of water rising and falling in it, can be very effective and far better than a third-rate concrete Cupid. What is more the birds will bathe and drink in the shallow bowl, giving added life and pleasure. Where the pool is designed for reflection, a sedate bubble fountain scarcely disturbing the water surface, will be more appropriate.

Sundials, Birdbaths and Other Objects The sundial is a useful pivot and center of attraction round which all kinds of garden patterns can evolve, but if one is honest and

thinks of it in these terms only, because its original use no longer applies, then its true relevance in the garden is doubtful. Better, perhaps, a birdbath of good design, preferably with small fresh water pipe laid on so that the water can be changed daily without resorting to buckets. This will bring far more life and interest to the garden than the silent dial. Apart from these obvious pieces there are other decorative possibilities, to be used with restraint and understanding. A sculptured plaque or the old carved keystone from a doorway set in a black piece of wall, urns or finials on tops of gate piers or seen against the sky on the parapet of a house, an old bust giving point to the end of a free-standing wall, all have their place in certain types of design. For those who wish to relive their childhood there are great quantities of gnomes, concrete or porcelain animals with colored eyes and other such things. But they belong to the world of the permanent funfair and have nothing whatever to do with gardens as such.

Seats and Furniture These items fall into two distinct classes, the permanent and the transient. Permanent seats and even tables can be both decorative and useful, either in natural wood or stone, or in painted wood or metal. The thing is to choose pieces which are not only pleasing in themselves but which reflect exactly the character of the place for which they are intended. One has only to experience the absolute absurdity of finding an elaborate white painted Victorian cast-iron seat beside a natural forest pool, to appreciate the importance of fitness for purpose. Where such permanent seats are to be used frequently they will need cushions kept easily to hand and covered in some plain dark colored or at least neutral fabric. Since flower color and the pattern of leaf or branch are what matters in the garden, obtrusive stripes, checks and vulgar florals should never be used. Where possible it is better to use cane, bamboo or woven willow furniture.

Structural Planting

Structure does not only imply walls and terraces but it also includes trees and shrubs, hedges and grass which together form the natural masses and voids, vertical and horizontal elements. It is important at this point to realize that planting can be structural or decorative and that the two purposes should not be confused nor should they necessarily be combined. Failure to understand this basic principle has resulted in too many weak and shapeless gardens, lacking in character and purpose.

Trees These are the largest structural element in the garden, providing shade, wind shelter and a degree of privacy. Not many small gardens need or have room for large wind-breaks, but a group of trees can filter the wind or reduce the impact of drafts between buildings. In any type of structural planting it is the structure which comes first, so that even in a small garden a group or a curved line of trees providing shelter and privacy should consist of one variety of tree only. Choose the right tree where form, habit, coloring and cultural requirements fit that position and stick to it. The result will be visually and practically far more satisfactory than an ill-assorted collection of odd specimens, some of which will flourish better than others. Trees can also be used formally to provide architectural green elements on a large scale. Grown as espaliers or cordons they have long been familiar in the vegetable garden but standard trees planted 8–10 ft apart, with their branches trained out espalier fashion above the top of the wall or fence, can soon provide privacy in small gardens. When the branches meet they are stopped and the ensuing twigs are trimmed to form what amounts to a hedge on legs. This training or pleaching of trees has been employed for hundreds of years in Europe, although it is more often encountered now in France than in England. The same basic method can be used to form open tunnels, arbors or complete pergolas of trees, trained out on wooden frameworks while their branches are supple. But such constructions require quite a lot of maintenance. Feathered trees of suitable varieties, that is those with branches all the way down the trunk, before the nurseryman makes them into standards, can also be planted 3 ft. apart or so in lines and with careful trimming can be induced to form tall hedges. They will need careful support in the early stages, before they grow together.

Hedges The first thing to decide is the purpose for which the hedge is to be planted. If it is to be green architecture, a neatly trimmed expression of geometric shapes, then the hedging material should be chosen with that in mind, since certain plants clip more neatly than others. Again, if the hedge is to form a background to decorative planting it is essential that its tone should be dark and its texture matt. For such purposes yew would be ideal, while the loose growth, pale shiny foliage and coarse texture of cherry-laurel would be utterly unsuitable. If the hedge is to be largely free growing and is

to be decorative in itself, then provided the growth of the chosen shrub is neat, well-furnished to the ground and suitable for growing in lines, the field is open for experiment both with evergreen and deciduous shrubs. However, if you wish to hide something it is pointless to try to do so with material which is in itself eye catching. If you think of those lines of Lombardy poplars which simply draw attention to the industrial developments which they are intended to hide, you will understand what is meant.

Shrubs A certain amount of structural shrub planting in the garden is often needed in addition to the backbone of trees and hedges, to give the required sense of form. But such shrubs must have the inherent quality of structure. Their solidity, form, habit of growth and tone value are of much greater consequence than the detail of flower or berry. Indeed, as a general rule all kinds of structure should be recessive in character, forming a background to the decorative objects and planting placed within it.

Grass This is almost the only structural planting on the horizontal plane and as such plays a very important part in many gardens. Where grass is hard to grow much greater thought must be given to the design and use of grass areas. Grass will not withstand a great deal of hard wear and continue to look attractive, so the first requirement is to design the grass shapes in such a way that they are not over used and that they are easy to maintain. To fulfil its function as a unifying, green matt textured carpet, holding together and flowing through all the other elements, the grass must be kept cut and, where appropriate, the edges trimmed. Simple forms and uncluttered shapes are, therefore, best. Do not try to achieve precise architectural forms with grass banks–the idea is attractive but in the long run the neat angles and sharp planes are impossible to maintain unless they are hand cut with shears, an almost impossible task. Where you are dealing with large areas, good use can sometimes be made of the contrast between smoothly mown grass and grass cut less frequently which can provide a home for bulbs and wild flowers of all kinds. Beautiful interlocking abstract shapes in two tones of green can be achieved in this way, although a very careful program will have to be evolved for cutting the longer grass, to ensure that the various bulbs and flowers it contains can all flower unharmed.

Plants as Decoration

'Isn't it pretty, I simply must have one of those' is a phrase which has rung the death knell of any number of gardens. Bought for some particular moment of flower or fruit, with no thought for the character or balance of the garden as a whole, any number of unrelated plants jostle in beds and borders, competing for our attention. The only effect

they achieve is of discord and unease. If only those same people would first decide on a general theme, and then work within these limits, they could have satisfying, even spectacular results with no greater expenditure of time and effort.

Plant Form Color photography has a great deal to answer for, since it is quite easy to take a pretty picture if the colors are harmonious, without thinking about composition, whereas with black and white work form, texture, light and shade are all important. All plants, if well grown, have a distinct outline which can be reduced to abstract shapes so that you see them as pyramids or circles, verticals or horizontals, or some combination of these elements. Not only do they have form, they also have texture so that they can be seen as coarse or fine, light absorbent or light reflecting and so on. Before deciding on any individual plant it is much better to evolve a thoroughly satisfying planting scheme in purely abstract terms as an arrangement of sizes and shapes, forms and textures. Only when this composition is correct should you try to translate these elements into plants, but even then it is better to think of those plants as though they were black and white photographs, so that you can appreciate their formal structure, the shadow patterns which they cast, the way they hold their leaves or flowers, and whatever other qualities they may possess, without being confused by the separate problem of color. And you must think of them at all times of year, the bare pattern of winter twigs as well as the heavy foliage of high summer, the hanging clusters of fall fruit as well as the delicate wreaths of spring flowers, so that your picture is properly balanced. Once you have got this far you must choose from among plants of suitable shape and habit, those which will grow in your particular conditions.

The Fourth Dimension In all garden work, time is a fourth dimension. No planting scheme is static and the effect next year, in five, ten, twenty-five, fifty years will all be different but must all be considered from the outset. Fortunately some plants mature quickly; others are very slow to reach maturity. So unless your outlook is very short term—and even then we should not think only of ourselves, but of those who follow—the slow growing shrubs and trees must be put in first, spaced at the proper distances, while the large areas between will contain shrubs and plants of moderate growth. Between these can grow annuals, herbaceous plants, bulbs and shrubs such as brooms and tree lupins which mature quickly and are equally short lived. Before making a final choice, always try to see the plants you are proposing to use, growing in some park or garden at various seasons of the year. Some may have very off periods which may make them unsuitable for your purpose. Never choose a plant, however apparently attractive from the sole evidence of a cut spray exhibited at a flower show as this can be very deceptive.

Color The vexed question of color, usually uppermost in people's minds, has been left deliberately until the last. To begin with, it is as well to remember that green is also a color, and that one could make very satisfying compositions in that color alone. Then there is the difference between the transient color of flowers and the longer lasting color of foliage, especially where conifers and evergreens are concerned, as they provide some of the brightest and most permanent color effects. Do not neglect, either, the color of tree trunks and young shoots which can do so much to cheer the winter landscape. The easiest way to handle color, particularly in a small area, is to have a single theme and to stick to one color at a time. For instance, a small garden, or part of a large one, planted in shades of yellow and gold only, in a general setting of gray foliage can be most exciting, and is comparatively simple to achieve. If this single color device is found too constricting, then it is best to keep firmly to one range of color. Flower and foliage colors are generally based on blue or yellow. In the blue range, beside blue and purple are all the purplish-reds, crimsons, bluish-pinks and whites which have no hint of yellow in them. In the yellow range are scarlet, orange, flame, yellow pinks such as salmon and apricot, creams and whites inclined to yellow. If you work within one range of color, setting it against a background of complementary foliage colors, the end result will still be very harmonious. Of course people with an eye for color can achieve exciting contrasts between the two ranges but unless you are in that class it is wiser to play safe. With care, you can have quite different color effects at different times of year, provided that the background planting is suitably neutral. The great thing to avoid is dotting little patches of unrelated color about the place, each one taking away from the impact of its neighbors rather than building up into a total effect. Bedding plants or bulbs in boxes of mixed colors should never be used unless a particular patchwork effect is required against a very plain setting. A single variety or perhaps two or three shades of one color are so much more useful. The blue quality of the light has an important influence on flower color as it brings out and intensifies the color of pale flowers giving them a life and character they could never have in a clearer less misty atmosphere. In the same way the blue light makes many of the bright color contrasts which appear so stimulating in the strong yellow light of other parts of the world appear merely tawdry and vulgar. Bright colors should always be seen in sunlight, pale colors and white flowers gain added quality in the shade or against a shadowy background. If the garden is going to be used at night, the ability of some pale flowers to glow in the dark can be used to create a new pattern quite different to the familiar daytime scene.

Making the Design

Practical Considerations At this stage it is as well to take a piece of tracing paper, place it over your survey and put down the basic facts about the way in which you use your garden in diagrammatic form. For instance there is an obvious desire line between the gate and the front door, back door, garage entrance. There is probably one sheltered place in which you like to sit in the sun (your designing can create any shade you may need). There may be other inescapable factors, such as the need to park a boat or trailer in a particular position, other desire lines from back door to back gate and so forth. Although some of these may be shifted slightly, you cannot ignore them and they will have an important bearing on the final

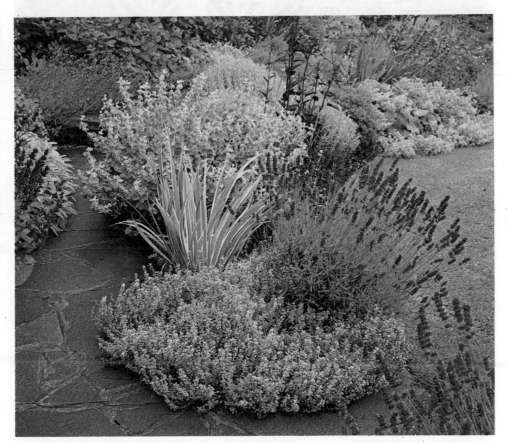

Left and above: The shades of red in these borders are subdued by the greens of the foliage
Far left: Trees, shrubs and hardy perennials, with different rates of growth, show how time must be considered as the fourth dimension when planting a garden. *Right:* The various shades of green can be used effectively. Among other plants shown here are thyme, lavender, ballota, and *Iris pallida variegata*

Top: A town garden can be made more interesting if full use is made of the different shapes of plants

Above: A corner of a paved garden in which various plant forms and colors are used effectively

solution. Obviously the garden should not only be attractive but convenient. Vegetable gardens are best near the kitchens they are to serve, so are small children's play areas. Areas for entertaining and general outdoor living must have good access from the house and should preferably not be approached by steps which make the carrying of chairs, cushions and loaded trays a hazardous undertaking. The service yard not only needs good access to all parts of the garden (and remember if you have steps, that barrows and mowers will need an alternative ramped approach) but also easy access to the road so that peatmoss, manure and other garden materials can be delivered without being carried through the rest of the garden. The tennis court must be on a north/south axis to avoid problems from low lying evening sun, whereas the swimming pool needs to catch as much sun as possible but is better kept out of sight of the house in northern areas of the country because of its dreary aspect in the winter.

Putting Thoughts on Paper The practical needs and the site factors such as views, movement of sun and shadow etc., will form a framework almost as definite as the boundaries of the garden, and between these two sets of conditions you will have to prepare your design. Certain objects of fixed size, such as a tennis court, can be drawn to the same scale as the survey and cut out, so that they can be moved easily about the plan, but for the rest you must begin to sketch out your ideas on thin sheets of tracing paper stretched over the original survey. At this stage do not worry too much about keeping your lines precisely straight or every detail of the work neat; there is something inhibiting in working with exact precision when the most important thing is to get ideas to flow. Possibly you will already have a design in mind, and if this works out easily when put on paper all well and good. If it does not fit in properly, then do not try to force the issue. It is very easy to get obsessed with some particular idea and then make everything conform to it, but the result is seldom satisfactory and always looks forced and contrived (which indeed it is).

Do not be afraid of discarding partly finished sketches which do not seem to work, but do not throw them away altogether as some further development of your ideas may solve the problem which prevented one of them from satisfying you completely. If you are absolutely stuck it is better to leave the work altogether and return to it again. Sometimes it is even helpful to reverse all the decisions you have made—put the sitting area in the shade, the compost heap by the living room and so forth. Although naturally your finished plan will not really be like this, the total reversal of all preconceived ideas will often free your mind so that designing in exactly the opposite way to your first intentions can provide a key to some problem which will allow you to proceed as you wished.

All the time you are sketching things on

paper, you must remember that the lines you are drawing represent real objects on the ground. It is important to visualize exactly how each element will look in that position. In your imagination you should be able to walk along the paths, mow the lawn, climb the steps, push a barrow round the corners and live at all times of day and all seasons of the year, in each projected design while you are drawing it.

If you can do this, you may well discover all kinds of faults and problems which are not immediately apparent. The path may not be wide enough to walk on with ease once the plants in the adjoining bed have grown to their full size, the curve of the lawn too tight for the turning circle of the mower, the corners too sharp for a fully loaded barrow, the steps steep and uncomfortable. This imaginative exercise is very important and can save making mistakes which would be difficult to remedy at a later stage.

Having satisfied yourself on paper that your scheme is a good one, you should draw it up neatly on tracing paper making sure that all the elements are exactly to scale, and that the shapes you are using are suitable for the materials you propose to use. For instance to design a $3\frac{1}{2}$ ft. wide path to be made with 2 ft. square slabs is obviously not practical. Any patterns you propose to make with different types of hard surface can also be worked out at this stage as can the positions of things such as water points and electric points for use with lights or electrical equipment, heating systems for the greenhouse, the useful luxury of a telephone point in a summer house or changing pavilion far from the house, and similar items.

Never use your original plan out of doors. In most towns there is a drawing office, art shop or similar place where dyeline prints can be made quite cheaply from your tracing paper plan. In this way you can have several copies made as you are bound to want to write in notes, mark distances and so forth on one, use another on the job where it will get wet and muddy, and keep clean copies for reference.

Before starting work you should always work out your whole design on the ground using pegs or bamboo canes and balls of cheap string. The most thorough way of doing this is to draw a grid on the plan, mark out the same grid full size on the ground, and then measure each point where the lines of the design intersect those of the grid on plan and transfer those measurements to the grid on the ground. In fact, it is seldom necessary to do this, as a certain number of measurements from known points such as the corners of the house, and measured positions on the boundaries, will generally suffice. At this point your paper scheme may need a little adjustment. However pleasing shapes may appear on plan, when translated to the ground and seen in perspective they do not look the same. Curves particularly look more extreme and may well need easing out to achieve the shape you intend. A garden hose can be very useful

EXTEND TO HERE & REDUCE HEIGHT OF SCREEN WALL TO 5'6" FROM TERRACE

The original rough plan, as shown on page 13, has now been completed. The narrow path in the front garden has been widened and the manhole cover in the lawn has been hidden. A decorative tree in the bottom right hand corner provides protection. Plants which will thrive in shady places have been planted in the cold, damp area near the house. At the back, bands of paving stones provide access to the

shed, garbage cans, etc, the poorly shaped forsythia has been removed, and a brick retaining wall has been built to raise the bed to the level of the terrace in drawing curves on the ground as it is heavy and solid enough to push into shape and will give the effect of the line more easily than a string which needs to be held in place with pegs.

Once the shapes are clearly marked out, do not rush to turn them into reality. A garden is a long term investment which may even go on to give pleasure to your children and grandchildren. Leave the pegs and strings in place for a few days. Look at the layout from the bedrooms, the bathroom, the kitchen as well as the living room. See how it strikes you as you arrive home at night and leave in the morning, what it looks like in sun and shadow, by day and night. A solution which perhaps looked clever and original when first drawn may seem more contrived than restful when you have seen it on the ground for a few days.

When construction is in progress, you can be thinking about the planting, deciding on the heights and general shapes needed for shrub masses, the exact position and outline needed for trees. Tall bamboo canes can be stuck in to represent tree trunks and looked at from every angle to ensure that when planting time comes no mistakes are made—nothing is more irritating to find, having dug a magnificent hole and put in a shrub or tree with infinite care, that it is not quite in the right place.

One should never think of the garden completely in isolation, because there is always an interaction to a greater or lesser extent between interior and exterior views. Some buildings – for instance ancient cottages with tiny crooked windows set comparatively high – exclude their gardens, creating a cosy, womb-like effect within their low-beamed rooms. But most other houses acknowledge their gardens to a greater or lesser extent and in the modern house with its wide windows, the garden becomes almost a part of the interior. When it comes to color, texture and shape, therefore, every effort should be made to integrate the furnishing of the house and the planting of the garden to create a total picture.

Not only color gives continuity, because different types of plant have very strong associations outside themselves. Laced pinks, auriculas, small moss roses, striped tulips and similar flowers with their air of Meissen bouquets belong to neat eighteenth century gardens with box edged beds and espalier fruit trees. Formal dark camellias, ferns, the roses 'Madame Pierre Oger' and 'La Reine Victoria', lilies-of-the-valley and certain other lilies are strongly Victorian in effect, while rhododendrons, hydrangeas, heavy-headed paeonies and swags of rambler roses or climbing roses belong to different kinds of Edwardian gardens.

One can give the garden a more contemporary feel by concentrating on trees, grass, shrubs and hedges rather than individual flowering plants. Beautiful effects can be obtained by the juxtaposition of differently colored trees and shrubs, ranging from light silvery-gray to dark green. Hedges of yew, box or other evergreens will provide a basic background against which perhaps one or two flowering plants, restricted to varying

Below left : It is not difficult to train laburnums over an archway to produce an effect like this, even in a small garden
Above : Roses and clematis on a pergola. Varieties can be chosen to flower at different times to ensure long continuity of color

shades of one color, can be grown. If you have a very large garden, it is possible to achieve the effect of a wilder landscape by allowing trees and plants to grow naturally without a formal arrangement.

To sum up briefly then: decide exactly what kind of garden you need for your particular family and way of life, and consider how best this garden can be expressed in materials and shapes which will accord with your house and its surroundings. Make sure that everything down to the last plant and cushion has a definite part to play in the picture you are trying to create, and never think of any one element as an object in its own right. Remember the pleasure you can give to others who see your garden from the outside only, and do not be in too much of a hurry. It may take fifteen to twenty years to obtain the finished garden if you have planted a large number of slow-growing plants and shrubs, although during this period there will still be many beautiful things to enjoy as the plants develop. A garden is never really finished: as plants die and others are grown to take their place its aspect is always changing, but the general layout of the garden will remain the same. Some of the things you build and plant will last a century or more.

Right : A traditional English-style garden

Bulbs, Corms & Tubers

Bulbs, corms and tubers are the specially modified resting stages of certain plants which enable them to live, dormant (e.g. not actively growing), through some adverse climatic condition (usually drought). They all contain a store of concentrated food, and dormant buds, some of which in the bulbs and corms may have embryo flowers already formed inside them, so that when suitable growing conditions recur, the leaves and flowers are produced in a very short time. Because they are not actively growing they can be dug up, transported and sold in shops with little check to the future growth of the plant.

Bulbs contain their food reserve in either special swollen scale-like leaves, loosely packed round the new bud, as in a lily bulb; or in tightly packed leaf bases encircling the bud, as in daffodil, tulip or onion (allium). In the second type the outside of the bulb is protected by dry, often skin-like, leaf bases. All parts spring from a very flattened stem area known as the 'plate', from the underside of which the roots grow.

Bulbous plants are members of either the lily family or the amaryllis family or of the genus *Iris*.

Corms differ from bulbs in that it is the stem, often flattened, which contains the food reserve. The main bud arises from the center of the upper surface; other buds may often be seen at the sides. Protective scales are dry. Roots form around the edge of the scar of the previous year's corm.

Each bud is capable of making a new corm and so small cormels arise around the main corm and spread the plant. The plants producing the corms we are considering all belong to the Iris family.

The swollen area of a tuber may arise from a stem or from both root and shoot, but although a stem tuber will produce roots when it starts to grow it is rarely that a root tuber which has lost its shoot (bud) will grow another. Tubers may have scale leaves but more usually lack these. Tubers are not a method of propagation as small ones are not formed from them, as in bulbs and corms.

Tuberous begonias, dahlias and gladiolus are dealt with in the section on Favorite Garden Flowers.

When to Look for Bulbs, Corms and Tubers in the Shops The main outdoors planting season for bulbs, corms and tubers is in the fall with bulbs on sale from mid-August to late November.

Lilies have a very long growing season and, if they have had to be transported over great distances, may not arrive in time for the fall selling season. Buy them as soon as they arrive and plant immediately. If soil conditions are very bad pot them and plant out when conditions are good in the spring, do not store them.

Many corms, though dormant during the winter, are not completely hardy and are liable to be killed in the soil before growth can start in the spring. These are stored in frost-proof conditions and sold from late January to the end of April, for planting as soon as the soil (not the air) is frost-free. If potted up in a frost-free greenhouse they can be had in flower much earlier. Treated in this way they can be planted out as soon as air frosts are unlikely, but must be hardened off first.

There is a small group of plants which flower in the fall, often well before their leaves, the main growth of which is not till spring. They have a short summer dormant season and are sold in July-August.

Bulbs are sometimes marked 'prepared'. This means either that they have been heat treated so that they will flower before their normal season, or that they have been cool stored past their normal flowering season so that they flower later. These are available in August-September and should be planted immediately for growing indoors for Christmas flowering.

Greenhouse bulbs include those which are available in the fall but make their growth during the winter, e.g. ixias, *Gladiolus nana*. These can, of course, be planted outside in mild districts, and in any case can be put out by the spring. Holding them dry until the spring is not always a success. They also include those plants which while they can be grown quite successfully outside can be obtained much earlier by growing in a cool house. Varieties of narcissi and tulips which

Mixed crocus

will stand this treatment are often marked as 'forcing' varieties.

True greenhouse plants are those which need a higher temperature than is likely to be experienced outdoors, especially during the period September to May. Their planting seasons vary enormously and depend not only on the season of flowering or growth but also on the amount of heat that can be supplied.

How to Select Bulbs, Corms and Tubers in a Shop Is the shop temperature suitable? If it freezes at night half-hardy bulbs may be damaged and go soft on the outside. If it is too hot (e.g. near the radiator or other source of heat), the bulbs will wither or start to grow shoots prematurely without root growth, and some fungal and bacterial diseases will attack bruised tissues. Tubers liable to wither, such as dahlias, should be prepacked in polyethylene. See that this is intact. Embryo buds are damaged by withdrawal of water during withering and also by high temperatures. Prepared bulbs lose the effect of the treatment in such conditions. Expensive bulbs should be in wood shavings, sawdust or peat moss.

Are the bulbs etc. clean? Dirty stock can carry soil-borne diseases and is likely to prevent you looking for bruising and other troubles. Is the stock well housed and properly labelled with variety name and grade as well as price? Narcissus bulbs can be single-nosed, double-nosed or mother bulbs. The more 'noses' the more main growths, each with a flower. Is a mother bulb, with three noses going to give you a better display than three single-nosed bulbs–compare the prices. Single-nosed bulbs are best for using with a bulb planter, as they will not stick in the hole, but fall to the bottom. Bulbs for naturalizing should not contain a lot of very small bulbs which will not flower the same year.

Corms are sold by size, the cms denoting the circumference of the corm. Very big corms have fewer advantages than big bulbs, e.g. it is usually better to have one good spike per gladiolus than one and a small one. Exhibition growers choose medium size corms. Large cyclamen corms have fewer years ahead of them and often take longer to settle than small ones.

Hyacinths of medium size give one good spike against one and a small one of the very large bulb. It may pay you to pick off the small one when it starts to emerge to keep the good spike from growing lop-sidedly.

If you can handle the stock before pur-

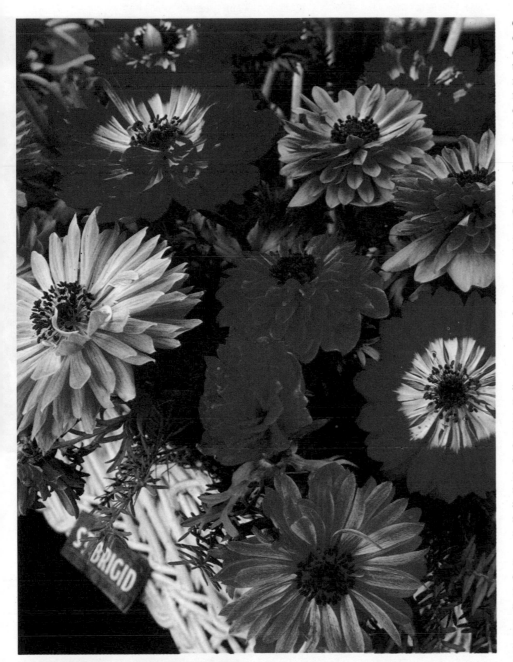

chasing do so carefully. If a sample of daffodils or irises has some bulbs which are obviously underweight and are soft to the touch leave the lot as it will be impossible to make sure you are not introducing narcissus fly larvae (maggots) or other pest which has eaten out the interior. If when you carefully move a scale leaf or two you find a fungal disease and you are prepared to dip the bulbs in a fungicide before planting, hyacinths may still be all right to buy, but irises with ink disease (black patches) are to be avoided and so are tulips and gladioli with scabby patches (tulip fire and gladiolus scab). Why buy trouble? Show the shopkeeper and he can report to the grower who should not legally be selling diseased stock. Lily bulbs which have the scales falling off probably have basal rot. A similar disease may cause narcissi to have a faulty base plate without a complete ring of roots. Such bulbs spread their diseases to the soil and to other bulbs. They should be burnt.

The only other troubles likely to affect bulbs are not readily seen at this stage. They are best avoided by buying from a reputable source. Virus diseases may cause striped or yellowing foliage or broken color in the flowers (desired in some tulips). There is no cure for virus diseases. Aphid eggs may be on the bulb scales of small irises and aphids may attack any bulb in growth; especially susceptible are the fleshy leaves of lachenalias. An aphid spray or (indoors) aerosol should be used as soon as they are seen, as aphids may spread virus diseases.

In the shop it now remains to see that the assistant knows how to handle the stock and does not shovel up corms and tubers with a metal scoop that can remove the buds, and also be sure that each bag is properly labelled. It is maddening to have to wait until the bulbs flower to know that the hyacinth you thought was the blue one is in fact red.

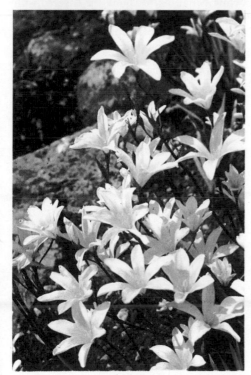

Above: St Brigid anemones, available in brilliant colors, make fine cut flowers
Right: Sinningias, better known as gloxinias, are among the most decorative of greenhouse plants
Left: Tritonia crocata, Saffron Tritonia, is a close relative of the montbretia

Below: Bulb planting chart

General Cultivation

Outdoors Although bulbs, corms and tubers carry their own food supply it is only good for one year at most and if you wish to have flowers year after year it is essential that they should be well fed. This is especially true of the highly-bred hyacinths, tulips and crocuses and some of the smaller irises. Always prepare the whole of the area to be planted in a bed, do not just dig out the holes, as these may act as drainage sumps in heavy ground, rotting the bulbs. Bonemeal and coarsely ground hoof and horn meal should be added to the soil, and also peatmoss and sharp sand if the soil is very heavy. It is worth making up plenty of such a mixture for putting round the bulbs or corms wherever they are to go. When the ground has been prepared scatter the bulbs on the surface where they are to go and then dig out hole by hole with an ordinary trowel or a specially marked bulb trowel, planting and covering as you go. In this way you will not be digging where you have just planted. In formal planting mark out the distances along a trench.

If the bulbs are to go in turf this can be cut out with a special bulb planter after scattering the bulbs in drifts. If the bulbs are small and the turf close it is easier to lift the turf with a turfing iron or flat spade and place the little bulbs on the soil underneath, sprinkling the peatmoss, sand and bonemeal mixture around them before replacing the turves carefully. Do not beat the turf down hard, but it can be watered to settle it.

Depth of planting Roughly speaking and if no special instructions are given the depth at which to plant a bulb is not more than twice its depth of soil above it and not less than its depth. Some bulbs make droppers (short stems) to take the new bulb to the optimum depth, others make contractile roots which pull the new bulb down. It may be possible to protect a half-hardy bulb outside from the effects of frost by planting it deeply, but some do not remain there but work their way to the surface.

Indoors, plants can be grown in pots filled with ordinary potting compost, in bowls or other undrained containers filled with a specially prepared bulb fibre, which is usually a fibrous or sphagnum peat with crushed shell and small pieces of charcoal, to prevent the fibre from becoming sour as a result of water collecting in the undrained bowl. The fibre has little feeding value, though the bulbs can be fed very carefully with a liquid feed. If grossly overwatered the roots in a bowl will drown for lack of air. If you think a bowl has been overwatered tilt it very carefully, holding the fibre in with one spreadeagled hand and drain off such water as appears.

Bulbs usually require a well–drained media and a general compost consisting of 2 parts of loam, 1 part of peatmoss, 1 part of sharp sand, plus 1 lb of bone meal per bushel of mix will suit the majority of bulbs we use for

Planting bulbs to flower indoors
1. A good layer of moist bulb fiber is placed in the container. 2. The bulbs are placed in position. 3. More moist fiber is pressed around the bulbs, leaving the tips exposed. 4. The container is placed in a polyethylene bag before being plunged under sand, ashes, etc.

indoor decoration. However, it is often more convenient to use a compost based on peat-moss, which is cleaner and lighter.

Plants for the house should be started into growth in a cool dark place such as a cold closet or a plunge bed in the garden. This is merely a flat area on which the pots can be stood and covered completely with about 2 in. of moist peatmoss, sand or washed ashes. These will fill in the spaces around the pots as well and keep the temperature very even. Boards or bricks can be placed round the outside or the bed can be made in a cold frame. Do not put bowls in a plunge bed out of doors or they may be flooded by rain. It may take as long as eight or ten weeks in a plunge bed before the pots are ready to bring into a warm place. By this time the bulbs or corms will have made a good root system which can take up enough water and food for the emerging shoot. If put into the warm straight away the shoot will often grow faster than the roots can feed it and the plant will collapse. Specially prepared hyacinths can generally be brought into the warmth after six weeks in the cool. The narcissi 'Paper White' and 'Soleil D'Or' do not seem to be any the worse for being brought straight into the warm if the bulbs have been properly ripened.

The planting depths for outside should not be followed inside. Large bulbs are usually planted with little or no compost over the last $\frac{1}{2}$–1 in. If the neck of the bulb is above the surface take care not to water into it. Plant the bulbs close, but not actually touching, and choose a bowl deep enough to contain all the roots which will otherwise come out at the surface, or through the drainage holes of too small a pot. Pack the compost down round the

bulbs which will shrink as the food is used up and may need top-dressing later on. Leave a space at the top to take the water.

A very fine display of daffodils can be obtained by planting a double layer in a large, deep pot. Plant the lower layer about half way up the pot and cover all but the tips of the noses with compost, then stagger the top layer above them so that all the noses have a straight run to the surface. Cover the top bulbs as usual.

Bulbs in the Greenhouse These are planted in pots often with sharp drainage below. Small bulbs should be covered with their own depth of soil and large ones may be only half submerged. Bulbs near the surface are more likely to need careful staking.

Bulbs being forced for cutting are often planted in deep flats as appearance is not usually so important. Otherwise they are treated as bulbs in pots.

Bulbs for the alpine house or cold frame are usually small; they are often planted in pans but if a plant needs a deep root run a pot should be used. Very good drainage is necessary.

Tulip 'Engadin'

Lilium 'Cinnabar'

Anemone blanda

Feeding Throughout the time that the plant is growing actively it should be fed. In pots there may be enough fertilizer in the compost to feed the plant for six weeks, but after that liquid feeds should be given every two weeks. If a plant makes most of its growth during the winter it will need feeding during this season, even if you normally stop feeding in the fall and do not begin again until spring. Generally speaking the fertilizer used should be one with a rather high potash content to assist ripening which is very important in many bulbs from warm parts of the world. Never feed a plant in dry soil, always water it first.

Watering Many bulbs fail completely if they become dry at any time when they are growing, but only plants which are growing strongly need much water in winter as less is lost by evaporation than in summer, and such plants should be watered on the soil only as water on the leaves causes too sharp a drop in temperature and can lead to fungal infection becoming serious.

Ripening This is the name given to the complex chemical processes which occur inside the plants both before and after the leaves die down. Potash appears to be essential for these changes, as are the gradual withdrawal of water and, in many but not all, baking by sun heat. The plants most in need of this are those which experience drought during their resting period, e.g. nerines.

It is important with plants needing sun ripening to ensure that they do not get smothered with other plants, including weeds. Internal changes continue during the resting period and can be adversely affected by incorrect storage temperature.

Resting When the leaves of a bulb start to turn yellow watering must stop and the bulb be rested, unless experience shows otherwise. All the bulbs, corms and tubers listed here have a definite resting period. Many can stand being dried right out; tulips like a thorough baking.

As far as many greenhouse pot plants are concerned the bulbs or corms are best left in the soil in the pot until it is time to start them into growth again. This prevents them withering as much as they would do in the open air and keeps them relatively safe.

Plants in the garden should be left to finish their growth before lifting, cleaning and sorting. If they are not to be lifted it may be wise to mark the site.

Grass with bulbs in it must not be mown until the foliage turns yellow, nor should the foliage be picked with the flowers. The leaves make the stored food.

Bulbs in bedding schemes may need to be moved before it is time to rest them. They can be lined up in trenches to finish their growth. Bulbs which were started in pots and plunged up to their rims in the formal beds are easier to cope with.

Bulbs which have been forced for use in the house or for cutting should not be used again for this purpose the following year.

Starting into Growth Bulbs still in pots can be put into fresh compost like new bulbs, or some of the old compost can be removed and replaced by fresh, or the whole pot ball can be transferred to a larger pot and top dressed. It is usually, but not always, necessary to water the soil to start growth. If a pot shows signs of growth it must be watered, but the amount given at first is usually modest.

Suitable sites There is some bulb, corm or tuber suitable for growing in almost any place you can name, though most prefer a sunny position. The following are some possibilities:

(1) Display beds devoted to nothing else: Hyacinths, greigii tulips, dahlias

(2) To grow through other bedding plants: Darwin tulips through wallflowers or forget-me-nots, Cannas through summer bedding plants or annuals

(3) To edge beds: Dutch crocuses, short alliums, muscari, zephyranthes, chionodoxa, scillas, puschkinia

(4) In clumps (groups) in mixed borders. Tall alliums, crocosmia, daffodils, summer snowflakes, crown imperial, camassia, some lilies, galtonia, dahlias, tall tulips

(5) In beds for cutting: gladioli, dahlias, narcissi, irises (Dutch, English and Spanish), St Brigid and Du Caen anemones, some alliums

(6) Naturalized in long grass: Narcissi (daffodils)

(7) Naturalized in short turf: Tiny daffodils, fritillaries, muscari

(8) Naturalized under deciduous shrubs or trees: Anemone blanda, eranthis, cyclamen, showdrops, colchicums

(9) Naturalized in thin woodland: Some alliums, English bluebells, erythroniums, ornithogalum, Galanthus nivalis

(10) On rock gardens: Chinodoxas, choice fritillaries, small irises, small narcissi, crocus species, some alliums

(11) Grown in alpine houses or cold frames: Winter-flowering crocuses, small irises, cyclamen, Anemone blanda, small fritillaries, fall snowflakes, small South African corms

(12) Tender bulbs for outdoor planting in favorable localities: Ixias, nerine, amaryllis, pancratium, babiana, sternbergia, sparaxia, crinum

(13) In warm but moist places: Tigridia, ranunculus, chincherinchee

(14) Grown in cool borders among evergreen shrubs: Most lilies, galtonia, colchicums

(15) Grown in pots or vases on a terrace: Hyacinths, daffodils, begonias

(16) Grown in pots or bowls indoors: Hyacinths, daffodils, early tulips, crocuses, muscari, scilla, dwarf irises, hippeastrum, vallota

(17) Grown in pots in a cool greenhouse: Begonias, gloxinias, lachenalias, veltheimias, nerines, hymenocallis, eucomis, some lilies and begonias in hanging baskets

(18) Grown in pots or boxes in a cool greenhouse, but for cutting: Gladiolus colvillei. Dutch, Spanish and English irises, ixiolirion, freesias, tulips, narcissi, tritonia, chincherinchee, acidanthera

(19) In an intermediate greenhouse: Cyclamen, gloxinias, smithianthas, vallota, gloriosa as a climber, and achimenes in baskets

Achimenes (Gesneria family) These greenhouse plants require a growing temperature of at least 60°F (16°C). Their fragile stems can be supported by twigs or allowed to fall out of a hanging basket. The small trumpet-shaped flowers, freely produced, are in shades of pink, violet blue and purple. The tubers are small scaly rhizomes, best started into growth in a box of peatmoss and sand and then transferred to the hanging baskets when growing. In 5–6 in. pots space them 2–3 in. apart in a compost of 2 parts loam, 2 parts peatmoss, and 1 part sand, and cover by $\frac{1}{2}$ in. They can be started into growth from February to April for succession of bloom. Once in growth never allow them to dry out and keep the atmosphere humid by spraying or red spider mite may attack. Pinch out growing points to cause branching, especially when in hanging baskets. When in flower transfer to a cooler place will ensure a longer display, as will shading from direct sunshine. Dry slowly after flowering and store in their soil in a dry place at a temperature of 50°F (10°C).

Plants can be increased by soft cuttings in spring in a warm propagator, by seeds sown in March, in a temperature of 65–70°F (18–21°C), or by removing scales and sowing them like seeds. Forking tubers can be divided.

Acidanthera (Iris family) *A. bicolor murielae* is a half-hardy corm with $2\frac{1}{2}$–3 ft. spikes of fragrant white flowers with maroon in the throat. These plants require a long growing season and in the northern part of the country this can be overcome by starting them in pots in a cool greenhouse in spring and planting them out in late May or June. Alternatively they can be grown in beds in a cool greenhouse. Stake to prevent wind damage outside and lift before frost occurs. Where the weather is mild, corms may be planted outside where they can remain.

Allium (Lily family) The ornamental onions are bulbs which produce heads of small flowers in soft colors on stems ranging from 3 in. to 4 ft. There are good plants for naturalizing in thin woodland, but most need a sunny site on the edge or in the body of a mixed border, on a rock garden or scree or even the protection of an alpine house. Many make good cut flowers. Some have a strong onion smell when bruised, therefore plant these where they will not be brushed against. The wild ramson *Allium triquetrum* (white) can be naturalized.

Amaryllis (Amaryllis family) (belladonna lily) This plant can only be grown outdoors in mild areas of the country. It requires a well-drained but well-fed border such as under a south-west wall where it receives the maximum amount of sunshine.

The large heads of fragrant, trumpet-shaped flowers are soft pink, but there is a good white called 'Hathor' and various deep pink forms. Flowers appear in September on 2–3 ft. stems before the leaves.

The bulbs are very large and work their necks out of the soil, but it is wise to start them just below the surface and to mulch in the fall. Leave them to form dense clumps before lifting and replanting.

Anemone (Ranunculus family) *A. coronaria* hybrids, the poppy anemones, have large flowers, on 8–12 in. stems, in bright red, violet, lavender and purple, some shaded with white, single in De Caen varieties and semi-double in St Brigid. In mild districts flowers can be had in succession by planting the irregularly shaped tubers at any time. In colder areas they may be planted in the fall in frost-proof cold frames to provide cut flowers. They require a rich moist well-cultivated soil.

A. blanda has little tubers. Soak the tubers before planting in the fall $1\frac{1}{2}$ in. deep in a sunny position, or under deciduous shrubs pruned off the ground. White, pink, blue, violet and carmine forms occur.

Babiana (Iris family) (baboon plant) *B. stricta* makes an excellent cool greenhouse pot plant. It has 1 ft. high spikes of magenta, blue, purple or sulfur-yellow flowers and

Allium roseum flowers in June

Name	Height in feet	Flower Color	Type of head	Flowering	Suitable site
aflatuenense	$2\frac{1}{2}$–4	rosy-purple	dense, globular	end May	border, cutting
albopilosum	2	lilac	large, globular starry flowers	June	sunny border, cutting
beesiana	$\frac{3}{4}$–1	bright blue	hanging head	July	rock garden
caeruleum (syn. azureum)	1–2	blue	globular	June–July	sunny border
cernuum	1–$1\frac{1}{2}$	pink	hanging head	June	border, strong smelling
cyaneum	$\frac{3}{4}$–1	turquoise	loose heads	July–August	rock garden
elatum	$2\frac{1}{2}$–3	rosy-purple	globular	end May	border
flavum	$\frac{3}{4}$–1	yellow	loose heads bell flowers	July	border edge
giganteum	3–4	lilac–violet	large globular	July	border, cutting
karataviense	$\frac{1}{2}$–$1\frac{1}{4}$	white–pale pink	large globular	July	border, cutting
moly	$\frac{1}{2}$–1	yellow	dense heads, starry flowers	June	naturalizing, border edge
narcissiflorum	$\frac{3}{4}$	rose	hanging head, bell flowers	July	alpine house, scree in peaty compost
neapolitanum	1	white	loose heads	April–May	cool greenhouse, cutting
var. cowanii	$1\frac{1}{4}$	white	loose heads	March–April	finer form
oreophilum var. ostrowskianum	$\frac{1}{2}$–$\frac{3}{4}$	rose	globular	May	rock garden, border edge
pulchellum	$1\frac{1}{4}$–2	rose purple	loose heads, pointed in bud	July–August	border, cutting
rosenbachianum	2–$2\frac{1}{2}$	lilac	large, globular	May	border
roseum	$\frac{3}{4}$–1	pink	loose heads	June–July	sunny edge, rock garden
schubertii	1–2	rose red	loose heads	April–May	border
siculum	2–3	dull red, striped blue-green	large, loose heads	May–June	border, cutting, flowers O.K. rest smells
sikkimense	$\frac{1}{2}$–$\frac{3}{4}$	dark blue	tiny heads	June–July	alpine house
sphaerocephalum	1–2	purple	globular	June–July	border
stipitatum	$2\frac{1}{2}$–3	rose purple	globular	July	border, strong smelling

Amaryllis belladonna needs a warm situation to produce its colorful flowers

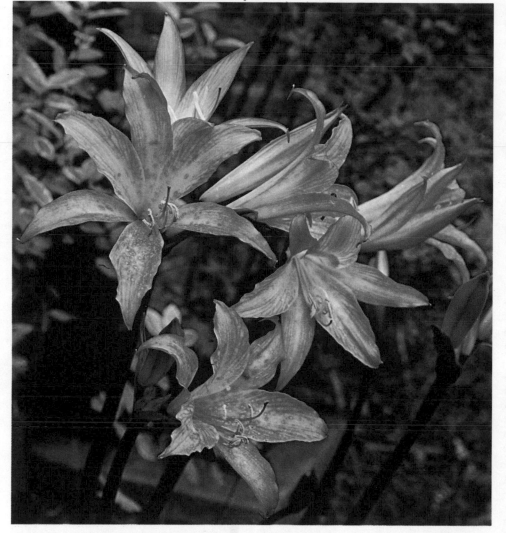

The Indian Shot, *Canna indica*

Propagation methods

All kinds of bulbs and corms normally increase in number naturally. Thus a double-nosed daffodil will produce at least two bulbs which may in turn have more than one nose. Gladiolus corms frequently produce large numbers of cormels around the new corm. If left in the soil in a frost-free place these would quickly make flowering size corms. If the corm is lifted the cormels can be detached and grown on in a frame. Some bulbs make many small bulbs instead of one or two flowering size ones. Tulips need specially good feeding to prevent this happening too frequently.

Some lilies, e.g. *Lilium tigrinum*, make bulbils in the axils of the stem leaves. These can be collected and grown on when ready to drop to the earth. Sparaxis make small bulb-like cormels at the lower leaf nodes. These can be collected and grown on.

Most lilies can be increased by detaching the bulb scales and pushing them, bottom edge down into a pan of sand and peatmoss; in a close propagating frame tiny bulbs will form on the lower edges.

Tubers are not so easy to increase as bulbs and corms and if the tuber is not of a shape that allows it to be cut into two or more pieces, each with a growth bud as well as some stored food it may not be possible to increase the plant other than by seed. Some are regularly grown from seed, e.g. cyclamen, others also from cuttings during the early stages of growth, e.g. dahlias, smithianas. When buying tubers it is sense to buy small ones which have only recently been grown from seed, as these will have a longer life.

Some bulbs can be grown to flowering size from seed in little over a year, but they are the exceptions. Most of the South African corms and many lilies flower in the third year, but tulips and daffodils may take as long as seven years to produce a flowering size bulb from seed.

can be grown in sheltered borders in milder parts of the country.

In the greenhouse treat all these like freesias grown from corms but plant babianas deeper or they will make droppers to pull themselves down. Outdoors they flower in June, but in pots are earlier.

Camassia (Lily family) *C. quamash* varies in flower color from purplish-blue to creamy-white. It likes good soil and produces fine clumps of flowers 2–3 ft. high. It flowers in June–July, but all the flowers on a spike come out at once, so giving it a rather short but striking flowering season. *C. leichtlinii*, with rather larger individual flowers on 3 ft. stems, has the same color range and is very fine in its cream forms. All have large bulbs which need planting at least 4 in. deep.

Canna (Canna family) (Indian shot) Cannas have swollen rootstocks which will withstand drying right out during their resting period, October to March, though they do best if packed in just moist peatmoss or left in the soil in their pots, only being knocked out to re-pot in fresh rich compost. The varieties and hybrids of *C. indica* produce large, brilliantly colored flowers, mainly yellow, orange or scarlet, often spotted with a darker red, on 2½–3½ ft. high stems, with broad green or dark red leaves.

Cannas are tender and need cool house temperatures even when at rest. Brought into leaf by moderate watering in March and kept growing steadily, in good rich soil, they will flower from June until the fall. If used outside, bring in before hard frosts occur. When necessary split up the clumps carefully before planting.

Chionodoxa (Lily family) (glory of the snow) *C. luciliae* produces its bright blue, white centered starry flowers in March or April, several on a 6-in. stem. It enjoys sunny places but does not object to some shade after the leaves have died down. It should be fed moderately. Plant in the fall 2 in. deep and leave the bulbs until they are overcrowded. It can also make a useful pan for indoors, planted in the fall and treated like hyacinths in pots.

Colchicum (Lily family) (autumn crocus) The earliest to flower is the European wild *C. autumnale*, the rosy-lilac buds pushing up without any leaves. A whole group of 2-in. flowers is usually produced from each bulb and each flower flops over as soon as it has finished.

The best to grow are *C. byzantium* and *C. speciosum*, and their hybrids which have much bigger flowers rather like rose-pink or white tulips on stalks about 9 in. to 1 ft. high in September. Some like 'Water-lily', are double flowered. Others have chequered markings like fritillaries.

The big bulbs need planting during their short dormant season, in July for *C. autumnale*, and August for the later ones.

No leaves are produced until the following spring, when *C. byzantium* and *C. speciosum* produce big pleated leaves, which are much too dominant for the edge of most borders. They are best planted in front of shrubs or as a border to a vegetable plot where they enjoy the rich, limed soil.

Crinum (Amaryllis family) *C. × powellii* is a hybrid, hardier than either of its South African parents. It is a large bulb, up to 1 ft. high, which can be grown in tubs and wheeled out of a cool greenhouse during the summer, or planted permanently under a sunny wall in mild places. Its 2½–3 ft. stem has several buds on top which open successively, each flower being a large trumpet. It may be had in flower any time from July to September and varies from pure white to deep pink.

Spring planting is best; the necks gradually work out of the soil and need protection during cold weather.

Crocosmia (Iris family) The montbretias (*C. × crocosmiiflora*) are hybrids; the common form is hardy in milder areas. It has 2–3 ft. branching stems of small, trumpet-shaped, orange-red flowers, produced freely, even in poor soil, during August. They appreciate a sunny situation and moderate feeding. There are named hybrids with much bigger flowers which have the merit that they do not have long spreading stolons.

C. masonorum, 2½–3 ft., has arching growth. The deep orange-red flowers, produced in July, all face upwards.

Corms of choice varieties can be lifted in October and replanted in spring, but are best kept in slightly moist peatmoss.

Crocus (Iris family) The large-flowered Dutch hybrids flower in March, and the little species crocus, by careful planning, will give flowers from September to March. The fall and winter flowering ones are available from July to August and need to be put in immediately, as some will flower almost at once. The rest can be planted at any time during the fall. The Dutch varieties are fine for edging beds and naturalizing in grass and the tiny ones are for alpine house or rock garden or, in many instances for planting under deciduous shrubs, or even for naturalizing in short grass (try *C. zonatus, C. speciosus, C. aureus* and *C. tomasinianus* for this). Plant the corms with not above 1 in. of soil over them. The flowers of the fall flowering ones will come up before the leaves. Do not cut grass with crocus naturalized in it until the leaves have died down. The corms like to be well sun baked during the summer. All may be grown in pans, the Dutch ones in bulb fiber also, but must not be brought into a warm place until the flowers are nearly out.

Cyclamen (Primula family) The tubers of cyclamen get bigger each year but do not make other small tubers, which are only obtained from seedling plants, the sole method of increase. The large greenhouse cyclamen obtainable around Christmas have been raised from seed. Unlike most of the small 'hardy' cyclamen the best display is from the

new plant raised from seed after about 16 months in a warm greenhouse, and although the corm such a plant forms can be saved and grown for many more years it is not usual to do so.

Species cyclamen are sold either in leaf or as dry corms; the latter should be treated with great care as the loss of the dormant buds sets the plants back permanently. Corms should be lightly covered with sieved leaf mould or peatmoss with some sharp sand and bonemeal, and should not have this pressed down. Similar compost should be used as a top-dressing every fall before the flowers or leaves appear.

All cyclamen have the characteristic swept-back petals, many have a color range from white through pink to carmine, often with throat markings of carmine on the pale flowers, and many have beautiful marbling on their leaves.

Endymion (Lily family) (bluebell) The English bluebell is *E. non-scripta* and the Spanish bluebell, *E. hispanicus*. The latter have stiffer, heavier-looking flower spikes and are usually sold mixed in color, deep blue, sky-blue, lilac pink and white. Both flower in May and can be naturalized in thin woodland, but the bulbs of the Spanish bluebell are more frequently planted in groups in mixed borders or naturalized with daffodils in grass. All do best deep planted in the fall and should not be disturbed unless necessary.

Eranthis (Ranunculus family) (winter aconite) *E. hyemalis*, produces bright yellow flowers in February–March on 3–4 in. stems, each ruffled with green bracts. It forms excellent ground cover if planted 2 in. deep under deciduous shrubs or trees and will naturalize by seed. The tubers are obtainable in August and should be planted without delay. The plants divide successfully immediately after flowering.

Other kinds occasionally available are *E. cilicica*, with finely cut bronzy foliage, and *E. × tubergenii*, which lasts in flower longer but does not spread by self-sown seed.

Erythronium (Lily family) *E. dens-canis*, the dog's tooth violet has spotted leaves and nodding pink or white lily-like flowers on 6-in. stems in March–April. Plants do well on soil containing lime and in light woodland, where they can be naturalized. They can also be grown in short turf or among shrubs, but must not become dried out in hot weather. Plant about 3 in. deep in fall.

Other good erythroniums are *E. revolutum* 'White Beauty', to 2 ft. high, white marked with brown, April–May; *E. hendersonii*, pink with purplish markings stem, April; *E. tuolumense*, light yellow with bright green unspotted leaves; its best hybrid is 'Pagoda', 1–1½ ft. All appreciate top-dressing with sieved leaf mold.

Eucomis (Lily family) (pineapple flower) Eucomis are cool greenhouse plants with thick stems which, in July and August, have small greenish-yellow flowers round the top foot or so of stem, which ends in a tuft of leaves – pineapple fashion. The best known is *E.*

CROCUS
Dutch varieties: * = good forcer.
*Yellow Giant, early; *Vanguard, lilac, early; *Jeanne d'Arc, Kathleen Parlow, white; King of the Striped, lilac on white; Pickwick, lilac on purple; Queen of the Blues, lavender; Paulus Potter, reddish purple; *Purpurea grandiflora, violet.
Fall and Winter flowering species*:
zonatus, September, pale lilac, good naturalizer; *leucopharynx*, September, lavender with white throat; *speciosus*, September–October, blue, veined violet, all are good naturalizers; *albus*, white; Artabir, lavender; *aitchisonii*, china blue, pointed petals; Oxonian, deeper blue; Cassiope, October, blue; *cancellatus cilicicus*, September, lilac with purple veins; *sativus cashmeriana*, September–October, rosy lilac, the saffron crocus; *longiflorus*, October–November, lilac, striped purple, must have sunny spot, scented; *medius*, October–November, lilac-purple; *ochroleucus*, November–December, cream with orange base; *laevigatus fontenayi*, December–January, violet-blue, striped brown outside.
Spring flowering species:
imperati, January–February, lilac, striped buff outside, good naturalizer; *ancyrensis*, orange yellow, January–February, many flowers per corm, good indoors; *sieberi* Hubert Edelsten, January–February, vigorous, bluish-violet with yellow throat and white shading; *aureus*, January–February, yellow spreads well by seed; *chrysanthus*, this has many named varieties, mostly excellent in pans; Blue Bird, purple and white; Blue Pearl, silvered blue; Cream Beauty, short, cream; E. A. Bowles, yellow, striped bronze; Ladykiller, purple and white; Snowbunting, lilac and white; Zwanenburg Bronze, deep yellow bronze outside; *tomasinianus*, January–February, variable shades of lavender, good naturalizer, seeds freely. Whitewell Purple is a dark selection; *balansae*, February–March, orange-yellow, pans; *biflorus weldenii*, February–March, white or blue and white; *etruscus* Zwanenburg, February–March, lavender blue, pans; *susianus* (Cloth of Gold), February–March, orange, striped bronze, pans, beds; *versicolor picturatus*, March, white, striped purple, beds.

CYCLAMEN
The following can be grown outdoors*:
August–September flowering:
C. europeaum, fragrant with round leaves, *C. neapolitanum*, very hardy, marbled leaves.
September flowering: *C. graecum*, velvety leaves. **October–November flowering:** *C. cilicium*, young leaves red beneath, marbled on top. **December–March:** *C. coum* (including *atkinsii, hiemale, ibericum, orbiculatum* and *vernum*) hardy and very variable, flowers small on short stalks. **February–March:** *C. creticum* must be in shade, white flowered, fragrant, leaves red beneath. **April–May:** *C. repandum*, requires deep planting in sheltered woodland.
Cool house kinds include *C. cyprium*, October flowering, fragrant, as are *C. balearicum* and *C. pseudibericum*, February–March flowering and *C. persicum* March–April flowering, *C. libanoticum*, one of the loveliest, needs an alpine house.

Left: *Crinum powellii* is one of the most beautiful of summer-flowering bulbs. In milder gardens it may be grown outdoors. Otherwise, it is a fine plant for a cold greenhouse or conservatory, in a large pot or tub. *Bottom left:* The large-flowered Dutch crocus, available in a good color range, are excellent for naturalizing in grass. The grass should not be cut until the crocus leaves have died down. *Below:* *Colchicum speciosum*, one of the autumn crocuses, produces its flowers in September. The large leaves do not appear then, but in the following spring. It is a plant for naturalizing towards the front of a shrub border. Plant the large bulbs in August. *Bottom:* *Crocosmia masonorum*, a relative of the montbretias, grows to 3 feet tall and has large, upward-facing, orange-red flowers.

Top: The winter aconite (*Eranthis hyemalis*) flowers in early February, or even earlier in a mild winter. *Right: Fritillaria imperialis,* the crown imperial, flowers in April or May. *Far right: Erythronium revolutum,* Mahogany Fawn Lily, a native of the west coast

comosa, (syn. *E. punctata*). In parts of the country where the weather is milder Eucomis may be grown outdoors. The large bulbs are best planted in 5-in. pots in February or March. Rest dry in the pots from November to February, in a frost-free place.

Freesia (Iris family) These are usually offered as colored hybrids, the funnel-shaped flowers of which may be white, cream, yellow, orange, pinks, blues and mauves. The newer hybrids are usually scented whatever their color. The wiry, arching stems may reach 2 ft. They are excellent for cutting from February to May.

Plant 7–9 in a 6-in. pot of compost composed of 2 parts loam, 1 part peatmoss, 1 part well-rotted manure and 1 part sharp sand in August, cover to a depth of 1 in., and put into a cool plunge bed under damp peatmoss for a month until roots are well formed. The greenhouse must be well ventilated, with as dry an atmosphere as possible, with a minimum temperature of 45°F (7°C). The leaves must be supported. After flowering they can be kept growing, and when the weather is

fit, transferred to a north-facing frame till leaves die down when they should be stored in their pots, dry, until August. Specially prepared corms can be planted outdoors in April for flowering in late summer.

Seed sown in flowering size pots in a propagating frame at 65–70°F (17–21°C) in February–March and grown on cool without any disturbance can be had in flower in November, by bringing them into the greenhouse (minimum 45°F (7°C) in September.
Fritillaria (Lily family) *F. meleagris,* the snake's head fritillary will grow in most garden soils, especially in thin woodland, but must not dry out completely. It has hanging, wide, bell–like flowers, often white with green markings or purplish–pink, often chequered, on 1–1½ ft. stems in April.

F. imperialis, the crown imperial, may reach 3 ft. and has a ring of orange or yellow flowers high on the stem, which is topped with a tuft of leaves. The large bulbs are less liable to rot if started on their sides.
Galanthus (Amaryllis family) (snowdrops) The common snowdrop, *G. nivalis,* has many varieties which extend the flowering period from January–February to as early as October with *reginae–olgae* which flowers before its leaves, to the end of March with 'Straffan'. The most readily obtainable are *atkinsii,* about ten days earlier than the usual type and

much taller (6–8 in.); 'Arnott's Seedling', another vigorous kind, and the double form. All grow well in thin woodland and should be planted 3 in. deep in the fall.

G. elwesii is best grown in full sun and should be given a chance to ripen without being overgrown by vegetation. The leaves are broad and the flower stems 6–8 in. long.
Galtonia (Lily family) (Cape Hyacinth) *G. candicans* produces 3–4 ft. spikes of greenish-white, hyacinth-type flowers in summer. It makes fine groups in the middle or back of mixed borders. The large bulbs are best planted 5–6 in. deep in spring in mild areas, and when the weather is fit, transferred to a north-facing frame and once established can be mulched instead of being lifted in the fall. They do best in rich, moist soil.
Gloriosa (Lily family) One of the lily family's few climbing plants, this needs a warm greenhouse, 70°F (21°C) minimum from February to August. The large tubers should be planted 2 or 3 in 8-in. or larger pots of compost consisting of loam, peatmoss, well-rotted manure and sand in equal proportions, or in warmer parts of the country, planted out in the border. Cover with 2 in. of soil.

G. rothschildiana has long-stalked, bright red flowers like a Turk's cap lily, often with a yellow throat. The leaves have tendrils at the

Right: Gloriosa rothschildiana

Leucojum vernum, popularly known as the spring snowflake, has white, green-tipped flowers which appear in February and March, on 6–8 in. stems, with bright green foliage. The bulbs should be planted in September, about 3 in. deep in sunny or partially shaded situations

tips and these enable the plants to cling to whatever support is provided.

Other varieties of *G. rothschildiana* and also *G. superba*, the glory flower, are sometimes seen with yellow flowers. All need moist, but well-drained soil and a humid atmosphere in summer. *G. superba* can be grown in an intermediate house. From September to January, when completely dry, all can be housed at 55°F (13°C).

Hippeastrum (Amaryllis family) *H. pratense* is the hardiest of these tender bulbs and can be grown outside in warmer areas, or where the weather is more severe in a cool greenhouse. It makes a good pot plant, producing 1 ft. stems topped with 2 or 3 deep red trumpet-shaped flowers with yellow throats in spring or early summer.

The better known large greenhouse hybrids–sometimes incorrectly called amaryllis – can be had in flower practically any month of the year in the greenhouse or indoors depending on their treatment. Bulbs put on sale from August onwards have been prevented from spring flowering and should be planted as soon as available, when they can be had in flower from November onwards. (These may be described as 'prepared bulbs'.) They are followed by normally early-flowering varieties which carry the flowering season through to April. Later varieties carry the bloom round to July or even September if the bulbs are planted in succession.

The 3 ft. stems are usually topped with four enormous trumpet flowers which open in quick succession; there are frequently 2 or more stems per bulb. The bulbs are very large. Place them half into 4- or 5-in. pots with a cane at the side. The flower stems may come up before the strap-shaped leaves or with them. They must be fed liberally. Any small bulbs which have formed may be removed and should be grown on without any drying off. Dry out the big bulbs as the leaves yellow, store the pots on their sides in a temperature of 50°F (10°C), and leave them thus for about three months before starting the bulbs into growth. In warm parts of the country, bulbs may be planted outdoors.

Hyacinths (Lily family) The Roman hyacinths usually have several slender, loosely packed spikes per bulb; the more spectacular, stiff spiked 'Dutch' ones have the flowers closely packed. Both are very fragrant.

The Dutch hyacinths may be bought 'specially prepared' and these should be planted as soon as available to give flowers in the greenhouse or indoors by late December or early January. They force well.

For indoors they may be grown in water only, in special hyacinth glasses (discard the bulb after flowering); singly in 3½-in. pots,

or close packed in larger pots or bowls, with their 'noses' just uncovered. Use bulb fiber for bowls and start these in a garage or shaded frame so that they are not drowned by rain; pots may be plunged in a cool place outdoors. Do not bring them into the warmth until the roots are well developed and the shoot is starting to grow (usually from 8–10 weeks). Then keep in full light.

Unprepared bulbs which flower about 3 weeks later may be planted in succession to flower from January to April.

Outdoor hyacinths should be planted in rich soil at least 5 in. deep in October–November. Use only unprepared bulbs. If used for formal bedding they should be replaced each season, but if fed well will make good clumps among shrubs.

The Roman hyacinths, which are white, pink or blue, are sometimes used on rock gardens, but are at their best indoors.

After flowering allow the leaves to die down naturally.

Ipheion (Amaryllis family) *I. uniflorum* (sometimes listed as *Brodiaea, Tritelia* or *Milla uniflora*), is a small South American, early-flowering bulb producing white or pale bluish-mauve funnel-shaped flowers 6 in. above the mass of grassy leaves. It needs well-drained soil in a sunny place. Plant in the fall 1½ in. deep. *I. uniflora* is hardy to Zone 8 but may be grown further north if given protection in winter.

Ixia (Iris family) (African corn lily) These corms may be grown outdoors where the weather is favorable and make interesting cool greenhouse plants flowering after the first spring rush. They are sold in mixed colors including deep carmine, white with red or yellow or purple center, orange or yellow sometimes bronze outside, on 2 ft. tall arching stems. The flowers close in dull weather but when open fully make a wonderful display. Pot the rather small corms fairly close together and covered with at least 2 in. of soil. Ripen well after flowering.

I. viridiflora, an arresting plant, has blue-green flowers, darker at the centre, in May–June. It needs cool greenhouse treatment and proper ripening. It should be given bonemeal and protected from slugs and small snails.

Ixiolirion (Amaryllis family) *I. montanum* is a slightly tender bulb worth growing as a cut flower in a cool greenhouse in the north or outside in mild areas. The flowers, on 15–18 in. stems, are in shades of blue, sometimes with violet banding, and bloom in May or June, *I. ledebourii* being earlier than the darker *I. palasii*. Plant in the fall in well-drained compost.

Lachenalia (Lily family) (Cape cowslip) These cool greenhouse bulbs flower in early

spring in airy conditions. Plant 5–7 close together in 5-in. pots in August–September, cover with ½–1 in. of compost and cover with moist peatmoss in a plunge bed until growth starts. Then place the pots in a well-ventilated cool greenhouse.

L. aloides nelsonii has spikes of golden-yellow flowers tinged with green; other varieties have paler yellow flowers and may have red markings. *L. bulbifera* (syn *L. pendula*) has coral red or salmon tubular flowers marked with purple and green.

Lachenalias often have pleasantly mottled foliage. Their flower spikes are long lasting if kept at 45–50°F (7–10°C), but if brought indoors into 65°F (18°C) or more, the plants soon suffer. Ripen well after flowering by standing on a shelf under the ridge of the greenhouse, and reduce the water until the bulbs are dried out.

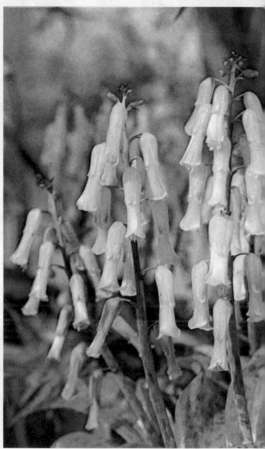

Above: Lachenalia tricolor nelsonii, a fine bulb for the cool greenhouse
Below: Ipheion uniflorum makes a good spreading clump, with grassy leaves, smelling of onions when crushed
Right: One of the many beautiful hippeastrums

Leucojum (Amaryllis family) (snowflake)
L. aestivum, the summer snowflake, flowers
from April to May. It has heads of white,
green-marked flowers on 1½–2 ft. stems and
dark green strap-shaped leaves, and its large
bulbs increase rapidly to make big clumps if
planted in fairly damp soil. Plant 5 in. deep.

L. vernum has only one or two good sized
flowers per 8 in. stem, but very fine bright
green foliage and flowers that are out in
February–March.

L. autumnale is less hardy but often does
well in a sunny, sheltered border. The flowers
on 6–8 in. stems are very delicate looking,
tinged with pink (not green) and usually come
before the leaves. Plant 3 in. deep.

Lilium (Lily family) (lily) Lilies are often
sold packed in peatmoss or wood shavings to
retain their moisture and protect them. They
should be planted as soon as available, from

HYACINTHS

Some recommended Dutch varieties:
Those marked with an asterick will force
satisfactorily, even though some are late
flowering.
White: *Arentine Arendsen; *L'Innocence;
Mme Sophie (double); Carnegie (late);
Ben Nevis (double). **Yellow and salmon:**
*Yellow Hammer; *Prince Henry; *City of
Haarlem (late); *Orange Boven (Salmonetta)
salmon. **Pink–pale shades:** *Anne Marie
(Ann Mary); *Princess Irene; *Lady Derby;
Chestnut-flower (double). **Pink–deep
shades:** *Pink Pearl; Queen of the Pinks.
Red: *Jan Bos (not for bedding); Eclipse
(double); *La Victoire; Victory Day (double);
Mme du Barry; Scarlet Perfection (double).
Pale Blue: Bismarck (unreliable forcer);
*Delft Blue; *Myosotis; Queen of the Blues.
Dark Blue: *Ostara; *Marie (Mary); King of
the Blues. **Purple:** Amethyst, lilac mauve;
General Kohler, double lavender.
Multiflora hyacinths are specially treated
Dutch varieties which produce several small
spikes in place of one large one.
Roman hyacinths are sold by color,
though 'Rosalie', a soft pink, is often
available.
Species for rock garden: *Hyacinthus
amethystinus*, 8 in.; *H. azureus*, 8 in. Both
flowering March–April.

RECOMMENDED LILIES (Liliums)
Height in feet: 'C' indicates lime tolerance
Cup-shaped flowers (upward facing)
croceum (2½–4) June–July: deep orange;
dauricum (2–3) July–Aug: yellow, orange,
spotted maroon or black; **hollandicum
(umbellatum)** (2–2½) June–July: yellow to
orange-red; **Mid-Century Hybrids** (2–4)
June–July: lemon yellow to crimson, some
reflexed.

Bowl-shaped flowers (outward facing)
auratum (4–8) Aug–Sept: gold rays on
white, crimson spots, fragrant. Good pot plant;
Crimson Beauty (4–5) August: crimson rays
and spots, otherwise similar. Good pot plant;
Imperial Silver (5–6) August: all white with
vermilion spots, petals reflexed at tips;
Imperial Gold (5–6) August: yellow rays and
maroon spots, petal tips reflexed.

Trumpet-shaped flowers (outward or
partly downward facing)
Aurelian hybrids (4–5) July: yellow,
apricot, pink or white colored centres;
Black Magic strain (5–6) June–Aug:
white, heavily shaded purple outside, fragrant;
brownii (5) Sept: white, heavily shaded
maroon, slightly fragrant; **canadense** (3)
July: orange-yellow, rather bell-shaped, long
flower stalks. C; **candidum** (4–6) June–July:
white, fragrant, the Madonna lily. C;
Golden Clarion strain (3–5) July; yellow to
gold, selected from the Aurelian hybrids, C;
Limelight (4–6) July: Chartreuse yellow,
shaded green, fragrant; **Olympic hybrids**
(4–5) July: white, soft pink or pale green,
shaded outside, fragrant. C; **Pink Perfection
strain** (5–7) July: fuchsia pink, fragrant;
regale (3–4) June–July: white, shaded
yellow within and purple outside, fragrant. C;
rubellum (1–1½) June: pink, 2–4 flowers
only, fragrant, likes shade.

Reflexed Pendent Flowers (the most
reflexed are known as Turk's cap lilies).
amabile (2–3) July: orange-red, black spots,
pungent smelling, grow among shrubs. C;
Bellingham hybrids (3–6) July: yellow,
orange, red with maroon to black spots, some C.
Shade, Shuksan (3–4) orange spotted maroon
is a named variety; **Bright Star** (3–4) July:
almost flat, nearly outward facing flower in
which the petal ends only are reflexed, white
with orange star-shaped centre; **cernuum**
(1–2) June–July: rose, spotted purple,
fragrant. Flowers from seed in 3 years. Plant
on rock garden or with low cover;
Chalcedonicum (2½–3½) July: scarlet.
The red Turk's cap lily. C.; **Corsage** (3–4)
June–July: outward-facing soft pink and
cream with maroon spots. Anthers sterile,
producing no pollen, so useful as a cut flower.
Will force; **davidii** (4–5) July–Aug: orange-
red, spotted brown, likes partial shade. C;
Fiesta hybrids 3–5 July: yellow, orange to
dark red with maroon or black spots;
hansonii (4–5) July: light orange, spotted
brown, some shade. C; **Harlequin hybrids**
(4–5) June–July: pink, lilac, old rose, purple,
white and cream, spotted maroon. C; **henryi**
(5–6) August: yellow-orange with brown
spots, dark purple stems, prefers lime. C;
martagon (3–4) June–July: light purple to
wine red, spotted purple, strong smelling. C;
martagon album (3–4) June–July: the
white form. Both naturalize in grass or light
woodland; **monadelphum** (3–4) June:
yellow, spotted maroon, fragrant. Good on
marls. C; **Mrs R. O. Backhouse** (4–5)
June–July: orange yellow, spotted maroon;
Paisley strain (3–5) June: white, yellow,
orange, tangerine, pink, mahogany red with
maroon spots. C; **pardalinum** (4–6) July:
orange shading to red, maroon spots. Prefers
damp, but well-drained soil with some sun.
The panther lily. Bulbs formed on rhizomes
which spread out from the base of the plant. C;
pyrenaicum (2–3) May–June: greenish
yellow, spotted black, strong smelling.
Naturalizes. C; **speciosum** (3–6) Aug–Sept:
a very variable species with many named
selections, good for forcing in cool greenhouse.
Usually white suffused with more or less pink
or crimson, often with deeper spots. There is a
pure white form; **testaceum** (4–5) June–
July: apricot-yellow, an old hybrid which likes
lime. C; **tigrinum** (4–5) July–Sept: orange-
red or lemon with black or maroon spots. Does
not set seed, but produces bulbils on the stems.
Tiger lily. C.

Cardiocrinum giganteum, formerly known
as **Lilium giganteum**, is closely related to the
lilies and forms spikes upwards of 6 feet, with
fragrant white flowers, in July, and broad
green leaves. It does well in light woodland.

'Golden Splendour' is the name given to a
modern strain of hybrid lilies with
trumpet-shaped flowers

Lilium 'Fire King' a modern Asiatic hybrid lily

Lilium tigrinum produces small bulbils in the leaf axils

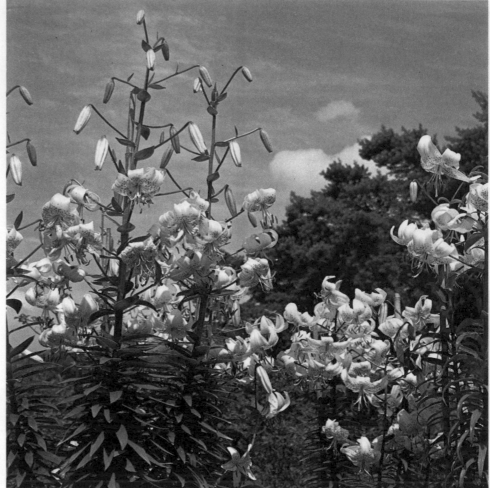

September to January, except for *L. candidum* and *L. testaceum* which are usually moved 'green', i.e. while still in leaf, after June–July flowering. Any lily can be moved successfully immediately after flowering if care is taken to keep the soil on the roots. As some flower in the fall these may not be on sale until soil conditions outside are far from ideal. In this case pot them immediately and plant out later when conditions are correct.

With the exception of *L. candidum* and other European lilies such as *L. martagon* which make roots from the base of the bulbs only, lilies should be planted with soil at least twice the depth of the bulb above it, thus a 2 in. deep bulb would need a hole 6–7 in. deep. This is because many lilies make roots from the stem in the first few inches of soil, in addition to those below the bulb. Sites for such lilies must be weed free, for hoeing near them is disastrous. Many lilies grow wild in the company of low-growing shrubs, the roots of which help to drain the soil, and others are found on steep slopes where moisture is flowing under the surface for much of the year, but all are on well-drained sites, and if necessary special beds must be made with extra peatmoss and sharp sand to retain moisture but allow free drainage. Beds or even hummocks of such soil which will raise the roots and bulbs above the winter water table may make all the difference between success and failure. Some lilies will tolerate lime and others die if given it. Most lilies like to have their flowering stems in the sun,

at least for part of the day, and grow well with a ground cover of low shrubs, or even annuals to protect their roots.

Lily bulbs should be examined to make sure there is no basal rot present, as this will cause the scales to fall away. Such bulbs should be burnt. The bulbs can be dusted with a fungicide to prevent the spread of the fungal disease which causes death of leaves and even of the whole shoot. Once the plants are growing they can be protected from this disease by spraying with a systemic fungicide. Virus diseases are incurable, but their spread can be checked by spraying plants with a systemic insecticide which kills aphids which spread virus diseases. Some lilies are comparatively tolerant of virus diseases, but grow better without them, and others are killed by them. The easiest way to get virus-free stock is to raise the plants from seed and keep them sprayed. This works for most species but garden hybrids will not come true to form or color. However, if 'strains' of lilies are bought rather than named varieties these will have been raised from seed, whereas the others will have been propagated from offsets, bulbils and by rooting scale leaves, and the risk of virus is greater with these.

Most lilies can be grown from seed, in fact *L. formosanum* and *L. philippinense*, white trumpet, cool greenhouse lilies, can be had in flower within a year of sowing the seed. However, many take three or four years and *L. martagon* takes six or seven to reach flowering size. *L. regale* flowers after two or three years.

In selecting lilies for gardens only species with similar cultural requirements to the garden hybrids have been chosen.

The garden hybrids are officially classified according to their breeding, but the shape and position of the flowers are more readily recognized in a garden and these are considered here.

Muscari (Lily family (grape hyacinth) *M. armeniacum* is the kind most frequently offered for sale. It makes little heads of honey-scented deep blue flowers on 6–8 in. stems, with lots of narrow, grassy leaves. Varieties are 'Heavenly Blue', deep blue; 'Cantab', paler blue; and a white form, though the white commonly sold is *M. botryoides alba*. *M. armeniacum* makes fine sheets of color in April–May under deciduous shrubs and small trees and also looks well as an edging plant, but soon spreads. It will also naturalize in short turf. *M. botryoides* makes a good rock garden plant as it is not so invasive; its heads of little bells are smaller and a paler blue.

M. comosum is not so often seen as its variety *monstrosum*, the feather or tassel hyacinth. This has curious heads of dark violet-blue threads on 12–15-in. stems in May–June.

M. tubergenianum has pale and dark blue flowers on the same head. It is best grown on the rock garden where it will flower in March–April.

Plant *M. armeniacum*, *M. botryoides* and *M. tubergenianum* 3 in. deep and the others 4 in. deep in any good soil in a sunny position. They will all grow on limy soil. Split clumps

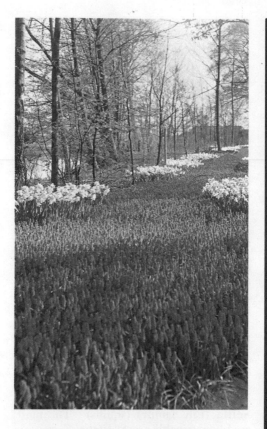

Left : The magnificent flower spikes of *Lilium* 'Sutter's Gold', another modern hybrid strain
Above : A closely-planted 'river' of grape hyacinths (*Muscari armeniacum*)

as necessary after flowering.

Narcissus (Amaryllis family) (daffodil) In gardens the narcissi are best divided into the large hybrids–for use naturalized in long grass, in beds for cutting and display, and in pots outdoors and in–and the small species and their hybrids–for use in short turf, on rock gardens, in pans in the alpine house or indoors. The official classification is based on flower color and form, the relative length of the petal-like central ring or corona (which may be a trumpet, cup or eye) being of importance. The term daffodil is often restricted to the large trumpet forms, the others being called narcissi.

The bulbs of the small species are tiny; those of the garden hybrids are large and sold graded according to the number of 'noses' (growing points). Plant single-nosed bulbs with a bulb planter as there is no danger of them sticking half-way down the holes. The double and triple-nosed bulbs are fine for planting in borders or in pots where a close display of flowers is wanted in the first year.

Grass planted with daffodils must not be cut until the foliage has yellowed, nor should leaves be picked with flowers, for the foliage builds up the bulb with next year's flowers. If the grass is treated with normal lawn fertilizers there is no need to feed the bulbs (other than with bonemeal at planting), but bulbs in short turf must not receive lawn fertilizers as this will encourage the growth of coarse grasses with which the small bulbs will be unable to compete.

NARCISSUS

Varieties specially recommended for forcing are marked *.

In the following list of recommended varieties (separated into those above and below 12in. in height) the sequence of flowering is indicated by letters (VE very early, E early, M mid-season, L late, VL very late). Actual dates from year to year and place to place vary, but the sequence remains relatively constant even when a warm spell following cold weather telescopes the sections.

Yellow perianth, yellow trumpet : Dutch Master (17) VE; *Golden Harvest (18) VE; *King Alfred (19) E; Kingscourt (16) M; Irish Luck (18) M; *Rembrandt (18) E; Unsurpassable (19) E.

White perianth, yellow trumpet : *Queen of Bicolors (18) M; *Trousseau (18) E.

White perianth, white trumpet : *Beersheba (14); *Cantatrice (16) M; Kanchenjunga (14) M; *Mount Hood (18) M; Mrs E. H. Krelage (16) M.

Yellow perianth, large cup, orange, yellow or red : *Carlton (17) E, yellow; Aranjuez (19) M; *Fortune (19) E, orange; Carbineer (18) M; *Red Devon (18) M; *Rustom Pasha (18) M, orange, edged red; *Scarlet Elegance (16) E, red.

White perianth, large colored cup : Green Island (16) M, white, edged yellow; Brunswick (18) E; Penvose (18) E; Polindra (20) M, yellow; Flower Record (16) M; Spencer Tracy (20) M; Sempre Avanti (18) M, orange; Eddy Canzony (17) M, orange red; Mrs R. O. Backhouse (15) L; Louise de Coligny (17) M, pink.

White perianth, large white cup : *Ice Follies (16) M.

Reverse bicolor, large cup : Binkie (16) M; Spellbinder (20) M, deep lemon cup, pale lemon parianth

Narcissus 'February Silver', a dwarf hybrid

Yellow perianth, small colored cup : *Edward Buxton (19) E, orange, edged red; Chungking (17) M, red.

White perianth, small colored cup : Firebrand (19) L, orange; Barrett Browning (16) E, orange red; *Verger (16) M, red.

Double flowered, either one large or 2–4 small flowers per stem : Double White, *poeticus (albus plenus odoratus)* (14) latest of all narcissi (mid-May) white, fragrant; Golden Ducat (Double King Alfred) (18) M; *Inglescombe (16) M, yellow; White Lion (18) M, white and cream; Irene Copeland (14) E, white and apricot; Mary Copeland (14) L, white, lemon and orange; *Cheerfulness (19) L, cream, fragrant and *Yellow Cheerfulness (19) L; *N. pseudo-narcissus* Von Sion, double wild daffodil, (15) E, yellow and green.

Hybrids from Narcissus triandrus, which have several pendent flowers per stem; *Thalia (12) M; *Tresamble (14) L, white.

Hybrids from N. cyclamineus, with swept back perianth: *Charity May (12) M; *February Gold (15) VE; *Peeping Tom (14) VE, yellow.

Narcissus 'Actaea'

Hybrids from N. jonquilla, several small, fragrant flowers per stem; Cherie (14) L, white and apricot; Sweetness (17) M, deep yellow; *Trevithian (15) M, pale yellow.

Hybrids of N. tazetta, with many small flowers, usually fragrant and often producing foliage early in winter, which makes them tender but good for forcing: *Paper White (15) E; *Scilly White (15) E; *Soleil D'Or (18) E, yellow, orange, all tender: *Cragford (14) M, white, orange-red; *Elvira (18) L; Geranium (18) L, white, orange.

Hybrids resembling N. poeticus (the pheasant eye narcissus), white, red and green eye, scented: Actaea (20) M; Cantabile (17) VL; Horace (19) L; Red Rim (18) L; and *N. poeticus recurvus,* the poet's narcissus (20) VL (May).

Species or small hybrids like them : *N. asturiensis (minimus)* (2–3) VE, miniature yellow daffodil for pans, or turf; *bulbocodium,* hoop-petticoat daffodil (6) VE, yellow, wide trumpet, rushy foliage. Naturalize in turf. There are several forms; *canaliculatus (lacticolor)* (4) L, white, yellow, scented, small tazetta type, best on light soil; *N. odoratus* (12) otherwise similar; *cyclamineus* (14) VE (Jan–Feb) yellow, swept back perianth, likes damp position. Naturalize in turf or grow in pans. Small hybrids include Baby Doll (9) M, yellow; Beryl (8) E, primrose orange; February Silver (10) VE, white, lemon; Jack Snipe (5) M, white, primrose; Little Witch (9) E, yellow; *N. jonquilla* (12) L, deep yellow, fragrant; Baby Moon (12) VL, lemon, deep yellow; Bobbysoxer (8) L, yellow, deep yellow. *N. juncifolius* (3) M, yellow, flat cupped fragrant, rush-like leaves. *N. calcicola* (6) M. Flowers similar to *juncifolius,* but about 1 week earlier and with strap-shaped leaves; *N. nanus* (4) E, yellow trumpet. Good naturalizer in turf; *N. pseudo-narcissus* (Lent lily or wild daffodil) (6) E. Small bicolor for naturalizing, *W. P. Milner (10) M, better shaped flower, *pseudo-narcissus obvallaris* (Tenby daffodil) (10) VE, similar but earlier; *N. rupicola* (3) E, yellow, scented, rock garden or pans; *tiandrus albus* (Angel's Tears) (4) L, creamy white, 2–5 flowers per stem; *N. triandrus concolor* (4) L, golden yellow; hybrid with *N. jonquilla* April Tears (7) L, yellow, *N. watieri* (3) similar to *N. rupicola,* but white and unscented, pans.

Narcissus cyclamineus, a dwarf species

Ornithogalum umbellatum, the Star of Bethlehem, does well in poor sandy soil, and is a good bulb to grow in a wild garden or in thin woodland. The greenish-white, star-shaped flowers are borne on 6–8 in. stems

Daffodils should be planted as soon as available, before hyacinths and tulips. Large bulbs require holes 6 in. deep and small ones 3–4 in. Bulbs in pots can be placed shoulder to shoulder with the noses just under or just above the surface. If intended for forcing they must be plunged in a cool moist place (with the exception of the variety Paper White) until the roots have developed well.

Nerine (Amaryllis family) These are South African bulbs although *N. sariensis* is known as the Guernsey lily. They may be grown outside in warmer areas of the country, but where winters are colder they must be considered a greenhouse plant. The lovely clear pink flowers appear from September to November, and there is quite a variation in flower shade and time of flowering. The leaves die off in late summer, leaving a short period in July–August in which the large bulbs can be moved. Plant them at least 6 in. deep; they will gradually work their way upwards until the neck is above ground level, when they must be well mulched in frosty places or put down lower again. They look well planted out in a bed in a cool greenhouse. Keep them well fed with bonemeal when they are planted and with liquid fertilizer during growth.

N. sarniensis is not so tall, vigorous or hardy. There are several hybrids in lovely shades of scarlet, salmon and wine shades as well as pinks and whites when grown in a greenhouse. Plant them singly in 4-in. pots with the neck of the bulb well out and never let the temperature fall below 45°F (7°C). Water the soil well only when growth starts. After flowering continue feeding well until growth ceases. Dry them out and ripen them near the glass. Divide them only when it is essential, as they all flower best in crowded conditions.

Ornithogalum (Lily family) The European *O. umbellatum*, the Star of Bethlehem, makes a fine wild garden or thin woodland bulb. It does well in poor, sandy soil, and has flattish heads of greenish-white, star-shaped flowers on 6–8 in. stems. *O. thyrsioides* is the chincherinchee, renowned for its longevity in water if picked in bud. It flowers in June–July, forming a long pointed head of white flowers. It is not quite hardy but can be treated like gladiolus (planted in March and lifted in October), or will grow permanently in milder areas of the country, planted 6 in. deep, or in a cool greenhouse.

O. arabicum is also suitable for pots in a cool greenhouse. It has black-centered white flowers in heads like *O. umbellatum*. *O. nutans* produces 1-ft. stems of translucent greenish-white flowers in April and will do well in a shady position.

Pancratium (Amaryllis family) (sea lily) These are more or less tender plants with flowers borne on top of a long stem like amaryllis. They are usually white with green markings, with long spidery petals from a tube and are often beautifully fragrant. They are suitable for planting in 5-in. pots in a cool greenhouse and can be stood outside during the summer in a sheltered place. Only in tropical areas of the country can they be grown outdoors.

P. illyricum flowers in May or June and may have up to a dozen blooms which open in succession on 1½-ft. stems.

The bulbs should be rested during the winter when the leaves die down, and kept cool but frost free and dry, but not bone dry, until the spring.

Puschkinia (Lily family) *P. scilloides* (syn. *P. libanotica*) produces 4–6-in. stems of pale blue flowers with a greenish stripe in March. There is also a white form. It makes a fine carpet planted 3 in. deep in the fall under deciduous shrubs or on a rock garden, especially in heavy soil. It also makes a good pan plant.

Ranunculus (Ranunculus family) The tubers of *R. asiaticus* (sometimes sold as *R. grandiflora*) should be planted in holes 2–3 in. deep, claws downward, in pots or in clumps in a sunny border or in a special bed for flowers for cutting. They can only be grown outdoors in districts where winters are less severe. Soak them for 24 hours before planting.

Plant carefully any time from October inside to April outside. They need well-drained, rich soil and produce large double flowers on stems 12–15 in. high, in shades of yellow, orange, pink and red. The normal season is May to June, but in a greenhouse they can be forced gently. They are normally sold mixed, but there are several strains differing in size, doubleness and height of flower and known as peony-flowered, French, Persian and Turban.

For cutting special beds are made with coarse rubble placed under about 1 ft. of compost containing coarse grit and also well-rotted manure, banked up like an asparagus bed. This ensures the necessary quick drainage and high level of feeding. They must not be allowed to dry out until the leaves die down after flowering. During August the tubers should be lifted and stored, preferably hung in paper (not polyethylene) bags in a frost-proof airy place until needed.

Scilla (Lily family) (squills) The most readily obtainable are *S. bifolia*, *S. sibirica*, *S. tubergeniana* and *S. peruviana*. The first three are spring flowering and *S. bifolia* and *S. tubergeniana* are worth planting in pans of quick-draining compost in a cold frame or alpine house for flowering in March and April respectively. *S. sibirica* does well in sunny borders or in short turf, and makes a good show indoors planted in bulb fiber. On 6–8-in. stems it bears deep bright blue flowers; there is also a white form. The flowers of *S. bifolia* are turquoise blue or pink or white. *S. tubergeniana* is almost white, but has a deep blue stripe down the centre. *S. peruviana* 8–10 in., has deep blue, lilac or white flowers massed in a 5–6 in. head, in May and June. It needs a warm border. Tender types can only be grown in the open in areas of the country that enjoy mild winters.

Sinningia (Gesneria family) (gloxinia) These warm greenhouse plants have velvety leaves and brilliantly colored purple, red, violet etc. flowers often with white throats to their trumpets, produced freely for many weeks. Tubers are planted, hollow wide up, singly in a compost consisting of equal parts loam and peatmoss, plus some well-decayed manure and sharp sand in 5-in. pots and covered with about 1 in. of soil, or they are pressed into boxes of moist peatmoss and sand until they have produced both shoots and roots. This is useful for checking shoot damage in newly purchased tubers. These tubers will flower in summer and fall the same year. The season can be extended by sowing seeds in June to flower early the following summer, or in January–February for later flowering the same year. Feed regularly. They need plenty of moisture throughout the year, but can be moved to slightly cooler conditions while actually in flower. Dry gradually and store at 50–55°F (10–13°C) in the pots.

Smithiana (Gesneria family) Once known as Gesneria or Naegelia, these require warm greenhouse treatment and are best grown from tubers planted singly in 5-in. pots in March in a well-drained compost. The flowers are in lovely shades of yellow, orange, apricot and red, set off by deep green velvety leaves which damp off if heat and ventilation are inadequate. From March to August the temperature should be 60–70°F (16–21°C),

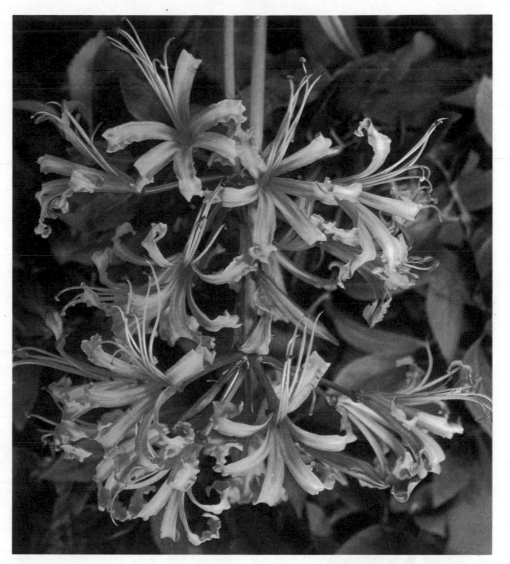

and once the tubers have started growing well plentiful water must be applied to the soil, not the foliage. The plants reach 1½–2 ft. and flower between July and November. During September and October the heat can be lowered slowly by about 10°F (6°C) and once flowering has finished they should be rested gradually and be stored in their pots, dry, at a temperature of 55°F (13°C) during the winter.

Particularly good plants are best increased by cuttings taken in early summer and rooted in a propagator.

Sparaxis (Iris family) (wand flower) These often have two or more colors per bloom in a wide range, including, white with yellow eye, bronze red with darker eye or with yellow eye, and purplish pink shades. They are best planted in March in a warm border where winters are less severe or grown in pots in a cool house, when they may be planted in the fall. The flowers appear in April to late May according to treatment. Feed and ripen well, but when cleaning off the dead foliage do not pull it out in handfuls, but cut it short as the lower nodes will be found to contain small cormels which if left are the means of rapid increase. Many of the more brilliant colors are the result of crossing sparaxis species with the related *Streptanthera*.

Sprekelia (Amaryllis family) (Jacobean lily) *S. formosissima* is an interesting flower, very

irregular in shape, looking like a 5-in. wide deep red orchid. The flowers are usually produced singly, occasionally in pairs. Plants are often grown in pots in cool greenhouses or in a frame, when they may flower as early as May, but in well-drained, sunny, warm sites in areas where the winters are warmer. flower in June. The large bulbs should be covered with their own depth of soil outside. Feed well and ripen thoroughly. Pot or plant when the foliage dies down.

Sternbergia (Amaryllis family) *S. lutea*, yellow star-flower, produces bright golden-yellow crocus-like flowers about 2½ in. high from late August. If the weather is bad at flowering time protect with a pane of glass, which will also assist ripening in a wet fall. The bulbs are best planted in sunny place in July and should have 4 in. of soil above them. In short turf they should be planted with a bulb planter, not by lifting the turves.

Tigridia (Iris family) (tiger flower) *T. pavonia*, a half-hardy Mexican bulb-shaped corm produces unusually brilliant flowers with the inner petals and bowl of the flower generally spotted red and making a tiger-face. The three petals which spread out flat are scarlet, cherry red, orange, buff or white; corms are usually sold as a mixture. The flowers last one day only but there are up to six on each 15–18-in. stem and they open in

Left: Scilla sibirica, the Siberian squill, is a fine bulbous plant for a sunny place, or may be grown indoors in pots or bowls

Top: Nerine bowdenii, a colorful fall flowering bulb for milder areas of the country.

Above: The smithianas (once known as gesnerias or naegelias) are beautiful plants for the warm greenhouse succession from June onwards. If treated like gladioli, planted 4–5 in. deep in spring when the danger of frost has passed and lifted before frosts, they usually flower in July. Where winters are less severe they can be left out if given a protective mulch. They need plenty of water and liquid feed during summer and then form good clumps.

Tritonia (Iris family) Tritonias are South African corms, and one only, *T. crocata* is freely available. The flowers are usually very brilliantly colored, orange, a pale coppery shade, yellow or white. They flower in late spring or early summer in a warm, frost-free border in areas where the winters are mild, or in pots in a cool greenhouse. They make good, long-lasting cut flowers. In pots treat them as freesias, planting them 7–9 in a 5-in. pot in a sandy compost, and provide light support. After ripening keep them in the same size pot but replace some of the soil

yearly in the fall until the pot is full of corms.

Tulipa (Lily family) (tulip) Tulips have been favorite spring bedding and pot plants in Europe since the mid-16th century. The flowers are in all colors except true blues, usually solitary, but also 3–4 per stem, the garden hybrids ranging in height from 4–34 in. Good bulbs can be guaranteed to give a fine, even display the first season, but except in warm situations on sandy loam rarely produce so many or such large blooms in later years, though feeding with bonemeal and proper ripening do help, and by this treatment the smaller species may become established on sunny ledges of the rock garden. The bulbs should be planted from 4–6 in. deep according to their size, but should not be put in before October for the April flowering kinds and November for the May flowering ones.

If used for spring bedding, either alone or

coming through a shorter ground cover of forget-me-nots, wallflowers or pansies, the bulbs will have to be lifted and allowed to finish their growth in trenches in a sunny position, unless discarded. Tulips in less conspicuous places should be allowed to die down before being lifted and placed in trays in a sunny place (cold greenhouse, frame or window) to complete their ripening. Only the large bulbs should be planted for display the following year, but small ones can be grown on to flowering size in a sunny frame. They take up to seven years to flower from seed.

Some varieties can be forced, but it is very important to grow the bulbs in a plunge bed until growth is well up (4–6 in.) and then to bring them gradually into light and moderate warmth. They do not respond well to high temperatures and must be forced slowly.

Vallota (Amaryllis family) (Scarborough lily) *V. speciosa* is a South African bulb for

Above: Tulipa tarda (dasystemon) is a low-growing species, about 3 in. high
Below: 'Rosy Wings', a Cottage tulip
Below right: 'Tol's Favorite', a Single Early tulip, flowering in April

Tulip species	Height in in.	Flowering time	Flower color	Use
acuminata (cornuta) (Horned tulip)	20	May	yellow, streaked red, long twisted petals	as cut flower, pots
batalinii	7	April	primrose or yellow flushed pink	rock garden or pans
clusiana (Lady tulip)	15	late April	outer petals cherry, inner ones white, violet base	border or rock garden
eichleri	12	March	scarlet, pointed petals, black base	pots, border
fosteriana	10–18	mid-April	scarlet, crimson within, black base, broad petals, large flower	Princeps 10 in. borders Red Emperor 18 in. pots
greigii	9	April–May	scarlet or orange, base black ringed yellow. Leaves mottled with chocolate, flat	borders, pots, as edging to beds, as leaves are decorative
kaufmanniana (Water-lily tulip)	8	March–April	large; cream tinged pink outside, white or cream inside	fine garden tulip
linifolia	8	April–May	scarlet, violet base; leaves narrow, red-edged, wavy margins, flat on soil	high in rock garden to show red stems
orphanidea	10	March–April	orange shaded bronze and green yellow base, pointed petals	rock garden
praestans 'Fusilier'	10	early April	vermilion, 4–6 on a stem	pot plant, rock garden
pulchella violacea	4	Feb–March	reddish purple, cup shaped, base black or yellow	alpine house, rock garden
saxatilis	10	April	1–3 on a stem, pale lilac, yellow base. Flowers best if crowded.	confine in sunny bed by slates as spreads rapdily by stolons. Leafs early.
tarda (dasystemon)	6	April	3–6 on a stem, white, yellow inside	rock garden, in paving pockets, edging beds
turkestanica	9	Feb–March	5–9 on a stem, white, orange centres	rock garden, alpine house

The Scarborough lily, vallota

the cool or intermediate greenhouse. Bulbs can be planted singly in $3\frac{1}{2}$-in. pots from May to July. Each year they should be moved into a larger pot without disturbing the clump. When they get grossly overcrowded and small bulbs are being squeezed up free from the mass it is time to divide and start afresh. Good soil should replace as much as possible of the old at each move and liquid feeding is essential to keep up the supply of flowering size bulbs.

The 3-in. trumpet-shaped flowers are rather like the smaller hippeastrums, but with more flowers in each head, on $1-1\frac{1}{2}$-ft. stems, and are normally a brilliant vermilion, though both pink and cherry-red forms are available. They flower in late summer.

Vallotas can be grown successfully in a sunny window in a rich well-drained compost. Water carefully during the winter and remove from frost danger at night. Bulbs may also be planted outside in areas where little frost occurs.

Veltheimia (Lily family) *V. capensis* (syn. *V. viridifolia*) flowers in early spring in a cool or intermediate house. The flowers form a red-hot poker type of spike but are straight sided, dull pink bells at the top of a speckled fleshy 15–18-in. stem. They are the sort of unusual flower color for off-beat flower arrangements, and last well in water. The bulbs are large and can be lifted dry when dormant in the summer. They should be planted in September in compost and be kept growing throughout the winter, which means good light and an adequate temperature. The dried up ends of the leaf bases which form the bulb should be kept clear of the soil and care should be taken to water the soil and not into the neck of the bulb.

Zephyranthes (Amaryllis family) (flowers of the western wind) These are bulbs from warm regions in Central and South America, so only a few can be tried outdoors in the mildest parts, though they make good pot plants in a cool house.

Z. candida, with single white flowers like crocuses and rush-like foliage, is the hardiest and the most readily available. It flowers in September–October and makes a good edging plant. Also occasionally available are *Z. citrina*, a bright yellow with a greenish base, which is not quite so big; and *Z. grandiflora*, rosy pink and slightly larger in flower. Both are too tender for anything but a cool greenhouse or areas that enjoy mild winters.

TULIPS

The following varieties (arranged as far as possible by time of flowering) are recommended: forcing varieties are marked with an asterisk. Height, in inches in brackets.

Late March–April
Kaufmanniana varieties and hybrids:
Alfred Cortot (8), scarlet, black base, mottled leaves; César Franck (8), red and yellow; Fritz Kreisler (8), flesh-pink, flushed rose, yellow base; Heart's Delight (8), carmine, edged rose and white, mottled foliage; Johann Strauss (6), cream with yellow base, flushed red, mottled foliage; Oriental Beauty (10), vermilion, mottled foliage; Shakespeare (6), salmon, apricot and orange; Stresa (7), deep yellow and orange-red; The First (6), red outside, cream edged, cream inside.

Early April
Greigii varieties and hybrids: These all have leaves beautifully marked with chocolate, which they have passed on to some of the *Kaufmanniana* hybrids. Mixed *T. kaufmanniana* × *T. greigii* are sold as Peacock tulips. Cape Cod (8), yellow, striped red, black base; Margaret Herbst (20), scarlet; Oriental Splendour (18), carmine on outside of lemon yellow, black base; Plaisir (7), carmine, edged sulphur, vermilion inside; Red Riding Hood (8), scarlet.

April flowering
Early singles: *Bellona (15), yellow, fragrant; *Brilliant Star (12), scarlet; Cramoisi Brilliant (14), scarlet; *Diana (12), white; *General de Wet (13), orange-scarlet, fragrant; *Ibis (14), rose, pale margin; Keizerskroon (15), scarlet and yellow; Mon Trésor (13), yellow, fragrant; Pink Beauty (13), pink and white; *Van de Neer (12), plum-purple.

Mid-Season (mid-April to mid-May):
Triumph (mid-April to mid-May); *Blizzard (19), white; Elmus (18), cherry and white; First Lady (16), violet, purple; Garden Party (16), white, edged pink; Sulphur Glory (22), light yellow.

Early doubles (about 7 days later): *Dante (10), blood red; David Teniers (12), violet-purple; *Electra (12), carmine, pink when forced; Maréchal Niel (12), yellow; *Murillo (10), pink and white; *Mr Van der Hoef (12), yellow; *Orange Nassau (12), orange-scarlet; *Peach Blossom (12), rose pink; Schonoord (12), white; Vuurbaak (12), scarlet.

Tulipa greigii 'Perlina'

Darwin Hybrids (end of April to mid-May): *Apeldoorn (26), orange-red, black base; Golden Springtime (26), yellow; *Gudoshnik (24), yellow, mahogany; Holland's Glory (20), scarlet; Oxford (24), orange-scarlet, yellow base.

Lily-flowered (reflexed petals; end April mid May): Aladdin (22), scarlet, cream edge, yellow base; Captain Fryatt (20), dark ruby, violet base; *China Pink (22), pink, white base; Mariette (22), salmon-pink; Maytime (20), mauve-lilac, white edge; Mrs Moon (28),

The Parrot tulip 'Estella Rijnveld'

deep yellow; Queen of Sheba (19), chestnut-red, orange edge; Red Shine (20), ruby-red, blue base; West Point (20), soft yellow; White Triumphator (26), white.

May flowering
Darwin Will not force before February: *Aristocrat (28), rosy magenta; Blue Aimable (28), heliotrope; Charles Needham (26), scarlet, blue base; Clara Butt (24), rose, flushed salmon; Farncombe Sanders (30), red, white base; La Tulipe Noire (25), maroon-black; *Nipheto (28), lemon-yellow; Pride of Haarlem (26), deep carmine, blue base, fragrant; *Prunus (26), deep rose-pink; *Queen of Bartigons (26), salmon pink; Queen of Night (28), purple-black; Scarlett O'Hara (26), scarlet, yellow base; Sunkist (28), golden-yellow; The Bishop (29), violet, blue base; Zwanenburg (29), white.

Breeder The old exhibition tulips of perfect globular shape, from which the Broken tulips known as Bizarre and Bybloemen arose: Dillenburg (26), orange; Louis XIV (30), purple, bronze edged.

Cottage or Single Late Advance (26), scarlet, blue base; *Carrara (22), white, (force from mid-Feb); Chappaqua (30), magenta; Inglescombe Yellow (21), yellow; Marshall Haig (26), scarlet; Mrs John T. Scheepers (24), soft yellow; Ossi Oswalda (26), cream, edged rose; Princess Margaret Rose (21), yellow, edged scarlet; Rosy Wings (22), pink, blue base; White City (Mount Erebus) (29), white.

Multiflowered with 3 or more flowers branching from one main stem; Claudette (22), ivory-white, edged rose; Emir (24), scarlet; Georgette (26), yellow, edged red.

Broken Colored These are tulips which are infected with virus disease which has caused the break up of the colours, causing them to appear in streaks and patches. They should be kept away from other tulips as the infection is spread by aphids which infest the bulbs in store. Rembrandt tulips are broken Darwin tulips, others are broken breeder tulips: Mme de Pompadour (24), white, flamed violet-purple (Rembrandt); Absalon (22), yellow, flamed coffee-brown (Bizarre); Mayblossom (22), cream, flamed purple (Bybloemen).

Parrot These are tulips in which virus has caused distortion and splitting (laciniation) of the petal edge. Similar, but shallower, division of the petal edge is known as 'fringed': Black Parrot (22), almost black; *Blue Parrot (24), violet and purple; Fantasy (22), soft rose, green markings; Orange Parrot (28), brownish orange, marked old gold, fragrant; Red Parrot (28), deep scarlet; Texas Gold (20), golden yellow, edged red, marked green; White Parrot (20), white; Fringed Beauty (12), red, yellow fringe; *viridiflora* (green tulips); *viridiflora praecox* (18), green, margined yellow; Artist (9), terracotta and green; Groenland (Greenland) (20), old rose, green and cream.

Double Late or Peony flowered: Eros (22), old rose; Nizza (16), sulfur-yellow, streaked red; Mount Tacoma (18), white; Uncle Tom (20), mahogany-red.

Annuals & Biennials

Seed is Nature's usual means of increasing plant life and it is also the simplest method for the gardener when it comes to raising annual, biennial and, in some instances, perennial flowering plants. Gardens of modern houses tend to get smaller and smaller, due to the high cost of land, therefore the thing to do is to grow only the best plants and to grow them well. Inferior seed takes just as much time to sow and grow, the results will never be first-rate and the saving of a few cents is false economy. Only the best is good enough for the experienced gardener, as he knows from years of trial and error.

Flower seeds, in common with vegetable and other crops, are bred with great care and the plant breeder maintains a stud-book in which he keeps the parentage of hybrid plants in the same manner as with race horses, pedigree dogs and the like. All this takes time and costs money, but the results are far superior to plants pollinated haphazardly by bees and other insects.

Vast numbers of plants are raised from seeds but as far as flowers are concerned they are known as hardy annual, half-hardy annual, biennial and perennial.

Hardy Annuals A hardy annual is a plant that is raised from seed, flowers, and dies a natural death within the four seasons, although gardeners often treat certain perennials and biennials as annuals. Given favorable weather a seed crop is harvested from such plants. However seed crops fail, or may be poor in some years, and it may take the seed grower a couple of years or longer to build up an adequate supply.

Half-hardy annuals These are sometimes raised from seed sown under glass and the seedlings planted out where they are to flower when the danger of frost is past. Many however may be sown in the open ground in spring, where they will provide a colorful display. Flowering will continue until the weather turns colder in the fall.

Biennials A biennial is sown one year, produces its flowers and dies the following year. Some biennials, the wallflower for instance, may prove to be short-lived perennials in some gardens, and the same applies to some half-hardy annuals, such as the antirrhinum, in a mild winter.

Perennials A perennial is a plant of any kind that lives for more than two years. It may be perennial in a greenhouse, others grown in the open are known as hardy perennials.

F_1 Hybrids Seed catalogues list many recent introductions as F_1 hybrids. This is the plant breeder's abbreviated way of recording that the seed is the result of a controlled cross of two known parent plants, or to the scientist,

the first filial generation. Such seed produces plants of superior vigor and uniformity and often the flowers are of more intense color and larger than ordinary hybrid seedlings. It is, however, a long and expensive process to obtain such seed, therefore it costs more per packet. Also the complicated breeding program has to be repeated, as seed saved from F_1 hybrids grown in the garden, would prove far from reliable.

Cosmos bipinnatus

Cultivation

Hardy Annuals Seed of hardy annuals may be sown in the open ground where it is to flower; it is as easy as that. The main requirements are an open sunny position and a well-drained soil. Obviously the condition of the soil will be reflected in the quality of the flowers produced and to get the best results the ground should be well cultivated in advance of sowing and, where the soil is poor, work in bonemeal to a depth of 2 or 3 in. and at the rate of about 2 oz. to the square yard. This is a fairly slow-acting fertilizer that will provide nourishment as the roots get down to it. Fresh manure is not a good thing for annuals as it encouraged much soft leaf growth and not flowers.

Before sowing firm and rake the soil level, removing large stones and hard lumps of earth. Most flower seed is small and does need a reasonably fine surface soil in which to germinate. Sow the seed broadcast or in drills and in any case sow thinly for germination of annual flower seed is usually good. This will reduce the wasteful job of thinning. Pelleted seeds make small seeds much easier to handle and thin sowing is easily achieved. This means that the seedlings will have sufficient space to grow without the check caused by thinning or transplanting.

Do not attempt to sow seed when the soil is wet and sticky, be patient and wait until it dries out. Seed sowing is controlled by the weather not by the calendar. After the seed has been sown cover it lightly with soil and water with a fine spray. Water it just sufficiently to make the surface soil moist.

To prevent the beds from becoming dried out they may be covered with lath screens or burlap which should be kept in place until germination takes place. Evergreen branches may also be used. In dry weather drills may be taken out and watered several times before the seeds are sown and covered with soil.

Where thinning of seedlings is necessary this should be done when they are about 2–3 in. high and a final thinning should leave sufficient space for the plants to develop. After each thinning water the seedlings to settle the soil around the plants. The seedlings that have been removed may be planted elsewhere in the garden, but this is not successful with all annuals. As a rough guide to thinning the distance between each plant should be about three-quarters of the plant's ultimate height; e.g. plants which will grow 1 ft. tall should be thinned to 9 in. apart.

In the south annuals are used principally for winter display. They should be sown in August and September to flower from January.

Half-hardy Annuals Many plants which we call half-hardy annuals are natives of much warmer lands where frost is unknown or a rare occurrence. Some are perennial in their native conditions. It is necessary therefore in some colder areas of the country to germinate the seed with the aid of artificial heat in a greenhouse or frame. It is also advisable to sow the seeds of plants that need a longer season of growth or have very fine seeds in this way.

Sowing should be carried out in February or March in flats, pans, or pots using a compost that is purchased ready mixed, or made up as follows, 2 parts loam, 1 part peatmoss, and 1 part sand. All soil used for seed sowing must be put through a fine sieve. The containers should first have a layer of crocks (broken earthenware pots) or stones placed over the drainage holes, covering these with a small quantity of peatmoss, or partly decayed leaves. Now add the compost which should be firmed with a flat piece of board so that there is a space of about 1 in. between the surface and the top of the container.

Sow the seed sparsely, then sprinkle a fine covering of compost over the seed (very fine seed will not require covering).

After sowing water larger seeds from above with a fine spray, very small seeds may be watered by placing the pots in water and allowing it to rise through the soil by way of the drainage holes, on no account should the surface be allowed to flood.

To aid germination cover the container with a piece of glass and a sheet of brown paper as shading.

Remove the glass daily, wiping off the condensed moisture and reverse the glass when you replace it. When the seed germinates remove the glass and paper and put the container in full light giving some protection from bright sunlight. On cold nights the seedlings should be protected with newspaper or may be moved away from the glass.

When the seedlings are large enough to handle, that is usually by the time they have developed two pairs of leaves, lift them carefully by levering up the soil with a dibber and prick them out into a flat, spacing them about 2 in. apart. Plant them firmly and water them into the compost. Keep them growing steadily under glass until the beginning of May. Remember that most annuals should have their growing points pinched out when they are 4–5 in. high to encourage bushy growth. If the weather is reasonably mild, stand the flats in the open for a week or so to harden the plants before they are planted out where they are to flower. If the flats have been in a frame it is a simple matter

Above: Choose a sunny position for the colorful South African gazanias. *Left:* Petunia hybrids make a bright show in summer. *Center:* Some of the eschscholzias or Californian poppies. *Below:* The best of the annual mallows, Lavatera 'Loveliness'

of just removing the frame light for this hardening-off process. Be sure that the flats are standing level, and on a firm base, otherwise some plants may lack water. Give the flats a good watering an hour or two before transplanting the seedlings so that they can be removed from the flats with plenty of moist soil attached to their roots. Water them again when they are planted out.

Among the half-hardy annuals which may be sown direct in the open where they are to flower are aster, cosmos, African and French marigolds, mignonette and zinnia. The last two resent transplanting and germinate better when the soil is made firm after sowing. May or early June is the time to sow half-hardy annuals in the open in a sunny position and in well-drained soil.

Biennials Seed of biennial plants may be sown straight into a seed bed in the open ground in May and June. As the soil is warm germination is not delayed, provided the seed bed is kept moist. When the seedlings are large enough to handle they should be transplanted in nursery beds and transferred in the fall to where they are to flower. In areas that have severe winters they are best moved to cold frames (protected with mats) where they should remain until spring. Another method is to sow in drills in a cold frame in March or April, or where only a small quantity of plants is required, to sow in pots or flats in a cold frame or cold greenhouse. With the frame light in position there should be sufficient warmth to encourage germination. Artificial heat is unnecessary for seeds of hardy plants, in fact, it is not usually desirable.

Whichever method is used, sow thinly and do not make the common mistake of covering the seed with too much soil. As a general rule cover the seed with its own depth of soil. Nature just scatters it on the surface and lets the rain wash it in, but Nature is very wasteful, and sows with abandon.

Where the seed is sown in a cold frame leave some ventilation or the frame may get too hot. Some shading on the glass will also reduce the need for frequent watering and the same applies to seed sown in pots in a cold greenhouse which should be covered with brown paper or newspaper until the seed germinates. These are small points which make all the difference between failure and

Nasturtiums

success. Biennials are sown one year and flower and produce seed the next, which completes their life cycle. Some will perpetuate themselves by self-sown seedlings, for instance, foxglove, forget-me-not, mullein, hollyhock, among many others.

The Uses of Annuals and Biennials

Beds and Borders Annuals are probably most widely used for filling gaps in borders, on the rock garden and elsewhere, for they provide splashes of welcome color in a matter of months. A bed or border devoted entirely to hardy annuals can make a splendid carpet of color during the summer months, but it does entail considerable work in weeding and watering in the early stages.

For a small garden or one of moderate size, a mixed border of hardy herbaceous perennials and annuals will provide interest and color from May to October without undue toil. With both types of plants it is possible, by making a careful choice, to include only such plants as require no staking and it is wise, in exposed gardens, to use low-growing plants that will not be battered by summer gales. (A list of such plants is given later.)

New Gardens One of the quickest ways of making a display in a new garden is by sowing hardy annuals, for seed sown in April and May where it is to flower will give a display from June onwards.

The choice of annuals is very wide and the color range all embracing, giving ample scope for those with bright ideas and those who like to try something different each year.

Containers For those whose gardening may be confined to window boxes, tubs or other containers on a roof garden or in a patio, half-hardy annuals are probably the best bet. These can be planted out as young plants in May and will soon start to flower. This is much more satisfactory, although it costs more than sowing seed of hardy annuals in window boxes which are usually too exposed for young seedlings to make good plants, even though the seed may germinate reasonably well in the first place. Suitable half-hardy annuals for growing in containers are antirrhinum, petunia, fragrant stocks, annual chrysanthemum, (heliotrope), lobelia, *Phlox drummondii*, African and French marigolds and other showy plants.

Hanging baskets are also most decorative when filled with heliotrope, trailing lobelia, free-flowering nasturtium, petunia and other summer-flowering plants. Their flowers and foliage will hang over the sides most attractively.

Edging and Paving Other uses of annuals are as dwarf edging plants for the front of a bed or border, or for sowing in crevices in paving. Among these is the low-growing *Limnanthes douglasii* with quite large white flowers with a yellow center, which seeds itself without becoming a nuisance, mesembryanthemum with gay daisy-like flowers

Above: Morning glory (Ipomoea)
Below: Nemesias are available in a very wide range of colors
Right: The most decorative variety of the annual corn cockle is *Agrostemma* 'Milas'

that thrives in well-drained soil and full sun, anagallis (pimpernel), and the creeping zinnia, *Sanvitalia procumbens*, with single yellow flowers with a black center on 6 in. stems. This curious little plant is like a miniature sunflower and never fails to attract interest.

Cut Flowers Annuals provide a splendid selection of flowers for cutting and with a little planning flowers can be available over a long period. By sowing hardy annuals in the open in the fall and making another sowing in the open in the spring a succession of welcome flowers will be assured. A list of annuals for cutting is given later.

Biennials are also most useful and effective in a border, particularly when planted in bold clumps. In milder areas wallflowers are probably among the most popular and there is a splendid range of color. The fragrance on a warm day in May is glorious. For small gardens the 'Tom Thumb' varieties, about 9 in. high, are most valuable and decorative. These and other biennials are best planted in their flowering positions in the early fall, but if necessary this can be deferred until March. In colder areas the plants should remain where they were sown through the winter and given the protection of salt, hay, or evergreen branches. They are then moved to their flowering positions in spring.

Another method is to sow the seed in frost proof frames in late summer and plant them outside in spring.

Groups of sweet Williams in well-drained soil and a sunny position are delightful in early summer, and they are also useful for cutting. Other popular biennials include Canterbury bell, the blue cynoglossum with forget-me-not-like flowers borne on incurling sprays, polyanthus and in many rich colors in milder areas, honesty with its large flat seed pods which make decorative material when dried, Iceland poppy (*Papaver nudicaule*) in areas where summers are cooler and not too humid, and many different violas and pansies.

Annuals and Biennials for the Cool Greenhouse

Raising plants from seed is a most economical means of providing a long-lasting display for the cool greenhouse. Where a minimum night temperature of about 45°F (7°C) can be maintained the choice of flowering and of decorative foliage plants is considerable. What is more many plants that we normally grow as annuals in the open may prove to be perennial when grown under glass, as they are in their native conditions.

For example, the fast-growing Mexican cup-and-saucer-vine, *Cobaea scandens*, has large purple and green cup-and-saucer flowers over a long period. This evergreen plant which clings by means of tendrils can make as much as 20 ft. of growth in a season, so it is too rampant for a small greenhouse but most decorative for a sunny wall in a large conservatory.

The popular morning glory (ipomoea or pharbitis) requires much less space, twining up supports to a height of about 10 ft. and bearing a succession of large sky-blue funnel-shaped flowers, as will the Chilean glory flower, *Eccremocarpus scaber*, which bears

clusters of bright orange flowers for many months. Even in the open, in milder parts of the country, the last named will sometimes seed itself when grown in a sheltered sunny corner, so it is easy enough to raise from seed. All these flowering climbers can be grown in a sunny greenhouse border or will flower happily when grown in pots or other containers.

Seeds of these plants, in common with many others, will germinate readily if sown under glass in March when the days are beginning to lengthen and to get warmer. An ideal temperature for germinating most seeds of this type is 65°F (18°C) and to maintain this as well as a moist atmosphere it will be found economical to have a propagating frame within the greenhouse. This need not be a costly affair, just four sides of a flat and a sheet of glass will suffice. Such a frame heated by electrical soil-warming cable is convenient and economical in that the whole greenhouse does not have to be maintained at this temperature.

With an electrically heated frame the thermostat can be set at a slightly higher temperature to encourage germination and when this has taken place the temperature can gradually be lowered. Whatever means of heating a greenhouse or frame is used the aim should be to keep the temperature as constant as possible and to avoid wide fluctuations of day and night temperatures.

Most seeds germinate best in the dark and it is wise therefore to shade the frame, or the pots and flats in which the seeds are sown, with brown paper. This will provide sufficient shade and at the same time reduce the amount of watering that may be necessary. The soil should be kept just moist in the early stages

1. A colorful hanging basket.

2. Squeezing surplus moisture out of the soaked moss before lining the basket. 3. Lining the basket with moist sheet moss. 4. The basket filled with compost gently firmed before planting. 5. Making a hole with a trowel to receive a plant knocked out from a pot.

49

after sowing, but as germination takes place a little more watering will be required, and as soon as the seed has germinated the shading should be removed. However, should germination coincide with a spell of really bright sunny weather it is as well to shade the tiny seedlings from the midday sun.

These days seed-sowing and potting composts, based on loam, or of the soil-less, peat-moss and sand type, are readily obtainable at garden shops in various sized polyethylene bags or cartons and are usually moist ready for use, which makes life easy in this respect.

While cyclamen are perennial tuberous-rooted plants they are often treated as biennials. They are easily raised from seed sown under glass in summer and will flower within about 15 months, that is by Christmas the following year, when an individual plant will be quite an expensive item. Seed germinates readily in a temperature of 60°F (16°C), which means that the house or frame will need shading to keep the temperature down in August, and the atmosphere should be kept moist in hot weather by spraying water around the pathway in the greenhouse. When the seedlings have made two leaves prick them out in seed trays, or singly in small pots, and grow them on in gentle warmth. Put the little corms into larger pots when necessary, but do not bury the corm when potting, merely making it firm in the surface potting compost. There are various excellent large-flowering varieties in shades of salmon, crimson, mauve and white, also a new double-flowered 'Kimono' strain of Japanese origin, in a pleasing range of mixed colors. After flowering, the corms can be discarded, or treated as perennials (see also the Part of this work dealing with The Greenhouse and Garden Frame). The dainty *Cyclamen persicum*, the parent of modern hybrids, has charming white or pink, sweetly fragrant flowers and is normally spring flowering.

Obviously one wants color in the cool greenhouse during the winter and early spring and cyclamen will help to provide this for a long period. Other decorative plants that are easily raised from seed include *Primula malacoides* with candelabrum-like

flowers on strong stems in shades of pink, lilac and mauve; the drum-head Himalayan Primrose, which is in fact a hardy perennial but easily raised from seed, will flower from February onwards under glass. The long-lasting heads of flower are in shades of purple, mauve or white. And don't forget fragrant polyanthus and primroses in many colors. These flower for months in cool conditions.

Cinerarias sown in June should provide bold splashes of color from February onwards. At this time the little *Limnanthes douglasii* should be a mass of yellow and white fragrant flowers and the sky-blue nemophila which also makes a charming pot plant for a partially shaded place in the cool house, should be in full flower. Schizanthus, butterfly flower, are available in an astonishing range of glorious colors – salmon, apricot, pink, yellow, mauve and purple. Many of the flowers have attractive markings. They thrive in cool house conditions as do calceolarias, but the latter do not usually start to flower until June, from seed sown the previous May.

The Chilean salpiglossis is remarkably beautiful, with a richness of color and splendid veinings on the trumpet-shaped elegant flowers. The color range includes rose, crimson, purple, cream and many blends. There are dwarf forms about 1 ft. in height and also large-flowered hybrids up to 3 ft. Seed sown under glass in August or September will make delightful flowering plants the following May.

There are numerous varieties of *Coleus blumei* which are grown for their decorative foliage. As they are natives of Java and Central Africa they like a warm, moist atmosphere which may make them a little difficult to accommodate in a cool greenhouse. Seed sown in warm conditions in February will provide large plants later in the year. While coleus are in fact perennial shrubby plants, given sufficient heat, they are more often treated as annuals. The leaves are in various shades of red-bronze, yellow, green and maroon. The spikes of blue flowers are best pinched out to encourage bushy, leafy plants.

Seed of *Celosia plumosa* sown under glass in March will provide summer-flowering annual pot plants of striking appearance with bright red, feathery tassels in summer. There is also a golden form. These fast-growing plants require a rich soil and plenty of light.

Some annuals which do not transplant easily may be sown thinly in pots in which they are to flower. After germination the seedlings should be thinned out to five or six plants to a pot, according to the size of the pot. It is as simple as that. Plants that can be treated in this way are the Californian poppy (eschscholzia), in shades of orange, copper, yellow, carmine and ivory; linaria, viscaria and the charming long-lasting mignonette (reseda), which is uniquely fragrant. Many other annuals can be sown in the normal way and will transplant quite readily when large enough to handle. A few pots of such plants will come in very useful to fill gaps in the sequence of flowering.

Other plants that will give a good display in a cool greenhouse are antirrhinum, brachycome, *Campanula isophylla*, of trailing habit and useful for growing over the edge of a shelf or in a hanging basket; *Campanula pyramidalis*, the chimney bellflower, with wide-open pale blue flowers borne on erect stems from 5–6 ft. in height, and clarkia sown in the fall will flower freely the following spring. There are annual and biennial stocks (matthiola) which may be sown at different times of the year to provide color and delicious fragrance for many weeks.

There is a wide range of hybrid petunias which are admirable as pot plants, in tubs or in hanging baskets. They are outstandingly colorful and long-lasting – large-flowered singles and doubles, compact bedding varieties, pendulous hybrids suitable for window boxes, some with fringed and ruffled flowers, bicolors and many self colors.

These are but a few of the flowering plants easily raised from seed which are so welcome in the cool greenhouse throughout the year.

Above: Colorful annuals form an edging to a border of hardy perennials
Left: The sweetly scented blooms of the flowering tobacco plant, *Nicotiana alata*

Right: A beautiful arrangement of bedding plants

Annuals for Special Purposes

Hardy annuals for Autumn Sowing in the open
Alyssum, Calendula (pot marigold), Centaurea (cornflower), Clarkia, *Delphinium ajacis* (larkspur), Eschscholzia (Californian poppy), Godetia, Iberis (candytuft), *Lathyrus odoratus* (sweet pea), *Limnanthes douglasii*, Nigella (love-in-a-mist), *Papaver nudicaule* (Shirley poppy), Saponaria, Scabiosa.

Hardy Annuals for Cut Flowers
Calendula (pot marigold), Centaurea (cornflower), *Delphinium ajacis* (larkspur), Gypsophila, *Lathyrus odoratus* (sweet pea), Nigella (love-in-a-mist), Saponaria, Scabiosa.

Annuals for Full Sun in Well-drained soil
(Hardy and Half-hardy)
Arctotis, Brachycome, Calandrinia, Clarkia, Dimorphotheca, Echium, Eschscholzia, Helipterum, Hibiscus, Linum (flax), Mesembryanthemum, Oenothera, Papaver (poppy), Portulaca, Salpiglossis, Sanvitalia, Sedum (stonecrop), Statice (limonium), Tagetes (African and French marigolds), Tropaeolum (nasturtium), Ursinia, Venidium, Zinnia.

Annual Climbers
Cobaea scandens, *Eccremocarpus scaber*, Gourds, Humulus (hop), Ipomoea (morning glory), *Lathyrus odoratus* (sweet pea), Maurandia, Quamoclit, Tropaeolum (nasturtium).

Annuals with Fragrant Flowers
Alyssum, Asperula, Centaurea (sweet sultan), Dianthus (pink), Exacum, Heliotrope (cherry pie), Hesperis (sweet rocket), *Lathyrus odoratus* (sweet pea), *Lupinus luteus* (yellow lupin), Matthiola (stocks), Nicotiana (tobacco plant), Oenothera (evening primrose), Reseda (mignonette), Tropaeolum (nasturtium) (Gleam hybrids).

Low-growing Annuals (from 9–18 in.)
Adonis, Anthemis, Centaurea (cornflower, dwarf forms), Collinsia, *Convolvulus tricolor*, *Coreopsis coronata*, *Coreopsis tinctoria*, Dimorphotheca, Eschscholzia, Gilia, Godetia (dwarf forms), Helipterum, Iberis (candytuft), Linaria, *Matthiola bicornis* (night-scented stock), Matthiola (ten-week stock), Omphalodes, Reseda (mignonette), Scabiosa (dwarf forms), *Tagetes patula* (dwarf French marigold), Ursinia.

Annuals for Moist Soil
Calendula (pot marigold), Helianthus (sunflower), *Limnanthes douglasii*, Linaria (toadflax), *Linum grandiflorum rubrum* (scarlet flax), Nemophila, Nigella (love-in-a-mist), Reseda (mignonette), *Saxifraga cymbalaria*.

A simple propagating frame for raising annuals

Adonis H.A., 1–1½ ft. Easily grown from seed sown in the spring in a sunny position, *A. aestivalis* bears small crimson flowers in June and July. The deep green, finely-cut leaves are also attractive.

Ageratum H.H.A., 6–18 in. This is a popular bedding plant with masses of fluffy little powder-puff-like flowers from July until fall frosts. The long-lasting flowers are mainly in shades of blue and retain their color without fading. Sow under glass in February or March and plant out in a sunny bed, window-box or other container towards the end of May. Dwarf kinds also make neat plants when grown in pots to flower in a cool greenhouse. Suitable varieties are 'Blue Mink', 6 in., powder blue; 'Blue Color', 6 in., mid-blue, early flowering; 'Fairy Pink', 6 in., pale pink. There are also white varieties. *A. mexicanum* has soft lavender-blue flowers on 18-in. stems.

Agrostemma (corn cockle) H.A., 1½–2 ft. Magenta-red single flowers are borne on slender stems freely throughout the summer. A more decorative variety 'Milas' has large rosy-lilac flowers with conspicuous dark lines along each petal. The long, stiff stems make it useful as a cut flower as well as for the border. Seed may be sown in the open ground in the fall or in the spring for later flowering.

Alonsoa (mask flower) H.H.A., 1–1½ ft. These South American plants thrive in a rich soil and in a sunny position. The most showy is *A. warscewiczii*, with bright scarlet flowers. There is also a dwarf form known as 'compacta', admirable as a pot plant for a cool greenhouse, where it is perennial. Sow in February or March under glass, in a temperature of 60°F (16°C) and plant out in May for a summer display.

Althaea (hollyhock) H.B., 4–5 ft. Easily raised from seed, the hollyhock may prove perennial, but is not long lived. Sow the seed in the open ground in May or June and transplant the seedlings to grow on, before putting them in their flowering sites in the fall or

early spring to flower in July and August. There are single and double varieties in shades of crimson, pink, yellow and white. There is also an annual form which should be sown outside in April to flower from July onwards.

Alyssum (sweet alyssum) H.A., 4 in. A popular plant for edging, *A. maritimum* grows well in paving and window boxes. It flowers freely throughout the summer and early fall and is easily raised from seed sown where it is to flower. Or seed may be sown under glass and the seedlings planted out about mid-May when the danger of frost should be past. The little heads of flower are sweetly fragrant. Recommended varieties include 'Carpet of Snow', white flowers; 'Rosie O' Day', deep rose-pink; 'Royal Carpet', violet-purple; 'Violet Queen', bright violet-purple.

Amaranthus (love-lies-bleeding) H.A., 3 ft. The long pendent tassels of crimson flowers are a curious sight from July to September. *A. caudatus* 'Viridis' has long greenish-yellow tassels. Sow in the open ground in April in well-drained soil and in a sunny position. It requires plenty of moisture during the growing season. In exposed districts it is best treated as a half-hardy plant. People either like it or it gives them the creeps.

Anagallis (pimpernel) H.H.A., 6–12 in. Seed of *A. linifolia* sown in the open in late May in well-drained soil on a rock garden or warm border will provide brilliantly colored flowers from July to September. Mixed packets will provide shades of scarlet and blue, or separate colors are available.

Antirrhinum (snapdragon) H.H.A., 9 in.–3 ft. These long-flowering plants are usually treated as annuals although in mild districts they are short-lived perennials. For bedding purposes seed is sown in flats or pots in a warm greenhouse in February or March. Sturdy plants should be ready for planting out in a sunny bed by mid-May. Seed may be sown in the open ground in April or May for

---

Notes on Plant Descriptions

H.A. Indicates that the plant is best raised as a hardy annual by seed sown in the open ground in the spring, or in some instances in the fall. This is stated where applicable. Such hardy annuals will withstand a normal winter in the open ground and will provide an earlier display than spring-sown seed.

H.H.A. Denotes a half-hardy annual which is a plant that is liable to damage by spring frost or may be withered by perishing winds in the young stage. Such plants are raised from seed sown under glass in a temperature of about 60°F (15°C), either in a greenhouse

or in an electrically heated propagating frame.

H.B. Indicates a hardy biennial that takes two years to flower from seed and then dies. The seed is usually sown in the open ground in the early summer, the seedlings later being transplanted in rows to grow on, before being moved to their flowering positions in the fall or early spring.

H.H.P. This refers to a half-hardy perennial plant which may live for a number of years but requires the protection of a frost-free greenhouse during the winter. Such plants are often used for summer bedding displays; sometimes exceptionally good plants are increased by cuttings.

Above: The common marigold, *Calendula officinalis*, seeds itself freely. But there are much improved kinds, with flowers of various forms, in a fairly wide color range. This one is 'Orange King'. *Below: Amaranthus caudatus* is popularly known as love-lies-bleeding. A half-hardy annual, seedlings should be planted out in late spring

flowering in late summer, but these cannot be compared with plants raised under glass. The range of color includes crimson, pink, orange-scarlet, yellow and white, and many subtle variations. The dwarf varieties are admirable for the front of a border or for window boxes and the taller varieties are useful for cut flowers. There is also a good selection of rust-resistant hybrids, which are advised where this disease is prevalent.

Arctotis H.H.A., 1–2 ft. These South African plants with daisy-like flowers require a well-drained soil and full sun. They are perennial in their native conditions but are easily raised from seed sown under glass in March in a temperature of 65°F (18°C). Harden off the seedlings before planting out in mid-May. The silvery-white flowers of *A. grandis*, 2 ft., have a mauve centre and a golden band. Young plants should be pinched back when about 6 in. high to encourage bushy growth.

Asperula (woodruff) H.A., 1 ft. A useful little plant for edging or for filling a gap at the front of a border. A native of Syria, *A. orientalis* is an easily grown plant producing fragrant, lavender-blue flowers from July onwards. It is of branching habit and is useful for miniature floral arrangements. It enjoys a moist soil and partial shade and should be sown in May where it is to flower.

Bellis (double English daisy) H.B., 6 in. *Bellis perennis* 'Monstrosa Flore Pleno' is a hardy perennial but is usually raised from seed sown in the open ground in early summer and transplanted to flowering positions in the fall. In colder areas plants should be planted in protected cold frames in the fall and transferred to the open ground in spring. The button-like flowers are in shades of crimson to rose and white and are effective among other spring bedding plants and tulips.

Brachycome (Swan River daisy) H.H.A., 9–12 in. In sheltered gardens *B. iberidifolia* a little Australian plant may be treated as a hardy annual, but it is usually sown under glass in March and planted out in May. Easily grown in a dry, sunny position, it flowers throughout the summer until the fall frosts. The star-like flowers are blue or white with a dark disk. As a pot plant it will flower for weeks in a cool greenhouse.

Calandrinia (rock purslane) H.H.A., 6 in. *C. umbellata* is a sun-loving plant from Peru which thrives on a rock garden ledge or on the top of a dry wall. The brilliant magenta-crimson flowers are borne in clusters from July to September, but do not open in dull weather. Sow the seed in April and May and thin the seedlings to 6 in. apart.

Calceolaria H.H.A., 1–1½ ft. The dust-like seed of the pale yellow *C. scabiosaefolia* is sown under glass in early spring and after hardening off the young plants are put out when the danger of frost is over. In a sunny position or in dappled shade they flower from July to September.

Calendula (pot or garden marigold) H.A., 1½–2 ft. These showy plants derived from *C. officinalis* are among the hardiest and easiest to grow in almost any soil and in full sun. They flower continuously throughout the summer and the fall. Particularly in light soil they seed themselves happily but modern varieties tend to deteriorate quickly when grown in this way. Sow in spring or the fall in milder areas where they are to flower. Young seedlings may be transplanted with success. There are numerous named varieties, many of American origin (F_1 hybrids), where they are known as the friendship flower. To get the best results purchase fresh seed each year. Good varieties include: 'First Lady', bright yellow, compact; 'Flame Beauty', deep orange; 'Golden Beauty', gold; 'Lemon Beauty', lemon-yellow; 'Radio', bright orange, ball-shaped flowers with quilled petals.

Callistephus (China aster) H.H.A., 1–2½ ft. The diverse and colorful modern asters have been developed from *C. chinenis* but some seedsmen find they are better known as asters –not to be confused with the perennial Michaelmas daisies. Seed should be sown in a cool greenhouse in March or April, or in warmer areas in the open ground in early May. There are both double and single flowers and the color range is all-embracing. Seedlings transplant quite readily when small. Grown *en masse* they make a splendid show in late summer and early fall. The short-growing varieties make bushy, decorative plants in window boxes. 'Ostrich Plume', and 'Princess', both 2 ft., are admirable for cutting.

Campanula (Canterbury bell) H.B., 2½–3 ft. An old favorite among gardeners, *C. medium* in shades of deep blue, lavender, deep pink and white is admirable in a mixed border in good soil and a sunny position. The cup and saucer varieties with large bell-like flowers and a saucer, or calyx, of the same color are among the most popular. Sow the seed in the open in May or June, covering it very lightly with fine soil, and plant out in the flowering position in early fall. They will flower the following June to August. Where winters are severe the plants should be transferred to frost-proof frames until the spring.

Celosia (cockscomb) H.H.A., 2 ft. The feathered forms of *C. argentea cristata* bear brilliant pyramidal plumes from July to September. The colors include shades of crimson, scarlet, orange and yellow and are seen to best effect with green foliage plants. Sow seed in a warm greenhouse in March, pot the seedlings individually and plant out in the open when the danger of frost is past. They thrive in a well-drained, light soil and in full sun. Seeds may also be sown outside in spring where the plants are to flower. They also make decorative pot plants in a greenhouse for summer display.

Left: The corn marigold, *Chrysanthemum segetum*, a hardy annual. *Below: Cleome* 'Pink Queen', a 3–4 ft. half-hardy annual, is known as the spider flower. It makes a very effective summer display. *Above: Cobaea scandens*, known as the cup and saucer vine, because of its Canterbury-bell-like flowers, is a vigorous, half-hardy annual climber. *Far right:* A dwarf cornflower, *Centaurea* 'Polka Dot'

Centaurea (cornflower, sweet sultan) H.A., 1–3 ft. The bright blue flowers of the cornflower, *C. cyanus*, are borne on tall stems and there are also pale blue, lilac, pink and white varieties, as well as dwarf varieties not exceeding 1 ft. in height. All are easily raised from seed sown from March to May, or in September in warmer areas, in a sunny position and in reasonably well-drained soil. The taller varieties are excellent for cutting. *C. moschata* (the sweet sultan) H.A., 1½ ft. is another popular annual with fragrant, fluffy heads of flower larger than those of cornflower, pale lilac in color. There are giant varieties in shades of mauve, purple, rose, yellow and white. The flowers are most useful for cutting and will last many days in water if cut young. Sow as for cornflower. Both do well on soil containing lime.

Cheiranthus (wallflower) H.B., 15 in. *C.* × *allionii*, is the Siberian wallflower with bright orange flowers in April and May. 'Golden

Bedder' is a more mellow golden-yellow variety. The common wallflower, *C. cheiri*, 1½ ft. is perennial in milder parts of the country, but both these wallflowers are best treated as a biennial and sown in an open seed bed in May, or mid-June for the Siberian wallflower, and transplanted to flowering positions in October. Plants should be overwintered in frost-proof frames where the winters are colder. The fragrance of wallflowers on a warm sunny day is glorious and they associate happily with tulips, forget-me-nots and polyanthus. The range of color is splendid–blood red, scarlet, purple, pink, yellow, ivory white.

Chrysanthemum H.A., 1–3 ft. *C. carinatum* (tricolor chrysanthemum), 1½–2 ft. *C. coronarium* (crown daisy) 2–3 ft. *C. segetum* (corn chrysanthemum) 1–1½ ft. There are many gay varieties of annual chrysanthemums, single and double. All have daisy-like flowers on good stems and often have rings or zones of color on white or cream petals. Among the best hardy annuals for summer flowering, they make excellent cut flowers. Seed should be sown in April in the open in a sunny position where they are to flower or in September for an early display the next year in milder areas. They do not transplant readily, so it is a waste of time to plant out thinnings. They are not fussy about soil provided it is not excessively wet.

Clarkia H.A., 2 ft. Double-flowered *C. elegans* hybrids are deservedly popular; their slender spikes bear numerous flower heads in shades of salmon-pink, carmine, rosy-purple and white. They are also most decorative as cut flowers. Sow in the open where they are to flower in March and April, or, in milder parts of the country in September to flower the following May and June. Clarkia does best in a light soil and will not tolerate heavy, wet soil. It is wise to support young plants with light twigs as they are liable to be broken off at ground level in a summer gale. For a spring display in a cold greenhouse sow the seed under glass in the fall.

Cleome (spider flower) H.H.A., 3–4 ft. The large, airy flower trusses are an attractive pinky-mauve and borne erect on rigid, thorny stems from July to September. The plants are most effective when grown in bold clumps in the border. Sow the seed in March in a warm greenhouse and plant out in May in rich, well-drained soil. They can also be sown directly outside where they are to flower. These fast-growing plants require ample moisture. 'Pink Queen' is an attractive apple-blossom pink; there is also a pure white variety.

Cobaea (cup and saucer plant) H.H.A., 10–20 ft. A vigoros Mexican twiner *C. scandens* bears large Canterbury bell-like flowers from July onwards on a warm wall. The flowers open green, becoming violet-purple. In a cool greenhouse it is perennial but requires ample space to spread. There is also a white variety. Soak the large seeds in water for a few hours before sowing and place them on their sides in the soil, not flat. Sow under glass in March and pot on, planting out in early June. Where the weather is warmer seeds may be sown directly outside.

Coleus H.H.P., 3 ft. These are ornamental foliage plants with attractive leaves in shades of green, copper, red and apricot, making them conspicuous for greenhouse or room decoration. They may also be planted outdoors in a sunny border as summer bedding plants. Sow seed of *C. blumei* or named hybrids in February under glass in a temperature of 75°F (24°C) and grow on without a check to obtain strong, showy plants. Particularly striking varieties may be perpetuated by taking cuttings, 3 in. long, of non-flowering shoots in August or March.

Collinsia H.A., 1 ft. The Pagoda collinsia is an attractive plant with white upper lip and lilac lower lip, 'Salmon Beauty' is a free-flowering delicate salmon-rose. It is a useful plant for partial shade, or for a woodland garden. Sow in the open ground in March or April, or in milder areas in September.

Convolvulus H.A., 12–15 in. *C. tricolor* (syn. *C. minor*) is a bushy plant and is not to be confused with the climbing convolvulus. It has large, funnel-shaped deep blue, yellow and white flowers throughout the summer and is easily grown in poor soil and in full sun. Sow in March or April where it is to flower.

Coreopsis (tickseed) H.A., 1–2½ ft. Sometimes listed erroneously in catalogs as calliopsis, this is easily grown even in poor soil. Plants bear large, broad-petalled flowers on slender stems from July to September, in shades of yellow, brown and crimson with pleasing markings in contrasting colors. Coreopsis are readily raised from seed sown in the open in a sunny position in April, or under glass in March for earlier flowering.

Cosmos (cosmea) H.H.A., 2–3 ft. This is a most decorative plant with fern-like foliage and large, single or semi-double, daisy-form flowers on slender but wiry stems which make it useful for cutting from July to October. The color range includes orange, yellow, deep rose to brilliant vermilion, red and white. Sow the seed under glass in February and March in a temperature of 60°F (16°C). Prick out the seedlings and plant out in May in light, well-drained soil and in full sun.

Cynoglossum (hound's tongue) H.H.A., 1½ ft. Although strictly biennial, *C. amabile* is usually grown as an annual, either sown under glass in March and planted out in May, or sown in the open in April for flowering in late summer. The fine seed should be sown thinly. The blue-green downy foliage and turquoise-blue drooping flowers, like large forget-me-nots, are charming. Plant in a

Annual dahlias

moderately rich, well-drained soil and sun or dappled shade.

Dahlia H.H.A., 1½–2 ft. Bedding varieties of dahlias are often treated as annuals as they are readily raised from seed. Sow the seed thinly in flats in February and March. In a warm greenhouse it should germinate within ten days. When they are large enough prick out the seedlings or pot them individually. Plant out in mid-May in a sunny position and in a fertile soil. Dahlias require ample moisture during the growing season. Any outstanding plants should be lifted in the fall after the first frost, and after the tubers have been washed and dried they should be stored in a frost-free place for the winter. They may be planted out the following spring and will start to flower in July. Or they can be put in a warm greenhouse in April to produce cuttings.

Delphinium (larkspur) H.A., 1½–3 ft. Seed of annual delphiniums sown in March or April will produce flowering plants by about mid-July. Seedlings do not transplant well, therefore sow where the plants are to flower. For earlier flowering sow in the open in the fall. The color range includes shades of pink, lavender, mauve, rosy-scarlet and white and there are dwarf varieties (1½ ft.). The 3 ft. tall kinds with branching stock-flowered spikes are admirable for cutting.

Dianthus (pinks) H.H.A., 9–18 in. Seed of the annual varieties of carnations and pinks, such as Chabaud carnations (*D. caryophyllus*) and the Japanese pink (*D. chinensis* 'Heddewigii') and others should be sown thinly in pots and lightly covered with sifted soil. Do this in February or March and place the pots in a warm greenhouse where germination should be evident in a week or ten days. Prick out the seedlings into boxes when they are large enough to handle and harden off before planting out in May in well-drained soil and a sunny position. A great many varieties of dianthus will be found listed in seed catalogs, including *D. barbatus*, the sweet William, H.B., 6–18 in., obtainable in a glorious color range. Sow in May or June; when 3 in. high transplant to nursery rows then to their flowering positions in October. Where winters are severe move the plants to cold frames and plant out in spring.

Digitalis (foxglove) H.B., 4–5 ft. The common foxglove (*D. purpurea*) makes a delightful picture in a woodland setting in partial shade in cooler parts of the country. The color range includes deep pink, purple, cream and white. There are several excellent strains; 'Excelsior Hybrids', with flowers carried horizontally all round the stem, revealing the beautiful markings within the

florets and 'The Shirley', are of outstanding beauty. Sow seed in the open ground from May to July and move to nursery rows when large enough to handle. Move plants to their flowering positions in the fall.

Dimorphotheca (star of the veldt) H.H.A., 1 ft. *D. aurantiaca*, a South African plant revels in a sunny position where it produces a succession of large, showy daisy-like flowers. In dull weather the flowers remain closed. It thrives in a light soil. Sow outside where plants are to flower in spring. In colder districts sow under glass in March and plant out in May. Colors include salmon, apricot, buff, orange with greenish-black center and the large 'Glistening White' of spreading habit 6–9 in. high.

Eccremocarpus (Chilean glory flower) H.H.A., 8–10 ft. *E. scaber* is a fast-growing, deciduous, climbing plant. In mild districts it is perennial and will seed itself happily. Sow under glass in March and plant out against a warm, sunny wall or fence when all risk of frost is past. The clusters of orange-scarlet, yellow-tipped tubular flowers are freely produced throughout the summer and fall.

Echium (viper's bugloss) H.A., 1–1½ ft. Compact little plants for the front of a border, echium hybrids bear many bell-like flowers in shades of blue, lavender, pink and white. They do well in poor, dry soil and in a sunny position. The cheerful heads of flowers withstand wind and rain remarkably well. 'Blue Bedder', bright blue, flowers from July to September and there are also good dwarf mixed hybrids.

Eschscholzia (Californian poppy) H.A., 1–1½ ft. These gay little poppies are easily raised from seed; in fact they seed themselves happily without being a nuisance. There are many varieties of *E. californica*, single, semi-double and double, in shades of yellow, orange, copper, carmine and ivory. For a hot, sunny bed there are few annuals of equal merit.

Felicia (kingfisher daisy) H.H.A., 4–6 in. Almost creeping in habit, *F. bergeriana*, is decorative on the rock garden or the front of a sunny border in light soil. Sow under glass in March and plant out in the open in early May, or outside where they are to flower. A profusion of small intense blue flowers is produced from June onwards. In dull weather the flowers open only partially to reveal the yellow center.

Gaillardia (blanket flower) H.H.A., 1½ ft. Perhaps not so well known as the perennial gaillardia, the annual *G. pulchella* has gay crimson-purple flowers tipped with yellow from July to October. The stiff, wiry stems

Above: Helichrysum monstrosum, an Australian 'everlasting' provides much color in the garden and may be cut and dried for winter decoration purposes
Below: Gazanias, otherwise known as treasure flowers, are among the most brilliant of all half-hardy annuals
Right: The 'Monarch' strain of godetias is low growing and consists of a variety of colors. The plants are suitable for bedding purposes but prefer cool conditions
Below right: One of a number of color forms of *Dimorphotheca* an annual popularly known as star of the veldt

Below: Sweet William *(Dianthus barbatus)*

make them useful for cutting. 'Indian Chief' is a striking copper-scarlet. Sow under glass in gentle heat in March, or in the open ground in April where plants are to flower. Choose a sunny position and well-drained soil.

Gazania (treasure flower) H.H.A., 6–9 in. These sun loving, broad-petalled, daisies from South Africa are popular in dry areas. They are easily raised from seed sown under glass in a moderate temperature in March. Seedlings should be planted out in mid-May in full sun and a light soil. The modern

hybrids are in shades of yellow, orange, brown, pink and ruby. The markings and zones of contrasting colors in the center of the flowers add considerably to their beauty.

Gilia H.A., 1½ ft. The blue, pincushion-like flowers and fern-like foliage of *G. capitata* are a delight from June to September. The dainty heads of *G. tricolor* (bird's eye) are in shades of lavender, pink and white with gold throat. *G. hybrida* (*Leptosiphon*) do not exceed 6 in. in height and are decorative on the rock garden or between flagstones in a

path. The small, star-like flowers are in a wide color range. Sow in spring in light, well-drained soil and a sunny position where the plants are to flower.

Godetia H.A., 1–2½ ft. Gay plants with big, colored cups, these are among the most popular of hardy annuals where summers are not too hot. There are dwarf and tall varieties, double and single, in shades of pink, mauve, salmon and white. The tall kinds make graceful cut flowers. Sow in March or April where they are to flower as seedlings do not transplant readily. They like a sunny position and a light soil.

Gypsophila (baby's breath) H.A., 1½ ft. The annual varieties are fast growing and when sown in the open in April will flower from June onwards. To ensure a continuity of flower sow at intervals of two or three weeks. Seed may also be sown in the fall for spring flowering in milder districts. *G. elegans* produces slender stems bearing dainty white flowers and 'Rosea' has pink flowers. They thrive in any good garden soil, preferably chalky. The flowers are admirable when used in arrangements with sweet peas, or to mask the stiffness of gladioli.

Helianthus (sunflower) H.A., 3–7 ft., or more. The giant sunflowers are useful for providing a quick screen and the seeds in the plate-like golden-yellow heads are a great attraction to birds in the fall, but there are other sunflowers of greater garden merit and of more reasonable height. Seed should be sown in the open in spring or in flats under glass and seedlings planted out in mid-May. They like plenty of sun and are not fussy about soil. Mammoth Russian is the largest of all with huge single yellow blooms, Italian white with dark centers and primrose petals.

Helichrysum (everlasting flower) H.H.A., 1½–3 ft. The Australian helichrysums are the best known of the so-called everlastings. They are decorative in the garden in full sun and in a light soil and when cut and dried they are welcome for winter arrangements. The double form 'Monstrosum' of *H. bracteatum* has a popular range of color – crimson, rose, silvery-pink, bronze and white. There are similar colors in dwarf, compact varieties which make bushy plants for the front of the border.

Helipterum H.A., 1–1½ ft. These Australian 'everlastings' are easily raised from seed sown in April where they are to flower. They do best in poor, well-drained soil and in full sun. The neat globular pink flowers are pleasing and there are also double pink and double white varieties.

Heliotropium (cherry pie, heliotrope) H.H.P., 15–24 in. These fragrant evergreen plants are really greenhouse perennials but hybrid varieties may be treated as half-hardy annuals. When sown in February in pots without a check, they can be planted out towards the end of May and will flower in the open from July onwards. The colors range from dark violet to lavender and white. 'Marine' is a splendid violet-purple; 'Marguerite' is dark blue with a white eye.

Iberis (candytuft) H.A., 6–15 in. *I. amara*, the rocket or giant-flowered candytuft, and *I. umbellata*, the common candytuft are most effective when sown in bold masses, but this does not mean sowing thickly. Sow in the open ground in September in milder areas for early flowering the following summer, or in March or April for flowering the same summer. Candytufts do best in moist, rich soil. The dwarf varieties are useful for edging and are obtainable in shades of lilac, rose and white.

Impatiens (balsam) H.H.A., 1–2 ft. The original species (*I. balsamina*) from which the camellia-flowered and other hybrids have been raised comes from India, therefore do not attempt to plant out while there is still a danger of late frost. Sow the seed in March in a warm greenhouse, or outside where the climate is milder. The dwarf and double varieties make attractive pot plants. The color range includes pink, salmon, scarlet and white.

Ipomoea (morning glory) H.H.A., 8 ft. or more. This free-flowering twiner is usually cataloged as *I. rubrocaerulea*, although the correct botanical name is *I. tricolor*; to many people it is convolvulus. Call it what you will the large sky-blue trumpets, 4 in. across, are a magnificent sight from July to September. Germination can be erratic, but it helps if the hard seed cover is carefully chipped with a sharp knife. It is worth taking a little trouble with this spectacular plant. Sow the seeds singly in small pots in a warm greenhouse in March and plant out in a warm sheltered place and in well-drained soil in late May, or

outside in the spot where the plants are to flower.

Kentranthus (often spelt centranthus) (valerian) H.A., 1–1½ ft. *K. macrosiphon* is easily raised from seed sown where it is to flower in a dry sunny position in spring. Blooms are produced from June to August. The gray-blue leaves and bright rose-pink, tubular flowers make this a showy plant.

Kochia (summer cypress, fire-bush) H.H.A., 3 ft. This neat, fast-growing foliage plant is burdened with the name *K. scoparia tricophila*. The finely-cut light green leaves turn coppery-red in the fall, hence the name fire-bush. Sow the seeds singly in small pots, or three seeds in a 3½ in. pot under glass in April, later thinning to one plant. Plant out in the open in late May. The little seedlings should be watered carefully in the early stages as they are likely to damp off.

Lathyrus (sweet pea) H.A., 1–8 ft. These fast-growing plants, derived from *L. odoratus*, make deep roots and therefore require a deeply dug, fertile, sunny site. They do not like excessive heat and grow better in cooler parts of the country. In milder areas the best results can be obtained by sowing the seed in pots or flats in the fall. To obtain the best results sow the seed in pots or flats in the fall and over-winter them in a cold frame (beware of mice). Plant them out in the open in mid-March or early April. They should start to flower in June and, provided fading flowers are removed, will continue in flower for a couple of months or so. Seed can also be sown in the open ground as soon as the weather is suitable in spring.

When planting out space the seedlings 1 ft. apart in the row and not less than 1 ft. between the rows. It is usual to have double rows growing up brushwood stakes, or they can be grown up tripods, or on netting firmly supported by strong metal posts, which may be used year after year. Seed catalogs list many fine modern hybrids in a diversity of color and height, including 'Bijou' (1 ft.), 'Knee-hi' (3–4 ft.) and the early-flowering 'Galaxy' strain, tall, and often producing eight flowers to each long stem. See also Favorite Garden Flowers.

Lavatera (mallow) H.A., 3–4 ft. Easily grown, the annual mallow, *L. trimestris*, has hollyhock-like flowers throughout the summer. Sow the seed sparsely, in March and April, where it is to flower, in a sunny position. 'Loveliness' is the best bright carmine-rose and there is also a pure white variety. Allow these plants adequate space for under good cultivation they may reach a height of 4 ft. and make a bush 3 ft. wide.

Limnanthes (meadow-foam) H.A., 6 in. Sow the seed of *L. douglasii* in an open sunny position in September, where it is to flower the following spring in mild localities, or in March to mid-May for later flowering. This cheerful little plant of spreading habit has shiny green leaves and bright yellow, fragrant, flowers, white at the tips, much loved by bees.

Linaria (toadflax) H.A., 9 in. Sow the seed of *L. maroccana* thinly in the open ground in March or April to obtain a display of snapdragon-like flowers from June to September. 'Fairy Bouquet' is of compact habit in shades of pink, yellow, lavender and salmon, with large flowers that last well when cut.

Linum (flax) H.A., 15 in. Sown in bold clumps in the open in a sunny position in spring, the scarlet flax, *L. grandiflorum* 'Rubrum', is a most effective summer-flowering annual. The common flax, *L. usitatissimum*, with pale blue flowers on slender stems is also delightful.

Lobelia H.H.A., 4–6 in. also trailing varieties. Seed of *L. erinus* and its varieties, is very small and it is easy to sow it too thickly, which means that it will damp off. Sow in pots containing a sandy compost, only lightly covering the seed with sifted soil. This should be done in February or early March in a warm greenhouse. Prick out the seedlings about a month later; these should become bushy plants ready to plant out towards the end of May. The trailing varieties are useful for window-boxes and hanging baskets but require ample and regular watering. Varieties are available in shades of blue; 'Rosamond' is deep carmine-red with a white eye, and there is a pure white variety.

Matthiola (night-scented stock) H.A., 1 ft. Sow seeds of *M. bicornis* in March or April where plants are to flower during the summer. The lilac-mauve flowers open in the evening and the fragrance on a warm summer night is delightful. Sown with candytuft there will be color by day and scent by night.

M. incana (ten-week stocks) H.H.A., 1 ft. Sow seed thinly under glass in March and prick out the seedlings when large enough to handle. Give the plants plenty of light and air and plant out 1 ft. apart where they are to

flower when they have made bushy growth. The color range is all embracing. In milder areas seed may be sown in borders where the plants are to flower.

M. incana (East Lothian or intermediate stocks) H.H.A., 1½ ft. Sow under glass in February or early March, otherwise treat as for ten-week stocks. East Lothian stocks are vigoros, branching plants flowering in late summer and fall. In milder parts of the country the East Lothians can be grown as biennials but are usually treated as half-hardy annuals. They are available in crimson, scarlet, rose, lavender, white, or in packets of mixed colors. *M. incana* cannot be recommended for areas where the summers are warm and humid.

Mentzelia H.A., 2 ft. *M. lindleyi* may still be found in some seed catalogs listed as *Bartonia aurea*. Sown in the open ground in March or April, in a sunny position, this easily-grown plant will flower from June onwards. The large, single golden flowers have an attractive mass of golden stamens.

Mesembryanthemum (Fig marigold) H.H.A., 6 in. Of South African origin, this annual, almost always sold under the name mesembryanthemum, but correctly known as *Dorotheanthus bellidiflorus*, requires the maximum sun and a rather dry soil. Of spreading habit it is most decorative trailing over a dry wall or growing in crazy paving. Sow under glass in March or April and plant out in May. Seed may also be sown directly outdoors where the plants are to flower. The star-like flowers are in a wide range of brilliant colors.

Mimulus (monkey flower) H.H.A., 6 in.–2 ft. Many mimulus are treated as half-hardy annuals although they may prove to be short-lived perennials. By sowing the seed under glass in March these quick-growing, moisture-loving plants will flower in the open in June and July. Seed sown in the open in partial shade in April will provide a later batch of color. The seeds are very tiny and should only be lightly covered with sifted soil. The large trumpet-shaped flowers are in shades of red and yellow with attractive markings and blotches.

Moluccella (bells of Ireland) H.H.A., 2 ft. Germination of seed of *M. laevis* is unpredictable; sown under glass in March or April in a temperature of 65°F (18°C) germination may be satisfactory, and on other occasions it may germinate in the open in early May, provided the soil is light and warm. The little white flowers are insignificant; it is the large pale green, white-netted calyces that are so unusual and a delight to flower arrangers. The flowers may be dried for use in winter.

Myosotis (forget-me-not) H.B., 6–12 in. These are easily raised from seed sown in the open ground in June. Transplant the seedlings when they are large enough to handle into the open ground or cold frames and plant them out in the fall where they are to flower, or plant them out in the spring. They are admirable when planted with tulips, wallflowers or polyanthus. They will grow in sun or partial shade and seed themselves happily. There are named varieties in several shades of blue and carmine-pink, and also white.

Far left: The Fig marigold, *Mesembry-anthemum criniflorum* (botanically known as *Dorotheanthus bellidiflorus*), is a half-hardy annual available in many bright colors
Left: The candytuft (*Iberis umbellata*) is most effective when sown to form masses of color
Above: In an annual bed, brilliant splashes of scarlet can be provided by sowing seeds of *Linum grandiflorum* 'Rubrum'

Mimulus cupreus, sometimes known as the monkey flower, is a moisture-loving plant which flowers in June and July from an early sowing under glass. It is a useful plant for a shady border or around the edge of a pool

Nemesia H.H.A., 8–12 in. Free-flowering little plants in a wide color range, the varieties of *N. strumosa* are among the brightest of the bedding plants. Sow the seed in mid-March in a cool greenhouse and grow them steadily without a check. Prick out the seedlings into flats and plant out in late May or early June. Be sure that the soil does not dry at any time. They may also be sown directly in their flowering positions when the danger of frost is over. For winter flowering under glass as pot plants sow the seed in August.

Nemophila (baby blue eyes) H.A., 6–8 in. *N. menziesii* is a useful spreading plant for moist conditions, in sun or partial shade. The feathery light green leaves and sky-blue flowers with a white eye make a cheerful picture for the front of a border or on a rock garden. Sow in the open in March or April, or, in warmer areas, in the fall. There is also a white-flowered form.

Nicotiana (tobacco plant) H.H.A., 1½–2½ ft. Fragrance is one of the chief attractions when the flowers usually open in the evening, although if grown in partial shade they often remain open all day. 'Sensation' is a strain with flowers of mixed colors that do remain open in daylight. 'Lime Green' has unusual greenish-yellow flowers, popular for floral arrangements. Sow under glass in a moderate temperature in March. Plant out, when the risk of frost is past, in rich moist soil which has been deeply dug. They flower from July to September. In milder parts of the country seeds may be sown outdoors as soon as the soil is suitable in spring.

Nierembergia H.H.A., 9 in. Although strictly a perennial, *N. caerulea*, from the Argentine, is usually treated as an annual and sown under glass in February or early March and planted out towards the end of May. The large, cup-shaped, lavender-blue flowers with an attractive yellow throat are freely produced from July to September. 'Purple Robe' is a selected form with deep violet-purple flowers, with golden anthers.

Nigella (love-in-a-mist) H.A., 1½–2 ft. *N. damascena* is a favorite among hardy annuals and is easily grown. Sow in the open in September in a well-drained soil and a sunny position for flowering from May onwards. Seed sown in March or April will provide a long season of flower. Seedlings do not transplant readily, therefore sow where it is to flower. 'Miss Jekyll', sky-blue with dainty feathery foliage is a fine variety; 'Persian

Jewels' is a pleasing mixture of pink, rosy-red, purple and mauve shades, also white.

Omphalodes (Venus's navelwort) H.A., 9–12 in. Resembling a forget-me-not, *O. linifolia*, bears masses of pure white flowers and gray-green leaves on slender stems from June to August. Sow in spring or early fall in a light, well-drained soil where the plants are to flower. It is a decorative plant for the front of a border or on a rock garden.

Papaver (poppy) H.A., 1½–2½ ft. Easily raised from seed, the diverse annual poppies should be sown in August–September or March, April and May where they are to flower. Shirley poppies, derived from *P rhoeas*, may also be sown in September to flower from May onwards. From the opium

Facing page: The brilliant color range of salpiglossis, a half-hardy annual. Salpiglossis thrives in a rich soil and a warm sheltered border
Left: Love-in-a-mist (*Nigella damascena*) is among the more popular annuals
Above: 'Pink Chiffon', one of the many varieties of *Papaver somniferum*, the opium poppy, has fully double flowers
Below: In *Nicotiana* 'Daylight', a flowering tobacco, the blooms remain open all day, instead of opening in the evening only

poppy, *P. somniferum*, have been raised many varieties, including double paeony-flowered and double carnation-flowered in many different colors. 'Pink Beauty' is a handsome double flower that shows up well against its gray foliage.

Penstemon (beard tongue) H.H.A., 1½ ft. Most penstemons are perennial but there is a hybrid race which is treated as an annual. In mild districts and in a well-drained soil they may survive the winter and start to flower earlier the following year. The elegant tubular flowers are borne on erect stems from July to September in mixed colors; pink, crimson, scarlet, mauve, white. Sow the seed under glass in March and plant out in a sunny place in May.

Petunia H.H.A., 9–15 in. Modern hybrid petunias are available in many different types; large-flowered singles and doubles, compact bedding varieties, pendulous forms suitable for hanging baskets or window boxes, bi-colors, self-colors, some with fringed and ruffled flowers. They are sun-loving plants, although some of the new varieties are colorful even in a poor summer. The vigorous F₁ hybrids with large trumpet-shaped flowers of uniform color are outstanding. Sow the seed under glass in March and grow the seedlings on steadily without a check. Prick out in flats when large enough to handle and grow them on in the greenhouse. Put them in a cold frame to harden off before planting out in late May or early June in a fairly light soil and full sun.

Phacelia (California bluebell) H.A., 9 in.–2 ft. *P. campanularia*, 9 in. has large bell-shaped brilliant blue flowers and grayish-green, red-tinted leaves, which make it a most desirable little plant of neat habit. Sow in the spring, or fall where winters are less severe, in a light well-drained soil and a sunny position, where it is to flower from June onwards. *P. tanacetifolia*, 2 ft. is a hairy plant with crowded spikes of lavender-blue flowers and is often cultivated by bee-keepers.

Phlox H.H.A., 6–12 in. *P. drummondii* is a popular, free-flowering bedding plant in shades of pink, salmon, crimson, violet and purple, many with a striking white eye; there are also pure white varieties. The compact varieties are about 6 in. high and the 'Grandi-flora' hybrids up to 1 ft. Sow the seed in gentle heat in March and plant out from mid-May onwards in a sunny position, to flower from July until early October. They can also be sown outside where weather conditions are milder. Keep the young plants well watered.

Portulaca (Purslane or sun plant) H.H.A., 6 in. The dwarf, spreading *P. grandiflora* from Brazil requires a hot, sunny position in light well-drained soil. Sow the seed in May where plants are to flower as seedlings do not transplant readily. Cover the seed lightly with fine soil and keep moist until established. Plants make an effective carpet from July onwards. They are usually offered in mixed colors—double and single—scarlet, deep pink, yellow and white.

Quamoclit H.H.A., 10 ft. *Q. lobata* is a fast growing twining plant with bright crimson flowers which change to orange-yellow and fade to cream. Sow the seed in small pots in a heated greenhouse in March or early April and move into larger pots when seedlings are well rooted. Plant out when the danger of frost is past in rich, moist soil. Seed may also be sown outside where the plants are to flower.

Reseda (mignonette) H.A., 9–12 in. This is a plant of great charm and delicious fragrance. Sow the seed in light, well-drained soil, preferably containing lime, in April and May, where the plants are to flower. Germination is improved when the soil is made firm after sowing and the seed is only lightly covered with fine soil. By making two or more sowings a succession of flowers will be ensured. 'Goliath' bears large, very fragrant, reddish spikes.

Ricinus (castor oil plant, castor bean) H.H.A., 4–6 ft. A decorative foliage plant, *R. communis*, has bronze-colored leaves up to 2 ft. across. The flowers are insignificant but the seed pods, covered with soft spines, contain large bean-like seeds from which castor oil is obtained. Sow the seed singly in small pots in March in a greenhouse with a temperature of 60°F (16°C). Pot on the seedlings and plant out in June. Seed may also be planted outside when the soil is suitable. Plants thrive in rich, moist soil but will probably need staking.

Rudbeckia (coneflower) H.H.A., 2 ft. The gay annual rudbeckias are easily raised from seed sown under glass in March and planted out in May in a sunny position, or sown outside where they are to flower. They are not fussy about soil. Listed in seed catalogs under *R. bicolor* 'Golden Flame' is a golden-yellow with a dark centre and 'Kelvedon Star' is deep yellow with a brown central disk and mahogany zone.

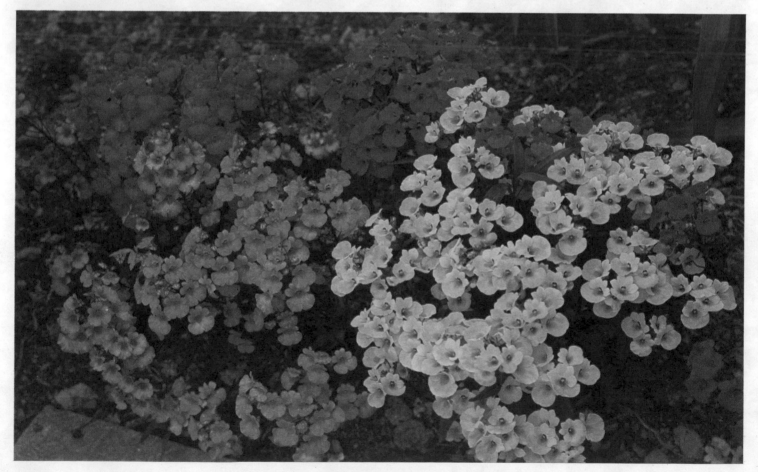

Salpiglossis H.H.A., 2–3 ft. The elegant, trumpet-shaped flowers, many of which are beautifully veined, are in a brilliant range of color. Sow the seed in a warm greenhouse in February or March. When large enough to handle prick out the seedlings singly into small pots and grow on steadily until they are ready to plant out in early June. They can also be sown outside when the danger of frost is past where they are to flower. They like a rich soil and a warm, sheltered border, and are admirable as pot plants in a cool greenhouse.

Salvia (sage) H.H.A., 1–1½ ft. The vivid scarlet *S. splendens*, the scarlet sage, is a tender perennial usually treated as a half-hardy annual. Seed should be sown under glass in February or March in a temperature of about 68°F (20°C). When seedlings are

March and planting out in May in a sunny border. The taller varieties should be supported with light twigs in good time or they may be damaged by summer gales. They are available in mixed colors and are admirable for cutting.

Schizanthus (butterfly flower) H.H.A., 1½–3 ft. Usually considered as highly decorative plants for the cool greenhouse, schizanthus hybrids may be also grown in the garden in a sunny position, sheltered as much as possible from wind. For this purpose sow the seed under glass in a warm greenhouse in March and plant out towards the end of May. There are several good strains, some with beautiful markings on the petals, in shades of salmon, apricot, pink, yellow, mauve and purple.

Senecio (groundsel) H.H.A., 9–18 in. A refined version of the common groundsel,

S. elegans can be quite effective when grown in a bold group. Sow in the open ground in April or May in a sunny position. Seedlings will transplant if necessary. It is usually obtainable in mixed colors—bright rose, lavender, pink, white with yellow center, in both single and double.

Silene (catchfly) H.A., 9–18 in. From southern Europe *S. armeria* has attractive blue-green foliage and rose-pink clusters of single flowers on erect stems in summer. More widely grown is *S. pendula*, of compact habit, with double flowers on 6–9 in. stems in shades of salmon-pink, rosy-purple, ruby-red and white. Seeds should be sown outdoors in August; when large enough to handle, the seedlings should be transferred to nursery beds or cold frames, and planted out in spring.

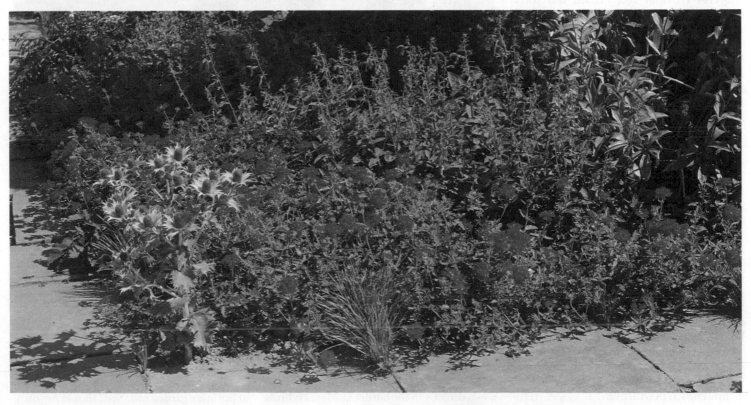

large enough put them into pots singly and grow them on steadily, hardening them off before planting out in a sunny bed in late May or early June. *S. horminum*, H.A., 1½ ft., should be sown in spring where it is to flower. 'Blue Beard' has attractive blue bracts.

Sanvitalia H.A., 6 in. Of prostrate habit *S. procumbens*. A Mexican plant, forms a carpet of small yellow flowers with a bold black center. There is also a bright yellow double form. Sow in the open where it is to flower in a sunny position and in a well-drained soil in late April or May. Or it may be sown under glass in March and planted out in May. Sowings can also be made outside in the fall where winters are less severe. Sown in a bold mass it can be most effective.

Scabiosa (sweet scabious) H.A., 1½–3 ft. Sown in the open in April or May, also in the fall, the annual *S. atropurpurea*, or pincushion flower, will make a good show from August onwards. It can be brought into flower much earlier by sowing under glass in

Opposite: The half-hardy annual nemesias are available in many bright colors
Above: The scarlet flowers of one of the half-hardy verbena hybrids, provide brilliant color at the front of this border
Below: Petunias, in various colors, are among the most reliable of half-hardy annuals

Above: 'Picador', an African marigold
Right: Dahlia-like Zinnias, one of their many flower forms

Tagetes (African and French marigolds) H.H.A., 6 in.–3 ft. These are easily raised from seed sown thinly in a cool greenhouse towards the end of March and planted out in a sunny position at the end of May. Seed can also be sown outside in spring. *T. erecta* is the bold African marigold which makes a branching plant up to 3 ft. in height. There are many modern F_1 hybrids in shades of yellow, orange and lemon. These are an improvement on the earlier rather harsh colors. There are also dwarf American hybrids (1 ft.). Very different are the petite French marigolds which make compact plants of symmetrical habit from 6–9 in. high. There are single and double varieties in shades of palest yellow, orange, gold and mahogany-red some with dark foliage.

Tithonia H.H.A., 4 ft. A vigorous, branching plant, *T. rotundifolia* bears large, orange-red, broad-petalled flowers in August and September. Sow the seed in March under glass, pot the seedlings and plant out in a light soil and full sun towards the end of May. Later blooms can be had from seed sown directly outside when the soil has become warm in spring.

Tropaeolum (nasturtium) H.A., 9 in., trailing and climbing. *T. majus* varieties are easily grown provided simple rules are observed. Do not sow too early as the seedlings may be ruined by a late frost; poor soil is preferable to rich which will only encourage leaf growth to hide the flowers. Late April is time enough to sow where they are to flower. There are single, semi–double and double flowered varieties in shades of glowing scarlet, golden-yellow, cherry-rose, mahogany-red and mixed colors. *T. peregrinum*, the canary creeper, is an attractive climbing species to 10 ft. from Peru, bearing fringed golden-yellow flowers from July onwards. This likes a rich soil and should be sown in sun or shade in late April or May.

Ursinia H.H.A., 9–15 in. Masses of daisy-like flowers and graceful foliage make these showy South African plants a welcome addition to the summer display. Sow the seed under glass in March and plant out in mid–May in full sun and in a light, well-drained soil. Sowing can also be carried out

in spring where the plants are to bloom. *U. anethoides*, 15 in., has large brilliant orange flowers with chestnut-red zone around the centre in July and August. *U. pulchra*, 9 in., suitable for the rock garden or front of the border, has rich orange flowers with a dark central zone. Several named varieties are obtainable, including 'Aurora', with a crimson-red center to the rich orange flowers, and 'Golden Bedder'.

Venidium (Namaqualand daisy) H.H.A., 2½ ft. Another sun-loving plant from South Africa, *V. fastuosum*, bears large orange flowers with a purple-black zone and shiny black center from July to September. Sow

under glass in March and plant out in mid-May in a good loamy soil. Seed can also be sown directly in the border in May. Hybrids are available in pleasing shades of yellow, straw, orange and cream, their petals attractively blotched at the base with darker colors.

Verbena (vervain) H.H.A., 6–15 in. The hybrid verbenas are easily raised from seed sown in a warm greenhouse in February or March. Germination may be erratic and can be delayed for several weeks. Prick out into flats and after hardening off, plant out in a sunny position in May. The compact varieties are admirable for window boxes or for the front of a border. The 3 in. clusters of flowers are freely borne from June to September. The color range includes scarlet, rose, salmon, deep blue, lavender, some with a white eye, and white.

Viola (pansy, viola) H.B., 6–9 in. Violas usually have smaller flowers than pansies, often self colored, are of tufted habit and are best treated as hardy biennials. Sow both kinds in flats in a cold frame or outside in well prepared soil in July or August, and keep the seedlings moist and shaded. When

large enough to handle prick the seedlings out in rows outside or in cold frames. Where winters are less severe the plants may be transferred to their flowering positions in the fall. In colder areas delay moving the plants and protect them with a light covering of salt hay or evergreen branches. Cold frames should have the sash in position during frost. Do not let them dry out at any time. They like a rich moist soil, in sun or partial shade. Sowing can also be done in March or April in the open where they are to flower later the same year. There are numerous special strains, also winter-flowering varieties.

Viscaria H.A., 6–15 in. Annual viscarias, mainly varieties of *V. oculata*, are easily grown in ordinary garden soil. Seed should be sown in March or April where plants are to flower. They are free-flowering plants, effective *en masse* at the front of a border, with showy five-petal flowers in pink, scarlet, crimson, blue and white, or as mixed colors. They are also decorative as cool greenhouse pot plants.

Zinnia H.H.A., 9 in.–2½ ft. Sow the seed in a warm greenhouse in April. There is nothing to be gained by sowing earlier as seedlings are liable to damp off during a cold spell. Prick out into flats when quite small, or singly into small pots. Harden off carefully in a cold frame before planting out in full sun and in a rich, well-drained soil in early June. Seed may also be sown outside where the plants are to flower as soon as the danger of frost is over. There is a diverse selection from giant-flowered and giant-dahlia-flowered varieties, up to 2½ ft. high, to 'Lilliput' and 'Pompon', 9–12 in. and the American raised 'Thumbelina' only 6 in. high. The range of color includes scarlet, pink, orange, lavender, yellow and white.

Roses & Rose Growing

Using Roses in the Garden

According to the archaeologists, roses have existed for 30 million to 70 million years. Ever since civilization began they have given pleasure. They are referred to in Greek poetry and mythology, the Romans crowned their heroes with them and Shakespeare, Herrick, Keats and other poets sang their praises in their verses. However, roses as we know them now date from the end of the 18th century, when rosarians turned their hand to artificial hybridization. Since then the beautiful complex modern rose has been developed. Because of the many crossings and intercrossings of types and varieties, our roses have become so involved that leading rosarians have sought a new classification, not to suit the botanists, but the gardeners, based on their qualities, degrees of flowering and their present-day uses in modern gardens.

Changing living conditions that have made small gardens more popular have created a new approach to roses, which will be assisted by these new classifications. Repeat-flowering is becoming an important factor in selecting roses, because prolonged color display is an essential in a restricted space. Whereas hitherto the choice has been largely confined to hybrid tea and floribunda roses, gardeners, particularly those with small gardens, should now look at the many other types that the vast rose family can offer and choose those that meet their needs. Gardeners should come to regard roses as flowering shrubs, which they are. Thus their use can be considered without inhibitions and their cultivation will be more easily appreciated.

Hybrid Teas and Floribunda Roses

These two types are the most commonly found in gardens. At one time, they were two very distinctly different sorts, with their own characteristics – the hybrid teas producing their flowers singly, or at most in threes, on each stem, and the floribundas, which were more usually single or semi-double, in clusters. However, rose breeders have, by crossing hybrid teas and floribundas, and further intercrossing, developed floribunda roses that have large clusters of perfectly formed hybrid tea-shaped flowers. Also hybrid tea roses have been bred that produce their blooms in large clusters in much the same way as the floribundas. Excellent examples of these are 'Pink Favorite' and 'Fragrant Cloud'.

These developments are of considerable value to modern gardeners who particularly wish to enjoy hybrid tea roses where their space is restricted. When gardens were larger, hybrid tea and, to some extent, floribunda roses were nearly always grown in formal beds, usually in part of the garden entirely devoted to them. It was an accepted rule that they could be grown only in formal surroundings, although floribundas were permitted to co-exist with other flowering shrubs and plants. Growing hybrid teas in formal beds is an excellent manner of dis-

playing them if space allows. Nevertheless, there seems to be little justification for this restriction. In fact, if there is not sufficient space to do otherwise, and they are to be enjoyed, hybrid tea roses must be mixed with other plants in shrub borders, mixed beds and anywhere else where they can be fitted in. Moreover, if it is true that floribundas are suitable for informal positions, then our modern hybrid teas, with their similar clusters of blooms must be equally suitable.

There is another feature, particularly of present-day hybrid tea roses, which renders them less appropriate to formal bedding than those of former days. This is their great vigor, which most of them have inherited from that wonderful parent, 'Peace', that causes them to reach $4\frac{1}{2}$ ft. in height, making them too unwieldy for formal beds, though they can be satisfactorily inter-mixed with shrubs in small gardens. Some of the very tall ones, such as 'Uncle Walter', make excellent specimens in the lawn. Fortunately there are still some low-growing hybrid teas available for those who desire a formal rose garden.

Polyanthas

A free-flowering group whose popularity has diminished since the introduction of Floribundas which have larger blooms and increased vigor. Never the less the dainty flowers have an appeal and are particularly useful where space is limited. Varieties include 'Cecile Brunner' (The Sweetheart Rose), 'Orange Triumph' and 'Little Lady'.

Miniatures

Even more diminutive are the miniature roses, ranging in height from 5 in. to 18 in. There are many varieties available in a wide range of colors. All have recurrent-flowering, minute blossoms, that are exact replicas of either hybrid tea or floribunda roses. They are excellent for forward posi-

A floribunda rose with blooms of hybrid tea shape

tions in borders, edging, and planting in rock gardens and containers. They are also available as standards and climbers.

Species and Shrub Roses

There are great opportunities for adorning modern gardens, with species and shrub roses. Many, such as *Rosa moyesii*, with its profusion of deep red blossoms, followed by large, bottle-shaped, red hips, and the *R. spinosissima* hybrid, 'Frühlingsgold', which is smothered with yellow flowers in May, are too large for most gardens, but there are other more modest growers, that can be planted as specimens in the lawn or among shrubs, as can the very beautiful *rugosa* shrubs, clear rose-pink 'Fraü Dagmar Hastrup', deep crimson 'Mrs Anthony Waterer', and the velvety, dark crimson, almost black, *gallica* shrub, 'Tuscany Superb'. There are also modern shrub roses that are repeat-flowering and not too large. These include the Kordes shrub roses, apricot-yellow 'Grandmaster', light crimson 'Elmshorn', and blood red 'Kassel', and the hybrid musk roses, 'Cornelia' and 'Felicia'. More recently developed are 'The David Austin New English Roses', which include among them the diminutive shrub type roses, crimson and purple 'The Knight' and warm pink 'The Wife of Bath', both under 2 ft. in height.

Rose Hedges

An excellent way of enjoying roses, particularly in a small garden, is to make a hedge of them. Suitable ones for this purpose are the white *rugosa*, 'Blanc Double de Coubert' (about 4 ft.), the hybrid musk, 'Penelope' (5 ft.), pink grandiflora, 'Queen Elizabeth' (6–8 ft.) and the hybrid tea rose, 'Peace' ($4\frac{1}{2}$ ft.).

Climbing Roses

The old-fashioned ramblers, such as 'Dorothy Perkins' and 'American Pillar', were once much cherished, but, because they flower once only in the summer, admittedly with a glorious display, and are so vigorous that it is essential that they are pruned and tied in immediately after they have flowered, present-day gardeners have little time for them. Fortunately, since 1930, when the pale flesh-pink, once-flowering 'Dr W. van Fleet', threw a sport, 'New Dawn', which was of the same color, recurrent-flowering, but far less vigorous, there has been bred from it a range of modern climbing roses, which are very suitable for present-day conditions. In a small garden they can be most effectively used to clothe fences, walls, trellis, etc.

Among the roses that have stemmed from 'New Dawn' are 'Bantry Bay', 'Parade' and 'Schoolgirl'. The German hybridist Wilhelm Kordes, has been responsible for raising another very attractive group of climbers, known as the Kordes climbers or pillar roses. They are all recurrent-flowering and modest growers. The best known are 'Dortmund', crimson with a white eye; crimson 'Hamburger Phoenix'; pale yellow 'Leverkusen', and red 'Parkdirektor Riggers'. Other mod-

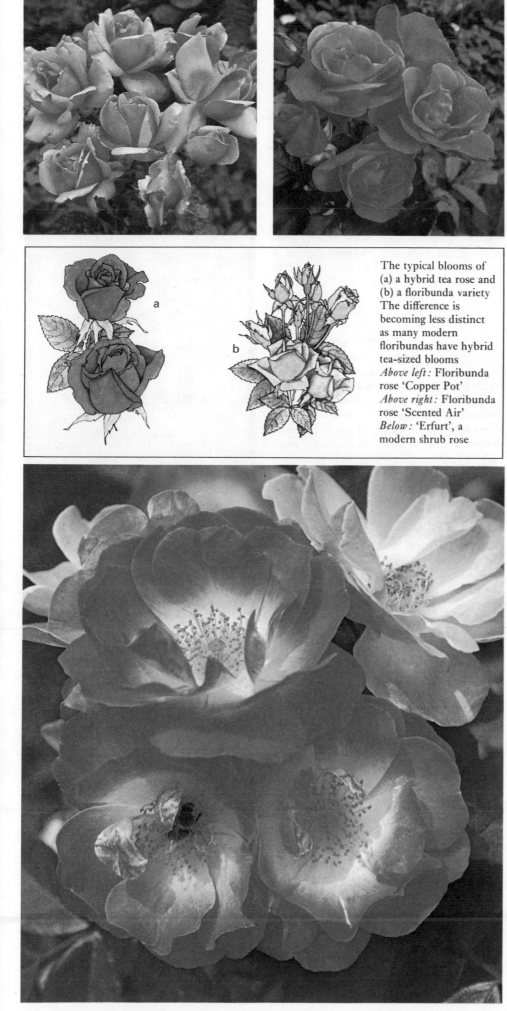

The typical blooms of
(a) a hybrid tea rose and
(b) a floribunda variety
The difference is
becoming less distinct
as many modern
floribundas have hybrid
tea-sized blooms
Above left: Floribunda
rose 'Copper Pot'
Above right: Floribunda
rose 'Scented Air'
Below: 'Erfurt', a
modern shrub rose

Left: Blooms of the floribunda rose 'Masquerade'

ern, charming climbing roses are vermilion 'Danse du Feu', 'Golden Showers' and scarlet crimson 'Soldier Boy'. All these are characterized by their modest vigor, variety of color and repeat flowering and have among them every form of flower that is found in all other types of roses. Mainly because of their long period of flowering, they have largely usurped the climbing sports of the hybrid teas and floribundas.

There are various ways in which climbing roses can be used. One trained up a post can form a very attractive specimen or make a colorful high point in a border. They are invaluable for clothing fences and walls, hiding sheds and covering dead tree stumps. They can be trained over archways, pergolas and draped ropes. An excellent use in a small garden is to form a hedge, by making them cover a post and wire fence, which is most space-saving, and with it little nutriment is sapped away from the surrounding soil. Some climbers when left untied, will sprawl over the ground and can be pegged down to cover ugly objects, such as manhole covers and boles of dead trees. 'Albertine', 'Excelsa', 'Max Graf', and 'Ritter von Barmstede' are excellent for this purpose.

They can also be trained to clamber into trees, which brightens them up at a time when they might be rather drab after their spring flowering has finished. This is an effective way in which to have one of the more vigorous climbers in a small garden. The selection of such roses can be made from the following: For trees up to 18 ft. high: 'Sander's White Rambler' and rosy-crimson 'Excelsa'; trees up to 30 ft. high: creamy yellow, tinged salmon, 'Lykkefund' and clear pink 'Climbing Cécile Brunner'.

Tree or Standard Roses These are usually hybrid tea or floribunda roses budded at the top of an upright stem about 4 ft. tall. Sometimes species or shrub roses are so treated, e.g. *R. xanthina spontanea* (Canary Bird). In addition, there are weeping standards, which are usually produced by budding ramblers, such as 'Excelsa'. These are particularly beautiful if planted as specimens in lawns. Standard roses are useful for giving height to a formal garden, but perhaps their greatest value is for planting in restricted areas, such as paved court-yards, patios and the like, where they can not only give the pleasure of having roses, but also allow other lovely plants to thrive at their feet.

Choosing and Buying Roses

The purpose for which roses are to be used is an important factor when making a choice. If possible, it is a good thing to make up one's mind regarding the requirements early in the summer. This gives plenty of time to see what best suits the need.

It is better to avoid making a final choice from a rose grower's catalog, because, good though the illustrations often are, the colors are not always true; this also applies to roses exhibited at flower shows, which take place before the normal flowering season, because the roses are produced under glass. It should also be remembered that roses growing in a nurseryman's fields are one year old do not always manifest their ultimate characteristics.

Before making a decision, it is best to see roses growing under garden conditions in friends' gardens, public parks, rose grower's demonstration gardens or the display grounds of the National and International rose test gardens. Always go to a reputable nurseryman, because he can be relied upon. Although bargains can sometimes be found, avoid cheap lines unless you are an expert. When buying you must see that the roses have several sturdy shoots emanating from at or near the union and at least three major roots and that they are free from pests, diseases and weeds.

Container-grown and pre-packed roses can be bought. They are a little more expensive than bare root roses. Although the choice of varieties is rather restricted, they are valuable for out-of-season planting. Container-grown roses are particularly useful for replacing dead roses in an old rose-bed.

Siting and Preparing Rose Beds

Conditions that Roses Like Fortunately roses are quite easy to accommodate. They have, however, several dislikes. These are poorly drained soil, deep shade, particularly when the roots of trees deprive them of nutriment, and very alkaline soil.

Choosing a Site The site should ideally be in an open position, sunny for most of the day, preferably with some shade during part of the time. There should be no overhanging trees, although smaller shrubs often give the correct amount of shade and help to keep their roots cool.

Good Drainage The soil must be well drained, because, firstly, roses strongly object to having their roots continuously in water and, secondly, in well-drained soil, air is sucked through by the water and it aerates the soil in the vicinity of the roots and thus stimulates the activity of the beneficial soil bacteria.

The drainage can be tested by digging a hole, 1 ft. deep and 1 ft. in diameter, and filling it with water. If it does not empty away within a day, it is necessary to improve the drainage. This can often be done effectively by raising the bed with soil well above the level of the surrounding ground or by digging a 2½ ft. deep trench across the bed and filling it with stones up to 1 ft. from the top and then with top-soil.

Roots of Roses Like other shrubs, the root system of a rose consists of two types of roots, viz., the tap-roots, which are long and strong so they penetrate well into the soil, giving good anchorage and a life line to more distant sources of water and nutriment, when they are needed; the surface roots, which emanate almost horizontally near the soil surface, collecting from the soil the rose's main supplies of moisture and plant foods.

The Ideal Soil for Roses Firstly, the top-soil must be friable so that the surface roots can pass freely through it, have a high fertilizer content, which is not easily washed away by rain and it must be able to retain adequate water to assist the absorption of the necessary plant foods. Secondly, there should be beneath it a porous sub-soil, which allows good drainage and which is sufficiently broken up to allow the tap-roots to penetrate without hindrance.

The above soil specification is that of a medium loam, but many gardeners have not got this and it becomes necessary for them to make whatever earth they have in their gardens as near to this as possible. Apart from soil with a good content of lime they normally have either clay soil or various degrees of heaviness or sandy soil. The practical difference between these is that sandy soil is very porous and allows rain to flow through it very quickly and is consequently poor, because the plant nutrients are rapidly washed away. On the other hand, clay soil retains the moisture, and, in extreme cases, is likely to become water-logged, but it remains fertile because the plant foods are not flushed out quickly. Thus to bring sandy soil nearer to the ideal, it is necessary to help it to retain water better; and, ideally to make clay more porous and so improve its drainage. Both objects can be achieved by adding humus-making materials, such as garden compost, rotted farmyard manure, peat, etc., although the addition of hydrated lime or gypsum to clay soil also helps. These materials also serve to improve the sub-soil.

Soil Preparation It is by digging that any soil can be conditioned. There are two main methods that are used in preparing rose beds, viz. double digging and plain or simple digging. Which is employed depends upon the nature of the sub-soil. If it is hard and compacted, it needs to be broken up and then double digging is carried out, but if it is stony or consists of gravel, it is readily penetrable and simple digging can be adopted.

The procedure to be followed for double digging is as under:

(1) Dig a trench about 18 in. wide and 1 ft. deep, across the width of the site. Transfer the excavated top-soil to the further end of the plot.

(2) Break up the exposed sub-soil with a fork to a depth of 10 in.

(3) Incorporate some humus-making materials in the upper layer of the sub-soil and place about 2 in. on its surface.

(4) Dig a second similar trench, adjacent to the first, using the excavated top-soil to fill the first.

(5) Break up the sub-soil and add humus-making materials as in (2) and (3).

(6) Proceed similarly with further trenches until the last is reached. This should be filled with the top-soil transferred from the first trench.

The procedure for plain or simple digging is as follows:

Climbing and rambling roses are easily trained over archways.
Firmly constructed trellis-work provides admirable support for climbing and rambling roses
Below: 'Chaplin's Pink Climber' is a popular variety

(1) Excavate a trench of similar dimensions as given above and transfer the soil to the further end of the site.

(2) Fill this trench with soil produced by digging an adjacent trench, incorporate copious quantities of humus-making material in the course of digging. Leave the sub-soil untouched.

(3) Continue this procedure until the last trench is reached. Then fill this one with the soil removed from the first.

Where the soil contains a lot of lime, it is best to incorporate copious quantities of humus-making material in the course of digging.

Renovating Old Rose Beds Sometimes, when restoring an old, neglected garden, it is necessary to replace some very old, weakened or dead roses. The soil in which roses have grown for perhaps ten years or more, for some reason which is not clearly understood, will not sustain new roses, despite the fact that established ones continue to flourish in it. This soil condition is known as 'rose sickness'. It is important, therefore, not to plant new roses in such beds, otherwise they will not thrive and after a year or so will very probably die.

There are two ways in which this situation can be dealt with. The soil in the old rose bed is removed to a depth of 18 in. and replaced by other soil in which roses have not been growing. The old excavated soil can be distributed anywhere in the garden provided it is not intended to grow roses in it, because other plants are unaffected. This method is the most satisfactory for a small garden or patio without any room to spare.

If the bed can be set aside for up to two years, another method is to 'green manure' the soil by sowing a succession of crops of mustard. Each is trampled down on maturing, moistened, covered with sulfate of ammonia and dug in.

When making a new garden, it is a wise thing to anticipate this possibility, by cutting beds in the lawn in such a position that if, after some ten years or so, it is desired to change the roses, it is possible to cut new ones adjacent to the old and to turf the latter over. It is important to make sure that this will not alter for the worse the general proportions and layout of the garden. A good way of ensuring this is to cut two original beds with enough lawn between to make two more if necessary.

Top: The floribunda variety 'Tip Top' is of dwarf, bushy habit
Above: 'Bonn', a modern shrub rose, trained against a wire support

69

Feeding, Maintenance and Pruning

Once roses are planted they are destined to give great pleasure for many years to come. It is well worthwhile, therefore, to take a lot of trouble at this stage to carry out this operation with care. Allow newly dug ground to settle for at least six weeks before planting anything in it.

Pre-planting Preparations Usually when bare-root roses are delivered from a nursery they are ready to plant, but if they are not the following should be carried out:

(1) Cut away all damaged and broken roots and shorten unduly long ones.

(2) Remove all immature, dead and diseased shoots.

(3) Tear away at their point of origin any suckers.

(4) If the roses are dry, with shrivelling stems, they should be immersed in cold water for twenty-four hours, after which they will be plumped up.

(5) If the leaves are left on, remove them in order to minimize the loss of moisture while the roses are waiting to be planted.

(6) To reduce the risk of attack by fungus diseases all newly delivered roses should be dipped in a fungicide consisting of 8 oz. of Bordeaux mixture mixed with $2\frac{1}{2}$ gals. of water, before planting.

A planting mixture should be made, consisting of a large bucketful of moist peatmoss, two handfuls of sterilized bonemeal and one of hoof and horn meal.

Roses must not be planted during a severe frost. They should be stored in a frost-proof place until it is warmer. If they are in a polyethelene bag, they will be all right for two to three weeks, but after this they should be unwrapped and kept covered with damp burlap to keep them moist. Roses packed in paper should be unwrapped immediately and treated similarly.

Roses should not be planted out in soggy ground. If it is very wet they should be placed in a trench in a sheltered spot, their roots well covered with soil and trodden in. They should be allowed to remain there until the ground dries up.

Time of Planting

The distance apart roses are planted depends upon their vigor. Generally speaking, most bushes are satisfactory when placed 20 in. apart, but for more vigorous ones, including species and shrub roses, this distance might be safely increased to 30 in.

upwards, according to their ultimate span.

Planting Procedure Roses either have roots growing centrally distributed uniformly round the central stem, or growing to one side. The technique of planting differs in each case. For bush roses with centrally growing roots a hole is dug of such a diameter that it is possible to spread the roots out in all directions. Its depth should be an inch or so greater than the distance between the top of the union, i.e. the enlarged portion on the stem, where the scion has been budded to the rootstock and its crown, which is the point from which the roots radiate. Two good handfuls of the planting mixture are then mixed with the soil in the bottom of the hole and heaped into a hump in the center of it. The crown of the rose is positioned on this and the roots parted and spread out, being sure that none are crossing. They are then covered with more soil and planting mixture and the rose gently moved up and down to eliminate air pockets. The hole is then about one-third filled with soil. Next the tip of the rose is held between the finger and thumb to prevent the union being lowered and this soil is gently trodden in, starting at the circumference of the hole, working inwards. The balance of the soil is then added, left loose and levelled off. If the soil is heavy or is very wet, treading in should be done very lightly, although it is better to avoid planting under the latter conditions.

For bush roses with side-growing roots a wedge-shaped hole, which has about the same width as that for a rose with centrally growing roots, is dug. One side of it should have a slope of about the same angle as the roots are to the vertical stem. The planting mixture is mixed with the soil on this slope and the rose placed on it in such a position that the union is just about in the earth's surface. The roots are then spread out without any of them crossing. A further quantity of planting mixture and soil is put on top of them. The hole is then about one-third filled with soil and trodden in. This time treading should begin above the tips of the roots and continue towards the stem. As before the top of the plant should be held to prevent it being lowered. The rest of the soil is then added, left loose and levelled.

Planting Climbing Roses Climbing roses are planted in the manner described for bush roses. If the position is at the base of a wall, the soil is usually dry there. It is better, therefore, to plant about 15 in. from it and train the shoots back to it. In addition a better choice for this purpose is a climber with side-growing roots, because they can be placed so that their ends are some distance from the wall, where more water will be available.

Planting Tree or Standard Roses The planting procedure for standard roses is exactly the same as that outlined for bush roses and again setting the plant at the correct depth and firming the soil around the roots is of prime importance.

As standards are liable to sway in the wind, they must be staked. A stake, which should

be 1 ft. longer than the distance between the crown of the rose and the union, is driven in between the spread-out roots, when planting, so that they are not damaged by being cut through, to such a depth that its top is just below the union. The stem is tied to the stake, using a special rose tie or tarred string with burlap or other fabric wrapped round the bark to protect it, at three different points. These are just below the union, just above the soil and midway between these two.

Feeding Roses

Roses need to be kept regularly fed, but like human beings and animals they do not want to be overfed, and certainly not with the wrong foods. What they like most of all is a well-planned diet given to them at the appropriate times of the season.

In addition roses are thirsty plants and need copious quantities of water. It is important to water whenever there is a dry spell, no matter how early in the season it might be, and not just during a heat wave, when their leaves are drooping, because by then it might be too late. Without a good supply of water roses are unable to manufacture their food, absorb the raw materials for this process from the soil and maintain the level of sap so that it can transport them to the places in the tissues, where they are converted.

Some gardeners think that organic or natural fertilizers are more beneficial to plants than inorganic or chemical ones. This is not completely true, because unlike animals, plants can only absorb plant food as simple chemical compounds. These are provided immediately by inorganic fertilizers, whereas the beneficial elements in organic fertilizers, which are complex substances cannot be taken up by the roots until they have been broken down into simple chemicals by the action of soil bacteria, which might take some weeks. Both types have their place in plant nutrition, because the organic fertilizers supply vital foods regularly over a long period and help to ensure their continuous presence in the soil, whereas the chemical fertilizers make supplies available to meet emergencies and special seasonal needs. Any nutritional advantages of organic fertilizers lie firstly in their soil-conditioning qualities as humus makers and the fact that they are sources of unspecified quantities of trace elements, required by plants in minute quantities. If inorganic fertilizers are used alone these have to be added.

Roses, like other plants, manufacture their own supplies of starches and sugar from carbon dioxide from the air and water from the earth through the agencies of the green coloring matter in the plants (chlorophyll) and sunlight. This is carried out in the vast majority of plants in the leaves. A good supply of moisture is necessary for this operation to be successful.

Apart from starch, however, roses need other vital substances if they are to flourish. Among these are proteins, chlorophyll, enzymes, nucleic acids and all sorts of other complicated compounds. These are all built up in the tissues from various elements that

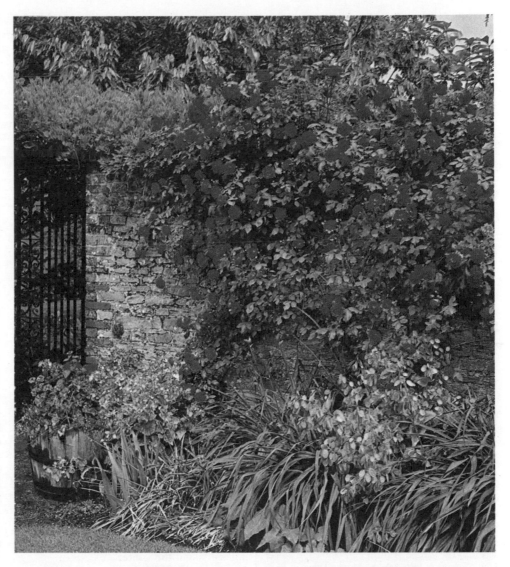

Left: Many climbing and rambling roses may be grown as pillar roses, rather than trained against walls or fences. Some of the more vigorous shrub roses may be treated in the same way. This makes it possible to take advantage of the height of such roses where a wall or fence is not available.
Below: Where space is restricted, as it is in this garden, it is often preferable to grow roses in a formal bed. *Above right:* 'Paul's Scarlet Climber' on an old wall, forming a backing to a border of perennials. Space should be left between the border and the wall.

for good health, these must be continuously available in the earth. To be sure of this, it is necessary to feed.

Plant Foods These are divided into two groups, the major nutrient elements, and the minor nutrient elements or trace elements.

Nitrogen is a constituent of many of the most vital substances used by a rose. It is, therefore, essential for the maintenance of good health, but too much is bad, because nitrogen encourages leaf-growth and if given lavishly, produces lush growth, which is often weak and falls an easy prey to disease and frost. Nitrogen compounds should not, therefore, be put down late in the season. In addition, excess nitrogen encourages roses to grow abundant foliage at the expense of flowers. Plants deficient in nitrogen usually look feeble and have yellowish leaves.

Phosphorus (Phosphate) is also a vital constituent of rose foods. It is beneficial by encouraging earlier growth, the ripening of the wood, hardening plants to resist winter conditions and improving the root systems. Its shortage is manifested by stunted growth and leaves that are tinged red.

Potassium (Potash) plays a leading part in plant growth. Without it, stems are brittle and roses are very vulnerable to disease and frost. Also parts of the plant, where winter food supplies are stored, such as roots and seeds, are poorly developed. Roses deficient

in this element usually have leaves that are yellow at their tips and round their edges.

Calcium not only helps to condition soil and keep it from becoming excessively acid, but is also important to roses because it is essential to the efficient working of the tissue cells. It is not very frequently deficient, but when it is, it is signified by malformation of the young leaves as they appear.

Magnesium is an important component of chlorophyll, which is essential to the food manufacturing process of roses. A severe shortage can be noted by the yellowing of first the older leaves and then the young ones.

Plant Foods Minor Nutrient or Trace Elements. Iron and Manganese are two of the most important trace elements because they are closely associated with the production of chlorophyll. Where they are deficient the younger leaves yellow, still leaving their veins green. (See Chlorosis.)

Other trace elements are copper, boron, molybdenum, and zinc.

A Feeding Program A program for feeding roses begins late in the winter after supplies of nutriments have become diminished. The first thing to do, preferably in early spring, provided the snows have gone, is to lay down foundations by distributing an organic fertilizer, which will break down over the ensuing months into simple chemical compounds and ensure that there is a

1. Where large, perfectly formed blooms of hybrid tea varieties are needed for exhibition or for other purposes, it is often necessary to disbud. Remove surplus buds, indicated by the red lines, as soon as they are large enough to handle.
2. The red lines indicate where both hybrid tea and floribunda roses should be pruned in their first spring to ensure ample new growth and a good shape. 3. This shows how hybrid tea roses are pruned in their second and subsequent springs. First cut out dead, diseased, weak and inward-growing shoots, then prune as indicated by the red lines.

4. Suckers, shown in dark green, should be torn away, not cut, from their points of origin on the roots. 5. This shows how to prune floribunda roses in their second and subsequent years. Cut out all dead, diseased, weak and inward-growing shoots as well as all spent flower heads from one-year-old growth (those shoots emanating from the base), at the second or third bud below the flower stalk. Shoots growing from old wood are cut back by half. Reduce lateral growths emerging just below the flower stalks (usually in the second year) to three or four buds. 6. Incorrect pruning: the cut is too long and may not heal properly. 7. Incorrect pruning: the cut has been made too close to the bud, which may in consequence be damaged. 8. Incorrect pruning: the cut has been made too far away from the bud and the shoot will die back. 9. The right way to prune: the cut is sloping, level with the base of the bud opposite to it, finishing $\frac{1}{4}$ in. above it.
Far right: Rosa foetida bicolor, the 'Austrian Copper Brier', has bright orange-red single flowers from midsummer onwards

basic supply that can be steadily absorbed by the plant. If it can be obtained, the substance to distribute is bonemeal at the rate of two handfuls per square yard.

Fertilizer is next applied in the spring, not earlier than April. This time it is a chemical fertilizer, which supplements the elements provided by the organic fertilizer, particularly when heavy rain has washed abnormally large quantities of a particular element away, or rapid growth, due to favorable weather conditions, has suddenly increased demand and so on. Generally, it is more satisfactory to put down a proprietary, ready-mixed rose fertilizer, of which there are several on the market. It is important to use one that is blended for roses and not a general fertilizer intended for vegetables, because sometimes the latter contains muriate of potash which is deadly to roses. Such rose fertilizer is distributed in accordance with the manufacturer's instructions. Usually these mixtures contain the trace elements that are needed by roses.

Although it is a lot more trouble, gardeners may mix their own fertilizer for roses. A recommended mixture is: Nitrate of potash 3 parts, Sulfate of ammonia $1\frac{1}{2}$ parts, Superphosphate of lime 8 parts, Sulfate of potash 4 parts, Sulfate of magnesium 1 part, Sulfate of iron $\frac{1}{4}$ part.

This is distributed at the rate of 2 oz. (about a handful) per sq. yd. once in April and again in May. Twenty pounds of this mixture is sufficient for 200 roses during the season.

It is important that no chemical fertilizer is applied after the end of July, otherwise lush growth might be produced, which will not withstand the winter.

Foliar Feeding This takes advantage of the fact that leaves absorb nutrients from liquids sprayed on them. It is not a substitute for the regular feeding program, but something that can meet an emergency. There are several good foliar feeds on the market. They are best applied in the early morning or in the evening, but never in hot sun.

Rose Maintenance

Apart from pruning and fighting pests and diseases, which are discussed later, the maintenance of roses is not an onerous task.
Spring Ensure that any roses loosened by the ravages of winter weather are well trodden in.

Make sure that any broken stakes, posts, trellis, etc. are replaced or repaired. Particular attention should be paid to renewing worn out burlap that is protecting the bark. This can often be done when the ground is too wet or too frosty to work.

Mulching helps to keep the soil moist, keeps its temperature steady, gives the roses a cool root-run. In addition, as the substances used for mulching provide humus they help to condition the soil and supply slowly-released plant foods. A mulch also keeps down weeds. It is also claimed that, because it prevents rain from splashing up from the ground on to the lower leaves of a rose bush, it reduces the spread of blackspot.

Rose beds should be mulched in May, when the soil has begun to warm up. A mulch is a layer, upwards of 2 in. thick, of an organic material. One of the best is well-rotted garden compost. Other suitable substances are moist peatmoss, buckwheat hulls and rotted farm-yard manure. Leave a small ring around the base of each rose, to avoid the risk of damage being done by the heating up of the mulch as it decomposes.

Summer Because weeds steal the moisture and plant foods intended for the roses, their suppression is important. The principal methods of doing this are: physical methods i.e. regular hoeing; mulching and chemical methods. The two main types of chemical weedkillers are:

(1) Contact: this type of weedkiller is watered on to the leaves of the weeds in spring and summer. The chemicals are absorbed and the weeds soon die.

(2) Pre-emergent: this sort interferes with the growth of the seedling leaves and they do not emerge from the soil. It is applied in the early spring.

Often during the spring, three shoots emerge from one bud center. As soon as they are large enough to handle, the outside growths should be pinched off, and the center one, which is usually the largest, should be allowed to develop.

Suckers are shoots that originate low down on the rose tree or beneath the ground. They grow from the root-stock and not the scion or budded variety. If they are allowed to remain, they sap nutriment from the main stems. The most satisfactory way of discerning a sucker is to note from which position it originated. If the shoot appears from below the union or from the root, it is a sucker and should be torn out, not cut away, at its point of origin, scraping away the soil, if it appears from below the ground. By tearing it out, the whole budding system is destroyed and there is little chance of it reappearing.

Some hybrid tea roses, instead of growing one terminal bud, develop three on a stem, while others grow their flowers in clusters. Disbudding consists in removing all the side-flowering shoots, when they are just large enough to handle, leaving one terminal flowering bud. Whether this is carried out is largely a matter of personal taste. Nothing should be done if a good, massed display of color is desired, but if large perfect individual blooms, say for showing, are required, it should be carried out (see figure 1).

If there is to be good repeat-flowering, removing the spent blooms as soon as they fade is essential. The stems should be cut off at the first outward-growing leaf with five leaflets to avoid removing too many leaves, which are important because they are part of the apparatus by which the plant produces its food from light (photosynthesis).

When watering, the blooms and the leaves should not be wetted, because the former will become blemished and moisture on the latter will encourage fungus diseases. The use of a perforated hose, turned upside down and interwoven among the plants avoids these possibilities.

Fall and Winter To prevent bush roses from being whipped by winds, cut back tall stems in November to halfway.

Roses should be sprayed, or watered, in December, where weather conditions permit, with 8 oz. of Bordeaux mixture mixed with $2\frac{1}{2}$ gals of water, to minimize the effects of fungus diseases.

Modern Ways of Pruning Roses

In recent years there have been conflicts of opinion on various aspects of pruning. There is little need, however, for worry if it is borne in mind that roses are flowering shrubs. As far as pruning is concerned these are classified as either plants that bloom on the new wood produced during the current season or they flower on last year's shoots. The first types are pruned in late winter or early spring and the second as soon after flowering as possible. All types of roses except true ramblers fall into the first class, while the ramblers bloom on the previous season's wood and must, therefore, be pruned immediately after flowering. True ramblers are not so numerous in gardens as they once were.

Most shrubs go on growing until they are mature, but roses grow shoots, which, when they get to a certain size, wane and ultimately die and are replaced by new ones. This is a form of natural pruning, but as these dying shoots sap nutriment from the younger vigorous ones and are also potential centers for diseases it is the practice to encourage the growth of new shoots by cutting back the old, spent and diseased wood annually.

There are additional reasons for pruning. Among these are (a) to shape and restrict the shape of the plants to fit in the space allotted to them (b) to control the habit (c) to maintain youthfulness by encouraging the growth of new shoots from the base and (d) to restrict the number of flower shoots, when large exhibition blooms are required.

The Technique of Pruning The most common pruning tool is a pair of hand shears. It is essential that they are always kept very sharp; blunt hand shears may crush the stem, giving an opening for diseases to attack. The better tool is a pruning knife, which should be kept sharp by continuous whetting. It is not difficult to use and it is worthwhile learning how to do so.

Long-handled pruners are heavy-duty cutters, used for removing tough and old wood. Pruning saws are of value for cutting out stout stems; a pad (keyhole) saw is a useful pruning instrument because of its great flexibility.

Because of the risk of spreading diseases when pruning dip tools in an antiseptic solution when a badly affected tree is pruned. One recommended is a 10% solution of tri-sodium orthophosphate.

When to Prune With the exception of true ramblers, roses are pruned during the winter or early spring. Exactly when depends upon the location and degree of exposure of the

garden. At this time, the cut will heal quickly, but in late spring or early fall, the shoot will bleed and, if a frost comes, damage is likely to be caused.

Ramblers are pruned in the late summer, soon after their flowers fade. So that they do not become unruly, the new shoots that remain should be tied in at the same time.

How to Prune If a rose of any sort is examined, it will be found that each of its shoots has buds, which alternately point in opposite directions, i.e., in a bush rose they are outwards and inwards towards its center. In pruning a bush rose, the cut is made just above an outward-pointing bud, as it is desirable to keep the center open with no inward-growing shoots crossing it, or where a horizontally-trained shoot of a climber is being pruned, it would be an upward pointing bud, because it is in this direction that growth is required.

The proper way to prune is to make a sloping cut, which begins level with the base of the bud on the side opposite to it and ends at a point on the same side as the bud, which is at a distance of $\frac{1}{4}$ in. from the base of the eye (see figure 9).

Unfortunately cutting is not always done properly and the following faults occur (see figures 6–8):
(1) The shoot is cut too far away from the bud. It then dies back and becomes exposed to fungus infection.
(2) The shoot is cut too close to the bud with consequential damage to the bud and malformation of the new shoot.
(3) The cut is too long, resulting in an excessive amount of pith being exposed, which prolongs the time of healing of the wound.

Bear in mind that if the cut is jagged the tissues will be damaged and may become a possible seat of infection.

Whenever a rose is pruned, always:
(1) Cut out all dead and diseased wood.
(2) Cut out all weak shoots, because while they remain they are using nourishment, that is required by the more robust ones.
(3) Remove all growth that is growing in the wrong direction.

Types of Pruning Three different types of pruning are practised by rosarians:

HARD PRUNING This consists in cutting a shoot back to three or four buds from its base; e.g. in a bush rose to an outward growing bud and at a point which is usually 5–6 in. from the ground.

MODERATE PRUNING In this form of pruning, a shoot is cut back by about half its previous year's growth.

LIGHT PRUNING Here there is very little cutting away; usually the dead flowers or hips are removed by cutting at the first or second eye below the flower-bearing stalk.

Left: Roses grown in formal beds. In such instances it is best to confine one variety to each bed. *Right:* A more natural effect is produced by growing roses informally

---

Pruning Hybrid Tea and Floribunda Roses in the First Year These should be hard pruned in the first spring after they have been planted, i.e. cut back to the third or fourth outward-growing bud from their base, to ensure that as many new shoots as possible spring from low down on the bush and that it grows into a well-balanced, compact shape. If this is not done, the bush soon becomes leggy and unsightly (see figure 2).

SUBSEQUENT PRUNING OF HYBRID TEA ROSES The present-day roses, which are very vigorous, a quality that many have inherited from 'Peace', do not take kindly to hard pruning. In the main, they should be moderately pruned, otherwise they do not bloom so plentifully in the summer.

It is the modern practise to prune hybrid tea roses moderately, i.e. to cut their shoots back by half their previous year's growth. However, because of their great vigor, many

soon become very tall and rather unwieldy for present-day small gardens. There are two ways in which this can be largely overcome.
(1) Moderate prune all shoots except two. These are hard pruned, i.e. cut back to two or three buds from the base of the bush. This procedure can be repeated in successive years.
(2) Hard prune the bush every three years. This method seems to keep its size under control without any serious lowering of its flowering-power (see figure 3).

The second method is the better.

Pruning Floribunda Roses Because the original floribundas stemmed from polyantha-pompom roses, they were first lightly pruned, i.e. only the clusters of dead flowers were removed. Because of their great vigor, this resulted in unwieldy bushes. When they were moderately pruned like modern hybrid teas, they lost their repeat-flowering, whereas with hard pruning they failed to grow and tended to die. The modern technique, aimed at keeping them in flower over a long period, is a combination of light pruning to produce early flowers and moderated pruning, which gives flowering shoots that produce color later in the season. During the first year they are hard pruned, but, the procedure in the second year is slightly different from that of

the third, which remains uniform for the rest of their lives. This modern technique is given below:

Pruning Floribunda Roses in their Second Year
(1) All the main shoots, which are the previous year's growth, and grown from the base of the tree, are lightly pruned by cutting out the clusters of dead blooms at the first and second eye, whichever is growing outwards, below their base.
(2) Secondary shoots which have developed below the clusters should be cut back to three or four eyes from the main stem.
(3) All other shoots, which are emerging from the shoots that were hard pruned in their first year, should be cut back to half their length (see figure 5).

Pruning Floribunda Roses in their Third and Subsequent Years
(1) All one-year-old wood, that emanates low

Right: 'Allegro', a floribunda rose variety

down on the bush, should be lightly pruned by cutting out the dead flower heads.

(2) All the remaining shoots are moderately pruned, i.e. they are cut back to about half their length.

Pruning Standard Roses Standard hybrid tea and floribunda roses are pruned in the same way as their dwarf counterparts. The object should be to preserve always an open center to the head. With hybrid tea standards, moderate pruning is usually the best.

Pruning Weeping Standards The most effective of these are Group 1 Ramblers (see under 'Pruning Ramblers and Climbing Roses'), that have been budded at the top of tall stems of the particular stock. All the old wood, that has flowered is cut out near to their base as soon as the blooms are spent in the summer. The current year's growth is allowed to remain and flower the following season.

Pruning Polyantha Roses After all dead, diseased, weak or inward-growing shoots have been removed, cut away clusters of dead flowers in late winter or early spring.

Pruning Shrub and Species Roses Apart from removing the dead blooms regularly, which enhances their power to repeat-flower, all that shrub and species roses require is to have cut away surplus growth to keep them in shape and their size under control. After some years, however, they tend to become bare at the base. This can be remedied by cutting one or two of the older shoots back to an outward-growing bud about 9 in. from the base. If this is done annually for two or three years, the roses will be completely rejuvenated.

Pruning Miniature Roses These roses, in the main, need to have diseased or dead wood and spent blooms only cut away, apart from any necessary thinning out and trimming to shape and size. Pruning is best done with a pair of nail scissors.

Pruning Ramblers and Climbing Roses There are four groups:

GROUP 1 RAMBLERS These climbing roses produce nearly all their new shoots from the base. The group includes 'Dorothy Perkins', 'Excelsa', 'François Juranville' and 'Sander's White Rambler'. All ramblers flower on the previous season's growth and it is necessary to prune them soon after they finish flowering in the summer. Pruning is done by cutting out all the old shoots at the base. At the same time it is equally as important to tie in all the new shoots, which will bloom in the following summer (see figure 10).

GROUP 2 RAMBLERS These mainly produce their new shoots at points on the old wood higher up the tree. Examples are the old ramblers 'Albéric Barbier', 'Albertine', 'American Pillar', 'Chaplin's Pink Climber', 'Easlea's Golden Rambler', 'Emily Gray' and 'New Dawn'.

The old wood is cut back to a point where a robust, young, green shoot emanates. This leading shoot is left and tied in ready for next year's flowering. All the shorter laterals are pruned back to a bud, 2 or 3 in. from where they originate. Old wood that has no new leading shoot should be removed to prevent overcrowding. This type of rambler tends to become bare at the base. This can be remedied by cutting one or two stems down to a bud 1 ft. from the ground (see figure 11).

GROUP 3 CLIMBERS This group contains the more vigorous climbing sports of the hybrid teas and floribundas, the stronger-growing large-flowering climbers, such as 'Casino' and 'Coral Dawn', and the climber 'Mermaid'.

The time to prune these is either late fall or winter, and not in spring after the new growth has appeared. None of last year's new shoots should be pruned unless they are damaged or are occupying too great a space. All exhausted wood should be cut away and the laterals that flowered last year reduced to the third eye from their points of origin.

Most of these roses, especially the climbing sports should not be pruned in their first year, because the latter are liable to revert to their dwarf stature.

GROUP 4 CLIMBERS Included in this category are the climbing sports of 'Iceberg', 'Korona' and 'President Herbert Hoover', the large flowering climbers, which are typified by 'Elegance', 'Golden Showers', 'Handel', 'Rosy Mantle', 'Schoolgirl' and 'White Cockade', the *Kordesii* climbers or pillar roses, 'Ritter von Barmstede' and 'Dortmund' and the Bourbon climber 'Zéphirine Drouhin'.

This group needs little attention other than a general clearing out of unwanted growth and pruning to control shape and size. During their first year remove only any dried out ends of stems, together with any dead wood and very twiggy shoots.

🌿 Keeping Roses Healthy 🌿

Roses are attacked by various pests and diseases. To fight them, it is important to be able to identify them and know what action to take.

Regular spraying with a chemical compound is important. Fortunately most sprays that are used today can be mixed together and can thus be used simultaneously, together, if desired, with a foliar feed.

There are several different types of sprayer available, but because of their cheapness and lightness, the pressurized plastic kinds are useful. For ease of handling, do not buy too large a one. Although it might have to be filled several times, a 2 pt. size is adequate for up to 150 plants.

Pests These can be divided into two categories, viz., *sap-suckers*, which include aphids and red spider mites and *leaf-and-bud-eaters*, such as caterpillars and sawflies.

Nowadays there are two types of insecticides: *systemic insecticides*, which enter the sap by absorption through the foliage and are used against the sap-sucking insects, and *contact insecticides*, which destroy leaf- and bud-eaters by direct contact with them. Systemics are of no value against the latter, because they do not imbibe sufficient sap to poison them.

The systemics are effective for about one month after spraying, whereas the contact types must be applied whenever the insects appear. A number of proprietary insecticides are mixtures of both.

Do not spray too soon, because the larvae of ladybugs, hover flies, lace-wing-flies and braconid wasps, which are the natural enemies of aphids, appear at about the same time as the caterpillars. It is better to hand pick and destroy them rather than spray them.

So that gardeners can detect hostile pests and diseases, their indications are given below.

Above: 'Mermaid' is a fine evergreen climbing rose which does well on a north wall. *Below:* In the right place, the old rambler, 'Dorothy Perkins' still provides a fine display of bloom. *Above right:* (**10**) Pruning Group 1 ramblers. All old shoots (marked x) that have flowered during the current summer are pruned to an outward growing bud near the base of the plant. The new shoots (marked y) that remain, are tied in at the same time. *Right:* (**11**) Pruning Group 2 ramblers. All old leading shoots (marked A) are cut back to the point at which a new leading shoot (B) emerges. The new shoots are all tied in. All laterals (marked D) on the main shoots remaining are cut back to the second or third bud from their point of origin

Pests: Sap-Suckers APHIDS These small insects breed rapidly and soon engulf the rose trees; they are sometimes pink, red or brown in color. By sucking the sap, they reduce the vigor of the plant, cripple the shoots and distort the leaves, which ultimately fall prematurely.

They must be dealt with expeditiously because not only do they damage the roses, they also exude a sweet, sticky fluid, honeydew, the natural food of the fungus, sooty mold, which by coating the leaves, interferes with their normal functioning. In addition, they are carriers of virus diseases.

THRIPS These small black or brown insects sometimes swarm all over roses, particularly in thundery weather. Their immature forms which are colored pale pink to reddish, suck the sap. If they are present, leaves become mottled in appearance, young shoots are malformed and affected buds produce damaged blooms.

RED SPIDER MITES These pests attack outdoor as well as greenhouse roses. They are very minute, red insects, that are so immobile that they may be mistaken for specks of dust. Their presence is shown by the development of a fine, silken web under the leaves, in which they live and breed. The leaves of infected roses become mottled and off-color. If badly attacked, they turn yellow and fall. There is also loss of vigor.

Leaf and Bud-Eating Insects CATERPILLARS These, the larvae of moths and butterflies, manifest themselves in various ways, which include holes in the leaves, skeletonizing of the leaves, rolling of the leaves and injured buds. Sometimes they exude a sticky fluid.

LEAF ROLLING SAWFLIES deposit their eggs on the leaves causing them to roll at the edges and hang down.

ROSE SLUG The larvae (grubs) of these insects usually devour the upperside of leaves and skeletonize them.

Diseases The principal diseases of roses are due to parasitic fungi, and do damage by stealing vital foods from their tissues.

BLACK SPOT This disease is well-known to all rose growers. Its attacks are at their worst in August and September. It is recognized by the appearance of black or dark brown spots on the leaves, often initially the lower ones. They gradually increase in size and join together. The remaining part of the affected leaf becomes yellow and eventually falls off, leaving the plants bare.

No garden roses are immune from attack from this disease, but there are some that are less susceptible. A list of varieties that have been found to be more resistant to fungus diseases is given on the following page.

Hitherto fungicides used against black spot have been contact types, which form a protective coat, which must be renewed at intervals of a week or so, with more frequent applications in wet weather. None of the compounds recommended is a complete

Left : The floribunda rose 'Orange Sensation', a very attractive variety with bright scarlet blooms. *Above :* 'Pink Parfait', another floribunda

12

12 : A rose cutting prepared for rooting

cure. Recently the first systemic fungicide has been introduced. It is claimed to be effective against both black spot and mildew.

MILDEW This starts with white or greyish white spots on the young leaves and eventually spreads all over the plants, making them look as if they have been dusted with flour. The leaves become distorted. Dryness at the roots often makes plants susceptible to mildew. Thus by keeping roses well-watered, the incidence of the disease can be reduced.

Fortunately there appears to be a few garden roses that are very highly resistant to attack. These are listed on the right.

RUST This has three characteristics: it only seems to attack roses in certain areas in this country, it often remains for two years or so and then disappears, and its spores need to be frozen to germinate and attack the following year. The last two might be connected, because a mild winter might prevent freezing. The disease appears in spring as rust colored swellings on the back of the leaves. In June, orange-colored spores develop. These germinate and the infection is widely spread. Later in August, they turn black and in this form they live over the winter.

DIEBACK AND CANKER A stem on a rose will often turn brown and die. This can be the result of several different things, including frost damage, lack of water, careless pruning,

causing jagged edges or being cut too high above a bud, the snapping of hardened shoots by high wind or rough handling, and by a fungus disease. The latter is true dieback; when the effect arises out of any of the other causes, it is commonly, but erroneously called 'dieback'.

Another fungus disease, stem canker, infects wounds, the cut end of stems after pruning, especially when blunt cutters are used, and dormant buds, which ultimately leads to browning and dying back. The first signs are yellow or reddish spotted or streaked, pimply or water-saturated portions of the stem. The brown area eventually extends some inches down the stem, usually terminating in a reddish-brown border where it abuts healthy tissues. Whatever may be the cause, the only remedy is to prune an affected stem back to a healthy bud, or cut it out altogether, if it has reached the union, otherwise the tree might die.

CHLOROSIS This is not a true disease, but an ailment, mainly caused by deficiency of iron and manganese. This can occur as far as the plant is concerned in soil in which there are ample quantities of these elements present, but where they are in a form in which they cannot be used by the rose, as often happens on alkaline soil. The symptoms are yellowing of the leaves and stems in springtime. They

often eventually shrivel up and drop off. Also growth is stunted.

This condition cannot be remedied by distributing ordinary, simple compounds of iron or manganese. If it is serious, the soil must be watered in spring with a proprietary formulation which contains chelates of iron and manganese in a form that can be absorbed by roses, together with active magnesium, which is another vital plant food.

A Selection of Roses that are More Resistant to Fungus Diseases

HYBRID TEA ROSES

Brandenburg, Color Wonder, Duke of Windsor, Colorama, Eden Rose, John S. Armstrong, Isobel de Ortiz, Peace, Pink

Favorite, Rose Gaujard, Silver Lining, Wendy Cussons.

FLORIBUNDA ROSES
Alliance, Arthur Bell, Chanelle, Elsie Devy, Elizabeth of Glamis, Mountain Haze, Masquerade, Orange Sensation, Pink Parfait, Queen Elizabeth, Scarlet Queen Elizabeth, Scented Air.

Propagating Roses

Because of the complexity of their pedigrees, roses other than the species cannot be grown true to variety from seeds. They are mainly propagated by budding, although they can be rooted from cuttings. They are, however, not so vigorous as those that are budded.

Growing from Cuttings Hardwood cuttings, about 1 ft. long and ¼ in. in diameter, are taken in the fall by making a cut horizontally below a lower bud at the top with a cut sloping downwards from above a bud. The lower leaves are removed and the eyes eliminated with a wedge-shaped cut, when they are likely to be below the ground level (see figure 12).

Place them 6 in. apart, in 2 in. of sand in a narrow wedge-shaped trench, which is filled with soil and gently trodden in, keeping them vertical. They should then be well watered. Rooting can be encouraged by wetting their lower ends and dipping them in hormone-rooting powder before planting.

In the fall of the following year the rooted cuttings can be transplanted to their permanent quarters.

Budding Roses Budding is the process of uniting the rose cell tissue to that of a related plant, which has well-developed roots. The latter is called a rootstock.

The budding knife is a razor-sharp, pointed knife, with a handle with a thin, wedge-shaped end for lifting the bark.

The seedling rootstocks are planted about 8 in. apart, preferably in a straight line in a spare plot in early spring. The neck, i.e. the part between the first green shoot and the root fork, should be about 1 in. above the ground. For convenience when budding, they should be put in sloping towards the spot where the budder will ultimately be working.

The shoot selected to provide buds should be one on which the blooms have just faded. As it should be fresh when the buds are taken, it should be left on the bush until the rootstock has been prepared.

In late summer, on a day following rain or copious overnight watering, the soil is scraped away from the neck of the rootstock and it is washed clean with water. Next the budder to assist him in his work, should press the rootstock down with his knee to give him good access to the neck.

About 1 in. above the root fork, a cross-cut, about ⅓ in. wide is made with the budding knife. Then from a point ¾ in. below it, a lengthwise cut is made to form a T-shaped incision with it. At the finish of making this

cut, the bark is carefully lifted slightly with a twisting movement of the blade. The bark along the whole length of the slit is raised, using the wedge-shaped end of the handle (see figure 13).

To take a bud the selected shoot is cut, the thorns removed and the leaves trimmed back.

The budding knife is inserted into the stem about ½ in. above a bud near its middle and the bark is cut thinly behind the bud until the blade is about that distance below it (see figure 14). The loosened bud is next gently torn away, taking a thin slip of bark with it (see figure 15).

Behind the bud there will be at this stage a thin layer of wood, which can be exposed by pulling away the strip of bark a little. This sliver of wood is removed, using the thumbnail, with a twisting movement (figure 16).

The bark containing the bud is next trimmed to form a wedge-shaped tongue on the side below it, so that the insertion into the incision on the rootstock is made easy (see figure 17).

Holding the small piece of leaf that has been left, the bud is next fitted into the T-cut

on the rootstock, with the wedge-shaped end downwards. The lifted bark of the rootstock is replaced and the portion of bark above the bud is trimmed off in line with the horizontal cut (see figure 18).

The bud is made secure, either by tying with two turns below and three turns above of raffia or plastic budding tape. If the remaining piece of leaf-stalk dies in about three weeks, it is a sign that the bud has taken. The fastenings eventually rot away (see figures 19, 20 and 21).

In the following spring, when the weather is dry and frost-free, the rootstock is cut away at a point about 1 in. above the bud.

Budding Standards Except that their buds are joined to the rootstock at the top of a vertical stem, the budding procedure is the same as with a bush except that the buds are inserted into side shoots when they have grown about 18 in. As the ties do not rot, they must be cut after four weeks. The newly-budded roses are ready for planting out in their permanent quarters in the following October, or thereafter in suitable weather conditions.

13: *Budding a rose:* A T-shaped incision is made in the bark and the bark is raised. **14**: Cutting out the bud. **15**: The bud is gently torn away, taking a thin slip of bark with it. **16**: The sliver of wood remaining is removed with a twisting action of the thumbnail. **17**: The strip of bark is trimmed off so that the end below the bud is wedge-shaped. **18**: The bud is inserted in the T-shaped incision, with the bark trimmed level with the horizontal cut. **19**: The bud is tied in with raffia or plastic tape. **20**: The bud fastened with the patented Fleischauer Tie, which consists of a patch of rubber fastened with a metal staple. The remaining leaf stalk is carefully cut away without disturbing the bud. **21**: The patented Fleischauer Tie

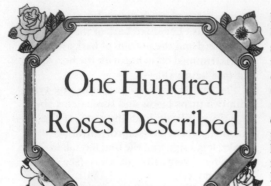

One Hundred Roses Described

To enable gardeners to decide whether a particular rose is suitable for a purpose, their heights and vigor have been included, but it must be remembered that under very good growing conditions, these are likely to be greater, and vice versa. The heights, unless specified, are graded as below: *short*: up to 2 ft. 3 in.; *medium*: 2 ft. 6 in.–3 ft. 6 in.; *tall*: 4 ft. upwards.

Hybrid Teas

Alec's Red This has large, full, perfectly formed, wonderfully perfumed cherry-red flowers, borne on strong stems. It is vigorous, a little under average height.

Alexander A 1972 introduction, a rose of promise, this has an outstanding brilliant vermilion color. The flowers are large. It is vigorous and tall and appears to be healthy.

Anvil Sparks A unique rose with sweetly scented coral-red blooms, punctuated with golden yellow stripes and spots. It grows as a low compact bush. It can be used both in forward positions in borders and for bedding and its blooms are good for floral decoration.

Blue Moon The silvery-blue, full, shapely flowers are very fragrant. It is vigorous, of medium height. Good for floral decorations. The best of the 'blue' roses.

Bonsoir The large, full, well-shaped blooms are deep apple-blossom pink in the centre, paling to shell-pink on the edges, highly fragrant. It is vigorous, of medium height.

Chicago Peace With its rich pink, canary yellow and copper tones, this has been aptly described as a 'polychrome'. It has large, well-formed, slightly perfumed flowers. It is vigorous and tall-growing.

Duke of Windsor This rose is brilliant orange-vermilion. It has very fragrant, full blooms of moderate size. It is vigorous, but forms compact, bushy plants that are not more than 2 ft. tall. It is a little prone to mildew.

Ernest H. Morse The blooms are a striking rich, turkey-red, full and of good form, very strongly scented. It is vigorous, upright growing tall and disease resistant.

Fleet Street A 1972 introduction of great promise. It has large, strongly perfumed, full blooms, deep rose-pink, slightly lighter on the reverse. It is vigorous, of medium height.

Fred Gibson The apricot and old gold blooms are large, very full and of excellent shape; fragrance slight. It is vigorous, grows tall and is normally healthy. An outstanding exhibition rose.

Grandpa Dickson Its lemon-yellow, very full, shapely, slightly scented flowers, fade to creamy yellow with a flushing of pink on their petal edges. Vigorous and tall, it is generally healthy. Long-lasting in water and excellent for showing and floral decorations.

Isobel De Ortiz The large, fragrant, very full, perfect blooms are deep pink with silvery-white reverse. Very vigorous and tall; a superb exhibition rose.

John Waterer This has deep rose-red, large fragrant, full flowers, borne either singly or several together. It is vigorous, branching and tall, with strong flower stems, making it excellent for cutting.

Message Pure white with a slight green tinge in bud. Large well-formed, full flowers, produced freely on long stems, excellent for cutting, slightly scented. A vigorous grower, medium height. It dislikes rain.

Mischief This has beautifully formed, fragrant, salmon-pink flowers, highly resistant to wet. It grows to medium height. Its flowers grow in trusses.

Mullard Jubilee Its strongly perfumed flowers, moderately sized and very full, are a striking cerise pink, borne in clusters, as well as singly. It is robust, of medium height, resistant to diseases.

Peace This famous rose has large, well-formed, slightly fragrant, creamy yellow flowers, edged with pink. It is exceptionally vigorous and tall, and although over thirty years old, it is still a bestseller. Excellent for cutting, showing and borders.

Piccadilly A lovely rose with flowers scarlet, flushed gold, with gold reverses, moderately full and high-pointed, slightly scented. It is vigorous and upright, of moderate height. It is the best bicolor.

Pink Favorite Deep rose in color, its flowers are large, full, perfectly formed and slightly perfumed, produced in large clusters, or, when disbudded, it produces excellent show blooms, and thus can be used for showing or grown informally. It is vigorous, of medium height, almost immune to diseases.

Red Devil This has very large, perfect, scented, very full blooms, crimson, with a slightly paler hue on the reverse. It is vigorous, healthy, tall, but objects to rain.

Royal Highness White with slight blush pink. It has large, perfectly shaped, sweetly scented blooms on strong stems. It is vigorous, growing just above medium height. An excellent exhibition rose.

Sante Fé This has large, full, rosy-salmon-pink flowers, lighter on the reverse. It is vigorous, of medium height. It is unaffected by bad weather.

Wanda Beauty A 1972 introduction. The fragrant blooms are brilliant deep yellow, well-formed and neat. It is strong growing, 2½ ft. tall. It flowers early.

Wendy Cussons The beautiful large, well-formed, cerise pink flowers come fairly early. It has a strong old-fashioned rose scent. It is vigorous, upright and tall.

Whisky Mac With its medium-sized flowers, very shapely, strongly scented and golden orange in color, this is an unusual rose of bushy growth, below medium height.

Floribundas

Allgold One of the best of the yellow floribundas, this has scented golden-yellow, well-formed flowers, semi-double and often 3 in. across. It is short and compact in growth.

Ama This produces large trusses of semi-double, bright scarlet flowers, about 3 in. in diameter. It is vigorous and grows tall, withstands bad weather and is healthy.

Arthur Bell This is another lovely yellow floribunda, with deep golden blooms, that change to creamy yellow with age. They are full, well-shaped, and very fragrant. It is vigorous, grows tall and upright and is usually very resistant to diseases.

Bangor A 1972 introduction. Its semi-double, large blooms are unfading carmine-pink. Vigorous and branching, 2 ft. tall. It appears to be healthy and weather resistant.

Bonfire Bright orange-vermilion, slightly lighter on the reverse, the moderately full, well-formed flowers of this floribunda are produced in shapely clusters. It is a compact grower, of medium height. The blooms are much appreciated by flower arrangers.

Copper Pot This has neatly formed, moderately full, coppery orange blooms, a color that is popular with flower arrangers. The fragrant flowers are often 3½–4 in. across. It is moderately vigorous but forms a tall bush.

Evangeline Bruce The flowers are yellow, edged and flushed with rose, with a predominance towards the latter. They are full and loosely formed, and borne in trusses of as many as twelve blooms. It is vigorous, reaching rather more than average height.

Evelyn Fison This has large clusters of

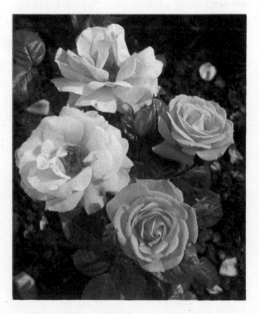

semi-double vivid scarlet flowers. It is vigorous, of medium height. Generally it is healthy, but a lookout should be kept for mildew. It faces bad weather well.

Grace Abounding This has plentiful, creamy white, double flowers, that open to show their stamens and are pleasantly perfumed. It is vigorous, of average height.

Heaven Scent This is outstanding for its delicious fragrance. It is deep pink-rose in color and its full, double flowers are well-shaped. It is a strong grower, on the short side in height. It flowers early.

Iceberg The blooms, carried in small or medium trusses, are full, pure white, but the buds are sometimes tinged pink and the flowers are spotted pink in cool weather. It is vigorous and grows tall, sometimes reaching 10 ft. and making a good hedge.

Meteor This rather older floribunda has withstood the test of time. It has brilliant vermilion, full flowers, 2½ in. across. Its growth is branching and short, and it is excellent for small gardens.

News This is a sensational shade of beetroot purple. Its moderately full fragrant blooms are brilliantly lit up by their bright golden stamens. Bushy and compact, it reaches medium height.

Orange Sensation The vermilion blooms are shaded orange at the base, moderately full and fragrant. It is vigorous and branching, a compact bush of medium height. It needs protection against mildew and black spot.

Picasso Its moderately full blooms rather prettily show their stamens in the centre of the beautiful multicolored petals. The whole ensemble might be likened to a pink, carmine and white pelargonium. It has a bushy, compact habit and a height of about 20 in. which make it suitable for small gardens. The beautiful blooms are excellent for floral decorations.

Satchmo The blooms are full, double and shapely, of the most outstanding, constant, vivid scarlet color. It is vigorous, but grows a little below average height.

Southampton This is a 1972 introduction, which during its trial period has been consistent and healthy. Its moderately full flowers are apricot-orange in color with a little flush of scarlet on the outside. It is very vigorous and a little over medium height.

Tip Top The large, full, salmon-pink blooms are borne in large trusses, produced freely and continuously. It is vigorous, but has a dwarf, bushy habit and is particularly attractive for use in small gardens.

Floribundas–H.T. Type

Courvoisier The strongly perfumed flowers are very full, ochre-yellow in color and often 4-in. in diameter, borne either singly, or several together, on a stem. It is of medium height, upright.

Irish Mist The reddish salmon-pink

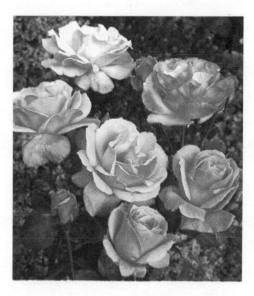

Below left: 'Arthur Bell' is a floribunda rose with deep golden-yellow, very fragrant blooms
Above: 'Queen Elizabeth', a floribunda rose, has blooms of hybrid tea type. It makes a very vigorous, upright plant
Below: The very fragrant flowers of 'Duke of Windsor', a hybrid tea which grows about 2 ft. tall

flowers are large well-formed and hybrid tea in shape. It is vigorous in growth, of medium height.

Lively Lady The large double, well-formed, bright vermilion blooms have a pleasant scent. It is healthy, of vigorous habit, growing to medium height.

Marjorie Anderson This was a 1972 introduction. Its full, high-centered, hybrid tea-form flowers are cerise-pink. They are produced freely and continuously in clusters and are fairly strongly perfumed. It is vigorous and bushy growing 2½ ft. tall.

Moonraker The flowers which are 4½ in. in diameter are cream, which turns white in hot weather, and which is flushed with honey to amber in cool. The vigorous growth produces a tall, branching bush.

Queen Elizabeth Introduced in 1955, this lovely rose, with its large, pink, moderately full, hybrid tea-shaped blooms, finds a place in many gardens. Its blooms are borne on almost thornless, stout stems, sometimes singly, sometimes in large trusses. Very vigorous and upright, it reaches 6 ft. or more. It makes an excellent hedge.

Violet Carson The flowers are a delicate soft peach with a silver reverse, full and of almost perfect hybrid tea-shape. Growth is vigorous, of medium height.

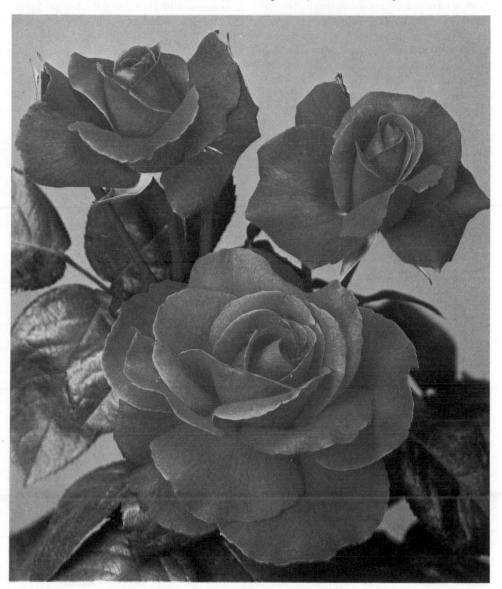

Polyantha Pompoms

This group, historically important, because its members are the fore-runners of our glorious present-day floribundas, has become neglected in more recent years. With the increasing popularity of small gardens, they could easily come into their own again, particularly because they are dwarf, rarely exceeding 2 ft. in height, and recurrent blooming, bearing their colorful, small blooms in delicate clusters. They are excellent for edging, forward positions and bedding.

Cécile Brunner This charming rose has tiny, pale pink, perfectly formed hybrid-tea type blooms, growing well-spaced in trusses. It is repeat-flowering. If it is lightly pruned, it makes a good specimen.

Eblouissant The large, scarlet crimson, semi-double blooms are 2 in. in diameter, borne in small clusters. It is very short.

Ellen Poulsen The small, deep pink flowers are very attractive. Growth is vigorous, spreading and height low.

Golden Salmon Supérieure This is an extremely bright, free-flowering rose, about 2 ft. high. Its blooms are a vivid golden-salmon.

Paul Crampel Free flowering, this has large clusters of small, orange-scarlet, semi-double flowers. It is moderately vigorous and makes a compact bush. It is excellent for more forward places in informal settings. Its color is exactly that of the geranium, 'Paul Crampel', and it is an excellent permanent replacement for that bedding plant.

The Fairy This is very free-flowering with full, pale pink flowers. Growth is vigorous, spreading and low in height.

Miniature Roses

These bijou roses have blooms that are diminutive replicas of the hybrid tea and floribunda roses. The bushes are tiny and the flowers are in proportion to their size. There is a wide range of varieties available, in heights from 4–15 in. They are ideal for small gardens, and rock gardens, sink gardens and window boxes, but should be given a minimum depth of soil of 1 ft. In patios and terrace gardens, they can be most effectively used to create a miniature rose garden in a raised bed. Those marked below with an asterisk are obtainable as standards and it is also possible to buy the following as climbers: 'Yellow Jackie', bright red, 'Magic Wand', bright, rich pink, 'Pink Cameo', and 'Showoff', buff-yellow flowers with red and orange touches.

Baby Masquerade An exact replica of 'Masquerade', with its deep yellow buds opening to pink and changing to deep red, this grows 10–12 in. high.*

Easter Morning This exquisite rose has large double ivory flowers. It reaches a height of between 9 and 12 in.*

Humpty Dumpty The rose-pink flowers are very full and 1 in. across. Height 4–6 in.

Little Flirt This has orange-red, reverse yellow, fragrant, full flowers. It is vigorous and reaches 12–14 in. high.*

Rosina (Josephine Wheatcroft) (Yellow Sweetheart) This has small semi-double, slightly scented, rich yellow blooms, in clusters. It grows 12–15 in. high.*

Scarlet Gem The flowers are very double and bright scarlet, on plants 9–12 in. high.*

Climbing Roses

Casino The hybrid tea-type, sweetly scented flowers are deep yellow in bud, soft yellow, when open. It is vigorous and grows to 10–12 ft. It is valuable for pillars and for covering fences. (Pruning Group 3.)

Copenhagen The recurrent blooms are large, full, scarlet and sweetly scented. Vigorous and compact to 8–10 ft., it is a good pillar rose. (Pruning Group 4.)

Coral Dawn This repeat-flowering climber has full, cupped, fragrant, pink flowers. Moderately vigorous, reaching 10 ft., it is a good pillar rose. (Pruning Group 3.)

Hamburger Phoenix This is repeat-flowering with large, rich crimson blooms. It is vigorous and grows to 9 ft. A good pillar rose, it is also valuable because it will flourish on a north wall. (Pruning Group 4.)

Handel This has moderately full, 3½ in. diameter, almost continuously flowering blooms, which are ivory with petal edges suffused a rich carmine. It is healthy, reaches 12–15 ft. and is useful for pillars and fences. (Pruning Group 4.)

Leverkusen A lovely rose, this has long sprays of golden, semi-double flowers, that are recurrent in summer and autumn. It reaches 9 ft. and is effective as a pillar rose, for walls and, because of its long stems, it can be used as a rambler. (Pruning Group 4.)

New Dawn The recurrent, shell-pink, delicately perfumed blooms are borne throughout the summer. It grows to 8 ft. and is useful for pillars, on a wall and as a hedge. (Pruning Group 2.)

Parkdirektor Riggers This splendid repeat-flowering climber, has 3 in. diameter semi-double, rich blood-red, velvety flowers with a golden center of stamens. Vigorous, to 7–8 ft. tall, it grows well on pillars and

north walls. (Pruning Group 3.)

Rosy Mantle The large, fragrant, hybrid tea-shaped, rosy-pink flowers are recurrent and last well when cut. Growth is vigorous, to 8–10 ft. It is a good pillar rose. (Pruning Group 4.)

Schoolgirl This is a recurrent climber in rich, soft copper-orange, with a spicy fragrance. It is vigorous, grows to 10 ft., a good pillar rose. (Pruning Group 4.)

Sympathie The hybrid tea-type flowers are bright red and very full. Vigorous, it grows to 9–12 ft., is useful for pillars and for a wall or fence. (Pruning Group 4.)

White Cockade The white, hybrid tea-shaped, pleasantly scented, recurrent flowers last well. It is vigorous and reaches 7 ft. It is a good pillar rose. (Pruning Group 4.)

Old-fashioned Shrub Roses

Blanc Double De Coubert (*Rugosa*) This has large, richly fragrant, snowy white, semi-double flowers with a buff and green center. It is repeat flowering. It grows vigorously to 5–6 ft. It is excellent for hedging.

Frau Dagmar Hastrup (*Rugosa*) This has single, pink blooms with delicate veinings, which show their large, creamy centers. It is very free- and recurrent-flowering, and the flowers are followed in the fall by large, rich red, tomato-shaped hips. It reaches 5 ft.

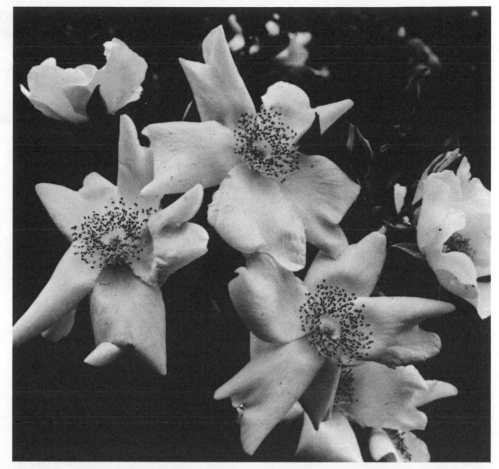

Below left: The cream climbing rose 'Mermaid'
Left: The single crimson, yellow-centered flowers of 'Cocktail', a modern shrub rose which blooms well into the fall
Right: 'Chanelle', an old-fashioned yellow floribunda variety

Mme Hardy (*Damask*) The exquisite, richly fragrant, large, white blooms are flat, perfectly cupped, with folded petals and a green button eye. Vigorous to 5–6 ft.

Mme Pierre Oger (*Bourbon*) This bears cup-shaped, very fragrant blooms, cream, flushed rosy pink, freely throughout the summer. Slender and erect, it reaches 6 ft. It makes an excellent specimen.

Tuscany (*Gallica*) A remarkable rose, with semi-double, intense dark purple-crimson, almost black, flowers, with brilliant golden stamens. It grows into a sturdy bush about 4 ft. tall. Popular with flower arrangers.

William Lobb ('Old Velvet Moss') (*Moss Rose*) The fully double, 3-in. diameter, richly-scented blooms are a medley of fuchsia purple and lilac with gray touches, giving them a shot-silk appearance. It grows vigorously to 7 ft. and is much appreciated by flower arrangers.

Modern Shrub Roses

Ballerina The masses of dainty, small, single, fragrant, apple-blossom pink flowers, with a white eye are borne in large clusters. It grows vigorously to about 5 ft.

Bonn The fragrant, moderately full, vermilion blooms are 3 in. across. It is vigorous, upright and tall and easily reaches 5 ft.

Buff Beauty This rose has buff or apricot-yellow, large, fully double, very fragrant blooms in large clusters. It is repeat-flowering and its blossoms become very plentiful as the summer advances. It has a vigorous, spreading habit and reaches 5 ft.

Cocktail This has single crimson flowers with a pale yellow center, borne in clusters. It is recurrent and free flowering. It grows up to 5 ft. high. Winter protection should be provided in very exposed gardens.

Cornelia The small, semi-double, very fragrant flowers are strawberry-pink, with a yellow base. It is repeat flowering. Growth is vigorous, to 5–6 ft. and it is excellent for hedging.

Elmshorn The small, fully double, light-crimson flowers, are produced almost continuously until December. Vigorous, upright and branching, it grows to 5–6 ft. and makes a good hedge.

Erfurt The large, semi-single, strongly perfumed citron-yellow flowers are edged brilliant pink. It is repeat-flowering. A very vigorous, bushy plant, it grows to 5 ft.

Fred Loads This is almost perpetual in flowering and produces masses of 4 in. wide, scented, single, vermilion flowers, in large heads. Very vigorous, upright and tall, it grows to at least 5 ft., makes a very good hedge and is excellent as a specimen.

Golden Chersonese A beautiful shrub rose, this has small, single yellow flowers, in May and June along the whole length of its shoots. It is very bushy.

Lavender Lassie A very charming, sweetly scented variety, this bears an abundance of huge trusses of lilac-pink, rosette-shaped flowers, up to 3 in. across. It is moderately vigorous in growth and reaches 4–6 ft. It is valuable for hedging and as a specimen.

Nevada The almost single blooms are creamy, sometimes tinged blush, with bright golden stamens. The flowers straddle the whole length of its arching, thornless branches, throughout the summer. Vigorous, to 8 ft.

Nymphenburg The pale salmon-pink blooms with gold tints are large, full and fragrant, produced periodically in clusters. Vigorous, it reaches 6 ft. and makes a colorful hedge.

Penelope Large, semi-double, very fragrant, creamy salmon-pink flowers are carried in large clusters. As the blooms age, they become off-white. It flowers freely and repeatedly throughout the summer. Moderately vigorous, it grows to 6 ft., and makes an attractive hedge.

The Knight This is another 'David Austin New English Rose'. It has the most beautiful, flat, full-centered carnation-like flowers not unlike those of the old *gallica* rose. The color is rich crimson with touches of varying shades of purple. A tough grower, reaching 2 ft.

The Wife of Bath This charming little rose is one of the 'David Austin New English Roses', suitable for modern small gardens. It has small cupped, old-fashioned rose-type, warm pink, fragrant flowers. It is vigorous, but reaches 20 in. in height only.

Wilhelm The flowers are semi-double, about 4 in. in diameter, velvety scarlet-crimson, borne almost continuously throughout the summer in great clusters. Vigorous, 6 ft. high, it makes a beautiful, strong hedge.

Species Roses for Modern Gardens

Rosa moyesii A splendid shrub, this has dusky red, single flowers with cream stamens. These are followed in the fall by large, bright red, bottle-shaped hips. The dainty, fern-like foliage is dark green. It is very vigorous and will grow to 12 ft.

R. rubrifolia The attraction of this species lies in its lovely bluish-gray foliage, tinged with a deep rosy shade, and its red stems. Its purplish-red flowers are insignificant, but they are followed by attractive dark red hips. It grows vigorously to 6–8 ft., and for the sake of its foliage, it is sought after by flower arrangers.

R. sancta This is massed with 4 in. wide, apple-blossom pink single flowers, fading to white. They have huge golden centers and buds are rich pink. It grows to 3 ft.

R. xanthina spontanea ('Canary Bird') A very lovely species rose with rich yellow, single blooms 2½ in. in diameter. In May or sometimes in April the flowers straddle the long arching stems. It makes a very attractive shrub, 6 ft. high and 6 ft. across.

Colorful Hardy Perennials

No single word or term has yet been accepted to cover garden plants, as distinct from bulbs and shrubs, which flower year after year.

'Herbaceous plants', 'hardy perennials', 'border plants' are all inadequate or inaccurate in some respect. Strictly speaking, the word 'herbaceous' denotes the decay of each season's growth, with the plant itself remaining alive, but dormant. Delphiniums, phlox and many others have this habit but several, including iris and kniphofia do not, because they retain winter foliage.

The time is happily past when hardy perennials were relegated in so many gardens because the rewards they gave were disproportionate to the trouble entailed. One reason was because post-war demands for labor saving forced a swing to shrubs. The conventional herbaceous border was largely at fault because of its long narrow shape with a backing wall, hedge or fence. The plants suffered from overcrowding, weak growth and excessive competition for light and air. Quite often such borders were too narrow in relation to the height of the plants. All this accentuated the main disabilities to which perennials are prone if not given a fair chance – difficulty of access to the plants and the need for supports. Harmful competition between the ranker and the less vigorous kinds, and indiscriminate selection and planting almost invariably lead to trouble.

Adaptability This calls for a fair-minded approach when one considers that nature herself has set the limitations. The majority of garden plants have their origin somewhere in the wild. An original type may have been improved upon by breeding and hybridization, but the varieties or cultivars retain their main parental characteristics, including those of adapatability. A species which for millions of years has been accustomed to certain conditions of soil, moisture, sun or shade can scarcely be expected to flourish so well where its natural preferences are lacking.

Most perennials are adaptable to ordinary garden conditions, but it would be as much a mistake to plant something which naturally prefers shade or moist soil into a dry open situation as it would the other way round. It would also be a mistake to plant something rank or invasive near something that is by nature of slow or lowly growth.

Light and Air The problem of overcrowding is linked to this. Plants need light and air and overcrowding and overhanging by trees or other taller growth, which reduce these inevitably leads to stem weakness. Plants in close competition for light and air become excessively tall and spindly. It is a vicious circle and is the major cause of untidiness and the need for staking in congested borders, or those backed by tall trees, shrubs, hedges, fences or walls. Usually where staking is necessary, it is not the fault of the plants but of the conditions under which they are grown.

Island Beds Some years ago Mr Alan Bloom, the well-known British nurseryman, who specializes in hardy perennials, experimented with 'island beds' and showed that not only were the plants shown to greater advantage, with all-round access, but very few needed staking, whereas the great majority had needed supports in the conventional one-sided borders. Although first-year growth was shorter, in succeeding years the growth was just as sturdy, with only such heavy spiked or headed plants as delphiniums and tall Michaelmas daisies needing support. Since then Mr Bloom has constantly advocated island beds as the best means of growing perennials. In the process, he has grown thousands of species and varieties.

Flanking Borders However, the small rectangular plot which most people have, with similar plots on either side, rules out the informality of island beds and such gardens admit of little choice but to go in for flanking borders. Even so in a small or otherwise inhospitable site, there are still ways and means of growing perennials successfully.

Selecting Plants The main thing is to select plants best suited to the place in which they are to grow. The range of available plants is sufficiently wide for this to be achieved, no matter how small the garden, or unkind the soil, so long as it is not completely hemmed in by tall buildings or overhung by large trees to exclude both light and air, and to compete for the available food and water. Even the conventional one-sided border with a high backing can be improved by growing kinds most suitable or adaptable to it. Such borders are usually far too narrow in relation to the height of the plants. Some plants are often invasive and attempts to grow shorter, choicer kinds as well have failed because of unfair competition. What is needed is a new approach, a new appreciation of garden worthiness and adaptability.

The range should include certain hardy bulbs or corms, such as crocosmia, which contribute greatly to the summer display, also certain dwarf perennials. If they are

An example of the type of island bed recommended for displaying hardy perennials to their best advantage
Stepping stones behind a backed bed allow for easy access to the climbers on the wall
A standard type of back garden, with two flanking beds
Above: The attractive flowers of *Aconitum septentrionale ivorene*

adaptable for growing in front of taller kinds, in ordinary soil conditions, then there are very good reasons for including them. Plants of, say, 6 to 12 in. tall are by no means out of place as frontal groups and in small gardens where beds have to be small, then dwarf plants are both desirable and necessary.

ଚ୍ଚ Sites and Soils ଚ୍ଚ

Those moving into a newly-built house must consider how to make the best use of the available garden space. It may be completely bare, a segment of farm or meadow land, and such factors as slope, exposure, drainage, and type of soil should be considered carefully.
Prepare the Site Bearing in mind the need to select plants best adapted to the site, the preparation of a bed or border for hardy plants should include drainage if the soil appears excessively wet or sticky in winter or

hard baked in summer. Thorough cultivation will usually suffice.

The fall is the best time for deep cultivation on heavy land as this will enable winter frosts to break down hard lumps and sods into a fine tilth for spring planting.

Eliminating Weeds There is a tendency nowadays to avoid manual labor, but there is nothing like hand digging. A spade is still the best tool for lighter soils, but for heavy or sticky soils a strong digging fork is best. Trenching, or double digging is necessary where there is a pan below the top spit. This will improve drainage and will enable surface-rooting weeds to be buried, but if the second spit is of subsoil then it should merely be broken up or turned over, not brought up to the surface. Perennial weeds, such as couch grass, must be eliminated, either by forking and raking during dry weather, or by weed killers. However, weed killers may be persistent, and they should never be used unless you know the long-term as well as the short-term effect they will have upon plant growth. Annual weeds are much easier to cope with. Contact sprays will kill them off quickly and leave the soil clear for plants within a few days. Normally perennial weeds that are deep rooted or spread by underground stems require drastic measures to kill them. If you are reluctant to use the lethal poisons which will ensure a complete kill, then it is best to fallow the ground rather than risk a permanent bed of hardy plants being ruined by perennial weeds.

Adding Humus On both light, poor soils and heavy clays, humus in the form of peat-moss, compost or well-rotted manure should be dug in. This will improve the texture, as well as the fertility of the soil, and give plants such a good start that nothing but occasional top dressings of fertilizer will be needed for years.

Grass-covered Sites This soil preparation applies to any site, new or old, but where the surface is grass covered, a cultivator can be useful. If the turf is not wanted elsewhere or is of poor quality it will improve the soil fertility if it is buried, provided it is chopped up first. If an open trench is dug across the narrow end of a bed or border, the loose, chopped-up turf can be pushed in, using a spade or digging fork to cover it well as the plot is dug, trench by trench. Large lumps of turf dug in often result in lack of consolidation as they slowly shrink during the much slower process of rotting. Grassland usually harbors wireworms, but a dusting of a wireworm killer, dug in with the turf or lightly forked in before planting will deal with these pests.

Making Borders Conventional styles in gardening are hard to change, but those who wish to give hardy plants a fair chance will see that there are quite a few variations open to them. There is no doubt that island beds give the best reward, just as narrow, hemmed-in borders give the least return, in terms of value for money and effort in maintenance. An island bed can be sited anywhere provided all-round access is possible, even if it is only a narrow path on one side or end. A backed border can be converted into an island bed provided there is sufficient width. No matter what the backing is, rear access can be provided either by a narrow grass path or paving used as stepping stones. If the backing is a wall, it can be used for vines and a strip allowed along the foot for bulbs or any of the wide variety of dwarf plants or climbers that like such a spot. The rear part of the bed itself should have as edging groups of dwarf early-flowering perennials such as bergenias, pulmonarias and epimediums, for even if the aspect is sunny, the taller perennials facing the adjoining groups will provide summer shading. This rear strip will prove a source of delight in spring and, even if color has gone by summer, you still have easy access to the rest of the bed for maintenance work, and there will be far less staking required, because the weakening effect of the backing is greatly lessened.

Width is, however, an important factor. So many conventional one-sided borders are too narrow and should either be widened, or, if this is impracticable, then the tallest plants should be avoided. Some old borders have a graveled path along the front – and perhaps a low hedge as edging. In most instances the graveled path is not necessary and could be dug up and incorporated as extra border width. The hedging could be removed, as it has little ornamental value and harbors slugs and snails.

Sometimes a border is flanked by a grass path or lawn and this presents no physical problem, if you wish to increase the width of a conventional border, whether or not it is to be converted into a semi-island bed. A curved edge could enhance the layout if the general lines of the garden lend themselves to this treatment. But irregular curves, or a scalloped edge would be out of place if straight lines prevail elsewhere in the garden.

In island beds plants grow more sturdily, are less marred by supporting sticks, and can be viewed from all angles at a more convenient eye level. One-sided beds have become anachronisms; only those on a small scale, where heights of plants are in keeping with the width of the border are worth considering. If the site is unsuitable for an island bed and you have to have a one-sided border, it will inevitably be more troublesome to maintain, unless you select the plants carefully.

Planning and Planting

Width of Border Whatever type of border you decide to plan and plant its success and potential interest will depend not only on a well-chosen site, well-prepared soil and the right selection of plants, but on its width. The narrower the bed, the lower the plants should be. Nothing looks more incongruous than plants flowering at 4 or 5 ft. in a bed only 4 or 5 ft. wide. They inevitably harm dwarfer, choicer plants growing beside them, regardless of aspect. A safe guide in selecting plants is to measure the plantable width of the border in feet, and halve it to arrive at the maximum height of plants it should contain. This restricts a 4 ft. wide border to plants of no more than 2 ft. tall, but a little latitude can be allowed for the erect, spikey plants, such as kniphofias, to exceed the limit by a few inches. This is a rule that can be applied to any type of border—island or one-sided, bearing in mind that an island borders the tallest plants are placed in the center, and in one-sided borders they are planted at the back.

Grouping should also be considered. Where space is very restricted and where variety is preferred, then there is a case for growing one plant only of each kind. But there is never any point in growing a single plant of the same kind in more than one position in the same bed or border. If the site is large enough, then plants should be grouped in threes, at least, in a bed of about 100 sq. ft. in area, and in groups of up to 10 to 15 in in the largest beds of a 1,000 sq. ft. or more.

Spacing Plants The space between plants in a group, should be less than that between the groups themselves. This is because the plants in a group will usually grow and mass together effectively when in flower. But they will probably differ in form and habit from neighboring groups, and will need extra space to allow for this as well as to allow for vital light and air to give sturdy growth and for access for maintenance. The average spacing should be about five plants to the square yard. If, for example, groups are of five plants of a kind, this gives a planting distance of about 16 in. from plant to plant within a group. But the space around the group, up to the outer plants in adjoining groups should be 20 in. Spacing depends on the vigor of the plant; a single plant may occupy a square yard or nine plants of a dwarf, slow-growing plant may occupy the same area.

Do not allow the more robust or rapid spreading kinds to overshadow or encroach on those that expand slowly. Those plants with a similar habit and vigor should be placed near to each other to avoid harmful competition. If you are prepared to plan your own bed or border, it is better not to use a stereotyped plan unless you are quite sure that the plants offered are suitable for the site. Making your own plan is not difficult. **Planning on Paper** First obtain a sheet of squared paper—each square inch subdivided into tenths. Using the most convenient scale that fits the paper, draw the outline of the bed or border. Within this outline, group spaces can be pencilled in faintly to begin with, once you have decided roughly on the area each group should occupy—depending on whether variety or a more massed display is preferred. A large variety of plants will call for smaller groups but a square yard at least will be needed if groups are to be large enough for massed color, depending on the total space available.

It is better to space each group by means of numbers. If there are to be, say, 36 groups in a bed, get the numbers one to 36 down on paper, spaced over the area, and when you are satisfied draw in the outline of each group as indicated on the sample plan. Using the list of plants you have already chosen, the placing of each one becomes a stimulating task, as you take account of height, spread, color and flowering season. At this stage it is useful to know something about the habits of the plants and here the descriptions of the plants which appear later will prove helpful.

Far left: The 3-ft. tall *Verbascum* 'Pink Domino', a modern hybrid suitable for an island bed
Left: Geranium psilostemon (G. armenum) is the most brilliantly colored of the true geraniums or cranesbills
Above: The deep pink, trumpet-shaped flowers of.*Incarvillea delavayi* open in May before the dark green leaves appear
Right: The large white flowers of the Christmas rose, *Helleborus niger*, are always welcome when they appear, usually in the New Year
Top: 'September Charm', a 3-ft. tall variety of *Anemone hypehensis*, flowers from August to October

Above: The bleeding heart, *Dicentra spectabilis*
Center: Hostas or plantain lilies are among the best of foliage plants

Below: Oenothera fruticosa, a good herbaceous perennial

If in the process of making a new bed or border, an error in placing occurs it will show up during the first flowering season. Perhaps a dwarf kind should have been nearer the front or vice-versa, or two colors do not blend well. This matters little, for a switch can easily be made in the fall or spring, provided a note is made when the error is seen.

When to Plant Generally speaking, fall planting is best – whether you are making adjustments or planting a complete new bed–provided the soil is in clean, friable condition. It may not be possible to obtain delivery of plants from a nursery in September or early October, the ideal time, but the whole of October is usually safe for planting except on heavy, sticky soils and in the coldest parts of the country. In warmer or drier districts and on well-drained soils, it is safe to plant in November too, except for a few kinds, notably *Aster amellus*, erigerons, pyrethrums, *Scabiosa caucasica*, nepetas and some of the grasses, which it is safer to plant in spring. In the fall the soil is still warm and new roots form quickly, so that in spring plants soon make up growth and do not lack for moisture. Watering in is seldom needed in the fall, but in spring it is often necessary.

Planting Planting a new bed poses few problems if you have a plan. When the consignment arrives, unpack and stand each plant or bundle upright, and sprinkle with water if dry. If the bed or border is all ready with its marker sticks or labels for each group in position, placing will be easy, but do not, if you can avoid it, lay out the plants too early lest sun or wind dry out the roots before they are safely covered with soil. If the soil is wet and sticky, move about the bed on one or two short planks, and do not tread in each plant too firmly. Lighter soils may be too dry, and if when you try to make a suitable hole with a trowel, you find that the soil tends to run back, then puddling is the answer. This is simply a matter of pouring water from the spout of a can, till the hole is almost full. The water will quickly soak away and then you can enlarge the hole sufficiently to take the plant and having inserted it with its roots well spread out, draw round some of the dry top soil and make a loose tilth round the plant.

Watering In spring, the soil is usually moist enough for planting until about mid-April, although even in March the soil can be so dry that puddling is necessary. If, after planting, plants show signs of distress, whether or not they were watered in initially, do not splash water over them. It is the roots that need moisture and a mere surface watering can be harmfully deceptive as it may erode the soil, expose the roots or cake the surface without soaking in. What the plants need is a fine spray; this takes longer, but will penetrate more readily to the roots, with far less waste of water. The same method, preferably using a sprinkler with a fine nozzle, should be used during a summer drought on established plants which are showing signs of distress; it is best done in the morning, and after each overhead watering, especially on a newly planted bed, it is worth hoeing or raking over the surface, as it dries out again, so as to retain a fine tilth, a top layer of loose fine soil ½ in. thick, which enables growth to keep fresh for much longer as water is drawn up from the soil below.

Mulching A new bed, with soil well-prepared will not need feeding for the first year or two if it is reasonably rich in humus. Sand, gravel, soils containing lime, are often shallow and lack humus. Although leaf mold is hard to come by, peatmoss is easy to obtain and apply, and is an excellent form of humus for such soils. It is useful by itself, either dug in or applied as a mulch that will retain moisture and keep down weeds. But if it is used in conjunction with an organic fertilizer it is most effective in promoting good growth. The best method where plants need both a feed and a mulch, is to apply the fertilizer in spring, at about 2 oz. per square yard and immediately hoe it in to the top 2 in. of soil.

The spring-flowering leopard's bane, *Doronicum plantagineum*

This is worth while on any bed or border after the second season, but if a mulch, too, is needed, this should be applied during April or May, depending on weather, type of soil and locality. The soil at this time is warming up, and to mulch too early in late districts may retard growth a little, though it will catch up later. The warmer the district the earlier you can begin feeding, hoeing and mulching. Before peatmoss is used as a mulch it should be thoroughly moistened (dry peatmoss can absorb up to eight times its weight in water); in this condition it is easy to spread over bare patches of earth between the plants to a thickness of ½ to 1 in. If you fork over a bed or border in the fall or winter, a peatmoss mulch applied in spring will largely disappear, though it will continue to do good, as a soil improver.

Winter Digging This also improves the soil structure, although there is always a danger of damaging the roots of plants. This can be avoided by using a flat-tined fork, rather than a spade; the flat tines will keep each forkful more or less intact so that annual weeds can be turned in. At the same time any pieces of perennial weed which may appear can be picked out. Couch grass, sorrel, thistle and the like are such nuisances that no effort should be spared to get rid of even the tiniest piece, even if it means taking up a border plant to do so.

Before winter digging begins remove last year's stalks. If you are not going to dig between the plants the dead stems may be cut back to ground level at any convenient time in the fall or early winter. This applies only to the truly herbaceous kinds, which lose each season's growth above ground and start growing again in spring. However, any foliage, for example that of kniphofias, that remains green over winter in mild areas should be left until new spring growth is about to begin and then it is a matter merely of tidying up the decaying or sere outer leaves.

Other Methods of Growing For most people, a bed or border appeals as a well-defined feature in a garden. But hardy perennials may be grown in other ways. Many kinds can be grown in company with shrubs so that both are enhanced. Such erect and troublefree plants as hemerocallis flower from midsummer onwards to add more than a touch of color to a background of shrubs. Apart from these, the wide range of ground-cover plants form a pleasing carpeting effect over what would otherwise be bare earth between shrubs, and most of these, too, will contribute color.

Right: Aster amellus, one of the types of Michaelmas daisies

Acanthus (bear's breech) Acanthus are best grown in isolated positions rather than in a mixed border. *A. longifolius*, *A. mollis* and *A. spinosus* will in time take up more than their allotted space as a group and then curbing becomes an annual task. *A. mollis* flowers less freely than the other two. All have long, jagged glossy green leaves and 3–4 ft. spikes of curiously hooded flowers, lavender-lilac tinged with white. They prefer a sunny place and well-drained soil, and a group by itself or in company with shrubs, can be very effective as they flower from early July onwards for many weeks. Needs protection where winters are severe.

Achillea (yarrow, milfoil) This genus includes a few good and showy plants, but also some of a weedy nature. All have flowers useful for cutting. *A. filipendulina* with plate-like heads of deep yellow on erect 4 ft. stems is deservedly popular. It is easily grown in any well-drained soil and needs the minimum of attention. It is usually offered under the name 'Gold Plate'. Stems cut at their best can be dried for winter decoration. *A.* 'Moonshine', 18 in. canary-yellow, with silvery leaves, is much dwarfer. It flowers from May to July. *A. millefolium* is the common yarrow. Deep pink, and almost red variants, such as 'Cerise Queen' make quite a brave show for a season or two, before they need curbing or replanting back into position. But heads on 3 ft. stems become top heavy and need support, as do the white achilleas, 'The Pearl' and 'Perry's White', both 3 ft. tall with double, button-type, white flowers in loose heads. All should be divided in early fall or spring.

Aconitum (monkshood) Aconitums are related to delphiniums, but have a hood over the upper part of the flower—hence the common name. Several are good garden plants, and most of them will stand unaided. The hybrid *A.* × *arendsii* is a first-rate late flowering plant with strong 4 ft. spikes terminating in a bunch of amethyst-blue flowers in September and October. *A. bicolor* has more openly branched spikes on wiry stems about 3½ ft. high and the blue-white flowers give a bright display for several weeks from midsummer onwards. *A.* 'Bressingham Spire', 2½–3 ft., grows rather like a well-foliaged tapering fir. The leaves are deep green and glossy and the terminal spike has violet-blue flowers, followed by secondary spikes, to cover the August to September period. The vigorous growing 'Newry Blue' flowers in June–July, but both this and the violet-blue 'Spark's Variety' have more open spikes, about 3½ ft. tall. Aconitums should not be left unattended for too long, and if the plants are not mulched, they should be divided and replanted in enriched soil after about three years. This does not apply to the hybrid 'Ivorine', 3 ft., very neat and shapely in growth, with ivory-white flowers from late May to July–August; a splendid plant for sun or partial shade.

Alchemilla (lady's mantle) *A. mollis* will grow in any but the driest, starved situations and in sun or shade, forming a neat, ground-hugging clump of pretty maple-shaped gray-green hairy leaves. From this loose sprays of tiny yellowish-green flowers spread out and up to about 20 in. for many weeks. The plant divides easily and sets seed freely.

Anchusa (alkanet) Bright though they are these are not reliable plants. The popular varieties include 'Loddon Royalist', 'Morning Glory' and 'Opal'. The black, fleshy roots send up large coarse leaves and 4 ft. spikes of small but intensely blue flowers from late May to July. They usually need supporting. After July, there is a somewhat blank space, and all too often plants fail to survive the winter, especially in wetter or richer soils.

Anemone (windflower) *A. hupehensis* (long known as *A. japonica*) can contribute so much to the late summer display that no garden should be without these delightful plants. Though shades of pink and white are the only colors, it is the way their flowers are borne that makes them so charming. Individual flowers ranging from 1½–3 in. across are like dog roses, with yellow-stamened centers. The wiry, branching stems are tipped by nodding flowers and close-set buds. Most varieties begin flowering in late July or early August and will continue until the fall. They need good drainage and a mainly sunny position and they are especially good on soil containing lime.

Anthemis (camomile) Most anthemis flower freely and for a long time, but they are short-lived plants, especially the varieties of *A. tinctoria*. The yellow, daisy flowers come on somewhat twiggy, not very erect plants, 2–2½ ft. high, from June to late August. If the woody rootstock fails to produce new basal growth in the fall plants will not survive. *A.* 'Grallagh Gold' is even trickier than the light yellow 'Wargrave' or 'Mrs Buxton', but the dwarfer species, *A. sancti-johannis*, 20 in., with deep yellow flowers, is more reliable.

Aquilegia (columbine) Very few aquilegias will come true from seed; for those who like a good range of color and large, long-spurred flowers, such strains as 'McKana Hybrids', about 3 ft. high and 'Beidermeier', 20 in. high, are delightful for a year or two, until replacements are needed. They are not fussy plants, and some will grow in shade.

Armeria (thrift) The common thrift is *A.*

maritima which has produced some varieties and hybrids of real garden value. 'Vindictive' makes an effective edging; it will make a continuous evergreen row 1 ft. wide within a year or two. In May and June, it is ablaze with 8 in. drumstick heads of bright carmine-pink flowers. The white-flowered variety *alba* serves a similar purpose. The tallest, largest flowered and brightest armeria is *A. latifolia* 'Ruby' (the color is in fact a deep rose). The central root stem just below ground is so bare, that division is seldom possible. Cuttings are not easy to strike but basal cuttings taken in the early fall or spring and inserted in a cold frame sometimes root. Armerias need full sun and a very well-drained soil.

Aster (Michaelmas daisy) The garden would be dull in the fall if no Michaelmas daisies were to be seen. New varieties have been churned out over recent years, and although decided advances have been made, enhancing the range of height, color and size of flower, it is a matter of personal preference when such a wide choice exists. One can only emphasize the need to choose varieties which do not need staking, and to replant every three years, using only the outer healthier shoots. Spring is the best time to divide asters.

Astilbe Astilbes grown in good moist soil are plants of incomparable beauty. They have attractive foliage and the plumed flower spikes are in every imaginable shade from white through pink, salmon and cerise to fiery red and deep red. Some are erect, others arch and droop, and heights vary from 6 in. to 6 ft. They do not need staking, are completely hardy and can be left alone for years, trouble-free and reliable, though they cannot stand hot, dry conditions. They appreciate a spring mulch to conserve moisture, and they can safely be divided when dormant. In general, the tallest astilbes are the strongest and least fussy about moisture,

but these do not include the brightest colors. One of the best of the taller kinds is *A. taquetii superba*, about 4 ft., with straight imposing spikes of an intense lilac-purple shade, in July and August. *A. davidii*, lilac-rose, and the varieties 'Tamarix', 'Salland', 'Venus', pale-pink, and 'Salmon Queen' are all tall and robust. Given the right conditions, the more colorful dwarfer hybrid astilbes, $1\frac{1}{2}$–3 ft. tall, will flower for much longer, between late June and mid-August. 'Cologne', deep carmine-rose, 'Dusseldorf', salmon-pink, 'Rheinland', early, clear pink, 'Deutschland', a fine white, 'Fire' is intense red shade and 'Red Sentinel' almost brick-red, are about 2 ft. high. 'Glow' at $2\frac{1}{2}$ ft. is stronger and 'Spinell' is another fiery shade. The $2\frac{1}{2}$ ft. 'Federsee' is a rosy-red variety, and 'Bressingham Pink' has fine clear pink spikes. 'Fanal', deep red, is barely 2 ft. high, and 'Irrlicht' is white. *A. simplicifolia* 'Sprite', a sturdy miniature, has very dark foliage as background to the 12 in. ivory pink spikelets.

Bergenia These are excellent space fillers for any but the hottest driest situations. The large shiny, almost evergreen leaves usually die off in late winter in readiness for the spring flowering period, when the stubby 9–12 in. spikes produce sprays of little bell-shaped flowers, usually pink – rather washy in older species, but deeper, bordering on red in such modern varieties as the dwarf 'Abendglut' (Evening Glow) and 'Ballawley', which is about the largest and finest of all. 'Silberlicht' is a free-flowering almost white shade. The value of bergenias is their bright foliage from May to March, and their ability to spread fairly quickly but unobtrusively in awkward places.

Brunnera *B. macrophylla* (formerly *Anchusa myosotidiflora*) differs from most anchusas by being a good reliable perennial, with less fleshy roots, forming clumps of rounded leaves which have weed smothering

Above: A vigorous example of *Salvia splendens*.
Left: The astilbes do best in moist soil.
Below: Old clumps of Michaelmas daisies are often tough and are best divided by using two garden forks, back to back. Otherwise, as shown on the right, young portions may be removed from the outer edges of the clump and replanted, to save digging up and replanting the whole clump. *Right:* The golden marguerite (*anthemis*) variety 'Grallagh Gold', which flowers from June to late August

properties all summer. From April to July the sprays of tiny brilliant blue 'forget-me-not' flowers are borne on 2 ft. branching stems. In good or moist soil, plants become fairly massive. A bright-leaved form *variegata*, is rather less robust; of its 6 in. wide leaves more than half is primrose yellow. It is best planted where hot sun does not scorch it.

Campanula (bellflower) This is an adaptable genus ranging from prostrate plants to those 5 or 6 ft. tall. With such diversity, recommendations will be easier to follow on the basis of height. The dwarfest, semi-prostrate hybrid 'Stella' can adorn not only a rock garden, a wall top, path edging or the front of a border, but makes a good pot plant for indoors or outdoors. It flowers from June to August, but if cut back, divided and re-vitalized it will flower again in the fall. Cultivation is easy in any reasonable soil, in sun or partial shade.

The varieties of *C. carpatica* are valuable for frontal groups. They are neat in habit, vary in height from 6–12 in. and have upward facing cup-shaped flowers, 1–2 in. across, from June to August. Colors vary from white to violet blue, and though easy to raise from seed, one must obtain named varieties to avoid mixed shades. *C. burghaltii* has long, near opaque smokey blue bells, dangling from 15–18 in. stems from June onwards. It is vigorous but not invasive. *C. van Houteii* is similar in habit with equally large pale blue bells. *C. glomerata* has many forms; the best of this top-clustered group is *superba*, 3 ft., with upturned violet flowers in June and July. *C. lactiflora* is also variable; the deepest colored named variety is 'Prichard's', growing erectly to $2\frac{1}{2}$–3 ft., with open clusters of bell-shaped flowers. The pygmy variety of this long-flowering species is 'Pouffe', which makes a green cushion for the light blue flowers from June to September. The tallest, 'Loddon Anna', reaches 6 ft., with heads of near pink; '*alba*' is only a foot or so shorter. All these are reliable plants and will grow happily in shade as well as sun. *C. latifolia* (syn. *C. macrantha*) which flowers in June and July, and it is similarly adaptable, has strong 4 ft. spikes with large blue bells. There is a good white form – *alba*; 'Brantwood' is deep violet-blue, but the near opaque 'Gloaming' is an entrancing pale-sky-blue.

Catananche (Cupid's dart) *C. caerulea* has cornflower-like blooms on wiry stems from June to August. It reaches 2–$2\frac{1}{2}$ ft. in well-drained soil. Its faults are lack of longevity and a tendency to loll over so that flowers droop rather than stand up to face the sky, especially in damp weather. It is grown from seed sown in May, or root cuttings taken in March.

Centaurea (cornflower) This genus includes coarse as well as choicer species with heights varying from 2 in. to 6 ft. or more. The deep pink variety *steenbergii* is a great improvement on the species *C. dealbata*; 'John Coutts' is another improved variety

Top: The valerians (*Centranthus ruber* forms) are excellent plants for growing in the crevices of walls. *Left:* *Bergenia cordifolia* is one of the earliest herbaceous plants to flower in spring.

Above: One of the best of all bellflowers for the border is *Campanula lactiflora*, 4–5 ft. tall, available in various color forms. *Below:* *Achillea filipendulina* 'Gold Plate'

with even larger flowers, of a lighter, clearer pink. Both reach 2½ ft. and flower freely in June and July. *C. macrocephala*, 5 ft. has yellow tufty flowers on more massive leafy plants. *C. hypoleuca* is charming with a profusion of clear pink flowers on compact gray-foliaged plants, with wiry, 1 ft. tall flowering stems from late May to July. *C. ruthenica* is distinctive for its shining foliage and gracefully slender 4 ft. stems carrying canary-yellow fluffy-headed flowers from June to August. All centaureas are best divided in early spring. They are easily-grown, vigorous plants, even in poor soil.

Centranthus (valerian) Many a garden would be the poorer without *Centranthus ruber* for it can colonize a neglected garden and can be seen naturalized on old walls as well as in old borders. Unwanted seedlings can be treated as weeds, leaving a group where it belongs to be self-replenishing. It grows 2–3 ft. tall and flowers freely. The usual deep, dull pink flowers are not specially attractive; the brighter red *coccinea* is better and there is also a white form, *alba*. If you consider it too common to grow among choicer plants, there is usually some odd dry corner where it can fill a need for color.

Chrysanthemum Strictly, this genus includes pyrethrums and also marguerites or Shasta daisies. The white-flowered *C. maximum* 'Esther Mead' is the best known, but other excellent varieties include 'Thomas Killin', 'Everest', large single white flowers; 'Wirral Supreme', double white, very large lacy-petalled single flowers; 'Cobham Gold', 'Moonlight', both flushed with yellow; 'Esther Read' and 'Jennifer Read', all doubles. But as a garden plant *C. corymbosum* is preferable. This has grayish foliage

and grows stoutly to 3½ ft. and bears hundreds of 1 in. wide white daisies from June to August. Even after Michaelmas daisies are over *C. uliginosum*, 5–6 ft., comes into flower; it has single white, yellow-centered daisies 2 in. across which add a last touch of summer to late fall.

Cimicifuga (bugbane) These are effective and easy plants given reasonably good soil that does not dry out too much. All have slender tapering spikes of small fuzzy, pearl-white flowers in later summer and fall. They need no attention for many years beyond an occasional mulch and feed. *C. cordifolia*, 3 ft. flowers in August and September; the variety Armleuchter of *C. racemosa* has large flower spikes and is very effective when even Michaelmas daisies are fading.

Coreopsis *C. grandiflora* is easily raised from seed in such varieties as 'Sunburst' and 'Mayfield Giant', but they deteriorate after one season's profligate show of deep yellow flowers, rather laxly carried on thin 2 ft. stems. The midget 'Goldfink', 8 in., smothers itself in deep yellow, maroon-marked flowers from June to September, and usually survives the winter. If odd plants exhaust themselves, those remaining divide easily in the spring to make replacements. The most reliable and distinctive coreopsis is *C. verticillata*, which forms shapely 18 in. bushes decked with 1 in. yellow flowers from June to late August; and var. *grandiflora* is slightly deeper in color.

Delphinium These majestic plants may be considered indispensable, but almost invariably they need staking in good time. They also need rich soil for best results and in some garden slugs can be a menace. From seed

sown under glass in spring it is possible for some plants to flower in late summer, otherwise sow outdoors to obtain stock to flower freely the following year after transplanting. Named varieties will not flower true from seed, which mostly produce mixed shades of blue. A few strains come reasonably true such as the shorter-lived 'Pacific Hybrids'. Belladonna delphiniums, less tall with more open spikes, are in their way as attractive as the large-flowered varieties, though it is in the latter that double flowers occur.

Dicentra (bleeding heart) The true bleeding heart, *D. spectabilis*, has few faults as a hardy perennial, and it is worth a little extra attention to ensure that it gives of its best. The lush foliage and the arching sprays of dangling red and white lockets are a gladdening sight in May and June. The fanged, brittle roots should be planted carefully in well-drained good soil, where some sun but not the worst of the winds can reach the plant. Division is tricky, but young shoots, with a good base will root in a cold frame.

Dictamnus (fraxinella, burning bush) *D. albus* is a deeply rooting plant that likes full sun and perfect drainage where it will live for years to send up 3 ft. spikes of lilac-pink flowers from June to August. Division is difficult, propagation by root cuttings in the fall or spring is better; plants grown from seed are slow to reach maturity.

Doronicum (leopard's bane) These easily-grown plants make a bright display of yellow in spring. The earliest to thrust up their widely-rayed yellow daisies are the dwarfest. 'Goldzwerg' reaches only 6 in. and flowers from late March to May. It is followed quickly by the 18 in. 'Miss Mason'. This is the height of the outstanding fully double-flowered variety 'Spring Beauty'. 'Harpur Crewe' is tallest, with wide-rayed flowers on 3 ft. stems. Doronicums are easy to divide (preferably in early fall) and respond to division and replanting every few years.

Echinacea (purple cone flower) *E. purpurea* (syn. *Rudbeckia purpurea*) has a special appeal, with its somewhat drooping petals accentuating the central cone on 3½ ft stems. Named varieties as well as variable seedlings are offered. A better plant than the best-known variety 'The King' is the erect 'Robert Bloom' in a much warmer red shade. This is one of the 'Bressingham Hybrids' which show only slight color variations. All flower from July to September. They like good deep soil, well drained but not too dry and can safely be divided in early spring.

Echinops (globe thistle) These deep-rooting plants are reliably hardy and perennial, but one or two are too massive for a small garden. All have grayish, jagged, slightly prickly leaves and branching stems which carry rounded flower heads of mainly light blue. *E. ritro*, 3 ft., is less troublesome than the taller kinds. Old plants are easier to divide than to dig up, and roots left in the ground will mostly sprout again.

Erigeron (fleabane) These useful members of the daisy family give a good display from May to August and some are useful for cutting. They are happy in open positions, in any well-drained soil and are best increased by division in spring. The most reliable include 'Darkest of All', 20 in., single-flowered, violet-blue, 'Foerster's Liebling', 20 in., near double, bright pink, 'Lilofee', 2½ ft., mauve blue, 'Prosperity', 20 in. light lavender-blue, almost double, 'Amity', 2 ft. lilac pink, 'Gaiety', 1½–2 ft., single pink,

Two varieties of erigeron

'Sincerity', 2 ft. mauve-blue, single, long-flowering, and 'Dignity', 2 ft. violet-blue.

Eryngium (sea holly) By comparison with most flowers the eryngiums are freakish, as all have flowers without visible petals. In some the stems are as brightly colored as the flower bracts and in others the flowers and leaves are green. Such species as *E. serra*, 6 ft., *E. bromeliifolium*, 4 ft. and *E. pandanifolium*, to 10 ft., grow from large green rosettes of vicious looking saw-edged leaves and send up stiffly branching spikes tipped with green spiny thimbles as flowers. *E. alpinum* is very handsome, with rounded green leaves and sturdy 2½ ft. stems crowned with large silver-blue flowers. *E. bourgattii* is reliable; it is very silvery with a tinge of blue in the 20 in. stems as well as in the terminal bract. *E. variifolium*, 2 ft., has marbled evergreen foliage. *E. giganteum*, 3 ft., is imposing, but only biennial. *E. planum* is easy, but the blue flowering tips are not as bright as in the widely-branching *E. tripartitum*, 3–3½ ft., which is the best of this group. Some eryngiums will grow well from seed, but the usual method of increase is from root cuttings in the spring.

Euphorbia (spurge) This vast genus includes a few good garden plants. All have bracts surrounding clustered flower heads. *E. charassias* and *E. veneta* (syn. *E. wulfenii*), are sub-shrubs, with year round blue-gray, somewhat succulent foliage, and build up

into imposing plants 3 ft. high or more till they burst into almost a fountain of sulfur-yellow heads of flower in spring. They look well with shrubs or on a wall. One of the best of all spring-flowering herbaceous plants is *E. polychroma* (syn. *E. epithymoides*), 20 in., a sturdy, compact plant which produces heads of bright sulfur-yellow bracts in April and early May. *E. griffithii* 'Fireglow', 2½ ft., produces deep fiery heads in May and June. Of the more vigorous species, which have their uses as ground coverers, *E. cyparissias*, 10 in., spreads rapidly and has bluish-gray foliage and heads of sulfur-yellow. *E. amygdaloides* and *E. robbiae* are similar, with deep green foliage and a reasonable spread, but are more suitable among shrubs than in a perennial border.

Filipendula (meadowsweet) These are, with one or two exceptions, moisture-loving plants, which will grow well enough in full sun, provided the soil is moist. *F. hexapetala plena*, which will grow where the soil is quite dry, has reddish stems, 18–20 in. and snow-white heads in profusion during June–July. *F. hexapetala grandiflora*, 2½ ft., is single flowered but has wide creamy-white heads. The remaining filipendulas are moisture loving. *F. digitata nana*, 9 in., has deep rosy-red flowers and *F. elegantissima*, 3 ft., hazy pink flower heads in June and July. Filipendulas can be divided in early fall or spring and benefit from an annual mulch.

Gaillardia (blanket flower) These are not very reliable perennials. They are easily grown from seed, though named varieties can only be propagated by root cuttings – easier from roots left in the ground after plants have been chopped off, than from actual root cuttings. They prefer poor soil and dry conditions. Flowers are borne profusely from June to August, when cutting hard back is helpful. Good named varieties are – 'The Warrior', mahogany colored, 'Ipswich Beauty', yellow with maroon cone, 'Yellow Queen', yellow, 'Wirral Flame', browny-red, all 2½–3 ft. 'Goblin' is a 9-in. miniature.

Geranium (cranesbill) True geraniums are hardy garden plants, easily grown in sun or shade. *G. armenum*, (syn. *G. psilostemon*), 3½ ft., makes a dense bush given ample moisture; the flowers, over 1 in. across, borne from June to August, are fiercely magenta. 'Bressingham Flair' is less intense, with more pink in the flowers. *G. endressii*, about 20 in., forms dense mounds of light green and its sprays of light or bright pink flowers make a good show in June and July. *G. grandiflorum*, 15 in., clear blue, spreads too quickly for what it gives in flowers, but 'Johnson's Blue', 18 in., is very good indeed. *G. ibericum*, 2 ft., has dark leaves and rich deep blue flowers. *G. renardii* has light mauve-blue flowers, marked with delicate crimson veins. *G. sanguineum*, 1 ft., spreads slowly and has a long succession of magenta-rose flowers. 'Holden Variety' or '*splendens*', is a good clear pink and there is a white form, *album*. *G. sylvaticum* 'Mayflower', 18 in., has light blue flowers in May and June. The uncommon *G. wlassovianum* has deeper blue flowers from July to September, and is worth a place.

Geum (avens) For reliability *G. borisii*, 1 ft., rates highly with its intense orange single flowers in May and June. The shortest lived are the popular double red 'Mrs Bradshaw' and double yellow 'Lady Stratheden'. These flower very freely, but after a couple of years they lose vigor and die. Other good hybrids which need replanting and dividing every two or three years are 'Fire Opal', orange-red, 'Orangeman', orange-yellow, and 'Red Wings', orange-red, April to June.

Gypsophila (chalk plant) The tallest, but still popular baby's breath, *G. paniculata*, is not an ideal border plant, because of its floppy habit. The double-flowered 'Bristol Fairy' can only be propagated by cuttings or longer-lived type. Both are charming in their way, with clouds of pure white flowers, but they need space, as well as free-drained soil, in which to make their expansive display from late June to September. But 'Bristol Fairy' can only be propagated by cuttings or grafting on to young seedlings of the single *G. paniculata*. There is a dwarfer, neater double-flowered variety, '*compacta plena*'. This grows 18 in. high and 2 ft. across and is to be preferred in a mixed bed or border. Two dwarfer double pink varieties are 'Pink Star', 18 in., with small pale pink flowers, and the more prostrate 'Rosy Veil'. All these will increase by cuttings in spring, and all are sun lovers and long flowering.

Helenium (sneezeweed) These are quite indispensable for providing a rich display of color, but neglect can cause some disappointment. They need dividing and replanting every three years or so, in early fall or spring, in enriched soil. Heleniums are very easy to grow in fully open positions. The tallest varieties should be avoided.

'Bruno', and 'Moerheim Gem', browny red and 'Butterpat', yellow, are in the 4 ft. range and flower from July to September. Earlier, sturdy varieties are 'Bressingham Gold', 'Coppelia', 'Gold Fox' and 'Mahogany', all with orange and browny flame shades. 'Golden Youth', about 2½ ft., is a fine clear color, and 'Wyndley', 2–2½ ft., is brown and orange.

Heliopsis (orange sunflower) These can be left alone for several years and relied upon to flower freely unsupported. All have basically yellow-green flowers as in 'Goldgreenheart', and the rich buttery-yellow 'Golden Plume', both semi-double. Good single varieties are 'Karat' and *H. patula*, both 3 ft., with 3 in. flowers from June to September. Divide in the fall or spring.

Helleborus (hellebore) The true Christmas rose (*H. niger*) has a never failing appeal even though it seldom opens in time for Christmas. But January and February flowering is exciting enough to make this a very desirable plant, though it is best placed in cool shade, not where it is over-hung or the soil is dry. Old plants do not move or divide easily; young seedling plants do best. Seed is slow to germinate and needs to be sown when fresh. *H. niger* is followed by the Lenten rose, *H. orientalis*, 12 to 18 in., and its hybrids, most rewarding plants, varying from white to deep pink and even plum purple. A few plants can fill permanently an odd corner even where it becomes quite dry in summer, so long as it is not sunbaked. Where it is moist enough, self-sown seedlings will appear, but mature plants can also be divided in the fall. *H. corsicus* has pale greenish-white flowers on 2 ft. stems in spring, and the 2 ft. tall *H. foetidus* with

Far left: The gaillardias are among the brightest of border plants, flowering from June to August
Left: Helenium 'Wyndley' grows 2–2½ ft. tall and flowers for many weeks from July onwards
Above: A pretty variety of *echinacea purpurea*, the purple cone flower
Right: Helleborus orientalis, is available in a range of colors, including the purplish-brown of this variety, *atropurpurea*

greenish flowers may become naturalized, even in dry shady places.

Hemerocallis (day lily) Many new varieties of this sterling garden plant have appeared in recent years. The rushy-leaved plants are robust without being invasive. They flower from June–August and are not pernickety about soil, shade or sun, but they respond to good treatment by giving a better, longer display of their richly-colored trumpet flowers. A wide range of color exists. Especially recommended are 'Petite Pink', 'Double Gold' and 'Whistling Swan'. Most varieties grow into very large plants. Divide in fall or spring.

Heuchera (coral flower) Heucheras have that rare combination of compact, well-foliaged evergreen growth and a show of brightly-colored flowers carried daintily on sprays or spikes for several weeks in early summer. On a well-grown plant hundreds of small, bell-shaped flowers are borne on wiry stems. Colors range from white to every shade of pink, and red including scarlet,

coral, salmon and coppery-crimson. Heucheras must have good drainage, and are best in sun or only partial shade. They flower better in rich soil, yet they are draught resistant. Every three to four years mulch deeply with soil or compost, or dig them up and replant them deeply, using only the most vigorous shoots. 'Bressingham Hybrids' is a mixed strain in a wide color range. They do not come true from seed and division is best after flowering ceases in July.

Heucherella 15 in., is a splendid plant for fairly good light soil, in light shade, and may produce its sprays of light pink flowers almost as freely in the fall as at its normal period of May and June. This and *H. tiarelloides* are hybrids between a *Heuchera* and a *Tiarella*. *H. tiarelloides* makes modestly spreading ground cover with slightly golden-leaves, producing in April and May 1 ft. spikes of pink flowers. It is easily grown in any but hot dry positions.

Hosta (plantain lily) These plants have come into their own of recent years, because of their hardiness, adaptability, reliable growth, good foliage and pleasing overall appearance. In any but parched or starved conditions they can be left for years to develop into solid clumps. They are happiest in cool shade. They vary in height from 8 in. to 4 ft. and can be used in a wide range of places from waterside to woodland conditions, for edging and for a mixed bed or

Left : Inula orientalis, one of the many daisy-flowered plants for the border, grows about 20 in. tall
Below : Many new day lilies (hemerocallis) have been bred in recent years and new colors have been introduced. This is 'Pink Damask'
Right : A bed of Russell lupins. These plants will grow best in a fairly sunny position

border. *H. crispula*, 3 ft., has handsome leaves edged with creamy-buff and lavender-mauve flowers from June to August. *H. fortunei* and its varieties flower earlier. The species has large pointed blue-green leaves and 2 ft. stems of pale lavender flowers. *H. f. picta* comes through in spring with bright and very attractive variegations which last until flowering at midsummer, before turning green. 'Honeybells' is a green-leaved variety, with 2½ ft. spikes of sweetly scented lavender trumpets. *H. lancifolia* has 20 in. lavender spikes in late summer. *H. rectifolia*, 4 ft., is a splendid free-flowering plant with lavender-mauve spikes. *H. undulata medio variegata* has brightly variegated leaves all summer and 12 to 18 in. spikes of deep mauve flowers. *H. ventricosa*, 3 ft., is easy and reliable. It bears its deep lavender trumpets freely in July and August and has bluish leaves; in its variety *variegata*, they are deep green and have streaks of yellow which make it one of the most attractive kinds. Hostas are best divided in early spring.

Incarvillea Once the deep fangy roots begin to sprout in early May, growth is rapid and startling. In two or three weeks, the exotic looking deep reddish pink trumpet flowers begin to open. The deeply-cut dark green leaves follow. In *I. delavayi* the stems reach 2 ft. or more before the last flowers fade in early June. *I. grandiflora* begins flowering almost at ground level and seldom exceeds 1 ft. Old plants can be carefully divided, or plants may be from seed. They need well-drained soil and sun. In colder areas some winter protection in the form of salt hay or dry leaves must be given.

Inula This is another genus with yellow daisy flowers. *I. barbata* spreads fairly quickly, and bears 1½ in. wide flowers many weeks from June onwards; *I. hookeri* is similar, but about twice as tall, at 2 to 2½ ft., with large flowers. 'Golden Beauty', 2 ft., is a neat plant flowering from June to September. *I. ensifolia compacta*, a most useful little plant for frontal positions, is long-lived and trouble-free. Though *I. orientalis* grows only to 20 in. or so, the flowers are 3–4 in. across and finely rayed. All are easily increased by division.

Iris The most popular irises, the *germanicas*, June-flowering flag irises, are available in a wide range of colors. There are others that help to spread the flowering season. *I. pumila*, under 1 ft., is at its best in April and May, in shades of yellow, blue and white. *I. foetidissima*, the wild Gladwyn iris, will grow in quite deep shade. One seldom notices it flower, but cannot fail to notice the vermilion seeds revealed in the fall as the pods open. For areas where the winters are less severe, there is an excellent variegated form as there is of the old *I. pallida*–sweet Iris. *I. sibirica* is a moisture lover, and where suited will flower for four or five weeks. The growth is erect and rushy, with stems rising to 2½ to 3½ ft. in shades of blue and purple as well as white.

Kniphofia (poker plant) All kniphofias like a sunny open position, and the range is now so wide that the five months from June to October can be covered, while heights range from 1½–6 ft. when in flower. The early variety 'Atlanta' makes massive broad-leaved plants with heavy red and yellow 3 ft. spikes. 'Bee's Sunset', deep orange, 'Gold-

else', 'Springtime', red and yellow, and *K. tubergenii*, light yellow, are all about 3 ft. and flower in June and August along with the salmon flushed ivory 'Jenny Bloom', and the white 'Maid of Orleans'; 'Bressingham Torch' and 'Bressingham Flame', also flower at this time. For late flowering–August to October, there are some of majestic stature, such as the brilliant flame 'Samuel's Sensation'. Division is best deferred until spring, although September is safe for early flowering varieties. Kniphofias need protection where winters are severe.

Liatris (blazing star) With erect or curving poker-like 3 ft. spikes of bright lilac purple flowers, these are showy, distinctive perennials. An unusual feature is that the fluffy flowers begin to open at the top of the stems, in contrast to nearly all spiky plants. The species *L. callilepis* is most often listed; *L. spicata* and *L. pycnostachya* are similar. Old plants are best dug up in the spring and rejuvenated by division and replanting in enriched soil.

Ligularia These thrive best in good deep soil and should not be planted in dry, windy positions. *L. clivorum* and its varieties have very large leaves and upright stems, 3–4 ft. high, carrying dozens of deep yellow, daisy-like flowers from early July to late August. 'Gregynog Gold' grows 3½ ft. tall; 'Desdemona' has purplish leaves and deep yellow flowers 2–3 in. across. These are all good waterside plants, spectacular when at their best, but they droop quickly in hot windy days. *L. przewalskii* is one of the easiest; its deeply jagged leaves do not spread widely and the 4–5 ft. spikes are slender but erect.

The black stems contrast well with the somewhat ragged yellow flowers which open close to the upper half of the spike. 'The Rocket' is even more attractive with brighter flowers. All will divide in fall or spring.

Limonium (*formerly Statice*) (sea lavender) The most reliable is *L. latifolia* which makes a large plant with a fair spread of shining green leaves and widely branching 2–3 ft. sprays of tiny blue flowers from July to September. For drying stems should be cut before the flowers begin to fade. The varieties 'Blue Cloud' and the deeper blue 'Violetta', have to be increased by root cuttings in spring. Plants do best in well-drained soil and open position.

Linum (flax) The blue *L. perenne*, 1½ ft., seldom lives beyond two summers. *L. narbonense*, 20 in., is much longer lived in well-drained soil and where it is happy it is one of the finest of dwarf border plants. The flowers are richly blue, 1 in. across. *L. dolomiticum*, 18 in., a compact plant, has wide clusters of bright yellow rounded flowers ¾ in. across, from mid June to late August. *L. campanulatum* (suitable for areas where winters are less severe) and *L. flavum* are similar.

Lupinus (lupin) With new varieties coming on to the market each year, the choice must rest with the purchaser, as far as named varieties are concerned. Many people prefer to have the cheaper seedling plants, even if they turn out to be a mixture of colors. Lupins grow better in neutral or acid soil rather than alkaline soil. These plants prefer cool summers and mild winters.

Lychnis (catchfly) *L. chalcedonica*, 2–3 ft., is a good perennial, with a head of small but intense red flowers from June to August. *L. coronaria* has silver-gray leaves and loose sprays of pink or carmine flowers for a long period. It grows best in a dry place. *L. viscaria*, 10 in., in the double form *plena*, has very bright pink flowers in June and July.

Lysimachia (loosestrife) These are mainly moisture-loving plants, robust enough to grow in drier soils. *L. clethroides* has white flowers and is very attractive with curved spikes in late summer. The yellow loosestrife, *L. punctata*, is very showy, with 3 ft. spikes of bright yellow flowers from June to August. Plants expand quickly and have to be curbed, but when small pieces are replanted, flowering is more prolonged.

Lythrum (loosestrife) These prefer moist soil. They flower freely from June to September. *L. salicaria* is taller and more robust than *L. virgatum*, and only named improvements of these wild types need be considered. 'Firecandle', 3 ft., has intense rosy red spikes, and 'Robert', 2½ ft., is a compact plant with clear pink flowers. *L. virgatum* 'Rose Queen', 2 ft., is light pink, 'The Rocket', 2½ ft., and has deeper, brighter flowers. All have a very tough woody root, but old plants will pull apart, and can be planted in fall or spring.

Macleaya (plume poppy) These easily grown plants make strong spikes up to 6 ft.,

Physalis franchetii (Chinese Lantern)

with powdered stems and pretty leaves, brownish beneath and bluish above, and large sprays of tiny flowers in late summer. In *M. cordata* the flowers are buff and it is an effective plant, by itself or against a dark background. *M. macrocarpa* has a wider branching flower spike, and the flowers are a brownish yellow; 'Coral Plume' is a slightly more colorful variation. The somewhat fleshy roots of macleayas tend to wander and shoot up among neighboring plants. They will grow in quite dry soils and do not object to shade.

Meconopsis (Himalayan blue poppy) Few plants have achieved such an aura as *M. betonicifolia* (*M. baileyi*) with its 3 ft. spikes of 2 in. wide sky-blue flowers. It is easily grown from seed. *M. chelidonifolia*, 2½ ft., is easy and fully perennial; it has 2 in. wide yellow flowers from June to August. All meconopsis prefer light leafy soil and some shade. These plants will not put up with hot dry summers but can be raised successfully in certain areas of the Pacific Northwest.

Monarda (bergamot) These are showy plants for the late June to September period. The flowers are of curious shape, having upward pointing petals, and come at the tips of the leafy stems which do not branch to any extent. These stems are however very profuse, and vary in height from 2½–4 ft. according to soil and situation. They revel in deep moist soil, and form quite wide mats of surface growth where happy. Such spread may need curbing and it is often necessary to dig over the centre part of a group and fill back with vigorous pieces which have spread away, as an alternative to a complete replant in early spring. Bright colors are available in such named varieties as 'Cambridge Scarlet' and 'Adam', and the salmon red 'Prairie Glow'. 'Croftway Pink' and 'Melissa' are both good pinks and for purple there is 'Prairie Night'. The leaves have a distinctive and not unpleasant odor.

Nepeta (catmint) *N. faassenii* (syn. *N. mussinii*), gives a long succession of lavender-blue flowers on 1 ft. spikes, from gray-leaved plants, from June to September. Though adaptable to sun and partial shade, winter losses occur where drainage is poor. Division is best done in the spring. 'Six Hill's Giant' has sprays up to 2 ft tall. 'Blue Beauty' has erect, 20 in. spikes of larger violet-blue flowers.

Oenothera There are several full perennial kinds that make a bright display with their big yellow cup-shaped flowers. *O. cinaeus* has bright leaves–buff, pink, purple-red in spring, fading to deep green as the loose sprays of rich yellow cups open. *O.* 'Fire-

works', 1½ ft., is a deep yellow, with purplish-green leaves, as is 'Yellow River', 2 ft., with green foliage, and these and the 2 ft. tall 'Highlight', can easily be divided in early spring. The most distinctive is the virtually prostrate *O. missouriensis*, which from July to October bears 4 in. light canary yellow flowers. This needs sun and good drainage and can only be increased by seed.

Paeonia (peony) Among the longest lived of all perennials, paeonias should be planted with permanence in mind, space in which to expand in an open situation. They like a rich, deep soil and respond to mulching. Old plants can be divided, between August and October, carefully using a knife to separate the most vigorous chunks. Planting depth is important; the new buds should rest 1 in. below the surface. Varieties of the popular June-flowering Chinese peony (*P. lactiflora*) up to 3 ft. tall, have huge flowers in shades of pink, red, and white, single, semi-double and double. Some are more fragrant than others. Consult a reliable catalog for details of the numerous varieties. *P. officinalis* is a plant popular for many years, 2 ft. tall. with very fragrant flowers, usually double, in red, crimson, pink and white.

Papaver For size of flower, *P. orientalis*, the Oriental poppy, can easily compete with paeonias. For brilliance of color, they can excel them, but they are not so permanent. All flower from late May until late June. The most erect is the blood-red 'Goliath', 3–3½ ft., though the orange scarlet 'Marcus Perry' is nearly as erect. Other varieties include brownish-red, various shades of pink, also white. All like a very well-drained soil, not too rich. Their fleshy roots are brittle and any pieces left when old plants are dug out will sprout again. Propagation is by 3 in. long root cuttings in spring.

Penstemon The showiest kinds are the least reliable as hardy perennials. Some are used as bedding plants by taking cuttings in late summer or fall and keeping them under glass till planting out time in spring, when they quickly make bushy plants to flower from July to October. The trumpet-shaped flowers are borne on spikes up to 2½ ft. tall. In milder localities the deep crimson

Below: 'Gibson's Scarlet' is one of the best herbaceous potentillas
Right: A splendid display of rudbeckias

'Garnet' and the blood-red 'Firebird' (*P. schonholzeri*) will usually survive for several years, as will 'Pink Endurance'.

Phlox Among the brightest of border plants, phlox are happiest in light rather than heavy or alkaline soil. They should be divided every three years, or propagated by root cuttings to avoid attacks by nemotodes. The newest introductions do not necessarily supersede older varieties, and recommendations include older kinds which have stood the test of time. The best dwarf white is still 'Mia Ruya'; 'White Admiral' at 3 ft. is taller. 'Mother of Pearl', 3 ft., is a vigorous, weatherproof pink suffused white; 'Mies Copijn' is soft pink and 'Dodo Hanbury Forbes' is somewhat deeper, with 'Windsor' a carmine-rose shade. 'Endurance', salmon-rose, 'Brigadier', orange-salmon; 'Spitfire' and the intensely bright 'Prince of Orange' should not be missed. The most reliable deep red is 'Starfire', with 'Tenor' an early flowering blood red; 'Aida', 'San Antonio' and 'Vintage Wine' are in the magenta range, with 'The King', 'Parma Violet' and 'Marlborough' for violet purples. Lavender-blue shades include 'Skylight' and 'Hampton Court', while 'Balmoral' has a tinge of lilac.

Physalis (Chinese lantern) Though the showy orange seed bags of *P. alkekengii*, 1–2 ft., are excellent for floral decoration, as plants they are scarcely suitable among other perennials. The roots wander and the flowers are insignificant. Propagation by division is easy.

Physostegia (obedient plant) These are good reliable perennials for any soil, with tapering spikes, flowering from July to September. *P. speciosa*, 'Rose Bouquet', 2 ft., has a profusion of light rosy-lilac flowers; dwarfer 'Vivid', deep pink, flowers later, but the roots wander so widely that it pays to dig them up every spring and replant them where they belong. *P. virginica* 'Summer Snow' and the deeper rose-pink 'Summer Spire', are both about 3 ft. Physostegias have a vigorous rootstock of spreading, whitish crowns, which tend to fall apart when dug up, and in moist or rich soil need curbing after two or three years.

Platycodon (balloon flower) When the buds of *P. grandiflorum* expand, the petals are joined together to form a hollow globe of about walnut size, changing into a saucer-shaped, campanula-type flower. Platycodons have real merit; they are long lived, have fleshy roots, and need only well-drained soil. Heights vary from the 1 ft. tall variety *mariesii* in shades of light blue, to the 2 ft. of the tallest kinds of *P. grandiflorum* in white, blue and very pale pink. Seed-raised plants are variable in color, but old plants will divide.

Polemonium (Jacob's ladder) Some of these are short lived and seed about to become a nuisance. More reliable and seldom setting seed is *P. foliosissimum*, 2½–3 ft., a good perennial with a much longer flowering period, from June till September, with heads of open petalled lavender-blue flowers. Pole-

moniums are not fussy plants, and when old can be divided to rejuvenate them, especially the dwarfer kinds, such as the light blue 'Sapphire', 15 in., flowering in May and June and 'Blue Pearl', 10 in., which also flowers for several weeks in May and June. **Polygonatum** (Solomon's seal) *P. multiflorum* and its forms, with arching sprays of green and white flowers, are best naturalized; they need cool soil for their tuberous

roots to run and flower freely in June. They can be divided in fall or spring.

Polygonum (knot-weed) Most polygonums have poker-shaped spikes of tiny closely-set flowers. In the robust *P. amplexicaule*, the 4–5 ft. spikes top a rounded dense bush of pointed leaves, at least 3 ft. in diameter. The dull red variety *atrosanguineum* and the lighter, brighter red 'Firetail' can be recommended for reliability and for

a three-month flowering season where winters are less severe. The 3 ft. stems of *P. bistorta superbum* carry 4 in. long pokers of a clear light pink in May and June. *P. carneum* has smaller but deeper pink spikes in June and July and sometimes well into August.

Potentilla (cinquefoil) For rich colorings, long flowering and reliability many of the potentillas rank highly. They are mostly dwarf plants, easily grown in ordinary soil

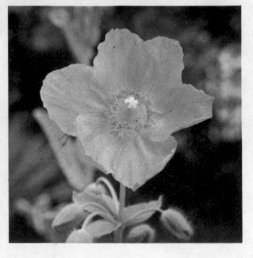

Facing page: Pyrethrums add much color to the border for some weeks from late May, and may flower again in the fall if they are cut back hard after they have first flowered
Above: The large blooms of *Paeonia lactiflora* 'Globe of Light'
Right: The numerous varieties of herbaceous phlox provide brilliant color for many weeks in summer and early fall
Far Right: Meconopsis betonicifolia, the Himalayan blue poppy, is renowned for its sky-blue flowers

and open positions, and all have green, gray or silvery strawberry-like foliage. *P. atrosanguinea* has silvery leaves, vigorous growth and sprays of bright red flowers, $\frac{3}{4}$ in. across. 'Flamenço', 2 ft., is similar, but with larger flowers and green leaves. Both flower from May to July, but from June to September the more prostrate but equally brilliant 'Gibson's Scarlet', 18 in., takes over. 'Firedance', orange salmon, 'Miss Willmott', pink and the good semi-double flowered 'Glory of Nancy', orange or red. 'William Rollison', flame orange and 'Yellow Queen', all grow about 18 in. Potentillas can be divided in fall or spring.

Pulmonaria (lungwort) These adaptable spring-flowering plants can be used effectively in places one can more or less forget when summer comes. *P. angustifolia aurea*, 9 in., has brilliant blue bell-shaped flowers from March to May; 'Munstead Blue' is a little dwarfer and flowers later. *P. saccharata* is much coarser, and this and the red-flowered 'Bowles's Red', take up space with their large rough leaves. Of those with prettily white-spotted leaves, which are effective even when flowering is over 'Pink Dawn', 1 ft., is worth while, its flowers pink at first, fading to blue, to give at times a two-color effect. All are easily propagated by division.

Pulsatilla (pasque flower) *P. vulgaris*, 9–10 in., is a deeply rooting plant, with gray-green ferny leaves, which in early spring sends up goblet-shaped flowers, surrounded by silvery gossamer calyces. Colors range from pale lavender to purple, and include white and ruby red, all with prominent golden stamens. The flowers are followed by prettily tufted seed heads. Seed, the only method of increase, must be sown when freshly gathered.

Pyrethrum The brightly colored daisy-type flowers of pyrethrums are decorative from late May until July, but unless they have ample light and air space, they need supporting, even though they are mostly under 3 ft. high. Well-drained soil and sun are essential, and they prefer alkaline soils. It is best to plant in spring and, other than in March and early April, old plants can be lifted and divided in late summer and early fall. Named varieties include single and double flowered white, various shades of pink, as well as rich salmon and crimson. Cut plants back hard after flowering.

Rudbeckia (cone flower) All the true perennial species are yellow, but their variations in form make all but the tallest of value. Tall kinds, varieties of *R. laciniata* include the well-known 5–6 ft. 'Autumn Sun'. 'Goldquelle', however, grows without support to a shapely 3–4 ft., bearing fully double chrome-yellow flowers 3 in. across from July to October. *R. deamii*, $2\frac{1}{2}$ ft., makes a wonderful show from August to October with its black-eyed, deep-yellow, black-centered flowers. The amazingly free 'Goldsturm', often begins in June or July and continues into the fall. No rudbeckias like to be in parched conditions and in good, reasonably moist

soil will flower for much longer.

Salvia (sage) The best hardy salvias flower from June to August. *S. × superba* makes erect stems, $3\frac{1}{2}$–4 ft. tall, topped with slender spikes of tiny lipped flowers which attract bees and butterflies. 'May Night', about 20 in., 'East Friesland', 1–$1\frac{1}{2}$ ft., both rather more compact and later, and 'Lubeca', $2\frac{1}{2}$ ft., are all good varieties, long-lived, hardy and easy in any well-drained soil, easily increased by division or by basal cuttings in spring. *S. haematodes* is best grown from seed. In some gardens it will survive for years, while in others it may live for three or four years only. It is a showy plant, 3 ft. tall., with open branching spikes of light lavender blue in June and July.

Scabiosa (scabious) *S. caucasica* is a firm favorite, splendid for cutting. Does not like cold winters and hot summers, preferring the cool climate of the Pacific Northwest. The flowers are in shades of blue and violet and there are also good white varieties, all about $2\frac{1}{2}$ ft. tall, flowering from June to September. Scabious dislike wet, especially in winter and survive longest in well-drained alkaline soils. The open saucer-shaped flowers on wiry stems need to be cut or dead headed to encourage long flowering. They are best planted or divided in spring, but can also be raised from seed. *S. graminifolia*, 10 in. makes a compact mound of silvery, grassy leaves and gives a long succession of rounded pincushion heads of light lavender blue, from June to September; the variety 'Pincushion' has soft pink flower heads 1 in. across.

Sedum (butterfly or ice plant) The taller herbaceous sedums include such well-established favorites as *S. spectabilis*, 1–$1\frac{1}{2}$ ft. tall, with wide heads densely packed with glistening pink flowers in late summer. The varieties 'Brilliant', 'Carmen' and 'Meteor' do not differ greatly from one another. 'Autumn Joy', 2 ft., is a sturdy plant with heads up to 12–15 in. across, opening light pink in September, changing slowly to salmon-rose. *S. heterodontum*, 9–12 in., is another easy, somewhat fleshy-rooted, compact plant with fuzzy heads of a burnt orange color and bluish foliage. The yellow-flowered *S. rhodiola*, the rose root sedum, is of a similar dwarf bushy habit. Plants are easily divided.

Sidalcea These graceful, spike-forming plants have mallow-like flowers in shades of pink to rosy-red between June and September. They are easy to grow in full sun with good drainage, and can be divided in spring. 'Mrs Alderson', 'Wm. Smith' and 'Rev. Page Roberts', to 4 ft., and 'Puck', $2\frac{1}{2}$ ft., have light pink flowers. Deeper shades are 'Rose Queen', 'Wensleydale' and 'Croftway Red', all 3–4 ft. After flowering the spikes should be cut back to promote new basal growth.

Solidago (golden rod) Many solidagos are far too tall and invasive and any that grow over 4 ft. tall should be omitted. 'Mimosa' will reach 4 ft., but the compact plants do not seed about after the handsome yellow plumes have finished in September.

Those growing less than 4 ft. are worth having; the color range varies from the deep yellow of 'Golden Mosa', 'Golden Shower' or 'Golden Falls' to the lighter shades of 'Lemore' and 'Leslie'. All grow to 2½–3 ft. and flower between July and September. 'Peter Pan', 3 ft., is earlier and has horizontal branches to the crested plume; 'Crown of Rays', 2 ft., is very bushy in habit, while 'Cloth of Gold', 18 in., has a vigorous outward spread. The neatest growing dwarfs are the miniatures, 'Queenie' and 'Golden Thumb', which form bright, almost golden-leaved bushes 9–12 in. high, flowering from August to October. These better solidagos are best planted or divided in spring.

Stachys *S. lanata*, with its felted silvery leaves, is an easily grown mat-forming plant, bearing thin spikes of small pink flowers in June and July. It is a good ground cover plant in quite dry positions; there is a non-flowering variety 'Silver Carpet'. *S. macrantha*, 2½ ft., is a charming plant with short spikes of rosy, purple-lipped flowers in June and July. *S. spicata rosea* has 1 ft. deep pink spikes, and in the ·variety *densiflorum* the flowers are closely packed on 15 in. stems. This is a showy plant, as is the sturdier 20 in. variety *robusta*. All these stachys are easily divided in spring or fall.

Thalictrum (meadow rue) Without exception thalictrums do best in rich soils and dislike drought. They all have pretty, tiny leaves. *T. minus* (syn. *T. adiantifolium*) is the easiest, but its 2½ ft. sprays of buff-green flowers are by no means showy. *T. angustifolium* has the fuzzy yellow flower heads on strong 6 ft. stems from June to August, as does *T. glaucum*, 5 ft., with light yellow fluffy heads and blue-gray leaves. The earliest to flower is *T. aquilegifolium*, 3–4 ft., with bluish-gray foliage on strong branched stems which carry fluffy flower heads in shades of mauve and purple in early June; there is a desirable pure white variety. *T. dipterocarpum* makes a much smaller rootstock but makes a vast amount of top growth. This consists of small-leaved, much-branched 6 ft. stems which need support. It bears mauve-blue flowers from early July to September. 'Hewitt's Double' is less vigorous and not so tall and needs rich moist soil to give of its best. Most species may be divided in spring.

Tradescantia (Spiderwort) *T. virginiana* has rushy leaves and stems up to 2 ft. carrying clustered heads of 3-petalled flowers up to 1 in. across in bright colors from June to August. Named varieties are available in white, light blue, mid and deep-blue as well as purple and magenta, and smaller flowered doubles exist as well. By August they may be looking tatty, and are best cut back. They grow in an ordinary soil in sunny or partially shady situations.

Trollius (globe flower) Though not for hot dry positions, these can add much to the garden scene in early summer. The vital period when plants need moisture is after flowering and for the rest of the summer. Mulching with peatmoss helps greatly and cuts down the need for watering. The 'globe' effect appears just before the buds open. *T. europaeus superbus*, 2 ft., is a reliable light yellow; 'Canary Bird' is paler and larger flowered. 'Goldquelle' has large mid-yellow flowers, while 'Orange Princess' and 'Fireglobe' are deeper yellow shades. The 3 ft. *T. ledebouri* is distinctive. The petals open to reveal an upstanding crest of stamens of egg yolk color. It flowers in June and July.

Verbascum (mullein) Although some of the brightest of these are not fully perennial or long-lived, a collection of perennials needs such spike-forming plants to break up uniformity. The most reliable have the stoutest rootstocks, thick and fleshy or tap rooted. *V. chairii* (syn. *V. vernale*) is a good yellow. It has strong spikes 4–5 ft., which flower from June onwards. *V. thapsiforme* (syn. *V. densiflorum*), 4 ft., has similar yellow flowers. 'Gainsborough', 3 ft., is a lighter yellow with wooly gray foliage, but dislikes winter wet. The bushy 2 ft. 'Golden Bush' is distinctive, reliable and long flowering. 'Pink Domino', 3 ft., has deep rose flowers. Verbascums do not need rich soil and do best in sandy or stony soil with perfect drainage to enable them to survive the winter. Increase named varieties from root cuttings in early spring.

Veronica (speedwell) This genus provides several good, easily grown plants. The varieties of *V. teucrium* are all blue and make a bright display in June and July. They include 'Shirley Blue', 1 ft., 'Crater Lake Blue', 15 in., 'Royal Blue', 18 in., 'Blue Fountain', 2 ft., all of mounded or bushy growth topped with short spikes. *V. gentianoides*, 2 ft., light blue, is at its best in May. Spikes come from mat-forming plants. *V. spicata*, 2 ft., bright blue, is also mat-forming, flowering in June and July. *V. spicata incana*, 15 in., has silver-gray leaves and violet-purple spikes. In the free-flowering 'Sarabande', the leaves are less silvery, as in the taller and less tidy 'Wendy'. Pretty pink-flowered 18 in. varieties are 'Barcarolle' and 'Minuet'. *V. exaltata*, 4 ft., light blue, is late flowering and sometimes needs support. This does not apply to the 4 ft. pale blue *V. virginica*, but both this and its pale pink variety *rosea* are soon over. By far the most attractive is the 5 ft. white-flowered *alba* which flowers in August and September.

Above: Sedum spectabile, the butterfly or rice plants. They grow 1–1½ feet tall, with wide heads densely packed with glistening pink flowers in late summer. Always attract butterflies
Right: The scabious, *Scabiosa caucasica*, available in various shades, mainly in the blue-violet range, provides excellent cut flowers. To encourage long flowering, the wiry-stemmed flowers need to be cut or dead headed. May be planted or sown in spring

Favorite Garden Flowers

Chrysanthemums

Originating in the cooler northern regions of the Far East, the chrysanthemum responded quickly to the efforts of hybridists when the first plants were introduced to Europe in the 18th century. Their attraction lies in four main characteristics; flowers may be obtained in various forms and sizes, in virtually every color other than blue; plants grow successfully over a wide area of the country, and are highly adaptable to soil, climate and treatment; by choosing suitable varieties, flowering can begin in the open garden in August and September, followed by the late-flowering types under glass from October to February. Perhaps the greatest attraction is the way the plant invites the grower's co-operation and intervention throughout the whole growing season.

Obtaining Plants The new grower should obtain his stock from a specialist nursery. In subsequent seasons it is possible to raise new stock from the stools of the previous year. A stool is what is left when the flowers have been cut and the main stem is shortened to about 12 in.

Propagation Though in many areas the chrysanthemum is hardy, it is better to take up the stools, wash them free of soil and then box them up in fresh compost. Keep the soil fairly dry throughout the winter and house the stools in a cool greenhouse or protected cold frame. In early spring the stool will send up young shoots and once growth has begun, give sufficient water to keep the soil moist. Growth can be hastened by applying gentle bottom heat but temperatures should not rise far above 50°F (10°C). Propagation may now proceed by either of two methods. If the shoots have roots already developed they may be taken off and boxed up to make new plants. For various reasons, better plants are obtained by taking cuttings.

Clean, healthy young shoots some 2-in. long should be cut or broken off and inserted 1 in. deep in a flat or bed of standard compost. A thorough watering is then given and the container placed in a simple frame covered with light cloth to shade the shoots from bright sunlight and to keep the air around them humid. This simple propagator may be placed either on the greenhouse bench or inside a cold frame. Since the optimum temperature for rooting is around 55°F (13°C) some slight warmth, particularly in the form of bottom heat, will help matters greatly. If rooting hormones are used, well-rooted plants should be produced in a month.

Most early-flowering varieties root easily in March and April but those which bloom during the later months in the greenhouse require an earlier start in January and February.

Growing On The young plants must be gradually prepared to face the outside conditions. Earlies are grown either in flats or in a bed of soil on the floor of the cold frame. Whichever method is used, they should be given plenty of room to develop and nothing less than 4-in. spacing will do. Since late-flowering plants are usually flowered in pots it is as well to start them in 3-in. pots, either clay or plastic, using a general compost, or a soilless compost. As the pots fill with roots it will be necessary to move the plants to 5- or 6-in. pots. A final potting will be needed later on into 8- or 9-in. pots using a compost consisting of 3 parts loam, 1 part peatmoss, 1 part sand, 1 part rotted cow manure plus 1 pint bone meal and 1 pint hydrated lime per bushel of mix and a small amount of charcoal. Make the compost little more than finger-firm so as to encourage rapid root extension. Late varieties can also be grown in the open garden and the plants lifted and replanted in the greenhouse in late September for flowering; the plants should be treated exactly as advised for the early-flowering varieties.

While plants are in the frame, guard against over watering, frost and drafts. Gradually increase ventilation so that plants are hardened off by late April.

Soil Preparation Ideally the soil should be well drained yet retentive of moisture; fertile without being over-rich and open to all the light and air available. A liberal dressing of manure or other humus-forming material should be dug in during the fall and the surface left rough. About mid-April a dressing of 4 oz. per square yard of a balanced fertilizer should be forked in to a depth of a few inches only, leaving the main body of the soil undisturbed. Raking to produce a good tilth is best left until a day or two before planting in May, the actual date depending on weather conditions.

A yellow late-flowering variety

Planting The canes should first be inserted and the plants placed close to them, each one secured by a loose tie and protected from slug damage by the application of bait.

Late-flowering plants in pots are moved out to their summer quarters at the same time. Insert a cane in each pot and set out the pots in lines, securing the canes to a wire stretched about 4 ft. above the ground. Leave at least 1 ft. between the pots and 2 ft. between rows to allow free access. Plants may also spend the summer in the greenhouse.

Bud development To obtain the best results it is helpful to understand the way in which a chrysanthemum plant develops. It begins with a single stem which extends until a flower bud appears in the growing point. This normally happens so early in the season that the bud fails to develop into a flower but forces the plant to break into lateral growth thus forming a bushy habit. This bud is known as the *break bud*. In their turn, the laterals extend and in due time form buds. According to the time of year, either a cluster of buds or one bud surrounded by leafy shoots will be produced. Such buds are known as *first crown buds*. Where leafy shoots are produced around this bud, they will grow on strongly and produce further buds known as *second crown buds* and if the grower does not intervene the result is a large first crown flower struggling into bloom at the base of a cluster of much smaller flowers, a rather unattractive effect.

It is best to ignore the break bud since it is usual to remove the growing point of the young plant before that bud appears and the resultant branching is just the same. Early-flowering types are usually flowered on first crowns so merely pinch out the growing point when the plant is well established in the garden (about June 1st). When lateral growths are a few inches long remove the strongest and weakest, aiming to leave four to six of equal strength. When the first crown buds appear remove the growths surrounding the central bud on each shoot and allow them to flower. Some late-flowering types give better blooms on second crowns and the procedure is as follows. Two dates are given in the catalog of varieties, which indicate (a) when the plant is to be pinched first, and (b) when the laterals arising from that first pinch are to be stopped again by the removal of the growing points. The result will be a further crop of side-shoots which are allowed to produce their buds to be dealt with as before by the removal of all buds except the central one. Two pinches will give far more stems than one but resist the temptation to flower them all. To obtain flowers of good size and quality the limit should be set at six to eight.

Sprays and pompon types are exceptions. These branch naturally and all you need to do is to encourage the development of laterals by one pinch only, when the plants are 9–12 in. high. Since the beauty of these plants is in the large number of small starry blooms carried in sprays, no disbudding need to be done. Nevertheless it may be wise to restrict the number of stems to ensure larger flowers.

Feeding By late May all plants will be growing away nicely in pots or the open garden and within some seven weeks the earlies will have to develop into mature bushes of up to eight stems each bearing its flower bud. Well-prepared, fertile ground will give fair results without further help but it is usually beneficial to give some added feed, firstly at the beginning of June to encourage quick establishment; secondly at the end of June to ensure that the plants are in vigorous health at the time the flower buds are being formed. Each time an application of a chrysanthemum fertilizer in powder or liquid form, is all that is required.

Where late flowering plants are grown in pots, feeding is more important. Liquid feeds are by far the best. It doesn't really matter what the label says so long as the relationship between the nitrogen and potash content is correct for the particular purpose. During the rapid development of leaf and stem there should be roughly twice as much nitrogen as potash. As the buds appear and are being dealt with, give only clear water but start feeding again when the buds have begun to swell, but now the nitrogen and potash contents must be roughly the same. Do not give heavy doses every ten days or so but give about a quarter the recommended strength every time you water.

Watering Correct use of the watering can is crucial to good growing but it is something which has to be learned rather than taught. With pots the safest rule is to apply water just before the plant threatens to wilt. Both the leaves and the soil surface will give clear indication when that point has been reached and enough water should be applied to moisten thoroughly the whole soil ball.

After care Throughout the period of rapid growth it is necessary to control the plants. Remove surplus branches and shoots as soon as they are seen; tie flowering stems loosely to the cane every 9 in. or so. Never tie too tightly but, to avoid breakages, allow branches to sway a little in the breeze. Watch out for and deal with early pest infestations; the best insurance against pest damage is to keep the garden free of weeds.

Housing plants Late-flowering types are flowered under glass. In late September, when the buds are beginning to show the first signs of color, it is time to house the plants that have been outside for the summer. Remove all old leaves to about one third

of the height from the pot, remove all surplus growths; tie up the plants securely and place extra canes if necessary. Spray with an insecticide and with a systemic fungicide to combat mildews.

The greenhouse must be thoroughly cleaned. Remove all debris and any growing plants before burning a sulfur candle. When the fumes have dispersed, wash the glass and every crevice with a jet of water from the hose. Test the heating apparatus and seal every leak in the roof.

Ideally there should be plenty of space around the plants inside but in practice one tends to pack them in rather tightly. In fact, it is far better to leave a few poor prospects outside so as to give the better plants more light and air. For the first ten days or so, leave doors and ventilators fully open. Watering will rarely be required for several days but it is good practice to give a little water say every two days rather than to wait until a pot is bone dry. In this latter condition the water will run all over the floor and cause damp air –the worst enemy of flowers indoors. After this the ventilators should be used in conjunction with the heating apparatus to main a dry moving atmosphere at a night temperature of around 50°F (10°C). Light shading may be helpful in bright weather.

Flowering Time This is not only the season of satisfaction and enjoyment, it also provides opportunity for planning future efforts. Look critically at the plants and their flowers with a view to choosing those which have exhibited both vigor and excellence. These should be clearly marked so that they can be retained for the propagation of new stock. In this way the collection can be kept at a high level of health. There is much to be gained by visiting the local shows so as to see what is new and to chat with fellow enthusiasts.

Cutting Blooms Chrysanthemum blooms will last longer if they are cut in the morning when the stems are full of sap. Place each stem in water immediately. Back at the house, bruise the lowest few inches of stem and remove all the leaves except the three or four beneath the bloom. Now set the stems in a deep container of water and place it in a dark, cool place such as a garage or outhouse, for about 24 hours. After this treatment the flowers will last for several weeks, particularly if any stems which are further shortened are again bruised at the base.

Outdoor plants need not be cut right down at flowering time; in a mild fall, it is not unusual to have a second crop of delightful sprays. Blooms may be small but the enriched color and profusion of the flowers will more than compensate for lack of size.

Neither early nor late-flowering types should be cut right down after flowering. It is better to allow the sap to run back for a few weeks before shortening the main stem to about 12–18 in. In this state the stools can be boxed as described earlier. A final shortening to a few inches can be carried out in the spring.

Types of chrysanthemum flower

Reflexed

Reflexed Decorative

Pompon

Incurved

Single

Thread-petalled

Incurving

Right: Well-grown, early-flowering chrysanthemums

Recommended varieties

The selection of chrysanthemum varieties is extremely wide and numerous novelties are introduced each year. The following recommendations are made on the evidence available at the time of writing. There are many other lovely cultivars but those listed can be relied upon to give the least trouble and the greatest satisfaction.

1. Outdoor types which respond to disbudding to give blooms of fine quality for cutting or may be allowed to carry large crops for border work.
Amber Bright: amber bronze (tall), October, large decorative
Bronze Giant: bronze (medium), September, large blooms
Bronze Song: bright bronze (tall), September
Full Moon: white (tall), October, one of the best white varieties for garden culture
Golden Arrow: deep yellow (tall), October
Golden Peking: deep yellow (medium), October, very prolific
Golden Promise: yellow (tall), September, good for cutting
Indian Summer: scarlet bronze (tall), September, large blooms
Pink Chief: deep pink (tall), October, large incurve
Pumpkin: orange, bronze (medium), September, semi-incurve
Real Gold: golden yellow (medium), September, large decorative
Red Skin: crimson red (medium), October, large flowers
September Song: pink (medium), September, semi-incurve
Silver Song: ivory white (medium), September
Touchdown: pink (tall), September, semi-incurve
Yellow Giant: yellow (tall), September, early flowering
Yellow Moon: yellow (tall), October, large incurve

2. Outdoor types requiring no disbudding. They produce a profusion of flowers in sprays which are excellent for vases.
Accolade: coral pink (tall), October, intermediate decorative
Carnival: orange red (medium), October, intermediate pompom
Dark Calumet: bronze (tall), intermediate pompom
Echo: white (tall), October, small pompom produces masses of flowers
Horizon: white (tall), October, intermediate pompom
Spellbound: lavender-pink (medium), September, intermediate decorative
Topflight: deep yellow (tall), October, small anemone
Yellow Calumet: yellow (tall), October, good quality intermediate pompom

3. Low growing types suitable for the front of a border but not giving stems long enough for cutting.
Golden Cushion: yellow, October, small decorative, cushion form of growth
Ruby Mound: crimson red pompom, September, cushion habit very prolific
Stardom: lavender pink, September, cushion habit, produces large amount of bloom
Sunburst Cushion: golden yellow, September, cushion habit of growth

Above: Pompon chrysanthemum Pepe

4. Late flowering varieties suitable for greenhouse decoration and cutting. The first mentioned in each color group will flower in October and may bloom happily in a cold greenhouse. The other will need slight warmth in late October and November.
White
Colonel Comfort: October, large semi-incurve
Dignity: October, large semi-incurve
Fred Shoesmith: November, semi-incurve, large blooms
Improved Mefo: November, incurved, good quality flowers
Yellow
Yellow Dignity: October, large semi-incurving blooms
Improved Indianapolis: yellow, October–November, medium incurve
Sea Foam: November, medium sized blooms
Yellow Shoesmith: November, large semi-incurving flowers
Bronze
Gambit: October–November, orange bronze, medium semi-incurve
Balcombe Perfection: November, medium incurve

Detroit News: November, large incurve
Onward: November, large vigorous habit of growth
Red
Festival: October–November, scarlet red
Mrs Roy: November, large incurve
Woking: scarlet, November
Pink
Escapade: October, light pink, semi-incurve
Promenade: October–November, large semi-incurve
Peacock: November, intense pink, good quality blooms

5. Late flowering varieties bearing flowers like large daisies.
Christmas Star: red
Merrymaker: red
Poinsetta: red, a striking variety
Spungold: light yellow

6. Varieties for the Christmas season
Acclaim: white pompom
Christmas Greeting: bronze red, intermediate decorative
Coronation: golden yellow, large decorative
Wintertime: white, large decorative

Right: Chrysanthemum 'Brown Eyes', a pretty bronze variety

Begonias, Fuchsias, Gladiolus, Irises

❧ Begonias ❧

Large-flowered begonias are usually grown from tubers, but they can be grown from seed and they will flower about eight months after sowing if sufficient heat is available. There are many other kinds of begonias with fibrous roots, and some with rhizomes. Typical of this type are the *B. rex* cultivars with multi-colored leaves. These will grow well along the edge of a greenhouse path, partly shaded by the staging. The most popular fibrous rooted begonias are those grouped under *B. semperflorens*, with green, bronze or variegated foliage, and white, pink or red flowers. Most have single flowers, but there are a few fully double varieties, chiefly grown as pot plants, while the single-flowered kinds are used for summer bedding. There are many others, some with silver spots on the foliage, many of which make good house plants.

Growing from Seed Sow seed of tuberous double varieties and *B. semperflorens* in January or early February, in soilless compost or general seed compost. Sow in a clay half pot or pan, and when using a soilless compost it should not be firmed down. Before sowing water the compost. Sprinkle the seed on the surface of the compost and do not cover it with additional compost, or with paper to exclude light. Place the pan in a heated propagator, and maintain a temperature of 60°–70°F (15°–21°C). The seed should germinate in 8–14 days, and the seedlings should be pricked out as soon as possible, into a similar compost, about 1 in. apart. Return them to the propagator if possible and, after a further 4–6 weeks, the seedlings should be touching each other, and they will then need spacing 2 in. apart. Return to the propagator again for a few weeks, but if this is not practicable, keep them as warm as possible and if it is dull or cool they will need very little water. By mid-May the seedlings should be hardened off in a frame prior to planting out in early June. They like some peat or similar material in the soil, and they can be planted in shade or full sun.

Greenhouse Cultivation Seedlings to be grown in pots in the greenhouse should be potted up into 3-in. pots in early May, in 1 part general potting compost, mixed with 1 part of soilless compost. After a few weeks the plants will need potting on into 5-in. pots, and for these and all larger pots use 2 parts loam, 1 part peatmoss, ½ part decayed cow manure, ½ part sand, plus a 4-in. pot of bone meal to every bushel of mix. The *B. semperflorens* varieties will flower in 5-in. pots but the tuberous doubles will need potting on into 6½–7½-in. pots. Clay pots are preferable as there is less danger of over-watering; if you use plastic pots add an extra part of coarse sand to the potting mix. In a greenhouse plants will need some shading from bright sunshine.

Begonias need cool conditions to produce sturdy plants with good blooms, and once all danger of frost is over the ventilators should be left open day and night to allow maximum circulation of air.

Disbudding Wherever you grow tuberous double begonias, it is best to remove the first flower buds. This allows the plants to become established before the strain of flowering and will result in larger and better formed flowers. Three blooms usually develop on each flowering stem, and with pot-grown plants the two outer blooms should be pinched off, leaving the larger double male bloom to open. The two outer blooms are usually females, and are always singles. The female blooms have a light green, three-winged seed capsule immediately behind the petals, but this is missing from all male blooms.

Feeding When in bloom tuberous double begonias will need a weekly feed with a weak tomato-type fertilizer, high in potash. Stop feeding in early September. Plants will need less water as the cooler weather arrives, but it is vital that the compost should be kept moist and no attempt should be made to force the plants into dormancy by withholding water. As top growth ceases moisture is needed at the roots to help build up a good tuber to survive the winter dormancy.

Winter Treatment Any green leaves retained by the end of October can then be removed, but the stems must not be forcibly pulled off. Stop watering as soon as all green leaves have dropped, or been removed, and the stems should drop off within a few days. The tubers can then be taken from the pots and cleaned up, but be careful not to damage the 'eyes' (axillary buds) on the top of the tuber as next year's growth will start from these. Store the tubers in dry peat in a frost-proof place until the following spring when they can be restarted. Plants in the garden should be lifted in early October with a ball of soil round the roots, placed on the floor of the greenhouse until all stems have dropped, then stored in dry peat.

(For begonias as house plants see the part of this work dealing with Indoor Plants.)

Recommended Begonia Varieties

Tuberous doubles: 'Roy Hartley'; 'Diana Wynyard' and 'Avalanche', white; 'Crown Prince', crimson; 'Guardsman', red; 'Harlequin', white ground picotee; 'Midas', yellow. Of the hundreds of different varieties of *B. semperflorens* 'Muse Rose' and 'Color Queen', are well worth growing.

Fuchsias

Fuchsias are shrubs and in mild districts the hardiest kinds, such as *F. magellanica* and its variety *riccartonii*, are used for hedges. But most of the hybrid forms grown are not so hardy and are treated as disposable bedding plants or plants for a 'cool greenhouse, apart from the warmer parts of the country. They are readily trained as bushes, cascades, standards and other more elaborate shapes. Their interesting hanging flowers are varied in size, form and color and there is a multitude of varieties, varying in habit.

Propagation Soft wood cuttings root readily. Those of hardy kinds are taken in spring, as are also those of greenhouse ones needed for making standards or pyramids or small plants to flower later the same year, but the bulk of greenhouse ones are made in mid-summer for growing through the winter in a minimum temperature of $55°F$ ($13°C$) to flower from May onwards. Soft wood cuttings are made by removing the top few inches of soft growing shoots. Ideally such a shoot should not have flower buds, but as the tip will be pinched out (stopped) soon after rooting this is not essential. The stem is cut with a razor blade straight across just below a node (leaf joint) and the bottom two pairs of leaves are carefully removed. The base is dipped in a hormone rooting powder and pushed into the cutting bed or pot, containing pure sand or a mixture of two parts of sand and one of peatmoss, which gives better results as the brittle roots are less liable to be broken when removed for potting. Cuttings will normally root in 3 to 4 weeks and should be potted singly into 3-in. pots of general potting compost or a soilless compost. As soon as they are growing again freely the top of each plant is removed, leaving only the two bottom pairs of leaves.

After care When the pots are full of roots the plants are moved into a larger size with a richer mixture, until by the end of the winter the summer-rooted plants will have reached their flowering size pots and be in a compost of 2 parts loam, $\frac{1}{2}$ part peatmoss, $\frac{1}{2}$ part dried cow manure, 1 part sand, plus bone meal. Standards and other top heavy plants must be in a loam-based compost to help keep them stable.

Stopping During the summer shoots may be shortened to two nodes again and again to make a bushy plant. However, as it takes six weeks from stopping to flowering on a side shoot, do not go on stopping too long.

Far left: Tuberous begonia, 'Diana Wynyard'
Center above: Varieties of *Begonia semperflorens*. *Center below:* 'Roy Hartley', a tuberous double begonia.
Left: Fuchsia 'Ting-a-ling', a single-flowered kind suitable for bedding out
Right: The delicate flowers of the fuchsia

Recommended Fuchsia Varieties

The sepal color is given before that of the petals. S = single, SD = semi-double, D = double

Hardy
For hedges: *F. magellanica riccartonii*, erect, branching, [S] scarlet, purple.
For rock gardens or window boxes: 'Alice Hoffman', cerise and scarlet; 'Tom Thumb', carmine and mauve; 'Lady Thumb', carmine and white; 'Peter Pan', red and purple; *pumila*, very small, scarlet and mauve.
For borders: 'Brilliant', very erect, [S or SD] scarlet and magenta; 'Chillerton Beauty', upright, [S] rose, violet; *corallina*, spreading, [S] scarlet and deep violet; 'Brutus', erect, [S or SD] cerise, carmine and purple; 'Lena', arching, [D] flesh pink, rosy purple; 'Madame Cornelissen', upright, [SD] scarlet and white, long buds; 'Margaret', erect, [SD] carmine and purple, very long flowering; 'Peggy King', erect [S] carmine and purple, large flowers; 'Susan Travis', erect, [S] rose pink.

Greenhouse
For bedding out: Singles: 'Bon Accord', white, lilac, held upright; 'Caroline', cream, pale magenta; 'Display', self pink, extending petals; 'Dutch Mill', rose and violet, curling sepals; 'Falling Stars', pale scarlet, brick-red; 'Forget-me-not', flesh-pink, light blue; 'Golden Dawn', flesh-pink, orange; 'Hindu Belle', flesh-pink, plum-purple; 'Lady Heytesbury', white, rose; 'Leonora', self pink; 'Major Heaphy', brick-red, scarlet; 'Marin Glow', white, purple to magenta; 'Mission Bells', red, dark violet, extended petals; 'Mrs Pearson', red, dark violet, large flower; 'Queen Mary', pink, rose, large flower; 'Rose of Castille Improved', flesh-pink, violet; 'Rufus the Red', turkey-red self; 'Sleigh Bells', all white, 'Ting-a-ling', all white, extended petals; 'Tolling Bell', scarlet, white, large bell.
Semi-doubles: 'Abbé Farges', carmine, light purple; 'Pink Flamingo', deep pink, curling sepals, pale pink; 'Satellite', white, shades of red; 'Snow Cap', red, white; 'Tennessee Waltz', rose, Parma violet.
Doubles: 'Emile de Wildeman' ('Fascination') waxy red, pink veined red; 'King's Ransom', crêpe white, purple; 'Lilac Lustre', carmine, lilac; 'Peppermint Stick', rose, striped white, purple, edged carmine; 'Prelude', white, purple, petaloids white striped purple; 'Royal Velvet', crimson, deep purple; 'Santa Cruz', crimson, dark crimson; 'Swingtime', red, white, veined pink; 'Tahoe', white, pink, mauve and blue; 'Torch', cream flushed salmon, salmon shading to red.
For foliage: 'Avalanche', bright yellowish green; 'Autumnale', coppery red; 'Sunray', cream and pink variegated; 'Thalia', red bronze
For standards: 'Cascade', [S] white, carmine; 'Coachman', [S] salmon, orange red; 'Flying Cloud', [D] white, veined pink; 'Jack Acland', [S] pink, rose, pointed buds; 'Mrs Marshall', [S] white, cerise; 'Native Dancer', [D] red and purple; 'Pink Galore', [D] self pink; 'Red Ribbons', [D] long red, white; 'The Tarns', [S] pink and lavender; 'White Spider', [S] white flushed pink, white.
Greenhouse necessary for good flowering: 'Billy Green', salmon self, olive foliage; 'Candlelight', [D] white, light purple to carmine: 'Carmen', [D] carmine, magenta; 'Chang', [S] orange tipped red, orange; 'Citation', [S] rose, white, petals extended; 'Curtain Call', [D] cream, rose to crimson; 'Gartenmeister Bonstedt', orange self, blue green foliage; 'Sophisticated Lady', [D] pale pink, white; 'Texas Longhorn', [D] very long, carmine, white; 'Winston Churchill', [D] pink, silvery blue, compact.

Cuttings destined to be trained as standards should be stopped once. The best side shoots are then tied to a cane, the others removed.
Standards The best standards are not made from the stiff upright types but from the vigorous growing pendulous ones, therefore the trunk of the standard needs to be tied in straight at all stages. To make a head on top of a given length of trunk grow the stem at least two or three further nodes and then rub out the top. The growths from these make branches from which the head is formed as if it were a bush. Side shoots which appear lower down should be rubbed out at once, but the leaves growing from the trunk should be left to make food for growth.

Half standards make good table decorations in a sun parlor, but fuchsias do not like being moved into overheated, draughty or poorly lit places and usually drop their flower buds. They are fine in window boxes and on terraces and patios, as well as bedded out, preferably in beds by themselves.
Hanging Baskets The pendulous varieties, known as basket or cascade forms, are stopped as for bushes, but put the pots on other inverted ones to keep the growth above the bench. Or the plants can be grown in hanging baskets suspended from greenhouse rafters, or from the rafters of patio, porch or pergola or a bracket from a wall.
Planting The soft growth of even the hardy fuchsias may be killed by frost in colder areas, but new shoots will usually shoot up from below ground the following spring. When planting scoop out a shallow depression in which to put the plant and after it is growing well gradually return the earth so that the base of the stem becomes covered, then in the fall put on a good top dressing. The small mound will help to protect the basal buds.
Housing Plants to be housed during the winter in a frost-proof place should be lifted immediately frost has cut the leaves, and stored almost dry until March when they will start into growth if moved into warmth and watered.

Fuchsia 'Tennessee Waltz', a
semi-double variety

Gladiolus

The gladiolus (correct plural gladioli in Britain, gladiolus in North America and elsewhere), is named from the bud-tip that breaks through the foliage and resembles the short broad blade of the Roman soldier's and gladiator's sword.

What is planted is not a bulb, but a corm, in which all parts of the eventual plant are present in embryo. Choose, therefore, large high-crowned corms feeling heavy for their width and with a small basal plate (root scar) underneath, indicating that they are young and vigorous. Ensure that these get a good start and are well fed from the beginning, since the number of buds to a spike is determined quite early. Grown mainly as cut flowers and for garden decoration, they vary from little over 1 in. to about 7 in. across the bloom.

Soils and Situations Gladiolus will grow on most soils, but prefer a medium to light well-drained loam with plenty of humus and some rich, moisture-retaining material from $1\frac{1}{2}$–2 ft. beneath the surface.

Preferably, they should be sited where there will be full sun for most of the day and not close to trees or hedges.
Where to Grow In the herbaceous border they make good tall plants, not merely for the back, but to vary the centre. Here the foliage-fans create useful green verticals, even when the plant is not in flower. Attractive patterns may be made by placing one central corm with a circle of from five to nine around it on a 6–9 in. radius. Diamonds of from three to five corms a side are effective; a small diamond inside a larger is even better. For continuous planting, avoid the straight line in favor of a zigzag of three to five corms to each 'tack'. Where there is sufficient room, three zigzags consisting of tall large-flowered at the back, medium-flowered 'Butterflies' and ruffled in the middle, and the dainty primulinus hybrids and 'Face-ups' in front would give more continuity of color.

Containers or small beds may be planted with circles and diamonds, but containers should be at least 15 in. deep. Underplanting with the usual range of low summer-flowering bedding plants works well, as they feed at a different level. Never let the containers dry out, but ensure there is ample drainage.
For Cutting For cut flowers, gladiolus are best grown in rows in the vegetable garden. Early saladings can be sown between corms (radishes, globe beets, cos lettuce, scallions, short carrots). These are harvested before the gladiolus need all the space between them.
Preparing the Site Dig in the fall, working plenty of water-holding material into the second spit or immediately below it. Rotted farmyard manure is best; but mature compost, leaf-mold, sedge-peat, or anything organic and moisture-retentive will do. Gladiolus like good drainage about the corms, but plenty of moisture at the roots.

For the smaller types, heavy feeding is not required.

Gladiolus grow best in neutral or slightly acid soil, so do not over-lime. In March make holes about 3 ft. apart throughout the patch, sprinkle a little naphthalene in, and cover immediately. The fumes will drive out wireworms. Avoid planting where root knot nematodes are known to be present, as these attack the corms and their roots. Douse the whole area with a weak solution of disinfectant, to which a liquid slug-killer may be added. Then sprinkle dry slug-bait on the soil.
Planting Grow your gladiolus in blocks of three or four rows each, with a 2-ft. path between for ease of access. The spacing between rows should be sufficient for easy hoeing, not less than 7 in. Larger-flowered kinds should be set about 9 in. apart, medium-flowered 6 in., small-flowered, primulinus, and nanus hybrids, 4 in. Plant in May. For the closely placed ones, dig a narrow trench about 6 in. deep. For the widely spaced ones it is quicker to trowel out holes; never use a pointed dibber that will create an air-pocket beneath the corm, as well as compacting the soil. On medium soils there should be $4\frac{1}{2}$–5 in. of soil above each full-sized corm, on light soils 5–$5\frac{1}{2}$ in., on heavy soils 4 in.

Have a bucket of sharp fine sand to hand, into which has been thoroughly mixed a fungicide and an insecticidal dust. Dust trenches or holes with bonemeal or steamed boneflour to promote root development. Then place a handful of the sand mixture where each corm is to sit, press the corm firmly into this, and pour a second handful over it. This ensures good drainage around the corm, easy, dry lifting, and a protective barrier against below-soil pests and fungus growths. Fill the hole with crumbled, stone-free soil.

Before planting each corm, strip any remaining leaf-husks and examine the top. If you want the maximum number of spikes with a multiplication of corms harvested, be careful not to damage them when pressing the corm into the sand. If you want one straight spike, especially for exhibition purposes, rub out all but the most central 'eye'. NEVER plant corms that are stone-hard, or squashy, or with large patches of brown, or with concentric circles of black where the old leaves joined. These will infect other stock with disease.
After care Hand weed close to the plants in moist conditions; hoe between the rows in dry weather. Mulching will reduce this labor, help the soil to retain heat and moisture, and suppress weeds. Mulch after the plants are showing and the larger-flowered kinds have been given a side-dressing of an organically-based fertilizer. Uproot and destroy any gladiolus showing yellow leaves with still-green veins. These are harboring *Fusarium oxysporum*, which is incurable.

Watch for budtips to appear and see these grow clear of the foliage without

Above: Gladiolus 'Peter Pears'
Below: A typical gladiolus corm, showing the base plate, the new corm and the cormlets, which may be grown on for propagation purposes. *Right:* Gladiolus 'Statuette'

new corm

base plate

cormlets

Recommended Gladiolus Varieties

The main types are primulinus hybrids (dainty hooded flowers on strong stems) and primulinus x nanus hybrids (less hooded, attractive throat-marks). These also have strong stems and both types are well suited to windswept sites; small- and medium-flowered, such as the 'Rufmins' and 'Butterfly' range (attractive as cut-flowers); and the large and giant-flowered (best suited for mixed borders and large displays).

1. Peacock and Coronado Nanus Hybrids in Mixture; Miniglads: 'Berta', lime-yellow, striped red; 'Celeste', lilac, blotched purple-green, picoteed purple; 'Lipstick', purple with violet lip-petals; 'Orla', tiny, pink tipped red, blotched strawberry; 'Tampa', smoky brown, striped gray.

2. Primulus Hybrids: 'Comic', reddish brown, lined yellow; 'Essex', bright red; 'Frank's Perfection', orange-scarlet; 'Hastings', light coffee; 'Pageboy', scarlet, picoteed gold; 'Pegasus', cream, darted rose-purple; 'Salmon Star'; 'Red Star'.

3. Ruffled small-flowered: 'Argus, gray-brown, veined red; 'Bluebird', blue-violet, blotched white; 'Camelot', pink; 'Greenwich', green-yellow; 'Foxfire', deep scarlet; 'Goldilocks' deep golden yellow; 'Little Slam', bright red; 'Mirth', pink; 'Parfait', salmon, red throat-marks; 'Rosy Posy', deep rose, plain-petalled, tall; 'Smidgen', dark red, picoteed gold; 'Statuette', yellow, red throat-marks; 'Tidbit', cream, flushed lavender, blotched purple on yellow; 'Towhead', creamy yellow, tall; 'Troika', lavender yellow rose.

4. Medium-flowered: 'Angel Eyes', white blotched blue-violet; 'Amusing', cherry red; 'Blondine', ivory, blotched white; 'Clio', deep purple; 'Confetti', scarlet, blotched yellow; 'Dream Castle', pale yellow, edged pink, blotched carmine; 'Madrilene', light apricot, red blotch on yellow; 'Sweet Fairy', mimosa yellow; 'Storiette', salmon-pink, blotched yellow; 'Sweet Song', bronzy-salmon, blotched apricot; 'Zenith', strawberry pink.

5. Larger-flowered: 'American Beauty', deep rose; 'Aurora', golden yellow; 'Blonde Beauty', pinkish buff, yellow throat; 'Cameo', creamy yellow, picoteed pink; 'Blue Smoke', mulberry salmon, smoky; 'Frostee Pink', pink and cream, sparkling; 'Isle of Capri', salmon-orange, tall; 'La France', pink and white; 'Landmark', cream, blotched dull yellow; 'Limelight', lemon; 'Mount Everest', white, tall; 'Orange Chiffon', robust, salmon-orange; 'Orchid Queen', pale rose-pink, blotched white; 'Pink Prospector', flesh-pink and yellow; 'Pompeii', deep pink, lavender smoky, silvery overlay, white throat; 'Salmon Queen', salmon and creamy white; 'Simplicity', tall, white; 'Spring Song', light salmon, blotched rich yellow; 'Thunderbird', deep salmon; 'Winnebago Chief', deep red; 'King David', blue-purple, picoteed white; 'Chintz Blue', pale blue-violet.

getting crooked. Stake with bamboo canes in wind-swept areas and always for the larger-flowered varieties, as soon as the direction of facing can be determined by the forward bend of the flowerhead. Tie in with *soft* material.

Cutting Cut in the early morning when the first bloom is partly or fully open, using a sharp knife down inside the foliage and then slanting it through the stem, to leave at least four leaves intact. Treat the plant as a grow-ing entity, so that about six weeks later you may lift the new corm plump and healthy.

Lifting Trim off all roots and foliage immediately and dry the corms thoroughly and quickly. A fortnight later the old corms will pull cleanly away from the new ones, which should be cleaned, further dried, dusted with an insecticide and fungicide mixture, and stored cool (but above freezing-point) where there is air circulation (dry) and preferably in the dark.

❧ Irises ❧

Of the large and varied family of irises cultivated today the bearded iris of the *germanica* type is the one most commonly grown. The original bearded iris, *I. germanica*, had purple flowers with a purple beard and 'falls' that hung down with rather a sad effect, but beautiful modern cultivars have come a long way since then and are available in a rainbow of colors. The poise and elegance of the bearded iris, its sword-like leaves that are excellent contrast for the soft foliage of other plants, and its wide range of colorings, make it a perfect gap-filler when tulips are over and border plants not yet at their best.

Colors These range from snowy white through cream to shell-pink and apricot, from butter yellow to flax blue, from deep sapphire to ruby red and purple. There are also browns, tans and near blacks as well as bicolors, and the plicatas have markings of another color etched on a paler ground. The upstanding portion of the flower, known as the 'standard' and the drooping tongue-like petal, known as the 'falls' are often different again, so that every conceivable combination of color exists somewhere in a named cultivar.

Heights The plants vary in height, from dwarfs a few inches high, through the intermediate irises, 16–24 in., to 4 ft. tall kinds. Dwarf bearded irises, forms of *I. pumila* or of *I. chamaeiris* and of many beautiful hybrids, can be used with great effect on rock gardens, in pockets in paving, on dry walls or in containers and troughs. Their flowers, on stalks a few inches high, resemble the tall flags. They flower during late March and April. They are vigorous and need revitalizing by division and replanting every year or two.

Intermediate Irises These, the result of crossing the dwarfs and the tall kinds, increase quickly and are less susceptible to rhizome-rot than the tall irises. Named cultivars come in a wide variety of colors. Though tall flags are better planted apart from other perennials which prevent the sun from reaching and baking their rhizomes, the intermediate irises are happy at the front of the border. Flowering in May, they prolong the season. They are rarely more than 2 ft. tall.

Tall Bearded Irises The tall bearded irises flower in late May and June. Though the blooms are individually short-lived, a succession of flower-buds ensures weeks of color. The modern kinds branch out, the better to display their numerous flowers.

Requirements Bearded irises are the most good-natured of hardy plants, provided their modest requirements are met. These are: 1. Proper preparation of the ground before planting. 2. A sunny site. 3 A well-drained soil containing lime, which should be deeply dug, and some humus-forming material incorporated before planting (on no account use animal manure).

Planting Always plant shallowly but firmly, barely covering the rhizome so that the sun can bake it. Artificial fertilizers are not necessary if the soil is fertile; excess of nitrogen tends to lush leaf growth and loss of flower. Plants must be hand-weeded, since hoeing can damage the rhizomes. Flower-stems should be removed as close to the ground as possible, but sound leaves should not be shortened until they die down naturally.

The best time for planting or dividing is from July to September, when congested clumps should be split up and only the young vigorous fans, each with a rhizome and strong roots, replanted. Space the tall irises 2 ft. apart; the dwarfs and intermediate kinds should be planted more closely. The most effective way for *all* bearded irises is to plant in blocks of one color; they look their loveliest grouped together, in island beds or standing alone, surrounded by stone paving, a perfect setting for their beautiful flowers.

Bulbous Irises Dwarf bulbous iris provide some of the most striking splashes of color in the winter garden. *I. danfordiae*, canary-yellow, and *I. histrio aintabensis*, blue, flower during spring and look well planted together. The brilliant blue *I. histrioides* 'Major', with flowers 4 in. across on short stems, flowers before the leaves appear. The bulbs of these tend to split up into tiny bulblets so that it is best to renew annually, potting on the little offsets until they reach flowering size. In February and March flower the sweetly scented, violet-purple *I. reticulata* and its cultivars, pale blue 'Cantab', reddish-purple 'J. S. Dijt' and dark blue 'Royal Blue'.

The Spanish, Dutch and English irises make good clumps in the border. The Dutch, at 2 ft., flower in May and June. The colors are white, yellow, mauve and blue. They are followed by the Spanish irises, *I. xiphium*, in a similar color range. Both are excellent cut flowers. Bulbs are so cheap that it is worth planting annually, though many will flower each year in a dry soil. The English irises, *I. xiphioides*, flower in June and July.

Recommended Iris Varieties
(height in inches)

Tall bearded irises: 'Big Day' (36), medium blue, white beard; 'Canary Bird' (38), lemon-yellow, white markings; 'Forest Hills' (36), blue-black; 'Golden Planet' (34), golden-yellow; 'Green Ice' (34), greenish-cream; 'Lady River' (30), apricot, falls bronze-violet, beard tangerine; 'My Smoky' (34), white, marked plum-purple; 'Happy Birthday' (34), pink, ruffled petals; 'Karachi' (33), purple-red, falls splashed white; 'Islander' (37), gentian-blue, ruffled petals; 'Foamy Wave' (32), sky blue.
Intermediate irises: 'Langport Honey' (26), orange, reddish falls, beard gold; 'Langport Chief' (16), purple-blue, beard gold; 'Langport Finch (18), medium blue; 'Langport Lady' (20), apricot-pink, tangerine beard.
Dwarf irises: 'Green Spot' (9), waxy-white, green spot on falls; 'Royal Contrast' (12), dark purple, white beard; 'Tinkerbell' (9), lobelia-blue; 'Path of Gold' (6), golden-yellow.

Left: A yellow variety of intermediate iris
Below: The parts of an iris flower. *Bottom:* Dividing an iris rhizome. *Right:* Dutch iris 'Blue Champion'

standards

falls

beard

Right: Delphinium 'Pacific Giant'

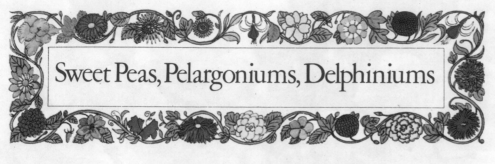

Sweet Peas, Pelargoniums, Delphiniums

Sweet Peas

A most popular annual, the sweet pea (*Lathyrus odoratus*) is not difficult to grow, though the richer the soil the better the results. Given good cultivation it will produce stems 2 ft. long bearing four, five or more florets. Elegant, graceful and fragrant, with the exception of yellow, it will provide every color of the spectrum and dozens of different tones or shades. It is a 'cut-and-come-again' annual; indeed, every other day blooms should be gathered to keep the plants in full production.

The 'Spencer' type, trained up canes in 'cordon fashion', will grow to a height of 14 ft. though this means that all side shoots need to be removed during the growing season and every few days there is the business of tying or ringing the thick haulms (stems), and once or twice during the growing season kneeing, or layering is called for. On the other hand, if the sweet pea is allowed to go its own way brushwood or wire to the height of 8 ft. will not be too tall.

Soils Land enriched with farmyard manure at the rate of one barrowful to each strip of 15 ft. by 4 ft., dug in the fall or early winter into the second spit of soil and fortified by $\frac{1}{2}$ lb. of bonemeal, will give the best results, or good garden compost at the same rate will serve. Failing that peatmoss may be used. A big bucketful to the square yard, fortified by a $\frac{1}{4}$ lb. of artificial fertilizer containing nitrogen, phosphates and potash in the ratio of 20.10.10, obtainable in granular form, has proved a very good substitute.

The whole area where the sweet peas are to be grown should be double-dug and the bottom spit treated as suggested. If the soil has been used the previous year for a crop that has been manured, nothing at all need be added. Acid soils should be given a light dusting of lime in early spring. Sweet peas revel in sunshine and dislike drafts, so give them a sheltered place.

When to Sow Where winters are less severe, seeds may be sown in November providing a covering of salt hay is given during the winter. In colder areas sow as early as possible in spring. A spring sowing may also be made in pots or flats in a greenhouse six weeks in advance of planting time.

Sowing Six seeds to a 6-in. pot, sown an inch from the edge is ideal; or of flats are used sow the seeds 2 in. apart each way. Sow $\frac{3}{4}$ in. deep. Use a moist compost of 3 parts of sieved loam, 1 part of peatmoss and 1 part of coarse sand. Cover the pots or flats with thick layers of paper to prevent drying out. Set a couple of mouse traps, for mice find the seeds irresistible. Inspect after a week and as soon as the shoots appear remove the paper. Water if necessary, and after a day or two start to give plenty of ventilation on all suitable days.

When the plants have four leaves pinch out the growing points to induce side shoots. When these are $1\frac{1}{2}$ in. long, harden off the plants by placing the pots or flats in a frame or under the south wall of the greenhouse.

When sowing directly outdoors the seeds may be sown $\frac{3}{4}$ in. deep, like garden peas. Always put down slug killer.

Planting Never plant out plants raised in the greenhouse until the soil on the plot has been reduced to a fine tilth. Then erect the canes if the plants are to be grown cordon style. A strong support at each end of each row will be necessary, with a cross-bar at a height of 5 ft. Double rows, 2 ft. apart, are best, as this helps when it is time to layer. Stretch strong wire from the end of each cross-bar, insert 8 ft. tall canes, 7 in. apart and secure them to the wire.

Using a trowel, make holes to receive the plants *on the outside* of each cane, to facilitate layering. If the plants are to be in circles, they should be planted *inside* the circle of brushwood. If a circle of netting is to be made, plant first and surround with the netting. Spread the roots and return the soil, so that it just covers the white collar of the plant. If a plant has a brown collar, reject it. It may grow to a height of 3 or 4 ft. and then collapse. Always surround each plant with small twigs. Black thread stretched across the twigs will deter birds.

The Climbing Plants May is a month of vigorous growth. The cordon plants by now will have been restricted to a solitary stem by removing the weaker of the side shoots, of which there may be three or more. Tie in the early stages, very loosely, using raffia. At 1 ft. in height the big sweet pea metal rings may be used. Pinch out side shoots and tendrils to channel the sap into the one stem.

When the plants are grown 'naturally' side shoots are left alone and the tendrils are not removed.

Watering Never allow the land or the plants to become dry. Water the former and spray the latter.

Bud-drop Early in the season buds which should develop into flowers sometimes assume a frozen appearance and drop off. This is not a disease and eventually nature will correct the trouble. It will even occur, on occasion, in the middle of the flowering

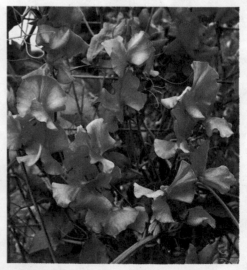

Left: Mixed sweet peas, Spencer type
Above: Sweet Pea 'Legend'
Right: Sweet Pea 'Bijou Mixed'

season. It is caused by hot days and cold nights, or excessive rain, and there is nothing to worry about.

Kneeing or Layering There is a task only for the cordon-growers, and a somewhat bewildering one for those who tackle it for the first time. If possible, it is best to visit a local grower and help him layer his plants. Broadly speaking, when the plants are 5 or 6 ft. tall, six plants are detached from their canes and drawn out at an angle of 45°, the next six, in order, are placed where the first six have been and so on right to the end of the double row, until there are six vacant canes left, for the first six detached to fill. This means turning the corners at the two ends of the row and great care is needed. But the growing point of each plant should rest near the cane up which you require it to climb.

The stems are laid in a row close to the line of canes. Each plant will lift up its head within a few hours and within three days it will be possible to start the tying process again. Flower stems at first will be twisted and should be cut off, but once the plants have grown a foot or so up the canes, if they are kept tied, the stems will be just as straight as previously, and there is still another 6 ft. or more of cane for them to climb.

The Natural Method Since only exhibitors require flowers with very long stems, the easiest method is to grow the plants much as garden peas are grown, with brushwood or netting for support. Four or five times as many blooms may be cut. Keep the plants weed-free, kill the aphids and, above all, keep cutting the flowers.

Feeding If the land was well prepared in the winter, feeding should hardly be necessary. However, if the flower stems are short, give the plants a liquid feed.

Exhibiting Special vases are filled to the brim, quite firmly, with thick bulrushes. The vase is thoroughly soaked in a bucketful of water. The stems of sweet peas are arranged in the shape of a fan. Exhibition sweet peas are straight of stem, and with four, five or six florets evenly placed. Gappy blooms should be avoided, as should any that have been marked.

Choosing Varieties The most popular sweet pea is the 'Spencer' which grows tall, has exceptionally long stems, and carries 4–6 florets per stem. 'Galaxy Hybrids' also tall-growing, will carry as many as nine or more florets per stem, but they are not so nicely placed. The shorter type known as 'Knee-Hi' grows into a nice bush, needs little support, and will reach a height of 4½ ft. with stems about 1 ft. long. Some dwarf types are less useful if cut-blooms are required; 'Little Sweetheart' varieties grow to 1 ft. and 'Color Carpet' 6 in. 'Bijou' and 'Dwarf Pigmy' will sometimes grow to a height of 3 ft. but the flower stems are short.

Recommended Sweet Pea Varieties

The following is a list of 'Spencer' sweet peas, good exhibition varieties and also splendid for decorative purposes, chosen from hundreds of named varieties. Where two or three of the same color are named there is not much to choose between them.
White: 'White Leamington'; 'White Ensign'; 'Majesty'. **Cream:** 'Hunter's Moon'; 'Margot'. **Picotee:** 'Selana'; 'Tell Tale'.
Pale Blue: 'Cambridge'; 'Larkspur'.
Mid-Blue: 'Noel Sutton'.
Deep Blue: 'Blue Velvet'.
Lavender: 'Leamington'; 'Harmony'.
Mauve: 'Mauve Leamington'; 'Reward'.
Salmon Pink *(white ground):* 'Splendour'; 'Superfine'. **Salmon Pink** *(cream ground):* 'Royal Flush'; 'Philip Simons'.
Almond-blossom Pink: 'Southbourne'.
Orange-Cerise: 'Herald'; 'Clarion'; 'Alice Hardwick'. **Scarlet:** 'Firebrand'. **Crimson:** 'Gipsy Queen'. **Maroon:** 'Milestone'.
Carmine: 'Rosemary Govan'.
There are not many 'Galaxy' or more dwarf varieties from which to choose; their colors are generally indicated by their names.

❧ Pelargoniums ❧

The pelargonium was introduced into Europe from South Africa towards the beginning of the 17th century; today it is one of the most popular of flowers. It is native to South Africa, Australia and Turkey, but is now widely grown in the temperate areas of the world.

Of the several sub-divisions of the genus the following six are the most popular.

1. **Zonals** (*P. hortorum*) Commonly but incorrectly known as 'geraniums', these are widely grown in beds, greenhouses, tubs, urns, borders, etc. Foliage may be zoned or plain, flowers single, double or semi-double, colors ranging from white through all shades of salmon and pink to reds and purples. Included in this section are Irenes, Deacons, Rosebuds, Cactus and Stellar varieties, detailed as follows:

IRENES This vigorous strain was raised in California and produces larger flower-heads in greater abundance than older varieties. Flowers are produced on long stems making them particularly suitable for arrangements and cut flowers, and are all semi-double. Spaced at not less than 18-in. intervals for correct development in beds and borders, the best results are obtained by planting first into 5-in. clay pots and sinking the pots into the ground. The following is a selection: 'Springtime', light salmon-pink; 'Trull's Hatch', coral-pink with paler center; 'Penny', neon-pink with blue overtones; 'Electra', deep red with blue overtones; 'Surprise', powder-pink; 'Modesty', pure white.

DEACONS (often known as Floribunda Geraniums) Derived from a cross between an ivy-leaf and a miniature, these are more compact than Irenes and produce many more smaller flowerheads. The development of the plant may be controlled by the pot size: for instance a plant in a 5-in. pot will grow to about 1 ft. in diameter, whereas one in a 15-in. pot may develop to about 4 ft. in diameter. Six of the most popular varieties, all double, are: 'Deacon Bonanza', neon-pink; 'D. Coral Reef', coral-pink; 'D. Mandarin', orange; 'D. Fireball', bright red; 'D. Lilac Mist', pale lilac-pink; 'D. Romance', purple-mauve with blue tinge.

ROSEBUD AND CACTUS VARIETIES The former bear relatively small flowers and the petals never fully open, thus looking like rosebuds. There are five varieties, three shades of red, one medium purple and one white with pink edges to the petals and a green center. Cactus varieties have narrow twisted petals rather like quills. Colors range through white, salmon and pink to red, orange and purple.

STELLAR VARIETIES, available in both single and double varieties, originated in Australia. The foliage is star-shaped (hence the name), sometimes zoned but often unmarked, and the flowers are carried on long stems. Plants will grow to over 5 ft. in Australia and California.

2. **Fancyleaf Zonals** These are mainly grown for their unusual leaf coloring, the

flowers often (but not always) being insignificant, usually red, single and sparsely produced. Popular for bedding schemes, they are also widely used for edging borders and to add variety to mixed groups. Leaf coloring ranges from green-and-black, various shades of green, yellow and bronze to red and copper in a variety of combinations. Because they are seldom as bushy as the Irenes or Deacons, a more impressive effect is produced by spacing them 8–9 in. apart. The following six will give an idea of the colorings available; 'A Happy Thought', mid-green leaves with cream butterfly mark in the center, flowers red, single; 'Mrs Pollock', red single flowers, leaves red, cream and bronze; 'Mrs Quilter', pea-green leaves with broad bronze zone, salmon-pink single flowers; 'Mrs Cox', leaves green, flowers red, purple and cream; 'Skies of Italy', green, cream, purple and orange foliage; 'Miss Burdett Coutts', leaves marked green, cream, bronze and pink.

3. **Regals** (*P. domesticum*) These are commonly known in Britain and Australia as pelargoniums and in USA as show or Lady Washington geraniums. They are mainly grown in this country as pot plants and greenhouse plants but they are suitable for outside beds, borders and tubs in sheltered but sunny positions. The older varieties flower for only two or three months of the year but the modern hybrids will continue to flower for at least ten months if grown under correct conditions. Flowering depends upon light to a large extent; if the quality of winter light is sufficient they can be flowered throughout the year; if the light is poor they will rest. In their natural environment show geraniums have no dormant period nor do they need one; dormancy is unnatural to them and is produced by adverse conditions.

Colors range from white to near-black through every possible shade and combination of shades (many being multi-colored), except yellow and pure blue. The flowers are usually larger than those of the zonals and the leaves are unzoned. However, there are now at least two varieties with colored foliage. 'Miss Australia' has silver-edged foliage and deep-pink flowers; 'Golden Princess', has gold and green foliage and white flowers. The following are among the most suitable for greenhouse or outside use: 'Georgia Peach', peach-pink with frilled petals (USA); 'Geronimo', blood-red with frilled petals (USA); 'Aztec', strawberry, white and chocolate with maroon markings (USA); 'Grandma Fischer', bright orange with brown marks on most petals (USA); 'Nhulunbuy', cerise, edged with white, very ruffled (Australia); 'South American Bronze', chocolate-maroon with white edge to petals (USA).

4. **Ivyleaf varieties** (*P. peltatum*) The fleshy leaves of these are shield-shaped. Flowers may be single, semi-double or double. These trailing varieties are mainly used in Britain for hanging baskets, tubs and urns, but are widely planted in other countries in bedding schemes for ground cover. Foliage may be zones or plain, and there are a few fancy-leaved varieties, including 'Crocodile', with a mesh-like pattern over the foliage in white or cream. Colors range through white, salmon and pink to reds and purple. The six modern varieties listed below are a vast improvement on the older ones: 'Sybil Holmes' ('Ailsa Garland'), rose-pink, double (USA); 'Blue Springs', mauve-pink double, upright habit (Continental); 'Cliff House', white rosettes with a touch of pink in the center (USA): 'Jack of Hearts', bright pink semi-double with scarlet mark on each petal, upright habit (USA); 'Malibu', crimson-cerise with maroon marks and orange flash, double (USA).

5. **Scented-leaf varieties** There are hundreds of these since they seed readily and produce many forms with only slight variations. The aroma is released when the foliage is brushed or gently pinched with the fingers. In California and South Africa they can make bushes up to several feet in diameter. The following six will serve as the basis for a collection: Pelargonium 'Crispum', lemon scented leaves; 'Dr Livingstone', finely divided leaves which are rose scented; 'Fragrans', nutmeg scented; 'Graveolens', leaves rose scented, flowers pink with purple veins; 'Lady Plymouth', rose scented leaves, flowers lavender marked with darker veins; 'Prince of Orange', orange scented with small pale mauve flowers.

6. **Miniatures and Dwarfs** These are mostly zonals, double, semi-double and single varieties in colors ranging from white through salmon and pink to reds and purples. This classification covers mature plants normally less than 8 in. high, chiefly grown as greenhouse pot plants but they can be used very effectively in bedding schemes, wall pockets and borders. Cultivation is as for other groups but over-potting should be avoided if maximum flower is desired. They can be flowered throughout the year under the correct conditions. The color range is as for zonals. There are a few miniature regals all with mauve or purple-and-white flowers, and two miniature ivy leaves–'Gay Baby', with tiny white flowers, and 'Sugar Baby' with pink flowers.

Among zonal varieties are 'Black Vesuvius', dark, almost black green leaves and scarlet flowers; 'Fournier', black green foliage, scarlet blooms; 'Kleiner Leibling', pink flowers; 'Pigmy', scarlet double flowers; 'Pixie', flowers pink with white centers; 'Venue', pink double flowers.

General Culture All pelargoniums prefer a sunny position, medium loam and shelter from north and north-east winds. They will withstand temperatures between 34°F (1°C) and 120°F (49°C), but will not survive frost. Propagation is by cuttings, 3–4 in. long, taken from green shoots, preferably in late July or early August (cuttings from miniatures will be shorter). Over watering should

Top left: Pelargonium 'E. B. Hoare'
Top right: The delicate blooms of the regal pelargonium 'Grand Slam'
Above: Pelargonium 'Maréchal McMahon', a fancyleaf variety
Far right below: Taking pelargonium cuttings.
1. A suitable shoot is cut from the parent plant. 2. It is cut cleanly below a leaf joint with a razor blade. 3. Prepared cuttings are inserted round the edge of a pot of cutting compost
Right: Delphiniums in the summer border
Far right above: Delphinium 'Blue Dawn'

be avoided; plants can easily be killed by an excess of water. Regular feeding with a balanced fertilizer is beneficial, but avoid high-nitrogen feeds including animal manures, which will result in lush growth and few flowers.

Delphiniums

These beautiful perennial plants require cool growing conditions if first class specimens are to be produced, and are well suited to the North West, although it is possible to obtain reasonable plants in other areas by raising them from seed at frequent intervals. They are used most frequently in herbaceous borders, mixed borders, and in front of shrubs. Few flowers are so pure a blue; there are also many varieties with mauve, purple, violet, lilac or white flowers. Early in the 1960s the first hybrid reds, pinks and yellows were bred by Dr R. A. H. Legro in Holland.

Generally described as hybrids of *D. elatum*, modern delphiniums are a mixture of more than half-a-dozen species. *D. belladonna* and its varieties are not so widely grown today. They produce several spikes on each main stem. *D. belladonna* tolerates light shade, but other delphiniums demand open, sunny positions, sheltered if possible from wind.

Soil Although a good garden loam is ideal, sandy or clay soils can be improved by digging in plenty of rotted manure, peatmoss, leafmold, rotted compost or spent mushroom compost. Dig 18–20 in. deep, mix in 4 oz. per square yard of a general fertilizer and let the ground settle for at least a month before planting.

Planting Spring and fall are the best times to plant, except in heavy, wet ground or where slugs abound, when spring is preferable. A space 2½ ft. across each way is sufficient in a border, but plants intended to produce spikes of exhibition quality deserve spaces 3–3½ ft. across. Young plants knocked from pots can be set with a trowel; those from open ground often arrive with their roots 'balled' in soil and then the roots must be spread out, keeping the crowns of the plants at surface level. Firm planting is essential.

Propagation Delphiniums are increased by seed, division and cuttings. Although seed does not come true; that from a blue-flowered plant may produce seedlings with mauve, purple and white flowers. However, the best quality seed produces excellent plants cheaply. Preferably sow freshly harvested seed in August or early September, in seed flats filled with seed compost. Stand the flats in a frame, greenhouse or sheltered spot outdoors. By late April or May seedlings are big enough to plant 1 ft. apart in a nursery bed outdoors and are moved later to their permanent positions. Seed may also be sown in April under cover or in May in open ground.

Named varieties will come true only when propagated by dividing clumps in early spring, when the shoots are 3–4 in. high, or by cuttings. The roots are teased apart and the crown severed with a knife so each new portion has roots and one or two shoots. Cuttings generally produce sturdier plants. They are made by choosing healthy shoots 3–4 in. high, scraping soil from around them before cutting them off close to the crown. Strip off their lower leaves, dip the lower ends of the stems in water, then in hormone rooting powder and set them with a dibber, about five in a 4½-in. pot of cutting compost. Bury one third of each stem, water the cuttings, and place them in a propagating case, or on a shaded greenhouse bench. They root in six to eight weeks and then are potted up singly in 3½-in. pots.

Cultivation In early spring crowns should be covered with ashes or coarse grit to keep slugs off the young shoots. Thin these out to leave the strongest four to six per plant, when 6 in. tall. Knock in a 6–8 ft. cane beside each shoot; tie the stems to the canes as they grow. Feed each plant with a general fertilizer in May, the same amount of general fertilizer in early June, and a tablespoon of sulfate of potash as the flower buds show color, watering in these plant foods. Keep the soil damp. Dead flower spikes should be cut back; secondary spikes sometimes develop and bloom in early fall.

Ten Reliable Delphiniums
'Blue Dawn', 5 ft, blue and pink with black eye; 'Butterball', 5 ft, cream with yellow eye; 'Skyline', 5 ft, blue with white center; 'Xenia Field', 5½ ft, lavender with lavender and white eye, a very strong growing variety; 'Blue Tit', 3½ ft, indigo with blue black eye; 'Cupid', 3 ft, sky blue with white eye; 'Lord Butler', 4½ ft, flowers blue with white centers; 'Peter Pan', 3½ ft, striking blue with dark eye; 'Purple Ruggles', 5 ft, purple double; 'Swanlake', 5½ ft, white with black eye.

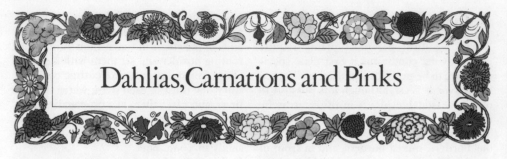

Dahlias, Carnations and Pinks

❧ Dahlias ☙

Dahlias are half-hardy perennials, originally from Mexico, and now very popular in the United States. Very adaptable, they grow well in any type of soil. They are versatile, being used for garden decoration, cut flowers, floral art and exhibition. Few flowers can match them for their wide range of brilliant colors, their wide variety of shapes and sizes, and their long flowering period. They tolerate extremes of climate and, even in a poor season, some kinds will produce over one hundred flowers.

Classification In height dahlias range from the Lilliput type, 1 ft. high, to the more normal types which can reach a height of over 5 ft., although the average is about 3½ ft. The sizes of the blooms vary tremendously, from about 1 in. across to over 14 in. There are fourteen groups as follows:

INCURVED CACTUS Fully double flowers with the margins of the majority of the floral rays fully revolute for ½ or more of their length and the tips of the rays curving toward the center of the flower.

STRAIGHT CACTUS Fully double flowers with the margins of the majority of the floral rays fully revolute for ½ their length of more, the rays being straight, slightly incurved or recurved.

SEMI-CACTUS DAHLIA Fully double flowers with the margins of the majority of the floral rays fully revolute for less than ½ their length and the rays broad below.

BALL DAHLIAS Fully double flowers ball shaped or slightly flattened. Floral rays blunt or round at tips and quilled or with margins involute for more than ½ the length of the ray in spiral arrangement, the flowers over 3½ in. in diameter.

MINIATURE DAHLIAS All dahlias which normally produce flowers that do not exceed 4 in. in diameter. Pompoms excluded, to be classified according to the foregoing description.

Miniature Single, Miniature Peony, Miniature Straight Cactus, Miniature Semicactus, Miniature Formal Decorative, Miniature Informal Decorative.

POMPOM DAHLIAS Having same characteristics as Ball Dahlias but for show purposes not more than 2 in. in diameter.

SINGLE DAHLIAS Open-centered flowers with only one row of ray florets with the margins flat or nearly so, regardless of the number of florets.

MIGNON Single flowers, the plants approximately 18 in. in height.

ORCHID-FLOWERING DAHLIAS Flowers as in single dahlias excepting that the rays are more or less tubular by the involution of the margins.

ANEMONE DAHLIAS Open-centered flowers, with only one row of ray florets, regardless of form or number of the florets, with the tubular disc florets elongated, forming a pincushion effect.

COLLARETTE DAHLIAS Open centered flowers with only one row of ray florets, with the addition of a different color, forming a collar around the disc.

PAEONY DAHLIAS Open centered flowers with two to five rows of ray florets with or without the addition of smaller curled or twisted floral rays around the disc.

FORMAL DECORATIVE DAHLIAS Fully double flowers, with the margins of the floral rays slightly or not at all revolute, the ray generally broad, either pointed or rounded at tips, with outer rays tending to recurve and central rays tending to be cupped; and the majority of all floral rays in a regular arrangement.

INFORMAL DECORATIVE DAHLIAS Fully double flowers, with the margins of the majority of the floral rays slightly or not at all revolute, the rays generally long, twisted or pointed and usually irregular in arrangement.

Site Dahlias prefer an open sunny position but will still grow well in a partially shaded spot, away from trees. They look glorious when massed in a bed or border by themselves. They also fit in well with other plants in the herbaceous border, if they are placed carefully to use their various heights and colors to best effect. The 1-ft. tall dwarf kinds will add summer color to the rock garden, or can be planted in a bed in a retaining wall or even in a window box. Planted in tubs or other containers, they will brighten up a patio, terrace or other paved area.

Soil Cultivation Single digging is all that is necessary. This should be done in late fall or early winter on heavy soil, leaving the ground rough for the snow and frost to break it down; light soils can be left until early spring. Every soil benefits from the addition of humus-forming material such as farmyard manure, peatmoss, horse manure, leaf mold, compost, straw, seaweed, etc., dug into the top few inches.

A month or so before planting, the soil should be broken down to a reasonable tilth and a top dressing of either bonemeal or a general fertilizer should be raked into the top couple of inches of soil.

Planting Out Dahlias can be grown either from tubers or green plants. Tubers are the roots which have formed at the base of a plant grown the previous season. They can

Collerette

Decorative

Ball

Semi-cactus

be planted from early May onwards. Space the tall types about $2\frac{1}{2}$ ft. apart, the dwarf bedding types $1\frac{1}{2}$ ft. apart, and the Dwarf types 1 ft. A stout 4 ft. stake or cane is needed for the taller types and these are put in position first. Plant the tubers 6-in. deep, just in front of the cane. On poor soil put in a couple of handfuls of a mixture of peatmoss and a little general fertilizer, into the hole and put the tuber on this, stem upwards, and fill in the hole with fine soil. Once the shoots appear above ground they are treated exactly as green plants.

Green plants are planted as soon as all danger of frost is over. Canes are put in position first and a hole slightly larger than the plant rootball is taken out just in front of the cane. A planting mixture of peatmoss and fertilizer will help to get the plants away to a flying start on poor soil. Place the plant in the hole and fill it in with soil. Tie the plant loosely to the cane with soft twine then water the plants in well. Place a few slug pellets round each plant.

Summer Management For the first three or four weeks after planting, hoe the soil between the plants to keep down the weeds. When the plants have developed five or six pairs of leaves, pinch out the growing tip to promote bushy growth. As the side shoots develop after this stopping they will need to be kept tied in to the cane.

The soil around the plants should never be allowed to dry out. Dahlias benefit greatly from the application of a mulch which will lessen the need for watering. Apply this in early July to a depth of about 4 in., completely covering the soil around the plants.

Flowering The first flowers should begin to appear about mid or late July. Better quality flowers can be obtained by disbudding, which means removing the two small side buds which appear either side of the main or terminal bud. Also remove the two side shoots which appear at the joint of the pair of leaves below the flowering bud. Left to themselves dahlias produce dozens of small poor quality flowers on short stems; a

little light disbudding and de-shooting makes an amazing difference.

Faded blooms should be removed to ensure continuation of flowering. This is particularly important with the single-flowering types which form seed heads very quickly. When cutting blooms for the house use a sharp knife, make a long slanting cut and plunge the stem immediately in deep water; cut in this way, dahlias should easily last a week. Cut as many blooms as you like, as often as you like.

Give the plants an occasional foliar feed. Make sure that all the plants to be saved for next year are clearly labeled with their name (if known), or type and color.

Lifting and Storing

Lifting The tubers which have formed at the base of the plants will need to be lifted and stored for the winter. After the frost has killed the foliage cut through the main stem about 6 in. above soil level. With a fork loosen the soil round the tuber then push the fork underneath and lift the tuber.

Remove surplus soil from the roots and place them stem downwards in a greenhouse, shed, garage, or spare room for about ten days to dry. While they are drying the tubers can be prepared for storage. Trim off the thin stringy roots from the ends of the tubers and cut the stem down to about 2 in. Any damaged ends of the roots should be trimmed away and the cut surface dusted with either green sulfur or a mixture of lime and flowers of sulfur in equal parts. Tie the label securely to the stem.

Storing If a frost-free garage, shed or spare room is available, place the tubers in shallow boxes of peatmoss or dry soil. A cool cellar makes an ideal storage place. Where frost protection cannot be guaranteed, protect the tubers by placing them in stout wooden or cardboard boxes filled with an insulating material such as dry soil, sand, ashes, straw or sawdust.

Inspect the tubers once or twice while they

are in store to make sure they are sound. Feel each tuber; if any parts are soft and brown this indicates rot which will have to be trimmed away and the cut surface dusted with sulfur/lime powder. Any tubers with a white fluffy deposit (mildew) will need to be wiped clean with a dry cloth and dusted with sulfur/lime.

Propagation

Dahlias are very easy to propagate, whether from seed, division of tubers, or by cuttings.

Sowing seed Plants will not reproduce true to type or color from seed, except for the single Coltness type and the semi-double dwarf bedders.

Sow the seed in March in a heated greenhouse, thinly, in pans or flats of general seed compost or one of the soilless seed composts, covering the seed with $\frac{1}{4}$ in. of compost. Once they germinate they should be pricked out 24 to a flat. Grow the plants on coolly and in April move them to a cold frame to harden off before planting them out in late May or early June.

Dividing tubers A dahlia tuber consists of a stem which is attached to the crown or collar where the eyes or buds are situated; swollen, potato-like tubers are attached to the crown. There are two types of tuber; the ground tuber is usually quite large and is formed at the base of a plant grown outdoors without restriction; the pot tuber is small and compact and is formed at the base of cuttings grown throughout the season in pots.

Before dividing the tuber the eyes must be visible and are coaxed into life by placing the tubers in moist peatmoss or compost in late March or early April in flats which are placed either in a greenhouse or cold frame or on a sunny windowsill in the house. Once the eyes are visible, cut down the center of the stem between the buds, right through the tuber. Further division may be possible, depending on the size of tuber and the position of the eyes, but each

Pompon

Cactus

Single-flowered

Anemone-flowered

piece to be planted must contain a portion of stem attached to a piece of the crown bearing an eye, and at least one portion of swollen root or tuber. The divisions can either be planted out in early May or grown on in flats in the greenhouse and planted out in late May.

Taking Cuttings Large numbers of cuttings can be taken from dahlia tubers; they root easily in a warm greenhouse in a minimum temperature of 60°F (16°C). If any tubers show signs of rot or mildew, treat them as described earlier. The tubers are boxed up in moist peatmoss or compost, or they can be bedded down on the open greenhouse bench, if possible, over some form of bottom heat. Keep the compost moist.

The cuttings are taken when the shoots are 3–4 in. long and are normally placed round the sides of a pot or pan or placed in a flat in rows.

With a clean sharp knife cut through the shoot just below the lowest leaf joint. Trim off the lower leaves, dip the end of the cutting in a hormone rooting powder then place the cutting 1 in. deep in the compost. Space the cuttings so that the leaves are just clear of each other and water lightly. Place the cuttings in a propagating frame, or bed the pots in moist peatmoss on the open bench and provide shade.

Spray the cuttings with a fungicide to prevent damping off and after a day or so allow them a free flow of air. To lessen the risk of flagging, spray the cuttings with tepid water twice daily until rooting takes place in about 14 days.

Pot the rooted cuttings singly into 3½-in.

Top left: Mixed varieties of dwarf double dahlias

Above left: A typical pompon dahlia, with perfectly formed, ball-like flowers, under 2 in. in diameter

Above: The giant decorative dahlia 'Hamari Girl'

pots of general compost or a peat-based compost. Keep the plants in a shady spot in the greenhouse for a day or so before placing them on a shelf near the glass, keeping the greenhouse well ventilated. In April remove the plants to a cold frame, keep the sash closed for a couple of days then progressively allow more ventilation until, towards planting out time in late May or, in the colder areas, in early June, the lights can be left off completely. At all times protect the plants from extreme cold.

Recommended Dahlia Varieties

Decorative Dahlias
Giant: 'Arthur Godfrey'. A strong grower with very large blooms which are red with orange shading; 'Hamari Girl', lavendar pink, easy to grow; 'Hollands Festival', orange with white tips; 'Ohcho', creamy-yellow very vigorous.
Large: 'Ben Hill', red blooms to top quality; 'Jacqueline Kennedy', rich purple; 'Leone', white suffused lavender with deeper lavender centers.
Medium: 'After You' produces masses of yellow flowers good for cutting or exhibition; 'Cherokee Charm', clear pink, flowers early in the season; 'First Lady', Dresden yellow, reflex shape; 'Golden Treasure', gold blooms, for cut flowers or exhibition; 'Purple Velvet', purple with a velvety sheen and outstanding exhibition variety; 'Sterling Silver', an outstanding white variety.
Small: 'Early Bird', purple and white, early flowering; 'Fete D'Orange', orange blooms which appear early in the season; 'Lions International', rose-pink and outstanding variety; 'Southern Beauty', white suffused purple, a good exhibition variety; 'Tammy Foondle', primrose yellow; 'Ventura', yellow, good for exhibition or cutting.
Miniature: 'Bobo', bronze suffused with scarlet at tips of petals; 'Silver Spring', pink, fine for exhibition; 'Treasure', pink.

Cactus Dahlias
Giant: 'Clarion Royalty', purple, strong growing, an excellent exhibition variety.
Large: 'Frontispiece', white; 'Goldie', golden apricot, an outstanding variety.
Medium: 'Alabama Melody', clear pink, early flowering, a good exhibition variety. 'Extravaganza', scarlet, early blooms of good quality; 'Krijnens Jubileum', yellow, strong growing and early flowering
Small: 'Dicky Bill', pink with red streaking, very early; 'Maude Crawford', yellow, flowers early and profusely; 'Orange Parfait', orange-red, low growing; 'Shawnee Lavender', early, flowers dark pink; 'Sonnet', yellow; 'Sundown', petals white tipped purple. A good cut flower

Semi Cactus Dahlias:
Giant: 'Arab Queen', coral pink flower, yellow center; 'Super', salmon red, one of the largest; 'Mary Elizabeth', dark red, strong growing

Medium: 'Extravaganza', scarlet, early flowering; 'Fair Lady', rose and white, good for cutting; 'Lady Elaine', white, good for exhibition; 'Mrs D. Bortels', orange, a prolific bloomer; 'Shawnee Dream', pink, a good exhibition variety
Small: 'Country Music', yellow; 'Herbert Smith', pink, an excellent show variety and first class for cutting; 'Poise', red and white, very striking color combination

Ball Dahlias
'Butterball', light yellow, strong growing; 'Clyde Carraway', very vigorous, golden streaked red; 'Pat'N Dee', white
Pompom: 'Bronze Beauty', bronze and orange, very strong growing; 'Clarisse', golden orange, fine for cutting or exhibition; 'Willos Violet', deep purple on lighter ground.
Anemone Flowered: 'Comet', deep velvet blood red; 'Vera Higgins', fawn and orange.
Colleretts: 'Coincident', cherry red and yellow; 'La Cierva', purple.
Paeony Flowered: 'Bishop of Llandaff', scarlet with dark foliage.
Single Flowered: 'Bright Flash', red, vigorous grower; 'Tango Century', bronze shades.

Above: Dianthus 'Jessie', an old-fashioned pink

❧ Carnations and Pinks ❧

The genus *Dianthus* is large, but the popular garden flowers are border carnations, growing about 2½ ft. tall, with exquisitely formed blooms and smooth-edged petals, and pinks in a wide variety of shapes, sizes and heights.

They need a sunny, well-drained position, but are not suited to areas which have severe winters. Any soil suits them, so long as it is not very acid, and they are very tolerant of lime. They can be planted during good weather in the fall or spring, setting them firmly but not deeply, burying the roots but not the stem, securing to a 6-in. stake if necessary. Planting distance for border carnations is about 12 in. and for pinks about 10 in.

To improve soil before planting, dig compost or well-rotted manure below the first spit, and hoe bonemeal at 4 oz. per sq. yd. into the top spit. In spring a side-dressing of sulfate of potash at 2 oz., or at 8 oz., per sq. yd. is good, but potash fertilizers should not be given in the fall as they make the stems brittle in winter. Plants in their second and subsequent years should have a side dressing of a balanced fertilizer.

Border carnations need staking with a 3-ft. cane, and they should be disbudded to leave one bud on the central stem and one on each side stem, removing the others when about the size of a small pea. Pinks are not disbudded, and rarely require staking.

Border carnations flower in July and August, and old-fashioned pinks in June, and apart from snapping off the old flower stems no special treatment is needed. Most modern pinks flower a second time, and should be thoroughly watered and then given a dressing of complete fertilizer.

Border carnations are propagated by layering in July and August. Select a good side stem and strip off all the leaves from the lower part, leaving five fully developed pairs at the top. Push a thin-bladed knife into the stem just below the lowest joint with leaves on. Cut downwards through the joint below and turn the knife away from the center of the plant so as to bring it out just below the joint. This leaves a tongue which opens out as the stem is bent down to the ground. If the stem is too stiff to bend down without snapping, bruise it between the joints with the thumbnail or a pair of thin pliers. Push the open tongue into the ground and secure it in position with a loop of wire. Prepare the ground beforehand by working in a mixture of equal parts of sharp sand and peatmoss.

After enough layers are put down, they are watered in and not allowed to become dry while rooting, which takes about six weeks. They are then cut away from the parent and left another week when they can be lifted. They can be planted out directly or potted up for two weeks before planting.

Pinks can be propagated in the same way, but usually cuttings are taken from late June to early August. Select strong side shoots for cuttings, and leave four or five fully developed pairs of leaves at the tip. Strip off the pair of leaves below this with a downward pull, exposing the joint. Cut just below the joint with a sharp knife or razor blade. The cutting is inserted in sandy soil up to but not above the next joint, in a pot in a cold frame, exposed to the sky but not the sun, watered and kept in a close atmosphere for three to four weeks, when top growth shows that it has rooted. The cuttings are then hardened off and potted up before planting.

Modern pinks sometimes send up the central stem to flower before proper side growth has been made, and if so they must be stopped. This is done when the plants have made ten to twelve joints. Hold the seventh or eighth joint in one hand, and bend the top sharply sideways when it should snap off, or cut it off cleanly just above the joint.

Border carnations should never be stopped, and stopping may delay the flowering of old-fashioned pinks for a season. However, a pink should never be allowed to flower unless it has good side growth.

Below: Pinks make a pretty addition to a garden

Some Definitions

Today, many people begin gardening, which often means tree and shrub planting, without the slightest previous practical experience and are therefore in many cases almost totally ignorant of the meanings of many of the terms and phrases used by more experienced gardeners.

A deciduous tree or shrub is one that loses its leaves in the fall (often after they have turned brilliant colors). On the other hand a tree or shrub which retains foliage throughout the whole year is said to be evergreen. Evergreens may be divided into two sections, broad-leaved, which include mountain-laurel, rhododendron, pieres, and camellias, and narrow-leaved evergreens represented by pines, firs, spruces, junipers, and yews, in fact all evergreen conifers belong to this group. It is interesting to note that the farther north we go the fewer native evergreen plants we are likely to encounter, because of this the importance of introducing evergreen trees, and shrubs to create winter interest in northern gardens cannot be over-stressed.

The term standard is applied to either a tree or shrub that has a clear stem of several feet from ground level to the first branches, many of our favorite flowering trees, including flowering cherries, and flowering apples, are grown as standards with 4–5 ft. clear trunks. Balled and burlaped refers simply to the fact that trees, or shrubs have been lifted with a ball of soil around their roots that is held in place with burlap, most evergreens and larger trees are treated in this way. Trees, and shrubs that are sold 'bare rooted' on the other hand have little if any soil attached to their roots. Before leaving this section on definitions it would be perhaps as well to consider the term shrub itself, for there is often some misconceptions about its meaning. It is in fact a plant deciduous or evergreen whose woody branches arise at ground level or just above ground level without forming a central trunk.

❧ Trees and Shrubs on a New Property ❧

Before planting any tree it is important to bear in mind that no matter how small it is, it will get larger, and in many cases one day grow to form a dominant feature of the landscape. Remember also that trees act as the chief unit of scale in the average garden, soften the hard outline of buildings, act as windbreaks giving protection in exposed positions, form an excellent sound baffle absorbing the noise of busy streets, function as air-conditioners and air purifiers, provide food and refuge for a large number of birds and animals, and give shade in the height of the summer.

From the practical point of view anyone planting trees or shrubs on newly acquired

Trees & Shrubs

property should first carefully study their placement to ensure that they are not positioned too close to buildings or neighboring property so that they may eventually cause damage or annoyance or their root systems interfere with proposed or existing drains. It is also important to study microclimatic conditions that might prevail in the area as well as soil depth, and soil drainage, as it would clearly be very unwise to plant subjects that need protection in natural frost pockets, or in exposed positions, likewise it would be folly to place deep rooting trees over rock ledges, or material that requires a well drained soil in a wet spot. Should there be trees already present on the site examine them carefully. If any appear to be unsound consult a qualified tree surgeon without delay. It must be pointed out that attention to these matters at an early stage may save a great deal of trouble and expense in years to come. The smaller the garden the more important this is.

Soil A great number of our native trees, both evergreen and deciduous, grow on the side of hills and mountains. This means that the rich, fertile soils of the valleys are not essential for their growth, but suggest that they do like good drainage. In other words a large number of trees, and shrubs on the market are well suited by the soil conditions to be found around our homes. There is one important qualification to this, there are certain trees and shrubs that will not grow in alkaline soil. In practice, if rhododendrons, azaleas, and other lime-hating plants are

Camellia chandleri 'elegans' is an old but still popular variety

growing in and around the new garden and the leaves do not look yellow, then you can grow all the trees and shrubs listed as lime haters. Even so, you can grow some of these when lime is present for example you can make a raised bed into which water from the surrounding soil does not drain and fill it with an acid soil (containing a good proportion of peatmoss). Or you can treat plants with a chemical, sequestrene, which helps to overcome the effects of lime, but its effect is not permanent and periodic applications have to be made.

Planting This very important operation is generally carried out, either in the fall, or in the spring as soon as the frost is out of the soil. In milder areas of the country planting may proceed at any time during the winter when conditions permit. Although if for some reason it is found necessary to move trees or shrubs during their active period of growth their chances of survival will be greatly enhanced if they are sprayed with an ANTI-DESICCANT before moving as this provides a coating over the leaves reducing water loss. Both trees and shrubs are available bare root, or balled and burlaped. Container grown plants are also becoming increasingly popular with home owners, one advantage being that by their use the planting season can be greatly extended through much of the summer. When transplanting evergreens make sure that the root ball is intact, failure to do so in most cases leads to disappointment. When purchasing trees or shrubs you can either order direct from a large supplier or go to one of the smaller nurseries in your particular area. One of the advantages of the latter course of action is that in many cases it is possible to select particular specimens, and one must also bear in mind that locally grown plants are at least acclimatized to prevailing climatic conditions. If it can be arranged it is advisable to plant both trees and shrubs as soon as possible after they arrive from the nursery. If the roots are found to be dry they must be thoroughly soaked with water before planting is attempted, and should there be a delay in planting operations they should be planted close together 'heeled in' in a sheltered shaded position and kept watered. At the time of planting take out a hole that is both wide enough and deep enough to take the roots, on no account must they be cramped. It is important to remember that planting should only take place when the soil conditions are suitable and must never be attempted if the ground is too wet or frozen.

When excavating the hole place the fertile top soil to one side for back fill infertile subsoil must be discarded and replaced with better quality media. If planting is to take place on poor land it is advisable to mix the excavated soil with well decayed humus, or manure on heavy soil add some sharp sand. Where the soil is totally unuseable new earth will have to be obtained. In any case since the tree or shrub will in all probability remain in its new position for many years it is wise to

Above: The brilliant scarlet young growths of the best forms of *Pieris forrestii* are as colorful as many flowers. The white flowers appear at the same time
Right above: 'Royal Red' is one of the best of the *Buddleia davidii* varieties
Right center: *Genista cinerea*, a good broom for dry soils and sunny places
Below: The 'japonica' (Chaenomeles) is one of the most brilliant of spring-flowering shrubs

fork in decayed humus, manure, or peat-moss into the bottom of the hole. Firm planting is essential, bare root specimens should have their roots spread out over the bottom of the hole before being covered with soil and damaged roots must be cut away and matted roots disentangled. Balled and burlaped material should be centered in the hole after which the root covering is carefully removed. Depth of planting is very important and care must be taken not to plant too shallow or too deep. The rule of thumb is to look for the soil mark on the stem which shows the depth at which the

tree or shrub was growing in the nursery, and plant to the same depth. When back-filling replace the soil in 6-in. layers working it between the roots of bare rooted specimens taking care to firm each layer by treading before another is added. After planting operations are completed loosen any compacted soil in the area, and form a depression around each tree or shrub for watering purposes. If there seems no likelihood of immediate rain, evergreens, and deciduous trees and shrubs in leaf must be thoroughly watered. A mulch of coarse grade peatmoss, well rotted manure, leaf mold or other suitable humus will help retain soil moisture and also protect surface roots from the sun in summer or frost in winter.

To protect the trunks of deciduous trees from sun and cold for the season following planting wrap them with burlap or with paper manufactured for the purpose. If a transplanted tree is fairly large and is in danger of falling over or being loosened by wind, it should be supported by staking.

Smaller bare rooted trees need only a single 4–5 ft. stake which should be driven into the hole at the time of planting after which the tree is set in position with its trunk against the stake. Care must be taken when securing the tree that the bark is protected by pieces of burlap where the ties are made. Support is given to balled and burlaped trees by three metal or wooden stakes of the appropriate height which are driven into the ground just outside the area of the root ball in the form of a triangle. The tree is secured to each of the posts with a length of wire stretched horizontally across the gap. A piece of rubber hose should always be used for protection against abrasion where the wire is in contact with the tree.

Finally it must be pointed out that there exists a relationship between the size of the root system and the amount of branches and leaves that a tree will carry. It follows therefore that some careful pruning after planting will help compensate for any damage done to the roots.

Pruning

As to the actual operation of pruning, the main objective is to make as clean a cut as possible, close up to the stem (but not damaging it) so that the bark can gradually spread over and heal the wound. Do not let the piece you are cutting come away and tear bark with it. If the branch you are cutting off is stout and heavy shorten it first to avoid its weight tearing it away then make three cuts in different places. The first cut is made on the underside about a foot from the trunk and extending about one-third of the way through the branch. The limb is then removed by cutting from the top 3–4 in. out from the first cut. Finally the operation is completed by taking off the stump flush with the main trunk. If the wound you leave is large–say an inch or more in diameter, it is well to paint with one of the special proprietary paints, in order to prevent infection, which can quickly take hold particularly in the growing season.

Suckers coming up from the bottom of a tree must always be removed; it is quite possible that they come from the quite different stock on which your tree was grafted or budded.

So much for young trees–except perhaps when two branches have grown together so that they rub, which is undesirable. The least important must be removed, to prevent damage to both trees.

When it comes to dealing with large branches on big trees, it is essential to leave this to a qualified tree surgeon. It needs most careful judgement to effect a good job and can be dangerous to an unskilled operator as well as, perhaps, causing damage to passers-by or neighboring property.

Pruning Shrubs When we come to the pruning of shrubs, to some extent the main principles apply. But the essence of a shrub is its growth which rarely arises from a leader but normally from a cluster of shoots at the base. There is the matter of pruning just to tidy up the shoots when they have become untidy–mere commonsense, bearing in mind that most shrubs send up new shoots naturally from the base.

There are, however, two underlying rules to follow when shrub pruning.

Firstly, some kinds flower mostly on wood that was produced and ripened in the past year; that wood must be retained, cutting out old flowered branches in the spring, usually after the flowering period.

Secondly, a considerable number flower on shoots that have grown during the current year–that is, you cut them hard back early in the spring.

These peculiarities are mentioned in the individual descriptions of shrubs and trees.

The craft of pruning is mostly easily learned by seeing examples of it that have been well done. Today, so often (but not always) this is carried out in local parks and public parks, visits to which are always worth while.

Always use sharp hand shears and well sharpened pruning saws.

The Waste Corner

Many gardens have awkward bits of land, often sloping and dry, perhaps shaded by trees when the sun shines and which drip when it rains. They are spots in which practically none of the ordinary run of garden plants, except a few snowdrops–will thrive.

However, there are several shrubby plants not exciting enough for the garden itself, that will grow quite happily in such places, spreading when once established, and giving quite a lot of interest.

Generally, in such places, all that grows naturally is rough grass. To establish plants, good patches of this are killed by spraying with one of the herbicides. As soon as the grass is killed, this ground is dug over and clumps of the following plants established. As this spot is sure to be dry, water them well until they have taken hold.

A good choice would be the Oregon holly grape, hardy to zone 5. This native of the Pacific Northwest has prickly evergreen leaves which color well in the fall. Its spikes of yellow flowers, opening in earliest spring, are followed by little purple grape-like fruit with a gray bloom. It is a shrub that will grow in poor soils and spreads quickly.

St John's wort, *Hypericum calycinum*, zone 6, is a low growing evergreen shrub that steadily spreads around by means of runners. Because it will thrive anywhere, under any conditions, it has been pushed into waste corners. If it was a new plant, the large yellow flowers which open at about

Basic Pruning Tools

Grecian saw

pruning saw

hand shears

pruning knife

1. Using notched shears to cut through thicker branches. 2. Right and wrong pruning cuts (a) is correct (b) the cut is too slanting and the top bud will be killed (c) the cut is too far away from the top bud and the snag left will die back (d) a ragged cut caused by blunt hand shears (e) the cut is too close to the top bud which will die. 3. A typical branch showing the terminal, lateral and dormant buds. 4. A *Buddleia davidii* in full flower before pruning. 5. The same bush after hard pruning. 6. Light pruning. 7. Harder pruning. 8. A typical tree. The side shoots on the trunk should be cut off as they form and the suckers on the right should be pulled off the roots. 9. Before cutting off a large branch make an undercut with the saw. 10. Then cut off the branch close to the trunk. 11. Failure to make an undercut will result in the branch tearing the bark of the main trunk. 12. Paint the wound with a fungicidal paint to prevent the entry of disease spores.

1

2

a b c d e

terminal

3

lateral

dormant

4

5

midsummer, would cause it to be all the rage.

In wild, rough places, another shrub, the snowberry, *Symphoricarpos albus*, zone 3 (sometimes called *S. racemosa*) will be found. This, an erect growing, slender, suckering, shrub of about 6 ft., is ideal for wasteland. The berries are fleshy, oval and white, ½ in. or so long, with a sparkling crystalline surface. They are a joy to flower arrangers in the fall, and follow the tiny pink flowers in June and July which one usually notices because of the myriads of bees collecting their nectar.

The dwarf *Cotoneaster dammeri* (*humifusa*) zone 5, needs a certain amount of light. This is an evergreen, of dense, twiggy growth with glossy green leaves about ½ in. long; self-sown seedlings often arise. But its value for the garden wasteland is that it lies flat on the ground, its shoots curving to conform with the contours. One plant will very soon cover a square yard and more.

Topiary for the Small Garden

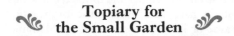

In olden times the cutting of evergreen trees and shrubs into every kind of fanciful shape was an important part of gardening in England. Although topiary is seldom seen in the United States occasionally an individualist will try his skill at clipping privets, yews and other plants into whatever shape takes his fancy. Large-leaved plants should not be used for topiary, instead stay with the old favorites, boxwood, Japanese,

and English yew, and in warmer areas, myrtle and pittosporum are suitable.

It is surely more fun to have the home-made, living frivolities than the many mass-produced plastic vases and bowls.

Traditionally, yew has long been the material from which topiary is usually formed. It long ago replaced the Mediterranean cypress from which the topiary of the ancients was formed for this tree is only hardy in mild parts of the country. The basis for a sizable piece of topiary may well be a mature yew in a garden, for yews will stand the most murderous pruning if it is not all done at once but spread over two or even three years.

Pyramids In this way a sizable tree can first be cut to form a pyramidal shape. A wooden template is easily constructed to press against the tree as a guide for working. Another step can be taken by cutting slices into this pyramid, right back to the trunk, so as to form a series of layers.

Finials Smaller yews can, again with the aid of a semi-circular template, be gradually cut to form balls that rest at the end of close-clipped yew hedges as finials. Or these may stand, as they do at Levens Hall, Westmorland, England, on solid blocks of yew, a simple and very effective design for a small garden.

Corkscrews Most ingenious and perplexing in its origin is the yew corkscrew, also a device suitable for a small garden. It takes the form of a yew spiral, broad at the bottom narrowing to a point at the top. The mystery

of its construction is quite simple. A young upright growing yew is placed beside a stout stake; all the side shoots are cut off or pinched out so that it grows on a single shoot. This shoot is, as it extends, wound spirally round the stake. Every side shoot is removed. So, as it thickens, it becomes rigid; the stake is removed and the center is, like a cork-screw, hollow.

Arches Fanciful topiary arches can be made. They too, are trained to wood frames which are eventually removed as the branches of the yew become rigid. Perfectly simple, rectangular, massive frames for elaborate wrought iron gateways are also very effective. The top consists of two leading shoots trained on a cross bar until they meet and thereafter thicken out.

Figures It is when we come to representation of living creatures–the peacock or the huntsman on his horse, that we become really excited. It is usually the result of some years of work by the owner of the small garden in which such marvels are displayed. A young vigorous yew is trained on bamboo canes. First, a branch is selected to form a bird's tail and two more trained to sticks placed fanwise for the tail. Consistently, all shoots extraneous to the design are pruned away; those that are to take part in it are led onwards as far as they are needed and allowed to thicken as required. The body is allowed to swell and clipped to its final shape.

Topiary work does not in fact take many years to reach completion. Yews, if well fed, grow surprisingly quickly.

6

7

8

feather

suckers

9

10

11

12

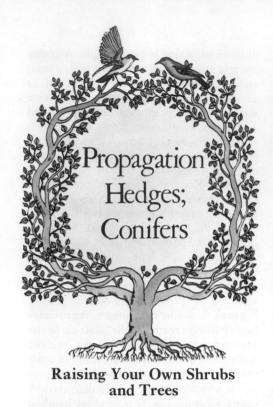

Propagation Hedges; Conifers

Raising Your Own Shrubs and Trees

Shrubs, and more so trees, are amongst the most expensive items in the plant world of the gardener. This is principally because they take much longer to produce than, for example, bedding out plants or perennials. Furthermore, the nurseryman, for commercial reasons, raises only things for which there is a regular popular demand, whereas the gardener may want something, say a tree, that he has seen in a friend's garden which he cannot find in any nurseryman's list or displayed at any garden center.

Propagation by Seed In the fall, the tree may be scattering (and wasting) large numbers of its seeds on the surrounding ground. Why not try raising the tree from seed? The general impression is that it takes too long. Yet, for example, from seed of a fine maple, it is possible to have a specimen 20 ft. tall, in ten years.

Sow the seed in a pot of seed compost, transfer the seedling after a couple of years into a bigger pot and then at about 2 ft. high plant it out in the garden. For the small garden, the Japanese maples are ideal. Lots of seed is usually produced. If you sow some of it, you can expect to get seedlings in two years 2 ft. high, big enough to plant out in a rock garden. A similar plant bought from a nursery may cost $8 to $12.

The usual way of sowing seeds of trees and shrubs is in pans of seed compost, standing them in a shaded cold frame. There is now a more effective way of doing it. You remove the husk or acorn cups, cut off the wings of maple seeds and, as soon as they are ripe, put them in a plastic bag, mixed with damp peatmoss. You then tie the neck of the bag with a bow of thin string. Put the bag in a dark, cool place. When spring comes, at regular intervals, untie the bow, tip the contents, seeds and peatmoss, on to a sheet of newspaper. You may find that some of the seeds have produced a small rootlet. If so, very carefully you put these seeds, with the

rootlet pointing downwards, in a small pot of seed compost, which you water and put in a shady place. You treat it as any seedling and in due course the leaves (with a bit of luck!) will appear. After extracting any seeds which have sprouted, you put the remainder, peatmoss and all (making sure that it is still damp) back into its plastic bag.

This operation can be repeated, going through all the bags say once every two weeks. Great care must be taken not to damage the rootlet.

In due course, those seedlings that grow should be put into large pots as soon as they have filled the smaller pots with roots and eventually planted in a nursery bed until they are big enough to go into their permanent positions. Usually one nearly always raises too many for one's own garden but the surplus is very welcome to friends and for charity sales.

Propagation by Layering Few shrubs are more desirable or more expensive than magnolias. These are quite easily reproduced by layering – as are rhododendrons. As it does little harm to an established plant, you can generally get a friend to let you operate on one that you covet. You choose a low-lying shoot and remove the leaves from its base. You then lightly fork the soil below it, working in some peatmoss. Then scrape away the soil and gently pull down the shoot into the hollow. When it is firmly embedded, you either by means of a stout wire hook driven into the ground or a good heavy stone laid on it, fix the shoot, firmly pressing it into the ground. And firm it must be, for your next operation is to bend the free end upwards as steeply as you can and tie it firmly to a stout stake that has been driven in beside it. Then cover the base of the shoot with peaty soil and press it down firmly.

Next you wait for a season's growth to take place, i.e., for a year after the layering. Then cut through the junction of your layered shoot with the main plant and then, after cutting the ties to the stake, very carefully, with a digging fork, remove the layer, which should have produced roots which must not be broken.

Sometimes the layered plant will have grown bigger and will be so well rooted that it can go into its final place at once. Otherwise it should be planted in a nursery bed and left there for a further year before it is again lifted and planted in its permanent position.

Most shrubs that have low-sweeping branches – particularly, as already mentioned, rhododendrons, can be propagated in this way. In fact, if you look and feel carefully round the base of an old rhododendron bush you may find naturally self-layered pieces which can be carefully cut away, forked up, and planted (preferably in the fall) with plenty of peatmoss worked into the fine root system. Layered plants when put into their final position must be well staked as the fine roots formed are only surface roots.

Propagation by Cuttings A great many trees and shrubs can be quite easily propagated from cuttings. All poplars (*populus*) and all willows (*salix*) grow freely from stout shoots cut in winter when they are dormant. Once the ground where they are to grow permanently has been cleaned and dug, they are driven in and the soil round them firmed, a crowbar or some similar tool being used to make a hole to receive them. They should be firmly staked. The shoots from the lower part of the sett – for this is what these stout cuttings are called – should be cut clean back to the stem. Very considerable branches of the popular weeping willow can be propagated in this way and a substantial tree can be produced in a few years. As a general rule willow cuttings need a moist situation.

Heaths (ericas and callunas) can also be propagated by cuttings quite easily, but in a quite different manner. The short, current year's growths are pulled gently off in August to November and dibbled into sandy soil in pans in a greenhouse propagating frame or in warmer areas in a cold frame. After a period many of them will have made tufts of roots and can be repotted in the following spring.

There is a number of trees the propagation of which is beyond the scope of the amateur unless he is capable of the skilled crafts of budding or grafting. These include apples, pears, cherries, apricots, quinces, medlars, damsons and other members of the rose family. Many of these produce fertile seed which will germinate but they are of hybrid origin and the seedlings will differ from their parent. Very, very rarely a seedling will arise that is better than its parent, but the chances are very much against this happening.

For the same reason, many modern shrubs do not come true from seed, but with the fine, dust-like seed of rhododendrons, which should be sown on a mixture of peatmoss and

Propagating a rhododendron by layering a branch is not a difficult process, although it may be a year before the layered branch has formed sufficient roots for it to be detached from the parent plant and replanted. The

Willows are among the easiest of all trees to root from cuttings. Even quite stout branches will root, if they are removed in winter when the tree is dormant. A suitable branch is shown at (**1**). Cut the branch below a bud (**2**). Then make a hole with a crowbar or similar instrument (**3**) and insert the cutting or 'sett' as it is known, firming the soil round it afterwards. To prevent wind rock, tie the cutting firmly to a stake (**4**)
Right: Berberis thunbergii, a good hedging plant

branch to be layered is bent down to the ground and held in place with a strong wire hook or a heavy stone. The free end of the branch should be tied to a stout stake, driven firmly into the ground beside it

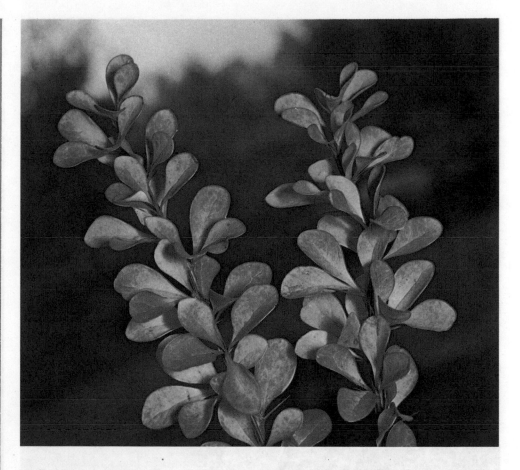

sand and kept carefully watered, there is a chance that something good may arise.

❧ Hedges ❧

Hedges are used to define the limits of property, as a barrier to keep people or animals in or out of a particular area, or as a feature, or to form a background to a particular display.

Nothing gives a more finished, indeed cosy appearance, to a small garden than a hedge, or even hedges–not of any great length or height but placed to give the appearance of an enclosed space making the garden a world of its own.

This is surprisingly easy to do with quite short lengths of hedging rightly placed. Do not in your enthusiasm have too much, as hedge-clipping (unless you have a mechanical trimmer) is tiring work (a good quality pair of shears is a splendid investment).

So many gardeners unfortunately get no further than the indestructible and deadly dull privet. But all sorts of plants, naturally of a variety of sizes and an even greater variety of shape, leaf color and in many instances of flower can be used; some of them are described in the list that follows. Privet (*ligustrum*) is omitted as not being worthy of the space it takes.

There are one or two rules that the hedge planter should learn.

The Site First must be the suitability of the plants used for the site. Most of the usual hedging plants and most of the unusual ones will tolerate a wide range of soil, provided they are well drained. Some are better when lime and chalk is present than others. Near

the seaside plants that will stand the salt-laden gales and protect the choicer plants that they shield are essential; several of these will not stand the harder frosts of inland districts.

When deciding to plant a hedge, apart from considering its position from the point of view of appearance, remember that a hedge has to be cut on two sides and make sure you are going to leave plenty of room on both sides, not only the one you will be looking at, to give easy access for this clipping.

Hedging plants are like other garden plants: the better their soil conditions the better they grow.

Planting A strip about a yard wide should be marked out where the plants are to grow and should be dug–it is a good idea to work in some compost.

A line should be stretched down the center and the young trees planted carefully against it. If the hedge is out of alignment it will take a lot of hiding later.

Except in really wet weather, always keep the young hedge well watered until it is established. The use of a mulch is a valuable help to the young trees.

Clipping Then, an important rule about clipping; always trim a hedge so that the bottom is wider than the top, that is, so that it tapers slightly from the base to the apex.

To ensure that a thick, well balanced hedge results, deciduous material should be cut down to within a foot of the ground after planting. Evergreens should not be treated in this drastic fashion but be allowed to reach their final height before pruning.

The planting distances given below are

approximate only; if the plants are a little wider apart, they will probably fill up in due course.

No suggestion is given of the height of the plants you should buy. Tell your nurseryman the purpose for which you will require them and remember that small plants will soon catch up the bigger and more expensive ones.

Old Favorites

Hawthorn (*Crataegus oxyacantha*) zone 4, is very popular in Europe. The shoots are stout and springy, and it is still unsurpassed for a boundary. It should be planted close, about 1 ft. apart. Winter is the usual time for pruning.

Beech The English beech (*Fagus sylvatica*) zone 4, is one of the most attractive and decorative of hedging plants. Happy on any kind of soil, including soil containing lime, provided it is well drained, it is a fresh green through the late spring and summer. Then in the fall the leaves turn russet color and hang on until May when the fresh new leaves break and push them off. If the young trees are planted about 1½–2 ft. apart, a good hedge soon results. The best time to clip the hedge is in summer when the leaves are fully unfolded. It can be clipped very hard and close so as to make, if so desired, a very narrow hedge, the growth being so twiggy that it becomes very dense.

To make a vari-colored beech hedge, seedlings of the copper and purple kinds may be mixed at random with the normal form.

Hornbeam Rather similar and particularly good on chalk soils, is European hornbeam (*Carpinus betulus*) zone 5.

Yew Both the English yew (*Taxus baccata*) zone 6, and the Japanese yew (*Taxus cuspidata*) zone 4, are widely used hedging plants, but seldom used as a purely protective hedge for outer boundaries but as an internal, formal division, the somber green making a fine background for flowers.

Young plants should be set about 2 ft. apart in October or April and during dry weather in spring watered freely. It is particularly important not to cut the leading shoot until it has reached the final required height. The sides should be clipped back hard on a slight slope so that the base of the hedge is broader than the top. Pruning can be done after the spring growth has finished.

Yew can be poisonous to animals, particularly the prunings, which should never be thrown where stock can get at them.

Box Another old favorite for evergreen hedges was box (*Buxus sempervirens*) zone 5. This is not an ideal material; it is subject to disease and has a wide-spreading, greedy root system. This is not the same as the dwarf kind, *B. sempervirens suffruticosa* used for edging, which must be placed close. The roots of this also rob the beds which it surrounds. Shrubs such as lavender are better.

Some Newer Kinds

The following are of comparatively recent introduction and are also suitable for hedges, particularly those that are informal.

Berberis Several of these prickly shrubs are quite often used for hedging. *B. stenophylla*, zone 5, and *B. thunbergii*, zone 4, are generally recommended. Neither stand pruning and in time become thin at the base.

Cotoneaster Various species are particularly useful as informal, decorative hedges that need no more than trimming to keep them tidy. All carry red or orange berries, eventually enjoyed by birds. *C. simonsii*, zone 5, is a semi-evergreen of close, erect growth which if pruned hard in spring will eventually form a quite rigid hedge some 5 ft. tall. As a contrast the evergreen *C. franchettii*, zone 6, is of close, bushy growth with arching branches which can be lightly pruned to keep it at about 7 or 8 ft. The leaves are green above, gray below. Both may be planted about 2 ft. apart.

Euonymus *E. japonica*, zone 7, is an evergreen shrub with glossy leaves, reaching about 10 or 12 ft., which is a valuable and fairly common hedging plant useful for seaside planting where it withstands the salt-laden gales. Plant at about 18 in.

Griselinia The large, leathery, evergreen leaves of *G. littoralis*, zone 7, can stand strong winds and salt spray but the shrub is hardy only in mild districts. It is often used for hedges, when plants are set about 3 ft. apart. It will grow about 8 ft. tall and needs little pruning. It will grow on soils containing lime.

Lavandula The gray-leaved, fragrant lavender, *L. officinalis*, zone 5, has for centuries been used as a low hedge reaching

Far left: Lonicera nitida makes a bright, colorful hedge.

Left: The golden-leaved form of Lawson's cypress, *Chamaecyparis lawsoniana lutea,* is sometimes used for making a tall screen.

Above: 'Tapestry' hedges are both colorful and interesting: this one is made up of *Prunus pissardii (P. cerasifera atropurpurea)* 'Purple Flash' and *Prunus cerasifera* 'Green Glow'.

Right: An example of a 'battlemented' yew hedge at Knightshayes Court, Devon, England.

Bottom: Although not an ideal hedging plant, the box (*Buxus sempervirens*) is readily clipped to shape

3 ft. It must have sun, likes lime and should be kept lightly clipped. It will grow by the sea. Plant 18 in. apart.

Lonicera *L. nitida,* zone 7, a very small-leaved evergreen honeysuckle (though no one would guess its relationship to the honeysuckle of our hedgerows), is quick growing and suitable for low hedges. It should be planted about 1 ft. apart and cut back hard afterwards. It needs good soil. It may be damaged in severe weather. Prune in summer at fairly frequent intervals.

Rosmarinus Rosemary (*R. officinalis*) zone 6, is another famous old garden plant which stands clipping well, September being the best month. It will grow well on lime and by the seaside. Treat it in the same way as lavender (Lavandula), setting plants about 18 in. apart and keeping them lightly clipped.

❧ Evergreen Conifers ❧

Chamaecyparis *C. lawsoniana,* zone 5 The well-known Lawson's cypress, is sometimes advised for evergreen hedges or taller screens, but is not ideal. Young plants must be used, as larger specimens may at first be rocked by wind. It does not like very rich ground. This particular evergreen prefers a mild moist climate and will only thrive in certain areas. Plant about 4½ ft. apart.

Cupressocyparis The Leyland cypress, *C. leylandii,* zone 6, is a splendid and adaptable tree. It is often recommended for hedges, but its rate of growth is so rapid that it will need cutting twice or more in a year, the last time in the fall. It is ideally suited for screens and windbreaks. Set the plants out 4–5 ft. apart.

Cupressus The Monterey cypress, *C. macrocarpa,* zone 7, has often been planted for hedges in the mildest districts. On all soils it is good. But even so, a particularly hard winter will kill isolated plants in a well established hedge, so destroying its previous regular appearance.

Thuya *T. plicata,* zone 5, the giant arbor-vitae, in its native habitat, is a large western American forest tree. However, it stands clipping extremely well and is a hedge plant of great merit with glossy-green fragrant leaves in fern-like sprays. Plants should be set out at about 4½ ft. apart.

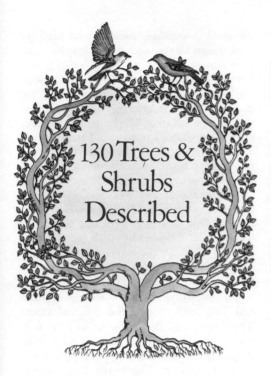

130 Trees & Shrubs Described

The following key letters will help you to pick out the different types.

D Deciduous
E Evergreen
F Valuable for decorative foliage
FL Valuable for decorative flowers
FR Valuable for decorative fruit
H High growing
L Low growing
M Medium growing
NL Will not grow on soils containing lime
S Shrub
T Tree

Omitted from the list are some highly popular trees which are unfortunately far too often planted in small gardens. Seen as attractive young nursery stock, they will, alas, in a few years occupy so much space that they will have to be removed. For instance, a common weeping willow, 3 ft. in diameter when planted, will cover a circle 18 ft. in diameter in 10 years. Conifers are described in a later section of this work.

Acer Of the shrubby maples, *A. palmatum* (S.M.F.) zone 3, the Japanese maple, with lobed leaves, is very decorative. It forms a low, rounded bush which after many years grows into a small tree. The form 'Atropurpureum' with purplish-bronze leaves is the most effective. Like all the *palmatum* maples, it does better in some shade and shelter from wind.

Amelanchier The shadblow or serviceberry, *A. lamarckii*, zone 4, (D.FL.M.) (sometimes cataloged as *A. laevis* and *A. canadensis*) can be grown as a large round bush or small tree from 20 ft. to 30 ft. tall, and eventually about the same across. It is densely covered with spikes of small white, scented flowers in spring which appear among the bronzy pink opening leaves. The fall color of the leaves is also good. It

will grow on any well-drained soil.

Arbutus The strawberry tree, *A. unedo*, zone 4 (S.E.FL.FR.) is a slow-growing evergreen shrub, or eventually a tree, with leathery, deep green leaves. The flowers, rather like those of lily-of-the-valley, appear in late summer and fall at the same time as the round fruit produced from the previous year's flowers ripen and turn scarlet. It is good in stony districts near the seaside and is happy on soil containing lime.

Berberis Of the many berberries, *B. stenophylla*, zone 5 (E.FL.S.H.) is one of the best. The dense, arching slender stems, up to 10 ft. tall, are covered with small orange flowers in April–May. It is excellent for tall, informal hedges. Prune in winter, only to restrict size as required.

Betula Several native birches (D.H.T.) with their white trunks and fine twiggy growth, are suitable for moderately sized gardens, particularly if grown in grass. If set in flower beds their greedy roots take the nature out of the soil. The weeping birch, *B. pendula youngii*, zone 2, with shoots that fall vertically, is one of the best weeping trees, slowly reaching about 20 ft. high. It needs careful pruning when in leaf, only to ensure a good shape.

Buddleia *B. davidii* (D.FL.S), zone 5, grows to 10 ft. tall and the long spikes of small, sweetly scented flowers attract butterflies during July and August. The long shoots should be cut hard back in early spring to encourage the production of new, flowering shoots. They are cultivars with purple, violet, pink and white flowers.

Calluna (E.L.NL.) zone 4   The Scottish heathers or lings (see also *Erica*) are varieties of the wild plant with mostly purple, pink and white flowers. There are many kinds, often grown with ericas to form heath gardens. Callunas must have light sandy soil without lime, to thrive, and benefit from leaf-mold or peatmoss worked in around their roots at planting time. Shear them over lightly in April to maintain a close, tufty growth, otherwise they tend to sprawl. They should always be obtained in and planted from pots. Foliage color varies from gold to deep green.

Camellia (E.F.FL.M.NL.)   The difficulty of growing these choice shrubs with rich glossy green foliage and ornate flowers in spring is often exaggerated. Many are not easy, but 'C. M. Hovey', zone 7, can be grown in most gardens on lime-free soil, giving a good crop of its semi-double pink flowers from March to April. Some shade is needed and protection from wind. Plenty of leaf-mold or peatmoss should be placed around the roots, and in very dry weather the shrubs should be watered. The only pruning needed is to keep the bush to a good shape. Camellias make very good house shrubs if grown in pots. The soil should have plenty of peatmoss mixed with it and at all times be kept well watered. During the winter months and while flowering they can be left in the house and later stand in a shady spot in the garden.

Caryopteris *C. clandonensis*, zone 5 (D.FL.L.), the blue spiraea, is a shrub with attractive gray foliage, which carries masses of small blue flowers from September onwards. It does well on light, sandy soils. Cut the bushes back hard in April, when growth is just beginning.

Ceanothus A group of shrubs, some evergreen and others deciduous. Many are liable to damage or may be killed in severe winters and so are often grown against walls. The hardiest and most reliable is 'Gloire de Versailles', zone 7 (S.D.M.FL.). This bears many clusters of powder-blue flowers in late summer. In about April all the shoots that flowered the previous year should be cut out to their base. It will usually grow well in the open, but is splendid when trained against a wall, where it may eventually reach 10 ft. The evergreen kinds, which flower in spring or early summer, need little pruning.

Chaenomeles zone 4. This is the shrub well known as 'japonica'. Of the various kinds, one of the best is 'Knap Hill Scarlet' (D.S.FL.L.), noted for its brilliant flowers in March and April. Other named kinds have white, pink and double flowers. All like a sunny position and do well in any fertile soil and on chalk. Pruning, after flowering, consists in thinning out some of the long, slender shoots to provide a framework of branches, and shortening the side-shoots on those that are left to leave two or three buds to provide flowering 'spurs'. The quince-like fruits that are sometimes formed may be left on until they ripen and made into jelly.

Choisya (S.M.F.FL.), the Mexican orange, *C. ternata*, zone 7, is an evergreen, rounded shrub reaching 6 ft. or more. The 5-petalled white flowers, sweetly scented like hawthorn, about 1 in. in diameter, are produced freely in spring and occasionally at other times. It is occasionally damaged by unseasonable frosts but is often unharmed in severe cold winters.

Cistus (E.FL.M.S.)   The rock roses are sun-loving shrubs, about 3 ft. tall, flowering in June or July, thriving on soil containing lime and not always hardy. The flowers are numerous, mostly white or pink, with golden stamens; the leaves of some kinds glossy green and sometimes sticky, while others have soft gray foliage. Most are easily raised from seed. Prune only to remove dead branches.

Self-sown seedlings often appear and are best left where they arise. One of the strong-

Cistus, the sun rose

Left: One of the forms of the Japanese maple, *Acer palmatum*

Above: One of the best of all small, slow-growing trees, *Acer pseudoplatanus brilliantissimum* has pinkish leaves in spring
Right: Erica carnea, a winter-flowering heather, is one of the few which will thrive on soils containing chalk or lime. 'Springwood Pink' is one of its varieties
Below: The beautiful pink and white blooms of a Deutzia, flowering in early summer
Far right: Eucryphia nymansensis makes an upright tree with beautiful white flowers in late summer

est is *C. laurifolius*, zone 7, with leathery dark green leaves, and white flowers up to 4 in. across.

Cornus (D.F.FL.M.S. and T.) The dogwoods are of two distinct kinds, those that are shrubby with decorative twigs and those that form small trees. Of the former, *C. alba*, zone 2, produces a mass of red stems, up to 9 ft. tall, very striking in winter. It thrives in wet or dry positions, and should be hard pruned in alternate years in March.

Of the small trees *Cornus mas*, zone 4, the cornelian cherry, is densely covered with small yellow flowers in February before the leaves open, followed by small red fruit; its form 'Variegata', the leaves margined with white, is attractive. It needs little pruning.

Cotinus (D.F.FL.M.S.) The smoke trees are large, sprawling shrubs flowering in June and July and giving good fall leaf color. They grow and flower better in poor soil, need little pruning, and grow 8–12 ft. tall. Probably the best is *C. coggygria* (syn. *Rhus cotinus*), zone 5. The many large flower spikes are pinkish, turning smoky gray later.

Cotoneaster This genus provides a wide range of shrubs of varying sizes and forms, notable for their berries which follow very numerous small white flowers. They are adaptable for all soils and situations. Two contrasting kinds are *C. franchetii* (E.FR.L.S.M.) zone 6, and *C. horizontalis* (D.FR.L.S.) zone 4. The former has arching sprays up to 8 ft. tall and makes a fairly wide bush with grayish-green leaves and brilliant red berries in the fall. The latter, a close-growing, spreading shrub with herringbone twigs and small leaves, usually grows pressed against the ground or a wall, with small green leaves which color well in the fall, and bright red berries.

Crataegus The common white hawthorn (*C. monogyna*) zone 4 and the red hawthorn (*C. oxyacantha* 'Coccinea Plena', zone 4) the double red may, are common throughout the British Isles. One of the best small garden thorn trees is the plum-leaved thorn, *C. prunifolia* (D.FL.FR.N.T.) zone 4. This has a broad rounded head, its leaves turn brilliant crimson in the fall. The flowers, larger than and the scarlet haws likewise are much larger. It needs pruning only to keep it in shape.

Cytisus The brooms are deciduous shrubs, mostly with insignificant leaves on slender stems, with pea-like flowers. All need full sun and thrive on light or peaty soils, growing well with heaths. Prune back the shoots that have flowered by about two-thirds after the blossoms fade—or they can be left unpruned if tall, leggy bushes are not objected to. The several kinds, some low and spreading, are excellent for furnishing a new garden. *C. albus*, zone 5, the white Portugal broom (D.FL.M.S.) with white flowers in May on arching 7 ft. sprays of gray-green foliage, is good. *C. praecox*, zone 5, which blooms earlier, on 6 ft. shoots with deep yellow and cream flowers, is another well tried and popular variety.

Daphne *D. mezereum* (D.FL.L.S.) zone 4, with small pink flowers is grown for its strong, sweet scent in earliest spring. The flowers are followed by red berries in summer. It likes some shade in summer and moist but well-drained soil. Several other kinds are attractive, but are often difficult to grow. Do not prune.

Deutzia (D.FL.M.S.) These are easy to grow and reliable on all but the poorest soils. The numerous small pink and white flowers are produced on young plants from May to June. The heights range from 5–7 ft. Cut out a proportion of the shoots after they have flowered. One of the best is *D. elegantissima*, zone 5, with deep rose flowers in May or June, on arching shoots reaching 6–7 ft.

Elaeagnus (E.F.M.S.) These valuable and hardy shrubs, eventually reaching 10–12 ft., have insignificant but scented flowers and handsome leathery leaves. They will grow in windy situations and beside the sea. No pruning is needed unless it is necessary to reduce their size, when it can be done in spring. *E. pungens maculata*, zone 7, with leaves splashed with gold is one of the finest of all variegated shrubs, less tall and more spreading than other kinds. Shoots that revert to green should be cut out.

Enkianthus (D.FL.M.NL.S.) Related to the heaths, *E. campanulatus*, zone 4, an erect-growing shrub will thrive on any lime-free soil, reaching 6 or 7 ft. In May it carries masses of hanging, small bell-shaped cream flowers with red veins. In the fall the leaves turn fiery red. No pruning is needed.

Erica There are many species and almost countless garden forms of the heaths. All like open situations and do best in lighter soils. They may be clipped over after flowering. Kinds can be had to flower in almost every month of the year. Some will grow on light,

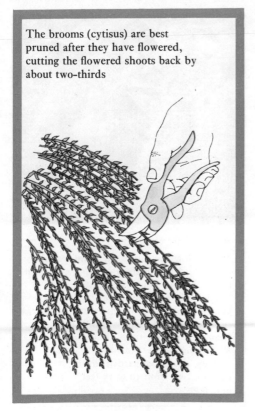

The brooms (cytisus) are best pruned after they have flowered, cutting the flowered shoots back by about two-thirds

acid soil only, while a few others will grow where lime is present.

The principal species, of which well-known variants are cultivated, are: *E. carnea* (E.FL.L.S.), zone 5, lime tolerant, flowering from early winter to early spring. The colors range from white through pink to purple; *E. cinerea* (E.L.NL.S.), zone 5, the twisted heath with flowers mostly ranging from white through pink to purple, from June to September.

The numerous forms of these will be more than adequate for most gardens and will provide color throughout the year. Those who wish to make a heath garden, will find that many other kinds are available.

Escallonia These close-growing, bushy small-leaved shrubs, often with arching branches, bear numerous small flowers, from white through pink to crimson over a long period, but at their best in June and July. They are most useful as isolated plants or as free-growing hedges in any type of soil and will thrive in windy conditions. Prune by shortening the flowered branches in July or allow them to make sizable bushes up to 7 ft. or so and prune only to give the requisite size. 'Apple Blossom' (E.FL.L.S.) zone 7, with pink flowers is one of the best.

Eucryphia (E.FL.H.NL.S.) zone 8. Tall, narrow growing shrubs or small trees, these have large white flowers, with central bosses of golden stamens, in late summer. They like fertile, fairly moist soil and some shelter. The most striking is 'Nymansay', flowering in August and September.

Euonymus Of the numerous kinds some carry the scarlet, fleshy fruit from which, when they ripen, the orange seeds dangle. Of these, the European spindle tree (*E. europaeus*) zone 3, is well known in hedgerows in England, particularly on soils containing lime, a fine form, 'Red Cascade' (D.FR.M.S.), about 8 ft., is well worth a place in any garden on account of its heavy fruiting on the arching branches. In contrast, the richly gold and silver-leaved (with some red in winter) *E. fortunei variegata* (E.FL.S.) zone 5, will grow flat against a rock or a wall and make a striking sheet of color throughout the year. It bears no berries.

Forsythia (D.FL.M.S.) This invaluable shrub, with its mass of bright yellow flowers in March and April, prefers sun, and will thrive on any reasonable soil. In some districts birds destroy the flower buds; black thread intertwined in the bush or one of the proprietary bird repellents may do good. Cut out a few of the oldest branches after they have flowered. The best form is *F. intermedia* 'Lynwood', zone 4, reaching about 5–6 ft. *F. suspensa*, zone 5, has paler flowers but a lax drooping branching system which enables it to be trained against screens or walls where it will grow much taller.

Fuchsia The genus includes many shrubs, a few quite hardy. The most reliable out of doors is *F. magellanica riccartonii* (D.S.M.FL.) zone 5, erect growing, to 4 ft., which carries scarlet and purple flowers from June to October. Plant so that the point from which the buds arise is 1–2 in. below the surface. In late spring cut back shoots now showing bud to near ground level.

Garrya *G. elliptica* (E.S.M.FL.) zone 8, should be planted in any soil, in a sheltered spot to protect the jade colored catkins borne in trails up to 9 in. long over a long period in winter. These are valuable for flower arranging. Prune after flowering only to shape the plant.

Genista (D.S.M. to L.FL.) The brooms are attractive, floriferous yellow-flowered shrubs which thrive in light soils even when lime is present. Many are quick growing and for their first two years staking and cutting back will help to get them firmly established; this does not apply to dwarf kinds such as *G. pilosa*, zone 5. One of the best for display is *G. cinerea*, zone 7, 6–10 ft., with masses of sweetly scented golden-yellow flowers in June and July.

Hamamelis The Chinese witch hazel is *H. mollis* (D.FL.M.S.) zone 5, one of the most delightful of winter flowering shrubs with many yellow flowers consisting of narrow, twisted petals, set in a crimson cup and scented like cowslips. These open from December to February on the bare shoots. The leaves color a good yellow in the fall. The bushes, up to about 10 ft. high, need no pruning other than to keep them shapely.

Hebe These shrubs (E.FL.L.S.) zones 7–9, known as shrubby veronicas and still sometimes listed under *Veronica*, will grow in any conditions, provided the situation is open, sunny and not wet. The small flowers range from white through violets and lavenders to purple. Clip the shrubs back in spring to keep them compact and tidy. One of the best is 'Autumn Glory', violet, flowering from June to August.

Hydrangea (D.FL.M.S.) All hydrangeas like rich, fairly moist but well-drained soil, and prefer light shade. Though ideal for pots and greenhouse culture, or in tubs, most are quite hardy. In general, blue kinds will only come true to that color in acid soil or when watered with a special blueing mixture. The pink and red kinds do best on slightly alkaline soil.

In the most popular kinds of cultivated hydrangeas, the 'Hortensia' varieties, zones 5–6, only showy infertile flowers are present, built up into globular large heads. There is a wide range of colors and sizes.

In the lace-cap hydrangeas the flower head is flat, with an outer ring of false petals at the center of which are small florets. One of the best and hardiest is 'Blue Wave', 4 ft. or 5 ft., the outer ring pink on soils where any lime is present, rich blue on acid soils. The central florets are always purplish blue.

Hypericum *H. calycinum* (D.FL.L.S.) Zone 6, St John's wort, a low, rapidly spreading shrub with yellow flowers at mid-summer is invaluable for carpeting dry shady situa- tions. The best decorative St John's wort is *H. patulum* 'Hidcote', zone 6, reaching 5 ft., bearing golden saucer-shaped flowers in August; this needs full sun. Cut hard back in early spring.

Kalmia The mountain laurel, *K. latifolia* (E.FL.M.NL.S.) zone 4, thrives in conditions suitable for rhododendrons. It slowly reaches 6 ft. and bears prettily shaped small pink flowers in June. No pruning is needed.

Kerria *K. japonica pleniflora* (D.FL.M.S.) zone 4, has a large number of small yellow pompon-like flowers carried on the slender, arching, bright green stems in spring and early summer. It will grow in most soils and situations and needs pruning only to train it.

Laburnum (D.FL.M.T.) This well-known tree often called golden chain, tolerant of most conditions, is grown for its small, golden pea-shaped flowers hanging in long chains during May and June. It can be grown as a bush or a standard and needs only the minimum of pruning to shape it. By far the best kind for gardens is the hybrid *L. vossii*, zone 5, with very long trails of flowers.

Lavandula (E.FF.FL.L.S.) The lavender, fragrant in all its parts, can be grown as a dwarf hedge or individually. Some give the name to the color lavender, others are shades of blue, purple, pink, or white. Heights range from 1–2 ft.; they flower in July. All need full sun and thrive in poor, light soil and like lime. Clip them over in the fall to remove the old flower spikes and again in spring for the sake of tidiness, but the old wood should not be cut. One of the best is *L. officinalis*, zone 5, with purple-blue flowers.

Leycesteria The Formosa honeysuckle, *L. formosa* (D.FL.M.S.) zone 7, will reach 5–6 ft. in almost any position or soil and is

Left: Belonging to the same family as the rhododendrons, *Kalmia latifolia*, mountain laurel, needs a lime-free, peaty soil
Above: The shrubby veronicas, correctly known as hebes, flower over long periods in summer and fall. This is 'Midsummer Beauty' with long trails of flowers
Right: Cotoneaster glabrata, a hardy, evergreen garden shrub which grows from 10 to 15 feet in height

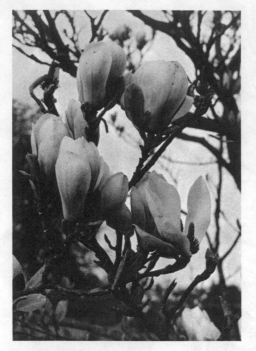

notable for its bright green stems from which hang reddish-purple leafy catkin-like growths containing small, pale pink flowers in late summer and fall. Cut out a few of the oldest stems in early spring.

Lonicera The winter flowering honeysuckle, *L. purpusii* (D.FL.M.S.) zone 5, is valuable for its scent and use in flower arrangements. In a sunny sheltered spot, the bare arching branches 6–7 ft. tall, are covered with creamy white flowers in early spring.

Magnolia All magnolias do best in moist, slightly acid soils, though many will do well when some lime is present. All prefer sunny, sheltered positions but several are tough and extremely hardy. All have fleshy roots and are best planted just before growth begins in spring, using plenty of peatmoss around the roots and watering well and staking firmly until they are established. The most reliable for a small garden is *M. soulangeana* (D.FL.M.S.) zone 5. This bears large, white-cup-shaped flowers with claret colored bases, from April to May; a pure white form ('Alba') and one with purplish flowers ('Rubra') are available. All have spreading, stout branching systems. They will flower when 3 ft. or so high and under ideal conditions will become small trees. Little pruning other than to shape the bushes is needed. None likes root disturbance – e.g. the forking of ground underneath them.

M. stellata, zone 5, is the smallest magnolia; it forms a compact shrub with very numerous white many-petalled flowers about 3 in. across in March and April. It is suitable for the smallest garden.

Mahonia The Oregon holly grape, *M. aquifolium*, zone 5, 3 ft. tall, with prickly leaves and small yellow flowers followed by small purple berries, is used effectively as a dense, decorative evergreen carpet under trees.

M. japonica (E.F.FL.M.S.) zone 7, is similar but on a much more magnificent scale with long, drooping spikes of small lemon-yellow flowers with the scent of lilies-of-the-valley, and is one of the finest late winter flowering shrubs. In a sheltered corner it may reach 5 ft., and will thrive in any reasonably good soil. Prune only to shape it.

Malus Crab apples are amongst the most beautiful of flowering trees, many producing highly decorative fruit that may be used to make jelly or preserves. A good variety for small gardens, 'Red Jade', has pendulous branches which are covered with white blossoms in spring, followed by red fruits which remain long after the leaves have fallen.

Another beautiful crab apple, 'Dorothea', which originated in the Arnold Arboretum, Boston, produces double pink flowers and quantities of yellow apples in the fall.

Olearia The daisy bush, *O. haastii* (E.FL.M.S.) zone 9, is a rounded evergreen with small, leathery leaves, sometimes reaching 6 ft., which is covered with small white daisies in July and August. It will stand seaside gales and town conditions; sometimes used as a hedge, it needs no pruning.

Osmanthus *O. delavayi* (E.FL.M.S.) zone 7, makes a most attractive rounded plant reaching 6 or 7 ft., with small, neat glossy leaves, that is thickly covered with small, sweetly scented white flowers over a long period in April. It is not particular about soil or situation and need not be pruned unless to keep it small, when shearing over flowering does little to prevent subsequent bloom.

Parrotia *P. persica* (D.F.FL.M.NL.T.) zone 5, is a small tree, eventually reaching 20 ft., of slender, open growth. In February and March the bare twigs may be covered with flowers in which the tassel-like clusters of anthers are crimson. In the fall the leaves turn a mixture of pinks, crimson, gold and orange. As the tree ages the bark becomes boldly marked like that of a London plane. It is at its best in a sunny, sheltered spot on lime-free soil.

Philadelphus Zone 4–6. This is commonly called mock orange and sometimes incorrectly syringa (which is the lilac) (D.S.M. FL.). Most kinds have stout, erect or arching shoots, covered with usually white, strongly scented flowers in June and July. All will thrive in any normal soils. Prune some of the oldest shoots from the base when flowering is over, which should be done annually when bushes are established. 'Frosty Morn' is very hardy, with fragrant double blossoms. 'Virginal' is a vigorous, erect growing form with white double flowers. There are many others.

Pieris (E.S.M.NL.F.FL.) These evergreen shrubs must have acid soils. Their attractive flowers, borne in April and May, are like small lilies-of-the-valley, but the main feature is the brilliant scarlet young foliage. 'Flame-of-the-Forest', zone 7, is among the hardiest and most showy, the leaves passing from flame color through pinks and cream to green. It will reach about 7 ft. and needs no pruning to maintain its shape.

Potentilla (D.S.L.FL.) Zone 2. The shrubby cinquefoils are most useful shrubs. Their brightly colored flowers like small single roses, in shades of yellow and white appear over a long period. They are tolerant of position and soil as long as drainage is good. In March some of the oldest twigs should be cut away at the base. *P. beesii*, 1½ ft., has silver leaves and buttercup yellow flowers from late summer to fall; 'Tangerine', 1½ ft., has yellowish-red flowers in late summer; 'Mandschurica', also dwarf, has gray leaves and white flowers.

Prunus (D.T.M.FL.) Under this name botanists and so, alas, nurserymen have to include trees and shrubs which the innocent gardener considers, particularly on examining their fruit, to be quite different. These are in alphabetical order: almonds, apricots, bird cherries, cherries (including the wealth of Japanese kinds), laurels (not included here) and peaches.

All like open, well-drained situations with plenty of sun and, except where stated, lime in the soil. The minimum of pruning is desirable. This should be done about midsummer or just after, otherwise the trees will 'bleed' their gum-like sap so that the wounds will not heal and fungal diseases may enter.

ALMOND *P. dulcis* (*amygdalus*) zone 6, is a small, rather gauntly branched tree, with large pink flowers on the bare stems in March or April. The large fruit with its downy skin does not contain edible almonds.

APRICOT *P. armeniaca*, zone 5, the kind usually grown for garden ornament, is a small tree opening its thickly clustered carmine buds in March and April to show the pink flowers. This does not produce fruit.

BIRD CHERRY *P. padus*, zone 3, is a medium-sized tree with narrow spikes, 5 in. or more long, of small white almond scented flowers

Left: One of the most reliable of all the beautiful magnolias for the small garden is *M. soulangeana*, of which various color forms are available
Above: 'Blue Diamond', a dwarf rhododendron, suitable for the larger rock garden or the front of a border
Right: One of the tall-growing hybrid rhododendrons derived from *R. fortunei*
Far left: Magnolia × soulangeana 'Norbertii', a beautiful variety of the flowering magnolia trees

in May after the leaves open. Small black berries follow.

ORNAMENTAL CHERRIES (including the Japanese kinds of which there are many); none normally produces fruit. A representative selection would include:

The variety 'Shirotae', zone 5, is a highly valued variety, with masses of white semi-double flowers, noted for its hardiness.

'Amanogawa', zone 6, is a tightly erect-growing Japanese cherry of narrow outline, like a dwarf Lombardy poplar. It has semi-double pale pink flowers in April or May. A little pruning to remove spreading branches may be necessary. It will occasionally and very slowly reach 20 ft.

P. avium 'Plena', zone 3, is a form of our native cherry making a handsome specimen larger than the Japanese cherries, which in mid-May is heavily laden with double white, long-lasting flowers. In the fall the leaves often turn crimson.

'Kanzan', zone 5, is the most popular and reliable of pink-flowered Japanese cherries.

When young the branches are stiffly erect but later spread. The large, purplish-pink double flowers open in April–May. The unfolding leaves are somewhat copper-colored; before falling, they turn a dull yellow.

P. sargentii, zone 4, is a round-headed tree. The opening leaves are bronzy-red, the flowers in March are single, pink in color and not as showy as in many kinds. Its principal feature is the brilliant red coloring of the leaves in the fall, often as early as September, and long-lasting.

'Tai-haku', zone 5, is a vigorous Japanese cherry notable for its very large dazzling white flowers opening among the copper colored young leaves in April–May. In the fall the leaves hang on late into the fall turning yellow and vermilion.

Pyracantha (E.S.M.FL.FR.) The firethorns are valuable thorny shrubs, with narrow evergreen leaves and hawthorn-like flowers in June, followed by red or yellow berries. They will thrive in any type of soil or situation including shade, and are thus often used for training against shady walls. They may be reduced in size by pruning when the berries are set, leaving untouched as many berry bearing shoots as possible. *P. atalantoides*, zone 6, has scarlet berries; its form 'Aurea' has yellow fruit. *P. coccinea lalardii*, zone 6, is of vigorous, rather erect growth, with orange-red berries.

Pyrus The orchard pears are large and beautiful trees but the kind most suited to gardens is the weeping willow-leaved pear *P. salicifolia* 'Pendula' (D.T.H.F.FL.) zone 4. A broad spreading tree, it reaches 25 ft. or more. The leaves are narrow, silvery green in color and quite unlike those of an ordinary pear. The clusters of small creamy-white flowers which open in late March or early April, have prominent crimson anthers. The fruit is insignificant. The only pruning needed is to keep the tree shapely. This can be done in winter.

Rhododendron (E.D.M.NL.FL.) In many modern catalogs, under this name (according to botanical rules) are included what we usually call azaleas (which are often, but not always, deciduous). Those we have long known as rhododendrons are evergreens.

None will tolerate lime and prefer sandy and peaty soils. Many appreciate some shade and in general all dislike drought, particularly the evergreen kinds. All prefer protection from strong winds.

The roots are fine and fibrous, and naturally form balls, making them easy to plant and transplant. Plenty of peatmoss should worked in round this ball when planting, and the young plants should be well soaked. If, when planted, the bush shows a tendency to rock, it should be tied to a stake for a year or so.

One of the best azaleas is *R. luteum* (*Azalea pontica*) zone 5, a medium sized shrub covered with very sweetly scented yellow flowers in mid-May, the leaves turning a rich red in the fall. Smaller growing, with a much wider variation in color, are the Mollis hybrids, zone 5, and the Exbury, zone 6, and Ghent, zone 4, hybrids, usually flowering in May and also giving good fall leaf color. There are also the much smaller evergreen Japanese azaleas, mostly in pinks and reds and some white, opening from April to June. All these of the azalea group are suitable for moderate and small gardens.

The true rhododendrons are even more numerous and vary in size from trees to little shrubs. The common *R. ponticum*, zone 6 (not to be confused with the so-called *Azalea pontica* mentioned above), is a large shrub with mauve to pink flowers. It is very common and is naturalized in places: there are many better kinds for gardens. A few well-known and reliable kinds are 'Pink Pearl', zone 7, large rose-pink flowers, April–May; 'Fastuosum flore-pleno', zone 6, semi-

Above left: Santolina chamaecyparissus 'Neopolitana', is grown for its finely divided foliage and its yellow, button-like flower heads
Above right: Sorbus pohuashanensis is a Chinese mountain ash with very large clusters of scarlet fruits. It is one of the best of this group for the smaller garden
Below: The pink flowers of the evergreen *Skimmia japonica* are followed by bright crimson berries

double flowers of an unusual bluish-mauve color, May–June; 'Cynthia', zone 6, deep rose with dark crimson markings, April–May; 'Britannia' fiery red flowers, April–May, and 'Mrs Furnival', soft-pink flowers with crimson blotches, May–June. These are all reliable and suitable for practically all gardens.

There are many other dwarf kinds suitable for the edge of borders or rock gardens, including 'Blue Tit', zone 6 (April–May), with blue flowers; *R. racemosum*, zone 5, thickly covered with small rose-pink flowers at the same season; 'Blue Diamond', zone 6, of erect growth with blue flowers in May and *R. campylocarpum*, zone 6, also May-flowering with yellow blooms.

R. praecox, zone 6, is an erect shrub up to 3 ft. tall, with pink flowers opening in February if the weather is mild, but which may be frosted unless protected.

Rhus (D.T. or S.M.F.) The stag's horn sumach, *R. typhina*, zone 3, is a small tree or large shrub of sprawling growths which suggest the antlers of a stag. They are covered with thick, close down when young. It is grown for its large, very handsome fern-like leaves which turn orange and red in the fall. There is a cut-leaved form, 'Laciniata'. Any old dead wood should be cut out. It needs sun and will thrive on poor, light soils.

Ribes (D.S.M.FL.) The flowering currants are very hardy and will grow almost anywhere. Their flowers are borne in tassels early in the year. The best known is *R. sanguineum* 'King Edward VII', zone 5, 6 ft. with deep crimson flowers in March or April. Prune by cutting out some of the old shoots from the base whenever the need arises.

Robinia (D.T.M.FL.F.) The false acacia, *R. pseudoacacia*, zone 3, with delicate foliage and pea-like flowers at mid-summer, is a quick growing tree that thrives in light sandy soils, but is too large for the small garden; its form 'Friesia' is smaller and has golden foliage which becomes paler in the fall before it drops.

Above: The large fragrant white flowers of *Romneya trichocalyx*, the Matilija poppy, are produced from July to September

Romneya The Matilija poppy, *R. tricho-calyx* (D.S.M.FL.), zone 9, is a remarkable shrub with white flowers of up to 5 in. in diameter with crinkled petals and a great boss of golden stamens at their center. These open from late July until early fall. The deeply cut leaves are silvery gray. It will reach 5 ft. and needs a sunny situation. Often slow to establish, the chances are that after apparently dying back at first it will recover. It likes a position adjoining paving or large stones and rocks under which the roots can run freely. Cut the shrubs right down to ground level in spring.

Rosmarinus *R. officinalis* (E.S.M.F.), zone 6. Rosemary, with its grayish, scented leaves and blue flowers in late spring, is one of our oldest garden plants. A sunny spot is essential and it is at its best on light soils. It can be used for low hedges. Under good conditions it will reach 6 ft. Plants should be clipped over lightly after flowering to retain a good shape.

Ruta Rue (*R. graveolens*) (E.S.L.F.) zone 4, is an old favorite evergreen grown for its blue foliage rather than its yellow flowers which open from mid-summer to August. It reaches 2 ft. or so. It prefers a light soil and sunny position. Some gardeners prefer to remove the flower spikes before they open. Otherwise, the previous year's shoots should be clipped back in spring.

Salix (D.T.M.FL.) The willows range from large trees, such as the white willow (*S. alba*) zone 2, crack willow (*S. fragilis*) zone 4, and the yellow-twigged weeping willow (*S. alba tristis*), all too large for most gardens, through the bushes, to dwarf shrubs suitable for rock gardens. The flowers are borne in catkins, the sexes normally on different trees. The males are showy, as they consist of the anthers covered with golden pollen. One of the best small trees is the male form of the European willow or goat willow (*S. caprea*) zone 4, which in Britain is widely cut as 'palm' at Eastertide. As far as propagation is concerned, a tree having been marked as of the right sex when in flower, a stout, leafless shoot, 3–4 ft. long is cut from it in early spring and the lower twigs entirely removed. The lower foot or so is then firmly

planted in the ground. This method can be used to propagate almost any willow.

Of similar size is the violet willow, *S. daphnoides*, zone 4, with purple-violet shoots covered with an almost white bloom. The large catkins open in late March.

One form of the white willow, *S. alba* 'Chermesina' has bright orange-scarlet shoots and makes a fine show in winter; it should be treated as a shrub and cut back hard every other year, in order to produce the colorful shoots.

Santolina *S. chamaecyparissus* (E.S.L.F.) zones 6–7. The lavender cotton is a dwarf shrub grown for its silvery thread-like foliage. It bears yellow flowers in late summer. It needs sun and prefers, poor, dry soils. If cut over in April to remove the previous year's growth this both keeps it tidy and prevents flowering, thus preserving its silvery appearance.

Sarcococca (E.S.M.F.FL.) Is a narrow-leaved shrub with small sweetly scented flowers in very early spring. *S. hookeriana digyna*, zones 5–7, is the best kind. It grows about 3½ ft. high and will cover the barest, completely shaded ground by means of suckers. It has purple stems.

Senecio *S. laxifolius* (E.F.FL.L.S.) zone 9, is a gray leaved, bushy, evergreen spreading shrub up to about 3 ft. high with clusters of bright yellow daisy-like flowers in June and July, or even later. It must have sun and is a good plant for a bank, as it needs sharp drainage.

Skimmia *S. japonica* (E.S.L.F.FR.) zone 7, grows from 2–3 ft. high. It needs shade but dislikes lime. It is grown for its foliage and bright crimson berries which last into winter. Male and female flowers grow on separate bushes and to achieve berries both must grow together. There is an exception, however; *S. japonica foremanii* which carries both sexes of flowers and usually produces some berries.

Sorbus (D.T.M.FR.FL.) This genus includes the rowans or mountain ashes with leaves consisting of numerous leaflets and the white-beams with entire (simple, undivided) leaves. All are moderate sized trees particularly suitable for gardens, with clusters of small white flowers followed by red (or sometimes yellow) berries. The leaves usually color well in the fall. All tolerate a wide range of soils, provided they are well drained, the white-beams being good on soil containing lime. Prune only to keep the stem clean. Young trees should be firmly staked after planting but are good in exposed places. All may be attacked by fire-blight where this is widely present on pear and other members of the rose family and it is advisable not to plant them in such districts.

ROWANS *S. aucuparia* 'Asplenifolia', zone 2, the fern-leaved form of the rowan, has deeply cut leaves and makes a very attractive small tree reaching about 25 ft. *S. cashmiriana*, zone 4, is another small rowan, with pink flowers in late May, followed by large, sparkling white berries that hang on far into the winter; it looks well if allowed to branch low and form two or three stems. *S. hupehensis*, zone 5, has rather large leaves with a distinctive bluish sheen, often turning a good yellow or sometimes red in the fall. Large hanging bunches of small white or sometimes pinkish berries follow the numerous flower clusters.

WHITEBEAMS *S. aria* 'Lutescens', zone 5, is a fine form of the common whitebeam which makes a stout tree reaching about 30 ft. The leaves are silvery when young and on developing become green above and gray below. The white flowers in June are followed by scarlet berries larger than in the rowan group. *S. intermedia*, zone 6, the Swedish whitebeam, is similar but with toothed leaves. It is very hardy.

Spartium The Spanish broom, *S. junceum* (D.S.H.FL.), zone 7, is one of the few brooms that will thrive on limy soils, and in any sunny situation. Reaching as much as 9 ft. it carries large, bright yellow pea-like flowers on the rush-like shoots from June until as late as October. Occasionally shorten some of the branches in April.

Spiraea (D.S.M.FL.) These useful shrubs do well under most normal conditions and carry large numbers of small flowers. *S. arguta*, zone 4, the garland spiraea, about 6 ft., is covered with small white flowers in late April. On established plants, cut out some of the old shoots when flowering is ended. *S. bumalda* 'Anthony Waterer', zone 5, is a dwarf shrub with flat clusters of crimson flowers from mid to late summer. Cut the stems back hard in spring.

Syringa (D.S.H.FL.) zone 3. The lilacs provide a wide range of color in their sweetly scented flowers opening from mid to late May. All prefer sun and good fertile soil, particularly if lime is present, but are tolerant of conditions. Newly planted bushes should be cut hard back to vigorous buds. When plants become dense and thicket-like, a few stout stems should be cut out down to the base as growth starts. It is worth removing the faded flower spikes for the first year or two.

Single flowers: 'Esther Staley', pink, mid-May; 'Maud Notcutt', white, late May; 'Souvenir de Louis Spath', reddish purple, late May.

Double flowers: 'Mme Antoine Buchner', rosy mauve, late May; 'Mme Lemoine', double white, late May; 'Paul Thirion', rosy red, early June.

Tamarix (D.S.H.F.FL.) The long, slender shoots are covered with minute flowers. The plants are quick growing and thrive in wind-swept places and by the seaside but will grow almost anywhere. To give their most graceful effect they should be cut almost to ground level in spring; unpruned they will form straggling, picturesque small trees. *T. pentandra*, zone 2, has rosy-pink flowers in July and August.

Ulex (E.S.L.NL.FL.) The double form of the common gorse, *U. europaeus* 'Plenus', zone 6, is covered with rich yellow flowers in April and May. It is good on poor, sandy soils in full sun, and should be clipped over after flowering to keep it tidy.

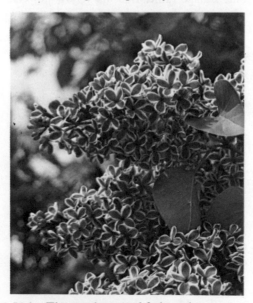

Right: The translucent red fruits and colorful fall foliage of the guelder rose, *Viburnum opulus*
Above: Syringa 'Sensation' has purplish-red white edged flowers

Viburnum (D. and E.S.M.FL.) These decorative shrubs, with clusters of small white or pinkish scented florets, thrive in any garden soil and are good on lime. Some are notable for flowering in winter; the remainder bloom in spring and early summer:

WINTER FLOWERING *V. fragrans* (*V. farreri*) zone 6, is an upright deciduous shrub with fragrant, white, pink-flushed florets opening from November onwards to February. The young leaves are a rich bronze color. Pruning is not needed. A sheltered, sunny position is desirable.

V. tinus, zone 7, the laurustinus, a rounded evergreen shrub, reaches 10–15 ft. and carries bosses of white flowers from October or November into spring. It is a fine, solid-looking specimen and is often grown in hedges.

SPRING FLOWERING *V. burkwoodii*, zone 5, has large heads of white, scented flowers in April and is one of the showiest of all viburnums. It will reach 6 ft. or more. Some of the rich green leaves may remain during the winter.

V. opulus, zone 6, has two forms, both valuable garden shrubs. The native guelder rose, *V. opulus*, a deciduous shrub to 10 ft. tall, will thrive under any conditions, with scented white flowers in May and June, followed by red translucent berries hanging among the red fall leaves. *V. opulus sterile*, the snowball bush, is an abnormal form in which all the flowers are large and infertile, giving a solid effect, at first greenish and then white like a snowball. The leaves color brilliantly.

Weigela These (also sometimes known as diervilla) (D.S.M.FL.) are shrubs heavily laden in May and June with flowers shaped like small foxgloves. They will grow under practically any conditions, including shade. Prune only to remove old, twiggy, worn out shoots after flowering. *W. florida variegata*, zone 5, one of the best, reaches 6 ft. with leaves edged with creamy white, and pink flowers–a most effective color scheme; 'Bristol Ruby' has ruby red flowers; 'Eva Rathke' is an old favorite with bright red-crimson flowers.

The Rock Garden
& Garden Pool

Rock Garden Plants

Traditionally, a rock garden is a place in which to grow alpine plants. Way back in Victorian days and before, such a place was usually referred to as a 'rockery', a word which, in these more enlightened times is very much out of favor with devotees of alpine gardening, who even eschew the word 'rock' and more often than not describe it as an alpine garden.

Even the word 'alpine' is suspect in this context, since many of the plants most fitted to be grown on a rock garden are far from having alpine origins. One must, however, have a brief collective description for plants which serve a specific purpose and it is convenient, and sufficiently accurate, to refer to all plants which one would associate with rocks and stones in the open air, as alpines.

There are more amateur gardeners today than there have ever been and the general interest in gardening is very evidently increasing, but it is gardening on a different scale from that to which our fathers and grandfathers were accustomed. It is much more a 'do-it-yourself' affair and this is good as it encourages a closer and more personal interest in plants.

Gardens are small and labor either unobtainable or too expensive. On the other hand, alpine plants are yearly increasing in popularity. So many of them can be grown in a limited space, and they respond so eagerly to individual attention that they offer an ideal form of gardening to those who come to love their jewel-like beauty and wish to grow as many of them as possible in surroundings which are often very restricted indeed.

That alpines are temperamental and difficult plants, needing very special care and attention is a myth going back to the bad old days, when 'rockeries' were made of ugly piles of stone heaped in unsuitable places—under the drip of overhanging trees, or in shaded and drafty corners. These were death traps for most plants and it is small wonder that alpines died in them and created the illusion that they were difficult to grow.

A select minority of alpine plants, mostly the true 'alpines' which come from great elevations and dwell in the rarified air and austere conditions of high mountains, demand skilled and knowledgeable care. It is to the cultivation of these that the novice progresses in gradual stages.

Although it is tempting to the beginner to attempt such plants as the delicious and exciting domes of alpine androsaces, or to 'have a go' at the exasperating but supremely beautiful *Eritrichium nanum*, wisdom should prevail and these delights postponed until the necessary skill has been acquired after experience with the many easy and lovely plants which are available.

One of the reasons for the avoidance of alpine plants by a few gardeners may well be the result of starting at the wrong end and trying to grow the rare and difficult minority. Failure with these will lead to discouragement and a disinclination to take further steps along what can be one of the most delightful paths into specialized gardening.

Those who are new to alpine gardening should start by growing the easier plants; those which will provide color and interest over as long a period as possible. Another criticism which has been aimed at rock gardens is that they are supremely beautiful and colorful in the spring and early summer, but deadly dull thereafter.

This is untrue; by choosing carefully from the immense variety of plants available a rock garden can be colorful from earliest spring until winter. There is, and always has been, a tendency to plant too many aubrietas, alyssums and arabis. These all blossom in the spring and are invaluable for providing masses of color, but if they are too generously used, there are wide blank spaces for the rest of the year.

Any such vigorous and space devouring plants must be employed in moderation and ample space left for later flowering specimens. The beginner would do well to seek among such genera as *Dianthus, Campanula, Phlox, Gentiana, Primula, Helianthemum, Achillea, Saxifraga, Geranium, Iris, Lewisia, Ranunculus, Polygonum, Sedum* and *Sempervivum* in order to secure a succession of flowers throughout the summer and fall.

A few really dwarf evergreen shrubs should also be grown. For this purpose none is better than the genuinely pygmy conifers. There is a trap here for the unwary however. Too often conifers are sold as dwarfs which will ultimately grow much too large for any rock garden.

It is fatally easy to be misled by the dainty and miniature appearance of such conifers as *Chamaecyparis lawsoniana fletcheri* when seen as young, immature plants and only guaranteed dwarfs should be planted. Ideal examples are the little juniper, *Juniperus communis* 'Compressa', any of the several pygmy forms of *Chamaecyparis obtusa*, and some of the tight, cushion-forming varieties of *Picea abies*.

One of the functions of the tiny trees is to create a sense of scale and proportion in the miniature mountainscape. The shape of the trees should be borne in mind when they are placed. Those of upright, columnar habit, such as the little juniper quoted above, should never be planted on high points. Place them lower down, against a small 'cliff' and reserve the prostrate kinds for the heights.

Plants for Special Purposes

The Alpine House Yet another aspect of alpine gardening is the cultivation of plants in an alpine house. There is a general impression that only the rarest and most tricky plants may be grown in such a structure. It is true that skilled growers keep their choicest specimens in such a house, but there is no reason why an alpine house, or a cold greenhouse, should not form a valuable adjunct to the rock garden.

There are many weeks during the year when gardening out of doors is far from being a pleasurable occupation and a select collection of plants grown in an alpine house can provide pleasure and interest at a time when other gardening activities are impossible and plants can be admired and cared for in comparative comfort.

There are specially designed alpine houses which differ from conventional greenhouses in having a lower pitched roof, and more ventilators. This is the ideal but is not essential. An ordinary house can easily be adapted and the only major modification likely to be needed is the provision of extra ventilation. No artificial heating is necessary, or even desirable and this is an economy.

By growing a number of alpine plants in pots and pans a constant succession of interest can be obtained. When not in flower the containers can be stood out of doors, preferably plunged to the rims in ashes or sand. Very early flowering alpine bulbs make a splendid beginning to the year and for this one would choose from the tiny narcissi, crocuses, snowdrops, snowflakes, winter aconites (eranthis), fritillaries, erythroniums, and aquilegios (columbines).

The gentianella, *Gentiana acaulis*

Above: A miniature waterfall will help to provide the right conditions for water-side plants. *Right: Caltha palustris* 'Plena', the double-flowered marsh marigold

After these come the early flowering saxifragas, particularly such kinds as *S. irvingii, S. kellereri, S. apiculata, S.* 'Cranbourne' and *S. burseriana.* Then come all the spring-flowering alpines of dwarf, compact habit, with campanulas and dianthus to follow on and some of the choicer sedums and late-flowering gentians.

The staging on which the pots and pans stand is best made of a solid base, not spaced wooden slats. If a layer of gravel or ashes is spread over the staging, this will help to keep the soil in the containers moist and cool and avoid the constant drying out to which the plants object.

In the summer, with some pots and pans outside those in the house can be spaced more widely. In the winter the entire population can be brought inside and stood more closely together. Fall potted bulbs can be stored on the floor beneath the staging until they begin to grow.

Pond and waterside plants The addition of water, and especially moving water, to a rock garden has several advantages. Not only does it widen the variety of plants which can be grown, but it adds life to the scene. There are now available several inexpensive types of submersible pump which can be used to circulate water from a pond at the lowest level to another higher up, from which it can be made to flow in a small stream, or a succession of small pools, back to its origin.

Pools and streams can be constructed with modern fibre-glass materials and with plastic sheeting, or they can be made more conventionally with concrete. Anyone with moderate abilities as a handyman can construct streams and pools without difficulty and at little expense.

By arranging for small overflows here and

Left: A beautiful crimson-flowered water-lily

there moist areas can be contrived by the pool or streamside in which to accomodate some of the plants which relish having their roots in wet soil. Do not ever imagine that, without making deliberate moist areas, the plants which enjoy them can be made happy by merely planting them at the waterside. The very edge of a stream or pond creates the illusion of dampness but can be very dry.

Appropriate plants for such damp situations would be all kinds of mimulus, moisture-loving primulus, for example *P. rosea, P. denticulata, P. frondosa* and, of course, all the candelabra primulas such as *P. japonica.* The double kingcup, *Caltha palustris* 'Plena' hangs its golden flowers attractively over the water and such plants as tiarella, astilbe, *Saxifraga aizoides* and the double ladies smock, *Cardamine pratensis* 'Plena' would help to create a pretty scene.

The site Whatever one does in a garden it is well to have an ideal at which to aim. It is not always possible to achieve perfection, but the very act of striving to attain it is rewarding and is certain to provide better results than aimless attempts.

The ideal site for a rock garden would be a gentle slope, on well-drained soil, falling to the south or west. Not many gardens will be able to provide such a perfect position, but there is no need to despair; many alternative situations will be quite satisfactory. Avoid if at all possible a due east aspect.

A sloping position is better than a flat one, but a rock garden built on the flat can be perfectly successful. The absolutely essential thing is good drainage. It is quite useless to construct a rock garden on soil which is likely to be flooded and waterlogged in the winter.

Alpine plants on the whole are extremely tolerant of widely varying conditions of soil, aspect and climate but they will not, under any circumstances, endure having their roots surrounded by sodden soil. Water they love, and need, and it does not matter how much there is, as long as it flows readily through and past their roots. The positions in which

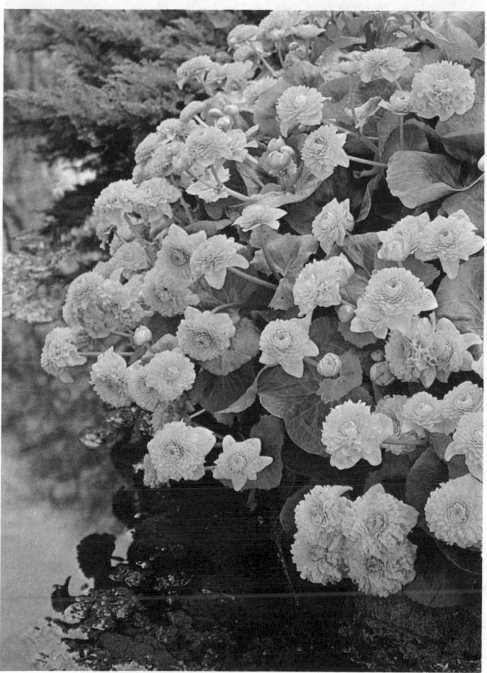

many of them grow naturally may appear to be dry, but water from melting snows flows constantly below the surface.

If the natural drainage is adequate little more preparation is necessary than deeply digging the area and removing all perennial weeds. It is a good idea to leave the area alone for a few weeks after it has been cleared and dug to allow weed seeds to germinate. These can then be destroyed by applying a post-emergence weedkiller. This will save a lot of later laborious weeding. Weedkillers which leave a residue in the soil and prohibit planting for some weeks or even months after application, should be avoided.

Site the rock garden right out in the open and never, if it can possibly be avoided beneath overhanging trees, or in narrow alleyways between adjacent buildings. The first will ensure a detested dripping of water from

The sort of compost to use is described below in the section devoted to cultivation, but make sure before you begin to build that you have available enough mixed soil. It always takes more than you expect and nothing is more annoying than to run out of compost halfway through the construction. Very roughly, you may estimate that, on a flat site, one cubic yard of soil will be needed for every ton of stone. A sloping site may need rather less as you can cut into the hillside to help fill the pockets.

If, after reading the above you feel that there is no possible position for a rock garden on your property, and if you still wish to grow rock plants, do not throw up your hands in despair and abandon the project. It may be a heretical statement, but it must be said that the great majority of rock plants can be grown very successfully without the

railroad ties, to a convenient height. Many who find the ground getting a long way away as the years advance discover in such raised beds a delightfully easy form of gardening. A good height to aim at is from 2–2½ ft. Fill the bottom half with good roughage for drainage and top up with compost and a perfect home is provided for alpine plants.

Cultivation There are two main divisions in the requirements of alpine plants. There are those which either like or will tolerate a soil containing chalk or lime and there is another, smaller but quite intolerant section, which cannot abide lime in any form.

The lime lovers will grow in limefree soil, but the lime-haters will not put up with alkaline soil. If, therefore, the natural soil contains lime, you must either refrain from growing the lime-haters, or make special provision for them. Unless you particularly

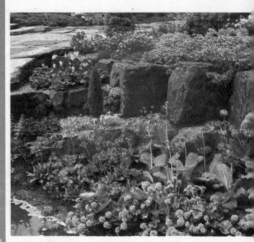

Left: One of the many desirable forms of aubrieta. *Below:* A well-planted rock garden. *Below center left:* After excavating the site for a plastic pool, put down a layer of sand. *Below center right:* The plastic sheet is held in place temporarily by bricks, while water is gently run in from a hose. *Bottom:* The pool complete

branches above and the latter will be draughty, and all plants hate draughts. Positions for plants which relish some shade can always be contrived in the construction of the rock garden. An outcrop of rocks running east and west will provide a warm south face and a cool north aspect on the other side.

Construction A detailed, stone-by-stone description of the making of a rock garden is almost impossible to write and quite impossible to follow in practice. So much depends upon each individual rock, the site, and what sort of scene it is desirable to create. One can really only set down some basic rules, which amount to a series of 'do's' and 'don'ts'.

Do not set the stones in isolation over a mound of soil. This only creates a Victorian 'rockery' and there will be constant erosion of soil from higher to lower levels. Do not set stones up on edges so that they erupt from the soil like fangs. Instead lay them on their longest edge and make sure that they join in pleasant complexes or outcrops much as they would in nature on a hillside.

aid of a rock garden; a rock garden is the ideal setting for them, but it is not essential.

Possible situations for alpine plants are between the cracks of paving stones. In fact, such a position provides everything that they like, such as a cool root run which does not dry out, their heads in the light and their collars protected from too much wet by the closely adjacent paving stones.

Retaining or free-standing walls provide excellent homes for alpines. Here too, they find perfect conditions. If all else fails, you have only to dig out a depth of soil in an open, sunny position, ensure good drainage and fill in with suitable compost and you have a bed which will grow a wide variety of them to perfection.

Many of the smaller plants will do well in old stone troughs and sinks. These little gardens are invaluable where space is really limited and it is astonishing how many different plants can be gathered into a small sink.

Finally, some people resort to a specially constructed raised bed. The sides can be built up in brick, stone or even planks or old desire to grow the lime-haters, many of which are very lovely plants, you need not be too sorrowful, for most alpines are tolerant. It is only the minority whose idiosyncrasies must be pandered to.

If you insist upon growing the lime-haters in spite of the lime in your soil, then you must make a special part of the rock garden for them. This should be on one of the higher places, so that lime-impregnated water does not soak into the soil from above. Many of the lime-haters are also plants which appreciate some shade so try to organize their special situation so that it is protected from full sun.

Dig out the natural soil to a depth of at least 1 ft. and fill in with prepared lime-free soil. This can be a mixture of lime-free loam, leafmold, or peatmoss, and sharp sand in the proportions, by bulk, of 3-2-1. Make sure if

Above right: Hypericum polyphyllum growing in a crevice. *Below:* Rocks should be placed in the mound of soil built up over a deep sump to ensure adequate drainage (important if the site is level). *Inset:* The wrong way to lay rocks. *Below right:* Rocks laid correctly, sloping slightly backwards

Above: A section through a pool. If marginal plants are grown, make raised 'platforms', on which such plants can be grown in containers. *Below:* The roots of plants to be grown on the bottom of the pool can be contained between bricks (or in baskets) to anchor them

leafmold is used that it is really lime-free. If made from the leaves of trees which have been growing where the soil naturally contains lime it is likely to have a lime-content. Peatmoss is safer, and it should be fine grade peatmoss. If there is any doubt about the lime-content of any ingredient test it with one of the inexpensive soil-testing outfits which are available.

Plants likely to demand this treatment are most heathers (except the lime-loving, winter-flowering forms of *Erica carnea*), cassiopes, andromedas, gaultherias, pernettyas, fall-flowering gentians such as *G. sino-ornata* and its allies, and most members of the family *Ericaceae* (which includes all rhododendrons). Most good catalogs quote the family to which plants belong and this can be a guide to their needs.

Drainage The first and most important basic need of alpine plants is perfect drainage and no time or trouble expended in ensuring this is wasted. Once you are certain that water will pass rapidly through the soil and will not linger around the plant roots you are more than halfway to success. On a naturally gravelly or sharply draining soil, little preparation will be necessary, but if you have to contend with a heavy, sticky clay, then some preliminary work is essential to provide the necessary drainage.

If the site on which the rock garden is to stand, or indeed, any position where alpines are to be grown, is flat, and if the soil is clay, or has a hard pan beneath, causing water to stand in puddles instead of draining away, then a deep sump must be excavated in the center of the site and filled with old clinker, rough stones, ashes, gravel, or any good draining material. The sump cannot be too deep and a minimum depth of 5 or 6 ft. should be the objective. Its width will depend to some extent upon the area of the site. A large area may demand two or even three sumps, but a small space, say 200 square feet, would be sufficiently served by one such excavation approximately 2 ft. in width. If it is decided to manage with only one sump on a larger site, it should be twice that width.

On a sloping site drainage is more simply provided. If necessary surplus water can be led away down the slope by a series of narrow trenches, in which agricultural tile drains can be laid, or the trenches filled with clinker or other rough material.

Soil mixtures Simplicity should be the aim of the beginner. Experts who delight in accepting the challenge offered by really rare and difficult plants will have 'cookery-books' of complicated soil recipes with which to pander to the tastes of individual plants, but 90 per cent of alpine plants (excluding the lime-haters) can be successfully grown in one basic soil mixture.

The three main ingredients of a desirable compost are loam, a good organic material and sharp sand or grit. Loam is either rotted turves or good top-spit soil containing an appreciable amount of fiber. Good, friable, well-nourished garden soil will serve very well.

The organic material will consist of either peatmoss, leafsoil or well-decayed compost: peatmoss should be of the finer grade, and sedge peatmoss should be avoided; leafsoil should be nicely rotted and broken down into a dark, friable material.

Sand is an important ingredient; its primary purpose is to ensure an open, freely draining compost. The soft yellow sand used for mixing mortar or cement is quite useless for alpines. The sand must be sharp in texture. If such sand is not available locally it should be replaced with any form of fine but sharp grit.

Measuring by bulk, the proportions of the three ingredients should be 3 parts of loam, 2 parts of organic material and 1½ parts of sand or grit. These must all be thoroughly mixed together, adding at the same time bonemeal in the proportion of 5 lb. to each cubic yard of compost.

Such a compost is ideal for the great majority of plants and no form of artificial fertilizer will be needed for at least the first two years. After that, a spring topdressing with similar compost is desirable in the fall and spring, scattered on the soil and gently forked into the top inch or so.

When filling the pockets and joints between the stones of the rock garden during its construction press the soil down firmly, using a blunt-ended wooden rammer to pack it well under and around the rocks. When building is completed leave the whole area unplanted for a week or two, to allow the soil to settle, which it will do after rain, or a thorough soaking. Some compost should be kept in reserve to top-up where necessary. It is better to do this first rather than have settlement after planting has been done, as this may result in unevenness.

Great care should be taken to ensure that all spaces and crevices between the rocks are well filled with soil. These are the crannies into which alpines delight in delving with their roots in search of the cool, moist conditions they need. Should they emerge into a soilless vacuum they may perish.

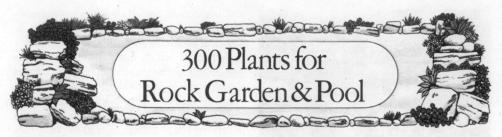

300 Plants for Rock Garden & Pool

Planting The two main planting periods are spring and fall. There are certain advantages in the early fall planting if it can be done while the soil is still warm. The plants can make growth and become well established, thus ensuring a reasonable display in the first spring and summer after planting. If it cannot be done before the soil becomes wet and cold it is as well to delay until the spring.

Alpine plants supplied by nurseries are always pot-grown and, if necessary, planting can continue during the summer months, although it will be necessary to water them and even shade them from the fiercest sunshine until they begin to take root and are able to seek their own moisture.

When alpines are knocked out of the pots or other containers for planting they will be found to have a firm rootball. If this is hard it should be gently pressed and loosened, without breaking it to pieces, before it is planted. Plant very firmly. Ideally the soil in which to plant should be just moist but not really wet. Do not plant in dust-dry compost, or in any which is saturated. After planting give the plants a really thorough soaking, using a fine-rosed can. This settles the soil nicely around them and provides them with moisture until the roots begin to seek for it further afield.

Watering Once plants in the open are firmly established watering should never be done unless it is absolutely necessary but, if, in a prolonged drought it has to be done, then do it very thoroughly; preferably in the morning rather than evening.

Top dressing When areas have been completely planted, and especially those occupied by the smaller, possibly cushion-forming plants, it is a good plan to top dress the whole area with small stone chippings, ensuring that the chippings are inserted beneath the foliage and close against the collar of the plant. This top dressing retains moisture in the soil, discourages the ravaging slugs and imparts a nicely finished appearance to the rock garden.

Cutting back Plants such as the cushion phloxes, helianthemums, aubrietas, arabis, alyssums, dianthus, veronicas, hypericums, iberis and geraniums benefit from being cut back quite severely after they finish flowering. This encourages new growth and often results in a further flush of late season blossom. It also maintains a tidy habit and prolongs the life of the plants.

Maintenance Normal maintenance and cultivation consists of controlling weeds, slugs and snails, and limiting the growth of the more vigorous plants which may tend to swamp smaller neighbors.

Winter care The average alpine plants with which a collection is started need no special winter care if they have been planted in suitable conditions as described above. If, during periods of excessive rainfall any which have very soft and hairy leaves seem to be suffering, they may be protected by a sheet of glass placed over them and held in position by easily contrived wire clips, but this is seldom necessary. The enemy of alpine plants is not cold, but wet. Most of them are accustomed to spend their resting period beneath a covering of snow. Where winters are very severe some covering of light material such as salt hay or even evergreen boughs is advisable.

Propagation Alpine plants can be increased by various methods. The usual means of propagation are seeds or cuttings but old plants may often be divided, usually in early spring or early fall, and a few plants may be increased by root cuttings.

The seeds of alpine plants germinate more readily if they are sown as soon as convenient after ripening. If they cannot be sown at once they should be cleaned and dried and stored in a cool, dry place until sowing can take place.

Sow the seeds in pans, pots, or flats, on a surface of finely sieved, rather gritty soil. Just cover the seeds with similar compost, stand the containers in a cold frame or greenhouse, or in a box out of doors and cover them with paper over which a sheet of glass is placed. As soon as they germinate they must be brought into the light.

The seedlings are ready for pricking-off separately as soon as they make the first true leaves which differ from the first, or cytyledon leaves. A standard compost is suitable to which should be added a little extra fine grit.

Cuttings of most alpine plants are made from soft tips of young growth which do not contain flower buds. They should be from $\frac{1}{2}$–$1\frac{1}{2}$ in. long. Trim off the lower leaves and, with a very sharp knife sever the cutting immediately below a node (leaf joint) and insert into pure gritty sand in pots or pans. Keep shaded and moist until the cuttings root, when they can be separately potted and grown on until well enough rooted to be planted out.

Divisions should be potted and treated in the same way as potted cuttings. Make sure that all portions have some root.

1: Sowing seeds of alpines in a flat
2: They may also be sown in pans. Before seedlings become overcrowded, they should be pricked out into a flat (**3**) spaced out well
4: Dianthus may be propagated from 'pipings', strip off the lower leaves first. **5**: Then insert the 'pipings' in a pot of cutting compost

Above right: Androsace sarmentosa chumbyi
Right: A variety of Ameria caespitosa

Three Hundred Rock Plants Described

Acaena (*Rosaceae*) (New Zealand burr) Carpeting plants native, mostly, to New Zealand, these are invasive but ornamental and are useful for crevices of paving and to clothe areas of poor soil where little else will flourish. All are for growing in mild areas. Their small flowers are carried in dense heads on very short stems and are often accompanied by brightly colored spines. They also make good ground-cover for dwarf bulbs. *A. buchananii* has pea-green leaves and yellow-brown flower heads; *A. glauca* has silky, blue-gray foliage; *A. microphylla* has bronze leaves and innumerable scarlet burr-like flower heads.

Achillea (*Compositae*) (yarrow) Many of these sun-loving plants are suitable for the rock garden. They flower in spring and early summer and possess beauty both of leaf and flower. They are easily grown in any well-drained soil. The following are unlikely to exceed 6 in. when in flower. *A. argentea* has intensely silver leaves and white flowers; *A. chrysocoma* has gray leaves and yellow flowers; *A.* 'King Edward' has soft gray-green leaves and lemon yellow flowers, and *A. tomentosa* green leaves and bright yellow flowers.

Aethionema (*Cruciferae*) (stonecress) Valuable dwarf, shrubby plants for places in full sun and any good garden soil, these flower from early summer onward. Propagate by seed or cuttings. *A. grandiflorum* makes a 9 in. bush of gray-green small leaves and has large heads of rose-pink flowers; *A. pulchellum*, similar but not so tall, has flowers the color of pink coconut-ice. *A.* 'Warley Rose' is a lovely, daphne-like shrub 6 in. tall with innumerable heads of rich rose-red flowers. As it is a sterile hybrid it has to be propagated by soft tip cuttings.

Allium (*Liliaceae*) This genus contains several fine rock garden plants; they mostly relish full sun and have no special soil requirements. *A. karataviense*, 9 in., has huge, handsome gray-green leaves and large 'drum-stick' heads of gray-white flowers in spring; *A. moly*, 9 in., is invasive but lovely. It has large heads of bright yellow flowers in spring; *A. narcissiflorum* has large, nodding wine-red flowers on 4-in. stems in spring.

Alyssum (*Cruciferae*) These easy-going, sun and lime-loving plants are very decorative in the early spring. They benefit from being cut back after flowering and can be increased from seeds and cuttings. They are splendid wall plants, especially when associated with arabis and aubrieta. They are mostly forms of *A. saxatile*, which has gray-

green leaves and many heads of yellow flowers on 9–12 in. stems; 'Compactum' is dwarfer and more compact; 'Citrinum' has sulfur-yellow flowers.

A. spinosum (*Ptilotrichum spinosum*) though not strictly an alyssum is usually included in the family. It is a 9 in. tall spiny bush smothered with white or soft pink flowers in summer.

Anacyclus (*Compositae*) (Mount Atlas daisy) *A. depressus* makes prostrate mats of gray, ferny leaves and radiating stems carrying large daisy-shaped flowers, crimson on the back of the petals and white in front. It is a plant for full sun and very well-drained soil. Propagate from seeds.

Androsace (*Primulaceae*) (rock jasmine) This large genus contains some of the most desirable rock garden and alpine house plants. They are all sun-lovers and, as most of them have densely hairy leaves they may appreciate some protection against winter wet. Propagate by seeds or by detaching rooted rosettes or by cuttings. All are spring and early summer flowering. *A. lanuginosa* should be planted in crevices from which it can hang its trailing stems, which end in heads of pale pink, crimson-eyed flowers; *A. primuloides* (*sarmentosa*) 'Chumbyi', 'Watkinsii' and 'Salmon's Variety' have neat, rounded, hairy-leaved rosettes and heads of deep pink flowers on 6-in. stems.

Anemone (*Ranunculaceae*) (windflower) Several species are admirable rock garden plants. They like well-drained, gritty soil, rich in humus and are increased by division or by seeds. All are sun lovers except where otherwise stated. *A.* 'Lesseri', a sterile hybrid has glowing rose-red flowers on 1 ft. stems in spring; *A. magellanica* has creamy

flowers in loose heads on 6-in. stems in spring and early summer; *A. nemorosa*, the wood anemone, likes partial shade and cool soil. The species has white flowers; the cultivars 'Allenii' and 'Robinsoniana' are blue. There is also a form with pretty, double white flowers; *A. vernalis* is one of the most beautiful of all alpines. It has huge opalescent flowers on 6-in. stems. It needs very gritty soil and sun.

Antennaria (*Compositae*) These easy little carpeting plants for sunny positions in any soil are invaluable for planting in crevices between paving stones. Propagate by division or seed. *A. dioica* has tiny gray leaves and fluffy heads of pink flowers on 3-in. stems in spring.

Aquilegia (*Ranunculaceae*) (columbine) Some of these are good rock garden plants. Few of them come entirely true from seed. They like sun and well-drained soil and flower in spring and early summer. *A. ecalcarata* has flights of elegant red-purple, spurless flowers on stems 9 in. tall. It comes true from seed; in *A. flabellata*, 9–12 in. tall, the large flowers may be blue or ivory-white; *A. glandulosa* has large blue and white flowers on 15-in. stems.

Arabis (*Cruciferae*) (rock cress) These sun and lime-loving spring flowering plants are easily grown in ordinary soil. Propagate by cuttings or seeds. Cut hard back after flowering. *A. albida* 'Coccinea' is the double white arabis, a valuable and showy spring flower; *A. blepharophylla* is very early flowering. It has pink blossoms on 6-in. stems.

Arenaria (*Caryophyllaceae*) (sandwort) These spring-flowering plants are easily grown. *A. balearica* loves shade. It is not hardy where winters are severe. It has a mere film of tiny leaves and clouds of dainty, tiny white flowers on 1-in. stems; *A. montana* is a spreading, sun-loving plant about 9 in. high, with innumerable large pure white flowers.

Armeria (*Plumbaginaceae*) (thrift) These decorative sun lovers will grow in any soil. All flower in spring. Propagate by division or cuttings. *A. juniperifolia* has tight tufts of closely packed deep green leaves and almost stemless heads of rich pink flowers; of *A. maritima* the best forms are 'Vindictive' deep red, 'Laucheana', crimson, and 'Alba', white.

Asperula (*Rubiaceae*) These flower in spring and have clustered heads of pink or white flowers. Propagate by division, seeds and cuttings. *A. gussonii* makes mats of dark green foliage and pink flowers. It will grow in any good soil; *A. odorata*, the woodruff, likes shade and cool soil. It has leafy 9-in. stems and heads of small white fragrant flowers; *A. suberosa* is an especially beautiful plant, but it needs gritty soil and a warm, sunny position. It produces soft carpets of gray leaves and clusters of tubular pink flowers. In wet areas it will appreciate shelter from winter rain.

Aster (*Compositae*) Those species suitable for rock gardens do well in open, sunny positions and in any good, well-drained soil. They may be increased by seeds or by division of old plants. Most flower in mid to late summer. *A. alpinus* has large blue and gold aster flowers on 9-in. stems. There is a nice white form and 'Beechwood' has large, more richly colored flowers, but is a little less 'alpine' in appearance; *A. natalensis* has flowers of gentian-blue on 6-in. stems.

Astilbe (*Saxifragaceae*) There are a few dwarf astilbes for cool, semi-shaded positions. Propagate by division of old plants. *A. chinensis* 'Pumila', 9–12 in., has stiff, dense spires of flowers the color of crushed raspberries, in August and September; *A. glaberrima* 'Saxosa' has dainty spikes of pink flowers on very short stems in late summer.

Aubrieta (*Cruciferae*) (rock cress) Aubrietas can be raised from seed and provided a mixture of colors. The best kinds are named and are propagated by cuttings or division. They are sun and lime-lovers and need to be heavily trimmed immediately after flowering to maintain their tidy habit and increase the length of their life. They flower in early spring, but do better along the cooler parts of the Pacific coast than where summers are hot. Any alpine plant catalog will provide a list of names and colors.

Calamintha (*Labiatae*) These are pretty plants with aromatic foliage and worthwhile flowers, easily grown in any good soil and full sun. All flower in summer. Propagate from seeds or by cuttings. *C. alpina* bears violet, white-tipped tubular flowers on 4-in. stems; *C. grandiflora* is a slightly larger plant with border pink flowers.

Campanula (*Campanulaceae*) (bellflower) Many campanulars are invaluable for the rock garden. Most flower in summer and late summer and are easily grown in good,

well-drained soil and sunny positions. Those mentioned may be regarded as the essential nucleus of a collection. Propagate by seeds, division or cuttings. *C. carpatica* has large, saucer-shaped flowers on 9–12 in. stems, its forms vary in color from white to blue and rich purple; *C. cochlearifolia* (*pusilla*) is a tiny gem with blue or white bells on 3-in. stems; *C. garganica* is a splendid crevice and wall plant. The spreading stems cling closely to the stones and carry multitudes of blue, white-centered starry flowers; *C. portenschlagiana* (*muralis*), 6–9 in., is one of the very best. It has sheets of rich purple flowers in dense masses and will grow and flower in light shade; *C. poscharskyana* is semi-prostrate, invasive but very handsome and flowers for a long period. It has star-shaped blue flowers on long stems.

Cerastium (*Caryophyllaceae*) The common snow-in-summer, *C. tomentosum* is too invasive to be permitted in any rock garden although it is a decorative plant for wild places. There is at least one well-behaved, easily grown species however. This is *C. alpinum* 'Lanatum', which has dense pads of woolly gray leaves and small white flowers in summer. Grow in poor, gritty soil. Propagate by seed, division or cuttings.

Chiastophyllum (*Crassulaceae*) In *C. oppositifolium* (*Cotyledon simplicifolia*) the golden flowers hang in slender chains from short leafy stems in spring. It likes a cool spot or light shade.

Chrysogonum (*Compositae*) *C. virginianum* is an easy plant for a not too hot place. It flowers the summer through. It has leafy stems and star-shaped yellow flowers. Propagate by division.

Cortusa (*Primulaceae*) *C. matthiolii* likes a cool position with moist soil. It has rounded lobed, softly hairy leaves and heads of pendent pink tubular flowers on 9-in. stems in summer. Propagate by seeds. Must be given protection where winters are severe.

Cotula (*Compositae*) These are invasive but useful for paving and poor, stony soil. The flowers are inconspicuous but the foliage is pretty. They are invaluable ground-coverers for areas where the winters are not too cold. *C. potentillina* has deeply divided bronze-green leaves in dense prostrate mats; *C. squalida* has green, almost fern-like tiny leaves in close mats.

Crepis (*Compositae*) These showy easy plants for sunny positions in any good soil flower in summer. Propagate by seeds. *C. aurea* has leaves like those of a dandelion and copper-red flowers on 4–6 in. stems; in *C. incana*, 9 in., the leaves are ash-gray and it has showers of soft pink flowers.

Cyclamen (*Primulaceae*) The hardy cyclamen are invaluable tuberous-rooted plants for cool positions in the rock garden. Of the many cultivated species the three described are of outstanding virtue. They love lime but do not demand it. Plant them as growing tubers, not stored and dried ones which take a long time to grow. Plant 3–4 in. deep in soil rich in humus. Propagate by seeds. *C.*

europaeum has marbled rounded leaves and pink fragrant flowers in summer; *C. neapolitanum* has beautifully shaped and marked leaves and deep pink–sometimes white–flowers in the fall; *C. repandum* bears long-petalled rose-pink flowers in early spring. The dark green leaves are marbled with white. It is not quite as hardy as the other two.

Daphne (*Thymeliaceae*) This genus contains some of the most beautiful dwarf rock garden shrubs. However, not all are hardy. They like sunny places but not dry conditions. The soil should be gritty and rich in peatmoss or leafsoil. They are sometimes slow to establish but are long-lived. Propagate by cuttings and seeds. *D. cneorum*, zone 4, is a low bush smothered in summer with

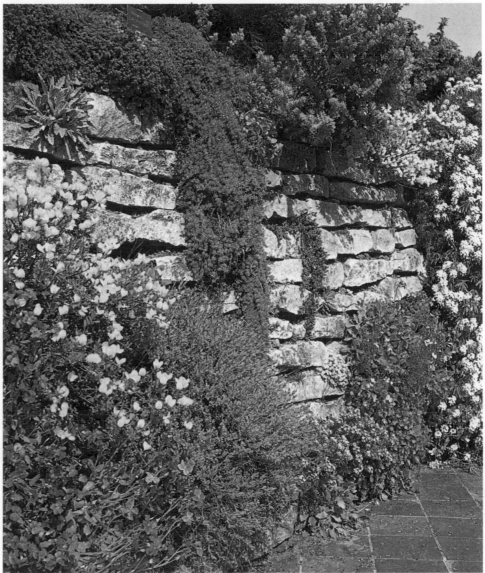

Above: The blue flowers are those of *Campanula portenschlagiana*, a vigorous bellflower for the rock garden. *Left:* Dwarf forms of the wallflower (*Cheiranthus cheiri*) provide color and fragrance in spring. *Below: Dianthus deltoides*, the maiden pink, a fine rock garden plant. Note how the surface soil is mulched with stone chippings which help to keep it cool and moist and discourage slugs. *Above right:* Many colorful alpines may be grown in the crevices of a dry stone wall

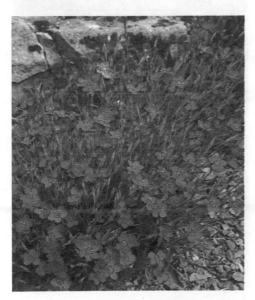

heads of rich pink, intensely fragrant flowers. If the stems become bare, fill up the plant with leafy soil; *D. collina*, zone 7, has red-purple fragrant flowers in spring and often again in late summer, on rounded 15-in. bushes; *D. retusa*, zone 6, makes a stiff, upright 2-ft., bush with sweetly scented purple flowers followed by large red berries.

Dianthus (*Caryophyllaceae*) (pink) This is a large and valuable genus of easily grown, lime and sun-loving plants. Their colorful, often sweetly scented flowers are borne in summer. Propagate by division, cuttings, and seeds of those which are not hybrids. Many are fertile hybrids; seedlings of these will not come true but may produce some worth while plants. *D. alpinus* makes low pads of dark green leaves and huge, almost stemless, rich pink flowers; *D. arvernensis* consists of ash-gray hummocks of leaves and 4-in. stems carrying rounded pink flowers. There is also a lovely white form; *D. caesius*. the Cheddar pink, has narrow gray leaves and large pink flowers on 6–9 in. stems; *D. deltoides*, the maiden pink, 9 in., makes sheets of flowers varying from light to dark pink; there is also a white form; *D.* 'Pike's Pink' is very dwarf with large pink flowers over flat cushions of gray-green leaves; *D.*

subacaulis forms green mats and has slender 4-in. stems carrying neat rose-red flowers.

Dodecatheon (*Primulaceae*) *D. meadia* likes a moist position or cool shade. It has pink and white, cyclamen-shaped flowers on 9–12 stems in spring.

Draba (*Cruciferae*) These spring-flowering plants are easily grown in sun and any good soil. Propagate by seeds. *D. aizoides* forms tufts of deep green pointed leaves and many yellow flowers in small clusters, on 3-in. stems; *D. dedeana* has gray-green leaves in huddled rosettes, and white flowers on 1-in. stems.

Dryas (*Rosaceae*) *D. octopetala* is a woody plant with trailing stems and tiny dark green leaves. The large white flowers are abundantly produced in summer on short stems. Plant in full sun. Propagate by division or by cuttings.

Epilobium (*Onagraceae*) *E. glabellum* is a sun-loving plant which flowers from May until the fall. It has showers of large white flowers on branching, slightly arching 1 ft. high stems and bronze-green foliage. Propagate by cuttings.

Erigeron (*Compositae*) There are a few dwarf erigerons suitable for the rock garden. They are easily grown and like open, sunny positions. They flower in spring and sum-

The blue, star-shaped flowers of *Gentiana verna* bloom in the early spring

mer. Propagate by seed or division. *E. aurantiacus* has rich orange flowers on 12 in. stems; *E. compositus*, 3 in. has tiny tufts of grayish leaves and soft lavender flowers; *E. karvinskianus* (*Vitadenis triloba*) bears profusions of white, pale and deep pink flowers from spring until winter, on 9 in. stems. It likes dry, poor soil.

Erinus (*Scrophulariaceae*) *E. alpinus*, 3 in., is an easy plant for sun or light shade, flowering in spring and delightful in rocky chinks. Propagate by seeds. It has soft pink flowers. There is a nice white form and several named forms of which 'Dr Hanelle', deep red, and 'Mrs Charles Boyle', rich pink, are the best. All naturalize freely but never objectionably.

Erodium (*Geraniaceae*) (heron's bill) These important rock garden plants flower over a long summer period, are long-lived and easily grown in sunny positions, and any soil. Propagate by seeds or cuttings. *E. chamaedrioides* makes prostrate mats of dark green leaves studded with short-stemmed white, pink-veined flowers. The cultivar 'Roseum' has rich pink blossoms; *E. chrysanthum* has tufts of ferny, silver-gray leaves and sprays of sulfur-yellow flowers on 9-in. stems; *E. corsicum* has gray, hairy leaves in neat 4 in. high tufts and rich pink flowers. It loves a sunny crevice.

Euryops (*Compositae*) *E. acraeus* is a good dwarf silver-leaved bush of about 15 in., studded in summer with multitudes of golden, daisy-shaped flowers. It needs a hot, dry place and will only grow in areas where the climate is mild. Propagate by cuttings.

Festuca (*Gramineae*) A few small alpine grasses are invaluable for filling chinks and crannies in the rock garden. Those described make neat, dwarf tufts, will grow in sun or shade and are propagated by division. *F. glacialis*, 3–4 in., has fine, gray-green leaves; *F. ovina glauca*, 9 in., has ornamental silver-gray foliage; *F. rubra*, 4 in., has bright emerald-green leaves.

Frankenia (*Frankeniaceae*) *F. laevis* our native sea heath, is worthy of cultivation, but *F. thymifolia*, a better garden plant, forms prostrate mats of gray-green leaves and sheets of bright pink flowers in summer. It needs a sunny, but not dry position. Propagate by division or cuttings.

Genista (*Leguminosae*) (broom) These dwarf shrubs are essential in any rock garden, they relish open, sunny positions and dry soil. Propagate by seeds or cuttings. *G. hispanica* 'Compacta' is a spiky 1 ft. high bush covered in summer with golden flowers; *G. lydia* rather large for the rock garden,

at 2 ft. high and 3 ft. in diameter, provides a sheet of rich yellow flowers; *G. pilosa* has prostrate woody stems covered with golden flowers in summer; *G. sagittalis* has curiously 'winged' stems which make low mats concealed in summer by yellow flowers.

Gentiana (*Gentianaceae*) (gentian) This is one of the most important genera of rock garden plants, where summers are cool. They are too numerous to describe in detail and only a representative list of the most useful can be given. Their needs vary considerably and are suggested in the descriptions. Most of them are increased from seeds. *G. acaulis* is the ever-popular spring and summer flowering blue trumpet gentian. Plant very firmly in good loamy soil and sun; *G. asclepiadea*, the willow gentian, likes a cool position. Its 3-ft. stems carry many pendent, tubular blue flowers in mid to late summer; *G. septemfida*, the 'everyman's' gentian, will grow in almost any soil and open, sunny places. Sheets of blue flowers are borne in clustered heads on 9-in. stems in mid-summer; *G. sino-ornata* demands lime-free soil and a cool spot. It makes sheets of azure flowers from late August until winter; *G. verna* has clear blue star-shaped flowers on 3-in. stems in early spring. Grow in gritty soil, rich in humus, and full sun. Raise fresh seedlings every two or three years.

Geranium (*Geraniaceae*) (crane's bill) Of this large genus several are admirable for the rock garden, in any good, well-drained soil and sunny positions. Propagate by division, seeds and cuttings. *G. pylzowianum*, 3 in., a

Above: The azure flowers of *Gentiana sino-ornata* are produced from late summer onwards for many weeks. It must have a lime-free soil

mat forming plant producing large purplish-pink flowers in early summer; *G. dalmaticum*, has erect 4 in. stems which carry shapely pink flowers in summer. The foliage assumes rich fall tints; *G. renardii*, 9 in., has lovely lobed leaves and pastel-lavender flowers; *G. sanguineum* 'Lancastriense' makes prostrate mats of deep green studded with large, saucer-shaped salmon-pink flowers; *G. subcaulescens*, 6 in., bears carmine, dark-eyed flowers all summer.

Geum (*Rosaceae*) (avens) At least one geum is an easily grown and showy alpine species, for full sun and any soil. Propagate by division or seed. *G. montanum* has large lobed leaves and huge golden, rounded flowers on 6-in. stems in summer.

Globularia (*Globulariaceae*) (globe daisy) These are sun-loving woody plants. Propagate by division, seeds and cuttings. *G. cordifolia*, a prostrate plant has tiny leathery dark green leaves and blue powder-puff heads of flowers on very short stems; *G. trichosantha* is larger in all its parts. It has quite large heads of blue flowers on 9-in. stems. Both flower in summer in milder areas of the country.

Gypsophila (*Caryophyllaceae*) (chalk plant) These easy and very showy plants trail effectively from walls and ledges. They are spring and early summer flowering. Propa-

Below: Erinus alpinus is a first-class plant for sun or light shade. It grows particularly well in the crevices between stones in the rock garden or dry wall. *Right: Geranium sanguineum lancastriense*, one of the most popular of the dwarf crane's bills, makes prostrate mats surmounted by salmon-pink flowers gate by cuttings. *G. dubia* has showers of clear pink flowers; *G. fratensis* bears rosy flowers in profusion; *G. repens rosea* has clear pink flowers and a trailing habit of growth.

Haberlea (*Gesneriaceae*) *H. rhodopensis*, 4 in., is a plant for cool, shady or north facing crevices. It has rosettes of deep green leaves and tubular lavender, gold-flecked flowers in spring.

Hebe (*Scrophylariaceae*) (veronica) This is the correct name for most of the evergreen shrubby plants often known as veronicas. It is a large genus and contains a number of valuable summer-flowering rock garden shrublets that may be grown in milder areas, particularly the Pacific Northwest. They are easily grown in any good soil and sun, but some are slightly frost tender and should be placed in warm positions sheltered from early morning sun. Propagate by cuttings. *H.* 'Carl Teschner' is a 9-in. tall bush sheeted with purple-blue flowers; *H. macrantha*, 18 in. tall is covered with very large pure white flowers. *H. pinguifolia* 'Pagei', 6 in., has gray leaves and myriads of small white flowers.

Helianthemum (*Cistaceae*) (sun rose) For a summer-long display of brilliant flowers the sun roses are unequalled, although they do require protection where winters are

severe. They appreciate full sun and sharply drained soil and it is essential to trim them quite severely as soon as the flowers are finished. This not only keeps them in good and tidy health but usually provokes a second display of blossom in the late summer. Propagate by cuttings. There is a multitude of named varieties of *H. nummularium*: *H.* 'Amy Baring', 6 in. with orange-bronze flowers, is the dwarf of the race. Others range in height from 6 to 12 in.; *H.* 'Ben Hope', carmine flowers with an orange center; *H.* 'Broughty Beacon', large flame-red flowers; *H.* 'Croftianum', silver foliage and apricot flowers; *H.* 'Golden Queen', rich yellow blossoms; *H.* 'Henfield Brilliant', glistening brick-red flowers, splendid new variety; *H.* 'Jubilee', double yellow flowers; *H.* 'Mrs Earle', double red flowers; *H.* 'Red Orient', glowing deep red flowers; *H.* 'Snowball', double white flowers; *H.* 'Wisley Pink', large soft clear pink flowers.

Helichrysum (*Compositae*) (everlasting, Immortelle) These are sun-loving plants for milder areas, some shrubby, others compact tufts. They have attractive gray or silver foliage and showy flowers. Propagate by division, seeds or cuttings *H. bellidioides* forms of gray mats of foliage and has white flowers in summer; *H. frigidum* has tiny silver tufts and daisy-shaped, golden-eyed

white flowers in summer; *H. milfordae* has mats of glistening silver leaves and white, scarlet-backed flowers in spring and summer.

Hepatica (*Ranunculaceae*) These delightful early spring flowering plants do best in cool positions and light shade. They like soil rich in humus and can be increased by seeds or division of old plants, although old plants should only be lifted when really necessary as they resent disturbance. *H. nobilis* (*triloba*), 4 in., has dainty clear blue flowers; *H. transsylvanica* (*angulosa*) has larger leaves and larger flowers of equally vivid blue. Both are sometimes included in the genus *Anemone*.

Hieraceum (*Compositae*) (hawkweed) This genus contains a few good rock garden plants. They are invasive and should be planted with this in mind. They do best in poor soil and full sun. Propagate by division or seeds. *H. aurantiacum*, 1 ft., has handsome heads of brilliant orange flowers in spring and summer; *H. villosum*, 1 ft., has lovely silver hairy leaves and yellow flowers from June to August.

Hippocrepis (*Leguminosae*) *H. comosus* 'E.R. Janes' is a delightful creeping, sun-loving plant which covers its carpets of green leaves with countless lemon-yellow flowers in spring and early summer. Increase by division or cuttings. It flowers more freely in well-drained poor soil.

Houstonia (*Rubiaceae*) (bluetts) *H. caerulea* has myriads of small clear blue flowers on 3-in. stems in spring. It loves cool shade and moist soil and should be divided and replanted every two or three years.

Hutchinsia (*Cruciferae*) *H. alpina* is a pretty little plant for a position where it is shielded from full sun. Tufts of dark green leaves are enlivened by clouds of snow-white flowers on 3-in. stems in spring. Propagate by seeds.

Hypericum (*Guttiferae*) (St John's Wort) These are semi-shrubby, summer-flowering, sun-loving plants. They flourish in any good well-drained soil. Their flowers provide brilliant color and they are long-lived, especially if trimmed fairly severely after flowering. *H. olympicum* has brilliant golden flowers on 9-in. bushes. There is a delightful form with lemon-yellow flowers; *H. poly-phyllum* is a neat, 6-in. bush with bright green leaves covered beneath multitudes of rich yellow flowers; *H. reptans* is completely prostrate with trailing, leafy stems set with orange-yellow flowers; *H. rhodopaeum*, 9 in., has softly hairy gray-green leaves and soft yellow flowers.

Hypsela (*Campanulaceae*) *H. longiflora* is a prostrate plant, excellent for crannies between paving stones. It bears small lilac and white flowers in summer, likes a cool position and soil which does not parch. Increase by division.

Iberis (*Cruciferae*) (candytuft) These sun-loving, spring and summer flowering plants are easy to grow in any good soil. *I. gibraltarica* has flat heads of white, lilac-tinted flowers on 9-in. stems; *I. aethionema coridifolium*, 6 in., bears large heads of white flowers turning to soft lilac as they age. It will flower until the fall; *I. sempervirens* 'Snowflake' is a spreading evergreen 9-in. bushlet, smothered with snow-white flowers. It makes a magnificent display.

Iris (*Iridaceae*) There are various dwarf species and varieties which are invaluable rock garden plants for various positions. They are best increased by division after flowering. Unless otherwise stated all those described are sun lovers and do best in a lime-rich soil. *I. chamaeiris* 'Campbellii' has large indigo-blue flowers on 4-in. stems in May–June; *I. innominata*, 9 in. has stiff, narrow leaves in dense tufts and, in summer, flowers which may be golden, pencilled with chocolate, or a variety of pastel shades; it will only grow in milder areas. *I. pumila* is grown in a variety of named forms, all usually less than 9 in. tall. The flower color varies from white to all shades of blue and purple. It flowers in early summer; *I. gracillipes* likes shade and lime-free soil. It has dainty lilac and gold flowers on branching 6-in. stems; *I. cristata* has lavender and gold flowers on 4-in. stems in late spring. It prefers a cool position.

Jasione (*Campanulaceae*) *J. perennis* is a pretty, blue-flowered plant but even better is *J. jankae*, which has large heads of clear blue flowers on 1-ft. stems from mid to late summer. It is an easy plant for any soil or situation. Increase by seed or division of old plants.

Leontopodium (*Compositae*) *L. alpinum* 6–9 in., is the famous edelweiss. It will succeed in any good and well-drained soil and a sunny place. The tufts of narrow gray leaves are surmounted in summer by the characteristic heads of flowers which look as if they have been cut out of gray flannel. Propagation is by seeds.

Leucanthemum (*Compositae*) *L. osmarense*, 9–12 in., is an alpine chrysanthemum of great merit. It requires a warm, sunny position in gritty but good soil, where it will make foaming masses of silver filigree foliage and carry innumerable large, white, golden-eyed daisy flowers throughout the summer. Increase by cuttings or seeds.

Lewisia (*Portulacaceae*) These are splendid spring and summer flowering rock garden plants which as a group are difficult to grow in the eastern part of the country. They prefer lime-free soil but will grow in alkaline soil if it is enriched with peat. They like sun and prefer to grow in crevices or on slopes rather than on the flat. Propagate by seeds and cuttings of side-rosettes. Keep plants dry after they finish flowering. They all have fleshy-leaved rosettes and when in flower vary from 9 to 15 in. in height. *L.* 'Birch Hybrids' range in color from pink to deep salmon and crimson; in *L. columbiana* 'Rosea' the wiry stems carry flights of red-purple flowers in abundance; *L.* 'George Henley' is a hybrid of great merit. It flowers from May until October with short, branching stems bedecked with brick-red blossoms; *L.* 'Rose Splendor' is another hybrid strain with very large flowers in which pale and deep pink predominate; *L. tweedyi* is perhaps the most splendid of the genus. It has lax rosettes of fleshy leaves and many large opalescent pink and salmon flowers carried singly on short stems.

Linnaea (*Caprifoliaceae*) *L. borealis* is the famous twin flower of the botanist (Carolus Linnaeus) whose name it commemorates. It is a woodland plant and creeps at soil level with wiry stems clad in tiny leathery leaves. The exquisite flowers, borne in spring, are clear pink bells carried two to each 1-in. high stem. It needs lime-free soil and shade or a north aspect. Increase by cuttings.

Linum (*Linaceae*) (flax) This genus contains dwarf shrubby plants and elegant perennials with tall stems and blue, yellow or white flowers. They all flower in summer and need sunny positions in good, perfectly drained soil. Propagate by cuttings or seeds. *L. flavum* is a stiff, 9–12 in. tall bush, with clouds of rich golden flowers; *L. monogynum*, 12–15 in., has large pure white flowers. It is a plant for areas where winter is less severe. *L. narbonense* bears huge funnel-shaped lovely flowers of gentian-blue on slender, arching 18-in. stems. *L. salsaloides* 'Nanum' makes prostrate mats of tiny leaves on woody stems and large white flowers on very short stems.

Lithospermum (*Boraginaceae*) The most widely grown and popular is *L. diffusum* and its forms. They are all lovers of hot, dry positions in full sun. They are propagated by cuttings. 'Grace Ward' has sprawling stems which carry myriads of vividly blue flowers throughout the summer. It makes a wide, semi-prostrate mat and must be given lime-free soil. With age the stems become bare, and then the plant should be liberally top-dressed with leafy soil.

Lotus (*Leguminosae*) *L. corniculatus* A native of Europe and Asia, the Bird's Foot Trefoil is too rampant a weed to be planted on the rock garden. The double form 'Plena', a desirable plant, makes a wide, flat mat, covered with golden flowers in the spring. It likes sun and sharp drainage and may be increased by cuttings.

Lychnis (*Caryophyllaceae*) (catchfly) Several species are excellent plants for the rock garden, easily grown in any good soil and sunny positions. Propagation is by division or seed. *L. alpina* is a tiny tuft of glossy leaves above which are carried, on 3-in. stems, clusters of small pink flowers early in the year. It is not long-lived and seeds should be sown every two or three years; *L. flosjovis* has gray hairy leaves and large carmine-red flowers on 1-ft. stems; *L. viscaria* 'Splendens Plena' 18 in., is too large for a very small rock garden, though it is a fine plant which deserves a place for the sake of its intense carmine-red flowers carried on 18-in. stems.

Maianthemum (*Liliaceae*) *M. bifolium* is a shade-lover and grows best in lime-free soil. It is a pretty plant, 3–4 in. tall, delightful in a cool corner of the rock garden. It creeps by underground stems and erupts into dense clusters of heart-shaped green leaves and fluffy heads of tiny white flowers in spring.

Margyricarpus (*Rosaceae*) *M. setosus* is a semi-prostrate shrub, 12–15 in. tall, its stems densely covered by small, pointed

dark green leaves. The inconspicuous flowers are followed by myriads of round, translucent white berries. It grows in any good soil and sun, but should not have a parched position or be attempted in colder areas of the country. Propagate by seeds or cuttings.

Mazus (*Scrophulariaceae*) These dwarf carpeting plants do best in cool rather than hot positions. They flower in mid to late summer and grow in ordinary garden soil. Propagate by division. *M. pumilio* makes green carpets studded with stemless blue and white flowers. It should be lifted, divided and replanted in fresh soil every so often; *M. reptans*, which is the hardier of the two, has bronze-green leaves and flowers of mauve, white and gold. It is rampant and must be given room to spread.

Mentha (*Labiatae*) (mint) There are a few mints which find a place among the alpines. They flower in summer and are increased by division or cutting. *M. requienii*, the Corsican mint, makes a mere film of soft green which spreads over the ground in moist or cool places and displays countless tiny, stemless lavender flowers. The whole plant is intensely peppermint-scented.

Micromeria (*Labiatae*) All the plants in this genus give forth a pungent but pleasant odor when the leaves or stems are handled. *M. corsica* likes a really hot, dry and sunny place and requires winter protection further north. It makes 6-in, spiky bushes of sharp

Left: Lewisias are among those plants which grow best in the crevices between rocks, or in cracks in a dry wall
Top: A relative of the anemones, *Hepatica transsylvanica* bears vivid blue flowers in early spring
Above: The bright yellow flowers of *Hypericum olympicum*, a 9-in. high semi-shrubby plant for the rock garden. *Right:* Helianthemums benefit from being clipped over quite severely after they have flowered
Far right: A pink variety of the sun rose (*Helianthemum nummularium*)

Left: Leucanthemum osmarense, a free-flowering dwarf chrysanthemum relative, covered with large, daisy-like flowers for many weeks in summer

Above: Trailing plants are always useful on rock gardens. *Oenothera missouriensis*, a relative of the evening primrose, produces its golden-yellow flowers over a long period

twigs and tiny gray leaves and carries many small pink flowers in summer. Propagate by seed or cuttings.

Mimulus (*Scrophulariaceae*) (musk) These easily grown and showy plants like moist or cool position shaded from full sunlight. Several are invaluable for places by the sides of pools or streams. They flower in early summer and are increased by seeds, cuttings or division. Most are fairly short-lived and should be re-propagated every two or three years. In *M. cupreus* 'Whitecroft Scarlet' the brilliant flowers are carried in abundance on 6-in. stems. Cut back after flowering. In colder areas treat as an annual. *M. primuloides* is a choice, tiny plant for a cool but not boggy position in the rock garden. It has gay yellow flowers on 2-in. stems. Divide and replant frequently; *M. radicans* likes a cool but not boggy position. It makes flat carpets of bronze leaves studded with stemless white and violet flowers all summer.

Minuartia (*Caryophyllaceae*) *M. verna* makes a delightfully neat little tuft of emerald green with gleaming white flowers on thread-like stems in spring. It is a splendid companion for *Gentiana verna*, which dislikes living in solitude. Grow it in full sun, in gritty soil and propagate by seeds. Needs protection in areas that have severe winters.

Mitchella (*Rubiaceae*) *M. repens*, the part-ridge berry, is a plant for cool shade and lime-free soil. A prostrate shrub, it makes a dense mat of interlaced slender woody stems. The pink bell flowers are followed by bright red fruits. Increase by means of cuttings or seeds.

Nierembergia (*Solanaceae*) *N. repens* (*rivularis*) is entirely herbaceous and disappears below ground in the winter, being hardy as far as N.Y. City. Further north it may be treated as an annual. Its underground creeping stems erupt in summer into bright green leaves amidst which nestle large, white stemless funnel-shaped flowers; it likes poor gritty soil and will flourish in a gravel path. Propagate by division in spring.

Oenothera (*Onagraceae*) (evening primrose) Several species are suitable for the rock garden. They are all sun-lovers with no special soil preferences as long as it is well drained. They have a long flowering season from late spring onward and, although the flowers of many last for one day only, there is a constant succession to continue the display. Propagate by seeds and cuttings. *O. acaulis* forms tufts of jagged-edged bright green leaves and has stemless clusters of white flowers which become pink as they age; *A. fremontii*, 9 in., has slender gray-green leaves and large bright yellow flowers; *O. missouriensis*, 9–12 in., a sprawling plant,

provides an endless succession of enormous deep yellow flowers; *O. pumila* (*perennis*), makes small tufts of shining green leaves and bears neat, cup-shaped yellow flowers in profusion on 6-in. stems over a period of many weeks.

Omphalodes (*Boraginaceae*) These are very early flowering plants for light shade or a cool north aspect. They are not fussy about soil. Propagation is by division. *O. cappadocica* has fresh green leaves and showers of clear blue forget-me-not flowers on 9-in. stems in March–April; *O. verna* flowers earlier, is not quite so tall and the flowers are of a paler blue. There is a delightful white-flowered form.

Oxalis (*Oxalidaceae*) Most of the species suitable for the rock garden are lovers of sun and warmth and good, well-drained soils. Propagation is by seeds or division. *O. acetosella* is one of the species which prefers a cool position. The cultivated form 'Rosea' rambles about in light shade and woodland soil, producing many rich pink flowers on very short stems in spring and summer; *O. adenophylla*, 4 in., has deeply cut silver leaves and countless funnel-shaped pink flowers in spring. Not to be grown where winters are severe. *O. enneaphylla* produces gray leaves and large pink, or sometimes white, cup-shaped flowers in spring. *O.*

Right: One of the colorful varieties of *Phlox subulata*

The alpine poppy, *Papaver alpinum*, provides a display of miniature poppy flowers throughout the summer

inops, 4 in., can be a weed, but it is a lovely one and should be spared a space where an invader is welcome. The large beautiful rose-red flowers are produced abundantly in summer; *O. lobata* sends up, from tiny, hairy bulbs, in early spring, clusters of emerald-green leaves. These soon die down, to reappear in the fall, accompanied by delicious golden flowers on 3-in. stems. It needs a warm corner and light soil; *O. magellanica* is a delightful plant for a cool position in milder areas of the country. Its minute dark green leaves make close mats and are studded with flat, pearl-white flowers in summer.

Papaver (*Papaveraceae*) (poppy) *P. alpinum*, the charming alpine poppy, is a short-lived plant but it perpetuates itself by means of self-sown seedlings in sunny places and light, gritty soil. The leaves appear in tiny tufts, surmounted throughout the summer by miniature poppy flowers which may be white, yellow, cream or shades of pink and red, on 4-in. stems.

Parochetus (*Leguminosae*) *P. communis* is a particularly lovely creeping plant which can only be grown in warmer areas in a warm, moist position. The leaves are clover-like and the plant spreads by trailing stems and carries, during late summer and fall, and often on into the winter, pea-shaped flowers of gentian-blue. Propagate by division or rooted runners.

Penstemon (*Scrophnlariaceae*) These dwarf shrubs like warm positions and protection from winds. A lime-free soil is preferable but not essential. They flower from spring until mid-summer. Propagation is by cuttings of soft tips taken early in the year. *P. davidsonii* (*rupicola*), 4 in. has leathery gray-green leaves and ruby-red flowers; *P. heterophyllus*, 1–1½ ft., has spires of blue flowers; *P. menziesii*, 1 ft. has small, thick and fleshy, toothed leaves and violet-purple flowers; *P. pinifolius* 9–12 in., bears scarlet flowers in profusion; *P. pulchellus* is quite prostrate and bears blue flowers on 3-in. stems; *P. roezlii*, 9 in., makes a stiff bush covered with red flowers.

Phlox (*Polemoniaceae*) In this large genus there are many important rock garden plants. The species, selections and hybrids, loosely grouped as 'cushion phloxes' provide invaluable color early in the year, are of neat habit, easily grown in any good, well-drained soil and benefit from being closely trimmed after they have flowered. Propagate by cuttings or division of old plants in spring or fall. The most popular are the forms of *P. subulata*. All are sun-lovers and,

although they will grow in light shade, they do not as a rule flower freely unless given full light. *P. adsurgens* is an exception in that it prefers a slightly shaded position. Its 3–4 in. mats are decorated by large, salmon-pink flowers. For milder areas *P. amoena* has 6-in. stems which carry heads of purple flowers. There is a form with pretty, variegated foliage. Should not be grown where severe winters occur. *P. divaricata* is of rather loose, untidy habit but the large lilac flowers are carried in loose heads on 12–15-in. stems; the forms of *P. douglasii* are of close, cushion-forming habit and carry carpets of almost stemless flowers. Among the best are 'Boothman's Variety', with clear mauve flowers, 'Rosea', rich pink, and 'Snow Queen', pure white; *P. stolonifera* 'Blue Ridge', 12 in. is a lovely phlox with heads of clear blue flowers; *P. subulata* has several forms and it should be plentifully represented on every rock garden. They are also excellent plants for growing in walls, crazy paving, or for tumbling over a path-edge. They all make wide, low cushions covered with flowers: 'G. F. Wilson', one of the oldest and still one of the best with mauve flowers; 'Alexandra's Pink', clear pink; 'Eventide', blue, very compact; 'Scarlet Flame', scarlet; 'Starglow', pale blue, very free flowering; 'Lilac Queen', lavender blue, are excellent varieties.

Phyteuma (*Campanulaceae*) Several species are worth growing in the rock garden in any good soil and an open position. Propagate by seeds. They flower in mid-summer. *P. hemisphaericum* has grassy leaves and heads of clear blue flowers on 6-in. stems; in *P. nigrum* the intense dark violet flowers are borne on 12-in. stems; *P. scheuchzeri* has rounded heads of deep purple-blue flowers on 12-in. stems.

Pimelia (*Myrtaceae*) *P. coarctata* is a prostrate tender woody shrub whose ground-hugging stems are clothed in tiny gray leaves. The plant is sheeted with small white flowers followed by translucent white berries. Propagate by cuttings or seeds. It needs very gritty soil and full sun.

Platycodon (*Campanulaceae*) (balloon-flower) This handsome plant, valuable for mid-summer flowering, needs only full sun and any good soil. Propagate by seeds. *P. grandiflorum* 'Mariesii' is the most usually planted form. On 12–15-in. stems it carries huge, inflated buds which expand into rich purple saucer-shaped flowers. The variety 'Apoyana', 6 in., is suitable for the small rock garden. There are also forms with white or soft pink flowers.

Above: A view of a small part of the famous rock garden in the Royal Horticultural Society's Gardens at Wisley, Surrey, England
Below: Plants of *Potentilla aurea* are almost hidden by the golden flowers in late spring and summer
Right: *Penstemon menziesii microphylla*, a dwarf kind suitable for the rock garden

Polygala (*Polygalaceae*) (milkwort) *P. cal-carea* loves chalky soil and sunny places where winters are less severe. It has tiny tufts of slender stems and 3-in. spikes of deep blue flowers in the spring; *P. chamae-buxus* likes a cool north aspect. It is a 6-in. evergreen shrub with clusters of cream and yellow tipped purple, fragrant flowers. Propagate by division in spring.

Polygonum (*Polygonaceae*) (knotweed) Two species at least are desirable: *P. tenui-caule* flowers in the very early spring, with short spikes of white flowers on 3-in. stems. Propagate by division; *P. vaccinifolium* is at its best from August until October. It forms dense mats of bronze-tinted green leaves on woody stems and has short spikes of heather-pink flowers. Both these plants should only be grown where winters are less severe. Propagate by cuttings.

Potentilla (*Rosaceae*) (cinquefoil) Some of these showy, easily grown sun-lovers should be on any well-planned rock garden. All flowers in spring and summer. Increase by seeds or division. *P. alba* is a sprawling plant, good for ground cover, with white flowers; *P. aurea* has sheets of golden flowers on prostrate mats of foliage. There is also a good form with double flowers; *P. megalantha* makes bold clumps of large, velvety leaves and huge golden flowers on 6-in. stems; *P. nitida* makes carpets of silvery foliage over which are set on very short stems pretty pink flowers. It needs very gritty soil; *P. verna* 'Nana', a prostrate plant continues to produce its golden flowers throughout the summer and well into the fall.

Primula (*Primulaceae*) These are mostly spring and early summer flowering. Propa-gate by seeds or division. The latter opera-tion yields the best results if carried out soon after flowering. Seeds should be sown soon after ripening. *P. acaulis* is the primrose, of which there are many double flowered and colored forms, all good rock garden plants. They all like a cool position and deep, rich soil; *P. auricula*, 4 in., the alpine auricula, loves a sunny crevice from which to display its charming yellow, fragrant flowers; *P. denticulata* is a plant for a moist place. It has great heads of purple, crimson or white flowers on 1-ft. stems; *P. frondosa* makes tufts of soft, meal-covered leaves and has rounded heads of pink flowers on 4-in. stems; *P. minima*, one of the smallest, has tufts of glossy leaves and large pink flowers on 1-in. stems. It needs gritty soil; *P. marginata*, 6 in., is a fine crevice plant with white powdered leaves and heads of lavender flowers; *P. rosea* loves a really wet position such as a bog garden or by the edge of a stream. In early March it produces vivid carmine-red flowers on 6–9 in. stems.

Pulsatilla (*Ranunculaceae*) (pasque flower) The spring flowering *P. vulgaris* (syn. *Ane-mone pulsatilla*) loves full sun and soil con-taining lime. There are many desirable forms, varying in color from white through shades of purple to pink and deep red. The finely divided leaves make a handsome foil to the large flowers carried boldly on 1-ft. stems. Propagate by seed, sown as soon as it is ripe in late summer, in light soil in an unheated frame.

Ramonda (*Gesneriaceae*) *R. myconii* demands a tight crevice between rocks with a cool, preferably north aspect. It has flat rosettes of leathery, wrinkled leaves and deep lavender, golden centered, flowers on 4-in. stems. Propagate by seeds or by very careful division.

Ranunculus (*Ranunculaceae*) (buttercup) Many species are valuable for the rock garden. They flower in spring and summer, thrive in sunny places and, in general are not at all fussy about the soil in which they grow as long as it is well drained. Propagate by seeds or division. *P. amplexicaulis* has large, flat-faced white flowers on 9-in. stems; *R. ficaria*, the lesser celandine is a pernicious weed but there are some good trustworthy cultivated forms, notably 'Aurantiacus' which has coppery-orange flowers on 4-in. stems; *R. gouanii* has huge, saucer-shaped golden flowers on short stems; *R. gramineus* has narrow, grassy leaves and elegant, branching 12-in. stems carrying golden buttercups; *R. montanus* 'Molten Gold', a gem of a plant, very easily grown, makes low mounds of large golden flowers on very short stems, seldom more than 3-in. high.

Raoulia (*Compositae*) These are completely prostrate plants with minute leaves. They make good ground cover for tiny bulbs or for carpeting the soil beneath pygmy columnar conifers. Recommended for milder areas. Plant them in full sun. Increase by division. *R. australis* forms mats of intense

silver leaves and has stemless golden flowers in the early summer; *R. glabra* makes green mats and has cream flower heads; *R. lutescens* is the tiniest of all, a mere film of gray-green which becomes golden with massed tiny flowers in early summer.

Salix (*Salicaceae*) (willow) Several delightful pigmy willows make entrancing little shrubs for the rock garden. They do not mind full sun, but like cool root conditions and will grow in light shade if necessary. They have fascinating gnarled woody stems and many of them bear pretty silver catkins in the spring. Propagate by cuttings. *R. arbuscula* a prostrate plant, has tangled woody stems and dark green foliage. It will spread over a considerable area; *S. reticulata*, another prostrate species, has lovely rounded leaves, netted with conspicuous veins, and silver-gray catkins.

Saponaria (*Caryophyllaceae*) (soapwort) *S. ocymoides* is a useful and decorative plant to trail down from a high ledge or crevice. The long leafy stems carry, in spring, sheets of bright pink flowers. It is easily grown in sun or light shade and any soil. Propagate by cuttings.

Saxifraga (*Saxifragaceae*) (saxifrage) This is one of the largest and most important genera of rock garden plants. The number of species, hybrids and forms is legion and there are kinds for many different soils and situations. They vary from 1 in. to 1 ft. or more in height. Unless otherwise stated they like open, sunny positions and sharply gritty soil. According to their kind they can be increased by seeds, division and cuttings; each will suggest by its habit and appearance

the appropriate method. Most of them flower in spring and early summer. Space permits mention of only a representative few of each of the many groups. *S. aizoon* is a large complex of slightly varying plants; the two most desirable varieties are 'Lutea' with soft yellow flowers and 'Rosea', soft pink. Both are about 6 in. tall; *S. apiculata* makes flat green cushions and has yellow flowers on 6-in. stems. There is also a good white form; *S. burseriana* is a choice plant of which there are many varieties. One of the best is 'Gloria' which has red stems and large white flowers on 3-in. stems over spiny cushions of gray leaves; *S. cochlearis* makes hard, humped cushions of congested gray rosettes and 9-in. pink stems carrying white flowers in summer; *S. fortunei* has large lobed leaves, red on the reverse, and 18-in. stems carrying flights of white flowers in the fall; *S. granulata* 'Plena' is the double meadow saxifrage. It dies down in winter but bears massed double white flowers in spring on 9-in. stems; *S. irvingii* makes hummocks of minute gray-green rosettes and stemless pink flowers in great profusion; *S. longifolia* forms magnificent rosettes of symmetrical gray leaves and very long spikes of innumerable white flowers; *S. oppositifolia* flowers in very early spring. It makes prostrate carpets of dark foliage and bears stemless red flowers; *S. urbium* (*umbrosa*), London pride, is an old garden plant, still a deservedly popular favorite. It also has some attractive miniature forms particularly suitable for the rock garden.

The so-called 'mossy' saxifrages are a separate group. They like a little shade or a

Left: Saxifrages are among the best of all dwarf plants for the rock garden. *Saxifraga apiculata* bears its yellow flowers on 6-in. stems in spring and early summer
Above: The Pasque flower, *Pulsatilla vulgaris*, has many different color forms. This is 'Rubra'
Right: 'Jersey Gem', a distinctive variety of the horned violet, *Viola cornuta*
Far right: One of the colored forms of the English primrose, *Primula acaulis*, which makes a fine display on the rock garden in early spring

cool aspect. They all make compact mats and vary in height when in flower from 3–6 in. Such kinds as 'Sanguinea Superba', deep red and 'Peter Pan', pink.

Sedum (*Crassulaceae*) (stone crop) Many of these easy, sun-loving plants are extremely decorative plants for the rock garden. Some species, of which *S. acre* and *S. album* are examples, are handsome but so weedy that they should be excluded from all but the wildest places. The few named below may be regarded as a nucleus of the best kinds. Propagate by division or cuttings. All are spring and early summer flowering unless otherwise stated. *S. album* 'Coral Carpet' makes flat mats of fleshy coral-pink leaves and soft pink flowers; *S. cauticolum* produces large heads of crimson red flowers on 6-in. trailing stems in late summer. *S. lydium* has tufts of small fleshy leaves, red in summer, green in winter. It bears white flowers in profusion, on 3-in. stems; *S. spathulifolium* has several good varieties of which the most decorative is 'Purpureum', with purple fleshy leaves and golden flowers on 3-in. stems. In 'Cappa Blanca' the leaves are densely covered with white 'meal'.

Sempervivum (*Crassulaceae*) (houseleek) These sun-lovers are best grown in poor, gritty soil. Very decorative and trouble-free, they carry quite good flowers but are valued most highly for the rosettes of fleshy leaves, often brightly colored. Propagation is by division; few of them breed true from seed. One hundred or more species, forms and hybrids are available. *S. arachnoideum* is the cobweb houseleek; the green and red rosettes are spangled with tangled white 'spiders-webs' of fine threads; *S.* 'Commander Hay' has large deep red-purple leaf rosettes; *S. tectorum*, the common houseleek, is often seen in great clumps on cottage roofs in Europe. It is very variable and various forms are available. The species has green, purple-tipped leaves.

Silene (*Caryophyllaceae*) (catchfly) These are easy plants for sunny positions, variable in color of flower and ranging from high alpine cushion plants to tall border plants. Propagate by seeds or division. They flower in spring and summer. *S. acaulis* makes hard humps of tightly packed tiny rosettes and stemless pink flowers. It needs very gritty soil; *S. schafta* produces sheets of pink flowers on 6-in. stems.

Sisyrinchium (*Iridaceae*) These sun loving, summer flowering, plants have tufts of narrow, grass-like leaves. They are increased by seeds or division. *S. brachypus*, 6 in. has bright yellow flowers; *S. angustifolium* bears bright blue flowers on 6-in. stems.

Soldanella (*Primulaceae*) These lovely, typical alpine plants like cool positions and gritty soil, rich in humus. They flower in earliest spring. Propagate by seeds or by very careful division. Guard from slugs. *S. alpina* has tiny rounded, leathery, dark green leaves and fringed lavender bells on 3-in. stems; *S. montana* has larger leaves and wider flowers of purple-blue, on 4–6-in. stems.

Thymus (*Labiatae*) (thyme) These summer-flowering aromatic plants present no cultural problems in sun and well-drained soil. *T. citriodorus* 'Silver Queen', a variety of the lemon thyme, makes an upright, 6-in. bush of green and silver leaves; *T. herba-barona* is prostrate, its leaves strongly scented of caraway. It has pink flowers. *T. drucei* (*serpyllum*) has many named forms, all invaluable carpeters. Flower color varies from white to deep crimson.

Tiarella (*Saxifragaceae*) *T. cordifolia* is a dainty, shade-loving spring and early summer flowering plant. It has elegant soft green leaves in neat tufts and fluffy spikes of white flowers on 9-in. stems. Increase by division.

Veronica (*Scrophulariaceae*) This is a large genus varying from dwarf kinds for the rock garden to tall plants best suited to flower borders. They all love full sun and grow well in any good garden soil. Propagate by seeds, division or cuttings. All flower in spring and early summer. *V. cinerea*, 1 ft., has gray leaves and long spikes of blue flowers; *V. latifolia dubia*, a low-growing plant, has several named forms providing low mounds of white, pink or blue flowers according to kind; *V. teucrium* 'Royal Blue' has deep blue flowers on 1-ft. tall stems.

Viola (*Violaceae*) *V. cornuta*, the horned violet, bears graceful long-spurred lavender-mauve flowers on 6-in. stems. Grow from cuttings or seed. It grows in any good soil and sunny place; *V. cucullata*, 4 in. loves shade and carries large white, lilac-veined 'violet' flowers in spring. Increase by division every two or three years.

Zauschneria (*Onagraceae*) (Californian fuchsia) *Z. californica*, 9–12 in., is a plant for the hottest, driest available position in milder areas, where it produces a riot of intense scarlet flowers over gray leaves in late summer and fall. Increase by cuttings of soft tips.

Fruit in Your Garden

Fruit should find a place in every garden. In the very smallest there must surely be room for a tree or two to be trained against walls of the house; even in the paved town garden or patio it might be possible to grow a few fruits in containers.

Fruit-growing is a part of gardening with a fascination all its own. As with vegetable-growing one has a useful end-product but in achieving that end one has quite different problems to solve and the interest of a quite different mode of growth. As a by-product, too, in many instances, one is rewarded by beauty of blossom, fruit and leaf color, which can add much to the general decorative effect of the garden.

The nutritional value of a plentiful supply of fresh fruit cannot be over-estimated and in these inflationary days an investment in fruit trees and bushes will make an ever-growing saving to your pocket.

For many gardeners, however, the greatest joy of home fruit-growing lies not so much in cash-saving, horticultural interest or visual effect, as in the enhanced flavor of fresh fruit eaten direct from the plant. One has to remember that all produce in a store is relatively stale as it began to lose flavor from the moment it was harvested. Moreover, commercial growers have to select the varieties they grow for the size of their yield, their ease of culture and their ability to withstand the rigors of handling, grading and transport, rather than for their flavor. The home grower can enjoy varieties of different kinds of fruit which are quite uneconomic to grow commercially—fruits he will never see in any store—and he can indulge his own personal preferences.

Choice of Site

Possible sites for fruit may be divided into three areas: (1) in a clean-cultivated area specially cultivated for the purpose just as a special plot may be provided for vegetables; (2) in the decorative part of the garden, e.g. beds cut out of the lawn; (3) against house or garage walls, or boundary fences or walls.

A Special Plot The provision of a special plot reserved entirely for fruit is the ideal. This enables you to group together fruits having similar manurial needs—gooseberries and red currants close to the apples, for instance, as these all call for much potash, and blackcurrants next to plums and pears, as these three require more nitrogen.

Having all your fruit in one place also simplifies spraying and makes it easier to provide protection from birds.

Although the fruit plot often has to border the vegetables it is unwise to mix the two if you can avoid it. Vegetables often need much richer soil than is good for fruit and dotting fruit trees among the vegetables leads to complications when spraying with toxic or leaf-searing sprays.

In the Flower Garden These same objections hold when fruit trees are planted in the flower garden. Perhaps the least objectionable is cutting out beds from the turf and planting trees in the lawn. When a grass-spoiling chemical is sprayed the adjoining turf can be temporarily covered with plastic sheets or burlap.

Trained trees (espaliers or cordons, see below) can be planted on either side of a pathway to form an avenue or arch and make a picturesque feature, the attractiveness of

which quite compensates for any spraying or feeding problems with the adjoining plants.

Against Walls or Fences The third possible site—against walls or fences—is one much too often neglected. A wall provides shelter and warmth and, therefore, sometimes enables less hardy fruits to be grown successfully. A tree trained against a wall can be more easily given temporary covering in the event of spring frost and can very easily be netted over to keep off birds. A tree growing against a house wall, being so close at hand, often receives better attention than those at the other end of the garden.

There are, however, certain points about the wall-training of fruits which must be borne in mind. This is an extremely dry situation and regular attention will always have to be given to watering. When planting, set the stem 9 in. away from the foot of the wall. In summer, red spider mites which thrive in the dry, may be a nuisance: occasional syringeing with clear water will discourage these pests.

If you are planting against a solid fence or boundary wall, think of the ultimate height of your tree. A fan-trained tree will soon reach to 10 ft. and an espalier, which can be restricted to the number of tiers for which there is space against the wall, may be a much better proposition.

If you intend planting against an open fence, remember that there are no protective benefits and if the fence forms a boundary, the pruning, spraying and picking of the fruit may put a strain on good neighborly relations.

Many kinds of fruit tree may be grown against a wall, and in colder areas this

Left: Bartlett pear is a popular dessert variety, at its best in September
Right: Cox's Orange Pippin apple
Above right: Fall harvest from the fruit garden

privileged position may be reserved for some of the choice fruits that will grow outdoors in the particular district, for instance, figs, peaches or nectaries.

The selection of fruits to grow against a wall should depend not only on the geographical situation but also on the aspect of the wall itself. House walls seldom face the cardinal points of the compass exactly, but the following recommendations may be used as a guide:

For east-facing walls: Early plums and pears. These are also suitable for north-east and north-west walls where winters are less severe, the fruits advised for north walls being a safer choice in the north.

For south-facing walls: Apricots, figs, gages, peaches and nectarines, pears, sweet cherries and grape vines. In colder and very exposed areas use such sites for pears and plums.

For west-facing walls: Apricots, early peaches and nectarines. In colder parts of the country, plant plums, early gages, pears.

For north-facing walls: Sour cherries, blackberries and loganberries, and, grown as cordons, red and white currants. These fruits, grown against a north wall, will ripen their crops later than the same varieties grown in a sunny position in the open garden and thus lengthen the season.

Fruit trees and bushes need sunshine for healthy growth. It is the action of sunlight upon the leaves which enables them to convert carbon dioxide and oxygen from the air and various minerals in solution absorbed by the roots into new tissue, including eventually the fruits which are your aim. Insufficient sunshine can result in weak growth, poor color in the fruit and indifferent flavor.

In small gardens it is not always possible to allot an ideal situation to all the fruit. Some, however, can tolerate partial shade better than others—the cane fruits (raspberries, blackberries, loganberries and other hybrid berries), gooseberries and red, white and blackcurrants—but these will crop later than those in full sun.

Remember that the trees you plant will themselves cast shadows and so the tallest specimens should be on the north side of the plot.

Shelter from wind is valuable but never plant close to a hedge or tree whose roots will spread into the soil and rob it of nutriment intended for the fruit. Exposure to biting winds in the spring can result in frost damage to blossom but, much more likely, this will be the cause of poor setting because the pollinating insects have been discouraged from flying.

What to Grow

Fruits are normally divided into two main classes:

(1) The soft fruits which include herbaceous plants such as strawberries, the shrubby ones, such as blackcurrants and gooseberries, and the cane fruits, such as raspberries and blackberries. All these are grown on their own roots. It must be pointed out that currants are alternate hosts for the white pine blister rust disease, and before planting them contact your state Experiment Station to find out if they can be grown in your area.

(2) The top or tree fruits. Apples, pears and plums are common examples. The named varieties you buy at a nursery have all been

half-standard

standard

pyramid

bush

cordon

double cordon

espalier

fan

The main types of trained trees

budded or grafted (mostly, the former) on to roots (known as the rootstock) raised separately and designed to impart certain desired characteristics to the behavior of the tree. Thus for garden planting apples are frequently budded on a weak-growing rootstock which will result in the tree starting to fruit early in life and never growing too big. See table of rootstocks.

Tree fruits may be pruned or trained to various different shapes or forms, e.g.

Standard This is the old-fashioned bushy-topped tree with a vertical stem of 6 ft. before the lowest branches arise.

Half-standard As above, but with a stem of only 4 ft. A half-standard, therefore, is only 2 ft. shorter than a full standard and both types are too large for most gardens. Not only do such trees eventually take up much space (30–40 ft. each way) but a ladder is essential for spraying, pruning and picking, and a good crop (possibly over 200 lb. of apples) is probably greater than any one family wants of one variety. Half-standard plums of the varieties whose branches tend to 'weep' downwards are sometimes planted in gardens but such a tree still requires from 15–20 ft. each way according to rootstock (see below).

Bush This is the most common form of tree, with a clear stem of from 1½ to 3 ft. below the branches. Soft fruits are also grown as bushes, the clear stem of red and white currants and gooseberries being about 6 in. Blackcurrants are grown as bushes but with no leg, the branches being encouraged to grow from as low down as possible. Apples are sometimes grafted or budded on weak-growing rootstocks which result in quite a small tree (see 'rootstocks' below). Dwarf bushes are very suitable for garden planting.

Cordon A single-stemmed tree without branches, fruiting spurs arising directly from the main stem. To induce early fruiting, cordons are frequently planted at an angle of 45° and are then referred to as oblique cordons. This is a useful type for the small garden and enables a range of different varieties to be planted in a small space, thus spreading the season of use and reducing the risk of poor cropping because of inadequate cross-pollination. Single vertical cordons are useful for growing against house walls, filling in comparatively narrow spaces between windows etc. Pears do well in such places.

Double Cordon This is formed by training the stem horizontally on both sides of the short vertical stem and then training up a single vertical stem or cordon from the extremity of each 'arm' so that the tree is U-shaped. In a similar way a triple cordon can be trained with three main vertical stems. The double or triple cordon shape is most often used with gooseberries and red currants.

Espalier A tree with a central vertical stem from which horizontal branches spring in pairs, one on each side. Apples and pears are often grown in this form along-side paths but espaliers are also useful for training against walls particularly where space for upward extension is limited.

Fan From a short vertical leg the branches are trained like the ribs of a fan, all in one plane. Fans are often trained against walls but they can equally well be freestanding but fastened to horizontal wires. Fans are most usually formed from peaches, nectarines, apricots, pears and plums, but apples can be trained in this form, against horizontal wires.

Pyramid A Christmas-tree shaped tree, with a central vertical stem from which the branches radiate. Apples and pear pyramids on dwarfing rootstocks are excellent for the small garden. Although there are no dwarfing rootstocks for plums, pyramid-training is gaining in popularity for keeping garden plum trees within bounds.

Family Tree This is not a shape but means that several varieties have been grafted together to form one tree. The 'family trees' sold commercially are usually in the form of bushes but this is not essential.

❧ Preparing the Site ❧

If your soil does not happen to be ideal for fruit-growing, you can do something to improve it and you can choose for planting the fruits least likely to be adversely affected.

Drainage The first and most important point of all is drainage. All fruits need good drainage for waterlogged conditions in winter kill the roots by drowning.

Sometimes it is possible to lay land drains in the direction of the fall of the land or to dig trenches at least 30 in. deep, spread 9 in. of rubble in the bottom and cover with inverted turves before returning the soil. Unfortunately this procedure is seldom possible in gardens because there is no outfall without which no drain can function.

Deep cultivation, however, will improve surface drainage and this should be carried out over as much of the garden as possible. If you only prepare individual sites for the trees, these become miniature sumps collecting surface water from their immediate vicinity.

It is also possible to mitigate the effects of bad drainage by planting on mounds or raised beds (see Planting).

Clay soil is, naturally, much more likely to collect water in winter than a light, sandy soil. To open up a clay soil, work in sandy or gritty material and vegetable matter such as well-rotted manure, peatmoss, garden compost, composted seaweed or leafmold. These same materials that will open a heavy soil will give 'body' to a very light soil.

As a general rule when preparing for fruit a piece of previously cultivated garden it will be quite unnecessary to add any manure. Over-rich soil will only encourage lush growth at the expense of fruiting. Soft fruits require a rather richer soil initially than the tree fruits and a soil containing plenty of vegetable matter which retains moisture well in the summer is invaluable.

Weeds Whether you are preparing a previously cultivated site or a piece of virgin meadowland, it is important to eradicate all perennial weeds. These can be a considerable nuisance in a fruit plot later and not easy to deal with when their roots are intertwined with those of the fruit. Where severely weed-ridden areas are concerned, it may be advisable to defer planting for a year to devote a whole growing season to fallowing the land and eliminating every weed to appear. Annual weeds can be easily dealt with by the application of a contact weedkiller. A total weedkiller such as sodium chlorate (dose: 2 oz. per sq. yd.), will make short work of all weeds but it will render the soil sterile for as long as a year, during which time it would be unsafe to plant anything.

Soil Acidity The degree of acidity of the soil is of much importance to the fruit-grower. All the fruits we grow, but two, flourish best in a slightly acid soil. The two exceptions are blueberries and cranberries which like very acid conditions.

Above: Large, well formed strawberry fruits
Right: 'Sparkle', a modern strawberry cultivar
Below: A hardy, free bearing variety of peach, ripening in late August

Although alkaline soils are not noted for fruit growing, one sometimes sees quite flourishing garden fruit trees and bushes in these areas. Some fruits will tolerate a certain degree of alkalinity better than others (see below).

When preparing ground for fruit it is prudent to test it for acidity or otherwise. Testing outfits for garden use are quite inexpensive. Make several tests, using distilled and *not* tap water, and take an average reading from the results.

One cannot in the garden control acidity within fine limits, nor is it necessary. Ideally we should like the test to show a pH scale reading between 6·0 and 6·5. But if the test shows a reading under 5·5 spread a 3 oz. per sq. yd. dressing of hydrated lime over the surface and lightly prick it into the topsoil. (The pH scale indicates the acidity or alkalinity of the soil. pH 7·0 indicates neutrality, readings below this indicate the degree of acidity, those above 7·0 indicate the degree of alkalinity. The scale is logarithmic, i.e. a reading of pH 5 shows that the soil is 10 times as acid as a soil which has a reading of pH 6 and one which has a reading of pH 4 is 100 times as acid as a soil with a pH 6 reading.)

It is not so easy to rectify matters if the test shows an alkaline reaction (over 7·0 pH scale). If the alkalinity is the result of over-liming in the past (old vegetable plots often suffer in this way), then of course you should not add any more lime. The addition of any humus-making material – farmyard or stable manure, garden compost or peatmoss – will all help to reduce the alkalinity. Refrain from using old mushroom compost manure because this usually contains chalk and is slightly alkaline. In future years fertilizers of an acid nature (e.g. sulfate of ammonia) should be preferred for the provision of nitrogen.

The reason why an alkaline soil is unfavorable for fruit-growing is that in such conditions certain trace elements – quite essential but required in tiny amounts only – become chemically unavailable to the roots. The minerals chiefly concerned are iron and manganese and in alkaline land fruit trees and bushes soon begin to show the deficiency symptoms of loss of leaf color between the leaf-veins and die-back.

Simply feeding extra iron and manganese is no remedy because the ordinary fertilizers soon become locked up, too. Chemists have circumvented this by producing these minerals in a form known as chelated or sequestered and one can now buy fertilizer mixtures containing both chelated iron and manganese for application as a liquid from the watering can or as a foliage spray. The use of chelated fertilizers has made fruit thrive in gardens where it has never been able to flourish before.

Soil preparation should be completed several weeks before planting so that the disturbed ground can settle properly. Early cultivation is important where manure has to be worked in (no manure should ever come into contact with the roots at planting time). Shuffling your feet over the cultivated soil will break up surface lumps and help to settle it.

Soil Needs of Individual Fruits

Apples These are tolerant fruits but they do not like bad drainage. They do best in deep, medium loam; on light soils they may suffer from potash deficiency. Their nitrogen requirements are moderate. They are liable to show serious signs of iron and manganese shortage on alkaline land.

Apricots These thrive on well drained sandy loams that are well supplied with organic matter.

Blackberries The stronger varieties will succeed in almost any soil but the weaker ones need a deep, well-worked moderately heavy loam for best results.

Blackcurrants A deep medium loam is best. Light soils should be enriched with manure. This fruit cannot be grown in areas that have hot summers. A host for the white pine blister rust disease, they are prohibited in many areas.

Cherries Cherries flourish best in deep medium loam. They will also prosper on a deep heavy loam, but will not tolerate poor drainage and soon show manganese deficiency on soils that are over alkaline. They require a moderate climate.

Figs Too good a soil results in growth rather than fruit and for that reason figs do well in a medium well drained loam. A light, sandy soil should be strengthened by the addition of peatmoss, to aid moisture-retention. Figs can only be grown outside all year round where winters are mild.

Gooseberries Its growth is prohibited in some areas because it is a host for white pine blister rust. It does best on a deep loam, hates poor drainage, and often shows potash deficiency on sandy soils. Shallow, light soils should be given plenty of humus to improve moisture retention.

Loganberries As for blackberries.

Peaches (and nectarines) These prefer a light well drained soil.

Pears These have requirements generally similar to those of apples but are slightly more tolerant of indifferent drainage. When on quince rootstock they are susceptible to iron deficiency on very limey soil.

Plums (and damsons and gages) These do best on a deep heavy loam; they will also succeed on a clay soil but it must be well-drained. Ex-vegetable plot soil (rich in nitrogen) is excellent. Light soil results in poor fruit quality, brittle branches and a short life. Plums are very susceptible to iron deficiency on a very alkaline soil.

Raspberries A well-drained deep loam is the ideal but raspberries will also flourish in a light soil if top and second spit have been liberally enriched with moisture-holding vegetable matter and the soil never allowed to dry out in drought. Good drainage is essential. Iron and manganese deficiencies can be serious on soil containing a lot of lime.

Red and White Currants These do best on a light loam but may show potash deficiency signs on a lighty sandy soil. They are less in need of rich humus content than other soft fruits and prefer only slight acidity. They are liable to iron deficiency on very alkaline soils. Hosts of the white pine blister rust, currants are prohibited in certain areas. They will only grow in a cool climate.

Strawberries A rich, well-drained medium loam is best. Light soils need the addition of plenty of vegetable matter to improve moisture-retention. Clay soils need plenty of vegetable matter worked in to lighten them and improve drainage. Winter waterlogging can cause serious losses. Iron deficiency is very liable to appear on soil containing a lot of lime.

Planting; Feeding; Growing Apples

The planting season for fruits other than strawberries (a special case and dealt with separately) extends, depending on the area, from September to early spring. Where winters are severe, planting must cease when the ground freezes.

For rapid re-establishment close contact is necessary between the particles of moist soil and the tiny root hairs. This is more likely to be achieved with the cool weather to follow, or in early spring. Another reason for early fall planting is that the soil then still retains sufficient warmth to encourage immediate root growth.

Fruits which start in to growth early (apricots, peaches and nectarines) are planted in late fall in milder areas. Where winters are severe planting should wait till spring.

It is one thing to plan to plant in the fall in the colder north, quite another to accomplish this. Rains may make the soil unsuitable, transport difficulties may hold up your new trees, the nurseryman may not have immediately just what you want or may be slow to deliver or frost may freeze the soil solid or the planting site may be deep in snow.

Should the fruit trees or canes arrive before you are immediately ready to plant them, heel them in temporarily. For this take out a slit trench with the spade with one face at an angle of 45°. The trench must be deep enough to take the roots when roughly spread out and so that they will be covered to the same depth as they were in the nursery (notice the soil mark on the stem). Lay the trees along the sloping side of the trench, return the soil, covering all the roots and firm it.

If the trees arrive during hard frost or snow so that planting is impracticable, unfasten the bundle and place the plants in the garage or a shed. Cover them and protect them from mice. If, when it comes to planting, the roots look dry, soak them in water for a couple of hours.

Staking and Tying Finally, stakes and tying materials should be obtained and prepared. In light land all posts should be sunk at least 2 ft.; in heavy soil 18 in. is sufficient. Above ground the stake must extend to just below the lowest branches. Strong stakes are necessary because they may have to do duty for many years. The underground part of the stake and at least a few inches above should be thoroughly soaked (not merely painted) in a copper-based preservative.

All tree fruits need to be staked on planting and those on dwarfing rootstock will need support for the whole of their life.

If a single vertical stake is to be used, this should be inserted before planting to obviate root damage. Some growers prefer a longer, oblique stake which is inserted at an angle of about 45° and pointing towards the prevailing wind. Such a stake must be long enough to cross the tree's trunk just below the lowest branches. Another method is to drive in two vertical stakes, one each side of the tree and at least a foot apart, then fix a crosspiece to these to which the stem will be fastened.

Apple or pear trees to be grown as oblique cordons require a system of horizontal wires. Preferably these should run from south to north and be 2, 4 and 6 ft. above the ground. Use gauge 12 galvanized wire and insert an adjustable straining bolt at one end of each wire to keep it taut. The end posts must be really stout (concrete or iron posts are often used) and should have angle struts facing down the row to take the strain.

Whether grown in the open or against a wall, fan-trained trees will require a system of horizontal wires about 6 in. apart.

Soft fruits such as currants and gooseberries do not require any support except where they are grown as cordons. Blackberries, loganberries and other hybrid berries need four horizontal wires at heights of 3, 4, 5 and 6 ft.

These preparations completed, planting may be carried out, provided that the soil is quite friable.

Take out a planting hole wide and deep enough for the roots of the tree, bush or cane to be spread out to their natural length. Clip off with the hand shears any damaged roots and shorten any one root which is substantially longer and stronger than the rest.

Break up the soil at the bottom of the hole with a fork and draw in a little topsoil to form a slight mound at the center so that the tree 'sits' on this. At this stage of the proceedings, an assistant to hold the tree is most helpful. When planting is completed and the soil firmed down, the tree should be at the same depth as it was in the nursery (the soil mark on the stem will probably be visible). Where tree fruits which do not grow on their own roots are concerned, it is essential that the join (known as the 'union') between the top part (the 'scion') and the rootstock should be quite clear of the soil, at least 4 in. above it. Most soft fruits should be at their previous, nursery, depth, except blackcurrants which should be slightly deeper than before.

Now, your helper holding the tree at the right depth (a stick laid across the planting hole will indicate the final soil level), begin to replace the topsoil round the roots. A little

Planting Distances for Tree Fruits

	Standard or half-standard	Bush	Dwarf bush	Pyramid	Cordon	Fan	Espalier
Apple	30–40	15	9	3½ × 7	2½ × 6	15	10–15
Apricot						12	
Cherry (Sweet)	30–40	30–40				20	
Cherry (Sour or Morello)	20	15				10–15	
Fig	12–18					12–18	
Nectarine	18					12–15	
Peach		18				12–15	
Pear	30–40	15	12	3 × 6	2½ × 6	12–15	12–15
Plum (including Gages)	15–20	12–20		10 × 10		12	

(All figures in feet)

moist peatmoss mixed with this soil as you proceed will aid rapid new root growth. Never add manure. Use your fingers to work the soil well in beneath and around every root. Firm it occasionally as you work. When ground level is reached firm with your feet and then just rake over the surface.

Finally, spread over the root area a 2-in. deep mulch of rotted manure, compost or peatmoss to preserve moisture and protect the roots.

Immediately after planting fasten the tree temporarily to its stake. Permanent fastening should only be done a few months later when the soil has had time to settle. Inspect and adjust the fastenings of all newly-planted trees frequently in their early years.

Patent plastic straps are excellent for fastening fruit trees because these incorporate a plastic buffer which prevents the stem from chafing against the stake and because they are so easily adjustable as the tree grows.

Alternatively, use soft string for tying a newly-planted tree, first wrapping a piece of burlap, old rubber hose or something similar round the bark.

Cordons should be tied with soft string or plastic tying tape to canes which, in turn, are tied to the horizontal wires. Similarly, espaliers and fan-trained trees should have their 'arms' tied to canes which are then fastened to the wires.

Oblique cordons should be planted at an angle of 45°, pointing to the north and with the scion part of the union on top of the rootstock part so that when the tree is bent down to a more acute angle this will tend to press the two parts of the union together rather than tear them apart.

Feeding Fruit

Like all other plants fruits have special need for the three major nutritional elements—nitrogen, potassium and phosphorus. They also require many other minerals in lesser quantities, some quite minute.

In the following pages the 'straight' fertilizers are recommended for the provision of the three major elements—sulfate of ammonia and ammonium nitrate for nitrogen, sulfate of potash for potassium and superphosphate for phosphorus. Natural manure provides all these three and all the minor elements.

Many excellent proprietary mixed manures are now on the market and these may be used with every confidence according to the makers' instructions.

The Care of Apples

Most gardeners plant two- or three-year-old trees which have already been pruned by the nurseryman into the required shape—bush, cordon, pyramid, espalier or fan. It is more interesting to start with a one-year-old tree (a whip) and carry out the shaping yourself: this is cheaper, but it does mean you have to wait longer before you can pick the fruit.

As soon as a new tree has been planted you must consider what pruning is necessary, according to the age of the tree. Winter pruning, carried out while the tree is dormant (not during periods of severe frost), promotes growth and in the early years, when the framework of the tree is being built up, can be fairly drastic. Later, when the branches to carry the crop have been developed, winter pruning should be more restrained, the aim now being to stimulate fruit bud formation rather than much more growth. Summer pruning encourages fruit bud formation and keeps trees within bounds.

Pruning Bush Trees FIRST WINTER: If a whip has been planted, the first pruning consists of beheading it at a point immediately above a growth bud about 18 to 24 in. above soil level. This cut determines the length of stem below the main branches.

SECOND WINTER: Select the three or four sturdiest of the resultant shoots made during the first summer. These should be evenly spaced round the tree and will form the main branches from which other branches will spring. The aim should be a goblet shape with an open center. Shorten each of the selected branches to between a third and a half of its length, making the cut beyond and close to a bud pointing to the desired direction.

Cut back any other shoots, not needed as main branches, according to vigor, the weak-

Far left (top): A six year old fan-trained apple on M.7 rootstock
Far left (bottom): An apple trained as an espalier on M.7 rootstock
Left: Young American crab apple

est to one bud and the strongest to five buds.

THIRD WINTER: Each of the three or four main branches will have produced one extension growth and a number of laterals. Cut back the leader by a half. Choose two or three of the strongest and best-placed laterals as new branches and cut these, too, back by half. Cut back other laterals over 5 in. long to the fourth bud and any laterals pruned in the second winter to one bud of the new growth. Any side shoots growing from the main stem of the tree should be removed entirely.

FOURTH WINTER: The stage has now been reached when, to encourage fruit production, pruning may be substantially less drastic. Subsequent treatment will depend upon the habit of growth of the tree in question. Most apples form fruiting spurs naturally or when their laterals are cut hard back. Some varieties, however, tend to make their fruit buds at the tips of young shoots and at or near the tips of older shoots. These are called tip-bearers. A few varieties bear their fruit terminally and on spurs. If tip-bearing varieties have all their leaders and laterals cut back, few if any fruit buds will be formed.

For the spur-forming majority of varieties only tip the leaders, removing about 2 in. and cut back new laterals to three buds and previously pruned laterals to one bud of new wood. Eventually the spur systems will become overlong and possibly congested. Remove a few entirely and shorten others by a half. Should growth be weak cut back branch leaders more than usual–by a half, even three-quarters of the new growth.

With all systems of pruning, a first step is to cut out entirely any dead or diseased wood and any shoots growing in an undesirable direction (e.g. congesting the center of a bush tree, directly towards the wall of a wall-trained tree) or crossing or chafing against another shoot.

If a shoot on a tip-bearing variety is left unpruned, it should develop a fruit bud at its end during the next year which, if still left unpruned, will produce fruit in the third year. If a tip-bearer is to crop well a good proportion of shoots must be left unpruned and the system known as renewal pruning is suitable.

Each year some fruited laterals are shortened to two buds so that two new shoots are produced the next summer. The remaining laterals are left unpruned to make fruit buds.

When a tip-bearer has begun cropping the tipping of leaders may cease.

Pruning Oblique Cordons FIRST WINTER: If a whip spur-bearer is planted, no winter pruning is necessary. Prune tip-bearers back by a quarter. Should there be any side shoots more than 4 in. cut these back to three buds.

MID-JULY: Cut back mature laterals (those which are becoming woody at the base and are more than 9 in. long) to the third leaf after the basal cluster. Leave immature laterals for similar treatment at mid-September. If, by mid-September there has been secondary growth from your first cuts, prune this back to one bud from the point of origin.

SECOND JULY AND SUBSEQUENT YEARS: Cut back mature laterals as in previous summer. Where sub-laterals have formed, and are mature, cut back to one leaf after the basal cluster. Deal with previously immature laterals and sub-laterals in September.

The leader of a cordon does not usually need to be cut until further height has to be restricted and then it should be shortened, as necessary, in spring. Before that, however, greater length can be accommodated by unfastening the cane to which the tree is tied and pressing it down to a more acute angle before refastening to the wires.

In time the fruiting spurs may become overlong and congested. They may be shortened or thinned out in winter.

Pruning Dwarf Pyramids The laterals and sub-laterals along the branches of a pyramid are pruned in summer in the same way as those on cordons and, accordingly, the spur-bearing varieties are much easier to deal with than those inclined to tip-bearing.

FIRST WINTER: Behead the whip at about 20 in. above soil level, just above a bud which will grow to provide further upward extension. Rub out the next bud below this (its growth would tend to compete with the leader). The next three or four buds should point out evenly round the stem. Rub out any buds pointing in the wrong direction (i.e. too close to their neighbor). The aim is a central leader growing vertically with three or four branches evenly spaced below it. The bottom three of these buds will be stimulated if you take a notch out of the bark immediately above each bud (see definitions). Side shoots more than 9 in. from the ground but less than 12 may be used to form the first branches: cut them back to about 6 in., to a bud pointing downwards.

FIRST SUMMER: Tie the leader to a bamboo cane if necessary to make it grow vertically. If more than four sideshoots have appeared, cut the surplus back to four leaves after the basal cluster in mid-July.

SECOND WINTER: Pruning now is designed to provide a second tier of branches to fill the gaps between the branches of the tier below.

Cut the central leader to a bud 12 to 18 in. above the previous winter's cut and to keep the central stem vertical, on the opposite side. Select suitable buds to form the branches, rubbing out unwanted ones and notching the two lowest. Prune back the leaders of the first tier of branches to downward-pointing buds about 9 in. from the point of origin.

SECOND SUMMER AND SUBSEQUENT YEARS: Treat laterals and sub-laterals as those on a cordon.

THIRD WINTER: Prune as in second winter. When the desired height limit has been reached defer pruning of the central leader until May and then cut it back by half. Thereafter cut new growth back to $\frac{1}{2}$ in.

Pruning Espaliers Espaliers are usually sold ready-trained with two or three pairs of horizontal branches. There is no reason, however, why you should not plant a whip

1: On heavy soil particularly, it is advisable to plant fruit trees on a mound of soil in the center of the planting hole, as shown. 2: A stick laid across the rim of the planting hole will enable you to ensure that the tree is planted at the right depth, according to the soil mark on the stem. 3: A whip is beheaded above a growth bud, about 1½–2 ft. above the ground, during the first winter after planting. 4: Branches will develop and these should be shortened during the second winter, as indicated. 5: Further growths which develop will need to be pruned in subsequent winters. 6: The system of wires, posts and straining bolts used for cordon and espalier trained fruit trees.

Left: Baskets of 'Winesap' apples

Rootstocks for Apples
M.9 Most dwarfing of all. A good stock for cordons and dwarf bushes. Usually too dwarfing for espaliers and pyramids.

M.26 Less dwarfing than M.9. For small espaliers, dwarf pyramids and for cordons and dwarf bushes where soil is not rich.

M.7 & MM.106 Semi-dwarfing, producing trees of moderate size on good soil, often used for pyramids. Will produce dwarf trees on poorish soil. Recommended for cordons or varieties which do not spur freely.

M.2 & MM.111 Vigorous stocks which make big trees on good soil. May be used for espaliers where there is plenty of space and good for cordons and pyramids where the soil is definitely poor.

Notes The letters refer to the research stations originally responsible for them. M = Malling; MM = Malling-Merton. When ordering espaliers, cordons and dwarf trees from a nursery, the rootstock may be specified.

Apple Varieties
Lodi, C; Melba, D; Early McIntosh, DP, BB; Gravenstein, DP; Wealthy, C, BB; McIntosh, DP; Cortland, DP; Cox Orange, D; Jonathan, D; Stayman, D; Golden Delicious, D, BB; Northern Spy, D, BB.

D = dessert; C = cooking; DP = dual purpose; BB = biennial bearing.

Notes There are of course many varieties of apple available and readers are urged to contact their state Agricultural Experiment Station for advice on varieties that are suitable for the area in which they live. The majority of apple varieties are self-unfruitful, meaning that they will not set fruit unless fertilized by pollen from a different variety. There are some varieties however whose pollen is sterile and therefore are not suitable as pollinators. These include: Baldwin, Gravenstein, Stayman, Winesap and Rhode Island Greening. It must also be noted that a red bud sport of any variety cannot be used to pollinate that variety.

Amongst varieties that are self-fruitful and require no pollinators are Golden Delicious and Rome Beauty. When planting a number of varieties together for the purpose of cross-pollination, it is important to ensure that the flowering times overlap.

Below: Cox's Orange Pippin, a dessert variety

tree and train your own espalier. Then you can have a single pair of branches or, if you wish, four, five or more tiers.

There is no rule as to the height of the first pair of branches or the space between subsequent tiers—usually about 15 in. is convenient. For preference plant a whip and cut back to a bud just above the lowest horizontal growth to carry the second tier of branches 15 in. higher in a year's time. Below the top bud look for a pair of buds as nearly as possible opposite each other. The growths from these will form the lowest pair of horizontal branches and to stimulate the lowest bud make a small notch just above it. Rub out any unwanted buds.

Tie the resultant shoots from the two lower buds to canes fastened to the wires at an angle of 45°. If one shoot grows more strongly than the other, lower it slightly to a more acute angle and raise its partner slightly, nearer to the vertical. Try thus to get equal growth in the two shoots. At the end of the first season lower both canes half way to the horizontal, then down to their permanent horizontal position at the end of the second season.

Treat any laterals and sub-laterals arising from these horizontal branches as those on a cordon. Year by year a further pair of new branches can be made as desired. Leaders need not be pruned until the limit of available space is reached unless growth is unsatisfactory—in which case in winter cut back the new growth of leaders by a half or more.

Pruning Fans Except in colder areas apples are not satisfactory when trained against a wall. However, an apple can be fan-trained, the ribs of the fan being fastened to horizontal wires.

The initial training follows the method adopted with peaches (see Peaches). Once established treat each rib as if it were a cordon, though when it reaches the limit of available space it cannot be bent down to a more acute angle and so the leader must be cut.

Fruit Thinning In good years failure to thin may result in a glut of undersized apples and put such a strain on the tree that it can produce little fruit the next year. In this way a habit of biennial bearing may be induced. Certain varieties are notorious for this alternate good and bad crop habit.

Timely fruit thinning will often check a tendency towards biennial bearing. Start thinning as soon as the fruitlets have set and you can form an idea of the possible crop.

With most varieties the central apple in each cluster is usually larger but does not in the end prove the best. So begin by removing any blemished fruitlets and then all the larger central fruits in each cluster.

Thin in about three stages, first reducing each cluster to one apple. Then continue until finally about one fruit remains for every 25 to 30 leaves. Dessert varieties should not be closer than 4 in. apart, cooking apples 6 in.

Watering Never wait until signs of distress are noticeable. Watering is particularly desirable in the spring for newly-planted and young trees and an equable moisture supply in the soil is always important.

Mulch trees in early spring with a 2-in. layer of rotted manure, garden compost or peatmoss to help maintain soil moisture and protect the roots.

Picking An apple is ready for picking as soon as it will easily part company with the tree, the stalk remaining on the apple. Pick by taking an apple in the palm of the hand, lift it to a horizontal position and give a very slight twist. If ready, the apple will come away quite easily. The picking season begins in late July and extends well into fall for late kinds. Early varieties of apple should be eaten quite soon after picking.

Storing Mid-season and late apples will only keep to their proper season (by which time only will their full flavor have developed) if they have not been picked too soon (which results in premature shrivelling) and if they have been stored in good atmospheric conditions and a low temperature.

A cool cellar provides the nearest to ideal conditions—moist air, adequate ventilation, darkness and an even temperature as near as possible to 40°F (4.5°C). If a shed has to be used, do not worry about an occasional drop in temperature to a few degrees below freezing but never handle the apples at such a time.

If you have a cellar or an insulated building, space the apples out, stalk uppermost on clean shelves. If space is short, wrap the apples separately in squares of newspaper or oiled apple wraps and put carefully into boxes.

Feeding Where apples have been planted on cultivated garden soil of reasonable fertility they are likely to need little feeding in their early years beyond an annual spring mulch of rotted manure or compost.

Always watch for signs of potash deficiency: fruits may drop excessively or be small, leaves may assume a bluish-green shade, developing paleness between the veins and eventually looking scorched at the edges. Dress with 1 oz. per sq. yd. of sulphate of potash.

In normal circumstances a suitable annual spring fertilizer dressing for established trees would be $\frac{1}{2}$ oz. of superphosphate and $\frac{3}{4}$ oz. of sulfate of potash per sq. yd. If no natural manure or compost is available for mulching, use peatmoss and add 1 oz. per sq. yd. of sulfate of ammonia to the fertilizer. If growth is slow, increase the sulfate of ammonia to 2 oz. per sq. yd.

Over-vigorous growth can be checked by sowing fine grasses up to within a foot or so of the trunk. Mow the grass several times during the growing season but always leave the mowings to rot *in situ*. When growth has steadied down the grass will need feeding with an annual dose of 2–4 oz. of sulfate of ammonia and $\frac{1}{2}$–1 oz. of sulfate of potash with $\frac{1}{2}$ oz. of superphosphate per sq. yd.

Various Fruits

The Care of Apricots

Apricots flower even earlier than peaches and can only be grown successfully where late frosts do not occur. They are self-fertile but unless flying insects are plentiful hand pollination is helpful (distributing the pollen with a camel's-hair brush or wisp of cotton-wool).

The Russian apricots are hardier than the larger fruiting varieties which are grown on the West Coast, and several varieties that are suitable for growing in the Great Plains area have been introduced by the South Dakota Agricultural Experiment Station.

In colder parts of the country apricots may be given the protection of a wall and trained as fans.

The habit of fruiting resembles that of the plum. Pruning of mature specimens consists of thinning of unwanted shoots and reducing the leaders to encourage the formation of spurs and young wood on which the fruit is borne. Older trees should be pruned harder to encourage the growth of new wood.

Apricots may be grown in the greenhouse but there should be no attempt to force growth, using the glass merely to safeguard from frost. Ventilate freely whenever possible.

The Care of Blackberries

Blackberries and other berry fruits are all very easy to grow. They fruit on canes produced during the previous year. After planting, cut down to a sound bud about 9 in. above the ground. Shoots which grow during the first summer will fruit in the second year. After picking, cut old canes to ground level and tie the new season's canes of trailing types against the horizontal support wires. It is sound practice either to spread out the old canes all to one side of the plant, tying the new ones in on the other side or to spread out the fruiting canes on both sides, but fairly low down, and fasten the new canes to the center and along the top. These schemes, by keeping the new canes separate or above the old ones prevent them from becoming disease infected by drip from above.

Recommended Varieties: Blackberries

Brainerd (August); Himalaya Giant (Aug.–Sept.) Extremely vigorous, large berries; Oregon Thornless (Aug.–Sept.), less vigorous. The absence of thorns is a great asset.

Hybrid berries: Loganberry (second half July). Thornless Loganberry. Similar to above but the canes are smooth; Japanese Wineberry (Aug.) Decorative. Very sweet, crimson berries; Malling Hybrid 53–16. Dark purple berries the pips of which are less trouble than raspberry pips in jam; Youngberry (late July–Aug.) Large purplish-black berries. Very vigorous, thornless.

Blackberries and their related hybrids are all self-fertile.

The Care of Blackcurrants

Because they act as alternate hosts to the white pine blister rust disease, black-currants cannot be grown in most states, and before any planting is carried out the local state Experiment Station should be contacted. The same regulations apply in fact to all currants and gooseberries.

Plant slightly deeper than the bushes were in the nursery, put down a 2-in. mulch of rotted manure, compost or peatmoss and at once cut all shoots down to within an inch of the mulch. The next winter cut down half of the new shoots; those which remain will give you your first crop. In subsequent years prune as soon as the crop has been picked, removing entirely about one third of the shoots which have just fruited. Black-currants yield most heavily on the young wood of the previous summer's growth but also on two-year-old and older wood. Try to keep the center of the bush from becoming congested.

Feeding Blackcurrants are gross feeders. Liberal dressings (5 lb. per sq. yd.) in winter or early spring with rotted farm or stable manure are best. Also scatter $\frac{1}{3}$ oz. of sulfate of potash and 1 oz. of sulfate of ammonia per sq. yd. in spring. Every third year add 1 oz. of superphosphate per sq. yd. Where no natural manure is available mulch freely with garden compost, lawn mowings or peatmoss, and double the sulfate of potash and treble the sulfate of ammonia dressings.

The Care of Cherries

Sweet cherries are not grown much in gardens because there are no dwarfing root-stocks yet available and because none is self-fertile you must have two trees. Fan-trained trees are a possibility but even root-pruning will probably be necessary to restrain vigor.

The Morello sour cherry is a different proposition because it is self-fertile and less vigorous. It can be grown as a bush or be fan-trained and as most fruit is borne on the previous year's growth pruning (in spring after the buds have broken) should be directed towards stimulating new growths, as with peaches, old fruited shoots being cut out and a few complete old branches being taken out each year from established trees.

Planting Distances for Soft Fruits

All figures in feet

	Between plants	Between rows
Blackberry		
Himalaya Giant	18	6
Other varieties	10	6
Blackcurrant	6	6
Gooseberry (bushes)	5	5
Gooseberry (cordons)	1¼	6
Loganberry and other hybrid berries	10	6
Raspberry	1½	6
Red & White Currant (bushes)	5	5
Red & White Currant (cordons)	1¼	6
Strawberry	1½	3

Left: The abundant berries of blackcurrent 'Blacksmith'
Below: Pruning a blackcurrant bush by removing about one third of the stems that have fruited after the crop has been picked

The Care of Gooseberries

The most usual way of growing a gooseberry is as a bush. The lowest branches should not be too low, however, or they may soon droop to the ground and if shoot tips take root, a tangle of growth results. To prevent this, start with a leg of at least 6 in. and prune branch leaders to upward-pointing buds.

Pruning Bushes Gooseberries bear their fruit both on wood of the previous year's growth and on spurs arising from older wood. The first few years' pruning should be fairly hard, directed to forming a good open framework of branches: cut branch leaders to half their length and laterals to three or four buds.

After three years confine winter pruning to removing crossing branches, those congesting the center and those drooping down to the ground. New upward growing laterals will then have to be selected to replace the old branches and these should be cut back half way to encourage growth. All laterals should be shortened to five leaves in late June.

Pruning could be done in the fall, as soon as the leaves fall, but it is often deferred until spring to discourage the birds which, in some districts, can do much damage pecking out the growth buds.

Protection against birds can, of course, be provided during the winter and in some areas may prove essential. It is not normally necessary to protect the berries while they are unripe but once ripening begins it is.

Trained Forms Gooseberries can be trained as standards as well as espaliers, fans or single or double cordons.

In pruning cordons cut back in winter the new growth of the vertical leader by a third (but never leaving an extension of more than 10 in.). In the second half of June cut back laterals to four leaves and when dormant shorten these laterals to two or three buds.

Feeding Give an annual early spring dressing of $\frac{1}{3}$ oz. sulfate of ammonia and 1 oz.

each of sulfate of potash and superphosphate, per sq. yd. Then follow this with a liberal mulch of manure.

Recommended Varieties: Gooseberries are self-fertile. Although English varieties were popular at one time, they are not now generally available. American varieties include: Clark, large, greenish-yellow; Downing, medium sized green; Poorman, large red; Pixwell, small pink, producing heavy crops.

The Care of Peaches and Nectarines

Peaches and nectarines (which are simply a smooth-skinned type of peach) may be grown successfully in many areas of the country. However, fruit production is severely affected by low winter temperatures.

Most peaches and nectarines are self-fertile and so a single specimen can be quite successful. The standard type of tree is the most popular, which by pruning can be kept at a height of 10–12 ft. Trees on dwarfing stocks are also available. It is also possible to train them against walls or give them the protection of a greenhouse in colder areas.

Pruning Standard Trees In forming a bush peach tree the aim should be an open-centered goblet-shaped tree, as with apples. Pruning should be carried out in early spring in cold areas, but in milder regions trees may be pruned at any time while they are dormant.

At the first pruning of a whip cut the central stem about 2 ft. above soil level. If any of the remaining side shoots have failed to break into growth at the extremity or have a dormant patch between the tip and point of origin, cut back to an outward-pointing shoot on the lower part where buds have broken vigorously into growth. The strongest of any side shoots, if well placed, may be selected to form main branches, the others being cut back to one bud.

In subsequent years pruning follows similar lines. Cut back any branch which shows die-back at the tip or down its length to a point immediately above the second strong

lateral. You have to remember with peaches (and nectarines) that blossom is carried only on wood made the previous year. Therefore your cutting is directed towards stimulating a continual supply of new laterals and, happily, the peach is naturally extremely vigorous. Any completely dead branches should be cut out at source and some may have to be removed or shortened to a sound bud because they cross others or cause congestion at the center.

Where a three- or four-year-old tree (standard or fan) is planted, remove any blossom the first season, and allow only a token crop to develop the second year.

Pruning Fans Although peaches and nectarines are usually grown as standards, they may in colder areas be given the protection of a wall or greenhouse, trained in the form of a fan with shoots tied to supporting wires or a trellis. The method described here takes more time but results in a more robust tree, which is more likely to fruit evenly.

Plant the whip as early in the fall as possible (if planting outdoors delay until spring in colder areas) and in early spring just before growth starts cut it back to a sound bud 2 ft. or slightly less from the ground. It is necessary to note carefully the difference between pointed growth buds and the rounded blossom buds. The cutting must be to a growth bud. If you are in doubt, cut to a triple bud – one of the three is always a growth bud.

Select, some 9–12 in. above the ground, a growth bud on either side of the main stem: from these the first two ribs of the fan will spring. Rub out all other buds and cut off any laterals flush with the stem. As a result of these operations the top bud will produce a vertical shoot and below it there will be a lateral on either side. When these two laterals are about 18 in. long tie each to a cane fastened to the horizontal wires at an angle of 45°. As in forming an espalier (see 'Pruning Espaliers' under 'The Care of Apples') lift or lower these arms to stimulate or check

Left: Gooseberry 'Clark' *Above:* Sour or Morello cherries

growth and keep the development of the two branches equal. On tying in these two main branches, cut out the central, vertical leaders entirely.

In the second year, in late winter, cut back these two branches to good buds 12–18 in. from the vertical leg. The buds to which you cut must be pointing either upwards or downwards, never towards the wall or away from it and from them further extension growth will be produced. As growth begins select two promising shoots from the top of each branch and one from below: allow these to grow on and form three more ribs of the fan on either side. Rub out all other shoots. When these six new shoots attain a length of about 18 in. they in their turn can be fastened to slanting canes fastened to the wires.

This process of trebling the number of branches or fan-ribs can be repeated year by year until the whole wall space available has been filled. Frequently this is achieved in three years and then fruit production may begin, laterals being allowed to develop along the branches, these fruiting the following year. Rub out any laterals which start growing towards the wall or directly away from it. Select suitable laterals at intervals of about 6 in., rubbing out all others, tying the chosen shoots in and pinching out their growing points when some 18 in. long. In subsequent years allow one or two replacement shoots to grow out from close to the base of the fruiting lateral. Rub out all others. Let the fruiting lateral grow until eight more leaves have appeared, then cut back to the fourth. After harvest, cut back the fruited lateral to the best replacement shoot.

Fruit Thinning Thinning is essential with wall-trained peaches to prevent overcropping and secure good fruit size. When the fruits are the size of marbles reduce all pairs to singles and then when walnut size has been reached remove further fruits until none is closer than a foot from its neighbor. Thinning is less essential with bush trees.

Feeding Mulch lightly with rotted manure or garden compost in early spring and fork this into the top few inches of soil in the fall. Only if growth seems to lag, and after cropping has begun, give an annual February dressing of 1 oz. of calcium nitrate and $\frac{1}{2}$ oz. of sulfate of potash per sq. yd. with an extra 1 oz. per sq. yd. of superphosphate every third year. If peatmoss replaces the manure or compost, double the quantity of calcium nitrate.

Greenhouse Culture Fan-trained peaches or nectarines are suited for growing along the back wall of a lean-to greenhouse. Do not pamper the peach but give free ventilation after harvest until growth is started in January. Aim at a temperature of 40°F (4·5°C), 50°F (10°C) in February, using the glass and heat, if any, to protect the blossom from frost rather than to force growth. Give plenty of water when growth begins.

Recommended Varieties: Peaches *Early* Dixigem, Redhaven, Golden Jubilee; *Midseason* Sunhigh, Golden East, Elberta, Valiant, Champion; *Late* White Hale, Afterglow, Rio-Oso-Gem.

Nectarines: Lexington Redchief, Garden State, Cherokee, Redbud, Nectaheart, Nectacrest, Nectarose, Rivers Orange.

It must be pointed out that there are a considerable number of nectarine and peach varieties available, all with their own particular climatic requirements. For rootstocks see under The Care of Plums.

The Care of Pears

Pears blossom a little earlier than apples and therefore there is a slightly higher risk of damage by frost or inadequate pollination because the weather discourages the pollinating insects from flying. They often take somewhat longer than apples to settle down and start fruiting. Although hardier than the nectarine and peach, pears will not tolerate very severe winters. Pears may be grown in any of the forms in which apples are grown.

Pruning Bush Trees At first prune as for apples but more lightly, but when regular cropping starts, pruning needs to be harder than for apples, leaders being reduced by two thirds to three-quarters, laterals to three buds and sub-laterals to one. Pears form natural spurs more readily than do apples but a few varieties are tip-bearers and these must be pruned much more lightly with all short laterals left uncut to form a terminal fruit bud.

Pruning Cordons, Dwarf Pyramids, Espaliers and Fans As for apples, except that the new shoots will mature earlier.

Fruit Thinning Generally less thinning of pears is required than for apples. Size of fruit will be improved and regularity of cropping aided if glut crops are thinned to one or, occasionally, two fruitlets per spur.

Watering In dry weather watering will be necessary, particularly when the trees are young. A spring mulch will help.

Picking The test for readiness to pick is the same as for apples, but pears need to be handled with even more caution as they year wood and on spurs which will develop without their assistance on older wood.

Pruning Pyramids The pyramid is the best form for plums in most gardens because it only needs 10 ft. of lateral space and can be restricted to a height of little more than 9 ft. You cannot buy plum trees already trained as pyramids so you must start with a whip which should be on St Julien A rootstock. Apart from size a great benefit with this type of tree is that branch breakage is substantially reduced and, with it, there is less possibility of silver leaf infection.

FIRST YEAR: In early spring behead the whip 5 ft. above the ground. Cut off at source any side shoots up to a height of 18 in., and reduce those above that point to half their length. When the growth of new shoots ceases cut back branch leaders to 8 in., pruning just beyond a bud pointing downwards or outwards. Shorten laterals to 6 in.

SUBSEQUENT YEARS: In April cut off two-thirds of the central leader's new growth. To keep the trees straight, cut to buds on opposite sides of the three each year. When new growth ceases cut branch leaders to 8 in. and laterals to 6 in. Once the tree has reached 9 ft. cut the central leader to an inch or less of new growth each. Should a new vertical shoot grow up to replace the central leader, remove it at source.

Pruning Fans Form the framework of the fan in the manner described for peaches. When the tree reaches fruiting age, however, the treatment has to be slightly different as the plum fruits on old and new wood and one does not, therefore, have to cut back a lateral as soon as it has fruited. Any new laterals not required to extend the tree or to replace old laterals should be stopped when they have made six or seven leaves. It may be necessary to 'go over' the tree several times during the growing season for this pinching. Also rub out entirely any shoots pointing at the support or directly away from it, doing this

bruise remarkably easily and the spurs are very brittle. The earliest varieties will be ready in late July or early August and should be eaten at once. Do not wait for pears to become soft before picking. Bartlett, for example, should be picked when still quite hard but will soon ripen.

Storing Polyethelene bag storage is not so successful with pears but they will keep indoors in a slightly drier atmosphere and higher temperature than apples. Be careful not to pick the late-keeping varieties too soon. They are better laid out separately on shelves rather than wrapped and stored in boxes. When almost ripe they should be brought into a living room to finish.

Feeding Pears often need more nitrogen than do apples and are less liable to suffer from potash shortage. Normally the ground around them should be clean cultivated and mulched in spring with rotted manure or garden compost. Where no natural manure or compost is available, mulch with peatmoss after first dressing with 1 oz. of sulfate of ammonia, 2 oz. of superphosphate and ½ oz. of sulfate of potash per sq. yd.

Above: Giant prune 'Burbank'
Below: Pears in a fruit store

The Care of Plums
Plums may be grown as standards, half-standards, bushes, pyramids and fans. They are unsatisfactory as cordons or espaliers. They do best on deep heavy loam or on a well-drained clay soil. Ex-vegetable plot soil (rich in nitrogen) is excellent. Light soil results in poor fruit quality, brittle branches and a short life.

Plums are extremely susceptible to a fungoid disease known as silver leaf which is most infectious during the winter months where this disease is prevalent. Pruning should be carried out during the summer, in spring or in early fall immediately after the crop has been picked.

Pruning Bush Trees. FIRST YEAR: If a whip is planted, behead it at about 3 ft. from soil level in spring just before growth starts. Existing side shoots may be selected for the fruit branches if well spaced. Plums are very liable to branch breakage and it is important to select as branches laterals with a wide angle to the main trunk, these being much stronger than those which are more nearly vertical and make an acute angle with the stem.

SECOND YEAR: In early spring cut back the selected branch leaders by a half.

THIRD YEAR: Again cut leaders by a half of the previous season's growth.

SUBSEQUENT YEARS: Remove crossing branches to open up the center of the tree. Cut out any dead wood. Some laterals may have to be cut out or shortened to avoid overcrowding but otherwise plum pruning is best kept to a minimum. Should growth be poor, cut back some laterals drastically to encourage new wood. Plums fruit on second-

Rootstocks for Plums, Peaches and Nectarines

Although there is some variance as to the hardiness within the various groups, European plums equate in hardiness to apples, and Japanese plums to peaches although some are quite hardy. American plums vary tremendously, some being suitable for northern areas while others will grow in southern states.

Plums of the European group are usually budded on to *prunus cerasifera* (Myrobalan plum). Japanese varieties can also be worked on to this stock or on to peach stocks. Seedlings of *prunus americana* are used widely as an understock for American plums.
St Julien stock is used occasionally for dwarf trees. *Prunus besseyi*, the native Sand Cherry, is also used for the same purpose.
Peaches and nectarines are usually budded on to peach seedling stocks. The St Julien and the Sand Cherry are sometimes used as a dwarfing stock.

Pear Varieties

Tyson, D; Bartlett, DC; Flemish Beauty, D; Seckel DC; Gorham DC; Conference, D; Sheldon, D; Dana Hovey, D; Beurre Bose, D; Winter Nelis, D.
D = dessert; DC = dessert or cooking.

Notes

Pear varieties are mostly self-unfruitful and need a different variety close by for cross-pollination purposes. Nearly all varieties will cross-pollinate each other. Seckel and Bartlett, however, will not pollinate each other.

Below left : 'Conference' is a good variety of pear for the small garden
Below right : Pear 'Doyenne du Comice'

Above : A fan-trained plum on St Julien A rootstock. Note the use of bamboo canes for training the ribs of the fan

as soon as these unwanted growths are noticed.

As soon as the crop has been picked cut back by half all the laterals previously stopped and either tie down towards the horizontal any vigorous shoots growing vertically or cut them out entirely allowing the tree sufficient space to promote strong new growth.

Fruit Thinning With glut crops on bush or pyramid trees, the thinning of plums not only increases fruit size but reduces the risk of branch breakage and the entry of silver leaf disease. Proper thinning also promotes regular cropping.

Thin gradually in two stages—early in June and, later, after the natural crop during stone formation. Break or cut the fruitlets off so that stalks remain on the tree, eventually reducing dessert plums to a minimum spacing of 2 in. to encourage the growth of good-sized fruit. Cooking plums may be slightly closer.

Feeding As advised for peaches. Be careful not to add too much nitrogen.

Choice for the One-plum garden

In many gardens there is room only for one plum tree and that must, therefore, be a self-fertile variety needing no other plum to pollinate it. It must be pointed out that there are few self-fertile varieties available. Some of the better known are given on the right:

Name	Class or Group	Color	Comments
Reine Claude	European	Greenish Yellow	Sweet, very high quality known as Green Gage in England
Italian Prune	European	Dark Purple	A good cooking variety
Yellow Egg	European	Yellow	Egg shaped large fruit with yellow flesh
Shropshire	European	Purple	A damson plum producing heavy crops of small fruit. Good for jam making
French Damson	European	Purple	Slightly larger fruit than Shropshire also excellent jam making
Beauty	Japanese	Red	Fruits very early in the season. Grown in California
Methley	Japanese	Red to Purplish	Large fruit of good quality
Santa Rosa	Japanese	Purple	Fairly hardy, fruit has red flesh

More Soft Fruits

The Care of Raspberries

Summer-fruiting raspberries bear their berries on new canes made the previous summer. This means you will get no crop the first summer but give the plants a chance to develop a good root system. No pruning will be necessary in the fall following planting and the canes produced during that summer will give you your first crop in the second summer after planting. Thereafter, prune as soon as the crop has been picked, cutting all fruited canes to ground level, tying in up to six of the strongest new canes and removing any others. In early spring tip the canes, reducing them to about 4 ft. 6 in.

Fall-fruiting or ever-bearing varieties crop on the new canes which grew during the summer. Thus new plants cut down in spring will try to fruit on the new canes the first year. This will put too much strain on the plants so be hard-hearted and cut off all blossom the first year. Subsequently delay pruning until winter or early spring and then cut all fruited canes to ground level (and in the first winter after planting that means cutting down the de-blossomed canes).

The summer-fruiting varieties must be protected from birds and netting over the whole row is most satisfactory. By the fall the birds have sometimes lost interest in this type of food and, in some areas at least, netting is unnecessary. Apart from this, and the time of pruning, summer and fall raspberries need similar treatment. Methods of support were described earlier under Staking and Tying.

Feeding Raspberries need a steady supply of nitrogen and potash. In the first year a mulch of manure (5 lb. per sq. yd.) put down in early spring will be sufficient but in subsequent years also give a dressing of 1 oz. per sq. yd. each of sulfate of ammonia and sulfate of potash in early spring. Every third year add 2 oz. per sq. yd. of superphosphate.

Plenty of moisture is essential throughout the growing period and the hose may well have to be used in summer. Keep weeds down but try not to disturb the surface soil more than is essential because this damages surface roots, for which reason a paraquat/diquat weedkiller is excellent. Such a weedkiller may also be used to destroy unwanted suckers which spring up away from the row.

Recommended Varieties. Summer-fruiting: Bristol, good quality fruit, a heavy cropper; Latham, widely grown, hardy variety producing heavy drops of larger berries; Newburgh, good variety for the home gardener. Very productive; Taylor, heavy yielding, quite hardy; Williamette, popular variety; ideal for canning and freezing.

Fall Fruiting or Ever-bearing: September, large good quality barries, one of the best varieties in this group; Heritage, ideal for the home garden, producing heavy crops of high quality fruit; Fallred, heavy cropper, excellent for canning and freezing.

Raspberries are self-fertile.

The Care of Red and White Currants

These are both grown in the same way and there are also but seldom seen, pink varieties. Their fruiting habit is quite different from the blackcurrant's and they, therefore, need quite different pruning. Red currants produce most of their fruit on short spurs on old wood and at the base of new growths. Little is borne on the new wood. As with gooseberries, birds can be a nuisance in winter pecking out the buds. Where this occurs it is preferable to give protection (see under 'Pests'): otherwise delay pruning until early spring when, after first signs of growth are visible, you can make sure of pruning to sound buds.

Pruning Bushes If a one-year-old bush is planted there may be three or four branches. Cut all back by two-thirds, to outward-pointing buds so as to secure an open-centered bush.

In the second winter again cut back hard, by two-thirds, and remove entirely any ill-placed laterals. Shorten other laterals, not required as branches, to one bud.

By the third winter the bush should have sufficient main branches. In this and subsequent years shorten branch leaders by a half, always to outward-pointing buds. Shorten laterals to one bud. If in later years growth continues to be vigorous the leaders need only be tipped; if growth is weak, cut back harder.

Trained Forms Red currants grow well as cordons and are sometimes used as single or double vertical cordons for filling odd spaces against walls or fences. The pruning is as for

Left: Mixed soft fruit. *Above*: Yellow raspberry 'Fall Gold'. *Right*: Redcurrant 'Red Lake'.

cordon gooseberries except that the laterals should be cut even more severely in winter – to one or two buds.

Picking It is easiest to use scissors, cutting off complete bunches at a time.

Feeding Give a spring dressing of ¾ oz. per sq. yd. of sulfate of potash and every third year add superphosphate at 1 oz. per sq. yd. Follow this dressing in late April with 1-in. deep mulch of rotted manure or compost. If the mulching materials are likely to be unavailable include 1 oz per sq. yd. of sulfate of ammonia in the spring dressing and mulch in April with peatmoss.

Recommended Varieties. Red Currants: Red Lake, large berries, very productive; Wilder, long established variety, heavy cropper.

White Currants: White Imperial and White Grape are two good varieties.

❧ The Care of Strawberries ❧

Weeds must be kept down in the strawberry bed but any hoeing must be very shallow to avoid root damage: it is better to use paraquat/diquat weedkiller as much as possible. However, one must be extremely careful not to let it touch the leaves of the strawberry plants.

Where winters are severe, strawberries must be given the protection of a mulch in the form of straw or salt hay, covering the plants lightly after the ground becomes frozen. The following spring the covering should be removed and left between the plants to keep the ripening fruit clean. In areas where this winter covering is necessary, straw or black polyethelene weighted down with stones may be put beneath the developing fruit trusses in spring.

Quite early in the season summer-fruiting strawberries start trying to propagate their kind by producing runners – cord-like growths on which tiny plants develop. These should always be cut off as soon as seen unless you wish to raise new plants. Unless you are very sure that your strawberries are quite free from virus disease infection (to which they are extremely prone) it is wiser to leave this job to the experts and buy new plants as required. It is never advisable to keep a strawberry bed for more than three seasons otherwise they may very easily become diseased. It is always most important to keep a close eye on the developing plants and fruit.

If you decide to raise your own plants, simply sink a 3-in. pot of good growing compost (general potting compost or soilless compost) into the ground by the parent plant where the plantlet on the runner can be bent down. Hold the runner in place with a stone or 'hairpin' of galvanized wire and pinch out the tip of the runner to prevent further growth. At the end of July the new plant can be separated from its parent and a week or two later lifted and replanted in suitable soil.

As soon as picking is finished, cut all the old leaves off with shears and deal with any weeds. In the early fall rake in ½ oz. per sq. yd. each of sulfate of ammonia and sulfate of potash and put down a mulch of well-rotted manure or garden compost (about 5 lb. per sq. yd.).

Greenhouse Culture The strawberry season can begin very much sooner if you force a few pots in the greenhouse. This method can be combined with the outdoors way and the season can thus be extended throughout the summer. Early-rooted runners are needed for this purpose – late July if possible. Plant in 9-in. pots using a well drained potting compost. Stand the pots in the open on a sheet of polyethelene until mid-November and then either turn them on their sides (to prevent over-watering) or put them in a cold frame. Towards the end of January transfer to the unheated greenhouse. When fresh growth becomes visible, start watering cautiously and turn on the artificial heat. A night temperature of 45°F (7°C) will be quite sufficient at first. Let this rise gradually to 50°F (10°C), when the blossom trusses are seen. Pollinate the flowers by hand, dusting their centers with a camel's-hair brush. When the blossom has fallen the night temperature may be permitted to rise another five degrees (F) to 13°C and gentle liquid feeding should begin and be continued until the berries color.

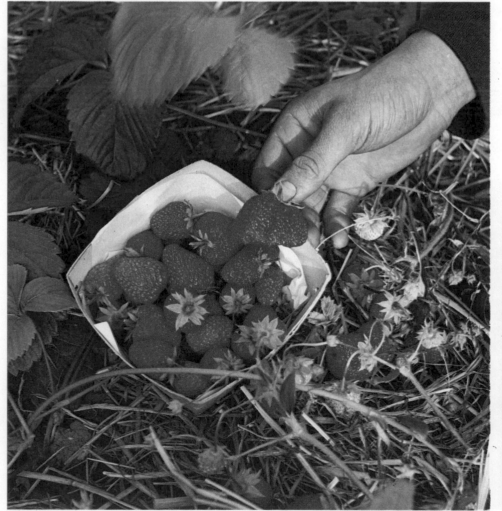

Left: A good crop of early strawberries
Below: Summer pruning a red currant bush, by shortening the new growth
By following the pruning instructions on page 175, an established, well-shaped bush should be obtained in 3 years

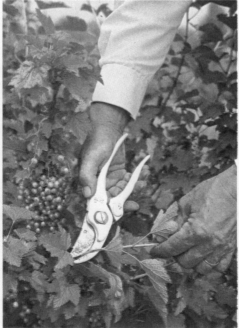

Polyethelene Covers The strawberry season can also be advanced two or three weeks by covering first-year plants with polyethelene covers in early spring. The extra warmth will encourage them to flower much earlier. Deal with all weeds before covering. Keep closed until the blossom opens and then open the covers by day to allow entry of pollinating insects. Close the covers again by 4 p.m. In April and May ventilate in sunny weather to prevent a dangerously high build-up of temperature. In dry weather watering may be necessary. Do this in the morning to let the plants dry before the ventilation openings are closed again. This is necessary so that pests and diseases are prevented as far as possible from damaging the plants.

Perpetual-fruiting Kinds These need slightly different treatment. In the first season, nip off all flower trusses which appear before June. In subsequent years all blossom may be allowed to develop. Some do not produce runners freely; where new plantlets appear they may be allowed to root and may flower and fruit the same season. After fruiting the first year cut off all old leaves but in subsequent years leave them to fall naturally. Always destroy strawberry leaves after removal; this is very important because otherwise their presence may encourage pests or disease to take hold, and these can be extremely difficult to eradicate, as they may penetrate well into the soil.

Your Strawberry Choice

Because of the tremendous variations in climate and soil types, those who are not sure of the varieties best suited for their particular area should contact their state Agricultural Experiment Station.

As a general guide, varieties that will grow in zones 4–8 are:

Darrow: Medium sized firm berries. Early.
Pocahontas: Large, good flavored fruit.
Catskill: Hardy, vigorous plants, producing large, firm, delicious berries mid-season.
Midway: Fine flavored large fruit. A heavy cropper. Very good variety and easy to grow. Late.
Jerseybelle: Fine flavored, very productive. Late.

Further north, Catskill Premier which is high yielding and early are suitable hardy varieties.

In Florida, the variety Florida Ninety is widely planted, while in southern California, Shasta and Lassen are suitable varieties.

Ever-bearing Varieties

Ogallala Hardy: Very productive.
Ozark Beauty: Good flavor and high yielding.

Alpine varieties

Baron Solemacher: Larger berries than wild strawberries and less acid than the cultivated summer strawberries. Does not produce runners. Rich flavor.
Alexandria and **Delicious:** Improved strains of Baron Solemacher with larger berries and better disease resistance.
Alpine Yellow: Golden yellow berries with excellent flavor.

Above: Strawberry 'Red Rich'
Below: A cage made from wire-netting, will protect various soft fruits from birds
Right: To save space and to provide decorative value, strawberries may be grown in a barrel

Birds Pests are, alas, always with us but thanks to modern specifics there is generally no reason why they should cause serious damage to our trees or crops. There is, however, one exception against which no easy defence has yet been discovered – the birds which, it must be admitted, often add much to the enjoyment of our gardens but can rob us of our reward for a year's care in a few hours.

As they begin to ripen, nearly all fruits are subject to bird attack but, worse than that, our chances of any crop at all can be destroyed the previous winter when birds turn to the dormant buds on gooseberries, currants, plums and other tree fruits as a source of food in hard weather. Which fruits are most liable to be attacked probably depends on the balance between the trees available and the local bird population.

To protect the buds one can apply a proprietary bird repellent spray. This can work well, for a time, but frequent renewal can be expensive and is a task easily forgotten. More lasting protection is provided by rayon web, the fine gossamer strands of which are teased out over the tree or bush. The birds hate this material but the individual threads are so fine and fragile they cause no injuries as cotton and, particularly, nylon thread can.

The only absolute protection against birds is provided by small mesh netting carefully draped over permanent or temporary supports. Plastic netting is available in many sizes and is rot-proof and very light in weight.

Both rayon web and netting will, of course, protect the ripening crops as well as the buds in winter.

Aphids Like birds, aphids always make an appearance sooner or later. If unchecked they can do serious damage to the tree fruits. Although they do little apparent harm to strawberries and raspberries, their sap sucking introduces virus disease which can be fatal. Aphids tend to attack growing points first and their activities frequently cause leaves to curl. Aphids eggs over-winter on the trees.

Woolly aphid

Caterpillars A number of caterpillars feed on various fruit trees and if left unchecked can do considerable damage to leaves, and in some instances to fruit. These include the fruit-tree leaf roller, red-banded leaf roller, tent caterpillar and cankerworm.

Plum Curculios These small beetles do considerable damage to stone fruits and apples by feeding on the leaves and making holes in the developing fruit to lay eggs.

After hatching, the grubs begin to feed inside the young fruit, causing them to fall prematurely.

European Sawflies These creatures lay their eggs in the flower of the apple or, less frequently, pear. The larva bores into the fruitlet. It will pass from one to another, spoiling each, and then fall to the ground. A mass of sticky frass (excreta) exudes from the hole where the pest enters the fruit.

Codling Moths This moth lays its eggs in early summer on leaves or fruit, and the grubs bore into the fruit to feed. These are the creatures you may find near the core when you come to eat the apple. Pears are less commonly attacked.

Apple sawfly

Plum sawfly

Spraying Program There are many other pests to spoil our fruit but the above-mentioned are those which do most damage. A drenching of the dormant trees and bushes in winter (but not during frost) with a dormant oil spray will do much to kill over wintering eggs but should only be used once in a season. Care should also be taken not to apply these sprays within a month of using a spray containing sulfur.

A minimum spray program starts at the green cluster stage (just before the flower bud breaks) of apples and pears to kill caterpillars and aphids. Give a second spraying at the pink bud stage (apples) or white bud stage (pears), for aphids, and a third spraying as soon as 90% of the blossom petals have fallen, to kill European sawfly and tortrix caterpillars. In mid-June spray to deal with codling moth and caterpillars, repeating this two weeks later. Two spraying are essential for plums – between bud burst and the white bud stage, to control aphids and caterpillars, when the petals have fallen and the fruitlets set, against sawfly. Curculios may be controlled by spraying when the young fruit are just forming.

Further sprayings, of course, must be given if pests are seen. Aphids may appear at any time and if the fruit is shortly to be eaten it is essential to spray with something which is non-toxic to humans – derris, for example.

There are dozens of pesticides on offer in the garden shops. The labels on the bottles or packets will tell you what pests they are intended for and when and how to apply them. The important thing is to follow those directions exactly.

Brown rot

Careful attention at all times to garden hygiene will do much to keep disease to a minimum. Indeed, one cannot 'cure' plant diseases and prevention must always be the policy. Always cut out any dead branches or shoots as soon as you notice them. Also burn any rotting fruits.

Scab This fungoid disease disfigures the skin of many apples and pears, especially in wetter and more humid districts. It is not likely to cause much harm if you spray regularly with captan at the green cluster, pink (or white) bud and petal fall stages.

Brown Rot Concentric rings of small pustules on ripe or ripening fruit are the outward signs of this fungus. It is very contagious. Burn all infected fruit and wash your hands immediately after touching them.

Silver Leaf This may attack all stone fruits (and sometimes apples) but is particularly virulent on plums. The leaves assume a silvery tinge and the diagnosis is confirmed by a brown stain inside the wood of infected branches or shoots. The disease is spread by spores entering wounds or cuts in the bark, usually between September and May. Do not, therefore, prune in winter and cut out any dead or infected wood in mid-summer. Pare all wounds smooth and cover with a protective tree-pruning paint.

Leaf Curl A very common trouble with apricots, peaches and nectarines, causing the young leaves to become puckered and curled. Such leaves become yellow, then reddish and develop 'blisters'. New growth is distorted.

The most likely means of control is to spray with lime-sulfur in late February or early March while growth is still dormant and just before the buds swell. Repeat in the fall just before the leaves fall. Once growth has begun in spring lime-sulfur must not be used; instead spray with captan.

Codling moth

Virus Diseases Of recent years a number of fruit troubles have been found to be of virus origin. Those most likely to come to the amateur grower's notice are those which attack strawberries and raspberries, drastically reducing crop yields. To avoid virus troubles only buy new stock from a nurseryman who sells virus-free stock, and sprays against aphids.

Early symptoms include various leaf markings but these can easily be mistaken for those caused by mineral deficiency. If you see abnormal markings on the leaves of strawberries or raspberries, give first-aid in the shape of foliar watering with a foliar feed containing chelated trace minerals just in case the trouble is due only to a lack of iron or magnesium or other trace element. Never use suspected plants for propagation. If cropping fails, dig up and burn the offenders.

Right: A yellow-fruited variety of the sweet pepper (capsicum)

Vegetables and Salads

The Seed Order

When deciding what to grow and when preparing your seed order consider what space you may have in your garden for each crop. Drawing a plan to scale is of help. It can prevent over-ordering. When planning for vegetables take into account the site of your vegetable garden. Few vegetables tolerate shade nor do they grow well if the roots of fruit trees and hedges rob the soil of nourishment. Plan so that your vegetables grow in good soil where the plants receive lots of sun.

Potatoes This is a useful crop to grow if you are starting from scratch. Potato plants are spreading in habit and smother weeds. A potato crop is often referred to as a 'cleaning crop' because the spreading habit and the cultivation carried out can eradicate many weeds.

Cauliflowers are greedy plants. Do not order cauliflower seeds unless you know your soil is very fertile. Planting cauliflowers in poor soil is a waste of time and garden space.

Onions are easy—from sets. A good crop of good-storing, maincrop onions is easily obtained if you start off with sets rather than by sowing seeds.

Vegetable marrow A close relation of squash and popular in Britain. Seed catalogs show varieties as *Bush* or *Trailing*. A bush plant is compact. Trailing plants may be trained on a wire mesh garden fence or on nylon netting.

Cucumbers For those with a greenhouse there is the European forcing cucumber, with a choice of varieties which bear male and female flowers or all female flowers. There are also the more popular outdoor cucumbers which include both slicing and pickling varieties.

Tomatoes Tomatoes not only come in very large, medium and small reds; there are also yellow, gold and striped tomatoes. The yellows and golds are excellent for mixed salads. 'Fireball' is one of the early ripening varieties. 'Tiny Tim' grows only 15 in. tall and is suitable for window boxes and pots.

Less usual vegetables There are many other vegetables not included in this seed list. You will find something about them under the heading *Fifty Vegetables and Salads*. Few are difficult to grow. If you have room in the garden why not order seeds of a few of them?

Some Useful Vegetable Garden Practices

Intercropping This is of great use in the small vegetable garden. A quick-to-grow and mature vegetable is grown between two rows of a slower-growing vegetable. A good example is radish sown between two rows of peas. Two somewhat slower-growing vegetables may be grown alongside each other. Thus lettuces may be grown in the vacant spaces left between two rows of peas. A later-to-mature vegetable may be planted in between or alongside rows of another vegetable which will shortly be harvested. Examples: cabbage plants set out among lettuces about to be cut for use; Brussels sprouts set out alongside rows of peas; broccoli planted between rows of dwarf bush beans.

Mulching Mulches are soil covers. Their use saves time in watering and weeding. All mulches are laid down when the soil is moist. They prevent a loss of soil moisture by evaporation. They also smother weed seedlings and usually inhibit the growth of more weeds. Most mulches disintegrate slowly and improve the garden soil. One only does not. This is black polyethelene sheeting.

Garden compost acts as a plant food as well as a mulch. The food is immediately available to plants mulched with compost. It may itself contain weed seeds. Well-rotted manure is excellent as a mulch for cucumbers, but must not be used as freely as garden compost around most vegetables. Granulated peatmoss contains little plant food but is the neatest mulching material. Lawn mowings are sometimes used as mulching material, but can attract slugs. Fall leaves should be partially rotted before being applied. Several sheets of newspaper make a useful but unsightly mulch. It is best covered with a little straw. Straw should not be used around seedlings because loose straw may blow over and on to them causing damage. Well-rotted or raw sawdust may be used only if the garden soil is highly fertile. Sawdust robs a soil of some nitrogen during decomposition. Wood shavings are liable to blow around at first. Use them only on very fertile soil. They are rather unattractive to the eye. Black polyethelene sheeting is ugly when laid in position but is camouflaged rapidly by growing vegetables.

Rotation A rotation of crops is very necessary in the vegetable garden. The main aim of rotation is as a preventive against pests and diseases. If cabbages and their kin are grown regularly in the same patch of ground there is the likelihood of the soil becoming cabbage-sick and infected with club root disease. Should onions be grown often in the same bed an outbreak of onion white rot may occur making the whole garden unfit for onion growing for several years. Where potatoes are frequently grown in the same patch or very near to it a build up of slugs may be expected. A secondary reason for crop rotation has more bearing on a less fertile rather than on a highly fertile soil. The theory is that because all vegetables do not utilize the same amounts of plant food in the soil it pays to rotate crops each season. The tomato is noted for its need of sufficient potash and lettuce plants need a lot of nitrogen. By rotating beans and peas in the garden the soil in which they grow is enriched with nitrogen.

For the medium-sized garden, the following three-year rotation is suggested.

First Season: *Potatoes.* Soil dressed with manure or garden compost in the fall, winter or early spring.

Second Season: *Cabbages and their kin.* Soil limed if necessary in winter or early spring. Where available apply manure or garden compost later. Alternatively, apply manure during late fall or winter when digging the garden. Apply lime where necessary in early spring.

Third Season: *Other vegetables.* No manure or garden compost need be applied for most other vegetables apart from such greedy feeders as cucumbers, squash and sweet corn.

In a larger garden the rotation may be based on a four-year plan. For this the garden is divided into four sections with planting as follows: *Section A:* potatoes. *Section B:* cabbages and their kin. *Section C:* peas and beans. *Section D:* root crops and other vegetables.

For the second season section A is used for root crops and other vegetables, potatoes are grown in section B, cabbages and their kin in section C, and peas and beans in section D. After the fourth season the rotation is complete.

Successional cropping This term covers two different aspects of vegetable growing. Successional sowings of the quick growing

Examples of successional cropping

Vegetable	Sown or Planted	Ground Cleared	Sown or Planted
Flava beans Peas (first early) Lettuce Potatoes (first early) Early cabbage Bush beans Potatoes (second early and maincrop)	March to May	July to August	Bush beans, Beet, Carrots, Lettuce, Winter radish Peas, Turnips

Left: Plan for a 4-year crop rotation

Below: The bounty of the fall from a well planned vegetable garden radish and fairly quick growing lettuce are made on and off between April and August. Successional planting means that no ground is left vacant throughout the summer. As soon as one crop has been harvested, the soil is prepared at once for a follow-on crop.

Certain vegetables have varieties which are earlier to mature than other varieties. The good gardener chooses, if he knows there will be available garden space for them, early and later varieties. There is then a succession of the same vegetable for use over a longer period than there would be were only either an early or a later variety grown.

In addition to choosing early and late varieties a greenhouse or an unheated garden frame can be put to use to extend the season itself. This leads to earlier than usual spring and summer vegetables and a greater choice of fresh vegetables from the garden in late fall.

F₁ Hybrid This term frequently appears on seed packets and in seed catalogs. It signifies that the variety is produced by crossing two selected parents. Plants of the two selected parents are grown in separate blocks. Pollen from the male flowers of one parent is transferred to flowers of the second parent. Self-fertilization of the flowers of the second (female) parent is prevented. Seed has to be produced afresh each year and the cross pollination is effected by hand. F_1 hybrid seeds are, therefore, usually dearer. In favor of F_1 hybrids is their outstanding vigor. The plants also have striking uniformity. This fact is worth noting if you exhibit at local or national shows. With ordinary, non-hybrids it is not easy to find several vegetables which are almost identical and just what is wanted for the show bench.

Pelleted Seeds These make sowing easier because the pellets may be handled separately and placed at a distance from each other in the seed drill. This replaces the old method of mixing such small vegetable seeds as carrots and lettuce with sand. Because pelleted seeds are evenly spaced, each seedling has room for good development. For the gardener there is far less tedious thinning of seedlings to be done.

Moisture must be present for the germination of all vegetable seeds. Where pelleted seeds are sown, even more moisture must be present to encourage the clay of the pellets to disintegrate quickly and permit rapid germination. Unless the soil is already very wet, always soak seed drills with water before sowing pelleted seeds.

Peas

Soil These vegetables will not tolerate heat and need a well drained soil. Should a soil test show acidity, apply lime (ground limestone) at the rate of from $\frac{1}{2}$ to 1 lb. per square yard in early spring. Simply sprinkle the lime over the cultivated soil. No manure or garden compost need be applied to the sites where peas and beans are to grow. Choose a site which was enriched with manure or garden compost for a different crop grown in the previous summer. Land in which potatoes or winter cabbage was grown is suitable.

Sorts of Peas There are two main groups of garden peas. Hardiest are smooth-seeded; slightly less hardy but with a reputation for their superior flavor are varieties with wrinkled seeds. There are many different pea varieties which vary in the time they

take to produce a crop and also the height they attain.

When to Sow The first sowing should be of an early variety, as soon as the soil is suitable for it in spring. Two or three more sowings at 10-day intervals, using later maturing sorts, will ensure a succession of the peas throughout the summer. Further plantings may be made in late summer to take advantage of cooler weather conditions.

Some Popular Garden Peas The height given is the average for the plant.

Alaska 18 in., extra early, smooth-seeded; Little Marvel 13 in. (F), early, extra sweet; Thomas Laxton $2\frac{1}{2}$–3 ft. (F), early maturing; Laxtin's Progress 13 in., early, good flavor; Freezonian $2\frac{1}{2}$ ft. (F), early, heavy cropper; Alderman 5 ft., good quality, matures later in the season; Green Arrow 2 ft. (F), exceptionally sweet, heavy crops; Lincoln $2\frac{1}{2}$ ft. (F), later cropper, high quality; Wando $2\frac{1}{2}$ ft (F), tolerant to heat and very prolific. F = suitable for the freezer.

How to Sow Garden peas are sown where the plants are to grow. Before sowing rake the soil surface level, removing all large stones and clods. A popular way of sowing peas is to take out an 8-in. wide furrow, using a draw hoe. Use a garden line to have a straight row and make the furrow no more than 1 in. deep in heavier soils; 2 in. deep, but no more, in light soils. Should the soil not be wet, flood the furrow with water. Start sowing after the water has drained away. Pea seeds are quite large. Sprinkle them fairly evenly on to the flat bottom of the furrow so that each seed is about $2\frac{1}{2}$ in. from the next. After sowing use a rake to draw soil over the seeds and to fill the furrow at the same time gently firming the soil.

Some birds will take pea seeds and will hunt for them after they have been sown; other birds peck at pea seedlings. For open garden sowings, several strands of black cotton stretched around and over the rows immediately after sowing provide full protection from marauding birds. Secure the cotton to short bamboo canes on either side of the rows.

A rough, ready and fairly accurate guide to the distance between rows is to space them to the height of the variety.

Do not waste large spaces between pea rows; grow lettuces or various members of the cabbage tribe in them.

Cultivation Where black cotton is used to prevent bird damage the cotton also serves as an excellent support for short growing (dwarf) peas. For varieties growing taller than 3 ft. augment the black cotton with brushwood or with strings tied to tall canes. Hoe between rows to prevent weeds. Pull out weeds growing in the rows by hand when the pea plants are young. In dry weather water often and water well. Pea plants which are short of water are prone to several disorders. One of the worst pests of garden peas is the pea aphid, which may be attracted to pea plants weakened by lack of moisture at the roots. Mulching pea rows with straw or other suitable material can reduce the amount of watering necessary in hot, dry summer weather.

Pick pods before they are drum-tight and cook the peas as soon as possible. Peas quickly lose their sugary flavor after harvesting. Pick peas regularly especially if you have a large crop all maturing at roughly the same time. If there is a glut, the majority of varieties are suitable for freezing.

Successional sowing chart

Vegetable	When sown or planted	Where sown or planted	Season of Use
Fava beans	March–April	In the open	July
Bush beans	May	Outdoors	July
	Late June–early July	Outdoors	August–September
Pole beans	May	Outdoors	July
	Early June	Outdoors	September–October
Peas (first early)	March–early April	Open garden	June and July
(second early)	Late June	Outdoors	September
(maincrop)	Mid May	Outdoors	July
Cabbage (early)	February–March	Greenhouse or garden frame	May–June
(mid-season)	April	Outdoors	June–July
	April	Outdoors	July–September
(late)	April	Outdoors	August–October
Lettuce	March	Heated greenhouse for planting outdoors as soon as danger of frost is past	June
	April	Outdoors	June
	May	Outdoors	July
	June	Outdoors	August
	July	Outdoors	September–October
	August	Outdoors	October
	NB Sowing may be made all year round in the south.		
Potatoes (first early)	March–May	Outdoors	Mid June–August
(second early)	March–May	Outdoors	July–August
(maincrop)	Early June	Outdoors	Dig and store for winter use in September

Beans; Salads; Tomatoes; Onions

Beans

Fava Bean This is the only hardy garden bean and is very popular in Europe. It is still common to place fava bean varieties into two groups—*Windsors* and *Longpods*. But newer varieties often have mixed ancestry. A true Windsor has short pods containing about four large seeds. A Longpod has longer pods with more but smaller seeds. Most fava beans are tall growers. Fava beans require cool growing conditions and do particularly well in the Pacific Northwest.

When to Sow Sow a single seed in each $3\frac{1}{2}$-in. pot in a warm greenhouse. Peatmoss pots are excellent for this sowing. Set plants outdoors as soon as the weather is suitable. Seeds may be sown outdoors as soon as conditions permit.

Some Popular Fava Beans (Seeds of which may be obtained from American or European distributors) Aquadulce (syn. Giant Seville); Aquadulce Claudia; Conqueror (syns. Exhibition Longpod, Colossal); Giant Windsor (syn. Giant Four Seeded White Windsor); Imperial Green Longpod; Imperial Green Windsor; Imperial White Longpod; Imperial White Windsor; Masterpiece Green Longpod; Red Epicure; The Sutton (syn. The Midget).

How to Sow Use a draw hoe to make an 8-in. wide, $1\frac{1}{2}$–2 in. deep furrow. Sow seeds in a double staggered way (see diagram) at 9 in. apart. Sow a few seeds quite close together at the end of the row; the seedlings may come in handy should any seeds in the row fail to germinate. The dwarf 'The Sutton' needs less space and seeds may be sown 6 in. apart. Leave $2\frac{1}{2}$–3 ft. between rows of tall varieties and 18 in. between rows of 'The Sutton'.

Pot-raised plants should be set at these distances at planting out time.

Cultivation Keep the plants free from weeds by hoeing. Water often and generously in warm, dry weather. Bean plants, particularly fava beans, are prone to an attack of black bean aphis. This pest favors bean plants which are short of moisture.

As well as watering when necessary, thwart black bean aphis by:

(1) Sowing as early as possible in spring; early sowings usually miss an aphis attack.

(2) Pinching out the growing point as soon as flowers have set and small pods are forming.

(3) Cutting off all tender young shoots around the base of plant.

(4) Spraying with soapy water, derris or pyrethrum in May before aphids appear. Continue spraying weekly. Spray in the late evening so that bees are not harmed. Do not spray at all if you see ladybug larvae devouring the aphids.

(5) Destroying any weeds which harbor the aphis.

In very exposed areas it helps to give tall growers supports of some kind so that plants are not blown down when cropping.

Harvest fava beans when the pods are well filled but before the seeds inside them are leathery and tough.

Snap or French Beans There are two forms—dwarf bush and climbing or pole beans. The bush form is the most popular. Although the pods of most varieties are green some bear yellow or mauve pods.

When to Sow At any time between late April and early June.

Seeds may also be sown in small pots in a warm greenhouse during April. The plants must not be set out in the open garden until all risk of a late spring frost has passed.

Some Popular Bush Varieties
Contender, Tendercrop, Bountiful, Greencrop, Sprite, Roma, Royalty, Dwarf Horticultural, French Horticultural. Wax Beans: Surecrop, Kinghorn Wax, Pencil Pod Wax, Cherokee, Honey Gold.

How to Sow Seeds should be sown in a similar manner to fava beans. Set out pot-raised plants 3 ft. between the rows.

Cultivation Keep down weeds and water often and well in dry weather from late May onwards. Healthy plants are seldom attacked by black bean aphis. Spray with soapy water, derris or pyrethrum should this pest appear on the undersides of the leaves. If dwarf plants topple under the weight of crop push brushwood alongside the plants to support them. Plastic garden mesh or wire mesh or plastic mesh fencing are modern supports.

Harvest French beans before the pods toughen. Many older varieties have pods which tend to be stringy when they age. Most new varieties, however, are stringless. Pick pods often and when of full size. Cropping continues over a period of about six weeks.

Pole Beans Most pole beans bear scarlet flowers; a few have white flowers and the seeds are white.

When to Sow Sow between early May and mid June in the open garden. Seeds may also be sown in pots in a warm greenhouse during April. The tender plants must not be set out in the open garden until all danger of frost has passed.

Some Pole Bean Varieties Kentucky Wonder, good for freezing; Romano, good for freezing; Blue Lake White Seeded, good for freezing; Scarlet Runner, widely grown in Europe. Its red flowers make it an attractive plant for the flower garden.

Seeds of pole beans may be grown in two different ways. The best method is to provide the plants with tall supports. These may be traditional bean poles or bean netting. Plastic or wire fencing is also very suitable. In very windy gardens pole beans may be grown as dwarfed plants.

Where plants are to have supports sow seeds at from 6–8 in. alongside them in a $1\frac{1}{2}$–2 in. narrow furrow made with a draw hoe. If plants are to be dwarfed sow as for fava beans. Leave from 4–5 ft. between rows of pole beans. Pot-raised plants should be set out at these distances.

Cultivation Hoe to prevent weeds and water well and often in dry weather. Spray with soapy water, derris or pyrethrum should black bean aphis show on the stems or on the undersides of the leaves. Permit plants on supports to reach the top of them. Then pinch out the growing point at the top of each plant.

Plants to be grown dwarfed are pinched back by a few inches when the plants are 1 ft. or so high. Lots of side growths are then made. Nip these back occasionally until the row of bean plants resembles a low, bushy hedge. If dwarfed plants topple, support them with brushwood or with strings tied to bamboo canes.

Soil which is enriched with manure or garden compost periodically is suitable. Where the soil is not highly fertile plants may be fed with a suitable fertilizer.

Harvest pods often and when they are young and tender. Never allow seeds inside the pods to plump up. Cropping should continue for two months.

Lima Bean Both bush and pole varieties of this popular bean are available. They include: (Bush) Fordhook, Hendersons, Bush, Burpee Improved Bush; (Pole) King of the Garden, Prizetaker, Carolina.

When to Sow Lima beans require warm growing conditions and should not be sown until the soil has warmed up in the spring.

How to Sow Seeds of bush varieties should be sown 3–4 in. apart in rows $2\frac{1}{2}$–3 ft. apart.

Pole varieties may be sown on small hills of soil drawn up around poles set 3–4 ft. apart. Several seeds should be set around each pole and thinned after germination so that 3–4 plants remain. Alternatively, sowings may be made against fences or trelliswork.

Cultivation Same as described for Snap or French Beans.

Salads

Lettuce There are three different types of lettuce: cabbage, cos or romaine and loose leaf. Cabbage lettuces are divided into two groups: *Butterhead*, e.g. 'Buttercrunch', 'May King'. *Crisphead*, e.g. 'Great Lakes', 'Iceberg'.

Sowing The sowing times are linked closely with varieties. The table shows when to sow for successional crops.

Sow fairly thickly in 1-in. deep drills, 9 in. apart if all the seedlings are to be dug up and the stronger plants transplanted. If the seedlings are to be thinned to leave strong plants at 1 ft. apart in the row, rows should be 1 ft. apart. Sow pelleted seeds 1 in. apart. Keep down weeds and water well in dry weather.

When to sow	Where to sow	When to transplant	Suggested varieties	When to harvest
March	Greenhouse or frame	May	Grand Rapids; Black seeded Simpson	June
April	Frame or outdoors	May/June	Black seeded Simpson; May King	June/July
May	Outdoors	Do not transplant	Great Lakes; Bibb; May King	June/July
June/July	Outdoors	Do not transplant	Great Lakes; Iceberg; Buttercrunch	August/September
Early August	Outdoors	Do not transplant	Grand Rapids; Iceberg	September/October
August/Sept.	Frames or outdoors	Give frame protection in colder areas	Bibb; May King; Grand Rapids	Late fall and winter
October/Jan.	Heated greenhouse		Bibb; May King	Winter and early spring

Above: Pole beans produce most attractive flowers as well as edible pods
Above right: Cos lettuces produce crisper leaves and whiter hearts if the plants are tied with soft string or raffia as they develop. *Right:* There are various ways of growing and training pole beans. The 'standard' method (1) consists in placing bean 'poles' on each side of a double row of beans. The same principle is employed in (2) where the plants are grown up strings, or netting. Where space is limited, the plants may be grown up a 'wigwam' (3) of strings or stakes, surrounding a central support

Radishes Those grown for summer salads vary in shape from round, ovate and long. Varieties are: 'Scarlet Globe', round; 'French Breakfast', tankard; 'Icicle', long; Fall/winter radishes are large; 'China Rose' and 'Black Spanish' are grated for salad use.

Sowing The first sowing should be made in spring as soon as the soil is in a suitable condition; thereafter for succession make a sowing every 10 days through the spring period. For fall crops, commence sowing again in August. Sow winter radish in late summer. Sow in fairly fertile soil, keep the plants moist and thin seedlings to 1 in. apart each way. Sow the large seeds of winter radishes 1 in. apart in 1 in. deep seed drills. Thin seedlings to 8 in. apart. Pull summer radishes as soon as some are sufficiently large for use. Pull winter radishes for use in the fall in cold areas. Harvest those remaining in late October. Cut back the foliage to an inch from the radish and store the roots in sand in a shed or garage.

Three modern ways of growing tomatoes in the greenhouse. *Left*: The 'Tom-Bag' system, in which a single plant is grown in each section of the bag of compost. *Center*: The 'ring culture' method, in which the plants are grown in plastic or clay 'rings'. *Right*: Plants grown in straw bales, previously partially rotted down. *Below right*: A cluster of well ripened tomatoes.
Bottom right: Various types of round radishes.

Tomatoes These vary very much in shape and size. 'Big Boy' averages from 8–12 oz. each; 'Gardener's Delight' measures no more than 1 in. in diameter. Most varieties produce tomatoes weighing 8 or 9 to the pound. Red is the usual color; white is rare, but yellow tomatoes, e.g. 'Tangella', are liked by some gardeners. 'Golden Boy' and 'Tiger Tom' are red tomatoes with yellow striping.

Plants may be trained to stakes or trellis (standards) or allowed to grow without support. There are also self-stopping varieties such as 'Spring Giant'. Varieties were and are bred for greenhouse cultivation; these include 'Tuckcross' and 'Vantage'.

Sowing Apart from the southern areas of the country, where sowing may be made outdoors, tomato plants are usually raised in the shelter of a greenhouse. Seeds should be sown 6–8 weeks before being set outdoors in a temperature of 65°F. After germination maintain day temperatures of 60°F, dropping a few degrees lower at night. For early greenhouse crops sow seed in mid-February for winter-maturing tomatoes. Seed should be sown in September or October.

Sow seeds about 1 in. apart in a well drained mix or soilless compost and cover with more compost. Firm gently, water thoroughly and cover with a sheet of glass and lay a sheet of newspaper over it. Turn the glass daily to rid it of excess moisture. As soon as germination is seen, remove the glass and paper. Two to three weeks later pot the seedlings into 3½-in. pots. Always hold seedlings by a seed leaf, never by the stem. A night temperature of at least 56°F (13°C) is best.

In the greenhouse border space the plants 18 in. apart and tie them as they grow to stout bamboo canes. The soil should be well drained and enriched with partially rotted strawy manure or garden compost. Plants must never be short of water. Good ventilation is necessary. Side shoots must be pinched out frequently, when they are small. When the plants have attained their full height, nip out the growing point.

There are four other ways of growing tomatoes in a greenhouse:
1. IN POTS Plants may be grown successfully in large pots filled with a suitable compost, housed on the greenhouse staging.
2. RING CULTURE Soil in the borders is removed to a depth of 6 in. and replaced by an aggregate (sieved clinker, ash or screened, washed, coarse gravel). Plants are grown in clay, plastic or 'rings', which allow the roots to grow easily into the aggregate.
3. STRAW BALE A 56 lb. bale of wheat straw will take two tomato plants. Lay bales in position on the greenhouse border and sprinkle a gallon of water on to each bale every day for 12 days. Then apply to each bale: 1 lb. of calcium nitrate, 1 lb. of potassium nitrate, ½ lb. of triple superphosphate of lime, ¼ lb. of magnesium sulfate (Epsom salts), 3 oz. of sulfate of iron. Water these chemicals in well. Fermentation of the straw occurs in a heated greenhouse and plants are set out in the fermenting straw when the temperature within the bales falls to 100°F (37°C).
4. THE TOM-BAG SYSTEM Bags filled with a suitable compost are laid down and panels of the bag are removed and one plant is set in each of the spacings. Using any of these methods it is necessary to feed with a tomato fertilizer.

Plants to be grown outdoors must be thoroughly hardened off before they are moved from a greenhouse to the open garden. Plant standard tomatoes 15–18 in. apart with 3–4 ft. between rows and push a bamboo cane alongside each one or erect a simple wire trellis to which plants may be tied periodically. Plants growing without support should be planted 3–4 ft. apart. Keep plants watered in dry weather, hoe to keep down weeds, de-shoot standard plants and stop them when they have reached the tops of their supports in late summer by pinching out the growing point.

Always leave tomatoes on the plants until they are really ripe. Pick unripe fruits on outdoor plants in late September; the larger fruits will ripen quickly in a warm room indoors. Small green tomatoes are excellent for chutney.

Tomato leaf mold, a fungal disease, is common on greenhouse tomato plants. Yellowish spots appear on the leaves with a pale grayish mold on the underside of the leaves. The foliage dies and the disease passes from plant to plant rapidly. Take care not to overspray with a copper-based fungicide. water, and provide ample ventilation. Never water in the evening. Pick off and destroy infected leaves. If the outbreak is severe

Tomato plants can suffer from several different disorders. Should flowers fall without fruits setting it may be that the plants are not receiving sufficient water. Overwatering or irregular watering are two possible causes of blossom end rot, which shows as a dark green patch at the blossom end of the fruit. The patch changes to brown or black and has a leathery texture. If the greenhouse temperature is very high but the soil itself is on the cold side the tomatoes may not ripen well, a condition known as blotchy ripening. Very strong sunlight can lead to a disorder known as greenback. The stalk end stays green or yellow but the rest of the tomato ripens well. Both early and late suffer from greenback. Both early and late blight can attack tomatoes and cause widespread destruction. Control by spraying at regular intervals with Bordeaux mixture or a copper-based fungicide. Plants are more at risk during warm, humid periods.

Cucumber There are three types of cucumber grown in the garden: European cucumber for greenhouse production (varieties include those which bear both male and female flowers and new all-female flowering kinds) and the garden cucumber and pickling cucumber, both of which are grown in the open.

Cucumber Varieties

1. *Suitable for greenhouse cultivation* (F = all-female flowerer): Bestseller (F_1) F, Fertila (F_1) F, Rocket (F_1) F, Bambina (F_1), Toska (F_1), Femspot (F_1), Brilliant (F_1), Telegraph.

2. *Suitable for outdoor cultivation:* Victory, Burpee Hybrid, Marketmore 70, Poinsett, Gemini, Marketer.

3. *Pickling varieties:* Ohio MR 17, Pioneer, Wisconsin, S.M.R.18, West India Gherkin.

Sowing For greenhouse cultivation sow in late March. Otherwise, wait until late April. A temperature of 75°F (24°C) is needed for rapid germination. Sow two seeds in a $3\frac{1}{2}$-in. pot. Later pinch off the weaker seedling.

The border soil must drain well and should be rich in organic matter. A framework of wires or of canes and wires is needed, to which plants may be tied. Set out plants 2 ft. apart and do not plant deeply. Stop the plants when they reach the top of the supports. Prevent fruits from setting on the main stems by pinching off flower buds. Tie side shoots to horizontal wires and prune back these shoots to the second leaf beyond the first small cucumber on each of them. Cucumber plants like a warm, moist atmosphere so keep plants well watered and spray with tepid water each evening in hot, sunny weather. In late July mulch the bed with a 1-in. layer of garden compost or strawy horse manure.

Outdoor Cultivation Seed of slicing and pickling varieties should be sown outside as soon as the danger of frost is over. A further sowing may be made 4 weeks later. For earlier crops of slicing types, seeds may be sown in small pots in the warmth of a greenhouse, or on a windowsill, about 4 weeks before planting out.

Cucumbers require a rich soil with plenty of humus. Small hills should be made 4–5 ft. apart on which are sown 8–10 seeds. After germination thin plants so that 3–4 remain. As the plants grow, keep down weeds, keep them well watered and give regular applications of liquid fertilizer. To save space plants may also be trained over a trellis or netting.

Ridge Cucumbers Plant these in early June, 18 in. apart. When plants have made seven leaves nip out the central growing point to induce branching.

Trellis Cucumbers Plant 1 ft. apart alongside a trellis 4–6 ft. high; a wire mesh garden fence or bean netting is suitable. Pinch out growing points when they reach the top of the supports. Water often in dry weather.

⟫⟫ The Onion Family ⟪⟪

Onions do best in a medium loam or reasonably light soil, provided that it does not dry out excessively.

Onions from Sets An easy way of growing maincrop onions is by planting 'sets' (small immature onions) during early spring. After cultivation rake the site level and simply press sets in the loose soil 9 in. apart, in rows 1 ft. apart.

Onions from Seed In areas where winters are milder, a sowing may be made in 1 inch drills in August. The young plants are left in seed bed until the following spring, when they are transplanted 9 in. apart in good rich soil. Do not plant deeply. Alternatively, in early spring, as soon as the soil is fit, sow seeds fairly thickly in 1 in. deep drills 1 ft. apart.

Varieties 'Southport White Globe', 'Southport Yellow Globe', 'Southport Red Globe', 'Early Yellow Globe', 'White Portugal' (Silver Skin), 'Yellow Bermuda', 'Sweet Spanish', 'Yellow Globe Danvers', 'Ringmaster', 'Ebenezer'.

Hoe and hand weed. Start thinning spring sown seedlings in June and continue doing so until mid-July. Plants left to bulb up should be around 9 in. apart.

The maggots of the onion fly burrow into young onions. The foliage withers and the plants die. Fall-sown onions and those grown from sets are unlikely to be affected, spring-sown seedlings are likely to be damaged in June and July. Prevent broken roots and foliage during thinning by watering beforehand if the soil is dry. Bury unwanted thinnings in the compost heap or the ground. Avoid breaking onion foliage when hoeing.

Hoe occasionally to keep down weeds. Water generously in dry weather. Liquid feeds may be given weekly when bulbs are swelling, but over-feeding will lead to onions which will not store well.

When in August the foliage yellows and topples over on to the soil, stop watering and feeding. When the foliage is brown, dry and brittle, just lift the onions off the ground. Hang the onions in bunches in full sun for a week when they are quite dry, rub off dead roots, dry soil and very loose scales. Store in a cool, dry, frost-proof place, in trays or, better still, roped.

Salad Onions Although thinning of spring-sown onions are of use in early summer salads, Southport White Globe and White Lisbon are grown extensively for salad purposes. Sow seeds quite thickly in spring and use thinnings as soon as they are large enough.

Pickling Onions (Shallots) These are generally grown for pickling, although they may be used in soups and stews. As soon as the soil is suitable in spring, push bulbs into it, 9 in. apart, in rows 1 ft. apart. Keep the rows weed free. Lift the clumps in July, separate the bulbs and spread them out to dry. Store in a cool place. Onions that may be grown for pickling include 'Silver Queen', 'White Portugal' and 'Yellow Ebenczcr'. Sow seeds quite thickly in March in a $\frac{1}{2}$-in. deep drill. Keep down weeds and dig the crop when the foliage withers.

Garlic Plant 'cloves' (segments of garlic bulbs) 6 in. apart, 1 in. deep in a sunny site during early spring. Dig the crop when the foliage dies. Hang clusters of bulbs to dry before storing them in string nets.

Leeks Sow seeds in early spring; keep down weeds and water well in dry weather. Dig up all the seedlings in late June and replant at once. Use a dibber to make holes 4 in. deep about 8 in. apart in rows 1 ft. apart. Drop a seedling into each hole and pour in a little water. Weed when necessary. Dig leeks for use at any time between November and late April.

For Tree Onion and Welsh Onion see Fifty Vegetables and Saladings; Chives see Herbs.

Cabbage Family, Root Vegetables, Squash

These do best in fertile, well-drained, alkaline soil. On acid soils spread lime at from ½–1 lb. per sq. yd., after the ground has been cultivated in winter or early spring. However, over-liming is dangerous; sufficient lime is added to most soils when garden compost is dug in or spread on to them; it is useful to sprinkle a little lime over layers of waste when a compost heap is being built. In a vegetable garden rotation (see Some Useful Vegetable Garden Practices) the plot where cabbages etc., are to be grown should be dressed with manure or garden compost.

Sow brassica seeds in a special bed of fertile soil, which, after it has been cultivated, should be raked level and firmed with the feet. Make 1-in. deep seed drills, 8 in. apart. If the soil is dry, fill the seed drills with water; allow the water to drain away before sowing fairly thickly. The seedlings will not remain in the bed for very long so that the ill effects of overcrowding will be minimal.

Varieties

Brussels Sprouts: Jade Cross Hybrid, Long Island Improved, Indra, Peer Gynt.
Cabbage (early): Golden Acre, Early Jersey Wakefield, Copenhagen Market, Emerald Cross Hybrid.
Cabbage (mid-season): Green Acre, Bonanza.
Cabbage (late): Penn State Ballhead, Premium Flat Dutch, Wisconsin Hollander.
Cabbage (Savoy, late): Chieftain Savoy, Perfection Drumhead.
Cauliflower (early): Super Snowball, Snow King.
Cauliflower (summer): Idol Original.
Cauliflower (late): Clou, Snowball-Y, Igloo.
Cauliflower (Purple): Purple Head.
Broccoli (Italian): Cleopatra, de Cicio.
Kale: Dwarf Green Curled, Green Curled Scotch, Dwarf Siberian.

Weed and water when necessary. In a frame you may have to water frequently. Remove the frame sash in May.

Brassica plants do best in firm fertile soil. The evening before transplanting water the seed bed well if it is dry.

Make holes with a dibber. If the soil is dry fill the holes with water and allow it to soak away. Pull seedlings out of the seed bed, choosing sturdy, straight specimens. Lower a plant into each hole until the lowest leaf is level with the surrounding soil. Push the dibber into the ground alongside, to press soil against the root and stem of the plant. Plant cauliflowers only to a depth at which the seedling was growing in the seed bed.

Cabbage root maggot is a fairly common pest. Eggs are laid alongside brassica plants often after they have been transplanted. The maggots bore into the roots. Plants are dwarfed or may wilt and usually die. The female flies find the plants by sense of smell. The scent from newly-planted brassica seedlings can be masked by setting out plants in firm ground mulched with garden compost.

Club root is a common and serious disease. Affected plants make poor growth and are often stunted, the roots are badly swollen and may smell nasty. Badly drained and acid soils favor the fungus. Regular heavy dressings of compost lower soil acidity and improve drainage. Dressing with lime also counteracts acidity.

Hoe and water often; plants weakened by drought are particularly prone to attack by caterpillars of the cabbage worm and cabbage looper. Strong, healthy brassica plants may be visited by cabbage white butterflies and by the cabbage moth. They are rarely a nuisance to plants making good, steady growth. If you spot any small caterpillars, pick them off. Spray with a weak solution of table salt and water. The best preventive measure is to ensure that the soil is fertile and that plants are never short of water in summer.

Start picking Brussels sprouts near the base of the stem in late fall/early winter. Continue harvesting until the top of the stem is reached.

Harvest cabbages when they are firm and tight. Cut cauliflowers and Italian broccoli when heads are well formed.

Pick side shoots of sprouting broccoli in winter and spring. Finally cut and use the central head, a loose collection of shoots. Cut the central, loose heads of kale for use in late winter or early spring. Side shoots will develop; pick these when they are still young and tender.

Calabresse This appears in catalogs as 'Green Sprouting Broccoli', 'Italian Sprouting Broccoli' or simply as 'Calabresse'. It is a winter/fall vegetable. Sow in April and set out plants in June. A green central head will form on each plant in August or September. Cut and use this as cauliflower. Thick side shoots are then produced; these may be cooked as asparagus, after removing the leaves and peeling the stems.

Red Cabbage This is often grown for pickling. Sow seeds in August and give the seedlings cloche protection until they are planted out at 18 in. apart each way in late March/early April. Seeds may also be sown in early spring and the seedlings then transplanted in June.

Transplanting dates and distances

Vegetable	Date	Between rows Inches	Between plants in the rows Inches
Brussels sprouts	May/June	30	30
Cabbage—early	April–May (depending on the district)	15–18	15–18
mid-season	June/July		
late	June–July		
Cauliflower—spring	Move plants from early spring greenhouse sowing to final positions as soon as weather is suitable	18–24	18
summer, late	July–August	24–30	18–24
Cauliflower, Purple	June	24–30	18–24
Broccoli, Italian	May–June	36	24–36
Kale (Borecole)	June/July	24–30	18–24

When to sow	Greenhouse or frame	Outdoors
Brussels sprouts	April	April
Cabbage—early	Feb–March (depending on area)	April–May (depending on area)
mid-season		May–June
late		May–June
Cauliflower—early	Feb–March (depending on area)	
summer		May
late		June/July
Cauliflower, Purple		May
Broccoli, Italian	March	May
Kale		April–May

Far left: A well formed summer cabbage
Center left: Club root of brassicas
Left: a clean root. *Right:* a root affected by club root disease. *Left:* Planting brassica seedlings. Use a dibber to make the hole, then push the dibber into the soil by the side of the seedling to firm it. *Above:* A large head of 'Early Golden Acre' cabbage. *Below:* Head of broccoli. *Right:* A well formed mid season cabbage

Root Vegetables

Root vegetables do well in fertile garden soil but there should be no hard band of gravel or clay beneath the top spit nor should the top soil contain a high percentage of large stones. Often some deep cultivation is necessary to prepare a garden soil initially for first-class root vegetables. No manure or garden compost should be applied to spots in the garden where root crops are to be grown that season. Grow root crops in soil in which manure or garden compost was applied for a different crop in the previous season. Where potatoes have been grown makes a suitable site for root crops. After cultivation of the whole vegetable garden in the fall or early spring just rake level and remove any large stones before sowing root vegetables.

Beet Beets may be round, cylindrical or long. Quick-to-mature beets for summer salads are round. 'Crimson Globe' is an example. Lutz Greenleaf may be grown for summer use and winter storing. Beet are usually deep red in color and bleed if cut. Burpees Golden Beet, however, has orange-red skin with yellow flesh and does not bleed like red beets.

Sowing For summer use seeds of globe type beet may be sown at 3 week intervals from the time the ground is workable in spring until July. Beet for winter storage are raised from seed down towards the end of June. Sow seeds thinly in 1 in. drills that are spaced 12 in. apart. Hoe between rows to keep down weeds. If you have sown too thickly, thin out some of the seedlings when the soil is damp. Do not thin seedlings too drastically; the small thinnings make delicious early greens.

Lift beet for storing in the fall before frost. Twist off the foliage and rub off any dry soil adhering to the roots. Store, sandwich fashion, in dry sand or peatmoss in boxes which should be housed in a cool but frost-free place.

Carrots For early use sow a quick-to-mature carrot (one that matures in 65–70 days) in spring as soon as the soil is workable. Where the ground is heavy and slow to warm up, the first sowing may be made in cold frames. For succession, sow every 3 weeks until early June. Maincrop varieties for winter storage should be sown in June.

If you are sowing in a frame make 1-in. deep seed drills at 6 in. apart. In the open garden allow 12 in. between rows. Do not sow too thickly. Mixing the small seeds with some dry sand or dry soil prevents a thick sowing. Carrot seeds are also offered in pellet form. Pellets can be sown at ½–1 in. apart. When sowing pelleted seeds the soil of the seed drill must always be quite wet. Flood seed drills with water should the soil be dry. Sow when the water has drained away.

Prevent weeds from developing by hoeing. Pull young carrots for use as soon as they are large enough. Maincrop carrots are thinned in July. Spread this job over several weeks, thinning so that finally carrots are about 4 in. apart.

Dig carrots for storage in late fall during dry weather. Cut back the foliage to 1 in. from the crown of each carrot. Store carrots in cool place such as a garage or basement, placing them sandwich fashion between layers of damp sand.

Parsnip Most gardeners favor a long rooted parsnip such as 'Hollow Crown Improved' and Harris Model. Shorter-rooted sorts are better where the garden top soil is shallow.

Sowing Parsnip seed may be sown as soon as the soil is workable in spring. Sow fairly thinly in 1-in. deep seed drills spaced at 12 in. apart. Pelleted seed is on offer. Sow pellets at 1 in. apart.

Hoe to keep down weeds. Thin parsnip seedlings twice, first to leave seedlings at about 1 in. apart and again in June when each plant left to grow on should be about 8 in. from its neighbors in the row.

Dig parsnips for use as and when wanted during winter and early spring. In colder areas the roots should be covered in the fall with dry leaves or straw, or they may be lifted and stored in a cool place between layers of sand. Any parsnips still in the ground in March may be dug up and heeled in a trench.

Rutabaga The vegetable is suited to the cooler parts of the country. American Purple Top, Laurentian and Long Island Improved are popular varieties.

Sowing Seed should be sown thinly in 1 in. deep drills, spaced 18 in. apart, towards the end of June. Hoe to prevent weeds from developing. Thin seedlings to 1 ft. apart. Pull Rutabagas for use in fall/early winter. Roots may be stored in a cool place in

Above left: Potatoes 'Pentland Crown'
Above right: Rutabaga 'Best of All'
Below: Stump-rooted carrots mature quickly for use in summer

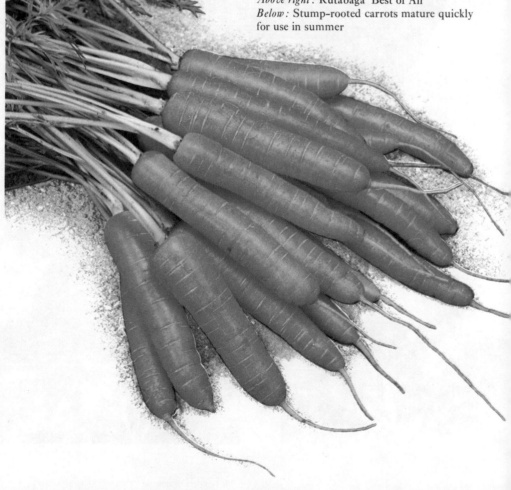

the same way as carrots.

Turnips grow better when the weather is cooler. There are two main classes. Those for spring sowing which are quick growing. Examples are Early White Milan. Early Purple Top Milan and Tokyo Cross. Purple Top White Globe is suitable for later sowing. For an abundant supply of turnip greens sow Shagoin and Just Right. Both of these varieties also produce fine roots.

Sowing The first sowings should be made as early in spring as possible. For fall and winter crops sow in July. For succession, make several sowings. Where winters are less severe, seed may be sown in the fall to provide greens.

Sow seeds thinly in 1 in. deep drills spaced 1 ft. apart. Weed and water often in dry weather. Thin seedlings to leave a strong plant every 6 in. Do not thin seedlings of turnips which are being grown solely for their edible foliage.

Flea beetles make holes in leaves of many seedlings – cabbage, radish, cauliflower, wallflower, alyssum, iberis and turnip. Damage is usually serious if seedlings are left to become dry at the roots. Frequent waterings lead to quicker growth and the seedlings recover from beetle damage. Dusting with derris at weekly intervals helps to control this pest. Strong growing seedlings, although holed by these beetles, do not appear inconvenienced.

Pull summer turnips when they are quite young and tender. Leave winter turnips in the ground and harvest as and when wanted. Where winters are severe turnips may be lifted and stored as carrots. When pulling turnip tops try not to take more than a couple of leaves at any one time from each plant.

For Hamburgh Parsley, Salsify, Scorzonera *see* Fifty Vegetables and Salads.

Potatoes The potato plant prefers a fairly cool climate and needs a well drained soil. For potato growing the texture of both light and heavy soils is greatly improved by regular dressings of strawy manure or garden compost. The site chosen for potatoes should always be dressed with either of these plant food-rich soil improvers during digging operations, but never limed.

Planting Seed potato tubers should be bought in winter and stood in trays to sprout. House the trays in a frostproof, light, cool, airy place.

The planting of quick maturing varieties should be carried out in spring some two weeks before the last killing frost. A further planting can be made about 2 weeks later. Late maturing sorts can go in 2 weeks after

Below: After the leaves have been twisted off, lay the beets on sand in a box and cover them with more sand

that. There are of course many varieties of potato available, both early and maincrop, but because climatic and soil conditions vary so much from one state to another it would be well to get in touch with your county agricultural agent if you have any doubts on the selection of suitable potatoes for your particular area.

Use a garden line to make straight rows and use a draw hoe to make 6-in. deep furrows.

Planting Distances	Distance between seed tubers in a row	Distance between rows
Early potatoes	12 in.	2 ft.
Maincrop	15 in.	2½ ft.

Discard any tubers which have not sprouted or which show decay. Plant so that the end of the tuber where most shoots are is uppermost. Rake soil over the tubers to fill the furrows.

Hoe between rows to keep down weeds. When the plants are 9 in. or so high, use a draw hoe to draw up soil around them. This practice is known as earthing-up. Some gardeners earth up again a few weeks later. After earthing up your potatoes do not use a hoe to remove weeds. Remove the few weeds which may appear by hand.

Late potato blight is one of the most feared diseases among potato growers. This fungus is unlikely to be troublesome in a dry summer and is a greater worry in western parts of the country than in the drier east. Where blight is a normal hazard of potato growing, regular sprayings with Bordeaux mixture, maneb or zineb are often necessary A power sprayer is needed to ensure that all of the foliage is well-coated with one of these fungicides. The varieties Kennebec, Essex and Sebago are resistant to the disease.

Early varieties may be lifted as required as soon as they are large enough to use, usually about 2½ months after planting. Dig only sufficient roots for immediate use. Continue digging on and off as and when potatoes are required in the kitchen.

By mid-August all first earlies may have been dug. Second earlies may then be dug as and when potatoes are wanted. Lift the rest of second earlies along with maincrop in September.

Do not dig maincrop potatoes until the plants are brown, dry and shriveled. Choose a dry, sunny day for digging the entire crop. Leave the tubers on top of the ground for an hour or so to allow them to dry.

Examine each tuber and put aside for immediate use any which are damaged. Store undamaged tubers only in boxes or trays in a dry, cool but frostproof place. Drape black polyethelene sheeting over the storage containers to prevent the potatoes from greening. Green potatoes are not edible.

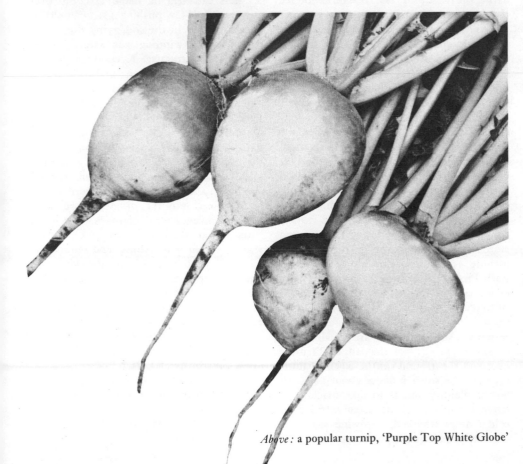

Above: a popular turnip, 'Purple Top White Globe'

Melon, Squash & Pumpkin

Fertile, well-drained soil is necessary for the good growth of these plants as they are greedy feeders.

Sowing The muskmelon, more popularly known by most as the cantaloupe melon, requires a long growing season. In milder areas of the country, seed may be sown directly outside as soon as the soil warms up in spring. Where the growing season is shorter it is wiser to make a sowing in small pots indoors or in a greenhouse about 1 month before the plants are to be transferred outdoors after the danger of frost is over.

Fill 3½-in. pots with the potting compost of your choice. Make sure the compost is moist. Then press two seeds into the compost in each pot. Water lightly, with a fine rose on the water can. Keep the pots moist but not over-wet. Germination takes about a week. When seedlings are forming the first true (triangular) leaf, pinch off the second, weaker seedling in each pot. Do not pull out this unwanted seedling. If you do, you may disturb the roots of the seedling you wish to retain. From now on until planting time keep the seedlings moist. Growth is very rapid. In colder parts of the country, melons may be grown successfully in cold frames or in a greenhouse.

Melon Varieties There are a wide selection of varieties available, including Hales Best, Hearts of Gold, Honey Rock, Pride of Wisconsin and Samson.

Melons grown outdoors should be set on hills which are spaced 4–6 ft. apart. If sowing directly in the open allow 4–6 seeds per hill; these are later thinned to leave one plant per station.

For greenhouse cultivation set out plants at 2 ft. apart. Erect a framework of bamboo canes and soft wires to which the plants may be tied loosely. Stop all side shoots when they are 1 ft. long and tie them to the horizontal wires. When the plants reach the top of the supports, pinch out the central growing points. To have a good set of fruits it pays to hand pollinate. You can transfer pollen from male flowers to females with a dry, clean camel's hair brush. Do this at around midday on bright sunny days. When four fruits have set on each plant cut off any surplus foliage and surplus fruitlets. Start feeding with liquid manure and keep the plants well watered. Allow plenty of ventilation. Stop all watering and feeding when it appears to you that the melons have stopped swelling. To prevent them from falling off the plants ripening melons are tied in string net bags. Knowing when the first melon is ripe is easy. A ripe melon emits a delicious aroma.

Various bacteria cause foot rot, a severe and killing disease of melon and cucumber plants. The soft rot occurs at or just above soil level. The trouble is caused by water collecting and remaining near the base of the stem. Prevent this from happening by setting out melon and cucumber plants on a slight mound. Ensure, too, that the soil ball is just above the surrounding soil after melon and cucumber plants have been planted out.

If you grow melons in frames each plant requires at least 2 sq. ft. of room. Plant during the second half of May and pinch off the growing point of each plant. Within a short time lateral shoots will be made. Retain four of them only. Pinch off the shoots when they reach the sides or corners of the frame. In July the plants will have made much growth. Prop up the frame light in warm weather to permit bees and other insects entry for pollinating the female flowers. As soon as you see the three melons (on plants of larger varieties) or four (on small varieties) have set, each on a sub-lateral shoot from a different main lateral, prune off surplus sub-laterals and surplus fruitlets. Place the melons you are retaining on to pieces of slate, tile or wood to prevent slug damage. Water often and apply liquid feeds occasionally. Stop watering and feeding when the fruits are of full size and ripening has started.

Squash Varieties Some varieties produce plants which are low, compact bushes, other varieties make long, trailing stems. Both early developing varieties (all bush) that are eaten when they are young, and winter squash which may be allowed to ripen and stored for winter use, are available. They include: (summer) Zucchini, Diplomat, Early Prolific, Straightneck, Cocozelle, Vegetable Spaghetti; (winter) Blue Hubbard, Buttercup, Waltham Butternut, Table Queen.

Sowing Although seeds are usually sown outside in spring when the danger of frost is over and the ground can be worked, seeds may also be sown indoors about a month before planting out is to take place. The latter method is to be recommended in colder areas where the growing season is shorter, but as squash plants are very sensitive to frost, on no account should they be transferred to the open until all danger of freezing is over.

Squash are usually grown on hills of fertile, well drained soil to which well rotted manure has been added. Stations for bush types should be 3–4 ft. apart depending on vigor, while those for trailing varieties are spaced at distances of from 8–12 ft. It is usual to sow 5–6 seeds per hill, which are later thinned to 3 plants. When sowing indoors plant 5 seeds to a 5 in. plant. After germination thin so that 3 plants remain. Trailers can also be made to climb over wigwams made by pushing 4 strong poles or bamboo canes in the soil, tying them near the apex and winding soft wire or string around the structure. Keep down weeds, water often in dry weather and if the soil is not very rich apply liquid manure feeds when squash are swelling. Fertilization of female squash flowers is usually carried out by pollinating insects. Some gardeners like to make sure of fertilization by doing the job themselves. To hand pollinate wait until midday. Then pick a male flower, strip off the petals and twist the single 'core' of the male flower into the divided 'core' of a female flower. Female flowers have small squashes at their rear. Summer squash should be cut when young and tender and when the thumb nail pierces the skin easily and to keep the plants producing, regular harvesting is necessary.

Pumpkin Treat pumpkin plants as if they are plants of trailing squash. Each plant will set and swell one or two fruits. Large pumpkins are obtained by giving liquid manure feeds generously and often.

Harvest pumpkins on a sunny day in fall when the skins are firm. Store them in a cool, dry place.

For Vegetable Marrows *see* Fifty Vegetables and Salads.

Above: Early Golden Summer Crookneck Squash
Right: A heavy crop of pumpkins harvested on a sunny day

50 Vegetables and Salads

Artichoke (Globe) A tender decorative, gray-leaved thistle-like plant, this grows 4–6 ft. tall. Plants can be raised from seed but superior varieties such as 'Vert de Laon' and 'Grand Vert de Camus' are propagated from suckers. Cut flower buds for use before the bud scales are fully open.

Artichoke (Jerusalem) This hardy perennial resembles a sunflower plant and reaches a height of 10 ft. Plant tubers 1 ft. apart and 6 in. deep, in spring. Lift roots for eating after tops turn yellow. Before winter freeze, lift remaining tubers and store inside in sand.

Asparagus Plant two-year-old plants in spring. 'Mary Washington' is a popular variety. Set plants on a ridge at the bottom of a 9-in. deep trench so that the crowns are 5 in. below the soil surface. Apply a 1-in. thick mulch of compost to the bed each spring. Do not harvest asparagus until the second season and when plants are well established. Sever the thick shoots well below soil level, using a sharp knife, during May and early June. Allow the foliage to grow naturally all summer but cut it down in late fall.

Beans (Shell) These beans are usually grown for drying. The variety Dwarf Horticultural may be used as a snap bean when the pods are young. Culture is the same as for bush beans. Allow pods to remain on the plants until late summer or early fall. After harvesting the dry pods place them in a sunny position to ripen off; when perfectly dry, shell them. Store the beans indoors in glass jars without lids.

Beans (Ornamental) Pole beans with colored pods, such as the Kentucky Wonder Wax which are curved and waxy yellow, make a decorative feature if trained over trellis-work. The pods may be picked when young and tender or used as shell beans or as dried beans.

Cabbage (Chinese) 'Pe-Tsai' and 'Mich-ihli' are the best known. Sow seeds in 1-in. deep drills 1 ft. apart in late June and July. Thin young plants to 1 ft. apart. Do not transplant any seedlings. The foliage is a lettuce substitute in salads or it may be cooked as cabbage. The mid-ribs may be cooked and served as asparagus.

Cabbage (Portugal) Sow seeds in April. Set out plants 3 ft. apart in early June. The edible portions are the thick, white mid-ribs of the leaves.

Capsicum or Sweet Pepper Sow seed in a greenhouse at a minimum of 60°F in spring, about 8 weeks before the plants are to be planted outside. When large enough transfer the seedlings to small pots. Keep them growing and when the soil has warmed up sufficiently plant in the open, 18 in. apart, in rows that are 2–3 ft. apart. Gather peppers when of full size and bright green.

Cardoon The plant is a 3-ft. high thistle-like plant. Sow seeds in a heated greenhouse in late March. Harden off plants before transferring them to the open garden, 18 in. apart. Keep them well watered. In October remove all yellowing leaves and tie the plants at the top. Then pile earth up and around them to blanch the stems, which takes about a month. Plants may also be grown in trenches in the same way as celery, but the earthing up is done in one operation. In milder areas seed may be sown directly outdoors.

Celeriac or Root Celery Sow seeds in heat in March or April, harden off the plants and plant them 1 ft. apart in the garden in May. Remove all suckers. Lift and store the roots in October. Store as carrots.

Celery There are three sorts–blanched,

Left: One of several kinds of capsicum or sweet pepper. Some kinds are bright green when ripe
Above: Cut asparagus shoots well below soil level
Below: The thick white midribs are the edible portions of the leaves of Portuguese cabbage

self-blanching and green. Sow seeds in trays or pots in a heated greenhouse in March. Harden off plants in a cold frame before planting outdoors in early June. Those which need blanching are set out in a trench; earth up plants slightly in mid-August, continue the operation two weeks later and finish it two weeks afterwards. Start digging blanched celery in late fall. A good place for self-blanching celery is a cold frame. Plant 9 in. apart. Remove the frame light in late June and in mid-July tuck straw around the plants to assist blanching. Lift plants for use in August and September. Green (Pascal Green) celery is grown in the same way as self-blanching celery but because it is eaten green there is no blanching to be done at all and plants may be grown in the open. Celery is grown as a winter crop in warm areas of the country.

Celtuce Sow and cultivate as lettuce. The plants reach a height of 2 ft. The thick stem is the edible part of the vegetable. Peel stems before use.

Chervil (Turnip-Rooted Chervil) Sow in April and cultivate as parsnips. Dig the roots as and when required in winter, or lift and store in moist sand in October.

Chicory Sow seeds 1 in. deep in spring and thin seedlings to 9 in. apart. In November dig up the parsnip-like roots and heel them in a trench over which a little straw should be spread. Take small batches for chicon production now and then during the winter. Trim roots back by a few inches and reduce the foliage to within 1 in. of the crown. Plant roots closely in the greenhouse border and cover with straw weighed down with dry soil. Inspect for chicons after a month or so. Alternatively, plant prepared roots in pails or pots and force chicons indoors or in a garage or shed. It is important that all light be excluded.

Chopsuy Green (or Shungiku) Sow seeds of this edible chrysanthemum in spring or in late summer. Cultivate as spinach. Harvest plants for use when they are from 4–5 in. high. It is used in Chinese dishes.

Corn Salad or Lamb's Lettuce Sow this useful lettuce substitute in August or in September in very shallow drills. Thin seedlings to 6 in. apart. Plants are ready for use when young so that thinnings may be added to salads. Pick leaves as and when required all winter.

Cress (Winter) Sow seeds between August and October in ½-in. deep, damp drills. Thin seedlings to 6 in. apart. A second sowing can be made in spring. It is a substitute for watercress.

Dandelion The cultivated dandelion is a selected French plant. Seeds are sown in April and the seedlings thinned to 9 in. apart. Roots are dug in November and are stored in sand. Batches of roots are taken out of store for forced, blanched foliage for winter salads. A heated greenhouse encourages the rapid production of blanched foliage.

Eggplant The eggplant requires warm conditions and will grow better in milder areas of the country. Seeds should be sown in a warm greenhouse in spring, about 8 weeks before the last frost. When the seedlings are large enough, transplant them in small pots. Transfer plants outdoors when the danger of frost is over and the soil has warmed up, in rows 3–4 ft. apart, allowing 2–3 ft. between plants. Harvest the fruits when they are glossy and softening.

Endive Sow and cultivate as lettuce. Hearts may be partially blanched by tying the plants with string. Full blanching is achieved by covering the plants with large pots so that all light is excluded.

Finocchio or Florence Fennel Sow seeds in shallow seed drills, 1 ft. apart in spring. Thin seedlings to 9 in. apart. The swollen stem bases are ready for use in late summer or early fall.

Garlic Plant cloves (segments stripped from garlic bulbs) 2 in. deep and 6 in. apart in early spring. Dig the crop in summer when the foliage yellows. Dry off the bulbs in a sunny place before storing them in a dry, cool but frost-proof place.

Gherkin For pickling gherkins sow and grow a few plants solely for this purpose. West India Gherkin is a good variety.

Good King Henry (Mercury) Sow seeds in April and thin the seedlings to 1 ft. apart. The leaves are a substitute for spinach. Young shoots poking through the soil in March or April may be cut when 4 in. long and used in the same way as asparagus.

Horseradish Plant root cuttings 1 ft. apart

Left: 'Gold Nugget', a winter squash variety grown for summer use or for storing
Above: A good head of Giant Pascal Celery

in spring. Dig up plants when required in the following fall and winter. Keep a few pieces of root for replanting elsewhere in the garden.

Kohlrabi Sow at any time between March and August. Thin seedlings to 9 in. apart. The thinnings may be transplanted. Harvest when the turnip-like swollen stems are no larger than a tennis ball.

The edible swollen stems of kohlrabi

Marrow (Vegetable Marrow) Closely allied to squash and a popular vegetable in Britain. Both bush and trailing types are available. Require plenty of humus in the soil and adequate water during growth. Cultivation is as recommended for squash. Marrows may be eaten young or allowed to mature for winter use.

Mustard Popular in the south, seeds may be sown in spring. Further sowings are made at intervals until summer. Sow again in August for fall use. Sow in drills 12–18 in. apart.

Okra or Gumbo A plant for milder areas. Sow seed in spring 1 in. deep in rows that are 4 ft. apart. Later thin plants so that they stand 2 ft. apart. The yellow flowers are followed by the edible pods which are harvested when still soft.

Onion (Potato Onion) Plant and cultivate as shallots.

Onion (Tree Onion) Plant small bulbs 1 in. deep 6 in. apart in rows 1 ft. apart as soon as the ground is suitable in spring. The tall stems need supporting. Clusters of small onions form at various levels on the stems. Harvest them for use between August and March.

Onion (Welsh Onion) Plant pieces taken from clumps in spring, 12–18 in. apart. Lift clumps for use in salads and cooked dishes.

Orach (Mountain Spinach) There are green, white and red forms. Sow seeds thinly in shallow drills between March and July. Thin seedlings to 15 in. apart. Use young leaves as a spinach substitute.

Parsley Sow in April in ½-in. deep drills. Thin the seedlings to 6 in. apart. 'Moss Curled' is a popular variety.

Parsley (Hamburgh Parsley) Sow and cultivate as parsnips. Cook roots as parsnips and use the foliage as parsley.

Pea (Asparagus Pea) Sow in a shallow drill in late May. Space the seeds at 6 in. apart and thin the young plants to 1 ft. apart. Give the plants some twiggy brushwood supports. Gather the pods when they are about 1 in. long.

Pea (Mangetout or Sugar Pea) Sow and cultivate as garden peas and provide the plants with supports. Harvest pods before the seeds inside them start to swell.

Pea (Pea Bean) Grow as pole beans but allow seeds in the pods to plump up. Pods may be gathered when green and the beans cooked as peas or the pods may be left to ripen and shelled for drying.

Pea (Petits Pois) Sow and cultivate as garden peas. Pick pods when very young and tender.

Popcorn Sow and cultivate as sweet corn but do not harvest cobs until they are dry and brittle, in the early fall.

Rhubarb A good variety is 'MacDonald'. Plant stools in late fall, 4 ft. apart. Do not pull sticks until the second season and always stop pulling at the end of June. Mulch the bed with compost or well-rotted manure each fall.

Salsify Sow seeds thinly in shallow drills in early spring. From then on cultivate and harvest as parsnips.

Scorzonera Sow, cultivate and harvest as salsify.

Seakale Plant thongs (root cuttings) 18 in. apart in early spring. Mulch with well-rotted manure or compost in May. Allow the foliage to die before lifting roots for blanching in winter. Plant roots in the greenhouse border and cover with dry straw weighed down with dry soil. Cut blanched seakale just below soil level with a small piece of the root attached.

Spinach Beet (Swiss Chard, Silver Beet) Sow seeds in shallow drills 12 in. apart between April and July. Thin seedlings to 12 in. apart. When plants are fully grown pick leaves as required. The thick white midribs may be cooked as a substitute for seakale and the green parts as spinach. There is a red form known as rhubarb chard or ruby chard.

Ruby chard, a red form of seakale beet

Spinach (Summer Spinach) (Round-seeded Spinach) Sow seeds in early spring and make successional sowings until early spring. Sow in 1-in. deep drills, 1 ft. apart and thin seedlings to 3 in. Keep plants well watered in dry weather. Harvest but a few leaves from each plant at any one picking.

Spinach (Winter Spinach) (Prickly-seeded Spinach) Sow and cultivate as summer spinach but wait until August or early September before sowing. In cold areas protect plants with salt hay or straw during the winter.

Spinach (New Zealand Spinach) Sow seeds in spring on small hills of rich soil, spaced 3 ft. apart. After germination, thin to leave 1 plant per station. Pick the tender side shoots as and when wanted. The leaves may be cooked as spinach or eaten raw.

Spinach (Perpetual Spinach) (Spinach Beet) Sow seeds in shallow drills 1 ft. apart in early April. Thin seedlings to 8–12 in. apart. Pick leaves as with summer and winter spinach, between July and winter.

Squash (Summer Squash) In American English the vegetable marrow is a summer squash. In Britain seedsmen and gardeners generally consider such differently shaped marrows as 'Patty Pan' (the custard marrow), 'Crooknecks' and 'Straightnecks' as summer squashes. Cultivate these as bush type vegetable marrows.

Squash (Winter Squash) Examples are 'Hubbard', 'Buttercup' and 'Golden Delicious'. 'Gold Nugget' is dual purpose and may be grown for summer use or for storing. Cultivate as bush or trailing marrows and harvest for storing in the fall.

Inspecting sweet corn for ripeness

Sweet Corn (Corn on the Cob) Place seed 3–4 in. apart in drills 1 in. deep. Rows should be 2–3 ft. from each other. It is advisable to have several rows in a block to ensure fertilization. After germination, thin plants to 1 ft. apart. Harvest cobs when the grains are full but immature in August. At that stage the 'silks' hanging from the cobs are dark brown to black in color and brittle.

Tomatoes (Ornamental) These are excellent in salads and are attractive in the garden, too. Grow as ordinary standard tomatoes. Ornamentals include Red and Yellow Cherries, Red and Yellow Plums, Red and Yellow Pears.

Watercress Choose a damp, shady spot and dig in plenty of peatmoss to retain moisture, leaving the surface of the bed a little lower than the surrounding soil. Sow in April and in August, protecting August-sown plants with a frame light between November and March.

Water Melon Water melons require a warm and humid climate and so are grown particularly in the south. Cultivation as for melons. No pruning is required.

Common Pests and Diseases

Vegetables growing in fertile, well-drained and well-cultivated gardens seldom suffer greatly from pests and diseases. The modern gardener accepts that all wildlife has a right to live. It is only when things get out of hand that any living creature causing damage to garden plants can be rated as a pest. It is up to the gardener to use his superior intelligence to outwit possibly harmful small creatures instead of polluting the environment surrounding his home. The labels of packaged pesticides should be read carefully. If the contents are dangerous to you, your children and your family pets consider carefully before you buy such substances. Always lock dangerous pesticides quite safely away from children. Do *not* mix dangerous pesticides with water and store them in beer or soda bottles. Your child may drink the stuff and be poisoned. The commonly recommended insecticide nicotine, for example, is a poison. As for chemical weed killers the long term effect of some modern kinds is as yet unknown. The older weedkiller, sodium chlorate, is liable to explode; it also runs in the soil and may not only kill your own choice plants but may kill plants in your neighbors' gardens. Many sprays and powders contain derris or pyrethrum. These are natural insecticides prepared from plants. They are harmless to all warm-blooded creatures but derris can kill fish. If you use derris pesticides, keep sprays and dusts away from your garden pool. Encourage natural predators, e.g. the toad, frog, ladybug, and wasps (in spring but not in summer).

Learn to distinguish between the helpful centipede, the less helpful millipede and the unpleasant wireworm. Most moths, butterflies and their caterpillars are on your side. The caterpillars of cabbage white butterflies and of the cabbage looper are not!

The following list gives some of the most common pests and diseases, the chief vegetables affected, the damage done, and lastly the control measures available.

Aphids *Vegetable:* all. *Damage:* they are sap suckers. Plants are weakened, leaves die and flower buds may be ruined. *Control:* allow plants sufficient space and do not grow vegetables in shade. Water well and often in dry, summer weather. Keep down weeds. Encourage ladybugs. Spray with derris or pyrethrum.

Birds *Vegetable:* seed beds and the seedlings of several vegetables. *Damage:* seeds are sought for and devoured; seedlings are pecked. *Control:* net or protect with black cotton. A scarecrow or strips of tinfoil may be tried.

Cabbage Root Maggot *Vegetable:* the cabbage tribe. *Damage:* maggots burrow into the roots; plants wilt and die. *Control:* set out transplants in firm soil and mulch with garden compost.

Carrot Root Fly *Vegetable:* carrot. *Damage:* grubs eat roots; plants yellow and die. *Control:* thin seedlings only when soil is moist. Bury unwanted thinnings and broken foliage.

Carrot Weevil *Vegetable:* carrot, celery, parsnip. *Damage:* grubs burrowing into roots and centers of plants. *Control:* rotation of crops.

Caterpillars *Vegetable:* the cabbage tribe. *Damage:* leaves are eaten. *Control:* Pick off caterpillars. Spray with derris or salt solution (50 gms [2 oz] of table salt to 5 litres [1 gallon] of water).

Club Root *Vegetable:* the cabbage tribe. *Damage:* the fungus causes swellings on the roots which decay. Plants are stunted and may die. *Control:* do not raise plants in soil known to be infected with the fungus. Rotate crops. Feed the soil with plenty of compost. Lime where necessary. Burn roots of affected plants.

Common Scab *Vegetable:* potato. *Damage:* scabby marks on the skin. *Control:* seldom serious and the flesh of potatoes is rarely damaged. Do not lime ground in which potatoes are to be planted. Rotate crops. Where this trouble is common surround seed tubers with peatmoss, leaf mold or lawn mowings at planting time.

Cutworms *Vegetable:* many. *Damage:* these soil caterpillars eat stems, leaves and roots. They often cut stems of seedlings at soil level. *Control:* destroy any found when digging. Hoe

cutworm

frequently and destroy any seen. Keep down weeds.

Damping Off *Vegetable:* many at seedling stage in greenhouse and in frames. *Damage:* a fungus which causes stems to shrivel. Seedlings topple over and die. *Control:* use sterile composts when sowing seeds. Sow thinly. Do not over-water, prick out early, ventilate freely. There are several chemical controls available.

Flea Beetles *Vegetable:* the cabbage tribe, radish, rutabaga, turnip. *Damage:* holes show in younger leaves. *Control:* proprietary slug killers with care. Some are harmful to pets and wild life. Prepare seed beds properly. Remove all rubbish. Keep seedlings well-watered in dry spring and summer weather. Dust seedlings with derris. This damage usually looks nastier than it is.

Grey Mold *Vegetable:* lettuce, squash, melon, cucumber, tomato. *Damage:* a fungal disease. Softening of plant tissue is followed by decay. Outgrowths of gray mold appear. *Control:* ventilate well. Clear away any debris. Remove side shoots when quite small. Prune cleanly so that no jagged stems are left. Allow plants sufficient room. Do not splash plants when watering. Dust with flowers of sulfur or spray with colloidal sulfur.

Harlequin Bug *Vegetable:* the cabbage tribe. A serious pest in the south. *Damage:* sap sucked from growing plants by insects in both the adult and nymph stage, causing wilting and death. *Control:* clean cultivation, hand picking, apply rotenone.

Leaf Mold *Vegetable:* tomato (in green-house). *Damage:* this fungus shows as yellow spots on upper surfaces of leaves with pale grayish mold on undersides. *Control:* ventilate

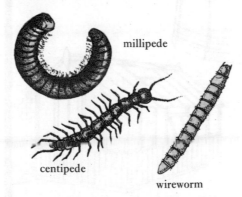

millipede

centipede

wireworm

well. Give plants adequate space. Do not over-water. Remove and burn infected foliage. Spray with zineb or a copper-based fungicide.

Mildew *Vegetable:* many. *Damage:* the fungus shows as a gray/white powder on foliage. *Control:* ensure that plants have sufficient moisture and ventilate frames and green-houses well. Dust with flowers of sulfur. Spray with zineb.

Millipedes *Vegetable:* all. *Damage:* roots are eaten. *Control:* destroy any found when digging and cultivating. Remove all rubbish to the compost heap. Trap by burying pieces of sliced potato or carrot on pointed sticks in the soil. This pest prefers roots already decaying. Do not confuse with beneficial centipedes.

Mosaic Virus *Vegetable:* cucumbers and squash. *Damage:* leaves show mottling and distortion. Plants are dwarfed. Crop is poor. Plants die. *Control:* prevent by spraying plants with derris or pyrethrum to deter aphids which spread the disease. Pull up and burn affected plants.

Onion Maggot *Vegetable:* onion, sometimes leek and shallots. *Damage:* grubs eat roots and below ground portion of plants. *Control:* avoid breaking or bruising onion foliage. Thin onion seedlings only when soil is damp. Bury broken onion foliage and unwanted thinnings.

Pea and Bean Weevils *Vegetable:* peas, beans. *Damage:* Leaves of seedlings are eaten. The bites show as 'U'-shaped notches. *Control:* hoe regularly around seedlings to disturb the pests. Break down clods under which they hide. Remove all rubbish to the compost heap. Dust or spray with derris.

Potato Late Blight *Vegetable:* potatoes, tomatoes. *Damage:* the fungus shows as brown/black markings on foliage. Potatoes and tomatoes decay. Plants rot and smell. *Control:* where this disease makes potato growing hazardous grow only early varieties. Certain varieties are available that show resistance to the disease. It seldom occurs on tomato plants in the greenhouse. Spray or dust with Bordeaux mixture or a fungicide from early June onwards.

Saddleback *Vegetable:* onion. *Damage:* underside of bulb splits. *Control:* never permit plants to become dry at the roots when bulbs are swelling.

Slugs and Snails *Vegetable:* all. *Damage:* these pests eat foliage, roots, tubers and fruits. *Control:* remove all rubbish. Search for possible hiding places and destroy the pests. Bait slugs by leaving cabbage and lettuce leaves on the soil at night. Encourage toads, frogs, and birds, slow worms and song birds.

Springtails *Vegetable:* beet, beans, cucumbers. *Damage:* insects feed on plants at ground level, particularly in damp weather. *Control:* remove dead leaves and other organic material from around plants.

Tomato Septoria Leaf Spot *Vegetable:* tomato. *Damage:* spots appear on leaves, having a water-soaked appearance at first, later turning darker. Lower leaves attacked first, but eventually spread to those higher up the plant. Leaves may be killed. *Control:* rotation of crops, keep down weeds, burn infected plants at the close of the growing season.

Wireworm *Vegetable:* all. *Damage:* grubs eat roots. *Control:* when starting a new garden do not dig in turves. Trap by burying cut pieces of potato or carrot on skewers. Search and kill any found when digging and hoeing. Grow less vulnerable vegetables such as fava beans and members of the cabbage family if this pest is present in quantity in a new garden.

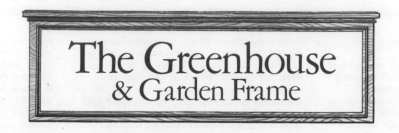

The Greenhouse & Garden Frame

❧ The Greenhouse ❧

Apart from the three standard types of greenhouse – the span or ridge, three-quarter span, and lean-to, recent years have seen the introduction of the circular house and the modification of the span types, often producing irregular designs.

The span type is an independent structure standing alone and the best for all-round purposes. Many of these are now produced with glass to the ground, instead of the traditional style with low walls of brick, concrete or wood. These walls help to preserve heat and do not allow the same violent changes of temperature as the all-glass house. Plastic is sometimes used as a glass substitute but must be regarded as of temporary value only.

Wood   Apart from cost, an important decision to make is whether the framework should be wood or metal. Wood is warmer, easier to repair and better for fitting shelves. Against this, wood needs periodic applications of wood preservative. There are two principal types of wood used in greenhouse construction: cypress and redwood, both of which are extremely durable. Teak is sometimes used but although it is very strong and remains sound for a very long time it is very expensive.

Wood is also used as roof bars when steel or iron is used to form the frame.

Metal   Steel and aluminum greenhouses are quite widely used, the latter material being easier to shape. Aluminum alloys are reasonably strong and provided they are well and firmly sited, they are satisfactory and in spite of their light weight, will stand firm. Points to watch for when selecting a metal greenhouse are absolute rigidity and provision for expansion and contraction without glass breakage or air leakage. Metal sashes are not glazed with putty; they need an elastic sealing compound. Steel needs painting, aluminum does not.

Concrete   Concrete greenhouses are also sometimes used. Less elegant than wood or metal, they are strong and durable especially since the concrete is usually reinforced with wire rods or frames.

Whatever type of greenhouse you decide to buy, make sure that all parts work properly, for ill-fitting joints, doors or ventilators can lead to trouble.

Guttering and leaders may be provided to prevent water pouring off the roof and down the wide panes, as well as making it possible to store rain water in butts or cisterns, although where winters are severe guttering may be detrimental by causing a build-up of snow and ice on the roof.

Choosing your Greenhouse   Buying a greenhouse is an investment, not only because it increases the value of your property but because of the all the year round pleasure it will give.

Since there are many kinds of greenhouse available, in various sizes and made of different materials it is important to choose the one that will best suit your needs. This will depend on a number of factors, including the site available, the plants you intend to grow and the price. Price will govern the size, although it is wise to buy the largest house you can afford to begin with.

It is a mistake to buy a greenhouse without

Types of greenhouse: 1: span type with low wooden walls. 2: a lean-to model with low wooden walls. 3: a span type greenhouse with glass to the ground. 4: a modern 'circular' greenhouse with glass to the ground. 5: a three-quarter span type. *Below:* The usual greenhouse staging is open slatted. However, many plants need humidity. One way of providing this is to cover the staging with corrugated iron or asbestos, which in turn is covered with ash or gravel and kept moist. *Right:* One of the many hippeastrums. *Far right: Columnea* 'Stavanger', a colorful trailing plant first deciding on what plants are to be grown in it. If you want to grow tall or rampant growing plants it is no use choosing an 8 × 6 ft. greenhouse. Modern materials and techniques have resulted in more glass and supports even in the largest greenhouses, resulting in better illumination which has greatly assisted the grower.

For pot plants such as cyclamen and primulas and for raising bedding plants, the usual span roof greenhouse is ideal. A structure with a brick or concrete base allows for staging but if you want to grow tomatoes or chrysanthemums, or lettuce on one side where they will need full light, it is possible to buy a type with glass to ground level – or to have one side with staging and one with glass to base.

If you are concentrating on orchids there are special houses for these plants. They are fitted with extra ventilators and often with two-tier staging, the idea being to stand the plants on the top lath staging, covering the lower staging with pebbles or old coarse ashes which are kept moist to provide the required humidity. A lean-to house is useful for taller plants while staging can be erected to accommodate colorful plants.

Make sure whatever type of greenhouse you buy is provided with ample ventilators of the right size. Ensure there are ventilators on both sides of a span greenhouse so that there is always one side against the leeward wind.

Siting the Greenhouse It is advisable to put the structure where it receives the maximum amount of sunshine, especially in winter. Avoid overhanging trees, because they cast shadows, and shed leaves and other deposits which can easily dirty the glass. Ideally the situation should be within easy reach of a water supply.

Avoid ground which becomes wet in winter and, wherever possible, choose a site where good paths can be made and which is not too far from your house.

The traditional alignment for a greenhouse is north to south, since in this position there is both a warmer and cooler side to the house. Some gardeners prefer an east to west siting, on the grounds that more light reaches the house. At all costs avoid windy situations, especially those exposed to north or east winds for these will bring draughts and some loss of heat, especially if north winds blow directly into the door. For preference, a lean-to should face south.

Erecting the Greenhouse: The Foundation A proper and permanent foundation is of paramount importance. Most greenhouse manufacturers supply a ground plan which must be strictly adhered to. A simple way of making a satisfactory foundation is to take out a 10-in. deep trench 1 ft. wide, with vertical sides. In to this is built a brick footing. Concrete blocks for footings and walls are also satisfactory. Cultivated ground needs stronger foundations since it is more likely to sink.

If the superstructure is to rest on brick walls the top of the concrete foundation must be 6 in. below ground level. If electricity is to be used lay the cables before the concrete is put in.

A solid or concrete floor can be made, but a soil base is an advantage, as it allows some crops to be grown in the 'floor'. In winter the soil can dry out, in summer it will help to maintain a humid atmosphere.

Glazing When putting in the glass, it is advisable to use putty for bedding it on the glazing bars. If the structure needs a coat of paint or preservative, put it on before the framework is glazed.

Glass should be dry when used. If wet, the panes stick together and they break more easily in cold weather. Make sure the woodwork can be securely fastened to the foundations so that subsequently, there is no movement as could occur in windy, exposed positions.

Plastic is sometimes used as a substitute for glass but is certainly not of the same value. Glass is easier to clean and the full quality of light is transmitted. Polyethelene or plastic houses are useful for providing summer protection and giving dappled light. While it does not break in the same way as glass, plastic does, however, need renewing from time to time.

❧ Heating Methods ❧

Hot Water The hot-water method is very satisfactory, since an evenly distributed warmth is produced without creating a dry atmosphere, and when used in conjunction with an oil-fired boiler involves very little work. (A big improvement on the old coal-burning units which required constant stoking.)

Electricity Electrical heating is time and labor saving and requires no boiler or fuel storage. With thermostatic control a predetermined temperature can be maintained, provided the right heaters have been chosen and there are no power cuts. There are various ways of using electricity for heating:

(1) By a wire grid over which air is blown by a fan.

(2) By a convector heater designed to produce warm air without a fan. Rapid warmth is produced, although distribution is not so even.

(3) By radiating tubes, plates or strips.

(4) By immersion heater used for hot-water pipes.

Soil warmth can also be produced by electric cables. This is used to provide bottom heat for propagating seeds or rooting cuttings and does not substantially increase air temperature.

Kerosene These heaters are sometimes used and, provided high quality fuel is used, there is little danger of poisonous fumes. This means keeping the burners clean so that incomplete combustion does not release harmful gases. For large houses, heaters with outside chimneys should be used. For small houses there are several portable models available which need little attention other than refilling. Choose one producing a blue flame which results from complete combustion of the oil.

Manufacturers usually indicate how long a heater will burn with one filling. More important, is how much heat is produced. Heat is lost through ventilation, but stagnant air encourages fungoid diseases and other disorders, and particularly with kerosene heating, a crack of ventilation is always needed, except during the severest weather.

What can be grown in a greenhouse largely depends on the temperature that can be maintained. At one time, in large private gardens, a range of houses was to be found, starting from the cold house and passing from the cool to the intermediate and hot or stove house. Today few gardeners can afford more than one greenhouse.

While many greenhouse owners like to specialize in particular types of plant, those less experienced, usually prefer to cultivate a range of plants. This means that one has to grow plants which need similar conditions.

Types of Greenhouse

The Cold Greenhouse This is one which is never heated by anything but the sun and a colorful display can be had without any artificial heat. In extra cold weather, some protection can be given by blinds which can be pulled down or let up at will. Outdoors, many plants are killed by winter dampness but if taken indoors they come through bad weather unscathed.

Where space is scarce the staging can be erected in tiers. Slatted wood is useful in that it allows air to circulate round the pots, helping to avoid atmospheric dampness in winter. Unfortunately, it also encourages pots to dry out quickly in summer.

The best plan is to place corrugated or asbestos sheeting over the staging and cover it with small shingle or stone chips. In summer the shingle can be kept damp to provide humidity, while from late fall onwards,

through winter it can be allowed to dry.

The Cool Greenhouse This is one where a minimum night temperature of 40°–45°F (4°–7°C) can be maintained. This must be controlled, which means adequate ventilation. It is, perhaps, plants in smaller greenhouses that suffer most when ventilation is wrong, especially if sufficient ventilators have not been provided. Fresh air is important but when the air vents are opened, this naturally lowers the temperature but equally important, it removes the stagnant dank air, leading to the buoyant atmosphere so vital for plant health.

The Intermediate or Warm House A winter night temperature above 48°F (8°–9°C) will allow a wider range of exotic plants to be cultivated. Such houses are usually sited where the benefit of all available sun is felt.

It pays to install automatic ventilation which acts according to outside weather conditions and inside temperature. Costing nothing to run, it is easily fitted.

A Hot (or Stove) House This is one where the winter temperature never falls below 60°F (16°C). As it is fairly expensive to run not many amateur gardeners can afford a house of this type. Except for the temperature difference and the fact that a wider range of tender plants, including many orchids, can be grown, the inside arrangements and attention needed, are the same as for the warm greenhouse.

Plants to Grow

In the Cold Greenhouse The success of plants in the cold greenhouse largely depends on the choice of the right kinds and the way they are looked after. There are distinct advantages in being able to provide just enough heat to keep the temperature falling below freezing point in winter. Failures are often due to overwatering in winter. In frosty weather, plants should be kept on the dry side.

Many alpine plants can be grown successfully in the cold house, where they can be raised from seed. These include: *Aster alpinus*, aethionemas, aubrietas, campanulas, dianthus, gentians, primulas, saxifrages and miniature cupressus.

Many bulbs do well as the protection provided leads to unblemished blooms. Among these treasures are crocuses, irises,

including the Dutch varieties 'Wedgwood', lavender; and 'Princess Beatrix', yellow. Dwarf irises are specially good, including *I. danfordiae*, yellow; and *I. reticulata*, violet, and its many forms. Narcissus, early tulips, fritillarias, liliums, scillas, tritonia and the early gladiolus produce a bright display. *Cypripedium calceolus* is handsome in flower. It likes a limey soil. Early flowering shrubs grown in pots taken in the greenhouse in December or January, soon produce a showy display. They include daphne, *Erica carnea*, forsythia, prunus and spiraea, while *Helleborus niger*, the Christmas rose, responds well.

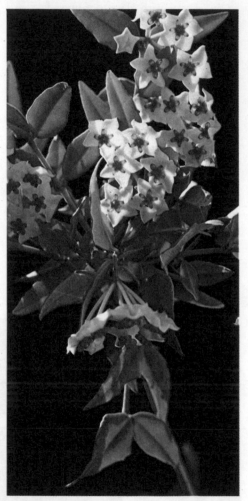

Left: Brunsfelsia calycina produces its flowers freely
Above: The wax flower, or honey plant, *Hoya carnosa*. It is a greenhouse climber
Right: the flowers and fruits of the Passion flower, *Passiflora caerulea*, another climber
Right above: Clivia miniata, a striking South African bulbous plant suitable for a warm greenhouse

In the Cool Greenhouse It is fascinating to see how quickly many exotic plants become acclimatized and grow in a cool greenhouse.

Daisy-flowered plants raised easily from seeds, such as arctotis, dimorphotheca, gazania and ursinia, will bloom continuously. *Gerbera jamesonii* has long lasting huge brilliant orange-amber flowers.

Erica hyemalis, the Cape heath, has long, white-tipped pink bells, while there are species with red, orange and yellow flowers.

Gardenias, daphnes, epacris and daturas are handsome shrubs.

Hoya bella, the wax flower, is flesh-pink. Ipomoea or morning glory, easily raised from seed, is in shades of blue. *Jasminum primulinum*, yellow; *Lapageria rosea*, rich pink waxy bells; *Passiflora caerulea*, the Passion flower; and *Thunbergia alata*, orange with a black throat are all interesting.

Foliage plants are indispensable. They include *Lippia citriodora*, the lemon-scented verbena, caladiums with beautifully spotted and veined leaves; *Eucalyptus globulus* with gray-green foliage; *Grevillea robusta*; *Maranta leuconeura*, with leaves curiously marked

and spotted; *Saxifraga sarmentosa*, fine for hanging baskets. Ferns and palms can be grown for temporary use in the living room.

Climbing plants can be grown in pots or planted in the greenhouse border. Among these are bougainvillea with brightly colored mauve bracts in summer; *Clematis armandii*, an evergreen with white flowers; *Cobaea scandens*, a fast climber of which seed is sown in March.

Carnations are among the important cool greenhouse flowers. Their cultivation is described later.

Fruit in the Greenhouse Although there are specially constructed greenhouses for the cultivation of fruit, few amateur gardeners are likely to buy a greenhouse solely for this purpose.

What can be grown depends on the space available and the amount of time that can be

spared. For further details see Fruit in Your Garden elsewhere in this work.

❧ Propagation ❧

Greenhouse and frame plants are propagated from seed or various types of cuttings. Seed sowing is often the easiest method although many plants must be propagated by cuttings, division, or off-sets.

By Seeds The majority of seeds germinate in a temperature of 60°–65°F (15°–18°C) but it is not necessary to keep the whole greenhouse to this required minimum. A propagator heated independently, can be used for seeds and cuttings.

Many seed failures are due to the use of unsuitable compost. Destructive damping-off diseases frequently result from the use of poor soil.

Whether trays, pans or flats are used the compost should be evenly compacted without being made hard. Thin sowing is essential. Very fine seeds such as those of begonias and gloxinias need not be covered but merely pressed into the surface soil. Larger seeds should be lightly covered. After watering place the flats or pots in a propagator and cover them with glass and paper. Once the seedlings appear remove the paper and glass, taking care to keep the surface soil just moist.

Early pricking out of seedlings is necessary. Keep the pricked out seedlings shaded for a few days until they are established. As the seedlings develop they will need potting up.

Stem Cuttings Many plants raised from seed can be increased from stem cuttings. These are usually made from young shoots or shoot tips. Only really healthy plants should be propagated and the cuttings should have two or three joints. Remove the lowest leaves and sever the stem cleanly just below a joint. The best results are obtained when the cuttings are inserted around the edge of pots filled with a moisture-retaining but fairly open mixture. Water in the cuttings, then place them in a heated propagator or polyethelene bag, closing it with a rubber band, but keep the plastic off the cuttings.

When the plants have rooted the propagating case should be gradually ventilated so that they become accustomed to greenhouse temperatures. Cuttings with hairy leaves are liable to damp off and should be rooted on the open bench where they should be shaded to reduce transpiration.

Leaf Cuttings Some plants, notably peperomias and saintpaulias, can be increased by leaf cuttings. Use healthy mature leaves and trim them so that the stalk is up to 1 in. long. Insert them in compost so that the leaf blades just touch the soil.

Rex begonias are treated rather differently. Slit the main veins in several places. Then peg down the leaves. Roots and plantlets will develop where the cuts are made.

Stem Sections Ficus, dracaenas and some other plants can be propagated from stem sections. The dormant bud in the leaf joint will develop into a good plant.

Leaf-bud Cuttings These consist simply of a leaf situated centrally on a piece of stem about ¾ in. long complete with a dormant bud. August and September are good months for the job since plants will be in full growth. Among plants that respond to this treatment are aphelandra, pilea and ficus.

Division Some plants such as chlorophytum and maranta can be divided in spring. Many bulbous plants multiply naturally by forming offsets which can be detached and potted separately.

Using Frames for Propagation Garden frames can, where required, be supplied with soil warming equipment. This will allow seeds and cuttings to be started. When used without heat, frames are useful for blanching endive and for growing a number of vegetable crops and salad plants.

The Garden Frame

Types The standard sash for the garden frame measures 6 ft. long and 3 ft. wide, although it is of course possible to have them custom built to whatever dimensions one requires. It is perhaps interesting to note that the standard English frame measures 6 × 4 ft., the Dutch 59 in. × 31¾ in. and the French 4 ft × 4 in. × 4 ft. 5 in.

Sectional frames of cast aluminum or steel are on the market, and there are many satisfactory portable frames with single or span roof, with sliding tops easily removed for ready access.

The size of frame you buy or make will depend on the purpose for which it is to be used, although the aim should be to have one as large, as space and pocket allow. Many frames are made with 3 ft. extensions, so that any length of run can be achieved.

Position Where possible place the frame due south and not under or too near trees. If it can be backed on to the greenhouse or other building to give protection from north winds, so much the better.

The body of the frame can be of tongued and grooved timber, bricks, concrete, or metal. Where frames are not permanent constructions make sure they are on a proper draft and damp-proof base. Provide a firm path round the structure, otherwise it will be difficult to attend to plants in winter or wet weather.

Keep the glass clean and free from cracks with puttying so efficient that rain drips cannot penetrate. Make sure the frame will open and shut properly without water getting between the panes or hinge joints.

Water with care to avoid excess moisture in the frame. An old-fashioned remedy for keeping out dampness is to place a lump of quicklime under each light. This takes up excess moisture from the air in winter and lasts for several weeks.

Heat escapes through the bottom of the frame into the surrounding soil. A 2–3 in. deep bed of cinders placed under the frame area before soil is added, greatly reduces the loss.

Propagating frames are used exclusively for raising plants from seed or cuttings. They can be a simple arrangement, such as a box on which a sheet of glass is placed, or a more elaborate structure with a wooden or metal base.

Use A garden frame can become an introduction to greenhouse culture, for with a frame you look after the plants from the outside, with a greenhouse you tend them from within, whatever the weather.

In summer greenhouse temperatures are likely to fluctuate rapidly; in a frame, plants can be kept cool easily, for as necessary, the glass can be completely removed.

Many small frames are available but none less than 4 ft. × 3 ft. gives much scope for growing worthwhile quantities of edible crops. An ideal soil depth is up to 2 ft. at the front, 2½ ft. or more at the back.

Hardening off Frames are invaluable for hardening off greenhouse-raised plants, summer bedding plants, which must be gradually acclimatized to outdoor conditions. At times greenhouses become overcrowded and the frame can be used to accommodate plants in different stages of development–an important matter when they are being grown for living room decoration.

Heating Frames can be electrically heated by soil cables which should be laid on 2 in. of sand and covered with another 2 in. before loamy soil is put on. Make sure there is no crossing or touching by different sections of the same heating element.

Ventilation Damp and drafts cannot be kept out simply by keeping the top closed.

Without air, mildew and rotting will occur. Ventilation is needed daily excepting in very cold or frosty weather. Never let cold winds blow into a frame; sliding lights are better than the hinged type since they can always be kept open away from the wind by using little blocks. Protective mats are valuable during frosty periods but should not be used when they are wet. It is an advantage to have duplicate mats so that the wet ones can be dried.

Forcing With heat you can force chicory, rhubarb and seakale, and in early spring, early potatoes can be planted. Lettuce sown in the fall will heart by Christmas, while partially grown lettuce, cauliflower and endive plants can be placed in frames to mature. Parsley transferred to frames in October will give winter pickings. Continuous supplies of mustard and cress may be had by successional sowings.

Drying Frames can be used for drying onions, potatoes and haricot beans, while they keep dry the ripening seed heads of onions and leeks.

Catch Cropping Where winters are less severe, you can use the frame for catch cropping; for instance early tulips planted 4 in. deep in early November overplanted with October-sown lettuce; 'Early French Breakfast' radish sown between the plants in January, will mature before the lettuce or tulips are very large.

A Greenhouse Annex Frames can serve as an annex to a greenhouse to accomodate flowering plants out of bloom and those for which the greenhouse would be too warm in summer, but still need protection.

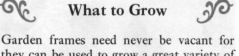

What to Grow

Garden frames need never be vacant for they can be used to grow a great variety of edible and ornamental plants.

Where winters are not too cold, cuttings of hardy plants and seedlings of fall sown sweet peas will benefit if covered with frames in winter, while frame-grown violets are always appreciated.

Bulbs Spring flowering bulbs in pots and bowls can be kept in the frame before being taken a few at a time into the living room thus ensuring a succession of bloom. Bulbs or

Five different types of frame

tubers such as hippeastrum, begonias, gloxinias and freesias can be placed in the frame in summer to ripen off properly before being stored for winter.

Bulbs in pots and bowls plunged in the frame in peat or leaf mold will make good roots before much top growth.

Greenhouse Plants Some popular plants used for greenhouse display can be sown in pots or flats in early summer and kept in a cool frame until September. These include

Provided the frame is properly ventilated, it may be used to house pot plants which would otherwise take up greenhouse space. *Right :* The range of plants for the cool greenhouse is very wide. Coleus dominate the foreground here

calceolarias, cinerarias and primulas.

In strongly made brick or wooden frames half-hardy plants such as geraniums, heliotrope and fuchsias can be over-wintered if there is just enough heat to keep the air buoyant and free from dampness.

Beans and Peas Dwarf bush beans, 'Masterpiece', sown in pots at intervals of three weeks from September to March will be ready for picking within 10 weeks of sowing.

For early peas glass covering without heat gives protection from cold winds and wet soil as well as keeping away mice.

Cucumbers Cucumbers are an ideal frame crop. To provide the high temperature and humidity this crop requires, make an 8 in. or 9 in. deep hot bed of fresh manure in March. Greenhouse raised seedlings will be ready for planting on the hot bed in April.

European Burpless cucumbers may be grown by making in early May, a trench 6–9 in. deep along the center of the frame and filling it with fresh grass mowings, old leaves and fermenting straw. Plants raised in a heated propagator can be set in the trench in early June.

The frame soil should consist of fibrous loam, old manure and leaf mold or material from the compost heap. One strong plant is sufficient for a frame of 6 ft. × 4 ft. Maintain a humid atmosphere and provide shade. Stop side-shoots when there are four leaves. Spread the resultant growth evenly over the frame area. Remove male flowers, otherwise fruits taste bitter.

Melons Cantaloupe melons can be grown in frames. For each plant, prepare a trench a foot deep and wide. Fill this with fermenting manure over which place a mound of soil on which plant the melon. Apply water and keep the frame closed for four or five days. Shade from hot sun and avoid excess moisture. Hand pollinate female flowers (those with an embryo fruit behind the flower) and spray with water in early mornings. Give liquid manure each week. Cut the fruit when a circular crack appears at the base of the stem.

Tomatoes Single, lean-to or double span roofed frames can be used for tomatoes. Fill the frame with a mixture of four parts of loam, and one part each of well-rotted manure (or compost), sand and mortar rubble or hydrated lime, plus a 3-in. potful of tomato fertilizer to every bushel of the other ingredients. If the frames are shallow excavate soil before adding the mixture so there is up to a foot of headroom. In spring set the plants 15–18 in. apart. Provide supports and keep side-shoots removed.

Year Round Interest

While a garden frame and a greenhouse used separately, will provide much interest and allow the production of many ornamental and edible crops, their value is greatly enhanced if they are used together. Whatever the size of one's greenhouse there never seems room enough to take in everything, which is why it is almost essential to use one or two frames in conjunction with the larger structures.

Many ornamental plants regarded as greenhouse specimens, can be placed outdoors in summer, in fact, they benefit from such treatment by making a better display the following season. It will not do to stand them in the open, or even in a sheltered position; they must have a place unexposed to winds and where water requirements can be met.

A frame is ideal for this purpose since pots can be plunged and the glass kept off the frames in reasonable weather. This applies to winter flowering plants such as azaleas, poinsettias and hydrangeas.

Frames are invaluable for propagating from seeds, cuttings, offsets and division, many highly decorative plants which will subsequently live in the greenhouse. Half-hardy bedding plants such as asters, antirrhinums, petunias, sweet peas and zinnias can be hardened off.

Viola cuttings can be overwintered, while bulbs in pots or bowls can be plunged in the frame for making a good root system before being moved to the greenhouse. In summer frames can be used for greenhouse plants that do not like high temperatures, while a shaded frame will hold calceolarias, cyclamen and primulas such as *P. obconica, P. malacoides* and *P. sinensis*.

Lady Washington pelargoniums and perpetual flowering carnations will benefit from being placed in sunny frames from June to mid-September. The sash can be taken off or the sides of the frames raised for tall plants. Frames can also be used to bring other flowering plants through cold periods.

Pans of alpines kept in the frame in summer can be transferred to the greenhouse for fall and winter display.

The use of a greenhouse and frames means that a kind of shuttle service is operated. Many young plants may be started in the greenhouse early in the year, moved to the frame in summer, and taken back into the greenhouse again in the fall.

One Hundred
Greenhouse Plants

Abutilon Half-hardy evergreen shrubs, the abutilons are also known as flowering maple.

Propagate in the fall or spring by cuttings of young wood, 4–5 in. long placed in trays of sandy compost in a temperature of 60°F (16°C). Cuttings of half-ripened wood can be taken in July and rooted under a bell-glass or in a frame. Use a compost of two parts of fibrous loam and one part each of peatmoss and sand. Sow seeds in pans in a warm greenhouse in March.

A temperature of 60–65°F (17°C) in summer and 40°F (4°C) in winter is suitable.

Species include *A. darwinii*, 4 ft., orange; *A. megapotamicum*, orange-pink, 2½ ft.; *A. striatum* var. *thomsonii*, 6–10 ft., mottled green and yellow foliage.

Acacia With their showy yellow flowers in spring, these shrubs or small trees, are often referred to as wattles or mimosas. Simple to grow, they need a minimum winter temperature of 45°F (5°C). Pot plants can stand outdoors in a sunny position from June to September, making sure the roots remain moist. Pruning and potting can be done after flowering. Cuttings of young shoots root well in a propagating frame during the summer.

A. dealbata is the most commonly grown species. Others are *A. armata*, 9–10 ft., and *A. drummondii*, which grows well in large pots.

Achimenes These belong to the same family as gloxinias and are first-class in hanging baskets, indoor window boxes, pots and tubs. If the shoots are stopped periodically, good bushy plants develop.

Plant the small tubers from the end of January in a peaty compost, in a temperature of 65–70°F (18–21°C). Provide a close, humid atmosphere, giving more ventilation once flower buds develop. After flowering is over dry off the tubers, keeping them in a light airy place, where the temperature does not fall below 50°F (10°C).

Seed provides a cheap and easy method of building up stock. In pans or flats of fine compost sprinkle the seed on the surface,

lightly firming it. In a temperature of around 70°F (21°C) germination occurs within two weeks. Move the plants into small pots and then into larger sizes as growth develops. A mixture of leaf mold, peatmoss, sand and some old manure is satisfactory. Leaf and stem cuttings root easily.

Anthurium These are often known as flamingo plants, on account of their ornamental foliage and brightly colored flowers which appear on long stems from April to August.

They flourish in a well-drained compost of equal parts of rough peatmoss and sphagnum moss. Shade them from direct sunlight and provide a minimum winter temperature of 60°F (16°C). A moist atmosphere is essential, and plenty of water is needed in spring and summer. Repot in March.

Species include: *A. andreanum* with heart-shaped leaves and orange-red flowers. There are forms with red, pale pink, rose and white flowers. *A. scherzerianum* produces scarlet flowers which show up well against the deep green leaves.

Propagate by division in March, or by seed sown in a temperature of 70°F (21°C).

*Anthurium
scherzerianum*

Aphelandra *A. squarrosa louisae* is a shrubby evergreen plant with handsome leaves and showy flowers and bracts. It does well in pots of peaty loam and likes warm conditions, although after flowering it succeeds in a temperature of 50°F (10°C), needing little water until spring. At that time, badly placed and weak growths should be removed.

Some of the resultant new shoots can be used as cuttings, especially if taken with a heel and placed in the propagating frame. When rooted, cuttings can be moved to 4- or 5-in. pots where, if left unstopped, they will produce flower heads the first year.

Asparagus These are invaluable for providing cut 'fern' and make attractive pot plants. They are not real ferns, but belong to the lily family. Use a well drained compost and keep the plant well watered, or the foliage becomes discolored. Sow seed in spring or summer in a temperature of 60°F (16°C). Move the seedlings to 3-in. pots, discarding those of slow or irregular growth.

A. plumosus nanus has long trails of fine foliage, ideal for cutting and useful for making up buttonholes in conjunction with various flowers. *A. sprengeri* is valuable for

hanging baskets as it produces bright green sprays 1–2½ ft. long.

Azalea One of the most popular winter flowering greenhouse plants, *A. indica* is correctly *Rhododendron simsii*, but is still widely known and sold as an azalea. Colors include shades of pink, red and white.

Make sure the roots remain moist. Plants are grown in a peaty mixture which is difficult to moisten if it dries out. Remove faded flowers to encourage the following season's flower buds. Repot as necessary in May and stand the plants outdoors in a sheltered place or bury the pots to their rims in the garden. Bring them into the greenhouse in September, maintaining a moist atmosphere. Frequent syringeings of water encourage the flower buds to develop. Avoid lime in the compost or in the water; it is best to water with rainwater.

Propagation is by cuttings of young shoots in summer or early fall, rooted in a propagating frame.

Begonia This beautiful genus consists of a number of groups each with distinguishing features. All like moist, peaty leafy compost, good light with liquid feeding when in growth. See Favorite Garden Flowers for further details.

Beloperone Known as the shrimp plant, *B. guttata* is an evergreen, shrubby plant from South America. It has inconspicuous pink flowers concealed by decorative pink bracts which color best when the plant is kept in the sun. Too much warmth hinders full coloring. They need fairly rich soil. Encourage a winter rest by keeping them dry and cool.

Cut plants back early in the year and ensure good drainage. Over-watering causes leaf drop. Propagate by cuttings of young growths in spring. They will root better if bottom heat is provided.

Boronia *B. megastigma*, a sweet-scented plant comes from Australia. Sow seed thinly and evenly in sandy compost in seed trays or directly into small pots in a temperature of not less than 55–60°F (13–16°C). Germination is slow, sometimes taking four to six weeks depending on temperature. When the seedlings are 1 in. high move them to 2½-in. pots and give more room as growth develops. Use lime-free, sandy loam. Occasional top dressings of leaf mold are helpful. Prune established specimens in spring, although if the blooms are cut this can be part of the pruning procedure. The maroon and yellow flowers are produced over a long period.

Bougainvillea These sub-tropical shrubs or small trees depend on their gaily colored flower bracts for their decorative value. Sun and good drainage with room to climb are necessary if there is to be a lasting summer display. Moisture and frequent liquid feeds are needed but avoid over-potting. After flowering, prune back side shoots to two buds, removing weak shoots. *B. glabra* and its form *sanderiana*, both pink, are free flowering, while *B. spectabilis* has mauve-pink bracts. Propagate by cuttings of young shoots in February in a temperature of not less than 75°F (23°C).

Boussingaultia The Mignonette vine, *B. baselloides*, a native of Equador and Peru, is a quick-growing, half-hardy perennial climber. The reddish stems bear wavy, heart-shaped fleshy leaves and scented white flowers in branched sprays in the fall.

Use sandy loam and peatmoss with plenty of moisture in summer. Dry off the tuberous roots in winter, leaving them in the soil, or lift and store as for dahlias. Seed or division of the tuberous roots and tubercles are means of increasing stock. Sowing and planting time is in spring, although seed-raised plants are slow to reach flowering size.

Bouvardia These evergreen plants provide a splendid display from September to January. They can be grown in small pots which should be watered and fed well in summer to build the following season's flower buds. Plenty of light, but shade from direct sun suits these plants. If growths are kept pinched out bushy specimens develop. Prune after the plants have been rested for a few weeks. Flowers form on new shoots. Propagation is by cuttings in spring, preferably in a temperature of 65–70°F (18–21°C).

Reliable species and varieties include: *B. humboldtii*, white and *B. triphylla*, scarlet.

Bromeliads The majority of these interesting greenhouse plants originate from Central and South America and have decorative foliage and in some instances colorful flowers. There are two main groups (1) the epiphytes, which live on boughs of trees, (2) the terrestrial kinds which grow on the ground or on rocks.

The leaves of most epiphytes form a rosette making a central depression or cup which collects water. If this cup is filled with water at greenhouse temperature, the plants will stand long periods of dryness. Keep the roots just moist. Liquid fertilizer in spring is all the feeding required.

The easiest bromeliads to grow include *Aechmea rhodocynea*, *Billbergia nutans* (Queen's tears) and *Neoregelia caroliniae tricolor*. *Cryptanthus bivittatus* is one of the best of the smaller kinds. It forms a star-shaped rosette of leaves which lie flat on the soil. These are prettily striped in shades of green and have crumpled edges. Side-shoots can be used for propagation. *C. zonatus* is broader leaved with silvery or yellow markings on a maroon-green background. *Vriesea splendens* flourishes in a temperature of 50°F (10°C). The pale green leaves are banded maroon. It likes semi-shade in summer; off-shoots can be used for propagation.

Brunfelsia These evergreen shrubs freely produce scented flowers in spring and summer. Good light, but not prolonged sunshine is helpful and they need well-drained rich soil. Cut out weak shoots in February and once growth is fully active, give plenty of moisture. A warm, moist atmosphere is best when the plants are growing. Propagate by cuttings of half-ripe shoots in a warm frame.

Top: A group of colorful foliage house plants. In front are bromeliads which have become very popular as houseplants. In nature, water collects in the central cup or 'vase' formed by the leaves. This should always be kept full, preferably with tepid rainwater. *Left: Bouvardia*, one of the plants which provide color in the greenhouse in the fall and early winter. *Below:* One of the many color forms of achimenes, the hot-water plant

Species include: *B. americana*, white; *B. calycina*, purple passing to white.

Cacti and other Succulents These bizarre plants are very popular and widely grown in greenhouses. Easy to cultivate, their extensive range of shape and habit plus in many species showy flowers, make them attractive. For fuller descriptions see INDOOR PLANTS elsewhere in this work.

Caladium These are tuberous-rooted perennials grown for their richly colored ornamental foliage. They like warmth, and 55°F (13°C) should be regarded as the minimum winter temperature.

Start tubers in March, in flats of peaty soil, giving frequent overhead syringeings. When the plants are growing well, move them to 5-in. pots of two parts of loam and one part each of peatmoss, decayed manure and sand. Water regularly while the plants are growing, but when leaves discolor, dry off the roots, keeping them in the warm. Propagation is by division in spring, occasionally from seed. Species to grow are *C. bicolor* and *C. humboldtii* and their forms.

Calceolaria These easily grown plants succeed in a temperature of 50–65°F (16–18°C). They form bushy plants with pouch-like flowers in yellow, red or brown, many being prettily freckled.

Sow seed in June and July, prick out seedlings early and pot on according to growth. The plants like light, rich soil which should be pressed firmly. The weakest looking seedlings often produce the best blooms. Keep the plants cool and shaded. Overhead sprayings produce the right atmosphere. If the pots are placed on a base of moist gravel, growth develops evenly. A winter temperature of 45–50°F (8–10°C) is sufficient and less moisture is needed then. As the flower buds develop, a rather drier atmosphere is required. It takes between eight and nine months for flowering sized plants to develop.

C. multiflora nana hybrids grow to 9 in. tall and the large-flowered 'Albert Kent' hybrids 15 in. There are newer strains including F₁ hybrids, as well as the shrubby *C. integrifolia* (*C. rugosa*), 3–4 ft. tall.

Callistemon A native of Australia, *C. citrinus*, the bottle brush, has leathery, grayish green leaves and dense, highly decorative spikes of yellow flowers near the end of the shoots. In the form *splendens* the flowers are bright crimson. The plants need ample sun, light and air. Use well-drained pots of peaty loam. Cut back shoots after flowering and give overhead syringeings of water. Repot every third year. Stand the pots outdoors during summer but never expose the plants

to low temperatures. Propagation is by cuttings of ripe wood rooted in a propagating frame in late spring or summer.

Camellia These shrubby plants are much easier to grow than is often supposed. They flourish in a temperature of 60–65°F (16–18°C) and like plenty of light and sun. Keep them in the same position, for when moved around the buds fail to open or fall prematurely. Sandy loam and leaf mold suits them. Frequent overhead syringeings from the time the buds begin to swell until color shows are helpful. Repotting with good drainage should be done after flowering. Do not feed until spring. As necessary, shorten long, badly placed shoots after flowering. Many named single and double varieties are available in shades of red, pink and white.

Propagation is by seed or by cuttings rooted in late summer in a warm propagating frame.

Campanula *C. isophylla*, an almost hardy, blue-flowered trailing plant is valuable for

hanging baskets and pots, giving a fine display from spring to fall. Specially useful for the cooler parts of the greenhouse, it can be grown outdoors in summer. Remove faded flowers. Cuttings of young growths root easily in spring or plants can be divided. Any good soil mixture is suitable. *C.i. alba* has white flowers.

Canna See Bulbs, Corms and Tubers.

Cantua *C. buxifolia* is a branching flowering shrub of easy cultivation. Treat it as a bush, or train the growth to the roof or greenhouse pillar. Clusters of six to eight large funnel-shaped flowers are produced in April and May. The bright red buds open a showy rosy-red, suffused yellow.

A compost of turfy loam, leaf mold and sand is suitable. Propagation is by cuttings made from half-ripened shoots placed in sandy soil in a temperature of 50–55°F (10–13°C), in summer.

Carex *C. morrowii variegata* is an attractive, decorative grass; the narrow green leaves have white edges. Keep the plants moist and away from bright sun, or they will dry out quickly. Peaty loam with a little bonemeal suits them, and they do best kept in small pots. Propagate by division in spring.

Carnation These can be grown with other plants, but are best by themselves. There are two main groups for growing under glass, the Perpetual Flowering and Perpetual Malmaison. A start can be made in spring by

A beautiful form of the Australian bottle-brush, *Callistemon citrinus splendens*. Plants grown in pots in the greenhouse may be stood out of doors in summer
Left: A sweetly scented bloom of the gardenia (*Gardenia jasminoides*), an evergreen shrub for the greenhouse, which blooms intermittently over a long period
Right: Some of the wide range of colors to be found in the cinerarias, which flower from December through to April. For the earliest show, sow in May, with further sowings at 14-day intervals

buying rooted cuttings or better still, established plants in 5- or 6-in. pots. Essentials for success include good ventilation and a fairly dry cool atmosphere; even in frosty weather a temperature of around 45°F (7°C) is sufficient. Avoid overwatering. For periodic feeding, use a carnation fertilizer. Catalogs of specialist growers list a wide range of varieties and also describe the stopping process.

Propagation is from cuttings or pipings taken in spring.

Celosia See Annuals and Biennials.

Ceropegia These fleshy-rooted plants of twining or semi-climbing habit grow best in full light with shading from direct sun. The finest results come from plants which have restricted roots. Use well-drained compost with plenty of peatmoss and some old manure or bonemeal. Free ventilation and a slight winter rest will prove beneficial. Propagation is by short cuttings, preferably rooted in a propagating case.

C. woodii is the most reliable species. Often known as string of hearts because of its manner of growth, it has small heart-shaped foliage and freely produced pinkish-purple flowers. It is ideal for hanging baskets.

Chrysanthemum No collection of fall and winter flowering greenhouse plants is complete without chrysanthemums. The range of varieties and their cultivation is described in FAVORITE GARDEN FLOWERS.

Cineraria These are indispensable for a colorful display from December to April. For the earliest show, sow in May, with further sowings at 14-day intervals. Transplant seedlings to small pots and keep them away from direct sunshine. Stand the plants in a shaded cold frame. Plant firmly, not bruising the stems or burying the crowns. Cinerarias flower well in 5-in. pots. In September move them to a cool temperature. When flowering stems show, feed with liquid manure. Watch for white fly and aphids; use derris insecticide to deal with these pests.

Good strains include *C. multiflora maxima nana*, 1 ft., compact and uniform; *C.* 'Moll' Strain, 1 ft., enormous heads on compact plants; *C. stellata*, star-shaped flowers in immense clusters. 'Gubler's Mixed' produces up to 70% double and semi-double flowers.

Citrus *C. mitis*, the calamondin, makes a branching shrub about 18 in. high with small oval, dark green leaves. The fragrant white flowers are followed by oranges up to 1½ in. in diameter. Specimens in fruit are attractive from December to April.

A minimum winter temperature of about 50°F (10°C) is suitable. If the pots are plunged in soil outdoors in a sheltered sunny situation, the wood will ripen and flower buds for the following season will develop. A moist atmosphere encourages fruit to set. Propagation is by cuttings rooted in spring

in a propagating frame.

Clivia See Bulbs, Corms and Tubers.

Codiaeum See Indoor Plants.

Coleus See Annuals and Biennials.

Columnea These evergreen trailing plants grow successfully where the winter temperature remains above 55°F (13°C). Use a compost of equal parts of peatmoss, sphagnum moss and coarse sand with a little charcoal. Water, warmth and a moist atmosphere are needed in summer, with regular applications of liquid manure. In winter keep plants cool and dry to encourage a resting period.

Left in the same containers for a few years they produce a striking effect in hanging baskets or cascading over greenhouse pillars.

Propagation is by rooting 2–3-in. cuttings of half-ripened shoots in a propagating frame in spring. Stop rooted plants a couple of times to ensure bushy growth and trailing stems 2–3 ft. long.

Species include *C. gloriosa*, scarlet and yellow, and *C. glabra*, orange-scarlet.

Cordyline See Indoor Plants.

Cuphea Although it can be grown outdoors in a sheltered spot *C. ignea* (*C. platycentra*), the cigar plant, makes a delightful pot plant. The red tube the flowers form, has a dark ring at the end which, with the wide mouth, produces an effect resembling a cigar. Flowers appear freely on 12–15-in. stems from July to September. Sow seed in flats or pans during March and prick out the seedlings into flats or small pots.

Cyclamen See Bulbs, Corms and Tubers.

Cypripedium This is one of the easier orchids which can be grown with other plants. A minimum winter temperature of 45°F (7°C) is needed. Avoid drafts and keep the plants from direct sunshine. Provide a humid atmosphere during spring and summer at which times the pots should be soaked every five or six days.

Use an orchid compost of which the base is osmunda fiber or sphagnum moss. Good drainage should be provided and the pots placed on gravel covered staging or inverted pots. Sphagnum moss round the plants is helpful. Necessary potting can be done from March to July.

C. insigne, with white, purple and brown flowers, and its many hybrids are especially reliable.

Datura The angels' trumpet, *D. suaveolens*, an impressive shrubby plant, is invaluable for cool greenhouse decoration with its large white pendulous trumpet-shaped blooms in late summer.

Give plenty of water in summer, but keep almost dry in winter and as growth develops keep from direct sun. Propagate by 6-in. long cuttings inserted in pots of light soil. The plant will grow 9 or 10 ft. high in time, but may be kept smaller by hard pruning after it has flowered.

Dipladenia This attractive twining plant likes a minimum winter temperature of 55°F (13°C). A moist atmosphere and plenty of water in summer are needed. Propagate by cuttings of young shoots in spring,

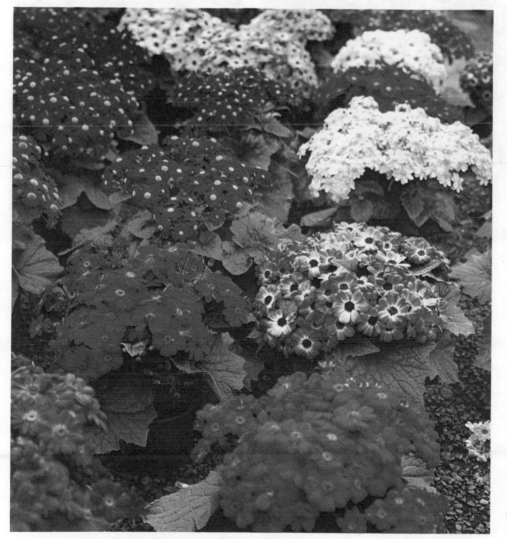

inserted in a peaty, sandy mixture in a warm frame.

The flowers are trumpet-shaped; in *D. brearleyana* pinkish-red, and in *D. splendens* pink, in large heads which open one flower at a time.

Dizygotheca See Indoor Plants (under Aralia).

Dracaena These splendid foliage plants thrive in a minimum winter temperature of 55°F (13°C). The species vary greatly in shape and color and should be grown in pots of rough peaty loam. Full light ensures that the leaves color well. Propagation is by pieces of stem placed in sandy peatmoss in a propagating frame, with bottom heat. Species include, *D. deremensis*, with silvery stripes; *D. godseffiana* with cream-spotted leaves; and *D. sanderiana*, the glossy leaves edged ivory.

tions of liquid manure.

Erica This very large genus, the heaths or heathers, contains the Cape heaths, excellent winter-flowering plants for the cool greenhouse. They require lime-free compost, regular pinching in early stages to ensure bushy growth, and a constant supply of moisture. Trim off the dead flowers and in summer stand the plants in a sheltered place outdoors.

Propagation is from cuttings of new growth taken in early November and inserted in a mixture of peatmoss and sand in a temperature of 60°F (16°C), preferably with bottom heat. Pot on and pinch out as necessary. *E. gracilis* and *E. hyemalis* and their varieties are the easiest kinds.

Eucalyptus Many species make excellent pot plants when young, the foliage assuming an attractive silvery shade. They flourish in

and yellow flowers.

Euphorbia The most popular and widely grown greenhouse species is *E. pulcherrima*, the poinsettia, which is so showy in the fall and winter. The large scarlet or pink bracts are very decorative.

Keep plants in full light and moderately watered. A temperature of 60–65°F (16–18°C) is ideal. Once the bracts expand less moisture is needed. After flowering gradually dry off the plants. At the end of April, soak the roots and cut back stems to 4 in. From these will develop three or four shoots, which can be used as cuttings. Dip the cut ends in powdered charcoal before inserting in a mixture of loam, peatmoss and sand. Provide a temperature of about 60°F (16°C) and when plenty of roots have formed, feed with liquid manure.

The 'Mikkelsen' strain has shorter, bush-

 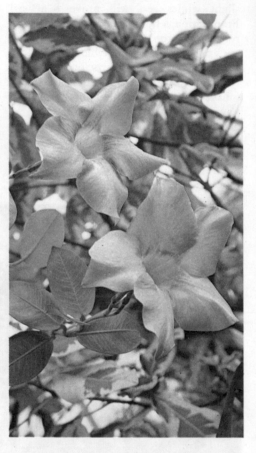

Eranthemum A beautiful winter and spring flowering shrub for the warm greenhouse, *E. pulchellum* (*macrocephalum*), 2–2½ ft., grows easily in a mixture of fibrous loam, leaf mold and sand. The flowers are an attractive bright blue, a color uncommon in winter-flowering plants.

Specimens reserved for propagation should be cut back after flowering. They then produce strong basal shoots suitable for cuttings. These soon root if inserted in pots of a mixture of equal parts of loam, leaf mold and sand. Once growing well, move them singly into 3-in. pots of a similar compost. Keep them in a temperature of not less than 60°F (16°C) and maintain a moist atmosphere. Once established and growing freely, plentiful supplies of moisture will be beneficial, together with occasional applica-

rich open compost and like plenty of water in summer but should be kept drier in winter. Propagate by seed sown in warmth in spring or by cuttings of side-shoots rooted in June in a propagating frame.

Eucharis These bulbous plants produce fragrant flowers in winter. Plenty of water is needed from March to September, less at other times, and a temperature of 60–70°F (16–21°C). Pot in a compost containing well-rotted manure, bonemeal and charcoal.

Propagation is by division. If necessary, pot the bulbs after flowering, although they can be left in the same pot for three years if top-dressed annually. Liquid feeding can begin once the flower buds begin to unfold. Gradually dry off as foliage discolors.

E. grandiflora amazonica, the Amazon lily has white flowers; *E. sanderi* has white

ier growth and the bracts remain in showy condition for a long time.

Eurya *E. japonica*, a splendid foliage plant for the cool greenhouse, has large leathery green leaves prettily edged with yellowish-scarlet. The flowers are insignificant. The plant has no special cultural requirements but will benefit if placed outdoors in a sheltered place in summer. Propagation is by cuttings taken in spring or summer, rooting them in a propagating frame.

Exacum These biennials will flourish in a winter temperature of 55°F (13°C).

Sow seed in early August in pots or flats of sandy compost. Little water is needed from November to February, when the plants should be moved to 5-in. pots.

E. affine, 6 in., with scented lilac flowers is the best known species; *E. macranthum*, 1½ ft. has deeper blue flowers.

Fatshedera *F. lizei* is a hybrid between fatsia and hedera. Tall-growing, it has five-lobed dark green leaves. There is a variegated form, *variegata*. Cultivation is as for Fatsia (below), except that propagation must be by stem cuttings rooted in spring.

Fatsia *F. japonica* is a tall shrub with large, dark green, 7- to 9-lobed leaves. It can be grown outdoors in warmer parts of the country but looks impressive in large pots. Propagation is by seed or by cuttings which root easily. The form *variegata*, with white leaf tips *must* be propagated from cuttings.

Ferns Ferns like occasional overhead sprayings of tepid rain water, but do not spray those species with hairy foliage. Moist, well-drained compost containing plenty of leaf mold plus some bonemeal, is suitable.

Dust-like spores form on the undersides

Sow seed in March, preferably with bottom heat. Prick off and pot up the young plants, in a compost of equal parts of sandy loam and leaf mold. Provide cool, airy conditions such as in a frame during summer, and bring the plants into the greenhouse in early fall. Little water is necessary in winter, but plenty during spring and summer.

Freesia See Bulbs, Corms and Tubers.

Fuchsia See Favorite Garden Flowers.

Gardenia *G. jasminoides* and its varieties, with fragrant white flowers, are splendid evergreen shrubs, worth a place in any greenhouse with a minimum winter temperature of 50°F (10°C). Watering plays a crucial part in obtaining good results. Too much or too little will cause the buds to fall before they develop. Syringe frequently in spring and summer, except when the plants are in bloom.

Never cut the flowers; pull them from the crown. Propagation is from seed, as fresh as possible. Sow thinly in a temperature of 65°F (18°C), preferably with bottom heat. When the seedlings can be handled, prick them into a sandy compost, subsequently transferring them to pots.

Various strains are available, but the 'Van Wijks' strain cannot be surpassed for size of flower, color range and constitution.

Gloriosa The glory lily, *G. superba* is a tuberous-rooted climbing plant. Its cultivation is described in Bulbs, Corms and Tubers.

Gloxinia See Bulbs, Corms and Tubers.

Grevillea *G. robusta*, the silk oak, an evergreen foliage plant, is easily grown in the average greenhouse. It has attractive, fernlike foliage in shades of green, bronze and almost red. It likes well-drained soil, free

Far left: The angel's trumpet (*Datura suaveolens*), a fine plant for the cool greenhouse, has long, trumpet-shaped flowers in late summer
Left: Twining plants are always valuable in the greenhouse as they can be trained up into the rafters to give height to the display. This one is *Dipladenia sanderi*
Below: One of the many bright color forms of the Barberton daisy, *Gerbera jamesonii*
Right: The poinsettia (*Euphorbia pulcherrima*) is one of the most colorful of greenhouse plants. It does well in a living room, provided it is not too cold, and is at its best in winter

of the fronds; when sown these form a prothallus, which contains male and female organs, which, in a temperature of 50–55°F (10–13°C), fertilize to produce the first leaf.

Specimens for the cool greenhouse include: *Adiantum cuneatum*, the maidenhair fern; *Nephrolepis exaltata*–for hanging baskets; *Pteris cristata* and *Davallia dissecta*.

Ficus See Indoor Plants.

Francoa A native of Chile, *F. ramosa*, the bridal wreath, has a stiff, erect main spike 2–3 ft. high, with numerous small subsidiary shoots, especially if the main stem is cut back after flowering. These are clothed with white or pinkish-red flowers throughout late summer. It succeeds in the cool greenhouse where the temperature is about 60°F (16°C) in summer and not less than 45°F (7°C) during the winter.

Prune into shape in February, when repotting can be done. Plant them in well-drained pots or beds of equal parts of loam, peatmoss, and decayed manure (or leaf mold) with a little charcoal, and shade them from direct sunshine.

Propagation is by cuttings of firm side-shoots taken from February to March, in a temperature of 70–75°F (21–23°C).

Gerbera The Barberton daisy (*G. jamesonii*) will flourish in a sandy soil containing plenty of humus. Free drainage is needed, but the soil should never dry out. It is best to grow plants in large pots or flats about 15–18 in. deep. Do not bury the crowns. Cover the surface soil with a layer of sand and shingle and plant so that the crown is just above soil level. Plenty of water is required in summer, but little during winter.

ventilation and plenty of water in summer. Repotting should be done in March or April. Plants are raised from seed sown in spring in a temperature of 65°F (18°C).

Heliotropium See Annuals and Biennials.

Hippeastrum See Bulbs, Corms and Tubers.

Hoya *H. carnosa*, the wax flower, has heads of flesh-pink flowers; *H. bella*, less vigorous, has flowers with crimson centers. Both are showy evergreen climbers suitable for pots or a well-drained border. Water freely in summer, moderately in winter. Frequent overhead sprayings when in growth are beneficial. Pruning consists in cutting out weak, badly placed shoots. Do not remove the flower stalks, since secondary growths develop from the base for further flowering. Propagation can be by layers or else by

cuttings of the current season's growth.
Humea *H. elegans*, the incense plant, is
best treated as a biennial and seed should be
sown in sandy soil in spring. Water carefully
during winter and grow the plants in rich
soil containing lumpy peatmoss. Well-
grown plants may reach 4 or 5 ft. high. The
feather-like flower plumes consist of many
small pinkish florets.

Impatiens The balsams have fleshy stems
growing 1–2 ft. high. Well-grown plants
often remain in flower over a period of many
months. *I. holstii* has reddish stems and pink
flowers; its hybrids are in shades of pale rose,
red and violet. *I. sultanii* has carmine and
rose flowers. Both are known as busy Lizzie,
because they flower so freely. The dwarf
'Scarlet Baby', which produces bright scarlet
flowers, and 'General Guisan', growing 5–
10 in. high with red and white blooms, are
particularly useful pot plants.

Sow seed in flats or pots from March to
May in a temperature of around 60°F
(16°C). Once the first rough leaf appears,
prick out the seedlings and pot up singly, in
a compost rich in peatmoss or leaf mold.

Kalanchoe These useful succulent plants
have interesting foliage and attractive flowers from March onwards. *K. blossfeldiana*,
bright flame red, is the best known. It has a
dwarf form, 'Tom Thumb', with bronze
leaves. *K. carnea* is pink, and *K. flammea*,
orange-scarlet.

A soil mixture of loam, leaf mold and sand
and a little old manure or bonemeal is ideal.
Keep plants in full light and water regularly.
After flowering is over pinch back the growing points to a pair of good leaves. This will
encourage bushy growth. If the plants are
kept in a temperature of around 60°F (16°C)
from the end of July, flower color will show
in October thus lengthening the time of
flowering. Propagation is by seed sown in
February and March or from summer
cuttings.

Lantana These evergreen shrubs have
large heads of verbena-like flowers over a
long period from spring to fall. Good
species include *L. camara*, yellowish-red; *L.
nivea*, white; and *L. selloviana*, mauve, of
trailing habit. They flourish in a rich soil
mixture, containing decayed manure or
bonemeal. Pot plants should be cut back in
February, to keep them bushy, shortening
each shoot to 3 in. In a temperature of 60°F
(16°C) new growths soon develop and, as
necessary, some of these can be taken as cuttings. Bottom heat encourages rooting.
Lantanas can also be raised from seed.

Lapageria *L. rosea*, with its bell-like, rosy-
crimson flowers, is one of the best evergreen

flowering climbers for the cool greenhouse,
standing a winter temperature as low as 40–
45°F (4–7°C). It can be grown in pots but is
best planted out in a well-drained compost
of very peaty loam plus a sprinkling of sand
and charcoal. Shade from strong sunshine
and give plenty of water in spring and summer with overhead syringeings until flower
buds begin to break.

Propagation is by layering of shoots in
summer. There are forms with white, rose
or red flowers.

Lasiandra *L. macrantha*, a native of Brazil,
produces large rich violet-blue flowers in
summer. It is an evergreen climber, excellent for covering walls or pillars. The flowers
are more freely produced when the plants
have a free root run. Well-drained peaty soil
is suitable. Trim the plants as necessary in
February. Well-rooted specimens like plenty
of water in summer. A winter temperature of
50°F (10°C) is needed. Propagation is by
cuttings in spring or from soft growth in
summer.

Lilium Many lilies make first-class pot
plants. A suitable compost consists of three
parts of fibrous loam, one part each of peatmoss (or leaf mold), sand and decayed
manure. For forcing, plant bulbs in October

and November. Use 6- or 7-in. pots and for
stem-rooting varieties, leave space in the
pots for topdressing later. Plunge the pots in
peatmoss or sandy soil in the cold frame or
place them in a cool greenhouse (at no time
must the bulbs be frosted), and bring them
into a temperature of 40–50°F (4–10°C)
early in the year, gradually raising the heat
to 60–70°F (16–21°C). Top dress when
growth is 5 or 6 in. high. Where little heat is
available, plant bulbs in February for flowering from May onwards. Good varieties for
pots include *L. auratum* and *L. speciosum*,
both stem rooting; *L. longiflorum*, the white
Easter lily; *L. formosanum*, white; and *L.
brownii*, creamy-white with brownish-red
markings.

Maranta *M. leuconeura* and its varieties are
handsome foliage plants which like warm
conditions with a winter temperature of 60–
65°F (16–18°C). Shade and humidity are
aids to good development. While plenty of
water is needed during spring and summer,
drainage must be perfect.

Propagation is by division of crowns in
spring. In the species the leaves have white
veins; the form *kerchoveana* has emerald
green leaves blotched red; it is known as the
prayer plant since the leaves move to an

Above: Easter lily 'Lilium longiflorum'
Left: Rehmannia angulosa

upright position at night.

Mesembryanthemum This is the name of a group of widely differing plants, all of succulent habit. Some are tall and bushy, others prostrate or creeping. The lithops group is sometimes known as 'living stones' on account of their thick round or angular shape and color.

There are many types to choose from as will be seen from the catalogs of specialists, and from the section of this work dealing with Indoor Plants.

Mimosa Often known as the humble or sensitive plant, the common names of *M. pudica* refer to the fact that the leaflets droop at the slightest touch. Although little spikes of blue-purple flowers are produced it is the foliage which makes this plant worth growing, always creating interest, particularly among children. Plants are raised from seed sown thinly in pots of sandy compost. An average temperature of 60–65°F (16–18°C) is quite sufficient.

Nerium An evergreen shrub with fragrant flowers, *N. oleander*, the oleander, thrives in pots, tubs or well-drained beds in the lightest and sunniest part of the greenhouse. A minimum winter temperature of 45°F (7°C) is needed. Repotting is done in February. Prune after flowering by shortening shoots of previous season's growth to 3 or 4 in. from the base. Propagation is from cuttings of firm shoots in early summer, placed in a temperature of 60–65°F (16–18°C).

The species has rosy-pink flowers; there are double white and red forms.

Opuntia These cacti are divided into several groups, those known as prickly pears being most decorative as pot plants. These have flat 'pads' which are really stem segments and not leaves. Opuntias are easy to grow, in sun and rich loamy soil with good drainage. Plenty of water is needed during the growing season but much less in winter. Propagation is easy by removing the pads and letting them dry for three days before potting them. Seeds can be sown in pots.

O. paraguyensis is a good flat padded species, with yellow flowers sometimes followed by purple fruits. See also Indoor Plants.

Palms There are several palms which can

The correct way to plant a lily bulb, leaving sufficient space for top dressing

be grown successfully in the cool greenhouse. They flourish under cool conditions but during the growing season like warmth and moisture. They do well in a compost of fibrous loam, sand, old manure and if possible, brick dust. Avoid overpotting. Frequent overhead syringeings in summer help the fronds to develop properly. An occasional spongeing with weak soapy water will keep off scale insects.

Useful palms include: *Cocos weddelliana*, particularly reliable for small pots; *Howea* (*Kentia*) *belmoreana*, *Phoenix dactylifera*, the date palm, and *P. roebelinii*. The latter has arching fronds and looks well in the greenhouse or living room in 5- or 6-in. pots.

Pancratium These handsome bulbous plants are suitable for pots in the cool greenhouse. They flower most freely when established and slightly pot bound. Repotting in spring is rarely needed more than once in three years. The bulbs flourish in a mixture of three parts of loam, one part of decayed manure or bonemeal, with a little sand. Water freely in the growing season but give little in winter when a temperature of 45–50°F (7–10°C) will be ample. *P. illyricum* and *P. maritimum* grow to 2 ft. high, and have fragrant pure white flowers.

Passiflora Vigorous climbers, the passion flowers will cover the rafters and walls of good sized greenhouses. They can be grown in tubs or large pots but are best in a well-drained border. A very rich soil encourages rampant growth at the expense of flowers and some form of root restriction is advisable. Transplant only in spring. A winter temperature of 45–50°F (7–10°C) is sufficient. Propagation is from cuttings of young shoots in spring.

P. caerulea, blue flowers and its white form, 'Constance Elliot' are best. *P. edulis* has bluish-purple flowers followed by fruits.

Pelargonium The so-called 'geraniums' are excellent greenhouse plants. Their cultivation is described in Favorite Garden Flowers.

Pilea These plants form close mats of foliage and are useful for growing towards

1: Space for top dressing. 2: A layer of compost above the bulb. 3: The bulb surrounded by compost. 4: A good layer of compost below the bulb. 5: Rough compost or lumpy peatmoss. 6: Broken crocks over the drainage hole.

the front of the staging or for draping tubs or troughs. They thrive in semi-shade but are sensitive to gas fumes. Propagation is easy by spring cuttings. In a moist atmosphere and a temperature of 50–60°F (10–16°C) growth is freely made.

P. cadieri has small, green shiny leaves with red and silver markings. *P. microphylla* (*muscosa*) is the artillery plant, so named because of the way it discharges its pollen when shaken.

Platycerium These fascinating ferns look well among the colorful cool greenhouse flowers. The common name stag's horn fern gives an idea of their shape. They are easy to cultivate in baskets or pots, but are a source of wonder when seen growing on a block of wood or a piece of bark which they encircle with their strong, infertile fronds. They can be grown in rough peatmoss and sphagnum moss kept damp. Light and a moist atmosphere should be provided. Propagate by division.

P. bifurcatum often makes fronds of 2 ft. or more; *P. grande* requires rather more heat.

Primula In this large genus there are species which are invaluable for growing under glass from which frost can be excluded. All can be raised from seed sown in spring. For sowing

and potting use a slightly acid compost.

P. obconica continuously produces clusters of large lilac, pink, crimson or white flowers. When some persons touch the foliage they are affected by a rash. The problem is overcome by wearing gloves. Sow from February to April. *P. malacoides* has dainty flowers produced in tiers. The color varies from lavender to deep rose or white, some strains being double. Sow in June. *P. sinensis* has large single purplish-rose or white flowers. When potting do not bury the centers of the plants or they will decay. Sow in spring. *P. × kewensis* has fragrant yellow flowers in winter or early spring. Sow in March or April.

Do not leave the plants in small pots too long or they will starve, resulting in irregular development. Keep the soil in the pots firm but not hard. Cool summer treatment, shade from strong sunshine, ample ventilation with no over watering and freedom from pests, encourage the plants to give a long-lasting display.

Rehmannia A half-hardy herbaceous perennial from China, *R. angulosa* grows 2–4 ft. high. Its large drooping pink flowers are somewhat like those of the foxglove.

Sow seed thinly from the end of May until

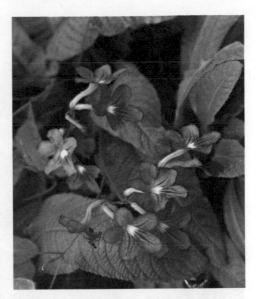

Above: 'Constant Nymph', one of the many varieties of the Cape primrose (streptocarpus), which enjoy cool greenhouse conditions
Below: A variety of colorful plants in a cool greenhouse, where many exotic plants quickly become acclimatized and grow successfully
For these plants to flourish, a minimum night temperature of 4°–7°C should be maintained, with good ventilation

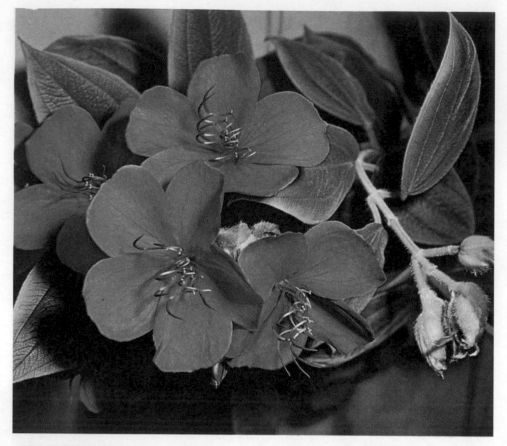

Above: Brazilian glory bush
Tibouchina semidecandra

Saintpaulia
leaf cuttings

August, using well-drained pans or flats, just covering the seed with fine compost. Prick out seedlings as soon as they can be handled and pot on gradually until the 6- or 7-in. size pot is reached.

Keep them in a cool greenhouse or frost-proof frame during winter. Water regularly in spring and summer, giving occasional feeds of liquid manure. As cut flowers, they are long lasting. Specially good plants can be used for propagation, taking basal cuttings in the fall.

Rochea These succulent plants have at various times been listed under crassula, kalosanthes and cotyledon. The 12-in. stems produce long, thickly arranged leathery leaves. In summer these stems are crowned with tubular scarlet flowers. Easily grown, a winter temperature of 45°F (7°C) is sufficient. Rich, well-drained compost is needed and plenty of water during spring and summer – much less for the rest of the year. After flowering, cut back the stems to keep the plants shapely. Propagation is by cuttings rooted in warmth in spring.

Roses Where sufficient space is available bush and climbing roses can be grown in the cool greenhouse, either in the border or in pots. Use a well-drained compost containing a good proportion of decayed manure with fibrous loam and bonemeal to ensure that food is available when needed.

Except where climbers are grown against the pillars or walls of the house, they should be potted in November and kept in the open until February and then be taken into a temperature of 45°F (7°C), given plenty of light and ventilation. In subsequent years, prune well before they start into growth.

Good hybrid tea varieties include older sorts such as 'Golden Scepter', 'President Herbert Hoover', 'Richmond'. 'Maréchal Niel', 'Dorothy Perkins' and 'W. A. Richardson' are reliable climbers.

The dainty, small-flowered red and pink Garnette roses are very long lasting, and are suitable for buttonholes or other decorative purposes.

Saintpaulia The African violet is not among the easiest of flowers to grow, but once its likes and dislikes are understood and acted upon, it responds generously. Light is important and plants should have all possible winter sunshine. Lack of blooms is caused by too little light, while anemic-looking foliage and short stems, are an indication of too much.

Temperatures are important. The aim should be to maintain warmth at 60–70°F (18–21°C) and at night 55°F (13°C) should be the minimum. Avoid drafts and stagnant air, but maintain humidity round the plant. Never attempt to grow saintpaulias where gas is used. Water with care; always use tepid water. Cold water splashes lead to leaf spotting.

Leaf cuttings are a ready means of increasing stock. Plants can also be raised from seed sown in a temperature of 70°F (21°C). While there is no need to cover seed with compost but merely to press it in, a little sand sprinkled over the surface helps to prevent damping off. Prick off and pot up in the usual way. Repot from February to May.

The only species grown, *S. ionantha*, has violet-blue flowers, but many single and double hybrids are available in shades of blue, pink and white.

Salpiglossis The netted and veined funnel-shaped flowers of *S. sinuata* are to be had in colors ranging from brown to deep violet, through to orange, yellow and white.

Sow seeds in late August for winter and spring display, and in February for summer color. A standard seed compost is suitable. Sow the seed thinly, in a temperature of 55–60°F (13–16°C). Cover with paper to prevent the soil from drying out.

Once the seedlings have made three rough leaves thin them to 2 in. apart or move them straight into small pots. Pot on as growth proceeds. Light supports are useful, also shade from direct sunshine. August sowings can be moved into the cold frame and the plants brought indoors when the cold weather comes.

Sansevieria Often known as Bowstring hemp or snake plant, this favorite foliage plant for the cool greenhouse or living room has narrow erect, pointed fleshy leaves. For details of cultivation see Indoor Plants.

Schizanthus The butterfly flower or poor man's orchid is a showy, easily-grown cool greenhouse plant. It is raised from seed sown in August and September in pots of standard seed compost placed in the cold frame. Once the seedlings can be handled move them singly to small pots and transfer to the cool greenhouse before frosts come. They like plenty of air and light but little water in winter. Pot in spring using 5- or 6-in. pots according to size of plants. Pinch out growing points as necessary and provide slender supports. Seed can also be sown in spring.

The hybrid *S.* × *wisetonensis*, 1½–2 ft., has large flowers on compact bushes; in the strain 'Dwarf Bouquet Mixed', 1 ft., colors range from crimson to apple-blossom pink.

Smithiana Once known as naegelia, this makes a beautiful pot plant. The rich velvety foliage is attractively marked or veined in contrasting colors. The flowers, like small foxgloves, are produced in spikes well above the foliage. Many named cultivars are obtainable in a good color range, including cream, pink, rose and salmon. Strong plants make a number of rhizomes which can be separated and used for increasing stock. Seed-raised plants take seven or eight months to come into flower. Sow the seed during the spring in a temperature of 75–80°F (24–27°C).

Right: Camellia reticulata 'Noble Pearl'

Start dormant tubers in spring in a temperature of 60–65°F (16–18°C) using pots of peaty compost, but do not bury them deeply. When flower spikes show, give liquid feeds at ten-day intervals. Keep water off the foliage or it will become marked.

After flowering, gradually dry off the rhizomes and store in a cool frost-proof place for the winter.

Solanum The bright orange-scarlet berries of the false Jerusalem cherry, *S. capsicastrum*, make it popular at Christmas time. From January onwards sow at 10 to 14-day intervals to provide a succession. Keep the flats or pans, in a temperature of 60–65°F (16–18°C) and cover them with glass and paper. Move the seedlings to other flats or pans before potting them separately. This encourages bushy growth. Plants should be ready for 3-in. pots by early May and later for bigger sizes according to growth. Keep them under cool conditions and subsequently move them outdoors to a sheltered place. Once the flowers begin opening overhead sprayings of clear water will encourage a good set of berries. Several dilute liquid feeds will encourage the berries to swell.

Take the plants indoors in September, shortening long growths. Avoid a dry atmosphere and if aphids or red spiders are seen, spray with insecticide to keep the foliage clean and fresh looking.

Stephanotis Sometimes known as the Madagascar jasmine, *S. floribunda* is a choice evergreen climber for the warm house, with white fragrant flowers. A minimum winter temperature of 55°F (13°C) is required. Not one of the easiest plants to manage it is, however, well worth any trouble. In the greenhouse border it will grow tall, but in a large tub or pot it can be restricted to 8 or 9 ft. It likes a peaty compost and plenty of moisture in summer but should be kept almost dry in winter.

Cut out weak shoots in spring and apply a top dressing of rich soil. Propagation is by cuttings of the previous season's growth taken in spring; a temperature of 75°F (24°C) is needed for good rooting, preferably with bottom heat.

Strelitzia *S. reginae*, the bird of paradise flower, is a showy plant with handsome, long-stemmed leaves and in summer, large purple and orange flowers resembling a bird's head. A well-drained loamy compost containing peatmoss and coarse sand is suitable. This should be kept moist in summer but water sparingly in winter when a temperature of 50°F (10°C) is quite sufficient.

Propagation is by detaching and planting up suckers. This is best done in late winter or early spring.

Streptocarpus The Cape primrose likes cool, humid conditions and the greenhouse should be ventilated on all reasonable occasions. The plants remain in growth well into

October when watering should be reduced so that the soil is on the dry side during winter but not dust dry. Repot in March, using a porous, moisture-retentive compost, plus decayed manure. Established plants benefit from feeds of liquid manure.

Propagation is by seed sown in succession to prolong the flowering period. From a December or January sowing, flowers appear between June and September, while from seed sown in June and July and over-wintered in a temperature of 50°F (10°C), plants will bloom from April onwards.

Various hybrid selections are available, many having flowers with unique throat markings contrasting with the dominant color, usually purple, violet and pink shades, or white, the large bell-like blooms measuring 2 in. at the mouth.

Streptosolen Evergreen climbers for the frost-proof greenhouse are always of value. *S. jamesonii* is doubly useful because of its showy clusters of orange-red flowers in summer. It grows well in pots or tubs or can be planted out in rich, well-drained soil in the greenhouse border. Regular watering and syringeing in summer help to maintain good growth. Prune as necessary when growth is dormant.

Propagation is by cuttings of young growth placed in the propagating frame.

Tibouchina The Brazilian spider-flower, *T. semidecandra*, is an interesting evergreen shrubby climber for the cool greenhouse where it can be grown in pots of rich compost, although it does best in the greenhouse border. It bears clusters of rich purple flowers, individually 4–5 in. across.

Use a mixture of equal parts of loam and peatmoss with a little silver sand. Keep the plants in full light and water and feed well in summer, with little moisture in winter. Prune established plants in February.

Propagate by half ripe shoots, preferably in a propagating case.

Torenia Usually treated as an annual, *T.*

fournieri, 1 ft., is a charming, free-flowering pot plant which thrives in a temperature of 60°F (16°C). It produces during July and August, large blue, antirrhinum-like flowers with a deeper blue and gold blotch.

Sow seed in March or April. Move seedlings to small pots and provide thin canes or sticks as support.

Trachelium *T. caerulea*, a half-hardy, shrubby perennial, known as the throatwort, is best treated as a biennial. Young plants are much more floriferous than older specimens. It likes light and sun and a compost of sandy loam and leaf mold. Heads of fragrant blue flowers on 18-in. stems appear from June to August.

From February to June, sow seeds thinly in flats or beds in the greenhouse or sheltered frame. Prick out seedlings early. Fairly slow growth ensures bushy specimens. Pot firmly and when plants are growing well, pinch out the leading shoots. In late September transfer plants to 5-in. pots and maintain a minimum winter temperature of 45°F (7°C).

Zantedeschia This popular plant has several names including calla lily, and arum lily and is sometimes listed botanically under *Richardia*.

Pot the roots in July, one in a 6-in. pot or several in larger receptacles, in a compost of equal parts of loam, sharp sand and well-rotted manure. Keep them outdoors until mid-September and water sparingly. As growth is seen, increase moisture with overhead syringeings. In the greenhouse, give free ventilation and keep the compost moist. A temperature of 45°F (7°C) is sufficient, but more heat brings earlier flowering. Once the flowers are over and foliage discolors the roots can be dried off. Propagate by suckers detached at planting time.

Z. aethiopica, the lily of the Nile, has white flowers; *Z. elliottiana* yellow. The latter requires a temperature of 55°F (13°C) and should be planted in spring. Both grow to approximately 3 ft. tall.

House plants are those plants that can be expected to spend all their life in a dwelling house. If you have a greenhouse you can grow a very large number of plants for decorating your rooms, but, once they have spent a certain time indoors, they are then returned to the greenhouse and kept there to recover. These are not house plants in the sense in which we shall be discussing them. Here we shall confine ourselves to plants that can be expected to thrive in the rather difficult conditions of a dwelling house.

Humidity Conditions in rooms are difficult for plants mainly because the atmosphere is very dry. The majority of house plants are evergreens from tropical countries and in the tropics you are only liable to find evergreens where the atmosphere is damp. In many parts of the tropics the atmosphere tends to be so wet that a number of plants have evolved, known as epiphytes, which can get all their nourishment from the atmosphere and have more or less dispensed with a root system. We do not want a moist atmosphere in our rooms, but it is possible to create a moist zone around our plants, by standing the pot or pots in some container, which will either contain water or will contain some substance such as peatmoss, which can be kept moist. You can put pebbles in a dish, nearly cover them with water and stand the pot on the pebbles, or you can get rather a deep bowl, plunge the pot in some moisture-retaining material, which can be peatmoss, or sand or moss and keep this surround always rather moist. Both these methods will ensure that water vapor will always be rising around the plant and the warmer it is the more vapor will rise, which is just what the plant likes. If the pot is stood on pebbles you should make certain that the base of the pot is clear of water.

Light Compared to even a rather shady situation outside the light in rooms is not very satisfactory. It is, naturally, at its best on the window sill and gets down to near impossible conditions in corridors and halls. Some plants have evolved to grow in extremely poor light conditions, but it is only in the very densest forests that you will find the dark conditions of parts of our houses. Apart from a few ferns, not much will grow in these very shaded conditions and even these will not grow so well as they do where it is lighter. This means that the choice of plants for these murky places is extremely limited and it is probably easiest to forgo plants altogether in this sort of situation, rather than to put plants in and see them slowly deteriorate. In reasonably lit situations, it is probable that the light will be

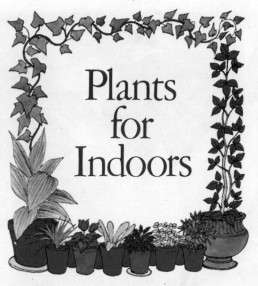

Plants for Indoors

coming from one direction only, unless you have a room with windows on all sides. Plants tend to grow towards the light, so if your plant is lit from one window only,, turn it slightly every week, so that all parts of the plant will be illuminated in turn. This will not only insure that all the leaves receive ample light (and without ample light the leaves will not function properly), but it will also mean that the plant stays symmetrical and does not grow twice as fast from the side nearest the light source. This should be done whether the plant is on the window sill or whether it is in the center of the room.

Leaves and Roots Most plants have two main feeding organs, the leaves and the roots. The leaves can take in plenty of nourishment and syringeing them with a foliar feed will have surprising results, but their main function is to make food for the plant. The roots will take up moisture and various chemicals from the soil. Normally neither can subsist without the other, but some plants do dispense with roots to a greater or lesser extent. A very few flowering plants dispense with leaves, but they can only do this by robbing other plants. Most plants require air, water and soil before they can function.

Air Apart from increasing the humidity of the air, there are other considerations. Drafts are appreciated by plants as little as they are by humans. A draft is a local-

ized stream of cold air, which will attack a portion of the plant only. This will first cause the leaves to drop and may eventually kill the plant, so a very drafty situation should be avoided.

Fumes from various forms of heating are another problem. Kerosene burners are normally fairly innocuous, although a few plants will shed leaves if placed near them, but if something goes wrong and the appliance smokes, you may well find many of your house plants dying. The fumes from gas fires used to be harmful to many plants, but the fumes of natural gas do not seem to damage plants. Coal fires seem to be harmless and, of course, central heating which maintains a more or less even temperature, is the ideal.

In the open air it is a safe assumption that the temperature will be lower at night than during the daylight hours. If you are out at work all day, and you do not have central heating, you will not light your fires until you come home, so that you may get the appalling conditions, from the plant's point of view, of a cold day and a hot evening. Many plants are very tolerant and can survive these unnatural conditions, but bear in mind that it is the daytime temperature that is the important figure to watch, as it is during the daylight hours that most of the growth is made. The fact that your room at night may be at a temperature of 70°F (21°C) does not mean that you can grow the plants that require this temperature, if it is liable to fall to 45°F (9°C) at midday. Minimum winter temperatures refer to the daytime readings, and these may fall a few degrees at night without any harm being done, so that you can air the room at night without qualms. During very frosty weather plants that are on the window sills should be brought further into the room, as it is quite possible for the window panes to be freezing, even though the rest of the room is quite comfortable and frost will certainly damage any house plants on window sills and will probably kill them.

Apart from frost many plants from warm climates will survive at temperatures that are lower than they require to make growth. For example, the popular *Philodendron scandens* will go through the winter quite happily with the temperature as low as 45°F (9°C), but it will be in a state of suspended animation. Not until the temperature reached 60°F (15°C) will it start to make any growth. The recommended winter temperatures for house

Left: To provide local humidity, place pebbles in the base of a bowl
Center: Cover the pebbles with water and stand the plant pot on the pebbles
Right: Or place the pot inside a larger one, filling the space between with peatmoss, kept damp

plants are usually about 10°F (5½°C) below the growth temperature, which means that if they are adhered to the plant will survive perfectly well, but will not be making any growth. The point of this is that growth made during the short daylight hours of winter is usually not very decorative. The stems are liable to become spindly and drawn, while the leaves will be small and a bad color. Indeed with foliage plants it is usual in the spring to nip out all the growing points and any bad growth that has been made in the winter, so that when the plant does start into growth again, the growth will be well-leaved and the plant will become bushy rather than drawn. However, there are available enclosed glass boxes with their own heating and illumination and in these it is possible to keep tropical plants growing evenly throughout the year.

It is customary to put house plants into three categories, Cool, Intermediate and Warm. The Cool group need a winter temperature of from 45°F–50°F (7°–10°C), while a few, notably ivies and fatshedera will tolerate even lower temperatures. The Intermediate group need winter temperatures around 55°F (13°C), while the Warm group need a temperature around 65°–70°F (18°–21°C). During the summer they will need at least 10°F (5½°C) more.

Soil Nowadays one has a choice of two sorts of compost, those containing loam and those without loam, known as soilless composts. A standard compost containing loam that can be used for growing the majority of house plants is as follows: 4 parts loam, 2 parts peatmoss, 1 part dried cow manure, 2 parts sand, plus 1 pint bonemeal per bushel of compost.

Good quality loam is hard to come by in large quantities and so the peat-based composts are now being increasingly used. These are mixtures of peatmoss and sand with added chemicals. Peatmoss and sand contain no nutrients so that when the plant has used all the chemicals in the soilless compost it will starve. With plants that are only going to be kept for a single season, for example, *Primula malacoides* this does not matter, but with plants that are going to be grown on from year to year, it is necessary to start replacing the chemicals as soon as the plant starts to use those already there.

Feeding Most house plants make their main growth between the end of March and the middle of September and this is the time to replace the chemicals by some form of feeding. There are various proprietary feeds, all of equal value, but it is necessary to follow the directions as to the amount and frequency of application. As the plant can take up only a limited amount at a time, little and often is better than large quantities at long intervals. Moreover any food not available to the plant is liable to be washed out during subsequent waterings, so it is not only potentially dangerous, but also wasteful to give too much food in any single application. Most of the feeds are applied to the soil dissolved in water and these should not be given when the plant is completely dry, otherwise the chemicals could damage the roots. Feeds are best applied about two days after the normal watering, when the soil will not be completely dry, but equally will not be sodden. It is also possible to apply foliar feeds to the leaves, by syringeing the plant

Codiaeum 'Mrs Iceton', one of the colorful crotons, which must be kept in a constant temperature, away from drafts

with a foliar feed solution. This is one of the best ways of feeding a plant, but it may not be convenient to syringe plants in your rooms. It is, however, usually possible to remove all the plants to your draining board and syringe them there.

Repotting As the plants grow, so do their roots and after a time it is necessary to move the plant to a larger pot. Most plants will want potting on yearly for the first few years.

The usual progression is from a 3-in. pot into a 5-in. pot and thence into a 6-in., 7-in. and finally an 8-in., in which pot it will probably remain, as plants in larger pots tend to be very large and unwieldy. Usually once you reach the 6-in. pot, it will probably suffice to pot on only every other year, so that it will be six years before you reach the 8-in. pot. Potting on should only be done when the plant is in full growth, so that May is usually the best month. If you tip the plant out of its pot (which is best done a day or so after watering) you can see if there are plenty of roots and if these are showing white tips. If the pot appears to be full of roots and these have their white growing tips, the plant is ready for potting on. This is best done when the plant is on the dry side, although it should not be dust dry, the soil may fall away from the roots when you take it out of its pot.

Take the plant out of its pot and lay it on the potting bench, or on the draining board. If you are using a loamy compost, put some coarse grit or broken crocks at the base of the

Right : The beautiful pink blooms of a winter-flowering cyclamen

new pot; with loamless composts this can be dispensed with. Now place some of the compost in the base of the pot and stand the old plant in the middle to see if you have enough in. In pots up to 3-in. there should be a gap of ½ in. between the soil level and the rim of the pot, while for larger pots the gap should be an inch. If the level is too high, you will not get all the soil moistened when you water, if it is too low, you will get too much water and also the plant will not have all the soil that it could have, so this is a matter worth paying attention to. When you have the right level, fill in around the old soil ball with the new compost, firming it down with your thumbs fairly heavily, otherwise you will find that after watering there will be a gap between the old soil ball and the new soil. The new soil you are using should be on the dry side and crumbly, but not dust dry.

Once repotting has been completed, give the plant a good watering, after which it should be allowed to dry out and only watered sparingly for the next week or so. Putting the plant in a warmer situation will encourage the roots to grow more rapidly into the new soil. No feeding is necessary until this new soil has been occupied by fresh roots.

Watering The most essential part in the successful growing of house plants is in the correct use of the water can and more plants are lost through drowning than through any other cause. When you do water, you should do it properly. Fill the pot to the brim. If you give less it may well not moisten the whole of the soil ball. It does no harm to make sure of

this and to turn out a plant a few hours after watering to see if the whole soil ball has been watered. If it has not, the only thing to do, if the plant is not in a state to be repotted, is to give two applications each time you water.

If you have some method of catching and keeping it, rain water is much to be preferred to tap water, but it is not always possible to obtain this. During the winter, very cold water will lower the temperature of the soil in the pot, perhaps to an excessive degree. Ideally the water should be at the same temperature as your room. You can get this either by mixing some hot water with the cold water, or by storing some water in your room for at least 24 hours before you use it. With most plants the temperature of the water is not very critical, but as far as African violets (saintpaulias), are concerned, if the temperature of the water is lower than 53°F (13°C) or higher than 60°F (15·5°C) you are liable to get unsightly blotches on the leaves. Always, during cold weather particularly, avoid using very cold water, or water that is more than luke warm, otherwise you can again damage the roots. Having watered the plant, give it no more water until it has used up all the water you have applied. The smaller the pot, the sooner the soil will dry out, so that plants of the same species in 3-in. pots will require rewatering sooner than plants in 5-in. pots. Plastic pots, not being porous, retain water for longer than clay pots. During the spring and summer the plant will absorb water much more rapidly than during the fall and winter, when growth is almost stationary and all the plant requires

to do is to replace any water it may have lost through its leaves. It will lose more in high temperatures than in lower ones, so the room temperature in fall and winter is also a factor.

There can be no hard and fast rules for watering plants, as, for example, once a week or every two weeks, but if you inspect your plants daily, you will notice when the soil dries out. Soil at the top of the pot may well be dry while the lower portion is still reasonably moist, so wait for 24 hours after the top soil looks dry and then water. In this way there is little risk of overwatering.

If, when you water, the water runs straight through the pot and out at the bottom, the soil must have become over dry and shrunk. This can usually be cured by firming the soil around the edge of the pot with your thumbs, but if this is not effective fill a bucket with water to the level of the pot and stand the pot in this water and leave it there for 2 or 3 hours, then remove it and firm down around the edge of the pot. Snake plant (*Sansevieria trifasciata laurentii*) is only watered once a month during the winter and this could well be excessively dried out when you want to give more water in the spring, so for this and similar plants the bucket treatment may be necessary.

Leaves wilting is usually a sign of a plant needing water, but it is not a certain sign. If a plant is dying as a result of overwatering, the leaves may well wilt, so that if you see wilting with a wet soil ball, you can be fairly sure that you have over-watered and that you must let the plant dry out (although your

Above: Repotting a house plant, using a loamless, peat-based compost. *Right: Cordyline terminalis*, one of the most colorful of all foliage plants. *Far right: Begonia rex* leaves are more colorful than many flowers; the color range is very wide chances of getting it to recover are pretty slim). Also leaves may wilt if they are in burning sunlight. They will immediately recover if placed in the shade or if they are given a light spray with cool water and this phenomenon is, in any case, only temporary; the leaves wilt to prevent excessive lack of water. If the leaves are wilting, inspect the plant and if it is dry, then watering is the answer, but do not water wilting plants unless you have made sure that they are dry.

Cleaning Leaves In towns and industrial districts, the air is liable to be polluted and some attention must be paid to the plant's hygiene. The plant 'breathes' through its leaves and if these get clogged up with dust, the plant will not grow well. It is, therefore, advisable to sponge the leaves once a week. Use a piece of cotton wool and luke warm water, but sponge the mature leaves only, as the young leaves are very soft and could easily be damaged.

Pest Control Insect pests are uncommon on house plants, but can be prevented from spreading by means of this weekly spongeing; even aphids can be removed in this manner. Aerosol insecticides are available to deal with any serious infection, but these are often poisonous, so they should be kept away from children and the aerosol should not be applied in the house, but in the open air or in an outhouse or garage in inclement weather.

Stopping Many house plants have a stem from which side branches emerge. With such plants, it is usually good policy to remove the growing point, as well as any unsatisfactory winter-made growth in the spring. This is known as stopping. Stopping will encourage the production of side shoots, so that you have a nice bushy plant as opposed to a rather thin lanky one. However, there is no use in stopping a plant unless it is well-rooted and making good growth. If it is not, all you will do is to get another growing point to replace the one you have removed and the plant will not bush out. With some very vigorous plants, such as the tradescantias, it may be necessary to stop two or three times during the growing season and sometimes with such plants not only the main growing point is removed, but the side shoots are also stopped when they have elongated sufficiently. Further details about whether or not to stop will be found under the descriptions of individual plants.

Propagation Some house plants can be easily propagated from tip cuttings in the home without any elaborate paraphernalia. For these you take a piece of the plant with the growing tip and some 2–4 in. of stem, depending on the ultimate size of the plant; low growing plants will not have much stem. Now make a clean cut with a razor blade at the lowest leaf joint. Then remove most of the lower leaves, if your cutting is very leafy, leaving only about a third of the leaves. Fill a small pot either with a ready purchased cutting compost (the soilless ones are very satisfactory) or with a mixture of equal parts (by bulk) of peatmoss and sharp sand, and then insert your cuttings to a depth of about $\frac{1}{2}$ in. Water them in and then enclose the pot in a polyethelene bag (or invert a glass jar over it). The pot should be stood in the shade.

The leaves of house plants should be cleaned from time to time to keep them healthy. Stiff, hard leaves may be washed to remove dust and grime; softer leaves must be treated very gently. *Below: Calathea makoyana*

The best time to take cuttings is between mid-May and mid-August and the worst possible time is during the winter when rooting will probably not take place at all. Rooting usually takes place between 3 and 6 weeks after taking the cuttings. If you see new leaves being produced, that is a fairly reliable sign of rooting. Another method is to give a very gentle tug to the cutting; if there is some resistance it is probably rooted, but if it just comes out, it must be reinserted and you must wait longer. Once the cuttings are rooted, remove the polyethelene bag or glass jar, and wait a week. Then knock the potful of cuttings out and pot each one up separately, taking care to damage the roots as little as possible. The newly potted-up plants should be put in a warm situation for a week or so and then they can be placed in their permanent situations. One or two plants require special treatment, but this is noted below. Some plants will root faster if the pot is placed in a warm closet; cuttings do not seem to mind being in darkness while they are making their roots, but once these are made, the cuttings must be brought out into the light and it is probably better to be patient and keep the pots outside. It is very important not to leave them outside, however, if there is any danger of frost, as this will kill almost any houseplant, particularly the flowering species.

Beloperone guttata,
the shrimp plant

warm enough, well into the winter.

During the winter the temperature should be 55°F (13°C) and the plants should be given as much light as possible. In the spring all the main growths should be cut back by a third, or the plant will tend to become rather leggy with a bare base. Once in a 5-in. pot it can remain there for two years, provided it is fed between mid-May and mid-September and the same period when it is potted on into a 6-in. pot. The plant should be kept moist all the year round, although it will require far less water during the winter months and it should be in a well-lit position that does not receive much direct sunlight.

If you keep your house very warm in the winter, beloperones may produce a lot of weak spindly growth, which looks unhealthy. Remove this in early spring. The plants should be fairly warm, around 65°F (18°C) between the spring pruning and the appearance of the first flowers and higher temperatures will do no harm. Once the flowers have appeared they will persist for longer under cooler conditions, but this sort of temperature adjustment is not very easy in the home and the plant will grow quite happily whatever the temperature is, within reason.

Foliage Plants There is a much larger range of plants with attractive foliage. Many of these plants are variegated. This variegation tends to be more marked in well-lit situations and most variegated plants need more light than the normal green-leaved forms. On the other hand many green-leaved plants will thrive in shady conditions which would be unsuitable for either flowering or variegated plants, so they have definite advantages. The only plant that will survive in very dark shade is the aspidistra. However, there are numerous situations where foliage plants will grow happily, although they would be too dark for flowering plants. Foliage plants also have the advantage that they look attractive throughout the year, while even the best flowering plants have some period when they are not flowering, so in many ways the foliage plant gives you better value for your money.

House Plants Described

Flowering Plants There are two flowering plants that will do well under the coolest conditions; these are the geranium (*Pelargonium* × *hortorum*) and the fuchsia.

These are such popular plants that their cultivation is fully described in Favorite Garden Flowers, elsewhere in this work. When grown in the house, pelargoniums should be given as much light as possible, preferably on sunny window sills. Fuchsias like a well-lit, but not sunny situation and will do perfectly well in the center of the room. They do not mind shade, provided it is not dark shade.

Busy Lizzie (*Impatiens walleriana*) is a popular flowering plant for rooms, but the purple-leaved *Impatiens petersiana* is better. This is like the old busy Lizzie with its scarlet flowers, which are produced freely in quite shady situations as well as in well-lit ones, but its dark purple leaves make it attractive even when it is not in flower. Cuttings root so easily, that all you have to do is to put them in water and roots will soon start to appear. As the season advances the plants tend to become leggy and the lower leaves drop off, so it is best to renew the plants at frequent intervals, with the last cuttings, that you intend to overwinter, taken at the beginning of September. If you do not want to start them in water, you can insert them in the usual cutting mixture, but there is no need to cover this with a polyethelene bag. It is practically impossible to overwater these plants during the spring and summer, and they require plenty during this period. During the fall and winter they must be kept just moist and they also require to be fairly warm, preferably around 55°F (13°C), although they will survive at 50°F (10°C). Stopping may encourage bushy growth, but they seem to do quite well without any

encouragement. Since the plants are normally only kept for the one season, soilless composts will be quite satisfactory without additional feeding.

One of the best and most easily grown house plants for continuous flowering is the *Cuphea hyssopifolia*. This makes a small, twiggy shrub with every twig covered with leaves, about 1 in. long and $\frac{1}{4}$ in. across. From the axils of these leaves emerge innumerable small purple trumpet-shaped flowers. Flowering starts in April or early May and will go on non-stop until November. During the winter a temperature of 55°F (13°C) is advisable, but if it falls below this occasionally, no harm seems to occur. Tip cuttings, which should not be too soft, root rather slowly in warm conditions, which probably means that you cannot take them until June, unless you have a heated propagating case. The plant should be grown on year after year, but when it is three years old it may be rather too large (although in this case you can prune harder) so occasional propagation is a good thing. At the end of March it should be pruned, shortening all the main shoots by about 2 in., but otherwise no stopping is necessary. The plant should be potted on every year in April and regular feeding from June until September will encourage more growth and flowers. It likes a well-lit situation and does not mind some direct sunlight, so long as it is not excessively burning, while during the winter it should be given a well-lit situation.

The shrimp plant (*Beloperone guttata*) is another small soft-leaved twiggy shrub, with heads of flowers at the ends of the branches. The flowers are concealed in the bracts, which form a shape like the body of a prawn and are either maroon-purple or, in the form known as 'lutea', a pale yellow. These are produced fairly continuously throughout the summer and fall, and, if conditions are

Impatiens walleriana variegata, the variegated Busy Lizzie

Plants for Cool & Intermediate Conditions

Plants for Cool Conditions

Some plants like cool conditions, with the winter temperature ranging between 45° and 50°F (7°–10°C). These plants will not enjoy higher temperatures, although many of those in the next group, needing a temperature of 55°–60°F (13°–16°C) will survive a winter either with lower or higher temperatures, without any ill effects. Plants that thrive in cool conditions will not necessarily like to be warm in winter, so choose other plants for your warm rooms.

The most notable cool-growing plants are the various ivies, the tradescantias, eucalyptus, chlorophytum, *Ficus pumila* and *Araucaria excelsa*.

The ivies are either small-leaved variants of the common ivy, *Hedera helix*, or of the larger leaved Irish ivy, *H. hibernica*, or of the large-leaved vigorous ivy, *H. canariensis*.

Both *H. hibernica* and *H. canariensis* are climbing plants and do best if they are trained up a stake or on trellis work. There are two forms of *H. canariensis* generally available, of which the most popular is the one with variegated leaves, with a wide silver margin and a dark green center. The other, 'Golden Leaf' has bright glossy green leaves with a yellowish patch in the center. These plants may be grown outdoors in milder areas of the country. They do not make their best impression until they are quite large. On the other hand many of the forms of the common ivy are satisfactory as small plants. They can be divided into two main sections, those that are self-branching and tend to make erect little bushy plants and those that are either trailers or climbers. The latter either have to be trained up some support or put in a hanging container, which may well look effective, but is a nuisance to water. The self-branching ivies will branch without any stopping, while the trailing forms require to be stopped in order to produce side shoots and will only do this if they are quite sizeable plants; smaller plants will just replace the original growing points and then grow on.

Among the self-branching ivies are 'Pittsburgh', 'Chicago', 'Minima', 'Minigreen', and 'Green Ripple', with plain green leaves, while among those variegated with silver are the 'Variegated Chicago', 'Little Diamond', 'Heisse', and 'Goldchild', which is more cream than silver. Among the trailers some good plants are 'Glacier', 'Eva' (sometimes called 'Little Eva'), and 'Maculata'. An unusual plant is 'Golden Jubilee', also known as 'Goldheart'. This has the center of the leaf a deep yellow and a dark green margin. Unlike the other ivies it needs as much light as possible and has the disconcerting habit of making a lot of new stem without any leaves; however patience is all that is required as eventually the leaves form. The other ivies will grow happily in quite shaded conditions, although the variegated forms look better in well-lit situations. During the winter you may get some unvariegated leaves coming at the end of the branches. These should be removed at the beginning of March. Ivies should be kept on the dry side at all times.

The so-called German ivy is in reality a climbing groundsel (*Senecio macroglossus variegata*). It has roughly triangular leaves of dark green and cream and is one of the few house plants that do not require sponge-ing, as the leaves are covered with a waxy secretion. It is a vigorous climber that will need frequent stopping and it is a greedy plant needing ample feeding.

The tradescantias and zebrinas are trailing plants with variegated leaves about $1\frac{1}{2}$ in. long and $\frac{3}{4}$ in. across. Some of the tradescantias are liable to revert to unvariegated leaves and any unvariegated shoot should, be removed as detected, as otherwise they will grow so much faster than the variegated portions that they will eventually swamp the plant. This danger does not apply to the zebrinas. Too deep a shade may suppress the variegation, otherwise they will thrive in any situation. Trails will root if placed in water and can be put several to a pot and watered in to make new potfuls. The plants soon become rather leggy and are best replaced every one or two years. You must make a hole in which to insert your cutting (which should be about 2 in. long) as they are rather brittle and might break if you just pushed them in. The compost must be kept fairly moist until the cuttings have rooted, which takes about two weeks. Tradescantias like plenty of water, but if kept dry the leaves will come small but quite well-colored. Side shoots appear whether you stop the plants or no, but, they will appear sooner, if you stop the main growths.

The eucalyptus most commonly grown as a house plant is *E. cinerea*, which could eventually make a small tree. It is very attractive with its white branches and blue-green leaves, which are nearly circular in young plants and lance-shaped when adult. To keep the plant within reasonable bounds it must be pruned hard every spring and the leading shoots that emerge at the top of the plant, must then be stopped, otherwise they will continue to grow and no lower growths will be formed. The plant should have a well-lit situation and be kept reasonably cool

Top left: Zebrina pendula

Above left: Tradescantia 'Rochford's Quicksilver'

A colorful group of house plants, grown for their foliage, though the aphelandra at the bottom right will also flower

Above right: Tradescantia purpurea

during the winter. Once in a 6-in. pot, it is advisable to keep it there, as otherwise the resultant plant might become too unwieldy. This entails regular feeding.

Chlorophytum comosum variegatum is sometimes known as the spider plant. It throws up a clump of grassy leaves, which are nearly a foot long, but which reflex to give a fountain-like effect. They are either cream colored with a thin green margin or else they have green margins and a cream center. The small white flowers are often replaced with a tuft of leaves and if this is pinned down into a pot, it will soon take root and the stem can then be severed, giving you a fresh plant. Keep these young plants somewhat on the dry side until they are well rooted, but well-rooted plants can take plenty of water during their growing season, although they are kept fairly dry from October until March. Small plants look rather grassy, but they grow rapidly and large plants are very impressive. They should be got into 5-in. pots as soon as possible and then potted on every other year.

Ficus pumila is a low creeping plant, producing aerial roots like an ivy and it can be trained up walls in the same way. The leaves are small, about 1 in. long and $\frac{1}{2}$ in. across, heart-shaped, and they completely cover the thin wiry stems. This plant thrives in shade and must, indeed, never be exposed to bright sunlight and similarly it must never be allowed to dry out completely, otherwise the leaves may shrivel and drop off. Overwatering is possible, particularly during the winter, but some moisture is essential even during this period. In mild parts of the country it will grow outside on a north-facing wall, so it has no objection to quite low temperatures.

Araucaria excelsa, the Norfolk Island pine is in nature a very large tree, but it is very slow-growing as a house plant. It makes a perfectly symmetrical pyramid, with a central stem, from which, after every year's growth, four branches radiate horizontally from the central stem and, in their turn, produce symmetrical side shoots, which are produced in opposite pairs all along these side branches. All these main and side branches are densely clothed with bright green needles. The plant must be rotated at regular intervals, so as to preserve its symmetry. The plant should never be pruned nor stopped and once in a 5-in. pot needs potting on every two or three years, and should be fed during the intervening period. The plant can be stood outside during the summer in a somewhat shaded situation, to great advantage. The plant must not dry out at any time, but on the other hand it does not require much water at any period, although more will be required when the new growths are elongating.

Other house plants that will thrive under cool conditions are two vine-like climbers, *Cissus antarctica*, the kangaroo vine, and *Rhoicissus rhomboidea*, while an attractive trailing plant is *Plectranthus oertendahlii*,

Chlorophytum comosum variegatum, known as the spider plant, is grown mainly for the sake of its cream-variegated, grass-like leaves

Hedera helix 'Eva' ('Little Eva'), one of a number of trailing forms of English ivy, with small, variegated leaves

with leaves that have the principal veins picked out in silver.

Plants for Intermediate Temperatures

With a constant winter temperature of from 55° to 60°F (13°–16°C), the choice is very much wider and many more colorful specimens may be grown. Perhaps the most gorgeous of all are the plants known in this country as the Ti tree, *Cordyline terminalis*. These are small palm-like plants with leaves up to a foot in length and 4 in. across, which first unfurl with the most brilliant colors in cerise, pink, or cream and pink and which gradually age to a purplish brown or a medium green with a red margin, but practically any combination of red, pink, cream and green can be found in the various cultivars. Unfortunately, these gorgeous colors do not appear until the plant has been growing some three years, so that they are not cheap to purchase. They are greedy feeders requiring a rich soil mixture and ample feeding. They should be potted on every two years. They must have a well-lit situation, but not in direct sunlight for too long and they require ample water, but should not be overwatered. Since the leaves are more brightly colored than a good many flowers, it can be appreciated that this is a fairly striking plant. It is never stopped.

The croton, *Codiaeum variegatum*, is equally colorful, but not quite so easy as it is very sensitive to drafts, which can cause the leaves to fall, and also to any violent fluctuations in temperature. If the temperature can be kept constant, the plant will thrive. The leaves vary in shape from nearly circular to almost grass-like and are in various combinations of brilliant colors. This can be kept somewhat on the dry side during the winter, but will take plenty of water during the summer. The plant contains a milky juice, which spurts out whenever the plant is damaged in any way, so this should be avoided. It requires ample light at all times and has no objection to direct sunlight. Potting on should take place every other year.

Very much easier are the rex begonias. These have roughly triangular leaves, which may be fairly regular or which may have very jagged edges; some are deep or rosy purple, others varying shades of green and silver; the choice is very large. They have no objection to shady conditions and will still keep their gorgeous colors in such situations. Begonias have very fine roots and are usually grown in a mixture composed mainly of leaf mold and sand, with only a little loam so that soilless mixtures will prove very satisfactory. They must not dry out at any time, but they do not require too much water either and should be watered regularly. Rex begonias spread outwards rather than upwards and they can be divided, if the plant is getting too large. The plants should be fed during the summer, but rather sparingly. The 'Iron Cross' begonia (*B. masoniana*) needs rather warmer conditions than the rex group and has bright green leaves with a maroon 'Iron Cross' in the center.

The zebra plant, *Aphelandra squarrosa louisae*, has an upright stem from which spring pairs of leaves, which may be 9 in. long and half as wide. These are a dark green, with the main veins picked out in bold ivory stripes. The original plants used to produce pyramidal heads of yellow flowers, but the later forms, known as 'Brockfeld' and 'Dania' flower very rarely. The plant needs repotting yearly and takes ample water during the summer and a certain amount in the winter. Side shoots can be detached and rooted in the summer, but a temperature of at least 65°F (18°C) is necessary and preferably somewhat higher. These plants need a

reasonable amount of light, but will grow in partly shaded conditions quite satisfactorily.

The various ficus are not particularly colorful, but they are impressive. The most popular is the indiarubber tree, *F. elastica*, which is offered either as var. *decora*, which has the immature leaf covered with a red sheath, or as var. *robusta*, which has very large leaves, somewhat rounder than those of *decora*. There are also some handsome variegated forms known as 'Schryveriana' and 'Tricolor', with their leaves blotched with cream, light and dark green, which are somewhat more decorative. The indiarubber plant can eventually make an enormous tree, so it is kept to reasonable dimensions by keeping it in a small pot, 5 or 6 in. in diameter, and feeding it during the summer to get the leaves a good size, but not to encourage much stem elongation. Their large leathery leaves must be sponged regularly on both surfaces to keep them glossy and to stop any possible infection with scale insect. They can be kept fairly dry in the winter and watered normally during the summer, when they will much appreciate the leaves being syringed during very hot spells. They will grow equally well in shade or sun, although they should be in the shade when the new leaves are unfurling, otherwise these will not be a good size. Ordinarily you do not stop at all, but if the plant gets too tall, it can be cut back in spring to about 6 in., when it will break again from the base. This is a messy job as the plants are full of milky latex (from which rubber can be obtained) and this will gush out and stain the plant. The cut surface should be sprinkled with powdered charcoal immediately to stop excessive bleeding. *Ficus benjamina* is another member of this genus, which makes a branching, thickly-leaved tree with long narrow leaves giving something of the effect of a weeping willow. Some of these leaves will be shed in the winter whatever you do, as it is their natural habit, but many more will be produced in the following spring and summer. This needs a well-lit but shady position and will take rather more water than *F. elastica*.

There are many philodendrons used as house plants; most of them are climbers, producing aerial roots, but one striking plant, *P. bipinnatifidum*, does not climb, but forms a rosette of long-stemmed very jagged leaves, which get larger as the plant grows and can end up a yard across. The leaves also get more jagged as the plant matures; the first leaves are heart-shaped. As the larger plants are handsomer, they are potted on yearly until they are in a 7- or 8-in. pot, in which they can then stay, being fed regularly each season. With these larger sized plants clay pots are better than the plastic ones, that are so light that a large plant makes them top heavy. This plant is never stopped. On the other hand the climbing species are stopped from time to time, although not necessarily every year. These climbers all require shady conditions, although these should not be too dark, whereas *P. bipinna-tifidum*, will grow either in shade or in full light, although the leaves seem to be larger in the shade. Ideally the climbing forms should have a very damp atmosphere from which their aerial roots can obtain nourishment, but they are often tolerant of quite dry conditions. They are sometimes trained on blocks of cork bark, to which the roots adhere and which is quite easy to moisten. The most attractive, but a delicate, rather difficult plant, is *P. melanochrysum*, with heart-shaped, dark green, iridescent leaves, 5 or 6 in. long. Much easier are the popular *P. scandens*, with green heart-shaped leaves, and two very similar species, *P. hastatum* and a plant called *P. 'Tuxla'*, both of which

have spear-shaped leaves about 7 in. long and 4 in. wide. They are a shining dark green, with some coppery sheen in the young leaves. These latter are fairly slow growers, whereas *P. scandens* is quite fast and benefits from a yearly stopping. If it becomes too tall you can bend the flexible main stem right over and tie it in at the base of the plant, whence it will start to climb anew. A plant needing similar treatment to the climbing philodendrons is *Monstera deliciosa borsigiana*. This has large serrated leaves, which are perforated with holes, giving a very exotic outline. In dark shade these perforations will not develop. It is best trained upright and the aerial roots carefully guided down into the soil in the pot. Stopping is not recommended unless the plant is getting too large, as it is slow to break again. Similar to *P. scandens*, but with gold variegated leaves is *Scindapsus aureus*, which needs more light than the philodendrons and requires a yearly stopping.

Aralia Dizygotheca elegantissima makes a slow-growing shrub with leaves like those

of a horse-chestnut in shape, but the leaflets are extremely thin in young plants, becoming wider as the plant ages. They are coppery red when they emerge but become very dark maroon, almost black. This may not sound very attractive, but the plant has enormous grace and charm, as much from its elegant habit as from its light, graceful leaves. It requires a well-lit position, but shade from much direct sunlight and the leaves should be syringed frequently during the summer and occasionally during the winter to discourage red spider. On the other hand the soil is always watered somewhat sparingly, particularly in the winter.

Snake plant, *Sansevieria trifasciata laurentii*, makes an upright plant, with its stiff,

Far left: Ficus elastica variegata and *Ficus benjamina* are two excellent but very different members of the fig family which make good house plants. *Left:* The striped leaves of *Calathea zebrina*, a plant which needs a warm, moist atmosphere and shady conditions. *Below: Philodendron* 'Burgundy', a large-leaved kind, grows fairly slowly as a house plant

fleshy leaves, which are mottled in light and dark green with a golden margin.

The plant usually produces only one extra leaf each year and this may turn up some way from the rest of the plant. There is a temptation to cut this out to form another plant, but this should only be done the year after it has appeared, as it does not produce any roots the first year and the plantlet would probably die. If, when the leaf is about 8 in. long, you can find the underground stem from which it rises and cut this half-way through with a knife, this seems to encourage rooting. This plant needs ample light and very little water. In the winter one watering a month is sufficient and even in the summer it should be allowed to dry out thoroughly between waterings. The new leaves are somewhat rolled in to start with and water should not be allowed to lodge in this hollow, otherwise the root could rot. Otherwise they are tough resilient plants, which will put up with almost any conditions and tolerate oil or gas fumes.

Peperomias are low plants, with a very

small root system. Some have trailing stems, but the most attractive throw up a tuft of leaves from a central point. The best are probably *P. griseo-argentia*, *P. caperata* and *P. sandersii*. *P. griseo-argentia* has heart-shaped leaves some 2½ in. long and 2 in. across, which have a quilted effect from the undulating surface. They are pale gray with olive green main veins. In the fall it produces flowers that look like white mouse tails. If a leaf is removed and inserted shallowly in a cutting mixture with the temperature not below 65°F (18°C) a small plant will arise from the base of the leaf. *P. caperata* has smaller corrugated leaves, the peaks appearing grayish, while the valleys have a purple tinge. The flowers are pure white. It is propagated the same way as *P. griseo-argentia*, but the stalk can be inserted a little deeper. Both these plants like shady conditions and never a great deal of water around the roots, although they revel in a moist atmosphere. The watermelon peperomia, *P. sandersii*, is the most handsome of all the peperomias, but is not very easy, requiring a winter temperature of 60°F (16°C) and great care in its placing as it is very sensitive to even mild drafts. The striking leaves, shaped like a watermelon, are silver with green zones around the main veins. Keep the plant as dry as possible in the winter; the leaves can flag before you need apply water as they come back without damage.

The calatheas and marantas all have very attractive leaves. They must have moist, shady conditions and the plants need ample feeding during the summer. They will probable need potting on yearly. If plants get very large, they can be divided. Although they will pass the winter happily at the temperatures recommended, they need about 10°F (5½°C) more during the summer to make proper growth. Direct sunlight can shrivel the leaves, so should be avoided. The plants are sometimes known as prayer plants, as they raise their leaves at night. *Calathea insignis* has elongated oval leaves, 4–9 in. long; they are yellowish green darkening towards the leaf margin and with dark green blotches along the midrib, while the underside of the leaf is a deep claret color. *C. mackoyana* is very striking with rounder leaves, about 6 in. long and 4 in. across. The main portion of the leaf is silvery in color with dark green blotches, underside rosy purple, so that the plant has a rosy glow. *Maranta leuconeura* is a variable plant, rather lower than the calatheas, its leaves usually about 4 in. long and 2½ in. across. The var. *massangeana* has leaves of soft green with the main veins picked out in white to give a herring-bone effect, while the var. *kerchoveana* has leaves that when young are emerald green with red blotches between the veins, while in older leaves the colors are dark green and maroon. The var. *erythrophylla* (*tricolor*) has larger, very dark green leaves, the main veins bright red, with yellowish-green blotches between them.

Cacti and other Succulents

Succulent plants are the camels of the vegetable world, storing up food and water to be used not on a rainy day, but during a period of prolonged drought. This may last for a few weeks or, in extreme cases, plants have survived without rainfall for over a year. This water can be stored in either the leaves or the stems of the plants, depending on the type. This gives rise to two distinct types of succulent plant, leaf succulents and stem succulents. The stem succulents usually have no leaves (except sometimes very small ones on young growth, soon falling off), and the green tissue of the stems takes over the work of the leaves to manufacture the food. Without leaves, the plants can reduce much of the water loss. The stems are usually very thick and full of water storage tissue, and are mostly either cylindrical or spherical in shape, sometimes being deeply ribbed. The ribs enable the plant to expand or contract as it absorbs or loses water.

Leaf succulents have plump, rounded leaves full of water storage tissue. They are often coated with wax, meal or hairs, helping to reduce water loss from their surfaces. Often these succulents have fleshy stems as well, but the leaves play the most important part in food manufacture.

The cacti, all belonging to one family, are the most popular group of succulent plants, but many other plant families have succulent members. Among the families whose succulent species are grown are the *Crassulaceae*, *Aizoaceae*, *Euphorbiaceae*, *Asclepiadaceae*, *Liliaceae*, and *Agavaceae*.

Cacti

The cactus family is native to America; plants found in Europe and elsewhere have been introduced at some time in the past. There are three distinct types of plant, the pereskias, the epiphytes and the desert cacti, and these require different treatment because of their differing 'home' conditions. Except for the pereskias, they are stem succulents, having either no leaves or small temporary ones. Cacti are not all spiny plants, some being strongly armed while others are quite spineless. All cacti have areoles, small pincushion-like structures scattered over the stems. Spines, when present, off-shoots, and branches come from these areoles. This is the way to distinguish a cactus from another stem succulent, such as a euphorbia, which does not have areoles. Also all cactus flowers have the same general design, while those of other succulents differ enormously between the various families.

Pereskias The pereskias must have a brief mention here, as they are so different from other cacti. They are obtainable from the specialist nurseries, but not likely to be found in the local florist. They are interesting in that they are the only cacti which are not really succulents, and have normal leaves, rather like those of a privet, but possess spines and, of course, the characteristic areoles. The flowers bear a superficial resemblance to the wild rose. They are bushes and climbers from the tropical regions of north and central America, where they are used as hedging plants, and can be grown as pot plants, but to be really successful they need to be bedded out in a large greenhouse, where they can scramble up a wall or over a support. They need a winter temperature of about 50°F (10°C) and to be kept moist all the year round. Most growers regard them as curiosities, and they are not very common in collections.

Epiphytic Cacti By contrast, the epiphytes are grown in this country very commonly, many being sold as florists' plants. In their native South American tropical rain forests, the epiphytic cacti are found growing in the debris caught up in the branches of trees. They grow among the other epiphytes, ferns, bromeliads, and orchids, which festoon the trees in these tropical regions. Although there is no shortage of water where the plants are found, the pockets of humus they are growing in dry out very quickly. Epiphytic cacti have no leaves, but flattened, slightly succulent stems, sometimes incorrectly called 'leaves'. These stems may consist of short segments, as in the familiar 'Christmas cactus' (schlumbergera), the flowers appearing on the ends of the segments, or the stems may be long and strap-like, as in the epiphyllums. In these latter, the flowers are usually carried on the sides of the stems. Owing to the beauty of their flowers, epiphyllums have received a lot of attention from the horticulturists. There are enormous numbers of beautiful hybrids on the market, in all colors except blue, while the wild species are not often grown as greenhouse plants owing to their large size and the difficulty of flowering them in cultivation. These hybrid epiphyllums, together with the short stemmed rhipsalidopsis and schlumbergeras are the ones in this group most often grown as pot plants. All require the same basic treatment.

They need a good, porous soil and a compost of equal parts loam, peatmoss or leaf mold, decayed cow manure and sand, plus some charcoal is suitable. Leaf mold is ideal if it can be obtained as it more closely resembles the natural soil of the forests. The soilless composts are also very suitable for these and other cacti, but for the epiphytes,

Areoles

the lime-free type of compost is best. It helps to add a teaspoon of bonemeal to each pot of compost. Re-potting should be done annually. These cacti will survive winter temperatures as low as 41°F (5°C), but flower much better if kept a little warmer. They should be kept moist all the year round. In fact, it is best to forget that they are cacti and treat them as normal pot plants. When in bud, epiphytes can be fed every two weeks with a tomato-type potassium fertilizer.

Because these epiphytic cacti grow among trees, they do not need full sunlight. They make very successful house plants if grown on an east-facing window-ledge, where they will receive the early morning sun, but are in shade during the heat of the day. They grow rapidly, and when a plant outgrows a 6-in. pot, it should be re-started. A stem is cut from an epiphyllum, or a few segments from the schlumbergeras and rhipsalidopsis. The cutting is allowed to dry for two or three days, and then potted up. This drying period for cactus and other succulent cuttings is always carried out to prevent rot from spreading into the fleshy stems. As they are succulents, they do not wilt during this period as other plants would. The best time of the year for taking cuttings is April–May, although it is quite possible at any time during spring and summer.

Desert Cacti The desert cacti are the spiny tall or round plants that we associate with the American deserts. Actually many are found growing on rocky mountain sides and in grassy areas, as well as in the sandy regions

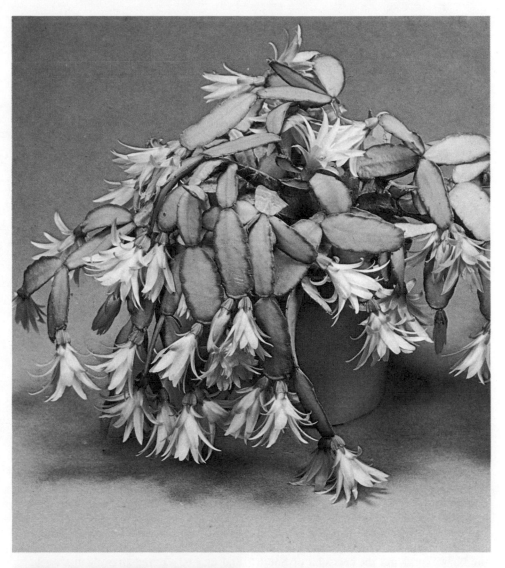

Left above: Agave hauchacensis
Left below: Areoles are distinctive features of a cactus plant
Below: Succulent-leaved aeoniums
Above right: Rhipsalidopsis 'Electra'
Right: A selection of succulent plants in the subtropical garden of Tresco Abbey, Isles of Scilly, Great Britain

of Mexico and South America. They all need the maximum amount of sunlight to flourish and flower freely. For this reason they do not make such good house plants as the epiphytes. If a greenhouse is not available, they should be kept on a south-facing window sill, and preferably stood outdoors from May to September.

A minimum winter temperature of 41°F (5°C) is adequate for most desert cacti. A well-drained compost is essential. One containing 2 parts loam, 2 parts peatmoss, 2 parts sand, 2 parts broken crocks, plus some charcoal and 1 pint bonemeal per bushel of mix, is suitable. Alternatively, a soilless compost may be used. Since the food content of the soil does not last forever, the plants should be repotted annually.

Many people seem to think that cacti need no water! This is far from the truth, although they will certainly survive a period of dryness (after all they are adapted to do just this). This means that it is not necessary to worry too much while you are on vacation (although seedlings will suffer). But without water they will just survive, not grow, and the plants should be kept more or less continually moist between April and October. The watering should be reduced after this and they should be left dry during December and January, if kept in a greenhouse. Watering can be restarted gradually as the light improves in February. If the plants are wintered in a heated house with a very dry atmosphere, more water will be needed during winter to prevent excessive shrivelling. Indoors, the ideal winter spot is an unheated room, but this may not always be possible. The reason for keeping them dry at this time is that if they grow in the poor light of winter, they are likely to become distorted and may well rot the following year. Also, flowering is very much affected by the previous winter's treatment.

Desert cacti are mostly very easily reproduced from cuttings. Some plants form offsets which can be removed and potted up, after the usual few days drying period. Some clustering plants will have rooted 'pups' (offsets) around the base of the parent; these can be removed and potted up directly. If the plant does not form offsets, a section of stem can be cut off and potted up after drying for about a week. The base of the parent plant can be kept as it will often sprout again, forming a number of offsets around the cut top. The best time to do all this is, as before, between April and June.

Other Succulents

As mentioned earlier, the other succulents fall into several different families, and since the cultivation varies somewhat for each, it is best to give a brief description of them.

Crassulaceae This family is very large, consisting of leaf succulents with almost world-wide distribution. The most beautiful members of the family are the echeverias of the New World and the crassulas of South Africa. Other attractive plants are the aeoniums and sedums, with plump, often highly colored leaves, arranged in rosettes. All should be kept slightly moist all the year round. Seed of these plants is difficult to obtain, but they can mostly be easily reproduced from cuttings which need little or no drying before potting up. Some species can even be grown from leaves, just laid on the soil, when they will root, and send out new shoots.

Aizoaceae This is a family of leaf succulents found mainly in Africa. They vary from small shrubs to plants about 1 in. high consisting of one pair of very succulent leaves. One of the main characteristics of this group is that most of them have distinct resting periods, corresponding to the dry season of their native lands. During this period, from about October to March, they must be kept completely dry. The old leaves will gradually shrivel away. Watering should not be re-started until the new leaves appear in spring. Popular plants are the fall growing conophytums, glottiphyllums and pleiospilos and the summer growing lithops and faucarias. This group is quite easily raised from seed, or heads of clustering plants may be removed, dried for a few days and potted up. June to July is a good time for this.

Euphorbiaceae This contains only one group, the euphorbias, commonly grown, but this is an immense group of world-wide distribution, many of which are not succulents. The succulent plants are most commonly found on the African continent. These are stem succulents, although during the growing period some species produce leaves on the new growth. Euphorbias vary enormously in size, some reaching tree-like proportions, closely resembling the giant cacti. Others are small, clustering plants only a few inches high. All have one thing in common, an irritating, sometimes poisonous, milky sap. Euphorbia flowers are usually small and insignificant, but often have a sweet lime-like scent. In some species the male and female flowers are on separate plants. Euphorbias are difficult to propagate from cuttings, but may be readily raised from seed, although it needs to be fresh for success.

Asclepiadaceae This family contains a large number of leafless stem succulents from the dry regions of the Old World. Where they occur, there are no bees and the flowers are pollinated by flies. To be attractive to flies, the flowers often have an unpleasant smell to us. However, the flowers are usually large (sometimes immense) in shades of reddish-brown or yellow, often covered with hairs. Stapelias are probably the best known in this group. We also have duvalias and carallumas. They are easily raised from seed, which germinates quickly but has a tendency to damp off equally quickly. Cuttings may be taken from June to August. They are best just laid on the soil and may be watered after about a week.

Liliaceae This family contains not only the lily bulbs of our gardens but a group of leaf succulent plants which are found mainly on the African continent. The most interesting plants are the aloes, gasterias and haworthias.

Aloes can reach a large size and bear a superficial resemblance to the American agaves, with their long strap-like leaves. There are also a number of small plants which are very attractive and will survive on a window sill. Aloes have long flower stems, but the rosette does not die after flowering.

Gasterias and haworthias are found growing in the shade of grasses and small shrubs in their native land. This makes them useful small plants for growing on window sills or under the greenhouse staging.

All the plants which form clusters may be reproduced by removing offsets. Otherwise they must be raised from seed.

Agavaceae This last family dealt with here, includes yuccas, sansevierias and agaves. It is the agaves that interest the grower of succulents. These are rosette-shaped plants with tough, strap-like leaves. Although many are far too large for the average grower, there are small species that are ideal for the living room, because the very tough leaves enable these plants to withstand the dry atmosphere. Many people are familiar with the large, rather coarse specimens of *Agave americana* found growing along the Mediter-ranean coast. These plants have at some time been introduced; the agaves are native to the southern U.S.A., Mexico, Central America, the West Indies, and northern South America.

Agave flowers are borne on stems many feet long, but only on very old specimens, and after flowering, the rosette dies, but by then there are usually offsets growing around the base of the plant. These can be removed and used for propagation. Agaves are very easily raised from seed.

Cultivation The cultivation of the other succulents is very similar to that of the desert cacti; any differences have been mentioned. They should be given plenty of water in summer and kept either dry or slightly moist in winter, depending on where they are kept. A suitable compost is that recommended for a Desert Cacti, with the exception of the *Aizoaceae* which are better with rather more grit, up to 50%. They all need the maximum amount of sunlight, particularly the *Aizoaceae*, which are not really suitable as house plants, but need the sunniest part of the greenhouse. A minimum winter temperature of 41°F (5°C) is adequate for most succulents although the stapelias and other *Asclepiadaceae* appreciate a little more.

Raising from seed Cacti and other succulents can be raised from seed in much the same manner as any other greenhouse plants. A good seed compost should be used; either a standard or soilless. After thoroughly moistening the compost, the seeds are just scattered on the surface. The container is placed in a plastic bag to conserve moisture. A temperature of 70°–80°F (21°–27°C) is needed for germination. If a propagator is available, early spring is the best time to sow, otherwise it is necessary to wait until later when the weather warms up.

Pests and diseases Cacti and other succuments do not suffer greatly from these, if they are carefully looked after. Small cotton-wool-like patches indicate mealy bugs which can be controlled with a malathion spray (but do not use malathion on *Crassulaceae*). Brown spots on stems (particularly epiphyllums) are usually due to too low winter temperatures, too much nitrogen in the compost, or otherwise faulty cultivation. Cold, damp conditions can cause plants to rot.

25 Cacti and Other Succulents

Chamaecereus silvestri (peanut cactus) is found growing among grass and low bushes in Western Argentina. The short, prostrate stems are freely branching, and covered with short, stiff white spines. The stems are pale green in winter, but turn violet in the hot sun. The furry brown buds open in May or June to large scarlet flowers. This cactus is hardy if kept dry, and may be wintered in an unheated cold frame in milder areas. Propagation is particularly easy by removing branches and rooting them.

Cleistocactus strausii from Bolivia, forms a tall, silvery column, which may reach a height of 5 ft. With age it branches from the base. The stems are covered with short white spines. Old specimens will flower; the narrow flowers are red and are formed at the top of the stem. However, if confined to a pot it will be many years before this plant becomes too large.

Echinocactus grusonii (golden barrel cactus) comes from the deserts of central Mexico. Young seedlings have tubercles which carry stout golden spines. As the plant gets larger the tubercles merge into ribs. Mature specimens of this cactus are about a yard across, but are very ancient as it takes about ten years for a specimen in cultivation to make a diameter of 6 in. The small yellow flowers are seldom produced under home conditions due to poor light intensity.

Echinocereus knippelianus is native to Mexico. The dark green, almost globular stem is about 2 in. across. It is divided by five ribs which carry weak, white spines. The pink flowers are produced profusely in May. This is a slow-growing plant and should be watered with care. Like most echinocereus, it is hardy in mild areas of the country if kept dry.

Echinocereus pectinatus is found growing in central Mexico. It has a thick stem about 3 in. in diameter, branching from the base, and covered very neatly with short white spines, arranged in a comb-like pattern. The pink flowers are 3–4 in. across and in some specimens are sweetly scented. The flowering period is about June. This is a slow growing cactus which is hardy in

Facing page: Echinocereus knippelianus, a cactus from Mexico. *Below left: Echinocactus grusonii*, the golden barrel cactus. *Above: Cleistocactus strausii*, an easily grown cactus from Bolivia. *Below:* One of the many beautiful epiphyllum hybrids. These are available in a good color range and often make large plants

winter where winters are less severe if kept dry; it needs particularly good drainage.

Echinopsis rhodotricha from Argentina, is an oval plant which in the wild can reach a height of 32 in. In cultivation it will flower when 6 in. high; the long-tubed, white fragrant flowers are about 6 in. long and 3 in. across. They are produced freely during the summer. They open in the evening. The stem is dark green, divided into ribs with stout brown spines. This is a fast growing plant and is hardy where winters are milder if kept dry. The best known is *E. eyrieseii*, but most specimens on the market are probably hybrids.

Echinopsis 'Golden Dream' is a *Lobivia × Echinopsis* hybrid, a vigorous and hardy plant. It has a globular plant body, up to 6 in. across, divided into ribs with short brownish spines. Offsets form around the base. The golden-yellow flowers appear in summer; they have long tubes and are 2 to 3 in. across and slightly scented.

Epiphyllum hybrids are examples of the 'jungle' type of cactus. They make largish plants with strap-like stems, often 2 or 3 ft. long. The flowers are 3 or 4 in. across, and appear on the edges of the stems, usually opening in the evening. Various un-named red hybrids are common; among the named specimens are 'Appeal' (red), 'Bliss' (orange),

Hamatocactus setispinus

'Cooperi' (white and scented), 'Exotique' (purplish), 'Gloria' (orange-red) and 'Sunburst' (orange).

Ferocactus acanthodes from southern California makes a cylindrical plant about 9 ft. high and 3 ft. across in nature. But such plants are very old. Seedlings and young plants make delightful pot plants; they are globular and have bright red spines, but are unlikely to reach flowering size in cultivation. The flowers, when produced are yellow and small for such a large plant, about 2 in. across.

Gymnocalycium bruchii is a miniature cactus from Argentina which eventually clusters from the base. The globular plant body is divided by twelve ribs, bearing neat white spines, covering the plant. The pale pink flowers open in May; these are over 1 in. long, and since the flowering plant may be less than 1 in. across, it often cannot be seen for flowers. This is a very easy plant to grow and flower.

Gymnocalycium baldianum is sometimes incorrectly named as *G. venturianum*. This native of Uruguay forms a plant body 3 in. across; it has nine ribs with yellowish spines. Old specimens form offsets. The flowers, produced in May, are usually deep red but occasionally specimens are found with beautiful intense pink flowers.

Gymnocalycium platense, a native of Argentina, is a globular plant, eventually 3 in. or more in diameter. The plant body is grayish-green and is divided into twelve or fourteen ribs. These carry short whitish spines. White flowers are freely produced in early summer. This is a very hardy, easily grown plant.

Hamatocactus setispinus is native to Mexico and southern Texas. It is a globular plant which can be as much as 5 in. across. Very old specimens cluster from the base. The stem is dark green and divided into thirteen ribs. The large satiny flowers are borne on top of the plant continuously through the summer. The petals are deep yellow with a red base. Again a very easy plant to grow and flower.

Lobivia jajoiana grows in Argentina at altitudes of up to 10,000 ft. It is a cylindrical cactus, slow-growing, 2 or 3 in. thick forming a few offsets. The plant body is dark green. The spines on the new growth are red but fade to brownish with age. The deep red flowers open during the summer; they are red with an almost black throat.

Mammillaria craigii is a native of Mexico. It is a globular plant, branching with age. Like all mammillarias, the plant body is covered with small protuberances (tubercles). These have yellowish-brown spines on their tips. The small, deep pink bell-like flowers form a circle around the top of the plant in spring.

Mammillaria spinosissima is a Mexican plant. It is very variable; the spines may be white, yellow, brown or red. One of the most attractive forms is the variety *sanguinea*, with red-tipped spines. The cylindrical stem is dark green; it may remain solitary, or cluster. The purplish-red flowers open during the summer, and may be followed by bright red berries.

Mammillaria prolifera is a widely distributed cactus, found in Texas, the West Indies and Mexico. It clusters freely, forming a 'cushion' of small heads about 1 in. across, covered with fine white spines. Creamy flowers appear in late spring and are often followed by orange-red berries, which are said to taste like strawberries. The heads are knocked off very easily, so the plant must be handled carefully.

Notocactus haselbergii grows wild in southern Brazil. It forms a silvery ball, about 4 in. across, covered with fine white spines. The tomato-red flowers are carried on top of the plant in early summer. This is a hardy cactus, easy to grow, but does not flower as a seedling. Flowering-size plants are about 2½ in. across.

Notocactus mammulosus, a native of Uruguay and Argentina, forms a large, globular plant, with stout yellowish spines. With age it forms offsets from the base. White, woolly buds appear at the top of the plant and open to golden-yellow flowers in early summer. It flowers profusely and will put up with cool conditions. The flowers are self-fertile and large quantities of dark brown seeds are formed.

Opuntia microdasys is a Mexican plant, and to keep it unmarked, the winter temperature should be at least 45°F (7°C). It has flat stem segments (or pads) up to about 6 in. long. These are dotted with little collections of fine barbed hairs (glochids), which may be white, yellow or dark reddish-brown, depending on the variety. These glochids (characteristic of the opuntias) can irritate the skin. This cactus is grown for the beauty of its form and rarely flowers as a pot-plant. Given a free root run in a greenhouse bed, it produces yellow flowers in May.

Opuntia basilaris spreads from northern Mexico to the southern U.S.A. It has pads about 8 in. long of a beautiful bluish color, dotted with collections of dark brown glochids. Branches form from the base, producing a large clump. The flowers are red, but it rarely flowers as a pot plant. There is a particularly beautiful variety, *cordata*, with heart-shaped, bluish-purple pads. This mostly branches from the base and remains one or two pads high.

Rebutia calliantha var. Krainziana is an example of the compact, very free-flowering South American rebutias. It will bloom when only 1 in. across. The globular stems are dark green, neatly covered with short white spines. The large orange flowers are produced in rings around the base of the plant in May. This is one of the easiest of the small cacti to flower and quite an old plant will only fill a 4-in. pot, but will be covered with flowers.

Rebutia miniscula var. violaciflora, from Argentina, is found growing about 10,000 ft. above sea level. It is a small clustering plant, and will flower when about 1 in. across. It is a light green in color with short ginger spines. The intense magenta pink flowers are produced from the base of the plant in April and May. They are self-fertile, and if left undisturbed, the plant will eventually be surrounded by dozens of little self-sown seedlings.

Above: Euphorbia beaumieriana, a spiny, cactus-like succulent, from Morocco.
In its native habitat it may reach 6 ft. in height; in cultivation it is much smaller

Rhipsalidopsis rosea is an epiphyte from the forests of southern Brazil. It is a small shrub about 9 in. high, consisting of dozens of stem segments about 1 in. long, with short bristles at the ends. The stems vary from green to dark red. The pale pink, bell-shaped flowers, about 1 in. across, cover the plant during May. After flowering the plant will look shrivelled, but after a few weeks it will come into growth again.

Schlumbergera 'Konigers Weihnachts-freude' is one of the many schlumbergera hybrids flowering in the winter which are often called Christmas cactus. It is an epiphyte and forms a shrub, becoming pendent with age, and can reach massive proportions if not broken up and re-started. The glossy green stem segments are up to about $1\frac{1}{2}$ in. long. The intense cerise-pink flowers cover the plant in the winter months, but not necessarily at Christmas. The common Christmas cactus, formerly known as *Zygocactus truncatus*, is very similar. It is now correctly called *Schlumbergera* 'Buckleyi', though still often listed under *Zygocactus*.

Right: Ferocactus acanthodes, a colorful cactus from California, has bright red spines
Below: Glottiphyllum arrectum, a succulent from Cape Province, has large golden-yellow flowers in the fall

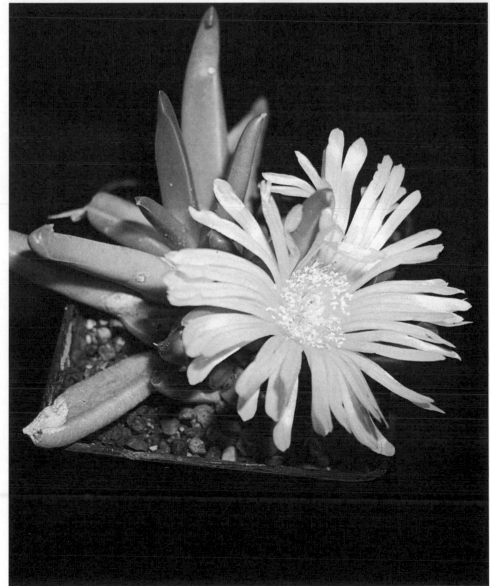

Other Succulent Plants

Aeonium domesticum (*Crassulaceae*) The aeoniums are native to the Canary Islands and are almost hardy. Beautiful specimens of these small shrubs may be found in dry warm areas of the country. *A. domesticum* has almost circular leaves covered with fine hairs; the yellow flowers are produced in summer. Aeoniums may be grown permanently as pot plants or planted out in a rock garden for the summer, and repotted and stored under the greenhouse staging in winter.

Agave filifera (*Agavaceae*), a native of Mexico, is one of the smaller growing agaves suitable for pot cultivation. It forms a rosette about 2 ft. across, consisting of long, narrow dark green leaves, with white threads along the edges. Agaves only flower when old, and the flowering rosette dies. But new ones are formed at the base of the old plant. The flower stem is over 6 ft. high and the flowers are greenish.

Agave parviflora (*Agavaceae*) is a rare plant in the wild, found in a few localities in southern Arizona and Mexico only. It forms a rosette about 8 in. in diameter, ideal for a pot plant. The dark green leaves have white markings and marginal threads. The flower spike is about 3 ft. high and the flowers are reddish. New rosettes are formed at the base of the old plant after flowering.

Aloe jucunda (*Liliaceae*) is a miniature aloe, native to Somalia. The small, flat rosettes are about 4 in. across and the bright green leaves have attractive white spots, and small teeth along their edges. The pink flowers, carried on a long stem, open in spring. This aloe clusters freely and the indi-

Left: The pale pink flowers of
Gymnocalycium bruchii
Above: The flat stem segments, known as
'pads', of *Opuntia microdasys*
Above right: The lithops, South African
succulents, closely resemble stones and are
often referred to as 'pebble plants'
Right: The Christmas cactus,
Schlumbergera 'Buckleyi', long known as
Zygocactus truncatus, produces its
cerise flowers in winter
Far right: One of the easiest cacti to
induce to flower is *Rebutia calliantha
krainziana*

vidual heads can be used to start new plants.
Aloe variegata (*Liliaceae*) (partridge-breasted aloe) a native of Cape Province, South Africa, forms a stemless rosette, about 1 ft. high; the dark green leaves have attractive white markings. The plant produces many offsets which are attached to the parent plant by underground stems. The small, orange, bell-shaped flowers are carried on a stout stem in March.

Caralluma europaea (*Asclepiadaceae*) is found around part of the Mediterranean coast, and also in South Africa. The thick leafless stems are grayish-green. This is a summer growing plant and the tiny flowers are stemless and produced in clusters. They are yellowish with brownish markings. The seeds are carried in long horn-shaped pods.

Conophytum flavum (*Aizoaceae*) comes from South Africa. The small plant bodies are green and rounded, freely clustering. The bright yellow flowers are usually produced in September or October, when they open in the afternoon. The plant should be watered when the old leaves have shrivelled, usually about August, and watering should be continued until November.

Conophytum salmonicolor (*Aizoaceae*) is a native of Namaqualand, South Africa. The green plant body is about 1½ in. high and consists of a pair of united leaves. The plant clusters quite readily, and with age, a woody stem becomes evident. Its apricot-colored flowers appear early in June. It should be watered when the old leaves have shrivelled (usually around the end of June) until the end of October.

Crassula falcata (*Crassulaceae*) spreads from Cape Province to Natal in South Africa. Because of its striking red flowers, it is a popular florist's plant. It is large, growing to about 1 ft., with bluish-gray leaves. The scarlet flowers are carried on a stout stem. It can be propagated from leaf cuttings.

Crassula teres (*Crassulaceae*) is a miniature plant from South-West Africa. The broad leaves are closely packed around the stem to form a short column. With age the plant clusters to form attractive groups. The tiny white flowers are stemless. It should be grown in a very open compost, placed in a sunny position and not over watered.

Duvalia radiata (*Asclepiadaceae*) is a smallish plant from Africa. The short, thick stem are prostrate and without leaves. The reddish-brown flowers are small and fleshy, but the horn-shaped seed pods are large and packed with numerous seeds, attached to tiny 'parachutes'. The growing and flowering period is summer.

Echeveria derenbergii (*Crassulaceae*) (the painted lady) is a dwarf plant from Mexico. It forms an almost stemless rosette about 3 in. across, which is soon surrounded by numerous off-sets. The leaves are plump and pale green with a white waxy coating. The reddish-yellow flowers open in the spring.

Echeveria hoveyi (*Crassulaceae*) from Mexico, forms a short-stemmed loose rosette which soon produces side shoots, making an attractive cluster. The long leaves are gray-green with pink and cream stripes. The coloring varies with the seasons; it is at its

most vivid in the spring. Full sun and not too much water help to maintain a good color.

Euphorbia aggregata (*Euphorbiaceae*) from Cape Province, is a shrub about 1 ft. high. It is a freely branching plant which soon clusters. The leafless stems are over 1 in. thick. The insignificant flowers are carried on thorn-like stalks which persist long after the flowers have died. This gives the whole plant a 'spiny' appearance, rather like a clustering cactus. The growing period is summer.

Euphorbia beaumieriana (*Euphorbiaceae*) comes from Morocco, where it can reach a height of 6 ft. It is, however much smaller in pots in collections. It is a cactus-like plant with ribs and spines. Like all euphorbias, it has milky sap, painful or even dangerous in the mouth or eyes.

Euphorbia obesa (*Euphorbiaceae*) is one of the more unusual plants from Cape Province, and is protected by the South African

Haworthia limifolia, a South
African succulent

government. It consists of a single spherical or slightly cylindrical stem, about 4 in. across, without leaves and reddish brown in color. It is divided into blunt ribs. The small, stemless yellow flowers appear all the summer; they are sweetly scented. The male and female flowers are carried on separate plants.

Faucaria tuberculosa (*Aizoaceae*) is native to South Africa. Very young plants are stemless, but with age, a woody stem is formed. When this stem becomes too obvious the plant should be re-started from cuttings, leaving a small piece of stem to each rosette. The thick triangular dark green leaves have small teeth along their edges and small knobbly protuberances on the upper surface; they are about $\frac{3}{4}$ in. long. Golden flowers are produced in the fall. The plant should be kept slightly moist throughout the year.

Gasteria maculata (*Liliaceae*) is a South African plant with long tongue-shaped leaves arranged in two rows. These are dark green in color, with white markings. Off-sets are produced by the plant, and these can be left to form a group, or removed and potted up individually. The reddish flowers are carried on a long slender stem.

Glottiphyllum arrectum (*Aizoaceae*) is from Cape Province, South Africa. The soft, tongue-like leaves are bright green in color and about 2 in. long. Young plants are almost stemless, but with age a woody stem appears. It is then best to cut up the clump, keeping a small piece of stem to each head. The large flowers are golden-yellow and almost hide

the plant's body in September and October. This plant has a short growing period and should only be watered from the beginning of July to the end of October.

Haworthia limifolia (*Liliaceae*) grows wild in South Africa. The stemless rosettes are about 4 in. across and consist of very dark green triangular leaves with ridges running across them. The plant forms many off-sets, attached to the main stem by underground runners. The tiny white flowers are shaped like narrow bells and are produced on a very long, slender flower stem in summer.

Lithops alpina (*Aizoaceae*) is one of the pebble plants. This little native of the Karroo, South Africa, closely resembles the stones among which it grows. The conical body is composed of one pair of stemless leaves with a fissure between them. These leaves are pale brown with dark brown markings. The bright yellow flowers appear from the fissure between the leaves, usually in June. Lithops are summer growing plants and should not be watered until the old pair of leaves has completely withered. The growing period is usually between April and September; the rest of the year the plants should be kept dry. The plant gradually clusters, forming a clump.

Lithops marmorata (*Aizoaceae*) is very similar to the above. The leaves are grayish-green with pale gray markings. The white flowers open in September.

Pleiospilos bolusii (*Aizoaceae*), from Cape Province, South Africa, is another of the mimicry plants, the thick, triangular leaves looking like pieces of granite. There is one

pair of thick purplish-green leaves, dotted with green. Old plants have woody stems, but younger plants are almost stemless. When the stem is obvious, it may be cut at about $\frac{1}{4}$ in. from the leaves and the plant re-started. The growing period is from late summer to autumn and the plant should be kept dry until the old pair of leaves has shrivelled completely. The large golden flowers open in October.

Sedum hintonii (*Crassulaceae*), like many of the beautiful tender sedums, comes from Mexico. It is a fairly recent discovery and consists of low rosettes, rapidly clustering. The furry leaves are egg-shaped and bluish gray in color. The white flowers appear in the winter, and, although an easy plant to grow in summer, it is very prone to rot in the flowering period. It should not be watered at this time, and if possible should be wintered in the dry atmosphere of a room.

Stapelia hirsuta (*Asclepiadaceae*), a typical 'carrion plant' is found growing in Cape Province, South Africa. The thick velvety stems are leafless and about 9 in. high. This is a summer growing plant and the large flowers start to appear about mid-summer. These are five-petalled, yellowish and densely covered with brownish hairs. Although these flowers have little odor to us, they are most attractive to flies, which may lay their eggs in them. The maggots hatch out and promptly die, for although the flowers may look like carrion, the larvae cannot live on them. In nature, attracted by the odor, the flies cause pollination of the flowers. The seed pods are large and horn shaped.

The first of January may be the start of the Roman calendar year, but as far as gardening is concerned it is only the beginning of the end, spring being more commonly regarded as the start for gardeners. However, in January in favored areas some plants begin to flower, snow-drops, winter aconites and winter heliotrope with its delicious fragrance; others such as Christmas roses, winter jasmine and witch-hazel may also provide some flower.

A wander round the garden on a sunny January day will point to seasonal jobs, in spite of its still being the close season for most plants. Bud pecking by birds, particularly of ornamental cherries, may be in full swing; one of the repellent sprays will help in milder areas. Supporting stakes and ties of shrubs and trees may be re-newed; snow should be shaken off branches, if possible, before they break; shelter and protec-tion of small or tender plants may need strength-ening. This is one of the worst times of the year for bark stripping by rabbits and mice, particu-larly in snowy weather, so make sure all is well. You can still plant woody specimens (shrubs and trees)where winters are less severe, when the soil is friable and crumbly, but not too cold nor too wet.

Borders can still be mulched. If you are a chrysanthemum fan, cuttings of winter flowering varieties need taking now, and of course will need some heat, in a propagating frame in the green-house; carnation cuttings can be put in as well. Bulbs for forcing, including tulips, hyacinths and narcissi that have been placed in the root cellar or plunged outside, may be brought inside at regular intervals.

Keep the greenhouse temperature up, the atmosphere not too damp, and ventilate slightly, even in severe cold; clean out rigorously all fallen vegetation, as botrytis (gray mold) thrives on this and is at its worst in cold, damp conditions.

But mostly the ornamental garden can be left to look after itself at this time of the year, and one can sit back in a comfortable chair by the fire and indulge one's self in dreams of sheets of color, from perfectly grown plants, superbly blended and covering every inch of the ground. Seed for this spectacle should be ordered now from the new catalogs. Annuals, biennials and bedding plants can all be ordered; some of the more easily grown annuals for quick display are echium, godetia, calendula, (pot marigold), limnanthes annual chrysanthemum, cornflower, nigella (love-in-a-mist), night-scented stock, forget-me-not, nasturtium, larkspur and a variety of ornamental grasses, for sewing in later in spring. Biennials for May and June sowing are foxgloves (the modern hybrids are delightful), sweet Williams, Canterbury bells and wallflowers (all good home garden plants). Pansies, honesty, sweet rocket and clary can be added, and a really striking and handsome plant is the mullein called *Verbascum bombyciferum*, with a rosette of great soft furry gray leaves, and a 5 or 6 ft. spire of white woolly buds unfolding to produce pale yellow flowers.

Left: Clematis 'Ville de Lyon' and 'Perle d'Azur'; hard prune in January or February

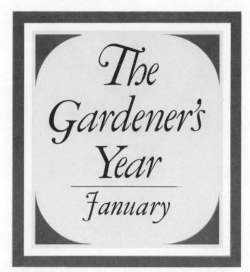

The Gardener's Year — January

The bedding plants can be started in February from seed–petunias, nemesias, ageratums, bed-ding dahlias, impatiens, lobelias, tobacco plants (nicotiana) and dwarf phlox are some to sow in a warm greenhouse.

Where weather conditions are favorable, apples and pears may be pruned, so can cherries and plums, provided there are no diseases about such as silver leaf or bacterial canker; otherwise the wounds are very easily infected, and such trees are best left uncut until summer. Redcurrants and gooseberries can have their summer pruning completed by cutting the remains of the year's new lateral shoots back to 2-in. stubs. Raspberry canes should be tipped and ties renewed where necessary. Dormant oil spray can be sprayed on to top fruit and soft fruit bushes to kill the over-wintering eggs of aphids and sap-suckers, spray-ing a drenching wash to run-off; it will clean off lichen and moss as well. In colder areas all these operations should be delayed until February or early March.

If peaches, almonds and nectarines are showing signs of bursting at the end of January, spray with a copper or sulfur fungicide to ward off leaf curl, again giving a drenching spray to run-off. Look for small mammal damage to bark of trunks; continue planting in suitable weather.

The vegetable front is the quietest, but even here there are jobs to be done where the ground is unfrozen. Cultivation and adding bulky organic materials such as well-rotted manure, compost and moist peatmoss, especially if you have a sandy soil, is one and, on a cold, sunny winter's day, taken easily, this is a not unpleasant task, and one finishes glowing with virtue as well as exer-tion. Dress with lime, but only if the soil is very acid and, in any case, not at the same time as the working in of the bulky organic materials; allow an interval of at least six weeks between the two.

Taking chrysanthemum cuttings

Decide on your plan of campaign for rotating your vegetable crops; this enables use to be made of all nutrients in the soil and avoids the build-up of such troubles as eelworms, clubroot, scab and so on. Rotating means what it says; every year one of three (or four) different categories of vegetables is grown on a given piece of ground; the following year those types grown on plot (A) are grown on a second piece and their place of the previous year taken by a second (B) collection. In due course the vegetables in collection (C) are grown on the original piece of ground, and so sets revolve round, using three different soil sites.

In general, vegetables for this purpose are con-sidered in the following categories: (1) brassicas such as cabbages, cauliflowers, sprouts, savoys, also lettuce, mustard and cress, and radish; (2) potatoes; (3) legumes, e.g. peas and beans; (4) root crops–carrot, turnip, parsnip, beet. Onions are left to themselves and can safely be planted in the same piece of ground for many years, where they seem to do better than if moved about. If there is not much space they can, however, be grown with the roots and legumes.

In a rotation, potatoes can be followed the next season by the roots and legumes, and they in turn are succeeded by the leaf crops, brassicas and salads.

There is no need to manure before planting potatoes, since the ground will have been dressed early the previous winter for the brassicas which will have just preceded the potatoes; it is, how-ever, a good idea in most instances to mix in a general compound powder fertilizer a week or so before putting out the sets. After the potatoes have been lifted, manure can be applied in the fall where peas and beans are to go in spring, but for the root crops potash only need be given, and that a few weeks before sowing or planting. For both again, a general fertilizer shortly before sowing or planting is advisable.

Tipping raspberry canes

In the third winter, compost or manure can be given before the brassicas, and by this time lime may also be necessary, allowing an interval of about two months between the two dressings. Since the leaf crops have such a large area of top growth, an application of a nitrogenous fertilizer while growing is advisable.

Tidying up vegetable debris, such as old Brussels sprout plants and cabbage tops is very necessary to keep pests and diseases at bay. Some vegetables can be sown in heat in the greenhouse: these include tomatoes, carrots, onions, leeks, radishes and bush beans, in a temperature of 60°F (15–16°C).

A fickle month which in many areas have cold weather to vie with that of January, but with warmer spells to show that spring is around the corner. But the days have steadily begun to lengthen, and the extra light—and sometimes warmth—will start plants into growth towards the end of the month in milder areas. Lawns may need topping, no more, on a mild day when the soil is not waterlogged or frozen. If it is very wet, spiking to a 4-in. depth with a garden fork is better treatment for the turf, and gives the grass roots a chance to breathe; later in the month worm casts may need sweeping off with a stiff broom.

In the south roses showing signs of breaking into leaf should be pruned quickly before they do; this applies of course to the hybrid teas and floribundas, and those climbers not yet cut back. Clematis, similarly, may actually be bursting. The early summer flowering varieties should be tipped back only, the late summer flowering kinds need cutting back hard to leave 3, 4 or 5 ft. of growth from ground level. They grow exceedingly vigorously in the next four months and such hybrids as the blue-purple *C. jackmanii*, pink 'Hagley Hybrid', 'Etoile Violette' and white 'Huldine' relish such harsh treatment and reward it with an abundance of flower. Further north these tasks must wait until March or early April. As in January, keep a vigilant eye open for bud-pecking, wind-rocking, bark-stripping and unsteady shrub and trees supports. After gales stakes and ties may need to be renewed, especially in exposed gardens. Be sure to firm the soil round wind-rocked plants.

Now is a good time to start repotting some of the permanent greenhouse plants. Included here are Ficus, Dracaena and Dieffenbachia. Use a standard compost and make sure that the new containers have been thoroughly cleaned.

Before the season really begins, a quick review of last year's pests and diseases will help in the battle against them this year. It is more than likely that some of the following will have appeared in the garden somewhere: white powdery mildew on roses, apple trees, chrysanthemums and herbaceous plants generally, gray mold throughout, rose black spot, scab on apples and pears, cankers on apple and rose shoots and branches, aphids on practically everything, caterpillars of various sorts, earwigs, red spider mite, and sooty mold where aphids have been feeding.

If so be prepared well in advance with such remedies as derris, malathion, BHC and trichlorphon insecticides, and benomyl, captan, dinocap, sulfur and copper for fungi. Spray with the appropriate deterrent as soon as leaves unfold, if there was trouble last season, otherwise leave the plants alone but keep a vigilant eye on them.

Very cold spells are another seasonal dismay, and the temperature may fall, quite unexpectedly, so listen to weather forecasts, follow your own knowledge and experience of local weather conditions, and prepare to increase the greenhouse heat accordingly. Many precious plants are lost by just one night's severe cold. But, unless this kind of Arctic climate is expected, always ventilate the greenhouse, so that gray mold does not ravage the plants and be ready to spray if troubles appear.

At this time of the year the greenhouse can be very colorful, with cinerarias and freesias in full spate, lachenalias, crocus, narcissus and hyacinths brought on early, haemanthus and hippeastrum joining them, and some of the shrubs, camellias, jasmine, boronia, browallia, abutilon and the shrimp plant (beloperone), and azaleas still just

The Gardener's Year
February

in flower. Primulas such as *P. obconica, kewensis* and *malacoides* will be in flower and are charming, especially the Kew hybrid, in lemon yellow, with grayish-white leaves; it is fragrant as well. Many of these plants may be brought into the living room while they are in flower and returned to the greenhouse once their flowers are over.

Begonia, achimenes, dahlia and gloxinia (sinningia) corms and tubers will all start to produce shoots if put into a bed of moist peatmoss. Another pleasant job for a dull February day is pruning many of the shrubby plants, for instance fuchsias, preparatory to topdressing or re-potting next month just as growth is starting. Flower seeds to sow are ageratum, impatiens, cobaea, canna, celosia, nemesia and petunia, in fact all sorts of half-hardy bedding plants for out of doors so that they can be brought on early and planted out at the end of May. Give them a temperature of 60°–70°F (16°–21°C); a propagating frame

Cineraria

Freesias

Chitting potatoes

which can be heated will be needed if the greenhouse is a cool one. Sweet peas may be sown for planting out later in the spring.

Hippeastrums, vallotas, clivias and lilies are some bulbs which can be started now, by watering a little and providing a little heat, to 50°F (10°C) or so. Watering of cyclamen, on the other hand, can be stopped, as flowers will have faded, the leaves will have fed the corms, and finished their useful life, and the plants can be gradually dried off and rested under the staging. More chrysanthemums can be footed from cuttings—the early-flowering kinds this month, as well as the winter ones, and so can perpetual flowering carnations.

Vegetables are an essential constituent of diet; home-grown ones are much better than store sold (or soiled) ones for flavor and nutrient content, crispness and general deliciousness. Where winters are less severe, sowing vegetable seed now will give crops much earlier than usual; for instance, bush beans, Brussels sprouts, cucumbers, carrots, radishes, tomatoes, leeks and lettuces, cauliflowers and fava beans will all germinate well in a temperature of 60°F (16°C) and more. Unusual vegetables are well worth considering; for instance celeriac seed can be sown inside, and Jerusalem artichokes and garlic can be planted in sheltered places and early gardens.

In milder areas, parsnips which have been left in the ground, as good a way of keeping them as any, will not remain dormant any longer, and should be lifted and stored in dry sand before they start to grow again. Seed potatoes can be chitted, that is, put in single layers in shallow boxes in a light, frost-proof shed, so that the eyes start to sprout; the heel should be uppermost. Early varieties will then be ready for planting out in March in mild gardens.

Good vegetables must be grown well—they will not tolerate poor soil. A steady supply of moisture, as well as nutrients, is always necessary, otherwise they will not grow or will bolt. So, manuring and digging operations should be completed as soon as weather conditions permit.

If one's stomach rules one's gardening, then fruit growing is another branch which will take up a good deal of time. Pruning of apples and pears (where weather conditions allow) should finish this month; spraying with dormant oil spray is still possible; peaches and allied fruits may need protective spraying against leaf curl, with lime-sulfur or a copper fungicide, timing the application for just on bud burst.

Red raspberries can still be tipped and fall fruiting kinds should have the old canes cut right out. Gooseberry and red currant pruning should be completed.

Clematis

Spring arrives officially this month, on the 21st, and by then the garden will be well on the way to a new season. The earliest shrubs will have started to bloom, *Mahonia japonica* with its bright yellow spikes of strongly scented flowers, *Daphne mezereum*, equally strongly scented but purplish-pink in flower, camellias, japonica, and that curious but attractively flowered shrub, *Corylopsis spicata*, in pale yellow, and acid-soil loving. These and other shrubs can be given a fertilizer dressing this month, watered in if the soil is dry; so, too, can herbaceous perennials, making the dressing relatively high in potash content if flowering is not all it might be. Rooted layers from shrubs can be detached and put in their permanent positions. Division of the border plants can also be undertaken successfully. Rose pruning will be in full swing; clematis pruning started last month should be finished by the middle of this one in milder parts of the country.

The Gardener's Year
March

hour of glory. A sunny, airy alpine house in the spring can be most colorful, and alpine plant cultivation one of the most satisfying and rewarding occupations. It needs a good deal of experience in gardening, on the whole; very well-drained composts are essential, and constant attention for most of the year. Small plants like these will be examined closely and need to be in first-class growth and flowering to be effective, so attention to detail is another 'must'. Some of the most easily grown and colorful plants for alpine houses, blooming in spring, are: the miniature narcissi, tulip species, scillas, *Aquilegia caerulea*, *Cyclamen orbiculatum*, *Anemone apennina*, grape hyacinths, primulas in variety, *Pulsatilla vulgaris* (the Pasque flower), iberis, *Gentiana acaulis*, and *Ramonda pyrenaica*.

In some parts of the country it is possible to sow seeds of herbs out of doors this month, but if the garden is a chilly one or the soil heavy, it is

Below: Protecting a newly-planted conifer with burlap
Center, above: Preparing and rooting dahlia cuttings

Below: Pans of colorful alpine plants
Center, below: Dividing a clump of herbaceous perennials

Evergreens can be planted this month, watered in well at the time of planting, and put in when the soil is moist. If in a windy position, give a temporary shelter of burlap or polyethelene, while they establish, as wind is one of the main causes of browning of foliage, particularly conifers. Moisture vapor is literally blown off the surface of the leaf, and the roots do not replace this until they take hold of the soil. If dry weather follows planting, spraying overhead with a drenching spray of clear water once or twice a day will do much to mitigate the effects of desiccation. Where winters are severe, delay the planting of evergreens until April.

Lawns can be given a spring clean, by first raking (provided there is no moss), then topping with razor-sharp mower blades, and following with spiking and the first feed. Where there is moss, spring is a good time to treat it with lawn sand, but a more long-lasting remedy is to improve the soil drainage or plant food content, so that the grass always grows strongly.

Lots of annuals can be grown out of doors, but do not be tempted too early in the month, and in cold gardens next month will be soon enough. Three or four very warm, sunny days often occur in March, deceiving one into thinking summer is on the way, but are followed by cold wet weather, when seeds rot in the ground. Annuals sown in patches, with some thought to color blending, are highly satisfactory; for instance; one might have all the blues, purples, lavenders and pinks together; or a patch of different shades of yellow.

The corms and tubers started into growth last

month in the greenhouse will be ready for potting; dahlias can have cuttings taken from them. Rooted chrysanthemum and carnation cuttings will need potting in 3-in. pots; pelargoniums rooted from fall cuttings will be growing and may need potting on. All sorts of pot plants can be turned out of their pots, the old compost removed, and replaced with fresh or, if they do not like root disturbance, the top 1½ in. can be scraped off and replaced with a topdressing.

Last month's seed sowings will need pricking out into flats 2 in. apart each way; the plastic seed trays seem to give earlier and stronger growth. If the seedlings can be moved with the rounded root tip intact, they will 'take' practically without a check; try not to leave them too long in the flats. Once past a certain stage in their growth, even if pricked out they will never make good plants—they should be moved as soon as they are large enough to handle.

Tomatoes sown last month can be pricked out when the first true leaf shows, burying the stem so that the seed leaves are just above the soil surface. They will need warmth of at least 50°F (10°C) to keep them growing on; a check to growth either by cold or drought is disastrous at this stage, or when they are young plants. The sweet peas sown last month can be hardened off ready for planting out.

If alpine plants occupy a large part of the greenhouse, this and next month will be their

better to sow in the greenhouse. Parsley is always said to be slow to germinate, but in warm soil it comes up just as quickly as the other herbs, and an out-of-doors sowing of it in April will produce more plants in the long run than a March one. Dill, coriander, sorrel, chives, sage, sweet marjoram and summer savory all germinate easily.

Parsnip can be sown this month; it is very hardy and needs a good long season to develop. Most of the rest of the vegetables, summer spinach, broccoli, spinach beet, sprouts, cabbage, cauliflower, early carrots, leeks, onions, lettuce, peas, radish and spinach beet can be sown outside later this month, but sowing must be delayed until April in colder gardens. Celery, celeriac, cucumbers, melons and more tomatoes can be sown in heat in the north.

Preparation of the soil for seed sowing will be the same as for annuals, broken down and raked to a crumb structure, and fed about 10 days before sowing. Seed is sown when conditions are moist, as warm as possible and preferably when rain is expected. Lining the drills with moist peatmoss, or sieved compost helps germination and subsequent growth in difficult soils and poor weather. Maincrop potatoes should be put to sprout.

From vegetables to fruit, bud pecking of gooseberries and red currants must still be watched for, as it is easy to lose an entire potential crop at this stage as a result of bullfinch attacks. Spur blight of raspberries is a particularly deadly fungus disease, which reduces production of new growth, and depletes fruiting of the older canes. Spray with lime sulfur or captan to control this, if present, as the canes begin to shoot. Strawberries should be cleared of dead leaves, accumulated during winter.

The traditional sunshine and showers of April, and rising temperature, bring the garden to life with a vengeance; time is at a premium. The spring-flowering perennials begin to color the border, blue lungwort with its white-spotted leaves; primroses and polyanthus, aquilegias in early gardens, aubrieta, alyssum, the Pasque

Below: Prick out seedlings carefully
Center: Spring tulips in variety

The Gardener's Year
April

next October onwards. Primula seed for next winter's display should be sown this month in carefully prepared, well-drained compost.

The vegetable seeds sown last month in heat, such as celery, cucumber, squash, eggplant and peppers, will need pricking out or potting. In the north, pole beans can be sown inside for May

Below: Remove the cloches from strawberries on sunny days to enable the flowers to be pollinated

flower, violets, brunnera, trollius and bergenia.

But the really blazing display is given by the bulbs, which have been growing away below the soil surface all through the winter and will have poked through in some places, and now burst out of their protective sheaths to unfold a rainbow of color. In many areas spring without the shining gold trumpets of daffodils is unthinkable, but there are so many other kinds that are lovely, in white, cream, combinations of white and yellow; some are double, some fragrant (the jonquils and narcissi), some with pink trumpets split into three and doubled, the 'split corona', Dutch hybrids.

Then there is the 'blue' group of bulbs, the grape hyacinths, scillas, puschkinias, and chionodoxa, with the magenta *Cyclamen orbiculatum* to blend; there is the sturdy crown imperial orange fritillary (*Fritillaria imperialis*), and the species tulips, *kaufmanniana, greigii,* and *dasystemon,* charming with their brilliant red and yellow flowers, and purple streaked leaves. St Brigid and du Caen anemones in blue, red, purple, lilac, white and pink will flower with abandon now; the yellow pheasant's eye, *Adonis vernalis,* unfolds its round yellow petals in their nest of ruffled green calyces—sometimes the 'eye' is green. *Erythronium dens-canis,* the dog's tooth violet, in rose-pink, adds itself to the scene, and the strange snake's-head fritillaries quietly unfold in grassy places. Hyacinths and leucojums (snowflakes), so like a large snowdrop, complete the parade.

There are summer and fall flowering bulbs, too and, provided there is good drainage, they will grow almost anywhere with little or no care; altogether it is rather difficult to fault the bulbs as garden plants. So make a mental note now, from what is seen in gardens, to order in time for planting in the fall; one of the arts of good gardening is to think ahead for next year.

All the annuals can be sown out of doors this month, and those that are best sown now and not earlier, can go in, nasturtiums, aster, tagetes, zinnia and salpiglossis. Border plants can be put out, pansies, sweet peas in warmer areas, montbretia, gladioli and antirrhinums can be put in their flowering positions, and annuals pricked out during the previous month in the greenhouse

can be put out and gradually hardened off.

The planting of deciduous trees and shrubs can continue. Leave evergreens until the end of the month; pruning of the late-summer kinds should be completed this month, and the very early spring and winter flowering kinds can also be tidied now. If feeding was missed last month, shrubs and perennials can still be treated, and roses can have their first feed. Spraying for rose black spot and mildew must be started, using captan, dinocap, sulfur or a systemic fungicide which gives a month's protection. Lawn cutting can start in earnest, and grass seed for new lawns can be sown now.

Weed control is a priority, either by hoeing, forking and hand removal, mulching or chemical treatment. The modern range of herbicides is wide, and includes paraquat and diquat for annual and shallow rooted weeds; selective hormone weedkillers containing 2, 4-D, 2,4,5-T or mecoprop for application to the leaves of broad-leaved weeds, and dalapon for top growth of couch and other grasses; simazine, sodium chlorate or dichlobenil for root absorption, and propachlor to stop weed seeds germinating. Lawn weeds are best treated with hormone herbicides. Whatever is used, however, read the directions first, and then follow them.

The greenhouse will be crying out for attention, to prick out seedlings into trays and boxes, to put out and harden off bedding plants and half-hardy annuals, to pot on or plant in the green-house border, chrysanthemums, carnations and pelargoniums, also tomatoes (the first three will want stopping if it has not already been done), and to pot on corms started last month. Water will be required in increasing quantities by all plants; very careful management of heating and ventilation will be necessary, with night frosts still about, even snow, and bright sun during the day alternating with showers and strong winds. Freesia seed can be sown where it is to flower, eight to a 7-in. pot or deep box, for flowering

planting out of doors and cropping in very early July. After the danger of frost is past, outdoor vegetable sowing can safely include late cabbage, maincrop carrots, lettuce, Brussels sprouts, peas, radish, savoy, spinach beet, beet, broccoli, cauliflower, globe artichoke, and all the herbs, including parsley at the end of the month, unless it is warmer than usual. Some of last month's vegetable sowing can be hardened off and planted out now, lettuce, leeks, onion and cauliflower. Chitted maincrop potatoes can be planted in milder areas. Any earlies which have already gone out may need frost protection. Asparagus beds and Jerusalem artichokes from last year can be given a general compound fertilizer.

In many areas pears, cherries and plums will blossom this month and if it can be carried out, a general aphids spray over all the fruit trees will save a lot of trouble and work later on. Apple and pear scab are fungus diseases which may defoliate the trees later in the year and will blemish the fruit with hard black spots which crack. It is important to cover both leaves and foliage with a protective covering of fungicide which should be put on at regular intervals from spring to mid-summer, but as the timing of such a spray program will vary according to the area, the advice of the local county agricultural agent or the state Agricultural Experimental agent. Captan lime sulfur, or collodial sulfur are used but directions as to sulfur-shy varieties must be heeded. A calm not windy day will result in good spray cover without browning and scorch of the leaves. McIntosh apples are extremely susceptible to scab while Baldwin apples are more resistant.

Strawberries will begin to come to life and should be weeded if not already done; red raspberries can be tied in, and both these and red currants can be mulched. If all the soft fruit is clear of weeds, a good way of keeping them down for the rest of the season is to put down straw as a thick covering. The soil will remain moist, too, except in dry summers or if very sandy or gravelly, and by the fall will be rotting in of its own accord. Moreover, it has the advantage of making picking easier and pleasanter. Peaches will have set, and may need frost protection; thinning can start towards the end of the month.

The warmth and wet of the last two months will, one hopes, have brought outdoor plants on fast, and flowering will really get under way. Border plants will shoot up and may need staking, particularly peonies. Annuals sown out of doors should be thinned. In the north, dahlia cuttings or tubers which have sprouted can be planted out at the end of the month, when frost is unlikely, also tuberous and fibrous begonias which have started into growth, with the same reservation. Gladiolus corms can be planted in sandy soil and a sunny place. Chrysanthemums may be set out, in pots, or in the soil directly, from mid May onwards, and freesias grown from seed can be placed in a shady position in late May.

The April-flowering shrubs can be pruned, especially clematis, and those flowering in early May, included will be forsythia, kerria, *Spiraea arguta, S. thunbergii* and berberis. Rhododendrons, azaleas and lilacs should be deadheaded as soon as the blooms have finished. Evergreens and tender shrubs can still be planted; hibiscus is likely to remain apparently lifeless after planting, until July. Planting of water plants can start now that the water is beginning to warm up.

Grass cutting should continue at five-day intervals, and a combined feed and weed application will do much good if applied now, when weeds are at their highest rate of growth. Lawns sown from seed last month will need topping this month.

Mulching can now be carried out. Biennials are sown this month for flowering next spring, e.g. wallflowers, Sweet Williams, Canterbury bells (*Campanula medium*)–the pink ones are unusual and pretty, and antirrhinums. Foxgloves, verbascums, pansies and polyanthus are also treated in this way.

This year's spring bedding will need clearing away, and spring-flowering bulbs can be lifted to make way for summer bedding. They are heeled in, that is, laid at an angle in a shallow trench, with the leaves exposed, but the bulbs covered with soil, to finish ripening, so that the embryo flower can form, ready for the next season. Sweet pea supporting and training, if grown as cordons, should start.

The compost heap will be growing daily; it is an essential to good gardening, and can consist of any green vegetative material, grass cuttings, weeds, soft shrub prunings, leaves and flower stems. Weeds should be pulled before they flower, otherwise the heap is likely to be full of weed seeds unkilled because of insufficient heat within the heap. A 6-in. layer of vegetation can be sprinkled with sulfate of ammonia, and the next layer dusted with lime. The heap can be built in

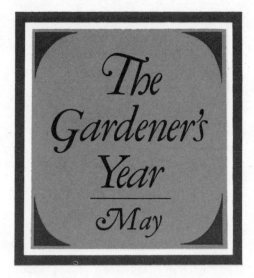

this way with lime and ammonium sulfate alternating, or calcium nitrate can be used to take both their places, at less frequent intervals. Quickly made heaps with plenty of green material in them will heat up high and fast, and kill weed seeds, fungus diseases and pests. Turning sides to middle is possible within a few weeks, and the heap can be ready to use in three months or less, but in any case not before it is dark and crumbly.

Hollyhocks are prone to rust disease and at the first sign should be sprayed with a fungicide containing benomyl. Now is also the time to spray iris with sevin against borers.

Indoors, the greenhouse will be emptying of the half-hardy bedding plants, and pricked out seedlings, but tomatoes, pelargoniums, and chrysanthemums will be coming on fast. Tomatoes sown in heat in February will have been planted or potted last month and will now need regular training and sideshooting. Pelargoniums should be stopped as soon as possible; peppers and eggplants can be sown this month, so can primulas and cinerarias.

The greenhouse may need shading this month, particularly if tomatoes, begonias and gloxinias are grown; the increasing intensity of the sun will send the temperature very high very quickly, so given plenty of air during the day, but continue to close down to some extent at night, remembering that frost is still possible. Damping down greenhouse staging, and paths in the middle of the day, will begin to be a routine task, to maintain a humid atmosphere, and discourage red spider mite. Humidity is essential for setting fruit and prevent bud drop before blooms unfold; it also prevents browning of leaf tips and leaf margins. Cactus plants should be given as hot and sunny a corner as possible; they revel in heat and light.

Where winters are colder, cucumbers, squash,

celery and melons brought on and potted last month, can go out at the end of the month, into rich, well-prepared soils, though cucumbers and melons can also be grown in the greenhouse. They will need strong supports in that case, and regular training and tying in with removal of unneeded sideshoots.

Vegetable seed sowing can continue, of beet, cucumbers, lettuce, radish, spinach, turnip, peas, pole beans and bush beans. In milder areas maincrop potatoes can be planted out and in some areas earlies will want ridging, unless grown on the flat, with a black polyethelene mulch. Weeds will need a good deal of keeping pace with, both among the vegetables and fruit, as well as ornamentals; they grow like wildfire this month. After cropping, the remains of vegetables should be cleared off before they can provide homes for pests and diseases which can infect growing vegetables. The larvae of the flies which attack onion, carrot and cabbage seedlings should be warded off with calomel dust on the soil around the plants, or trapped with baits of carrots and potato on pointed sticks.

Quickly growing vegetables, e.g. the leafy kinds, will want a feed now, or regular weekly feeding with a liquid fertilizer; remember to water if the weather is dry, or to mulch on to moist soil so that the water supply is continuous throughout the life of the vegetables. If the district is a bird ridden one, protective netting is essential, both for vegetables and soft fruit. The fruit will probably not need protection until next month, unless it already is for bud pecking, but vegetables should be guarded sometime this month.

In some areas, strawberries will be flowering and setting; frosted flowers will have blackened centers, as will those of apples. Gooseberries and (where they may be grown) black currants will generally finish setting early this month; if the flowering period is windy and cool, black-currants will 'run off', as bees will not work them in such conditions, and low temperatures inhibit pollination and fertilization. So give them a place sheltered from wind when planting, or put up a temporary barrier of burlap if the wind sets in from the north-east or south-west at flowering. There is still time to put straw on to clean ground. Spraying for aphids, caterpillars, apple sawfly and mildew should continue. If dry weather occurs towards the end of the month, irrigate the raspberries, otherwise the new crop of canes will be severely depleted. Remove any unwanted suckers from around the canes. These should be pulled away (not cut) to prevent further growths appearing.

Left: Planting gladiolus corms
Center: A selection of biennials
Below: A section through a compost heap

One of the nicest months in the garden, when the blend of color and fragrance can be enjoyed while the weather is yet relatively cool.

Plants of all sorts spill over with blossom, scent and foliage in June; shrubs come into flower thick and fast – depending on the area, kalmia, ceanothus, cytisus, berberis, escallonia, deutzia, weigela, genista, philadelphus, spiraea, lilac, viburnum and roses of all kinds.

The climbing plants begin to make walls and fences and screens brilliant with flower; they include roses, whether they are climbers of the large-flowered kind such as 'Blaze', brilliant red or the pink 'New Dawn' or ramblers of the small-flowered double 'Dorothy Perkins' kind, the tubular orange flowers of *Eccremocarpus scaber*, honeysuckle with its sweet scent, and white *Jasminum officinale*, sweeter still, and the large-flowered clematis, blue, red, purple, lavender, white and cream. All may want tying in and will need watering, particularly if they are growing up walls.

Perennials in bloom are delphiniums, campanulas, lupins, bearded iris, evening primrose, potentilla, poppies, peonies, verbascum, geranium, veronica, cimicifuga; the list is endless. But one can relax now that the first spring rush is over, and take time to wander round the garden, mark the gaps and note the plants doing badly, decide on new ones to fill them in or replace them; one sees clearly those that do not like their positions which will be the better for transplanting in the fall.

It is very important, this wandering round; it looks aimless, but in fact, the more one can do it the better. In the process a good gardener observes his plants and their reactions to his treatment and draws conclusions which result in better plants and an even more attractive interlocking of their habits of growth, color, leaf shapes and flowering. He sees the beginning of pest and disease attack, and the onset of weed infestation, the need for water, the appearance of deadheads and the over-luxuriant growth that wants pruning away.

Jobs to do, if one must, are staking border plants, pruning early summer flowering shrubs, tying or ringing sweet peas, liquid feeding annuals and bedding plants, mowing the lawn,

spraying for rose mildew, black spot, aphids and caterpillars. The last of the bedding plants should be out at the beginning of the month, together with dahlias and chrysanthemums. The latter should be stopped this month, in the first two weeks, and again at the end for second crown flowering, but if they are to flower at Christmas, stopping should be left until July.

Biennials can still be sown this month for next season's spring flowering. Watering is likely to be necessary constantly, particularly the lawn. The quick growing hedges can be given their first cut in early June, privet, *Lonicera nitida*, blackthorn and hawthorn.

Sweet peas may flower later this month, but in any case will be growing fast. They flower more prolifically if trained up supports, tied in, and their tendrils removed. Water copiously in hot weather as bud drop occurs when the soil is dry (and if they are growing on shallow soil); liquid feeding each week will help flower production.

Perhaps the plants most evocative of the summer scene are the old-fashioned shrub roses, and this month and July are the times to see them in nurseries, if they are not already in the garden. They need very little care, will be recurrent flowering with the right choice, and are exceedingly free from diseases, though they can be rather heavily smitten with aphids. They are loosely held together shrubs, of between 4 and 8 ft. tall, whose flowers range from single to very double, quartered blooms, in colors of white and yellow, pink and red to deep black-crimson, taking in red and white stripes on the

Far left: A climbing rose *Left:* Clematis. *Below left:* Rooting a soft tip shrub cutting. *Below:* Sweet peas grown on netting

way; they are mostly heavily fragrant, and have wildly romantic names; 'Belle de Crecy', 'Variegata di Bologna', 'Fantin Latour', 'Cuisse de Nymphe', 'Gloire des Mousseux', 'Tour de Malakoff', 'Zéphirine Drouhin' and 'Roseraie de l'Hay' are some of them. Deadheading is particularly effective in encouraging continuous flowering from June to October, and in some parts of the country it is even possible to pick the odd flower at Christmas.

The greenhouse will be almost too hot, but the cacti will be well suited, and so will the pelargoniums. Gloxinias, begonias, streptocarpus and achimenes must have shade, however, and frequent dampings down. Seedlings of cineraria and primula can be pricked out and potted, or sown this month, together with calceolarias. The big bulbs, hippeastrum, lily and clivia will be in flower and will need plenty of water; indeed watering will be a constant preoccupation, being necessary twice a day in really hot weather.

Soft tip cuttings of shrubs and greenhouse plants can be removed now and placed in sandy compost, three or four to a small pot, with a polyethelene bag over the top to keep the atmosphere moist and the cuttings shaded. The term 'soft' indicates that the top 3 in. of stem are used for the cutting, before the stem has time to ripen and harden.

Tomatoes which were sown in heat in February will be ripening this month under glass, and can be allowed to carry at least eight trusses before stopping, that is, breaking off the growing tip of the main stem just above a leaf. This prevents any more upward growth. Sideshooting and overhead damping should continue; if the yellow mottling of magnesium deficiency starts to show on the leaves, spray with Epsom salts at 2 oz. per gallon immediately the first faint yellowing begins to appear and repeat four or five times at two-week intervals. Cucumbers and melons growing inside will need further control of the excess sideshoots; the latter plants should be hand pollinated.

Squash can still be planted out at the beginning of this month, also outdoor tomatoes, celery, leeks, cauliflower, savoy cabbages, sprouts, broccoli, late cabbage, peppers and eggplants. Asparagus cutting should finish by mid-June in milder areas, early potatoes can be dug and maincrops will need earthing up. Vegetable seeds sown outside last month will need thinning, and more seed such as peas, lettuce, parsley, radish, summer spinach, spinach beet and shorthorn carrots can be sown outside.

The soft fruit season will start in about the middle of the month, and will continue for six weeks or so, with the earliest strawberries such as 'Earlidawn' followed by 'Darrow' and 'Catskill' and finishing with 'Jerseybelle' and 'Marlate'. Where raspberry fruit worm is troublesome, spray just prior to flowering with an insecticide containing methoxychlor. The first gooseberries may be ready at the end of the month and redcurrants will be ready for picking.

Apples and pears will be suffering the June drop at the end of June, when they thin themselves naturally; spraying for mildew and scab should continue. Also spray for apple codling moth caterpillars in mid-June, repeating 2–3 weeks later. Make sure that plums and peaches against walls do not run short of water, and finish peach thinning. Strawberry runners should be removed and the plants netted. At the end of all this, spare yourself some time to enjoy the fruits (literally) of your labors with clotted cream and sugar.

The perennial border comes into its own this month and, done well, carries a splendid display of color. With careful choice and blending of plants, however, it can be highly decorative for most of the year. The use of plants which have colored leaves, silver-gray, purple, and variegated, and using plants which are 'architectural' in form, so that their habit of growth and outline complements the flowering kinds, will make the border easy on the eye in or out of the flowering season.

Attention should be paid to the management of the soil, to provide a basis for good plants, and much of the work on this will be done in winter (see November, December). Then the choice of plants can come, and here it helps to note good plants at this time of year, in nurseries and other gardens, where one can see designs which need not necessarily be transferred complete, but can be modified to the pattern of one's own garden.

Herbaceous plants in flower are *Salvia haeflatodes*, kniphofias, hostas, day-lilies, veronicas, polemoniums, lilies, Shasta daisies, ligularias, rudbeckias, phlox, gaillardias, the blue thistle (eryngium) penstemons, and many, many others. Any high winds will mean attention to staking; thunderstorms also often beat plants down and so it is doubly important to make sure that they are securely supported. Deadheading helps the appearance of the border.

Bedding plants and half-hardy annuals, such as petunias, ageratums, fibrous begonias, nemesias, impatiens, nasturtiums, zinnias, dwarf phlox, salvias and lobelias, will be at their best in colder areas, and one begins to think they are worth the trouble of early sowing, coddling in the greenhouse in spring, pricking out, hardening off and finally planting out of doors. Sweet peas will continue to need training and layering by now. Chrysanthemums can be stopped the second time in mid-July if flowering is wanted at Christmas. They will also need disbudding every few days, as will dahlias, if really large flowers are wanted. Both will be the better for spraying to control aphids early in the month. Lawn watering should not be neglected; if no rain occurs for several days which are hot and sunny as well, start watering, as waiting until the lawn is obviously gasping for it is too late, and the grass will be irremediably weakened. Continue to mow.

Cut the fast growing hedges again, privet, *Lonicera nitida* and the thorns, also start on most of those which grow at a more normal speed, such as beech, hornbeam, euonymus, hazel, holly and pyracantha. Conifer hedges can also be cut now, such as yew, thuja, juniper, cupressus and chamaecyparis. The pruning of early summer flowering shrubs should be completed; the late summer flowering kinds can be enjoyed, such as hydrangea, hypericum, fuchsia, clematis, late honeysuckle, some philadelphus, hebe, Californian tree poppy and cistus. Wisteria can be summer pruned this month or next, cutting back sideshoots to leave five buds or leaf joints. The rock roses (helianthemums) are much the better for having straggling shoots cut back after flowering. New shrubs can be ordered this month for the fall delivery.

Hybrid tea roses should be deadheaded regularly, unless heps are wanted, and it is during this month propagation of roses by budding can start, at any time when the bark lifts easily, but not during dry weather. Continue to spray for rose black spot, mildew, aphids, red spider mite, caterpillars and thrips, especially the latter on gladiolus.

Bulbs, such as daffodils, tulips, bulbous iris,

The Gardener's Year
July

and hyacinth, can be lifted, cleaned, and stored. Biennials can still be sown, and seedlings of those sown last month should be transplanted to permanent positions or pricked out into flats. Fall flowering crocus, cyclamen, colchicum and sternbergia can be planted.

Greenhouse damping and watering are necessities; tomatoes will be ripening and feeding should continue. Primulas, cinerarias and calceolarias will need pricking out or potting on to 4-in. pots. Seeds of these can still be sown—it is not too late for flowering them next year. Freesias will want staking.

Soft tip cuttings of shrubs and perennials can be rooted in warmth, and half-ripe kinds will be rooted in a frame or cool greenhouse. Cyclamen can be retrieved from under the bench, so can Christmas cactus, watered and started into growth, and then repotted. Greenhouse plants in flower now are abutilons, achimenes, impatiens, begonias, bougainvilleas, calceolarias, *Campanula isophylla*, cannas, celosias, fuchsias, heliotropes, hoyas, ipomoeas, lantanas, lapagerias, neriums, passifloras, pelargoniums and crinums.

It is during July that the splendor of the lily is at its height; among the easiest to grow and the most magnificent is the regal lily, *Lilium regale*. Its great white trumpets, yellow-throated and centered with deep orange anthers, unfold in early July and waft a heavy fragrance over the garden. Once settled in well-drained, but not particularly fertile soil, provided it contains some leafmold, they will flower reliably every year without trouble. The Madonna lily, *L. candidum*, is another that is easily grown, and the clustered short white trumpets on stems 4 ft. tall were once seen in every cottage garden.

Right: Lilium candidum
(the Madonna lily)
Center right above: Lilium tigrinum (the tiger lily)
Center right below: Lilium martagon (the martagon lily)
Far right: Strawberry layering (above).
Tip layering a blackberry (below)

Others for this month are *L. amabile*, red; the 'Bellingham Hybrids', red, orange and yellow, with bell-shaped flowers; *L. martagon*, the Turk's-cap, in purple; *L. pardalinum*, orange and crimson; *L. tigrinum*, the orange tiger-lily and the 'Aurelian Hybrids' with such evocative names as 'Black Dragon', 'Golden Clarion', 'Green Magic', 'Limelight' and 'Pink Perfection'. All are easily grown in the soils that suit the regal lilies, except the Aurelians which mostly dislike lime in the soil and grow better in a slightly acid one. The lily fever is easily caught but not so easily lost.

In some areas, soft fruit picking will claim a good deal of time and with a deep freeze much of it can be preserved with its fresh flavor for winter; raspberries with cream or a blackcurrant pudding are particularly tasty out of season in the depths of winter. Strawberries will finish cropping this month; raspberries will come into ripening, and will finish by the end of July, and blackcurrants, redcurrants and gooseberries will also finish.

Strawberry runners should be removed as they appear, unless wanted for a fresh bed next year; pegging them down directly into the soil, if it is done early, seems to produce as good plants as the pot-grown kinds. Blackberries can be tip layered, that is the tips of new shoots are pegged down into the soil, where they will send out roots. Where melons are beginning to swell it is important that the plants are watered copiously. In some areas the first apples will be ready, such as 'Lodi', 'Melba' and 'Early McIntosh'.

Succession vegetables can be sown, lettuce, radish, parsley for winter, endive for blanching later in the fall. Winter vegetables to be planted cabbage, savoy and fall celery—the self-blanching kind will begin to be ready at the end of this month. On potatoes blight may be a trouble, particularly in warm wet seasons, so spray the foliage with Bordeaux mixture to give a protective covering before the disease infects.

Onions will be maturing and the tops should be bent down, if they are not already doing it of their own accord. Early potato lifting can finish and that of second earlies start. Herbs can be gathered and dried this month, storing for winter use. Keep the hoe going and the weeds under; if ground empties as a crop is lifted, sow a quick maturing green crop such as mustard, rape or annual vetch, to be dug in early September, before it flowers.

The Gardener's Year

August

Left: The leaves of onions bent over to hasten ripening. Onions are often stored 'roped', the withered leaves plaited together as illustrated
Right: Most chrysanthemum plants, except spray varieties, are disbudded to obtain larger blooms

Traditionally the month for vacations and merry-making, August is, in fact, one of the quieter months in the gardener's year; the production of new growth has slowed down, and the process of ripening and maturing is evident. One can relax a little and the ornamental garden can be left to itself to a large extent, merely removing dead-heads, replacing supports, and spraying for mildew. This is a fungus disease, characterized by a white powdery coating on leaves, stems and buds, and at this time can be a great nuisance on ornamentals, particularly if the soil is dry or the garden rather stuffy. Dinocap or sulfur dust, or in solution, will restrain its increase. Watch for it also on apples, roses and hedge plants.

Mowing the lawn and irrigating it continue in hot weather. Hedge cutting can continue, or start, if missed last month. Shrubs which flower this month, as well as those which started in July, are hibiscus, more hebes, ceanothus, caryopteris, ceratostigma, buddleias, species clematis and more hydrangeas.

In cooler areas heaths and heather come into their own. It is not strictly accurate to confine the color to purple as the modern hybrids and cultivars come in all shades of purple as well as pink, rose, and white, with foliage in gray, green, yellow, cream- or yellow-variegated, and red- or pink-tipped. Given an acid soil, preferably inclined to be peaty, but not fertile, heathers, once planted, will continue to be a carefree joy. Clipping the tops with shears when they have flowered, or in spring for those that bloom in late summer and fall, is virtually all that need be done. For extra plants, pull down outside shoots to ground level and cover their stems with soil. Eventually, roots will form and new plants (layers) can be detached.

A border of heathers really is a patchwork of color, and with the dwarf conifers in their equally varied foliage colors and silhouettes interspersed among them at suitable intervals, such a planting can only increase in beauty and effectiveness through the years. A heather collection could be started with the cultivars of *Calluna vulgaris*, which are in flower from August to October and later, such as 'Beoley Gold', acid yellow leaves and white flowers; 'Cuprea', copper-bronze leaves and purple flowers; rose-pink 'H. E. Beale', and purple 'Mrs Pat'; 'Silver Queen', lavender flowers and gray-white green leaves, and pink-lilac 'County Wicklow'.

Propagation of various plants by a variety of methods can continue; semi-ripe cuttings can be taken, and at the end of the month pelargonium cuttings can be started, also conifer heel cuttings, 2 in. long, placed in a cold shady frame in pure sand or a sandy compost. It is still possible to root soft cuttings, and layering may be started at the end of August. Disbudding of chrysanthemums continues, and the top bud of the outdoor ones can be secured this month. Biennials to bloom next year can be planted out.

Freesia corms for December flowering can be planted early in the month, about 2 in. deep, in pots put out of doors in a shady place. So can prepared hyacinths for Christmas, but after potting they should be put in a cool dark place for three months. *Iris reticulata* for January flowering, and winter flowering begonias, can be potted; Christmas cactus and cyclamen can be started this month, if this has not already been done. Cyclamen will have spent the last two or three months out of doors in a shady place, and can now be moved to a lighter one, watering thoroughly to start them into growth. If new compost is required, they should be repotted before watering, using a slightly acid compost, and removing all the old. The corm is replaced so that it is only half buried.

Watering and damping down of pot plants should continue, and routine tidying of fallen leaves, flowers and dying vegetation generally.

Out of doors self-blanching celery will be ready. Where winters are less severe, vegetable seeds which can still be sown outside include lettuce, radish, spinach beet, winter spinach and endive; young plants of broccoli, winter cabbage and savoys can all be put in.

Herbs are still good for picking and drying, on a warm day when the foliage is dry. Second early potatoes will be ready, and onions can be lifted and spread out in the sun in single layers in boxes to dry before storing. Vegetables and salads in season this month are pole beans, cabbage, carrots, lettuce, onion, peas, potatoes, spinach, spinach beet, squash (including courgettes), beet and garlic. Crops which have finished should be cleared out and the ground manured or not, depending on the rotation. Where broccoli, savoy,

onion and early summer lettuce are grown, manure helps.

August is the best time to clean up the soft fruit, removing the protective netting where this is temporary, as soon as the crop has been gathered. Strawberry beds that have finished fruiting and are to be retained for cropping next year should be cleaned of weeds and old foliage and given a general fertilizer.

Old fruited canes of raspberries should be cut down to soil level and removed, also poor new cane growth. The remaining new canes are tied in, and thinned if still too plentiful. Blackcurrants are pruned so as to remove most of the old fruited branches, either to the ground or to a well-placed good new shoot. Branches close to the ground should be removed, strong or not, as they only get pulled down by the weight of fruit and trampled underfoot by pickers.

Gooseberries and redcurrants can be summer pruned, that is cut back to just above the fifth leaf from the base, not counting the basal cluster of leaves, of the new growth that season. The new leading growths are allowed to remain until winter. Clean up all weeds, leave the straw mulch until the fall, and renew where the soil is showing through.

Apples and pears trained as cordons and espaliers or other formal shapes can also be summer pruned in early August, finishing the job in winter. Remove the new sideshoots back to just above the fifth good leaf, excluding the basal cluster, when the shoot has started to become firm and brown at the base, but is still green at the tip; leaders are left uncut. If pruning is done too early, it will result in secondary growth, which will use up the tree's energy unnecessarily, and will be cut back by frost, so providing an entry for disease.

Some branches may be breaking or about to break under the increasing weight of ripening fruit, and branch propping may be a necessary job. Woolly aphis may be apparent on apple trees, so spray with malathion under strong pressure, or scrub the patches with a wire brush dipped in methylated spirits if there is not too much of the pest and the trees are small.

In some areas plums will be ripening and a selection of reliable varieties are Allred, Premier, Superior Toka, Abundance, Beuty Methley and Shiro. The sour or English Morello cherry will also ripen in early August.

The Gardener's Year
September

The focus this month on work in the purely decorative part of the garden is on the lawn, as it is at this time that established lawns can be repaired and generally cared for, and seed can be sown to produce new ones.

Brushing, raking with a wire rake, and spiking all help to improve the penetration of air to the turf surface and the soil beneath. The mat of dead vegetation which is likely to form during summer is removed and so, too, are pests which may have been hiding in it, and fungus diseases which can damage the grass. Worm casts are brushed off at the same time.

Spiking can be done with an ordinary garden fork, at least $3\frac{1}{2}$ in. deep, and at intervals of a few inches all over the lawn, but hollow-tined aerators are even better, as they remove soil instead of compressing it; a further variation is the use of slitting tines which will cut the turf and break up a vegetative mat.

This can be followed by a fall feed with a compound lawn fertilizer high in potash and phosphate, and finally by a topdressing, made up of loam, peatmoss and coarse sand, varying the proportions of the ingredients according to the basic soil type on which the lawn is growing. Apply this topdressing at 2–4 lb. per sq. yd. It should be applied dry and worked in with a stiff brush. Mowing can continue, but at less frequent intervals.

In the north this is undoubtedly the best month to make a new lawn either by seeding or sodding. Clean, weed-free soil and the application of a pre-seeding general fertilizer ten days or so before sowing are advisable; choose a day when the soil is moist and rain is likely to follow, make sure there is a good tilth, and sow the seed evenly at $1\frac{1}{2}$ oz. per sq. yd. Patchy sowing leads to trouble with damping off disease.

Bald parts of established lawns should be scratched up to provide some sort of seedbed and sown with a seed mixture which matches the grasses already present. Breaking edges can be remedied by cutting the turf so that a piece a foot wide and of a convenient length is removed, to include the bad edge, turned round so that the edge is inside, and the turf replaced, filling in the gap now inside the lawn with compost and grass seed.

Fall flowering border plants come in all the flaming colors, red, orange and yellow, for instance, dahlias are magnificent, rudbeckias, heliopsis, gaillardias, the early flowering chrysanthemums, and solidagos, but purples and pinks are by no means out of the picture. There is a beautiful range of color in the named

Left: Repairing the broken edge of a lawn by reversing the turves. *Above right:* The correct way to pick an apple. *Right:* A modern device for spiking a lawn

varieties of Michaelmas daisy–'Marie Ballard' is a good blue, and 'Ernest Ballard' is an equally eye-catching crimson. Phlox, with their curious, slightly stuffy fragrance, the purple coneflower (echinacea), the magenta sedums, particularly the variety 'Brilliant', and liatris species (the Kansas gayfeather) all add a splendid burst of color to the season's end. Fall bulbs contributing to it will be *Cyclamen neapolitanum*, colchicum and fall-flowering crocus, nerines, crocosmia and montbretia.

For early blooms in May and June next year, some of the annuals can be sown now, such as godetia, larkspur, nigella, calendula, Shirley poppies, annual scabious and coreopsis. They are sown in the open and should be well established by the time the cold weather comes. Sweet peas can also be sown now and over-wintered in a frame, for flowering in June next year where winters are less severe or earlier. Mice can destroy them, however, so protect with small mesh wire netting.

Roses will be in bloom again, and the yellow flowered fall clematis species, *C. orientalis* and *C. tangutica*, also *C. rehderiana*, tubular and cowslip scented. Rambler roses are pruned this month, cutting the flowered canes out completely and tying the new ones of this season in to take their place. Shrubs in flower are ceanothus, caryopteris, ceratostigma, hibiscus, perowskia, and *Hamamelis virginiana*, the witch hazel which is used to supply that refreshing substance. More heathers (calluna and daboecia) will be in flower, and all the berrying kinds of shrubs will be changing the color of their fruit to red, orange, yellow, purple, blue and white.

Cuttings of half-ripe wood can still be taken and put in a cold frame; layers can be brought down to earth and encouraged to root, and planting of evergreen shrubs can be undertaken in milder areas, as well as the clipping of evergreen hedges, and the fast growing kinds given their final trimming. Mildew on all sorts of plants should be watched for and sprayed against where necessary.

Frosts are possible before the end of the month, so plants which may have to be taken into the greenhouse are chrysanthemums, azaleas, carnations, fuchsias, heliotropes and pelargoniums, cyclamen and Christmas cactus. Freesias also can go in at the end of the month in some areas and,

although they would survive a light frost, it would slow up flowering.

Greenhouse tomatoes should be cleared of their remaining fruit, and pulled out, and sweet peas will also be finished. The shading should be cleaned off the glass and the inside of the greenhouse washed down and sterilized if possible, removing the plants temporarily to do this. Watering can be reduced and many pot plants can be gradually dried off. Cuttings of zonal pelargoniums can be taken and rooted now. Seeds can be sown to flower in late winter and spring, such as the annuals, schizanthus and salpiglossis.

Fall-fruiting raspberries will be cropping so, too, will blackberries. Summer pruning of the soft fruit can be finished early this month, and strawberry runners may be planted.

Apple and pear picking will be in full swing; both are ready to pick if the stalk detaches easily when the fruit is lifted gently up in the palm of the hand. Pears to be stored should be picked just as the skin begins to turn yellow round the stalk but while the body of the fruit is still green, and then placed in single layers in a coolish room in the dark. The atmosphere should not be dry, otherwise they shrivel. Sometimes with late pears picking should be delayed until the weather deteriorates, but they must be picked then, even if the stalk has to be pulled quite hard to detach it. Apples will keep well in the same conditions, or can be put four or five in a polyethelene bag, with the opening closed, using fruit which is not injured and without signs of disease. Put in a dark, cool place, it will keep well, preserved in its own gases given off as maturing continues.

This time of year is both an ending and beginning for the vegetable garden; potatoes, beet, carrots, turnip and celeriac are lifted for storing, and onions are finally cleaned and hung up. Blanching of celery and endive should continue. Eggplant and peppers will be in full cropping. Pole beans, cabbage and lettuce, peas, cucumbers, squash and courgettes will be coming to an end. Once they have all been finished, the remains of the plants should be cleared away, and the ground cleaned of weeds. It is at this time that weeds seem to take on a new lease of life, and grow up behind one's back, just as the season seems to be over. If not cleaned off now, by the time spring arrives they will have gained complete control of the garden.

The atmosphere about the garden now is that of clearing up after the party; the guests have made their bow and graced the scene, they have been fed and watered and now they are leaving, and only the debris remains to be sorted and cleared away or used. The perennials will mostly have finished flowering and need cutting down, with the stakes and supports put away in a dry shed until next year. Now is the time to move and divide, and to act upon notes made during the season as to where plants should really be growing, and which ones will never do and can be thrown out. The large clumps can be split, and the best pieces from the outside replanted, the center being thrown away.

Edges of beds and borders can be straightened and re-cut, and the last remnants of the annuals and bedding plants lifted and put on the compost heap. Dahlias should be cut down after they have been blackened by the first frost, the tubers dug up and shaken free of soil, then labelled and stored in a dry cool place through the winter. In mild winters, they will live in the soil without lifting, to shoot again without difficulty next spring. Tuberous rooted begonias and gladiolus should also be lifted early in the month and cleaned, then stored in a dry, frostproof place.

This is the month for bulb planting, leaving it to the end, however, if the weather remains warm. Narcissi, hyacinths, scillas, snowdrops, crocus, grape hyacinths and chionodoxas (glory of the snow) can all go in. Leaves will need sweeping up everywhere, particularly from the lawn. Rambler rose pruning can continue. Most trees and shrubs can be planted now, although in the north tender types are best left till spring, and propagation of most shrubs, including roses, by hardwood or fully ripened cuttings, can be started, as soon as the shoots are mature, putting them in a trench out of doors or in a cold frame.

Where winters are less severe October is a suitable time to prepare the sites where shrubs are to be planted next month. This preparation is very important, and does a great deal towards ensuring that the new shrub will survive and thrive; so often it dies through being planted in badly drained soil that is starved of plant food, or short of humus, as well as being in all probability totally different to that in which it was growing in the nursery. The hole should be dug out two spade's depth deep and at least 4 ft. wide, the bottom forked up and well-rotted organic matter mixed with it. The excavated soil is then returned, making sure that the topsoil remains on top, and mixing with it all, more compost, manure and leafmold. A proportion of half and half is about right. Doing all this a month ahead gives the soil time to absorb the new material and settle after digging.

By now most of the top fruit will be picked and in store, if not already eaten, and now is a good

time to decide on possible new varieties to obtain a succession, and to grub up old, poorly fruiting trees, or those with fruit of poor flavor. Apples and pears can both be grown on dwarfing stocks, to produce small trees about 12–15 ft. tall and as much across. They can also be grown in restricted forms as cordons, pyramids, or espaliers. There are no dwarf stocks for cherries; plums and greengages do not grow very tall or large in any case, though they can be fan trained against walls. Peaches may be grown against sheltering walls in colder areas.

Fruit, like vegetables, is in a different class if eaten as soon as picked, rather than 24 or 48 hours later, as it so often is if store bought. The production of one's own fruit also ensures that one knows exactly what was applied in the way of spray chemicals to ward off various pests and diseases. Choice of top fruit should be carefully made, as it will last twenty-five years on average; strawberry beds are replanted every three or four years, raspberries, gooseberries and currants every 10–15 years.

The ground can be prepared as it is for shrubs, and new fruit trees planted. Strawberry runners can be planted, and the rooted tips of blackberries and loganberries can be separated from the parents, preparatory to planting. They should also have the old fruited canes taken away and the new put in their place. This is a very prickly job,

Left: Dahlia tubers lifted, dried, cleaned and being stored. *Center:* Using a bulb planter to plant daffodil bulbs in turf. The planter removes a 'core' of turf which is replaced and firmed after the bulb has been planted. *Right:* The winter cherry, *Solanum capsicastrum*

and gloves are essential, unless a variety such as 'Oregon Thornless' is grown. Peaches can be given a Bordeaux mixture or lime-sulfur spray just as the leaves start to fall, as the final protective covering against peach leaf curl.

Apples for picking, eating and storing this month are 'Jonathan', 'Northern Spy', 'Sweet Delicious', 'Winesap', 'Yellow Newton'; 'Winesap' in particular can be kept without difficulty in a cool shed in boxes with lids on, provided they are not infected with rot or any kind of fungus in the first place, and will keep so until the spring of the following year. Similarly pears will keep for a good part of the winter, in particular such varieties as 'Doyenne du Comice', 'Easter' and 'Kieffer'.

By this time the greenhouse will be filling up again, as plants come in early in the month for protection. These may include freesias, both from seed and corms – the former in flower by now – azaleas, cyclamen, Christmas cactus, poinsettias, orange and lemon trees, young plants of primula and cineraria, saintpaulias and the winter cherry, *Solanum capsicastrum*, and chrysanthemums for flowering in late November and December. Some good varieties for late flowering are 'Pink Champagne', 'Chattanooga', 'May Shoesmith' both white varieties; 'Bright Yellow May Shoesmith' and 'Balcombe Perfection', bronze. A little heat may be needed at the end of the month in the greenhouse if there is frost at night.

In the north, carrots, potatoes, beet and celeriac can be lifted; good sized roots of the latter will be about 6 in. in diameter. The first of the parsnips may be ready, and the last of the squash should be cut. Brussels sprouts, cauliflowers and leeks will be coming into season, also winter celery towards the end of the month; there may still be a few lettuces. Eggplant and peppers will come to the end of bearing. Cauliflowers should have the outer leaves bent over the curd to protect it.

Asparagus fern should be cut down to soil level, and the bed mulched with rotted manure or garden compost; if this is not available a light dressing of basic slag can be given. Asparagus does best in a limey soil, and if it is acid a dressing of lime in some form should be given every three or four years. Globe artichoke crowns should be protected with a heavy mulch after removing dead leaves.

Otherwise much of the work in the vegetable garden consists in clearing and cleaning of weeds, digging and rotavating, and manuring this month and next where brassicas, leaf vegetables and potatoes are to be planted next spring. Vegetable or animal manure should not be used where root crops are to follow, but for them wood ash can be forked in. Do not add lime at the same time as bulky organic material. Spring cabbage plants should be planted outside.

In milder areas, shrubs and all sorts of hardwood plants will be arriving from nurseries in November, provided they were ordered in good time, back in the summer, and will need planting. The site will have been prepared last month, and now, about ten days before planting, a light dressing of bonemeal can be scattered over the area to which the roots are likely to extend, and forked into the top 4 or 5 in. of soil. When the plants arrive, put them in as soon as possible.

Planting can be undertaken, provided the soil is moist but not frozen or really sodden; if it is, then put the plants back in their wrappings with a little air and leave them for three or four days, or heel them in a shallow trench in a place where they are sheltered from wind and least likely to be frozen, until the weather improves. They will be quite safe there for several weeks.

When they are planted, if bare root, the roots should be spread out to their full length–they are not mobile, and will stay put in any position, so that if doubled up or bent backwards, they cannot extend normally and may never grow. A small hump at the bottom of the hole encourages the roots to spread out and downwards as they naturally would, and staking before planting avoids damage to the roots. Firmness is essential to prevent wind rocking and to avoid pockets in the soil. Water the plant in, and rake the soil surface so that it does not remain smooth and collect water, and all should be well, unless the winter is unusually cold.

Hardwood cuttings of shrubs, including roses can still be taken and put in a trench out of doors in a sheltered place, lining the bottom with sand, and stripping the lower leaves off the cutting. Where winters are severe they should be tied in bundles and buried in sand in a cold frame for lining out in the spring. In milder parts of the country, climbing roses can be pruned, and ramblers should be given the finishing touches.

In the northern part of the country, established lawns will have had their final cut and fallen leaves should be raked from the surface.

In fact leaves should be removed constantly as they encourage worms and suffocate the grass so that it turns yellow. They make good compost, except the leathery ones, such as laurel, bay and holly; beech, oak, elm, linden and fruit tree leaves are all good, however.

Some plants will be coming into flower now, for instance *Mahonia* 'Charity' and *M. lomarufolia*, the autumn-flowering cherry (*Prunus subhirtella autumnalis*), some of the late varieties of *Calluna vulgaris* and *Erica carnea*, and *Jasminum nudiflorum* in sheltered places. Border digging and manuring can continue as weather permits. Tulips can be planted, and there is still just time to plant narcissi and hyacinths. Outdoor chrysan-

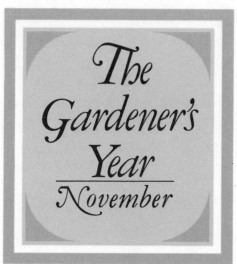

The Gardener's Year
November

themums will now come to an end and the stems should be cut back to leave a few inches, lifted and boxed into compost, and placed in a cold frame until mid December. The gray-leaved plants and any with woolly leaves will come through the wet of the winter better if protected now, with a cloche or covering of some kind which keeps off the wet but lets in air.

In the north, light becomes very short in November, and when it is there, is of poor quality, so the greenhouse glass should be as clean as possible, and should be scrubbed if necessary. Condensation should be avoided, as this cuts down light transmission, by adequate ventilation during the day. A little gentle heat will also dry things out and prevent too much humidity in which gray mold can thrive.

Young plants of primulas, cinerarias, polyanthus and calceolarias will need attention, and, in particular, should be watched for aphid outbreaks. The late-flowering chrysanthemums will begin to flower in succession, and freesias will be in full bloom, scenting the greenhouse gloriously. Azaleas, cyclamen and poinsettias will be coming up to flowering, so that watering and liquid feeding will be required.

Many plants will have been dried off and put under the greenhouse staging for their winter rest, and cacti need only be watered once a month, if that. Pelargonium cuttings which have rooted will no longer be growing and will need only just enough water to keep the soil moist; the same applies to potted fuchsias, which do not appreciate dust-dry soil.

As soon as the leaves have fallen, and the last of the crop is picked, the top fruit can be pruned this month and any time during the winter from now onwards if the weather is suitable, following with winter pest and disease spraying. Pruning is done to prevent shoots and branches becoming crowded and disease ridden, and to induce the production of new growth, which will crop well and regularly. Unpruned trees become a tangled jungle of growth, live and dead, full of pests and diseases, and bearing too much fruit which does not ripen or is too small when it does. Bud pecking by birds may start this month and proprietary bird repellents are advisable. Formally trained apples and pears can have the summer pruning finished now so as to leave stubs 2–3 in. long; the bush trees are better renewal pruned; be particularly careful to remove the shoot tips where mildew was a nuisance in the summer. Mulching can follow pruning and spraying.

If blackcurrant pruning was not done in August, it can be done now, and summer pruning of redcurrants and gooseberries can be completed as with top fruit. The old fruited canes of raspberries are cut out now, if not already done, together with those of the fall fruiting kinds. Strawberries should be well established, and may be thawed to prevent weed growth. In milder areas, established plants more than one year old may be treated with simazine as an alternative for weed control. Vegetable garden tidying can continue, together with digging and manuring. If lime is thought necessary, do not be too prodigal with it, and in any case time its application so that at least six weeks intervene between liming and manuring. Parsnips can be lifted now and stored in sand in a cool shed, though they will usually keep perfectly well through the winter if left in the ground protected with leaves or salt hay, and dug up only when wanted for cooking. Celery can be lifted, leeks should be ready–they are a useful vegetable as they will go on right through the winter. Spinach and spinach beet are equally obliging. Lettuce sown in the autumn and transferred to cold frames, if protected during periods of severe frost, will provide fresh lettuce until mid-winter.

Left: Gray-leaved plants and those with woolly leaves benefit from cloche protection in winter.
Right: Heeling in a tree when the weather is unsuitable for planting out

In many parts of the country, the garden will have one of two appearances: either it will be bare and clean, with branches and twigs silhouetted against the sky and the soil borders and beds nicely brown, or it will be completely white, with only the evergreens and the red berries and haws of holly, thorn, rose and cotoneaster to color it. Whichever it is, the gardener at any rate is now allowed a well-earned rest and a change as the end of the year and all its festivities comes. Indeed it is obligatory, however enthusiastic the gardener, that there should be some pause in the routine, otherwise the mind becomes set and the garden pattern reflects this and is static. Its owner needs to recharge his gardening outlook by letting it lie fallow, just as soil, left unused for a season, builds up its food content and repairs its structure.

For the first two weeks or so there are small jobs to do, for instance planting of shrubs, trees, fruit and roses can be continued or finished as the weather allows. Pruning and spraying of fruit can continue; digging and manuring of borders and vegetable plots can finish. It is advisable to do this before Christmas to give the soil time to absorb the fresh material, and to allow sufficient time before spring for the breaking up of clay soil by frost.

Slug bait may be needed round delphiniums, lupins, pyrethrums and other succulent shooted border plants. Watch for bud pecking of fruit and ornamental trees, such as cherry and forsythia. There may be trouble with bark stripping by rabbits and mice, and a wary eye can be kept open for this, particularly if the weather suddenly becomes very cold for a few days.

One now has time to overhaul the machinery used during the year, such as rotavators, lawn mowers and hedge cutters, to sharpen all cutting blades and to clean and oil all hand tools.

The greenhouse will be the pleasantest and prettiest place, with chrysanthemums, freesias, azaleas, cyclamen, forced hyacinths and 'Soleil D'Or' narcissi, saintpaulias, poinsettias and Christmas cactus in full flower. Heat will be needed; a night temperature of 60°F for tropical plants and 45°F for cool house subjects is ideal. Chrysanthemums boxed up and put in the frame last month can come in and be watered, in mid-December, so that they start to grow and produce shoots for cuttings. It is the shoots that come from below soil level that will grow into the best plants; those which sprout from the old stems will not be strong. Sometimes chrysanthemum crowns or stools will produce a tremendous number of shoots tightly clustered round the old stems, and when this happens it is a sign that the plant is infected with a bacterial trouble called crown gall, and should be discarded.

Sweet peas passing the winter in frames should be stopped at the fourth leaf, and looked at occasionally in case they need further protection from mice. Fruit in store should also be examined occasionally, together with dahlia tubers and root vegetables; remove any rotting specimens.

Stopping sweet peas

This is a good time, while the bones of the garden show, to re-design unsatisfactory parts of it where weather conditions permit, and to carry out new constructions. Concrete paths can be laid (but not in frosty weather), ponds excavated before the soil becomes really wet, pergolas and arches built and paving laid for terraces and patios. Rock gardens can be established, or improved in their lay out, new borders cut and old ones turfed or planted with such ground cover plants as ajuga, periwinkle, lamium, *Rosa paulii*, violets, hypericums and saxifrages. A pattern for a herb garden can be laid down, or a fruit garden planned; dry stone walls built and planted. Color groupings can be improved, planting a border with all the red tones or all the yellow ones, using leaves as well as flowers to give the effect. There is time to put any of these ideas into practice now, or to mull them over ready for carrying them out in the early spring.

Flowers for picking for Christmas celebrations will be in all the best gardens; depending on the area, there may be a few roses here and there, the hellebores (*Helleborus orientalis*) will be in bloom, so will laurustinus, winter jasmine, hamamelis, chimonanthus, mahonia, *Erica cinerea* and its varieties, primroses and violets in sheltered places, the occasional precocious 'japonica' bloom, sedums, pansies, to say nothing of the greenhouse offerings. *Iris reticulata* may be showing bud towards the end of the month and if picked and put in a vase in the warmth, will unfold its dark purple-blue, fragrant flowers.

Winter jasmine   Iris reticulata

The plants in pots, both flowering and foliage can go into the home for the time being for extra decoration, and all sorts of berrying shrubs will add to their color. The evergreens will retain their leaves, especially the conifers, if sprayed with the modern polyvinyl resin which lasts for several weeks, before or immediately after cutting, as it seals the pores and prevents the loss of water vapor.

Often, sadly, one of December's disasters is the death of expensive pot plants, acquired as Christmas gifts. Such plants include the azaleas, poinsettias, cyclamen, Christmas cactus and the zebra plant (*Aphelandra squarrosa*), at the height of their flowering season, covered in bloom and apparently in the best of health. They are in fact extremely fit, but the change from nursery greenhouse conditions to those of the home, particularly at Christmas time, is often too much for them. In no time, buds and flowers have dropped, leaves withered and fallen, and a few stark bare stems are all that is left of a once beautiful plant. One is so occupied at Christmas with other things that plants have all kinds of extreme and distasteful conditions to cope with, and it is no wonder that many succumb.

Smoky, dry atmospheres often predominate; although the temperature may be well up, it will be too high near radiators or fires. Conversely, window sills behind drawn drapes where pot plants are often put, can be death traps of freezing air, as the outside temperature drops swiftly to or below freezing, as it can easily do at this time.

In all the excitement nothing is more likely to be overlooked than watering, and an azalea in full bloom will want a big drink at least every day; cyclamen also flag extremely quickly with their leaves turning yellow, and the zebra plant will droop its leaves in no time, as it is another plant that must have a daily drink when flowering. Plants may also suffer from being given liquids other than water at this time of the year. Drafts are a further menace as doors constantly open with the arrival and departure of guests and family; one way and another, all pot plants have a hard time of it.

Try to remember at any rate, to review the water needs every day; bring the plants in from the window sills when the drapes are drawn. Spray them lavishly every day with clear water, or pack really damp peatmoss all round the container and keep it damp. Keep them somewhere out of the line of drafts and away from fierce heat.

Then leave the garden alone, except for the greenhouse, enjoy the holidays, hibernate a little as all sensible animals do in the short dark days, and come back to it with a refreshed mind in the New Year when the days begin to lengthen.

Aphelandra squarrosa

Index

Italicized references are to illustration captions.

ACKNOWLEDGMENTS

The publishers would like to thank the following individuals and organizations for their kind permission to reproduce the photographs in this book:
A–Z Botanical Collection 108 left, 120 right, 165; Bernard Alfieri 100 above, 112 right, 120 above left; Pat Brindley 2–3, 6–7, 51, 136 above; Burpee Seeds 192, 195 right; P. R. Chapman 223, 231 above, 232, 233 above and below, 234 left and right, 235 right; R. J. Corbin 35 below left, 73, 176 right; Derek Fell 11 left, 99, 107, 111 above, 166; Valerie Finnis 144 right, 145, 147 below, 149 below, 151, 153 above, 155, 159 right; Brian Furner 169, 176 left, 177 above, 183 left, 185 left, 188 left and right, 189 below, 191 below, 194 right, 196 centre and below; Iris Hardwick 21 below left, 22 below, 26 below, 32, 35 above, 89, 92 centre, 102 above, 129 above right, 130, 140 left, 201, 203; W. H. Hodge 163 below; Peter Hunt 17 below, 21 below right, 26 above, 30–31, 38 below, 39 below, 41 above left and below right, 44 left and right, 45 above right and below, 47 above, 56 below, 57 below, 59 right, 88, 100 below left, 101, 123 left, 132 above and centre, 136 below, 138 above and below, 144 left, 148–149, 206 below, 208 left, 213 below, 229 above and below left and right, 235 left; A. Huxley 11 right, 38–39, 39 below right, 48, 56 above, 58 left, 60 below right, 67 below, 92 below, 153 below left, 154 left, 156–157, 196 above, 209 left and right, 213 above, 214, 221 above, 224–225, 226; G. E. Hyde 47 below left, 50 below, 60 below left, 90–91, 92 above, 100 below right, 102 below, 103, 127, 140 right, 212 above and below; D. J. Kesby 47 below right, 50 above, 53 above, 54 right, 61, 90 below, 95, 123 above right, 134 right, 142, 207; Lord and Burnham 204; Elsa Megson 1, 29 below right, 43 below, 70, 71 above and below, 199 right, 200, 205 below left and right, 206 above, 211, 216 left and right, 222 below; E. Memmler 112 left; Ray Procter 20 above, 40, 96 below, 124, 164 above and below, 173 above, 177 below right, 182 left, 182 below right, 191 above; K. Scowen 8–9; Donald Smith 177 below left; Harry Smith Horticultural Photographic Collection 4–5, 10 above and below, 14–15, 15 above left and right, 16, 17 above, 18, 19 left and right, 20 below, 21 above, 22 above, 23 left and right, 24 above and below, 29 above and below left, 33, 35 below right, 36 above and below, 37, 41 above right and centre, 47 below centre, 49, 53 below, 54 left, 55, 57 above, 58–59, 60 above right, 64 above and below, 66, 67 above left and right, 68, 74 left and right, 75, 78 left and right, 80, 81 left, 82 left, 83, 85, 86 left and right, 87 left and right, 91 below, 93, 94 left and right, 96 above, 96–97, 106, 108 below right, 109, 110, 111 below, 113, 114 left and right, 116 above, 116–117, 117 above, below left and right, 120 below left, 121 above, 123 below right, 128 left and right, 129 above left and below, 132 below, 133, 134 left, 137, 139, 143 above and below, 147 above, 149 right, 150, 152, 153 below right, 154 right, 156 below, 157 below, 158, 159 left, 160 left and right, 161, 162–163, 162 below, 167, 168, 170 left and right, 172 above and below. 173 below, 174, 175 left and right, 187 above, 189 above, 190 above left and right, 199 left, 205 above, 208 right, 210, 218, 220, 221 below, 222 above, 224 below, 225 below left, 227 left and right, 231 below right, 236; (Downward and Crowson) 27, 42, 43 above, 45 above left, 62, 63, 69, 81 right, 82 right, 105, 108 above right, 115, 135, 171, 179, 180–181, 182 above right, 183 right, 185 right, 187 below, 190 below, 194 left, 195 left, 215, 225 below right, 228, 231 below left; Spectrum Colour Library 121 below, 193, 219; D. Woodland 138 centre.